Mar Caribe
OCÉANO ATLÁNTICO
Barranquilla
Cartagena
Maracaibo
Caracas
Barquisimeto
Río Orinoco
VENEZUELA
Medellín
Manizales
Bogotá
Cali
COLOMBIA
CORDILLERA DE LOS ANDES
Salto Ángel
Georgetown
GUYANA
Paramaribo
SURINAM
Cayenne
GUAYANA FRANCESA (Francia)
Quito
ECUADOR
Ecuador
Guayaquil
Cuenca
Islas Galápagos (Ec.)
Iquitos
Manaus
Río Amazonas
Belém
Fortaleza
Río Madeira
Cajamarca
Trujillo
PERÚ
Río Branco
BRASIL
Recife
Lima
Machu Picchu
Ayacucho
Cuzco
BOLIVIA
Lago Titicaca
Salvador
Arequipa
La Paz
Brasília
Cochabamba
Santa Cruz
Arica
Sucre
Belo Horizonte
Iquique
Desierto de Atacama
Potosí
PARAGUAY
Río de Janeiro
São Paulo
Santos
Trópico de Capricornio
Antofagasta
Salta
Asunción
Salto Iguazú
CHILE
San Miguel de Tucumán
ARGENTINA
Coquimbo
Río Paraná
Río Uruguay
Pôrto Alegre
Córdoba
Rivera
Rosario
URUGUAY
Valparaíso
Santiago
Mendoza
Buenos Aires
La Plata
Montevideo
Río de la Plata
OCÉANO ATLÁNTICO
Concepción
Bahía Blanca
Puerto Montt
OCÉANO PACÍFICO
Estrecho de Magallanes
Islas Malvinas (Br.)
Punta Arenas
TIERRA DEL FUEGO
Cabo de Hornos
OCÉANO PACÍFICO
I. Pinta
I. Fernandina
I. Marchena
I. San Salvador
Santa Cruz
I. Isabela
I. Santa Cruz
Puerto Ayora
Puerto Villamil
I. San Cristóbal
Puerto Baquerizo Moreno
ISLAS GALÁPAGOS (ECUADOR)
OCÉANO PACÍFICO
Cabo Norte
Volcán Katiki
Hanga Roa
Cabo Cumming
Mataveri
ISLA de PASCUA (CHILE)
América del Sur

CURSO ELEMENTAL

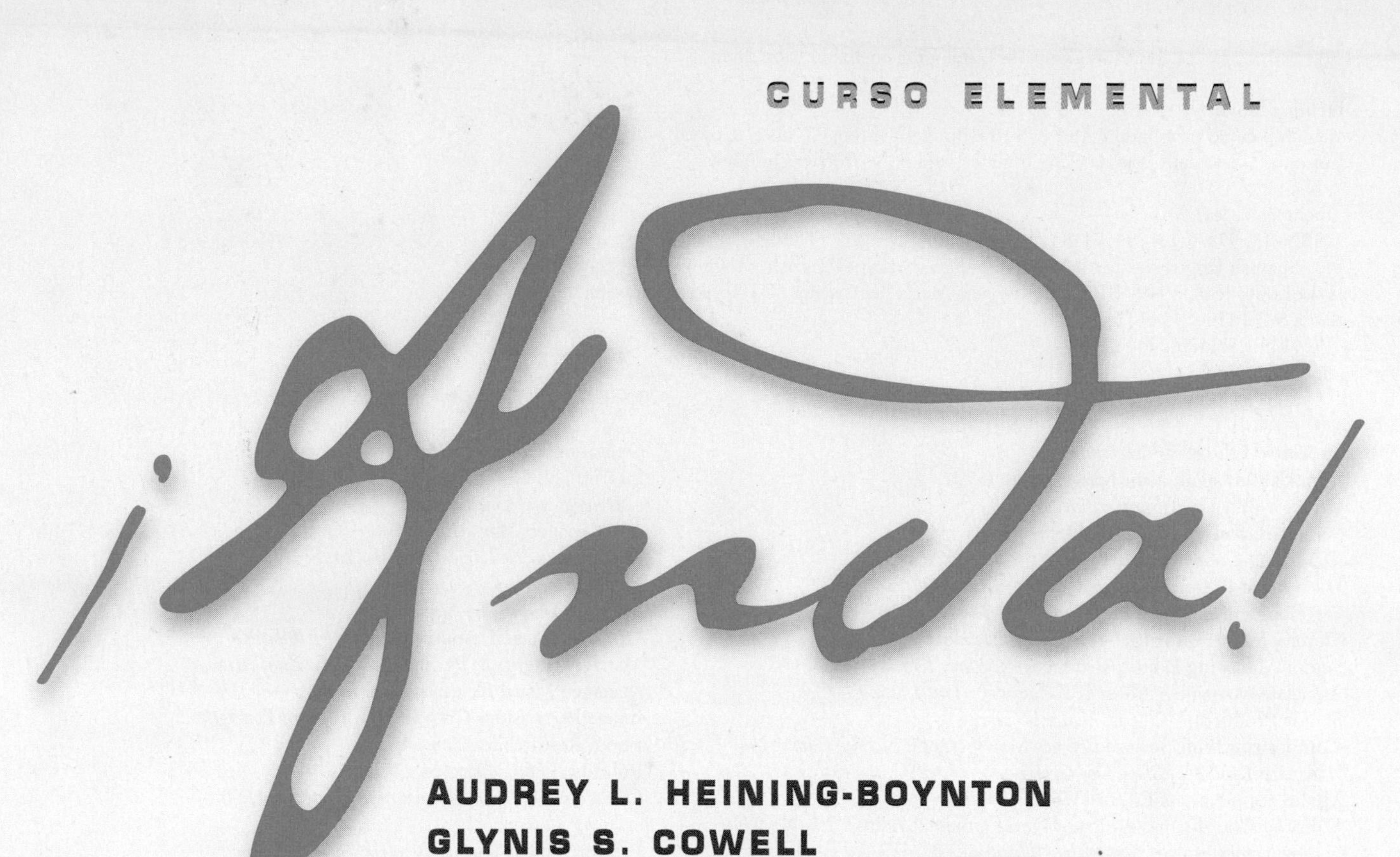

AUDREY L. HEINING-BOYNTON
GLYNIS S. COWELL
The University of North Carolina at Chapel Hill

WITH
Jean LeLoup
María del Carmen Caña Jiménez
Sonia Torres-Quiñones

UPPER SADDLE RIVER, NJ 07458

Library of Congress Cataloging-in-Publication Data

Heining-Boynton, Audrey L.
¡Anda! : curso elemental / Audrey L. Heining-Boynton, Glynis S. Cowell; with Jean LeLoup, María del Carmen Caña Jiménez, and Sonia Torres-Quiñones.
p. cm.
Includes index.
ISBN-13: 978-0-13-184571-8 (alk. paper)
1. Spanish language--Textbooks for foreign speakers--English. I. Cowell, Glynis S. II. LeLoup, Jean, 1949- III. Caña Jiménez, María del Carmen. IV. Torres-Quiñones, Sonia S. V. Title.
PC4129.E5H428 2008
468.2'421--dc22

2007046521

Executive Editor: *Bob Hemmer*
Editorial Assistant: *Katie Spiegel*
Director of Marketing: *Kristine Suárez*
Senior Marketing Manager: *Denise Miller*
Marketing Coordinator: *Bill Bliss*
Director of Editorial Development: *Julia Caballero*
Development Editor: *Janet García-Levitas; Guadalupe Parras-Serradilla*
Development Editor for Assessment: *Melissa Marolla Brown*
Senior Managing Editor (Production): *Mary Rottino*
Associate Managing Editor (Production): *Janice Stangel*
Senior Production Editor: *Nancy Stevenson*
Composition/Full-Service Project Management: *Natalie Hansen and Sandra Reinhard, Black Dot Group*
Media/Supplements Editor: *Meriel Martínez*
Editorial Coordinator/Assistant Developmental Editor: *Jennifer Murphy*
Senior Media Editor: *Samantha Alducin*
Senior Operations Supervisor: *Brian Mackey*
Operations Specialist: *Cathleen Petersen*
Interior and Cover Design: *Lisa Delgado, Delgado and Company, Inc.*
Art Manager: *Maria Piper*
Illustrators: *Eric Larsen; Andrew Lange*
Electronic Art: *Siren Design*
Maps: *Peter Bull Art Studio*
Director, Image Resource Center: *Melinda Reo*
Manager, Rights & Permissions IRC: *Zina Arabia*
Manager, Visual Research: *Beth Brenzel*
Image Permissions Coordinator: *Richard Rodrigues*
Photo Researcher: *Diane Austin*
Publisher: *Phil Miller*
Cover image: *Donald Nausbaum, Getty Images Inc. – Stone Allstock*
Printer/Binder: *Courier Kendallville*
Typeface: *10/12 Janson*

Credits and acknowledgments borrowed from other sources and reproduced, with permission, in this textbook appear on page A49.

Pearson Education LTD.
Pearson Education Singapore, Pte. Ltd
Pearson Education, Canada, Ltd
Pearson Education–Japan
Pearson Education Australia PTY, Limited
Pearson Education North Asia Ltd
Pearson Educación de México, S.A. de C.V.
Pearson Education Malaysia, Pte. Ltd
Pearson Education, Upper Saddle River, New Jersey

DEDICATION

To David
–Audrey

To John, Jack, and Kate
–Glynis

10 9 8 7 6 5 4
ISBN: 0-13-184571-3/978-0-13-184571-8

BRIEF CONTENTS

(The numbers next to the grammar and vocabulary sections indicate their location within the chapter.)

FIRST

	Capítulo Preliminar A **Para empezar**	Capítulo 1 **¿Quiénes somos?**	Capítulo 2 **La vida universitaria**
Vocabulary sections	**1** Saludos, despedidas y presentaciones **2** Expresiones útiles para la clase **4** Los cognados **7** Los adjetivos de nacionalidad **8** Los números 0–30 **9** La hora **10** Los días, los meses y las estaciones **11** El tiempo	**1** La familia **6** Gente **9** Los números 31–100	**1** Las materias y las especialidades **2** La sala de clase **5** Los números 100–1.000 **6** En la universidad **8** Emociones y estados **10** Los deportes y los pasatiempos
Grammar sections	**3** El alfabeto **5** Los pronombres personales **6** El verbo **ser** **12** **Gustar**	**2** El verbo **tener** **3** El singular y el plural **4** El masculino y el femenino **5** Los artículos definidos e indefinidos **7** Los adjetivos posesivos **8** Los adjetivos descriptivos	**3** Presente indicativo de verbos regulares **4** La formación de preguntas y las palabras interrogativas **7** El verbo **estar** **9** El verbo **gustar**
Pronunciation		Spanish vowels	Word stress and accent marks
Cultural readings and country focus	• Cómo se saluda la gente • ¿Tú o usted? • ¿Quién habla español?	• Los nombres en el mundo hispano • El español, lengua diversa	• Los estereotipos • Los deportes en el mundo hispano
		LOS ESTADOS UNIDOS	**MÉXICO**
Escucha		**Estrategia:** Determining the topic and listening for words you know	**Estrategia:** Listening for the gist
Escribe		Un poema	Una descripción
Ambiciones siniestras		**Lectura:** *Conexiones* **Estrategia:** Recognizing cognates **Video:** *¿Quiénes son?*	**Lectura:** *Las solicitudes* **Estrategia:** Skimming **Video:** *La aventura comienza*

SEMESTER

Capítulo 3 Estamos en casa	Capítulo 4 Nuestra comunidad	Capítulo 5 ¡A divertirse! La música y el cine	Capítulo 6 ¡Sí, lo sé!
1 La casa **3** Los muebles y otros objetos de la casa **4** Los quehaceres de la casa **5** Los colores **7** Los números 1.000–100.000.000	**1** Los lugares **3** ¿Qué tienen que hacer? ¿Qué pasa? **7** Trabajos y servicios voluntarios	**1** El mundo de la música **6** El mundo del cine	**Reviewing strategies**
2 Algunos verbos irregulares **6** Unas expresiones con **tener** **8** **Hay**	**2** **Saber** y **conocer** **4** Los verbos con cambio de raíz **5** El verbo **ir** **6** **Ir** + **a** + infinitivo **8** Las expresiones afirmativas y negativas **9** Un repaso de **ser** y **estar**	**2** Los adjetivos demostrativos **3** Los pronombres demostrativos **4** Los adverbios **5** El presente progresivo **7** Los números ordinales **8** **Hay que** + infinitivo **9** Los pronombres de complemento directo y la "a" personal	**Comunicación** Recycling of Capítulo Preliminar A to Capítulo 5
The letters **h, j,** and **g**	The letters **c** and **z**	Diphthongs and linking	
• ¿Dónde viven los españoles? • Las mujeres del mundo hispano	• Actividades cotidianas: Las compras y el paseo • La conciencia social	• La música latina en los Estados Unidos • La influencia hispana en el cine norteamericano	
España	**Honduras, Guatemala y El Salvador**	**Nicaragua, Costa Rica y Panamá**	**Cultura**
Estrategia: Listening for specific information	**Estrategia:** Paraphrasing what you hear	**Estrategia:** Anticipating content	
Un anuncio (*flyer*)	Una tarjeta postal	Una reseña	
Lectura: *El concurso* **Estrategia:** Scanning **Video:** *¡Tienes una gran oportunidad!*	**Lectura:** *Las cosas no son siempre lo que parecen* **Estrategia:** Skimming and Scanning (II) **Video:** *¿Quiénes son en realidad?*	**Lectura:** *La búsqueda de Eduardo* **Estrategia:** Anticipating content **Video:** *Se conocen*	**Ambiciones siniestras** **Y por fin, ¿cómo andas?**

(The numbers next to the grammar and vocabulary sections indicate their location within the chapter.)

SECOND

	Capítulo Preliminar B Introducciones y repasos	Capítulo 7 ¡A comer!	Capítulo 8 ¿Qué te pones?
Vocabulary sections	**Capítulo Preliminar A** **Capítulo 1** **Capítulo 2** **Capítulo 3** **Capítulo 4** **Capítulo 5**	**1** La comida **4** La preparación de las comidas **6** En el restaurante	**1** La ropa
Grammar sections		**2** Repaso del complemento directo **3** El pretérito **5** Unos verbos irregulares en el pretérito	**2** Los pronombres de complemento indirecto **3** **Gustar** y verbos como **gustar** **4** Los pronombres de complemento directo e indirecto usados juntos **5** Las construcciones reflexivas **6** El imperfecto
Pronunciation		The letters **r** and **rr**	The letters **ll** and **ñ**
Cultural readings and country focus	**Cultura**	• Las comidas en el mundo hispano • La comida hispana	• Zara: la moda internacional • Los centros comerciales en Latinoamérica
		CHILE Y PARAGUAY	**ARGENTINA Y URUGUAY**
Escucha		**Estrategia:** Combining strategies	**Estrategia:** Guessing meaning from context
Escribe		Un recuerdo (*memory*) (I)	Un recuerdo (II)
Ambiciones siniestras	**Ambiciones siniestras** **Y por fin, ¿cómo andas?**	**Lectura:** *El rompecabezas* **Estrategia:** Predicting **Video:** *¡Qué rico está el pisco!*	**Lectura:** *¿Quién fue?* **Estrategia:** Guessing meaning from context **Video:** *El misterio crece*

SEMESTER

Capítulo 9 Estamos en forma	Capítulo 10 ¡Viajemos!	Capítulo 11 El mundo actual	Capítulo 12 Y por fin, ¡lo sé!
1 El cuerpo humano **3** Unas enfermedades y tratamientos médicos	**1** Los medios de transporte **4** El viaje	**1** Los animales **2** El medio ambiente **4** La política	**Reviewing strategies**
2 Un resumen de los pronombres de complemento directo, indirecto y reflexivos **4** **¡Qué!** y **¡cuánto!** **5** El pretérito y el imperfecto **6** Expresiones con **hacer**	**2** Los mandatos informales **3** Los mandatos formales **5** Otras formas del posesivo **6** El comparativo y el superlativo	**3** El subjuntivo **5** **Por** y **para** **6** Las preposiciones y los pronombres preposicionales **7** El infinitivo después de preposiciones	**Comunicación** Recycling of Capítulo Preliminar B to Capítulo 11
The letters **d** and **t**	The letters **b** and **v**	Review of word stress and accent marks	
• El agua y la buena salud • Las farmacias en el mundo hispanohablante	• ¿Cómo nos movemos? • Venezuela, país de aventuras	• El Yunque: tesoro tropical • La política en el mundo hispano	
PERÚ, BOLIVIA Y ECUADOR	**COLOMBIA Y VENEZUELA**	**EL CARIBE: CUBA, PUERTO RICO Y LA REPÚBLICA DOMINICANA**	**Cultura**
Estrategia: Asking yourself questions	**Estrategia:** Listening for linguistic cues	**Estrategia:** Using visual organizers	
Un resumen	Un reportaje de un lugar turístico	Un anuncio	
Lectura: *¡Qué mentira!* **Estrategia:** Asking yourself questions **Video:** *No llores por mí*	**Lectura:** *¿Qué sabía?* **Estrategia:** Skipping words **Video:** *Falsas apariencias*	**Lectura:** *Celia* **Estrategia:** Using visual organizers **Video:** *El desenlace*	**Ambiciones siniestras** **Y por fin, ¿cómo andas?**

PREFACE

Why ¡Anda!?

> **andar** *vi* to walk; to move; to travel around; **¡Anda!** *excl* Come on! That's it!

In survey after survey, and focus group after focus group, Spanish instructors tell us that they are finding it increasingly difficult to accomplish everything they want in their elementary Spanish courses. Contact hours are decreasing. Class sizes are increasing. And students' lives are busier than ever. At the same time, course goals have become more and more ambitious. Instead of focusing only on grammar and vocabulary, instructors have made it clear that they want to give their students a thorough exposure to Hispanic culture and an opportunity to develop and practice communication skills. But there simply isn't enough time to do all of this as well as most would like, and the available elementary Spanish texts do little to address the problem. As a result, some instructors end up galloping through their text in order to cover all the grammar and vocabulary, omitting interesting cultural topics and limiting student speaking time. Others have made the awkward choice to use a text designed for first-year Spanish over three or even four semesters.

Based on this extensive research, you now have another option: ***¡Anda!***

¡Anda! has been developed to provide a practical response to the challenges today's Spanish instructors are facing. Its innovations center around three key areas:

1 Realistic goals with a realistic approach
2 Focus on student motivation
3 Tools to promote success

¡Anda! is ready to go! More of what you need … less of what you don't!

Realistic goals with a realistic approach

¡Anda! is the first college-level Spanish program conceived from the outset as a four-semester sequence of materials. The ***¡Anda!*** program is divided into two halves, ***¡Anda! Curso elemental*** and ***¡Anda! Curso intermedio***, each of which can be completed in one academic year.

Each volume's scope and sequence has been carefully designed, based on advice from hundreds of instructors at a wide variety of schools. Each volume introduces a realistic number of new vocabulary words, and the traditional first-year grammar sequence has been spread over two volumes so that it can be presented in four semesters rather than two. As a result, students have adequate time throughout the course to focus on communication, culture, and skills development, and to master the vocabulary and grammar concepts to which they are introduced.

Each volume of *¡Anda!* has been structured to foster preparation, recycling, and review within the context of a multi-semester sequence of courses. The ten regular chapters in each volume are complemented by *two preliminary* chapters and *two recycling* chapters.

Capítulo Preliminar A	Capítulo Preliminar B
Capítulo 1	Capítulo 7
Capítulo 2	Capítulo 8
Capítulo 3	Capítulo 9
Capítulo 4	Capítulo 10
Capítulo 5	Capítulo 11
Capítulo 6 (recycling)	Capítulo 12 (recycling)

- *Preliminary Chapter A* is designed with **ample vocabulary** to get students up and running and to give them a **sense of accomplishment** quickly. Many students will already be familiar with some of this vocabulary. It also has students reflect on the question "why study Spanish?".
- *Preliminary Chapter B* is a **review** of Preliminary A through Chapter 5 and allows those who join the class midyear or those who need a refresher to get up to speed at the beginning of the second half of the book.
- *Chapters 1–5* and *7–11* are **regular** chapters.
- *Chapters 6 and 12* are **recycling** chapters. No new material is presented. Designed for in-class use, these chapters recycle and recombine previously presented vocabulary, grammar, and culture, giving students more time to practice communication without the burden of learning new grammar or vocabulary.

Each regular chapter of *¡Anda!* has also been developed with the goal of providing a realistic approach for the achievement of realistic goals.

- New material is presented in manageable amounts, or **chunks,** allowing students to assimilate and practice without feeling overwhelmed.
- Each chapter contains a **realistic** number of new vocabulary words.
- Vocabulary and grammar explanations are interspersed, each **introduced at the point of need.**
- Grammar explanations are clear and concise with many supporting examples, followed by practice exercises and activities.
- Practice begins with **mechanical** exercises, for which there are correct answers, progresses through more **meaningful,** structured activities in which the student is guided but has some flexibility in determining the appropriate response, and ends with **communicative** activities in which students are manipulating language to create personalized responses.

Focus on student motivation

Many of the innovative features of *¡Anda!* have been designed to help instructors generate and sustain interest on the part of their students, whether they be of traditional college age or adult learners:

- Chapters are organized around themes that reflect **student interests** and tap into students' **real-life experiences.**
- Basic **vocabulary** has been selected and tested through *¡Anda!'s* development for its relevance and support, while additional words and phrases are offered so

that **students can personalize** their responses and acquire the vocabulary that is most meaningful to them. Additional vocabulary items are found in *Vocabulario útil* boxes throughout the chapters as well as in Appendix 3 (*También se dice…*).

- Exercises and activities have been designed to foster active participation by students. The focus throughout is on giving students opportunities to speak and on allowing instructors to **increase the amount of student "talk time"** in each class period. The majority of activities **elicit students' ideas and opinions,** engaging them to respond to each other on a variety of levels. Abundant pair and group activities encourage peer editing and help to create a comfortable arena for language learning.
- **No assumptions** are made concerning previous experience with Spanish or with language learning in general.
- Each exercise is designed to begin with **what the student already knows.**
- A **high-interest mystery story** runs through each chapter. Two episodes are presented in each regular chapter, one as the chapter's reading selection, the other in a corresponding video segment. Characters from the story are also integrated in the *Escucha* boxes.
- Both **"high" and "popular" culture** are woven throughout the chapters to enable students to learn to recognize and appreciate cultural diversity as they explore behaviors and values of the Spanish-speaking world. They are encouraged to think critically about these cultural practices and gifts to society.

Tools to promote success

The ***¡Anda!*** program includes many unique features and components designed to help students succeed at language learning and their instructors at language teaching.

Student learning support

- A **"walking tour"** of the *¡Anda! text and supplements* helps students understand their language program materials and the language of language learning before they use them.
- Explicit, systematic **recycling boxes with page references** help students link current learning to previously studied material in earlier chapters or sections.
- **Periodic review and self-assessment** boxes (*¿Cómo andas?*) help students gauge their understanding and retention of the material presented. A final assessment in each chapter (*Y por fin, ¿cómo andas?)* offers a comprehensive review.
- **Student notes** provide additional explanations and guidance in the learning process. Some of these contain cross-references to the English Grammar Guide and other student supplements. Others offer learning strategies (*Estrategia*) and additional information (*Fíjate*).
- An **English Grammar Guide,** available separately, explains the grammatical concepts students need in order to understand the Spanish grammar presentations in the text. Animated English grammar tutorials are also available within *MySpanishLab.*
- ***MySpanishLab™*** offers students a wealth of online resources and a supportive environment for completing homework assignments. When enabled by the instructor, a "Need Help" box appears as students are doing online homework activities, providing links to English and Spanish grammar tutorials, e-book sections, and additional practice activities—all directly relevant to the task at hand. Hints, verb charts, a glossary, and many other resources are available as well.

- A **Workbooklet,** available separately, allows student to complete the activities that involve writing without having to write in their copy of the textbook itself.

Instructor teaching support

One of the most important keys to student success is instructor success. The *¡Anda!* program has all of the support that you have come to expect and, based on our research, it offers many other enhancements!

- The **Annotated Instructor's Edition** of *¡Anda!* offers a wealth of materials designed to help instructors teach effectively and efficiently. Strategically placed annotations explain the text's methodology and function as **a built-in course in language teaching methods.**
- **Estimated time indicators** for presentational materials and practice activities help instructors create class plans.
- Other annotations provide additional activities and suggested answers.
- **The annotations are color-coded** and labeled for ready reference and ease of use.
- A treasure trove of **extra activities,** known as the **Activity Cache,** allows instructors to choose additional materials for in-class use.

The authors' approach

Learning a language is an exciting, enriching, and sometimes life changing experience. The development of the *¡Anda!* program is the result of many years of teaching and research that guided the authors independently to make important discoveries about language learning, the most important of which center on the student. Research-based and pedagogically sound, *¡Anda!* is also the product of extensive information gathered first-hand from numerous focus group sessions with students, graduate instructors, adjunct faculty, full-time professors, and administrators in an effort to determine the learning and instructional needs of each of these groups.

The Importance of the National Foreign Language Standards in *¡Anda!*

The *¡Anda!* program is based on the *National Foreign Language Standards.* The five organizing principles (the 5C's) of the Standards for language teaching and learning are at the core of *¡Anda!:* **Communication, Cultures, Connections, Comparisons,** and **Communities.** Each chapter opener identifies for the instructor where and in what capacity each of the 5C's are addressed. The **Weave of Curricular Elements** of the *National Foreign Language Standards* provide additional organizational structure for *¡Anda!* Those components of the **Curricular Weave** are: **Language System, Cultural Knowledge, Communication Strategies, Critical Thinking Skills, Learning Strategies, Other Subject Areas,** and **Technology.** Each of the Curricular Weave elements is omnipresent and, like the 5C's, permeates all aspects of each chapter of *¡Anda!*

- The *Language System,* which is comprised of components such as grammar, vocabulary, and phonetics, is at the heart of each chapter.
- The *Comunicación* sections of each chapter present vocabulary, grammar, and pronunciation at the point of need and maximum usage. Streamlined presentations are utilized that allow the learner to be immediately successful in employing the new concepts.

- *Cultural Knowledge* is approached thematically, making use of the chapter's vocabulary and grammar. Cultural presentations begin with the two-page chapter openers and always start with what the students already know about the cultural theme/concept from their home, local, regional, or national cultural perspective.
- *Communication and Learning Strategies* are abundant with tips for both students and instructors on how to maximize studying and in-class learning of Spanish, as well as how to utilize the language outside of the classroom.
- *Critical Thinking Skills* take center stage in ***¡Anda!*** Questions throughout the chapters, in particular tied to the cultural presentations, provide students with the opportunities to answer more than discrete point questions. The answers students are able to provide do indeed require higher-order thinking, but at a linguistic level completely appropriate for a beginning language learner.
- With regard to *Other Subject Areas*, ***¡Anda!*** is diligent with regard to incorporating **Connections** to other disciplines via vocabulary, discussion topics, and suggested activities.
- Finally, *Technology* is taken to an entirely new level with ***MySpanishLab***™ and the *Ambiciones siniestras* DVD. The authors and Prentice Hall believe that technology is a means to the end, not the end in and of itself, and so the focus is not on the technology *per se*, but on how that technology can deliver great content in better, more efficient, more interactive, and more meaningful ways.

By embracing the *National Foreign Language Standards* and as a result of decades of experience teaching Spanish, the authors believe that:

- A **student-centered classroom** is the best learning environment.
- Instruction must **begin where the learner is**, and all students come to the learning experience with prior knowledge that needs to be tapped.
- All students can learn in a **supportive environment** where they are encouraged to take risks when learning another language.
- **Critical thinking** is an important skill that must constantly be encouraged, practiced, and nurtured.
- **Learners** need to **make connections** with other disciplines in the Spanish classroom.

With these beliefs in mind, the authors have developed hundreds of creative and meaningful language-learning activities for the text and supporting components that employ students' imagination and engage the senses. For both students and instructors, they have created an instructional program that is **manageable, motivating**, and **clear.**

The Authors

Audrey Heining-Boynton

Audrey Heining-Boynton has been a Professor of Education and Spanish at The University of North Carolina at Chapel Hill, where she has taught Spanish and education courses for many years. She has won many teaching awards including the prestigious ACTFL Anthony Papalia Award for Excellence in Teacher Education, the Foreign Language of North Carolina Teacher of the Year Award, and The UNC ACCESS Award for Excellence in Working with LD and ADHD Students. Dr. Heining-Boynton is a frequent presenter at national and international conferences; has published more than seventy articles, curricula, textbooks, and manuals; and has won nearly $4 million in grants to help create language programs in North Carolina and South Carolina. Dr. Heining-Boynton has also held many important positions: President of the American Council on the Teaching of Foreign Languages (ACTFL 2005, The Year of Languages), President of the National Network for Early Language Learning, Vice President of the Michigan Foreign Language Association, board member of the Foreign Language Association of North Carolina, committee chair for Foreign Language in the Elementary School (FLES) for the American Association of Teachers of Spanish and Portuguese (AATSP), and an elected Executive Council member of ACTFL.

Glynis Cowell

Glynis Cowell is the Director of the Spanish Language Program in the Department of Romance Languages and Literatures and an Assistant Dean in Academic Advising, General College and Arts and Sciences, at The University of North Carolina at Chapel Hill. She has taught first-year seminars, honors courses, numerous Spanish language courses, and team-teaches a graduate course on the theories and techniques of teaching foreign languages. Dr. Cowell received her M.A. in Spanish Literature and her Ph.D. in Curriculum and Instruction, with a concentration in Foreign Language Education, from The University of North Carolina at Chapel Hill. Prior to joining the faculty at UNC-CH in August 1994, she coordinated the Spanish Language Program in the Department of Romance Studies at Duke University. She has also taught Spanish at Davidson Community College in North Carolina. At UNC-CH she has received the university Students' Award for Excellence in Undergraduate Teaching as well as the Graduate Student Mentor Award for the Department of Romance Languages and Literatures.

Dr. Cowell has directed teacher workshops on Spanish language and cultures and has presented papers and written articles on the teaching of language and literature, the incorporation of information technology in language teaching, and teaching across the curriculum. She is the co-author of two other college textbooks.

The Development Story

At the beginning of the 21st century, it was clear that things had changed in language classes all across the country. At most institutions, there were more students per classroom than ever before. There were more schools where language classes met three or fewer times per week than there were with classes meeting four or five times per week. More students were working than ever before: The American Council on Education reported that 78% of students worked while they were enrolled in college, and that the average time worked was nearly thirty hours a week. At the same time, research shows that language instructors were clearly trying to do a better job of exposing students to the target culture, to spend more time practicing communication skills, and to establish a balance of four-skills practice. In short, with less time and fewer resources on the one hand and a desire to broaden the scope of language study on the other, something had to give. But what?

In 2004, 2005, and 2006, the authors and their editors surveyed hundreds of Spanish instructors. This is what we learned:

- When asked about the grammatical scope and sequence, 85% of instructors said that the most important thing to them was to have a text that had realistic goals about what students could accomplish in one year.
- When asked about the basis they used for making text decisions, 77% said that the text should be "based on good pedagogical practices."
- When asked if they would like to slow down the pace of grammar instruction to allow more time for communicative practice and coverage of cultural topics, 74% said yes.
- When asked if they would like to spread the traditional grammar syllabus over four semesters of instruction, 65% said yes.

With this information in hand, we developed a plan for a textbook series and supplements package that would address these salient preferences issues. To refine the plan, we enlisted the help of hundreds of instructors at a wide variety of schools (their names are listed on the following page). They gave us feedback on the plan through online surveys and traditional manuscript reviews. They attended focus groups on their local campuses or in other locations. Nine instructors attended a two-day reviewer conference in New Orleans to help us make decisions on issues where consensus had not yet been reached. The scope and sequence, the chapter structure, the mystery story, the page design, even the cover and the title—all benefited greatly from the many valuable suggestions made by these instructors.

Along the way, we also consulted students. Some 359 of them gave us feedback on their preference for art styles.

The results are for you to judge, but of one thing we are sure: The entire development of ***¡Anda!*** was driven by instructors and students and dedicated to providing contemporary solutions for the needs of today's language students and teachers.

To the many instructors and coordinators who dedicated countless hours helping us understand their and their students' needs, we are grateful. You will see your comments and suggestions reflected throughout the text. Thanks to you all!

Faculty Reviewers

James Abraham, *Glendale Community College*
Martha Aguilar, *Bronx Community College*
Pilar Alcalde, *University of Memphis*
Renee Andrade, *Mount San Antonio College*
Rafael Arias, *Los Angeles Valley College*
Mary Jo Arns-Radaj, *Normandale Community College*
Andrea Bacorn, *Montgomery College*
Angela Bagues, *Shippensburg University*
Amanda Baron, *Southeast Community College*
Roberto Batista, *Valencia Community College, East Campus*
Robert Baum, *Arkansas State University*
Rosa Bird, *University of Central Oklahoma*
Beatrice Bongiorno, *Bellevue Community College*
Mary Boutiette, *North Hennepin Community College*
Patrick Brady, *Tidewater Community College*
Cathy Briggs, *North Lake College*
Greg Briscoe, *Utah Valley State College*
Elaine Brooks, *University of New Orleans*
Karen Brunschwig, *University of La Verne*
Elizabeth Buckley Sánchez, *University of Tulsa*
Linda Burk, *Manchester Community College–Manchester Connecticut*
Isabel Bustamante-López, *California Polytechnic State University at Pomona*
Ana Caldero, *Valencia Community College (West Campus)*
Lisa Calvin, *Indiana State University*
Paul Cankar, *Austin Community College*
Karen Cárdenas, *South Dakota State University*
Morris Carson, *J. Sargent Reynolds Community College*
June Carter, *University of South Carolina Spartanburg*
Samira Chater, *Valencia Community College, East Campus*
Carmen Chávez, *Florida Atlantic University*
Robert Chierico, *Chicago State University*
Maritza Chinea-Thornberry, *University of South Florida*
Carrie Clay, *Anderson University*
Carmen Coracides, *Scottsdale Community College*
Steve Corbett, *Texas Tech University*
Manuel Cortes Castañeda, *Eastern Kentucky University*
José A. Cortes-Caballero, *Georgia Perimeter College*
Xuchitl Coso, *Georgia Perimeter College/Lawrenceville*
Judith Costello, *Northern Arizona University*
Dale Crandall, *Gainesville College*
José Cruz, *Fayetteville Technical Community College*
Julio de la Llata, *Austin Community College*
Aída Díaz, *Valencia Community College*
Héctor Enríquez, *University of Texas, El Paso*
Luz Escobar, *Southeastern Louisiana University*
Janan Fallon, *Georgia Perimeter College*
Mary Fatora-Tumbaga, *Kauai Community College*
Carmen Ferrero, *Moravian College*
Estelle Finley, *Spelman College*
Luz Font, *Florida Community College at Jacksonville*
Elizabeth Fouts, *Saint Anselm College*
Carmen García, *Texas Southern University*
José Manuel García, *Florida Southern College*
Rodolfo García, *Metropolitan State College of Denver*
José M. García Sánchez, *Eastern Washington University*
José García-Sánchez, *Eastern Washington University*
Pamela Gill, *Gaston College*
John Gladstein, *Howard College*
Julie Glosson, *Union University*
Olympia González, *Loyola University*
Yolanda L. González, *Valencia Community College*
Roberta Gordenstein, *Elms College*
Sergio Guzmán, *Community College of Southern Nevada*
Peggy Haas, *Kent State University*
Terry Hansen, *Pellissippi State Technical Community College*
Mary Harges, *Southwest Missouri State University*
Ana Lucy Hernández, *William Rainey Harper College*
Yanina Hernández, *Texas Southern University*
Ann Hills, *University of La Verne*
Kristi Hislope, *North Georgia College & State University*
Michelle Horner Grau, *Christopher Newport University*
Alexis Indenbaum, *Reading Area Community College*
Luis Jiménez, *Florida Southern College*
Valerie Job, *South Plains College*
Dimitrios Karayiannis, *Southern Illinois University at Carbondale*
Jacoba Koene, *Anderson University*
Ruth Konopka, *Grossmont College*
David Korn, *Anderson College*
Marianna Kunow, *Southeastern Louisiana University*
Andrea Labinger, *University of La Verne*
Edwin Lamboy, *Montclair State University*
Felipe Antonio Lapuente, *The University of Memphis*
Rebecca Leigh, *Williams Coastal Carolina University*
Jorge O. López R., *University of Tennessee at Martin*
José López-Marrón, *Bronx Community College–CUNY*
Margaret Lyman, *Bakersfield College*
Domenico Maceri, *Allan Hancock College*
Carlos Madan, *SUNY Plattsburgh*
Anne-Marie Martin, *Portland Community College*
Janie McNutt, *South Plains College*
Joseph Menig, *Valencia Community College*
Sandra Merrill, *Central Missouri State University*
Silvia Milosevich, *Butte College*
Deborah Mistron, *Middle Tennessee State University*
Libardo Mitchell, *Portland Community College, Sylvania*
Joshua Mora, *Wayland Baptist University*
Daniel Nappo, *University of Tennessee at Martin*
William Nowak, *University of Houston–Downtown*
Marcela Ochoa-Shivapour, *Cornell College*
Cecilia Ojeda, *Northern Arizona University*
Milagros Ojermark, *Diablo Valley College*
Dale Omundson, *Anoka-Ramsey Community College*
Ann Ortiz, *Campbell University*
Ruth Owens, *Arkansas State University*
Hannah Padilla, *Normandale Community College*

Diane Parmeter, *Clinton Community College*
Edward Pasko, *Purdue University Calumet*
Peggy Patterson, *Rice University*
Inmaculada Pertusa, *Western Kentucky University*
Todd Phillips, *Austin Community College*
Mirta Pimentel, *Moravian College*
Joyce Pinkard, *Fresno City College*
Harriet Poole, *Lake City Community College*
Enrique Porrua, *University of North Carolina at Pembroke*
Comfort Pratt, *Texas Tech University*
Marcie Pratt, *Black Hills State University*
Cheryl Reagan, *Sussex County Community College*
Claire Reetz, *Florida Community College-Jacksonville*
Marilyn Reit, *Shasta Tehama Joint Comm. College*
Robert Rice, *Austin Community College*
John T. Riley, *Fordham University*
Jennifer Robertson, *Valencia Community College*
Karen Robinson, *University of Nebraska at Omaha*
Vicki Roman-Lagunas, *Northeastern Illinois University*
Ana Romero, *Arkansas State University*
Francisco Ronquillo, *Albuquerque–TVI*
Sandra Rosenstiel, *University of Dallas*
Cecil J. Roth, Jr., *Jamestown College*
Linda Roy, *Tarrant County College–South*
Cecilia Ryan, *McNeese State University*
Carmen Salazar, *Los Angeles Valley College*
Elizabeth Sánchez, *University of Tulsa*
Edgard Sankara, *LaGrange College*
Robert Shell, *Missouri Western State College*
Virginia Shen, *Chicago State University*
Gregory Shepherd, *William Paterson University*
Eugenia Simien, *Southeastern Louisiana University*
Roger Simpson, *Clemson University*
Victor Slesinger, *Palm Beach Community College (Central Campus)*
David A. Smallwood, *Southeast Missouri State University*
Anita Smith, *Pitt Community College*
Ruth Smith, *University of Louisiana at Monroe*
Oscar U. Somoza, *University of Denver*
Irena Stefanova, *Santa Clara University*
Melissa Stewart, *Western Kentucky University*
Stuart Stewart, *Southeastern Louisiana University*
Jonathan Stowers, *Salt Lake Community College-Redwood*
Michael Tallon, *University of the Incarnate Word*
Pam Taylor, *University of North Carolina–Greensboro*
Mercedes Thompson, *El Camino College*
Sue Ann Thompson, *Butler University*
Richard Tooke, *South Dakota State University*
Stephanie Traynor, *Widener University*
Rene Vacchio, *Austin Community College*
Irma Valdez, *Blinn College*
Salvador Valdivia, *Shasta College*
Gloria Vélez-Rendón, *Purdue University Calumet*
Kathy Vestal, *Rowan-Cabarrus Community College*
Olga Vilella, *St. Xavier University*
Carlos Villacís, *Houston Community College*
Francisco Vivar, *The University of Memphis*
Geoffrey Voght, *Eastern Michigan University*
Gloria F. Waldman, *York College–CUNY*
Chris Weimer, *Oklahoma State University at Stillwater*
Bruce Williams, *William Paterson University*
Helga Winkler, *Moorpark College*
Gloria Yampey-Jorg, *Houston Community College*
Francisco Zermeno, *Chabot College*
Theresa Zmurkewycz, *Saint Joseph's University*

Faculty Focus Groups

Claudia Acosta, *College of the Canyons*
Clementina R. Adams, *Clemson University*
Sara Aguirre, *Reedley College*
Karin Alfaro, *Northeastern Illinois University*
Carlos Arce, *Cerritos College*
Rafael Arias, *Los Angeles Valley College*
Norma A. Arizpe, *Blinn College*
Rosalind Arthur, *Georgia Perimeter College*
Letvia M. Arza, *Georgia Perimeter College*
Jennifer Austin, *Rutgers University–Newark*
Marisol Ballester, *Broward Community College–North*
Enrique Barquinero, *Florida Community College, Jacksonville*
Erika Barragán, *Tarrant County College–NE*
Roberto Batista, *Valencia Community College*
Paul Begin, *Pepperdine University*
Tracy Bishop, *Hofstra University*
Julián Bueno, *Southern Illinois University–Edwardsville*
Susan Byrne, *SUNY–Oneonta*
Froylán Cabuto, *Cerritos College*
Alejandro Cáceres, *Southern Illinois University, Carbondale*
Ana Caldero, *Valencia Community College*
Marla A. Calico, *Georgia Perimeter College*
José A. Caraballo, *Blinn College*
Beth B. Cardon, *Georgia Perimeter College*
Dinora Cardoso, *Pepperdine University*
Norma I. Carrero Román, *Blinn College*
Samira Chater, *Valencia Community College*
Carmen Chávez, *Florida Atlantic University*
Robert J. Chierico, *Chicago State University*
Kathy Chonez, *Southern Illinois University, Carbondale*
Alicia Class, *El Camino College*
Daria Cohen, *Rider University*
Mary Cooley Lorenzo, *Blinn College*
Al L. Cooper, *Pima Community College, East*
José A. Cortes, *Georgia Perimeter College*
Mayra Cortés-Torres, *Pima Community College, East*
Xuchitl N. Coso, *Georgia Perimeter College*
Darren Crasto, *Houston Community College*
Patricia Crespo-Martin, *Foothill College*
Ivana Cuvalo, *South Suburban College–Cook Co.*
Aleta Davis, *El Camino College*
Susann M. Davis, *Western Kentucky University*

Ana María de Barling, *West Valley College*
Elizabeth Dowdy, *Manatee Community College*
James P. Dowdy, *Manatee Community College*
Kyle Echols, *Florida Community College, Jacksonville*
Nilsa O. Ehresman, *Blinn College*
Rhonda Eisner, *Los Angeles Valley College*
Margaret Eomurian, *Houston Community College*
Nora Erro-Peralta, *Florida Atlantic University*
Dina Fabery, *Valencia Community College*
Janan Fallon, *Georgia Perimeter College*
Ronna Feit, *SUNY–Nassau Community College*
Marino Fernández, *Valencia Community College*
Ruth E. Fernández, *Broward Community College*
María Rosa Fernández de Bell, *Southern Illinois University, Carbondale*
Patricia Figueroa, *Pima Community College, East*
Luz Font, *Florida Community College, Jacksonville*
Tom Fonte, *El Camino College*
Deborah Foote, *Columbia College–Chicago*
María Elena Francés-Benítez, *Los Angeles Valley College*
Ronald A. García, *Nova Southeastern University*
Luisa García-Conde, *CUNY–Queensborough Community College*
Nereyda Garza-Lozano, *Fresno City College*
Eddy H. Gaytán, *Chicago State University*
John S. Geary, *Northeastern Illinois University*
Robert Geraldi, *Palm Beach Community College-Boca Raton*
Beatrice Giannandrea, *Valencia Community College*
Scott Gibby, *Austin Community College*
Yolanda L. González, *Valencia Community College*
Esther Greenstein, *Broward Community College*
Mercedes Guadalupe, *Valencia Community College*
Scott Harris, *Clemson University*
Hiltrud A. Heller, *El Camino College*
Librada Hernández, *Los Angeles Valley College*
Julio F. Hernando, *Indiana University-South Bend*
Ana M. Hnat, *Houston Community College*
Michael Horswell, *Florida Atlantic University*
Patricia Houston, *Pima Community College, East*
Dimitrios H. Karayiannis, *Southern Illinois University, Carbondale*
Caroline Kreide, *Merced College*
Todd Lakin, *City Colleges of Chicago–Richard J. Daley College*
Jeffrey N. Lamb, *Solano Community College*
Stephanie Langston, *Georgia Perimeter College*
Carlos A. Lebrón, *Northeastern Illinois University*
Sonia Lenk, *Western Kentucky University*
Susana Liso, *The University of Virginia at Wise*
Susan Lister, *De Anza College*
Eder F. Maestre, *Western Kentucky University*
April Marshall, *Pepperdine University*
Delmarie Martínez, *Nova Southeastern University*
Linda Martínez, *Chicago State University*
Renato Martínez, *Fresno City College*
Sergio Martínez, *San Antonio College*
Melissa McClennen-Davis, *Blinn College*
Natasha J. McClure, *Western Kentucky University*
Mary Yetta McKelva, *Grayson County College*
Nancy Membrez, *University of Texas at San Antonio*
Joseph A. Menig, *Valencia Community College*
Dora Cecilia Mezzich Kress, *Florida Community College, Jacksonville*
Iván Miño, *Tarrant County College–SE*
Natasa Momcilovic, *Southern Illinois University, Carbondale*
Mónica Montalvo, *Valencia Community College*
Lizette S. Moon, *Houston Community College*
RoseAnna Mueller, *Columbia College–Chicago*
Araceli Muñoz, *Chicago State University*
Sonia Navarro-Milano, *Valencia Community College*
Ofélia R. Nikolova, *Southern Illinois University, Carbondale*
Gustavo Obeso, *Western Kentucky University*
Milagros Ojermark, *Diablo Valley College*
Carmel O'Kane, *Northeastern Illinois University*
Elma Orozco-Félix, *Fresno City College*
José J. Osorio, *CUNY–Queensborough Community College*
Mercedes Palomino, *Florida Atlantic University*
Isaías Paz S., *Fresno City College*
Carolina Pérez, *El Camino College*
Inmaculada Pertusa, *Western Kentucky University*
Joyce P. Pinkard, *Fresno City College*
Ramona Rendón, *Florida Atlantic University*
Sheila Rivera, *Valencia Community College*
Patricio Rizzo-Vast, *Northeastern Illinois University*
Anthony Robb, *Rowan University*
Cathy A. Robison, *Clemson University*
María T. Rocha, *Houston Community College*
Mónica Rojas, *Clemson University*
Amalia Ruiz, *Florida Atlantic University*
Daniel L. Russo, Jr., *Pima Community College, East*
Carmen Salazar, *Los Angeles Valley College*
Elena Sánchez, *Florida Atlantic University*
Rafael Sánchez-Alonso, *The University of Southern Mississippi*
Rhoda Segur, *Blinn College*
Virginia Shen, *Chicago State University*
Roger K. Simpson, *Clemson University*
Victor E. Slesinger, *Palm Beach Community College–Central*
Maggie Smallwood, *Clemson University*
María Jiménez Smith, *Tarrant County College–NE*
Eva Solano, *Florida Community College, Jacksonville*
Marguerite Solari, *Oakton College*
Lidia C. Stahl, *Southern Illinois University, Carbondale*
Edward Stering, *City College of San Francisco*
Melissa A. Stewart, *Western Kentucky University*
Greg Taylor, *Southern Illinois University, Carbondale*
Silvina Trica-Flores, *Nassau Community College*
Cristóbal Trillo, *Joliet Junior College*
Irma O. Valdez, *Blinn College*
María Gladys Vallieres, *Villanova University*
Fernando Vidal, *Valencia Community College*

Carlos Villacís, *Houston Community College*
Lisa M. Volle, *Central Texas College*
Luz E. Wright, *Georgia Perimeter College*
Gloria Yampey-Jorg, *Houston Community College*

Student Reviewers

We asked students to give us comprehensive feedback on the art that is used in Spanish textbooks. A total of 359 students from the following 21 colleges and universities responded to questions about the kinds of art they like, what they dislike, and what they find useful for each of the major sections of the text (e.g., grammar, vocabulary, and culture). The results are what you see in ***¡Anda!***

Colleges and Universities

Citrus College
Clemson University
Coastal Carolina Community College
Florida Atlantic University
Florida Community College at Jacksonville
Georgia Perimeter College
Harper College
Rowan Cabarrus Community College
South Plains College
The University of North Carolina at Chapel Hill
The University of Texas at Austin
Tidewater Community College
University of Cincinnati
The University of California, Los Angeles
University of Evansville
University of Central Florida
University of Florida
University of Louisiana at Monroe
University of Nevada, Reno
University of Texas at El Paso
Western Kentucky University

Students

Brenna, Kacy Cunningham, Grace M. Lear, Elyse Magdule, Jay Jacobson, Katey Jayne, Jenny Russo, Tabitha Potter, Alex Luft, Manuel Hernandez, Kelly De Stefano, Griselda Luna, Shaun Davis, Lamore Hanchard, Tiffany Lumpkin, James Shelton, Ryan Furkin, Yonel Roche, Nicole Holman, Riley O'Connell, Zenyth Propst, Katie Tucker, Jason L. Seward, Carolyn Buck, Brian Dunne, Jessica Hatter, Samantha Williams, Mike Williams, Elizabeth Clary Jocys, Kellie Shanahan, Tiffany Mills , Kate Lepley, Tara Schmidt, Danielle King, Jared Anderson, Josh Beasley , Kelli Clements, John Ponce, Miso Jang, Casey Cowan, Amiee, Jesse Belcher, Michael Lynch, Tim Falconbury, Ryan Cremeans, Latonya Sholar, Christopher Campbell, Beard, Erik Belford, Ashley Skinner, Dylan Nielson, Michael Dickson, Tim Powers, Morgan Crosby, Saera Kim, Nathaniel Baker, Jade Wallace, Kristen Moore, Armando Delima, Traci Bird, Megan Guffee, Michelle, Erin Hunter, Lindsey Wheeler, Emmalyn Cochran, Julia Young, Crystal Washington, Trevor Seigler, Nick Johnson, Griselda Luna, Paul Loiodice, Kelly Dwight, Kristian Morales, Kristian Morales, Warren Giese, Lauren Johnson, Jacklyn Johns, Haneen Sayyad, Brittney Green, Randall Lee, Andy Robling, Ashley, Felicia Blackwood, Venessa Chandra, Jon Tuminski, Andrea Newsome, Jessica Collins, Thomas Russell, Everet Macias, Carrie Gray, Tamara Clarke, Sarah Harrington, Susie, Grace Aaron, Shelley Lewis, Margie, Haley, Joseph Fisher, Kelley Daoust, Rebecca Brown, Eric Dean, Anna Woodlock, Audrey Clark, Travis Greene, Emily Schultz, Jessica D. Taylor, Douglas Glenn, Ashley Pate, Anna Browning, Melisa Gonzales, Kara Murphy, Natalie Hood-Kramer, Jessica Johnson, Jayson Vignola, Gretchen Pegram, Tanya Aboul-Hosn, Brittney Martin, Matt Harlow, Leah Gibson, Leah Gibson, Clint Darter, Nkechinyere Nwoko, John H. Gagnon, Bernadette, Rachel, Larry James Reeder II, Ny'Sheria Sims, Nicholas Robino, Deanna Caniff, Michael Baker, Elizabeth Morgan, Brooke Swinson, Ian King, Seaqn Kaye, Mekisha F. Smith, David Hahn, Susan, Keri Britcher, Jean Henn, Bonnie Swift, Lisa Carrizales, Cori, April Michaud, Gailen Field, Stephanie Hoock, Nicole Rivera, Kristin Durant, Maria Melanie Meyer, Mallory Erford, Chris Banks, Sam Srour, Kate Glover, Madison Dunn, Jillian Murphy, Jose Quintanilla, Stephanie Lenk, Matthew Hoag, Femi, Laura Anderson, Jared Zirkle, Laura Yoder, Genna Offerman, Leigh Cash, Amy Creighton, Susannah Federowicz, Candice Mccarty, Mary Beth Whitmire, Annie Quach, Robert Burnside, Bryttne Lowden, Emily Hankinson, Sarah Gerald, Sarah Baber, Lawrence Lander, Amanda Carrington, Mariah Jimenez, Jordana Fyne, Thomas Giannini, Pamela Okeke, Dominique Brown, John Norton, Patrick S. Lockett, Jill Meinrath, Jenny Seifert, Jennifer Pritchett, Christine Reppa, Joshua Gorney, Vishal, Joseph Marker, June Clark, Jenny Forwark, Tara Hush, Whitney Schlotman, Daniel Zainfeld, Matthew Cross, Katiria Robles, Magdalena J. Semrau, Neal Ward, Barry Lacina, Katie K, Shawntavia Smith, Kati Payne, Brian Carter, Deanne Grantham, Sarah Hendrix, Kira Seward, Christin Huether, Chelsea Harp, Meaghan Jones, Rachel Blakely, Nicholas Emerick, Ramiro Tey, Rebecca Adams, Danielle King, Martina Blatterspiel, Greg Longstreth, Sarah Longtin, Jessica Torres, Sarah, Kimberly Deuble, Rachel Hopkins, Sara Tapia, Katherine Chudy, Sarah Kopp, Carmen Gilbert, Lynn Greco, Jen Robinson, Laura Busch, Mandie K. Rios, Sean Santoscoy-Mckillip, Lindsay Dewitt, Raquel Krauss, John Stroud, Stephanie Humphrey, Elaine Ellis, Carrie Ziegenmeyer, Bryan J Sykes, Tracy Delzeith, Matt Cherry, Yadira Anglin, Filipp Lassman, Lauren Barker, Terrilyon, Angela Schuch,

Betsy Ortiz, Heinz Landeck, Nash T. Bermudez, Curt Neichter, Arielle Goldberg, Kelli Walker, Yeong Oh, Brandon Cody Goehring, Jessica Irving, Alfonso Ontiveros, Jessica Davis, Marcus Donahue, Ashley Moeller, Kyle Milos, Toni Mcnair, Candace Lau, Jenifer, Jenessa Cottrell, Jessica Pollock, Ronni Rancich, Charla Mcdaniel, Laura Scullin, David Emery, Alex Montgomery, Kelly Mccafferty, Michael Lara, Angela Sehon, Alleene Strickland, Erika Maldeney, Jessica Elizondo, Jason Boone, Kellen Voss, Jessica Elley, Sara Bochiardy, Stephen Hopper, Garrett George, Mistoria Brown, Ian Singer, Christine Yau, Victoria Ng, Racquel Rolle, Jeremy Jacob, Matthew Korte, Josh Duran

Teacher Annotations

The teacher annotations in ***¡Anda! Curso elemental*** fall into several categories:

- **Methodology:** A deep and broad set of methods notes designed for the novice instructor.
- **Section Goals:** Set of student objectives for each section.
- **National Standards:** Information containing the correlation between each section with the National Standards as well as tips for increasing student performance.
- **Warm-up:** Suggestions for setting up an activity or how to activate students' prior knowledge relating to the task at hand.
- **Suggestion:** Teaching tips that provide ideas that will help with the implementation of activities and sections.
- **Note:** Additional information that instructors may wish to share with students beyond what is presented in the text.
- **Expansion:** Ideas for variations of a topic that may serve as wrap-up activities.
- **Cultural Background:** Information on people, places, and things that aid in the completion of activities and sections by providing background knowledge.
- **Additional Activity:** Independent activities related to the ones in the text that provide further practice than those supplied in the text.
- **Alternate Activity:** Variations of activities provided to suit each individual classroom and preferences.
- **Heritage Language Learners:** Suggestions for the Heritage language learners in the classroom that provide alternatives and expansions for sections and activities based on prior knowledge and skills.
- **Recap of *Ambiciones siniestras:*** A synopsis of the both the *Lectura* and *Video* sections for each episode of *Ambiciones siniestras.*

A guide to instructor icons

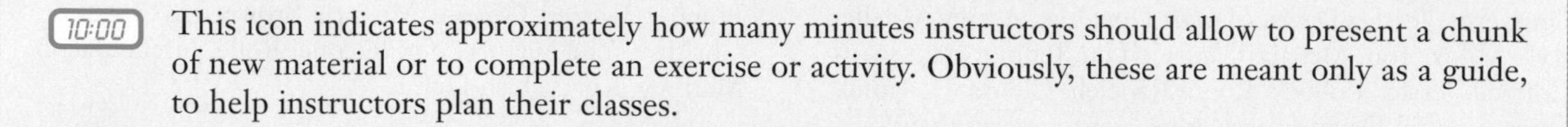

This icon indicates approximately how many minutes instructors should allow to present a chunk of new material or to complete an exercise or activity. Obviously, these are meant only as a guide, to help instructors plan their classes.

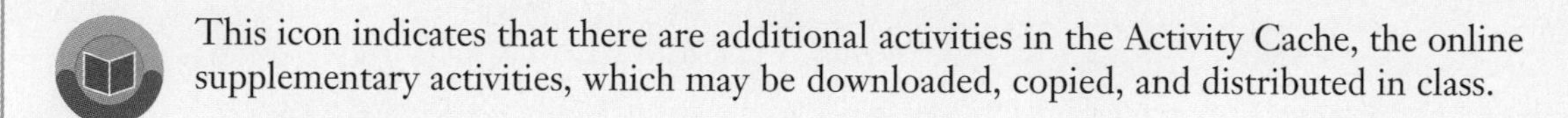

This icon indicates that there are additional activities in the Activity Cache, the online supplementary activities, which may be downloaded, copied, and distributed in class.

This icon indicates that there is a PowerPoint presentation available on the topic under discussion.

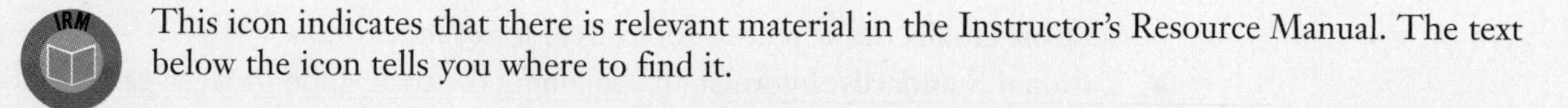

This icon indicates that there is relevant material in the Instructor's Resource Manual. The text below the icon tells you where to find it.

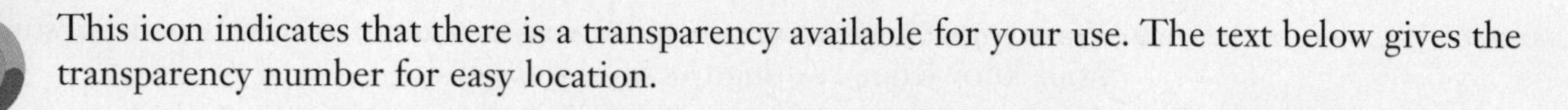

This icon indicates that there is a transparency available for your use. The text below gives the transparency number for easy location.

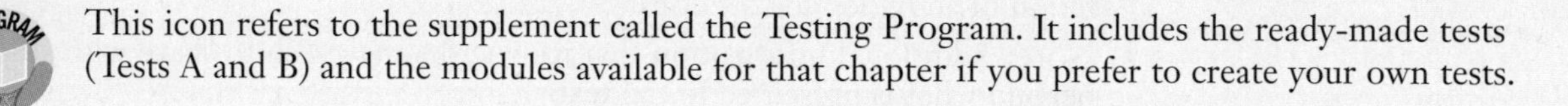

This icon refers to the supplement called the Testing Program. It includes the ready-made tests (Tests A and B) and the modules available for that chapter if you prefer to create your own tests.

ACKNOWLEDGMENTS

The first edition of ***¡Anda! Curso elemental*** is the result of careful planning between ourselves and our publisher and ongoing collaboration with students and you, our colleagues. We look forward to continuing this dialogue and sincerely appreciate your input. We owe special thanks to the many members of the Spanish-teaching community whose comments and suggestions helped shape the pages of every chapter—you will see yourselves everywhere. We gratefully acknowledge and thank in particular our reviewers for this first edition.

We are especially grateful to those who have collaborated with us in the writing of ***¡Anda!*** In addition to contributors such as Jean LeLoup, María del Carmen Caña Jiménez, and Sonia Torres-Quiñones, there are others whom we wish to recognize and thank.

We thank Josefa Lindquist for her work on the *También se dicé…* appendix. We also thank Taryn Ferch for bringing her experience and contributing to the instructor annotations, as well as to both Taryn and Douglas Jensen for writing some of the student notes. We owe many thanks to Megan Echevarría for her superb work on the Student Activities Manual. Thank you also to Sharon D. Robinson for the Service Learning and Experiential Learning Activities and to Dolores Durán-Cerda for the Heritage language learners materials. Special thanks are also due to Luz Font, Cheryl McDonough, Patrick Brady, and María Mónica Montalvo for all of their work on the Testing Program, to Patricia Moore-Martínez for writing many of the activities in the Electronic Activities Cache, to Ignacio Pérez-Ibáñez for his work on the Instructor's Resource Manual, and to Virginia Shen for the Sample Syllabi and Lesson Plans. Additional thanks to the many talented contributors for the development of the web site materials to accompany the first edition.

All of the previously mentioned contributors have played an important part in this program, but equally important are the contributions of the highly talented individuals at Pearson Prentice Hall. We wish to express our gratitude and deep appreciation to the many people at Prentice Hall who contributed their ideas, tireless efforts, and publishing experience to the first edition of ***¡Anda! Curso elemental.*** First of all, a very special thank you to Bob Hemmer, Executive Editor, who has guided and supported us through every aspect of this exciting project. His intelligence, talent, and complete commitment to ***¡Anda!*** have helped us to realize our vision. Additionally, we are especially indebted to Janet García-Levitas, our Development Editor, for all of her hard work, suggestions, attention to detail, and dedication to the text. Her tireless efforts, support, and cheerful spirit helped us to achieve the final product we had envisioned.

Special thanks are due to Samantha Alducin, Senior Media Editor, for helping us produce such a superb video and for managing the creation of ***¡Anda!*** materials for MySpanishLab™ and the Companion Website. Thanks also to a/t Media Productions for their work on *Ambiciones siniestras.* We would also like to thank Melissa Marolla Brown, Development Editor for Assessment, for the diligent coordination between the text, Student Activities Manual, and Testing Program; and Meriel Martínez, Media Editor, and Jenn Murphy, Assistant Development Editor, for their efficient and meticulous work in managing the preparation of the other supplements. Thanks to Debbie King, Assistant Development Editor, and Katie Spiegel, Editorial Assistant, for their hard work and efficiency in obtaining reviews and attending to many administrative details.

We are very grateful to Kristine Suárez, Director of Marketing, who led the market development efforts for ***¡Anda!*** Her terrific work helped to connect us to the needs of students and instructors. Thanks too to Denise Miller, Senior Marketing Manager, and Bill Bliss, Marketing Coordinator, for their creativity and efforts in coordinating all marketing and promotion for this first edition. Many thanks are also due to Nancy Stevenson, Senior Production Editor, who guided ***¡Anda!*** through the many stages of production; to our Art Managers, Maria Piper and Gail Cocker-Bogusz; and to Siren Design for the creative reproductions of realia. We are particularly indebted to Andrew Lange and Eric Larsen for the amazing illustrations that translate our vision. All students will enjoy their artwork as they learn. Thanks to Lisa Delgado for her gorgeous interior and cover designs. We thank our partners at Black Dot Group for their careful and professional editing and production services.

We would like to sincerely thank Phil Miller, Publisher; Julia Caballero, Director of Editorial Development; Mary Rottino, Senior Managing Editor; and Janice Stangel, Associate Managing Editor; for their support and commitment to the success of ***¡Anda!*** We are also very grateful to Glenn and Meg Turner of Burrston House for the special care and attention they gave our project during the development stage.

We also thank our colleagues and students from across the country who inspire us and from whom we learn.

And finally, our love and deepest appreciation to our families for all of their support during this journey: David; John, Jack, and Kate.

Audrey L. Heining-Boynton

Glynis S. Cowell

A Walking Tour

¡Hola!
¡Bienvenidos!

I'm Audrey Heining-Boynton

We are the authors of **¡ANDA!** and we were thinking that when you visit a new place, one of the best ways to get to know your new environment quickly is to consult your guidebook before you take the trip! We thought it would be a good idea for you to join us on a "walking tour" of your new Spanish textbook and supplementary materials because we know from experience that language texts have a unique organization that is different from other textbooks... They use terminology that you might not be familiar with, and lots of the material is written in the language you don't know yet. So let's get on with the tour!

and I'm Glynis Cowell

Here it is!

The doorway to ¡ANDA! What does the cover tell you about what you'll find inside? No, it's not a spring break brochure to a Spanish-speaking country!

Think about it.

Check out the "map" of your book!

Scope and Sequence. You can think of the Scope and Sequence as the roadmap of the book. The scope tells you what is covered, and the sequence shows you the order of those topics. In other words, the Scope and Sequence tells you where everything is! It's a very useful tool for navigating **¡Anda!**

Semester 1
Preliminary A
This chapter gets you up and running quickly. You will learn many easy-to-learn words that will allow you to begin speaking in Spanish very quickly. You should feel good about how much Spanish you can use after studying the preliminary chapter.

Chapters 1–5
These are the main textbook chapters. Each chapter has an overall theme—like food, for example—and teaches you the words to use (vocabulary) and how to put them together in a sentence (grammar) so that you can talk about that subject. You'll also focus on the four skills (speaking, listening, reading, and writing) as well as culture.

Semester 2
Preliminary B
This chapter reviews the basic vocabulary and grammar from the first half of the book. Maybe you need this; maybe you don't. Maybe you are joining this class from another school or from high school and you need a little refresher. That's what this chapter is for!

Chapters 7–11
These are typical chapters, just like Chapters 1–5 above.

SCOPE AND SEQUENCE • SCOPE AND SEQUENCE • SCOPE AND SEQUENCE • SCOPE AND S

(The numbers next to the grammar and vocabulary sections indicate their location within the chapter.)

FIRST

	Capítulo Preliminar A Para empezar	Capítulo 1 ¿Quiénes somos?	Capítulo 2 La vida universitaria
Vocabulary sections	1 Saludos, despedidas y presentaciones 2 Expresiones útiles para la clase 4 Los cognados 7 Los adjetivos de nacionalidad 8 Los números 0–30 9 La hora 10 Los días, los meses y las estaciones 11 El tiempo	1 La familia 6 Gente 9 Los números 31–100	1 Las materias y las especialidades 2 La sala de clase 5 Los números 100–1.000 6 En la universidad 8 Emociones y estados 10 Los deportes y los pasatiempos
Grammar sections	3 El alfabeto 5 Los pronombres personales 6 El verbo **ser** 12 **Gustar**	2 El verbo **tener** 3 El singular y el plural 4 El masculino y el femenino 5 Los artículos definidos e indefinidos 7 Los adjetivos posesivos 8 Los adjetivos descriptivos	3 Presente indicativo de verbos regulares 4 La formación de preguntas y las palabras interrogativas 7 El verbo **estar** 9 El verbo **gustar**

SCOPE AND SEQUENCE • SCOPE AND SEQUENCE • SCOPE AND SEQUENCE • SCOPE AND SEQ

(The numbers next to the grammar and vocabulary sections indicate their location within the chapter.)

SECOND

	Capítulo Preliminar B Introducciones y repasos	Capítulo 7 ¡A comer!	Capítulo 8 ¿Qué te pones?
Vocabulary sections	**Capítulo Preliminar A** **Capítulo 1** **Capítulo 2** **Capítulo 3** **Capítulo 4** **Capítulo 5**	1 La comida 4 La preparación de las comidas 6 En el restaurante	1 La ropa
Grammar sections		2 Repaso del complemento directo 3 El pretérito 5 Unos verbos irregulares en el pretérito	2 Los pronombres de complemento indirecto 3 **Gustar** y verbos como **gustar** 4 Los pronombres de complemento directo e indirecto usados juntos

Chapter 6

We call this a recycling chapter. This means that you will be given the opportunity to reuse everything that you learned from Preliminary A through Chapter 5. No new information is presented in this chapter so that you can get some time to practice and internalize Spanish. It also helps you prepare for the final exam!

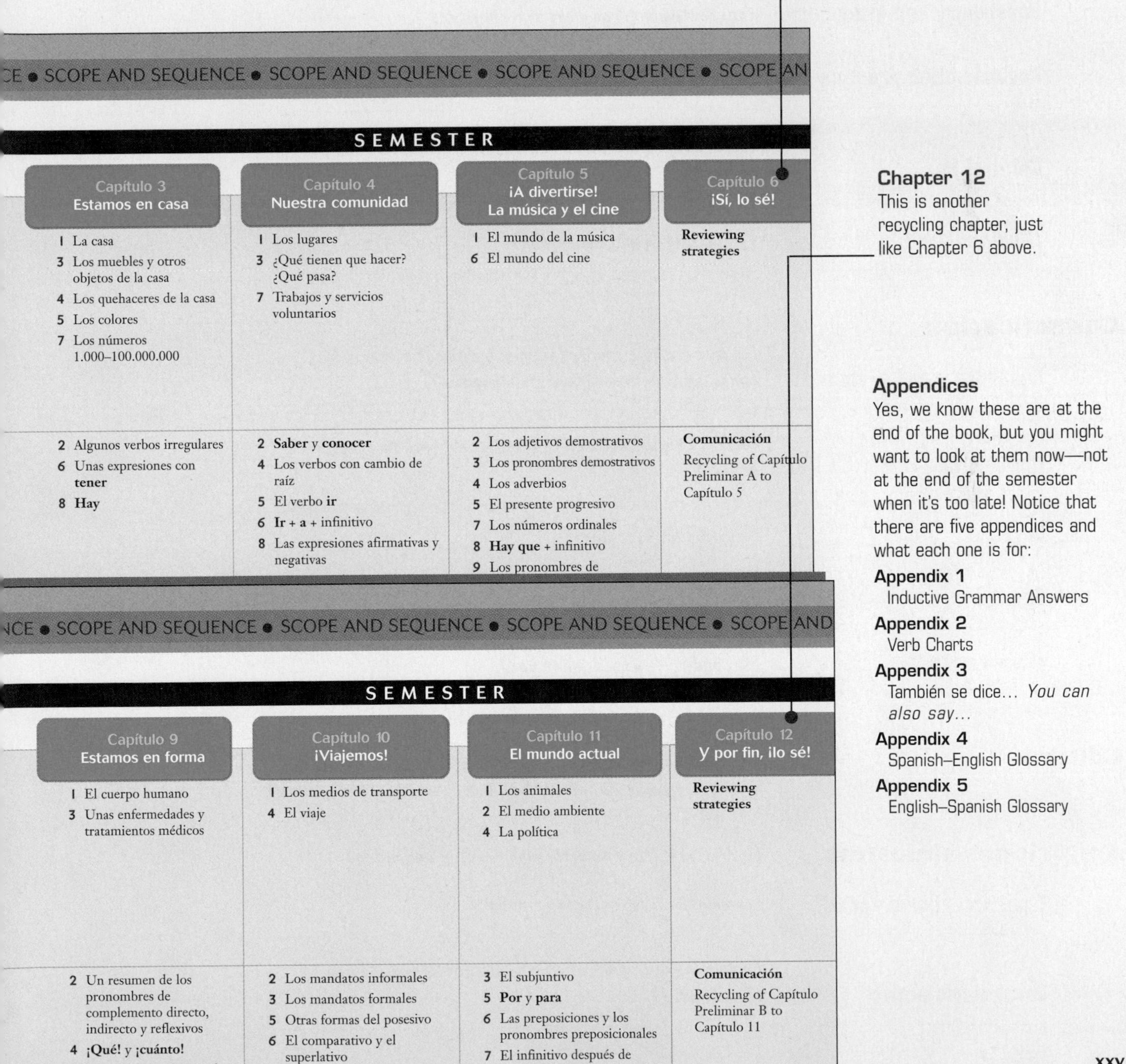

CE • SCOPE AND SEQUENCE • SCOPE AND SEQUENCE • SCOPE AND SEQUENCE • SCOPE AN

SEMESTER

Capítulo 3 Estamos en casa	Capítulo 4 Nuestra comunidad	Capítulo 5 ¡A divertirse! La música y el cine	Capítulo 6 ¡Sí, lo sé!
1 La casa 3 Los muebles y otros objetos de la casa 4 Los quehaceres de la casa 5 Los colores 7 Los números 1.000–100.000.000	1 Los lugares 3 ¿Qué tienen que hacer? ¿Qué pasa? 7 Trabajos y servicios voluntarios	1 El mundo de la música 6 El mundo del cine	**Reviewing strategies**
2 Algunos verbos irregulares 6 Unas expresiones con **tener** 8 **Hay**	2 **Saber** y **conocer** 4 Los verbos con cambio de raíz 5 El verbo **ir** 6 **Ir** + **a** + infinitivo 8 Las expresiones afirmativas y negativas	2 Los adjetivos demostrativos 3 Los pronombres demostrativos 4 Los adverbios 5 El presente progresivo 7 Los números ordinales 8 **Hay que** + infinitivo 9 Los pronombres de	**Comunicación** Recycling of Capítulo Preliminar A to Capítulo 5

NCE • SCOPE AND SEQUENCE • SCOPE AND SEQUENCE • SCOPE AND SEQUENCE • SCOPE AND

SEMESTER

Capítulo 9 Estamos en forma	Capítulo 10 ¡Viajemos!	Capítulo 11 El mundo actual	Capítulo 12 Y por fin, ¡lo sé!
1 El cuerpo humano 3 Unas enfermedades y tratamientos médicos	1 Los medios de transporte 4 El viaje	1 Los animales 2 El medio ambiente 4 La política	**Reviewing strategies**
2 Un resumen de los pronombres de complemento directo, indirecto y reflexivos 4 **¡Qué!** y **¡cuánto!** 5 El pretérito y el imperfecto 6 Expresiones con **hacer**	2 Los mandatos informales 3 Los mandatos formales 5 Otras formas del posesivo 6 El comparativo y el superlativo	3 El subjuntivo 5 **Por** y **para** 6 Las preposiciones y los pronombres preposicionales 7 El infinitivo después de preposiciones	**Comunicación** Recycling of Capítulo Preliminar B to Capítulo 11

Chapter 12

This is another recycling chapter, just like Chapter 6 above.

Appendices

Yes, we know these are at the end of the book, but you might want to look at them now—not at the end of the semester when it's too late! Notice that there are five appendices and what each one is for:

Appendix 1
Inductive Grammar Answers

Appendix 2
Verb Charts

Appendix 3
También se dice... *You can also say...*

Appendix 4
Spanish–English Glossary

Appendix 5
English–Spanish Glossary

Organization of a chapter

Have you ever used a Spanish textbook before? Do you know what each section is about? Do you know what you're being asked to read, memorize, practice, and why? Here's an outline of a typical chapter in **¡ANDA!**, followed by some actual chapter sections so that you can see what they look like. And we couldn't resist... we made lots of notes for you!

Comunicación

Vocabulary and grammar	*(in manageable chunks, as needed, each numbered consecutively throughout the chapter)*
Pronunciation practice	*(after first vocabulary list)*
Cultural box	*(brief, contextualized readings, relevant to chapter theme)*
¿Cómo andas?	*(first self-assessment box)*

Comunicación

Vocabulary and grammar	*(in manageable chunks, as needed, each numbered consecutively throughout the chapter)*
Cultural box	*(brief, contextualized readings, relevant to chapter theme)*
Escucha	*(a focus on listening)*
Escribe	*(a focus on writing)*
¿Cómo andas?	*(second self-assessment box)*

Cultura

(a focus on one or more Spanish-speaking countries—what the people do, what they make, and how they think)

Ambiciones siniestras

(a mystery story told through reading and video)

Y por fin, ¿cómo andas?	*(cumulative self-assessment box)*
Vocabulario activo	*(a two-page list of all of the essential vocabulary of the chapter)*

Chapter opener

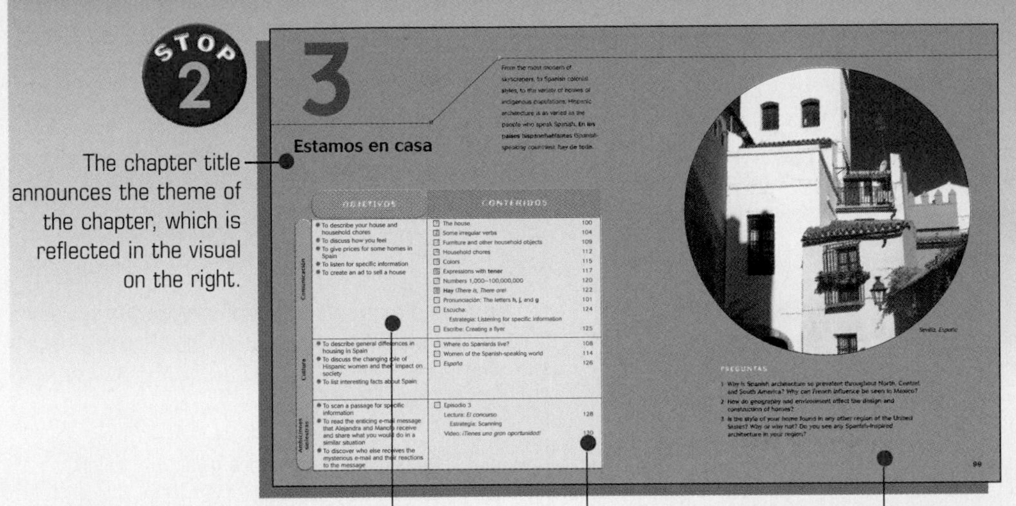

The chapter title announces the theme of the chapter, which is reflected in the visual on the right.

The questions are designed to get you to think about the topic for the chapter—not to get you to search for THE right answer. Bringing the topic to the forefront of your mind will help you make educated guesses about the meaning of Spanish words. Remember the topic as you work your way through the chapter.

There is a list of goals for the communication, culture, and mystery story sections under *Objetivos*. Notice how the goals relate to the chapter theme!

The content related to the goals is listed under *Contenidos*, with page numbers. It's in English so that you can understand it clearly!

Comunicación

Comunicación is divided into manageable chunks of what you need to learn: vocabulary (the words you need) and grammar (the structures that you use to put the words together). Vocabulary and grammar are two of the most important tools for communication! By the way, we didn't invent this—research indicates that the best presentation of language separates vocabulary and grammar for a manageable progression especially when combined with recycling and reintroduction of previously studied material—more on that later.

Communicative goals are listed for each *Comunicación* section.

The vocabulary sections are numbered consecutively throughout the chapter.

The vocabulary chunks introduce new vocabulary through art.

A lot of the vocabulary is presented without translations so that you can try to figure out the meaning of the Spanish word.

Vocabulary lists with translations are given for those words that are hard to illustrate and, therefore, hard for you to guess the meanings.

Pronunciación indicates the right way to make the sounds of the language. Pronunciation practice and activities, with new and recycled vocabulary, follow the first vocabulary chunk.

Vocabulary activities immediately follow each vocabulary presentation.

Grammar

The grammar sections introduce new grammar concepts.

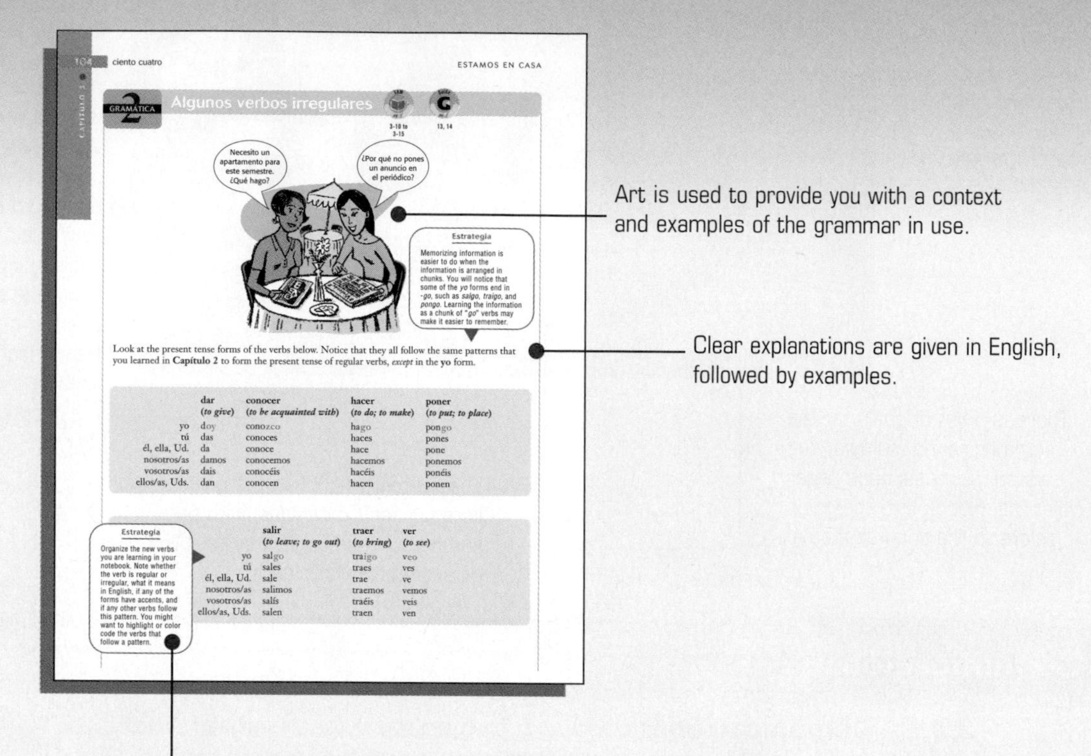

104 ciento cuatro ESTAMOS EN CASA

CAPÍTULO 3

GRAMÁTICA 2 Algunos verbos irregulares

3-10 to 3-15 13, 14

Estrategia

Memorizing information is easier to do when the information is arranged in chunks. You will notice that some of the *yo* forms end in *-go*, such as *salgo*, *traigo*, and *pongo*. Learning the information as a chunk of "*go*" verbs may make it easier to remember.

Look at the present tense forms of the verbs below. Notice that they all follow the same patterns that you learned in **Capítulo 2** to form the present tense of regular verbs, *except* in the **yo** form.

	dar (*to give*)	**conocer** (*to be acquainted with*)	**hacer** (*to do; to make*)	**poner** (*to put; to place*)
yo	doy	conozco	hago	pongo
tú	das	conoces	haces	pones
él, ella, Ud.	da	conoce	hace	pone
nosotros/as	damos	conocemos	hacemos	ponemos
vosotros/as	dais	conocéis	hacéis	ponéis
ellos/as, Uds.	dan	conocen	hacen	ponen

	salir (*to leave; to go out*)	**traer** (*to bring*)	**ver** (*to see*)
yo	salgo	traigo	veo
tú	sales	traes	ves
él, ella, Ud.	sale	trae	ve
nosotros/as	salimos	traemos	vemos
vosotros/as	salís	traéis	veis
ellos/as, Uds.	salen	traen	ven

Estrategia

Organize the new verbs you are learning in your notebook. Note whether the verb is regular or irregular, what it means in English, if any of the forms have accents, and if any other verbs follow this pattern. You might want to highlight or color code the verbs that follow a pattern.

Art is used to provide you with a context and examples of the grammar in use.

Clear explanations are given in English, followed by examples.

Student notes help you with your learning. They provide additional background information, interesting facts, and strategies that help you learn!

Icons indicate when to work in pairs or groups, and also refer you to other resources (e.g., CD tracks for audio, corresponding activity numbers in the Student Activities Manual) when you need them.

Recycling boxes also point out when we have deliberately reused materials from a previous chapter—or from earlier in the same chapter—to help you build upon what you have already studied. Page references are provided so that you can return to that section of the book if you need and/or want to.

You'll find a blend of activities that practice individual words and verb forms, as well as activities in which you focus on putting everything together to use the language for purposes of communication.

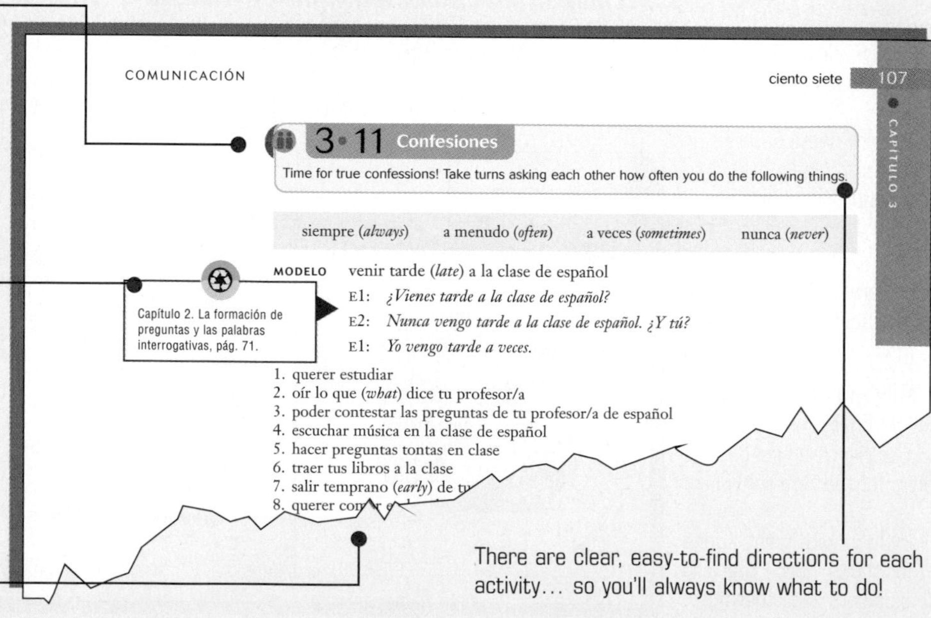

COMUNICACIÓN ciento siete 107

CAPÍTULO 3

3-11 Confesiones

Time for true confessions! Take turns asking each other how often you do the following things.

siempre (*always*) a menudo (*often*) a veces (*sometimes*) nunca (*never*)

Capítulo 2. La formación de preguntas y las palabras interrogativas, pág. 71.

MODELO venir tarde (*late*) a la clase de español
E1: *¿Vienes tarde a la clase de español?*
E2: *Nunca vengo tarde a la clase de español. ¿Y tú?*
E1: *Yo vengo tarde a veces.*

1. querer estudiar
2. oír lo que (*what*) dice tu profesor/a
3. poder contestar las preguntas de tu profesor/a de español
4. escuchar música en la clase de español
5. hacer preguntas tontas en clase
6. traer tus libros a la clase
7. salir temprano (*early*) de tu
8. querer com

There are clear, easy-to-find directions for each activity... so you'll always know what to do!

Listening, writing, and self-assessment

The second **Comunicación** provides listening comprehension **(Escucha)** and writing activities **(Escribe)** prior to the self-assessment check **(¿Cómo andas?)**.

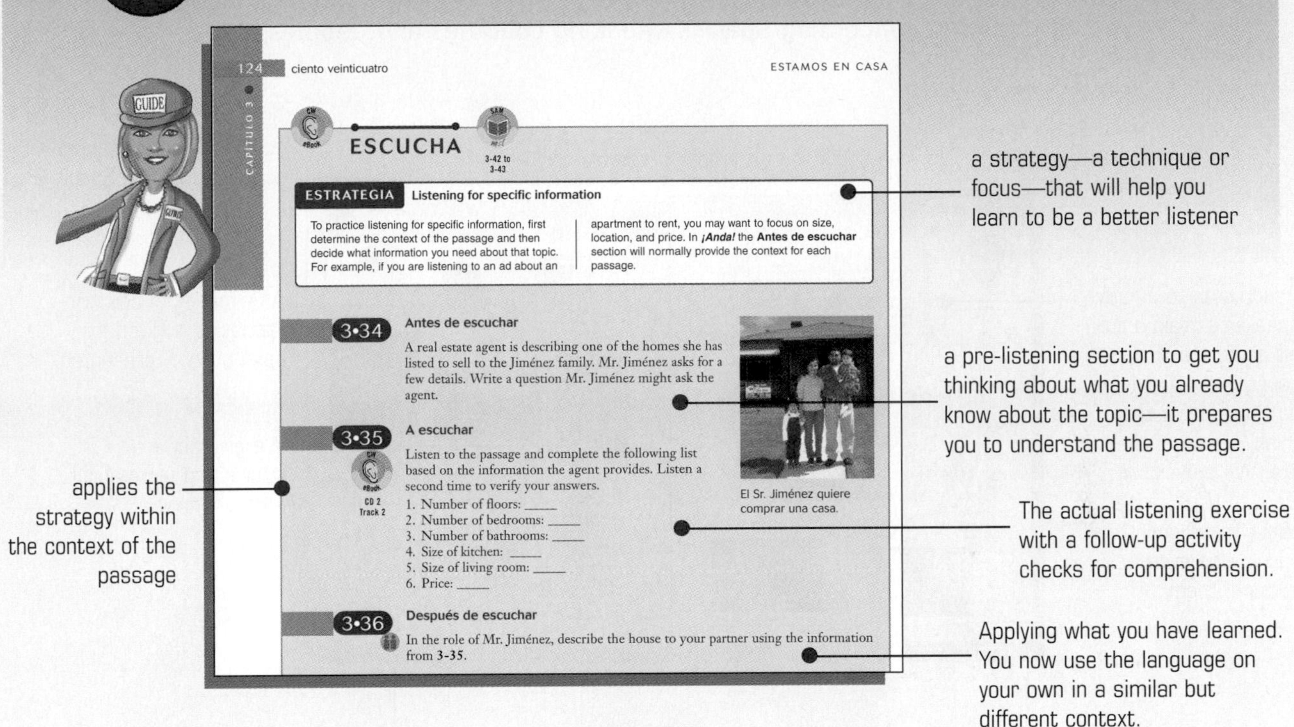

a strategy—a technique or focus—that will help you learn to be a better listener

a pre-listening section to get you thinking about what you already know about the topic—it prepares you to understand the passage.

applies the strategy within the context of the passage

The actual listening exercise with a follow-up activity checks for comprehension.

Applying what you have learned. You now use the language on your own in a similar but different context.

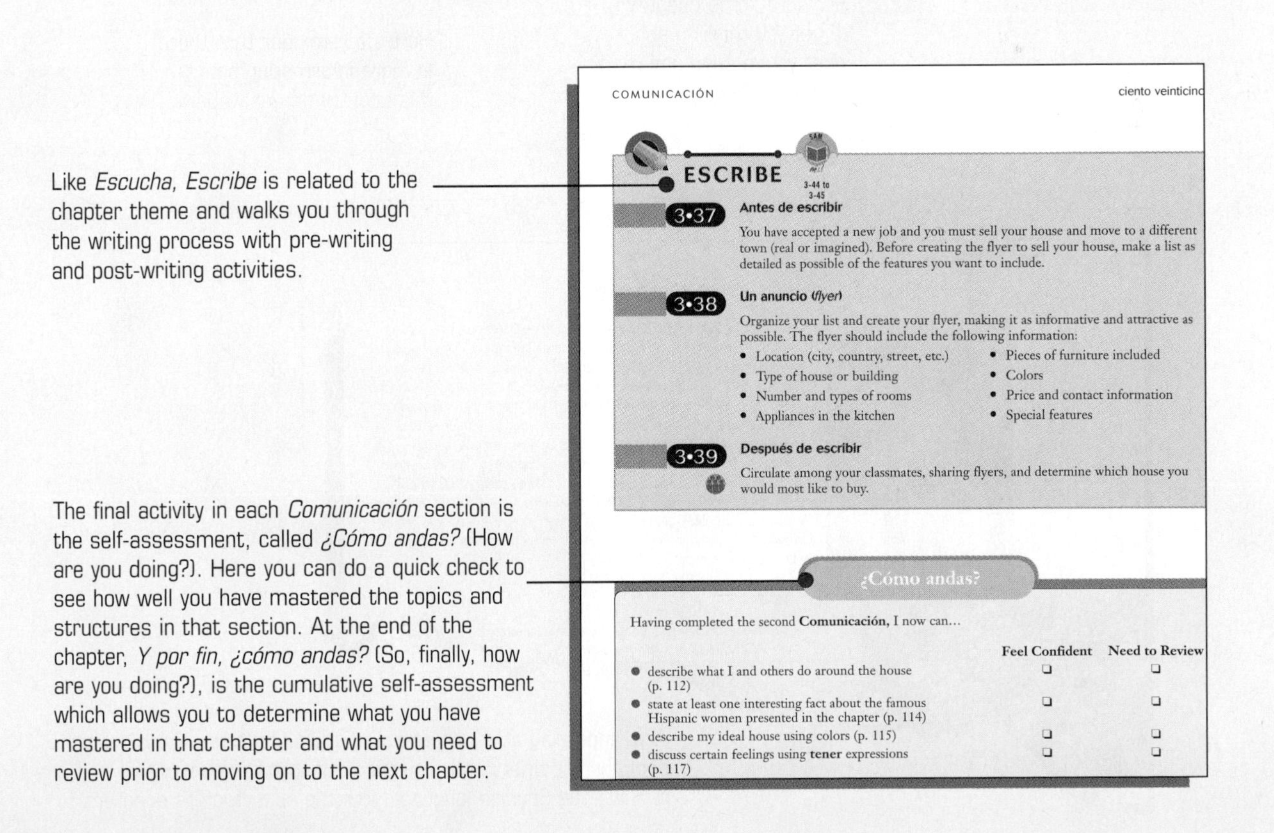

Like *Escucha, Escribe* is related to the chapter theme and walks you through the writing process with pre-writing and post-writing activities.

The final activity in each *Comunicación* section is the self-assessment, called *¿Cómo andas?* (How are you doing?). Here you can do a quick check to see how well you have mastered the topics and structures in that section. At the end of the chapter, *Y por fin, ¿cómo andas?* (So, finally, how are you doing?), is the cumulative self-assessment which allows you to determine what you have mastered in that chapter and what you need to review prior to moving on to the next chapter.

Time for a break to grab a cup of **café con leche**?

Between the second **Comunicación** and **Ambiciones siniestras** (the ongoing mystery story) is **Cultura**, designed to provide key facts and high interest information concerning Spanish-speaking countries and peoples.

A map gives you an idea about the geography of the country.

You'll find lots of photos with short captions in Spanish.

Read/listen to a native speaker explain a little bit about his or her country. . . what folks do there, what they think, and what they like. We hope you'll want to learn more about these countries and maybe even visit some of them.

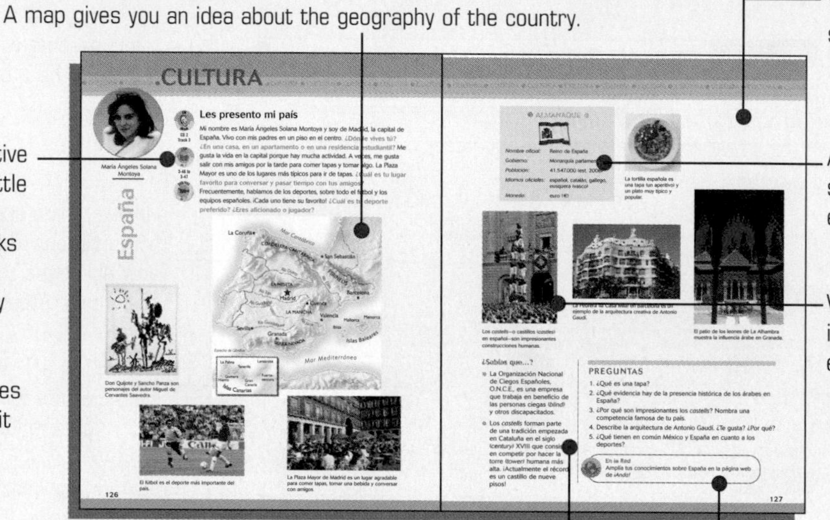

An almanac of country statistics is given for each country presented.

We give some interesting facts about each country.

Here are some questions to get you thinking about what you've seen and read.

Here's a reminder that there is more information about this country on our website.

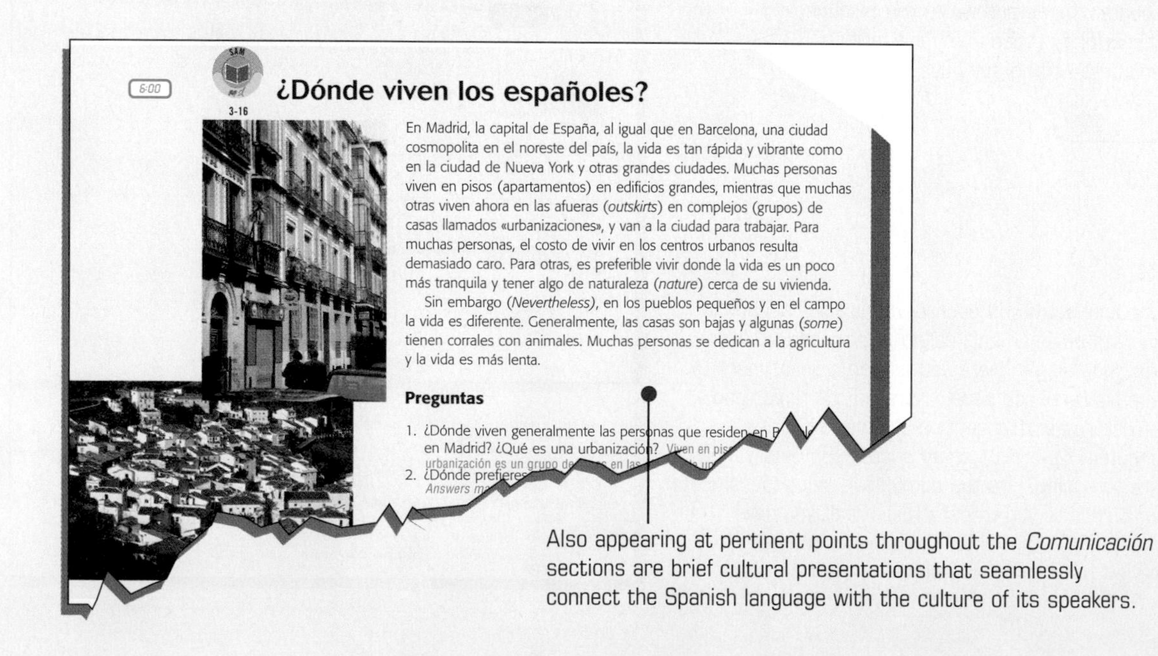

¿Dónde viven los españoles?

En Madrid, la capital de España, al igual que en Barcelona, una ciudad cosmopolita en el noreste del país, la vida es tan rápida y vibrante como en la ciudad de Nueva York y otras grandes ciudades. Muchas personas viven en pisos (apartamentos) en edificios grandes, mientras que muchas otras viven ahora en las afueras (*outskirts*) en complejos (grupos) de casas llamados «urbanizaciones», y van a la ciudad para trabajar. Para muchas personas, el costo de vivir en los centros urbanos resulta demasiado caro. Para otras, es preferible vivir donde la vida es un poco más tranquila y tener algo de naturaleza (*nature*) cerca de su vivienda.

Sin embargo (*Nevertheless*), en los pueblos pequeños y en el campo la vida es diferente. Generalmente, las casas son bajas y algunas (*some*) tienen corrales con animales. Muchas personas se dedican a la agricultura y la vida es más lenta.

Preguntas

1. ¿Dónde viven generalmente las personas que residen en ... en Madrid? ¿Qué es una urbanización? *Viven en pis...* *urbanización es un grupo de ... en las ...*
2. ¿Dónde prefiere... *Answers ma...*

Also appearing at pertinent points throughout the *Comunicación* sections are brief cultural presentations that seamlessly connect the Spanish language with the culture of its speakers.

Reading and video

STOP 7

A mystery story called **Ambiciones siniestras** is presented through readings and videos. It re-uses many of the grammar structures and vocabulary words presented in the chapter.

The pre-reading activity helps you prepare for what you are about to read. It gets you thinking about topics that will be presented in the story so that the context will help you figure out what is going on.

Strategies give you ideas and techniques to help you become a better reader.

The reading activity asks you to apply the strategies to the reading.

The post-reading activity helps you check your comprehension.

The sequence of activities for the reading is the same: pre-, during, and post-. The story that was started in the reading is continued in the video. To understand the story, you'll have to read first and then watch the video.

Meet the cast of the video:

Alejandra

Cisco

Manolo

Eduardo

Marisol

Lupe

Sr. Verdugo

Vocab summaries

The **Vocabulario activo** section at the end of each chapter is where you have all the new vocabulary from the chapter in one place. The words and phrases are organized by topic, in alphabetical order.

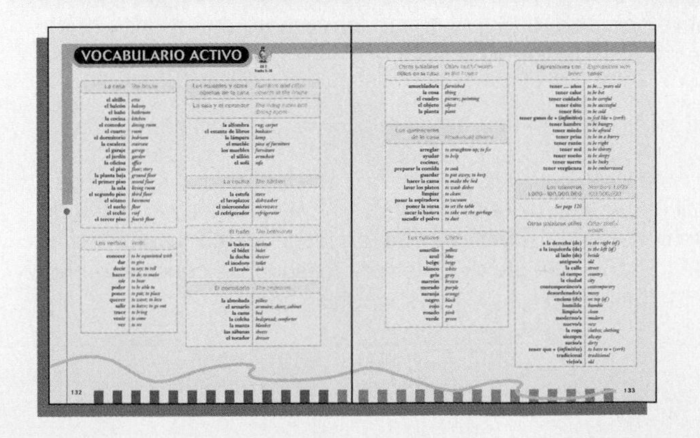

Supplementary materials

Before we finish our walking tour, we want to walk through the many supplements that we provide. Your instructor may have selected some of them to be used in your course.

Student Activities Manual (paper)	The *Student Activities Manual* (SAM for short) contains practice activities that were designed as homework to reinforce what you learn in class. Although instructors may use the SAM in different ways, one thing is constant; the SAM is assigned as homework. So we make no assumptions… we know you probably won't have an instructor around to answer any questions when you're doing your homework at 2:00 A.M.!
Answer Key to Accompany the Student Activities Manual	Some instructors want their students to have this answer key; other instructors don't. We'll sell you the answer key only if your instructor requests it.
Workbooklet	We know that most students don't want to write in their textbooks, but we also know that writing is a great method for helping you to learn Spanish! So, we've created a *Workbooklet*, in which we have reproduced all of the activities in **¡Anda!** where writing is an important part of the activity (e.g., you need to gather information in writing from classmates and then report back to the class orally).
Ambiciones siniestras DVD	The DVD of *Ambiciones siniestras* allows you to watch or rewatch the video at any point during your busy 24/7 life. This is a great tool for helping you practice your comprehension and listening skills!
Audio CD to Accompany the student text	This audio CD contains the listening passages that correlate with sections of your textbook. A listening icon appears in your text with a cross-reference to help you locate the audio.
Audio CDs to Accompany the Student Activities Manual	These audio CDs contain the listening passages you'll need for some of the activities in the SAM.
English Grammar Guide	After taking a Spanish class, most students say they learned as much about English grammar as they did about Spanish grammar. Here's a helpful pocket book that explains the English grammar points that will be helpful when studying Spanish. An icon cross-references the necessary grammar points in the guide for each of the Spanish grammar concepts presented in the text.
Vistas culturales DVD	If you want to listen to native speakers of Spanish and learn more about each of the Spanish-speaking countries, this is the DVD for you!
Companion Website	Extra practice available for free: you can find it online at www.prenhall.com/anda.
MySpanishLab™	*MySpanishLab*™ contains all of the above supplements and more. It's a state-of-the-art learning management system, designed specifically for language learners and teachers. You'll need an access code to get in, but the price is very reasonable, considering how much you get. For more information, go to www.myspanishlab.com.

Signposts!

When traveling, it's always helpful to watch out for the signposts. Here is a list of signposts that we've used in ¡Anda!

Accompanying the activity instructions, this pair icon indicates that the activity is designed to be completed in groups of two.

This group icon indicates that an activity is designed to be completed in groups of three or more.

The ear indicates that an activity involves listening and that the audio is provided for you on the Audio CD, on the Companion Website (CW) or, if you are using *MySpanishLab*™, in the eBook.

Activities that ask you to write have been duplicated in a separate *Workbooklet* so that you don't have to write in your text if you don't want to. This icon indicates that an activity has been reproduced in the *Workbooklet*.

The activity references below this icon tell you which activities in the *Student Activities Manual* (SAM) are related to that particular section of the textbook. You may have the printed SAM or the electronic version in *MySpanishLab*™.

One of two video icons, this icon tells you where to find the *Ambiciones siniestras* video: on DVD, VHS (instructors only), or *MySpanishLab*™.

The other video icon, this one tells you where to find the *Vistas culturales* video: on DVD, VHS (instructors only), or *MySpanishLab*™.

This icon means that the activity that it accompanies requires you to use the Internet.

The numbers accompanying this icon indicate which English grammar points are related to the Spanish grammar topic that you are studying. The *English Grammar Guide* is available to users of **¡Anda!**

Back to the cover

So what do you think the cover image represents? We see those footsteps on a clear path, heading toward the horizon… to clear goals, a clear path, a bright and sunny future, blue skies, and clear sailing! ¡Anda! was designed to keep you motivated and on a stress-free learning path.

¡Que disfruten! **Enjoy!**

The top five world languages	
Chinese	1,075 billion
English	514 million
Hindustani	496 million
✔Spanish	425 million
Russian	275 million

Para empezar

You are about to begin the exciting journey of studying the Spanish language and learning about Hispanic culture. Learning a language is a skill much like learning to ski or playing an instrument. Developing these skills takes practice and in the beginning, perfection is not expected. Research has shown that successful language learners are willing to take risks and experiment with the language. What

	OBJETIVOS	CONTENIDOS
Comunicación	• To greet, take leave of, and introduce people • To understand and respond appropriately to basic classroom expressions and requests • To spell your name in Spanish • To identify cognates • To name the subject pronouns in Spanish • To state your nationality • To say the numbers 0–30 • To tell the time and date, and state weather conditions • To state basic likes and dislikes	1 Greetings 4 2 Useful classroom expressions 8 3 Alphabet 9 4 Cognates 10 5 Subject pronouns 11 6 The verb **ser** (*to be*) 13 7 Adjectives of nationality 14 8 Numbers 0–30 16 9 Telling time 18 10 Days, months, and seasons 20 11 Weather 23 12 The verb **gustar** (*to like*) 25
Cultura	• To give at least two reasons why it is important to study and be able to communicate in Spanish • To compare and contrast greetings in the Spanish-speaking world and in the United States • To explain when to use the familiar and formal "you" in Spanish • To name the continents and countries where Spanish is spoken	How to greet people 7 **Tú** or **Ud.**? 12 The Hispanic world 16

is essential in learning Spanish is to keep trying and be willing to risk making mistakes, knowing that the practice will garner results. *¡Anda!* will be your guide and provide you with key essentials for becoming a successful language learner.

Why should you study Spanish, or for that matter, any language other than English? For some of you, the answer may be quite frankly, "because it is a graduation requirement!" Bear in mind, however, that Spanish is one of the most widely spoken languages in the world. You may find that knowledge of the Spanish language is a useful professional and personal tool.

If you have never studied Spanish before, this preliminary chapter will provide you with some basic words and expressions you will need to begin to use the language in meaningful ways. If you have already learned or studied some Spanish, this preliminary chapter can serve as a quick review.

PREGUNTAS

1 Why is it important to study Spanish?
2 How might Spanish play a role in your future?

Comunicación

VOCABULARIO 1 Saludos, despedidas y presentaciones

SAM A-1 to A-3

Los saludos	*Greetings*
¡Hola!	*Hi!; Hello!*
Buenos días.	*Good morning.*
Buenas tardes.	*Good afternoon.*
Buenas noches.	*Good evening; Good night.*
¿Cómo estás?	*How are you?* (familiar)
¿Cómo está usted?	*How are you?* (formal)
¿Qué tal?	*How's it going?*
Más o menos.	*So-so.*
Regular.	*Okay.*
Bien, gracias.	*Fine, thanks.*
Bastante bien.	*Just fine.*
Muy bien.	*Really well.*
¿Y tú?	*And you?* (familiar)
¿Y usted?	*And you?* (formal)

Las despedidas	*Farewells*
Adiós.	*Good-bye.*
Chao.	*Bye.*
Hasta luego.	*See you later.*
Hasta mañana.	*See you tomorrow.*
Hasta pronto.	*See you soon.*

—¿Qué tal?
—Bien.

—¿Cómo estás?
—Bien, gracias.

—Hasta mañana.
—Adiós.

Las presentaciones	***Introductions***
¿Cómo te llamas?	*What is your name?* (familiar)
¿Cómo se llama usted?	*What is your name?* (formal)
Me llamo…	*My name is…*
Soy…	*I am…*
Mucho gusto.	*Nice to meet you.*
Encantado/Encantada.	*Pleased to meet you.*
Igualmente.	*Likewise.*
Quiero presentarte a…	*I would like to introduce you to…* (familiar)
Quiero presentarle a…	*I would like to introduce you to…* (formal)

- The expressions **¿Cómo te llamas?** and **¿Cómo se llama usted?** both mean *What is your name?*, but the former is used among students and other peers (referred to as *familiar)*. You will learn about the differences between these *familiar* and *formal* forms later in this chapter. Note that **Encantado** is said by a male, and **Encantada** is said by a female.
- Spanish uses special punctuation to signal a question or an exclamation. An upside-down question mark begins a question and an upside-down exclamation mark begins an exclamation, as in **¿Cómo te llamas?** and **¡Hola!**

A•1 Saludos y despedidas

Match each greeting or farewell with its logical response. Compare your answers with a classmate.

1. ______ ¿Qué tal?
2. ______ Hasta luego.
3. ______ ¿Cómo te llamas?
4. ______ Que lo pases bien.

a. Me llamo Julia.
b. Bastante bien.
c. Igualmente.
d. Hasta pronto.

A•2 ¡Hola! ¿Qué tal?

Greet five classmates and ask how each is doing. After you are comfortable with one greeting, try a different one.

MODELO
E1: *¡Hola! ¿Cómo estás?*
E2: *Bien, gracias. ¿Y tú?*
E1: *Bastante bien.*

A•3 ¿Cómo te llamas?

Introduce yourself to three classmates.

MODELO
E1: *¡Hola! Soy… ¿Cómo te llamas?*
E2: *Mucho gusto. Me llamo…*
E1: *Encantado/a.*
E2: *Igualmente.*

A•4 Quiero presentarte a…

Now, introduce one person you have just met to another classmate.

MODELO
E1: *John, quiero presentarte a Mike.*
MIKE: *Mucho gusto.*
JOHN: *Igualmente.*

A•5 Una fiesta

Imagine that you are at a party. In groups of five, introduce yourselves to each other. Use the model as a guide.

MODELO
AMY: *Hola, ¿qué tal? Soy Amy.*
ORLANDO: *Hola Amy. Soy Orlando. ¿Cómo estás?*
AMY: *Muy bien, Orlando. ¿Y tú?*
ORLANDO: *Bien, gracias. Amy, quiero presentarte a Tom.*
TOM: *Encantado.*
E4: …

Cómo se saluda la gente

How do you generally greet acquaintances? Do you use different greetings for different people?

When native speakers of Spanish meet, they greet each other, ask each other how they are doing, and respond using phrases like the ones you just learned. In most of the Spanish-speaking world, men usually shake hands when greeting each other, although close male friends may greet each other with an **abrazo** (*hug*). Between female friends, the usual greeting is a **besito** (*little kiss*) on one or both cheeks (depending on the country) and a gentle hug. The **besito** is a gentle air kiss. When men and women greet each other, depending on their ages, how well they know each other, and what country they are in, they either simply shake hands and/or greet with a **besito.** While conversing, Spanish speakers may stand quite close to each other.

Preguntas

1. How do your male friends generally greet each other? And your female friends?
2. In general, how much distance is there between you and the person(s) with whom you are speaking?

VOCABULARIO 2 Expresiones útiles para la clase

The following list provides useful expressions that you and your instructor will use frequently.

Preguntas y respuestas	*Questions and answers*
¿Cómo?	*What?; How?*
¿Cómo se dice... en español?	*How do you say... in Spanish?*
¿Cómo se escribe... en español?	*How do you write... in Spanish?*
¿Qué significa?	*What does it mean?*
¿Quién?	*Who?*
¿Qué es esto?	*What is this?*
Comprendo.	*I understand.*
No comprendo.	*I don't understand.*
Lo sé.	*I know.*
No lo sé.	*I don't know.*
Sí.	*Yes.*
No.	*No.*

Expresiones de cortesía	*Polite expressions*
De nada.	*You're welcome.*
Gracias.	*Thank you.*
Por favor.	*Please.*

Mandatos para la clase	*Classroom instructions (commands)*
Abra(n) el libro en la página...	*Open your book to page...*
Cierre(n) el/los libro/s.	*Close your book/s.*
Conteste(n).	*Answer.*
Escriba(n).	*Write.*
Escuche(n).	*Listen.*
Lea(n).	*Read.*
Repita(n).	*Repeat.*
Vaya(n) a la pizarra.	*Go to the board.*

In Spanish, commands can have two forms. The singular form (**abra, cierre, conteste,** etc.) is directed to one person, while the plural form (those ending in **-n: abran, cierren, contesten,** etc.) is used with more than one person.

Estrategia

When working with a partner, always listen carefully. If your partner gives an incorrect response, help your partner achieve a correct response.

A•6 Práctica

Take turns saying which expressions or commands would be used in the following situations.

1. You don't know the Spanish word for something.
2. Your teacher wants everyone to listen.
3. You need your teacher to repeat what he/she has said.
4. You don't know what something means.
5. Your teacher wants students to turn to a certain page.
6. You don't understand something.

A•7 Más práctica

Play the roles of instructor (I) and student (E). The instructor either tells the student to do something or asks a question; the student responds appropriately. Practice with at least **five** sentences or questions, using the expressions that you have just learned; then change roles.

MODELO I: *Abra el libro.*
E: (Student opens the book.)
I: *¿Cómo se dice* "hello"?
E: *Se dice "hola".*

Estrategia

To learn Spanish faster, you should attempt to speak only Spanish in the classroom.

El alfabeto

A-9 to A-12

CD 1 Track 1

The Spanish alphabet is quite similar to the English alphabet except in the ways the letters are pronounced. Learning the proper pronunciation of the individual letters in Spanish will help you pronounce new words and phrases.

LETTER	LETTER NAME	EXAMPLES	LETTER	LETTER NAME	EXAMPLES
a	a	**a**diós	**n**	ene	**n**oche
b	be	**b**uenos	**ñ**	eñe	ma**ñ**ana
c	ce	**c**lase	**o**	o	c**ó**m**o**
ch	che	**Ch**ile	**p**	pe	**p**or favor
d	de	**d**ía	**q**	cu	**q**ué
e	e	**e**spañol	**r**	ere o erre	seño**r**a, ca**rr**o
f	efe	por **f**avor	**s**	ese	**s**aludos
g	ge	lue**g**o	**t**	te	**t**arde
h	hache	**h**ola	**u**	u	**u**sted
i	i	señor**i**ta	**v**	ve o uve	nue**v**e
j	jota	**j**ulio	**w**	doble ve o uve doble	**W**ashington
k	ka	**k**ilómetro	**x**	equis	e**x**amen
l	ele	**l**uego	**y**	i griega	**y**o
ll	elle	Sevi**ll**a	**z**	zeta	pi**z**arra
m	eme	**m**adre			

A•8 En español

Take turns saying the following abbreviations in Spanish, helping each other with pronunciation if necessary.

1. CD-RW
2. IBM
3. CNN
4. MTV
5. MCI
6. UPS
7. WWW
8. QVC
9. CBS
10. ABC

A•9 ¿Qué es esto?

Complete the following steps.

Paso 1 Take turns spelling these words for a partner, who will write what you spelled. Then pronounce each word.

1. hola 2. mañana 3. usted 4. igualmente 5. que 6. noches

Paso 2 Now spell your name for your partner as he/she writes it down. Your partner will pronounce your name, based on your spelling.

MODELO E1: *de, a, ve, i, de; ese, eme, i, te, hache*

E2: (escribe y repite) *D-a-v-i-d S-m-i-t-h*

Los cognados

A-13 to A-16 CD 1 Track 2

Cognados, or *cognates*, are words that are similar in form and meaning to their English equivalents. As you learn Spanish you will discover many cognates. Can you guess the meaning of the words below?

inteligente **septiembre** **familia** **universidad**

A•10 Práctica

Take turns giving the English equivalents for the following words.

1. importante
2. animal
3. programa
4. mapa
5. atractivo
6. favorito
7. especial
8. fantástico
9. famoso
10. diferente

A•11 ¿Hablas español?

Read the classified ad and make a list of all of the cognates; then answer the following questions.

1. What job is advertised?
2. What are the requirements?
3. How much does it pay?
4. How can you get further information?

Administrador/a

Departamento de Servicio Público.

Hospital General de Mesa Grande, AR.

Experiencia necesaria.

Fluidez en inglés y español.

$45,000–$60,000.

Teléfono: 480-555-2347

Los pronombres personales

A-17 to A-18

6, 7

Can you list the subject pronouns in English? When are they used? The chart below lists the subject pronouns in Spanish and their equivalents in English. As you will note, Spanish has several equivalents for *you.*

yo	*I*	**nosotros/as**	*we*
tú	*you* (familiar)	**vosotros/as**	*you* (plural, Spain)
usted	*you* (formal)	**ustedes**	*you* (plural)
él	*he*	**ellos**	*they* (masculine)
ella	*she*	**ellas**	*they* (feminine)

Tú

Generally speaking, **tú** (you, singular) is used for people with whom you are on a first-name basis, such as family members and friends.

Usted

Usted, abbreviated **Ud.,** is used with people you do not know well, or with people with whom you are not on a first-name basis. **Usted** is also used with older people, or with those to whom you want to show respect.

Spanish shows gender more clearly than English. **Nosotros** and **ellos** are used to refer to either all males or to a mixed group of males and females. **Nosotras** and **ellas** refer to an all-female group.

¿Tú o usted?

Languages are constantly evolving. Words are added and deleted, they change in meaning, and the use of language in certain situations may change as well. For example, the use of **tú** and **usted (Ud.)** is changing dramatically in Spanish. **Tú** may now be used more freely in situations where **Ud.** was previously used. In some Spanish-speaking countries, it has become acceptable for a shopper to address a young store clerk with **tú.** Just a few years ago, only **Ud.** would have been appropriate in that context. Nevertheless, the traditional use of **tú** and **Ud.** still exists. Regarding your choice between **tú** or **Ud.,** a good rule of thumb is: *When in doubt, be more formal.*

There are a few regional differences in the use of pronouns. Spanish speakers in Spain use **vosotros** ("you all") when addressing more than one person with whom they are on a first-name basis. Elsewhere in the Spanish-speaking world, **ustedes,** abbreviated **Uds.,** is used when addressing more than one person on a formal or informal basis. In Costa Rica, Argentina, and other parts of Latin America, **vos** replaces **tú,** but **tú** would be perfectly understood in these countries.

Preguntas

To understand how Spanish is changing, consider what has happened to English over the years.

1. What new words have been added to the English language in the past twenty years?
2. What are some words and expressions that we do not use in English anymore?

A•12 ¿Cómo se dice?

Take turns expressing the following in Spanish.

1. we (all men)
2. I
3. you (speaking to a friend)
4. they (just women)
5. we (all women)
6. you (speaking to a professor)
7. they (just men)
8. they (fifty women and one man)
9. we (men and women)
10. they (men or women)

A•13 ¿Tú o Ud.?

Determine whether you would most likely address the following people with **tú** or **Ud.** State your reason, using the categories below.

A respect
B family member
C someone with whom you are on a first-name basis
D someone you do not know well

1. your sister
2. your mom
3. your Spanish professor
4. your grandfather
5. your best friend's father
6. a clerk in a department store
7. your doctor
8. someone you've just met who is older
9. someone you've just met who is your age
10. a child you've just met

GRAMÁTICA 6 El verbo *ser*

A-23 to A-26 7, 11, 12, 15

You have already learned the subject pronouns in Spanish. It is time to put them together with a verb. Consider first the verb *to be* in English. The *to* form of a verb, as in *to be* or *to see* is called an *infinitive*. Note that *to be* has different forms for different subjects.

Fíjate

The subject pronoun *it* does not have an equivalent in Spanish.

to be

I	**am**	we	**are**
you	**are**	you (all)	**are**
he, she, it	**is**	they	**are**

Verbs in Spanish also have different forms for different subjects.

ser (*to be*)

Singular			Plural		
yo	**soy**	*I am*	nosotros/as	**somos**	*we are*
tú	**eres**	*you are*	vosotros/as	**sois**	*you are*
él, ella, Ud.	**es**	*he/she is, you are*	ellos/as, Uds.	**son**	*they are, you are*

- In Spanish, subject pronouns are not required but rather used for clarification or emphasis. Pronouns are indicated by the verb ending. For example:

  Soy means *I am.*

  Es means either *he is*, *she is*, or *you* (formal) *are.*

- If you are using a subject pronoun, it will appear first, followed by the form of the verb that corresponds to the subject pronoun, and then the rest of the sentence, as in the examples:

  Yo **soy** Mark. **Soy** Mark.

  Él **es** inteligente. **Es** inteligente.

As you continue to progress in **¡*Anda!***, you will learn to form and respond to questions, both orally and in writing, as well as have the opportunity to create longer sentences.

A-14 Vamos a practicar

Take turns saying the forms of the verb **ser** that you would use with the following pronouns. Correct your partner's answers as necessary.

1. nosotras
2. Ud.
3. yo
4. él
5. ellas
6. tú
7. Uds.
8. ella

A·15 "Ser o no ser..."

Take turns changing these forms of **ser** to the plural if they are singular, and vice versa. Listen to your partner for accuracy and help him/her if necessary.

MODELO E1: yo soy
E2: *nosotros somos*

1. usted es
2. nosotros somos
3. ella es
4. ellos son
5. tú eres

VOCABULARIO 7 Los adjetivos de nacionalidad

SAM A-27 to A-28

Nacionalidad	Estudiantes				
alemán	Hans	**español**	Rodrigo	**mexicano**	Manuel
alemana	Ingrid	**española**	Guadalupe	**mexicana**	Milagros
canadiense	Jacques/Alice	**francés**	Jean-Paul	**nigeriano**	Yena
chino	Tsong	**francesa**	Brigitte	**nigeriana**	Ngidaha
china	Xue Lan	**inglés**	James	**estadounidense (norteamericano/a)**	John/Kate
cubano	Javier	**inglesa**	Diana	**puertorriqueño**	Ernesto
cubana	Pilar	**japonés**	Tabo	**puertorriqueña**	Sonia
		japonesa	Yasu		

In Spanish:

- adjectives of nationality are not capitalized unless they are the first word in a sentence.
- most adjectives of nationality have a form for males, and a slightly different one for females. (You will learn more about this in **Capítulo 1.** For now, simply note the differences.)
- when referring to more than one individual, you make the adjectives plural by adding either an **-s** or an **-es.** (Again, in **Capítulo 1** you will formally learn more about forming plural words.)
- some adjectives of nationality have a written accent mark in the masculine form, but not in the feminine, like **inglés/inglesa** and **francés/francesa.** For example: **Mi papá es *inglés* y mi mamá es *francesa*.**

A•16 ¿Cuál es tu nacionalidad?

Describe the nationalities of the students listed on page 14. Form complete sentences using either **es** or **son** following the model. Then practice spelling the nationalities in Spanish with your partner.

MODELO
E1: china
E2: *Xue Lan es china.*
E1: chinos
E2: *Xue Lan y Tsong son chinos.*

1. francesa
2. japonés
3. estadounidenses
4. canadiense
5. mexicanos
6. alemán

A•17 ¿Qué son?

Take turns naming the nationalities of the people listed. Make sure you use the correct form of **ser** in your sentence. Follow the model.

MODELO
E1: Yena
E2: *Yena es nigeriana.*
E1: Yena y Ngidaha
E2: *Yena y Ngidaha son nigerianos.*

1. Jacques
2. Xue Lan y Tsong
3. Ingrid
4. Brigitte
5. Kate
6. Hans
7. Javier y Pilar
8. Jean-Paul
9. yo
10. mi familia y yo

8 VOCABULARIO Los números 0–30

SAM A-29 to A-32

0	**cero**	7	**siete**	13	**trece**	19	**diecinueve**	25	**veinticinco**
1	**uno**	8	**ocho**	14	**catorce**	20	**veinte**	26	**veintiséis**
2	**dos**	9	**nueve**	15	**quince**	21	**veintiuno**	27	**veintisiete**
3	**tres**	10	**diez**	16	**dieciséis**	22	**veintidós**	28	**veintiocho**
4	**cuatro**	11	**once**	17	**diecisiete**	23	**veintitrés**	29	**veintinueve**
5	**cinco**	12	**doce**	18	**dieciocho**	24	**veinticuatro**	30	**treinta**
6	**seis**								

A-18 ¿Qué número?

Take turns saying what number comes before and after those below. Your partner will check your accuracy.

1. 2
2. 5
3. 8
4. 11
5. 15
6. 17
7. 20
8. 23
9. 24
10. 26

A-19 ¿Cuál es la secuencia?

Take turns reading the number patterns aloud while filling in the missing numbers.

1. 1, 3, 5, ______, 9, ______, 13, ______, ______
2. 2, 4, ______, 8, ______, 12, ______, 16, ______, 20, ______
3. 3, ______, 9, ______, 15, ______, 21, ______, 27, ______
4. 1, 3, 6, ______, 15, ______, 28

El mundo hispano

¿Sabías que...?

- Spanish is an official language of the European Union. Approximately 15% of the EU population speaks Spanish. It is the third-most-taught foreign language in the EU.
- The United States is the fifth-largest "Spanish-speaking country."
- There is no official language written into the U.S. Constitution.

PAÍS	POBLACIÓN
ARGENTINA	39.921.833
BOLIVIA	8.989.046
CHILE	16.134.219
COLOMBIA	43.593.035
COSTA RICA	4.075.261
CUBA	11.382.820
ECUADOR	13.547.510
EL SALVADOR	6.822.378
ESPAÑA	40.397.842
LOS ESTADOS UNIDOS	31.933.531
GUATEMALA	12.293.545
GUINEA ECUATORIAL	300.000
HONDURAS	7.326.496
MÉXICO	107.449.525
NICARAGUA	5.570.129
PANAMÁ	3.191.319
PARAGUAY	6.506.464
PERÚ	28.302.603
PUERTO RICO	3.927.188
LA REPÚBLICA DOMINICANA	9.183.984
URUGUAY	3.431.932
VENEZUELA	25.730.435

*CIA Fact Book, July 2006

Fíjate

When you see numbers or statistics presented in Spanish, the decimal point (.) represents a comma. In English, commas (,) are used to separate numbers.

A-33

¿Quién habla español?

Jennifer López es actriz, cantante y compositora puertorriqueña.

Omar Sosa es un músico cubano.

Rigoberta Menchú Tum es una activista maya guatemalteca.

Óscar Arias es un Nobel Laureate y presidente costarricense.

Many terms are associated with people from the Spanish-speaking world, most commonly *Hispanic* and *Latino*. While there is some controversy around the use of these terms, typically *Hispanic* refers to all people who come from a Spanish-speaking background. *Latino*, on the other hand, implies a specific connection to Latin America. Whichever term is used, the people denoted are far from homogeneous. Some are racially diverse, most are culturally diverse, and some do not even speak Spanish.

A·20 El mundo hispano

Use the map and chart of the Spanish-speaking world on pp. 16–17 to answer the following questions in Spanish. Compare your answers with your partner.

1. Fill in the chart with the names of the Spanish-speaking countries in the appropriate column. How many countries are there in each of these areas? How many are there in the world?

AMÉRICA DEL NORTE	CENTROAMÉRICA	EL CARIBE	AMÉRICA DEL SUR	EUROPA	ÁFRICA

2. How many continents contain Spanish-speaking countries? What are they?
3. How many countries have a Spanish-speaking population of 25,000,000 or more? Name them and their continent.

La hora

A-34 to A-36

Es (la) medianoche.

Es (el) mediodía.

Es la una.

Son las diez y cinco.

Son las tres y cuarto.

Son las seis y media.

Son las nueve menos cuarto.

Son las diez menos veinticinco.

La hora	***Telling time***	**¿A qué hora...?**	*At what time...?*
¿Qué hora es?	*What time is it?*	**... de la mañana**	*... in the morning*
Es la una./Son las...	*It's one o'clock. It's...o'clock.*	**... de la tarde**	*... in the afternoon*
A la.../A las...	*At...o'clock.*	**... de la noche**	*... in the evening*

When telling time in Spanish:

- use **Es la...** to say times between 1:00 and 1:30.
- use **Son las...** with all times after 1:30.
- use **A la...** or **A las...** to say *at* what time.
- use the expressions **mediodía** and **medianoche** to say *noon* and *midnight*.
- use **la** with **una** (**a la una**) and **las** for hours greater than *one* (**a las ocho**).
- **de la tarde** tends to mean from noon until 7:00 or 8:00 P.M.
- **cuarto** and **media** are equivalent to the English expressions *quarter* (fifteen minutes) and *half* (thirty minutes). **Cuarto** and **media** are interchangeable with the numbers **quince** and **treinta**.

A•21 ¿Qué hora es?

Look at the clocks and take turns asking and responding to **¿Qué hora es?**

MODELO

E1: *¿Qué hora es?*

E2: *Son las nueve de la mañana.*

1. 

2. 

3. 

4. 

5. 

6. 

7. 

8. 

A•22 Tu horario

Think about your daily schedule. Then take turns asking and telling your partner at what times you do the following activities.

MODELO go to sleep
E1: *¿A qué hora?*
E2: *a la una y media*

1. wake up
2. eat breakfast
3. attend your first class
4. eat lunch
5. finish classes for the day
6. study
7. eat dinner
8. exercise
9. go to bed

A•23 ¿Y el fin de semana?

What is your schedule for the weekend? Take turns telling your partner at what times you plan to do the activities from **A-22** this coming weekend.

Los días, los meses y las estaciones

A-37 to A-43

Los meses y las estaciones (*Months and seasons*)

la primavera

marzo, abril y mayo

el verano

junio, julio y agosto

el otoño

septiembre, octubre y noviembre

el invierno

diciembre, enero y febrero

Los días de la semana	*Days of the week*	Expresiones útiles	*Useful expressions*
lunes	*Monday*	**¿Qué día es hoy?**	*What day is today?*
martes	*Tuesday*	**¿Cuál es la fecha de hoy?**	*What is today's date?*
miércoles	*Wednesday*	**Hoy es lunes.**	*Today is Monday.*
jueves	*Thursday*	**Hoy es el 1 (primero) de septiembre.**	*Today is September first.*
viernes	*Friday*		
sábado	*Saturday*	**Mañana es el 2 (dos) de septiembre.**	*Tomorrow is September second.*
domingo	*Sunday*		

Unlike in English, the days of the week and the months of the year are not capitalized in Spanish. Also, in the Spanish-speaking world, Monday is considered the first day of the week. On calendars the days are listed from Monday through Sunday.

A·24 Antes y después

Which days come directly before and after the ones listed? Take turns saying the days in Spanish.

1. sábado
2. lunes
3. viernes
4. domingo
5. jueves
6. miércoles

A·25 y los meses

Now do the same activity as **A-24** with the months listed here.

1. octubre
2. febrero
3. mayo
4. agosto
5. diciembre
6. junio
7. septiembre
8. enero
9. octubre
10. marzo

A•26 ¿Cuándo es?

Look at the activities included in the **Guía del ocio.** Take turns determining what activity takes place and at what time on the following days.

GUÍA DEL OCIO MADRID

MÚSICA

Sábado 4

- **XVI Festival de Jazz:**

Joe Henderson
La Riviera. 21 h.

- **Alonso y Williams**
La Madriguera. 24 h.

Domingo 5

- **Pedro Iturralde**
Clamores. Pases: 22.45 y 0.45 h. Libre.

Lunes 6

- **Moreiras Jazztet**
Café Central. 22 h.

CINE

Las vidas de Celia
(2005, España)****
Género: Drama
Director: Antonio Chavarrías
Interpretación: Najwa Nimri, Luis Tosar…
Najwa Nimri da vida a una mujer que intenta suicidarse la misma noche que otra joven es asesinada.

Mujeres en el parque
(2006, España)*****
Género: Drama
Director: Felipe Vega
Interpretación: Adolfo Fernández, Blanca Apilánez…
Una película llena de pequeños misterios, donde los personajes se enfrentan a lo difícil de las relaciones personales.

Volver (2006, España)*****
Género: Comedia dramática
Director: Pedro Almodóvar
Interpretación: Penélope Cruz, Carmen Maura…
Se basa en la vida y los recuerdos del director sobre su madre y el lugar donde se crió.

EXPOSICIONES

- **Museo Nacional Centro de Arte Reina Sofía**
Santa Isabel, 52.
Metro Atocha
Tel. 91 4675062
Horario: de 10 a 21 h. Domingo de 10 a 14.30 h.
Martes cerrado.

Un recorrido del arte del siglo XX, desde Picasso. Salas dedicadas a los comienzos de la vanguardia. Además, exposiciones temporales.

- **Museo del Prado**
Paseo del Prado, s/n. Metro Banco de España.
Tel. 91 420 36 62 y 91 420 37 68
Horario: martes a sábado de 9 a 19 h. Domingo de 9 a 14 h.
Lunes cerrado.

Todas las escuelas españolas, desde los frescos románicos hasta el siglo XVIII. Grandes colecciones de Velázquez, Goya, Murillo, etc. Importante representación de las escuelas europeas (Rubens, Tiziano, Durero, etc.). Escultura clásica griega y romana y Tesoro del Delfín.

Upper right: The Art Archive/Picture Desk, Inc./Kobal Collection.

MODELO E1: el lunes por la noche
E2: *El Moreiras Jazztet es a las diez.*

1. el sábado por la tarde
2. el miércoles por la mañana
3. el domingo
4. el sábado por la noche
5. el martes por la tarde

VOCABULARIO 11 El tiempo

A•27 ¿Qué tiempo hace?

Take turns asking and answering what the most typical weather is during the following seasons where you go to school.

MODELO E1: ¿Qué tiempo hace… en (el) otoño?
E2: *En (el) otoño hace sol.*

¿Qué tiempo hace…?

1. en (el) otoño
2. en (el) invierno
3. en (la) primavera
4. en (el) verano

A·28 España

Take turns answering the question **¿Qué tiempo hace?** based on the map of Spain.

MODELO E1: ¿Qué tiempo hace en Sevilla?
E2: *Hace calor.*

1. ¿Qué tiempo hace en Mallorca?
2. ¿Qué tiempo hace en Pamplona?
3. ¿Qué tiempo hace en Barcelona?
4. ¿Qué tiempo hace en Madrid?
5. ¿Qué tiempo hace en Córdoba?

A·29 y América del Sur

Take turns making statements about the weather based on the map of South America. You can say what the weather is like and also what it is not like. Follow the model.

MODELO E1: *Llueve en Bogotá.*
E2: *No hace frío en Venezuela.*

Fíjate

To make a negative statement, simply place the word *no* before the verb: *No llueve en Caracas. No nieva en Buenos Aires. No hace calor en Punta Arenas.*

Gustar

A-47 to A-49

To express likes and dislikes, you say the following:

Me gusta la primavera.

No me gusta el invierno.

Me gustan los viernes.

No **me gustan** los lunes.

1. To say you like or dislike one thing, what form of **gustar** do you use?
2. To say you like or dislike more than one thing, what form of **gustar** do you use?

Check your answers to the preceding questions in Appendix 1.

A•30 ¿Qué te gusta?

Ask your partner if he/she likes or dislikes the following things.

MODELO la primavera

E1: *¿Te gusta la primavera?*

E2: *Sí, me gusta la primavera.*

1. el otoño
2. el invierno
3. el verano
4. los lunes
5. los sábados
6. los domingos
7. los viernes
8. la clase de español

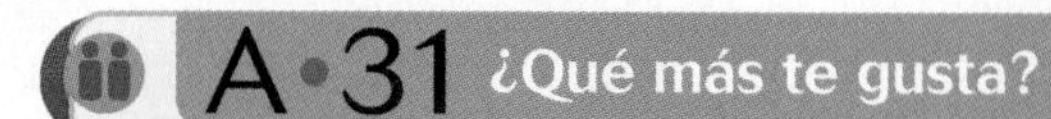

A•31 ¿Qué más te gusta?

Take turns asking your partner about the following places and things.

MODELO las hamburguesas

E1: *¿Te gustan las hamburguesas?*

E2: *No, no me gustan las hamburguesas.*

1. Nevada
2. la guitarra
3. los autos Ford
4. la pizza de Domino's
5. Los Ángeles y San Francisco
6. San Antonio
7. los teléfonos celulares
8. el béisbol y el fútbol.

Y por fin, ¿cómo andas?

Each of the coming chapters of *¡Anda!* will have three self-check sections for you to assess your progress. A **¿Cómo andas?** (*How are you doing?*) section will appear one third of the way through each chapter, another will appear at the two-thirds point, and a third and final one at the end of the chapter called **Y por fin, ¿cómo andas?** (*Finally, how are you doing?*). Use the checklists to measure what you have learned in the chapter. Place a check in the *Feel confident* column of the topics you feel you know, and a check in the *Need to Review* column of those that you need to practice more. Be sure to go back and practice because it is the key to your success!

Having completed this chapter, I now can...

	Feel Confident	Need to Review
Comunicación		
• greet, say goodbye, and introduce someone (p. 4)	❑	❑
• ask and respond to simple questions when meeting or greeting someone (p. 5)	❑	❑
• understand and respond appropriately to basic classroom expressions, and requests (p. 8)	❑	❑
• spell my name using the Spanish alphabet (p. 9)	❑	❑
• identify cognates (p. 10)	❑	❑
• state the subject pronouns (p. 11)	❑	❑
• use the verb **ser** to say who I am and talk about some nationalities (p. 13, 14)	❑	❑
• say the numbers 0–30 (p. 16)	❑	❑
• tell time (p. 18)	❑	❑
• say the months, days of the week, and seasons (p. 20)	❑	❑
• talk about the weather (p. 23)	❑	❑
• state some things that I like and dislike (p. 25)	❑	❑
Cultura		
• state at least two reasons why it is important for me to study and be able to communicate in Spanish (p. 2)	❑	❑
• state the similarities and differences in greetings between the Spanish-speaking world and the United States (p. 7)	❑	❑
• know when to use **tú** and **Ud.** (p. 12)	❑	❑
• name the continents and countries where Spanish is spoken (p. 16)	❑	❑

Estrategia

The *¿Cómo andas?* and *Por fin, ¿cómo andas?* sections are designed to help you assess your understanding of specific concepts. In the *Capítulo Preliminar,* there is one opportunity for you to reflect on how well you understand the concepts. Beginning with *Capítulo 1* there will be three opportunities for you to stop and reflect on what you have learned. These checklists help you become accountable for your own learning, and help you determine what you need to review. Also use the checklist as a way to communicate with your instructor about any concepts you still need to review. Additionally, you might also use your checklist as a way to study with a peer group or peer tutor. If you need to review a particular concept, more practice is available on your *¡Anda!* web site, where you will find quizzes online.

VOCABULARIO ACTIVO

CD 1
Tracks 3–16

Los saludos	*Greetings*
Bastante bien.	*Just fine.*
Bien, gracias.	*Fine, thanks.*
Buenos días.	*Good morning.*
Buenas noches.	*Good evening.; Good night.*
Buenas tardes.	*Good afternoon.*
¿Cómo está usted?	*How are you?* (formal)
¿Cómo estás?	*How are you?* (familiar)
¡Hola!	*Hi!; Hello!*
Más o menos.	*So-so.*
Muy bien.	*Really well.*
¿Qué tal?	*How's it going?*
Regular.	*Okay.*
¿Y tú?	*And you?* (familiar)
¿Y usted?	*And you?* (formal)

Las despedidas	*Farewells*
Adiós.	*Good-bye.*
Chao.	*Bye.*
Hasta luego.	*See you later.*
Hasta mañana.	*See you tomorrow.*
Hasta pronto.	*See you soon.*

Las presentaciones	*Introductions*
¿Cómo te llamas?	*What is your name?* (familiar)
¿Cómo se llama usted?	*What is your name?* (formal)
Encantado.	*Pleased to meet you.*
Encantada.	
Igualmente.	*Likewise.*
Me llamo…	*My name is…*
Mucho gusto.	*Nice to meet you.*
Quiero presentarte a…	*I would like to introduce you to…* (familiar)
Quiero presentarle a…	*I would like to introduce you to…* (formal)
Soy…	*I am…*

Expresiones útiles para la clase — *Useful classroom expressions*

Preguntas y respuestas	*Questions and answers*
¿Cómo?	*What?; How?*
¿Cómo se dice… en español?	*How do you say… in Spanish?*
¿Cómo se escribe… en español?	*How do you write… in Spanish?*
(No) comprendo.	*I (don't) understand.*
Lo sé.	*I know.*
No lo sé.	*I don't know.*
No.	*No.*
Sí.	*Yes.*
¿Qué es esto?	*What is this?*
¿Qué significa?	*What does it mean?*
¿Quién?	*Who?*

Expresiones de cortesía	*Polite expressions*
De nada.	*You're welcome.*
Gracias.	*Thank you.*
Por favor.	*Please.*

Mandatos para la clase	*Classroom instructions (commands)*
Abra(n) el libro en la página…	*Open your book to page…*
Cierre(n) el/los libros.	*Close your book/s.*
Conteste(n).	*Answer.*
Escriba(n).	*Write.*
Escuche(n).	*Listen.*
Lea(n).	*Read.*
Repita(n).	*Repeat.*
Vaya(n) a la pizarra.	*Go to the board.*

Las nacionalidades — *Nationalities*

alemán/alemana	*German*
canadiense	*Canadian*
chino/a	*Chinese*
cubano/a	*Cuban*
español/a	*Spanish*
francés/francesa	*French*
inglés/inglesa	*English*
japonés/japonesa	*Japanese*
mexicano/a	*Mexican*
nigeriano/a	*Nigerian*
estadounidense (norteamericano/a)	*American*
puertorriqueño/a	*Puerto Rican*

Los números 0–30 — *Numbers 0–30*

See page 16.

La hora — *Telling time*

A la…/A las…	*At… o'clock.*
¿A qué hora…?	*At what time…?*
… de la mañana	*… in the morning*
… de la noche	*… in the evening*
… de la tarde	*… in the afternoon*
¿Cuál es la fecha de hoy?	*What is today's date?*
Es la…/Son las…	*It's… o'clock.*
Hoy es…	*Today is…*
Mañana es…	*Tomorrow is…*
la medianoche	*midnight*
el mediodía	*noon*
¿Qué día es hoy?	*What day is today?*
¿Qué hora es?	*What time is it?*

Los días de la semana — *Days of the week*

lunes	*Monday*
martes	*Tuesday*
miércoles	*Wednesday*
jueves	*Thursday*
viernes	*Friday*
sábado	*Saturday*
domingo	*Sunday*

Los meses del año — *Months of the year*

enero	*January*
febrero	*February*
marzo	*March*
abril	*April*
mayo	*May*
junio	*June*
julio	*July*
agosto	*August*
septiembre	*September*
octubre	*October*
noviembre	*November*
diciembre	*December*

Las estaciones — *Seasons*

el invierno	*winter*
la primavera	*spring*
el otoño	*autumn; fall*
el verano	*summer*

Expresiones del tiempo — *Weather expressions*

Está nublado.	*It's cloudy.*
Hace buen tiempo.	*The weather is nice.*
Hace calor.	*It's hot.*
Hace frío.	*It's cold.*
Hace mal tiempo.	*The weather is bad.*
Hace sol.	*It's sunny.*
Hace viento.	*It's windy.*
Llueve.	*It's raining.*
la lluvia	*rain*
Nieva.	*It's snowing.*
la nieve	*snow*
la nube	*cloud*
¿Qué tiempo hace?	*What's the weather like?*
el sol	*sun*
la temperatura	*temperature*
el viento	*wind*

Unos verbos — *Some verbs*

gustar	*to like*
ser	*to be*

1

¿Quiénes somos?

What makes us who we are? What makes each of us unique? We may come from different geographical locations and represent different cultures, races, and religions, yet in many respects we are much the same. We have the same basic needs, share common likes and dislikes, and possess similar hopes and dreams.

	OBJETIVOS	CONTENIDOS	
Comunicación	• To talk about your family • To describe yourself and others • To give telephone numbers in Spanish • To write a poem in Spanish	1 The family 2 The verb **tener** (*to have*) 3 Singular and plural nouns 4 Masculine and feminine nouns 5 Definite (*the*) and indefinite (*a, an, some*) articles 6 People 7 Possessive adjectives (*my, your, our,* etc.) 8 Adjectives 9 Numbers 31–100 Pronunciación: Spanish vowels Escucha: Estrategia: Determining the topic and listening for words you know Escribe: Writing a poem	32 35 37 38 39 41 42 44 48 33 50 51
Cultura	• To explain how Hispanic last names are formed • To state several regional and national differences in both the English and Spanish languages • To discuss the size, location, and makeup of the Hispanic population in the United States	First and last names in the Spanish-speaking world The diversity of the Spanish language Hispanics in the United States	34 48 52
Ambiciones siniestras	• To meet the six protagonists in the continuing mystery story, *Ambiciones siniestras* • To begin to recognize cognates when reading • To view the video to learn more about the classes the protagonists in *Ambiciones siniestras* are taking and more about their lives	Episodio 1 Lectura: *Conexiones* Estrategia: Recognizing cognates Video: *¿Quiénes son?*	 54 56

PREGUNTAS

1. List the personal characteristics that make you unique. Which of the characteristics do you share with members of your family? Whom do you resemble most in your family?
2. How does where you live affect who you are? What social factors have contributed to the development of the person you are today?
3. What are some different nationalities and cultures you encounter on a regular basis in the United States? What do you have in common with them?

Comunicación

- Describing family members

VOCABULARIO 1 La familia

SAM 1-1 to 1-4

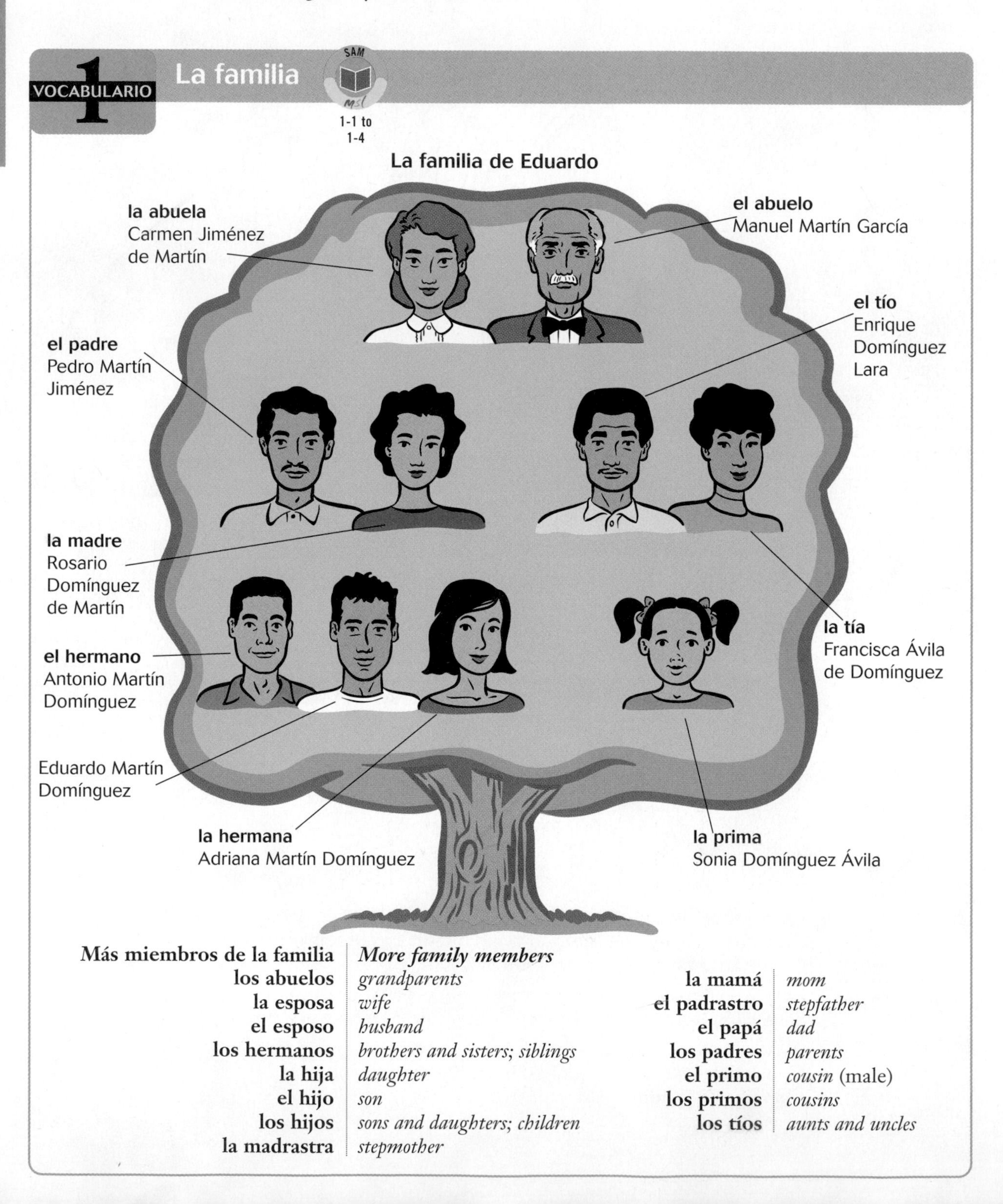

Más miembros de la familia	*More family members*
los abuelos	*grandparents*
la esposa	*wife*
el esposo	*husband*
los hermanos	*brothers and sisters; siblings*
la hija	*daughter*
el hijo	*son*
los hijos	*sons and daughters; children*
la madrastra	*stepmother*
la mamá	*mom*
el padrastro	*stepfather*
el papá	*dad*
los padres	*parents*
el primo	*cousin* (male)
los primos	*cousins*
los tíos	*aunts and uncles*

CD 1
Track 17

SAM

1-5 to 1-7

PRONUNCIACIÓN

Spanish vowels

The vowels, *a, e, i, o, u,* are nearly always pronounced the same way. Their pronunciation is crisp and shorter than in English. For example:

a like the "a" in *father* but shorter
e like the "e" in *hey* but shorter
i like the "ee" in *meet* but shorter
o like the "o" in *zone* but shorter
u like the "u" in *rule* but shorter

1•1 Las palabras

Practice pronouncing the following words and focus on the vowels.

1. la madrastra
2. la hermana
3. el esposo
4. el primo
5. inteligente
6. los hijos
7. el otoño
8. Uruguay
9. uno

1•2 Las oraciones

Pronounce the following sentences, paying special attention to the vowels.

1. Mi primo es mexicano. Es inteligente y simpático.
2. Me gusta la primavera y el otoño. No me gustan los lunes.
3. Mis hermanos son cómicos. Su música favorita es la música clásica.

1•3 Los dichos y refranes (*Sayings*)

Now pronounce the following saying (**dicho**), focusing on the vowels.

¡A, E, I, O, U, el burro eres tú!

Capítulo Preliminar A. El verbo *ser*, pág. 13.

1•4 La familia de Eduardo

Look at Eduardo's family tree and state how the following people are related to him. Share your answers with a partner.

MODELO E1: *¿Quién es* (Who is) *Antonio?*
E2: *Es su* (his) *hermano.*

1. Francisca
2. Carmen
3. Enrique
4. Manuel
5. Pedro
6. Rosario
7. Sonia
8. Adriana

Estrategia

¡Anda! has provided you with recycling references to help guide your continuous review of previously learned material. Make sure to consult the indicated pages if you need to refresh your memory about the topic.

1•5 Mi familia

Paso 1 Draw and label **three** generations of your own family tree, or create a fictitious one. Share your information with a partner, following the model. Please save your drawing! You will need it for actividad **1-10.**

MODELO E1: *Mary es mi* (my) *hermana.*
E2: *George es mi papá.*

Paso 2 Write **five** of the sentences that you shared orally with your partner, or **five** different sentences about your family members. Follow the **modelo** in **Paso 1.**

MODELO ________ ________ mi ________________.
(Subject) *(verb)* *(family member)*

Estrategia

For additional vocabulary choices, consult Appendix 3, *También se dice...*

1-8 to 1-9

Los nombres en el mundo hispano

In Spanish-speaking countries, it is customary for people to use both paternal and maternal last names (surnames). For example, Eduardo's father is **Pedro Martín Jiménez** and his mother's maiden name is **Rosario Domínguez Lara**. Eduardo's first last name would be his father's first last name (**Martín**); Eduardo's second last name would be his mother's first last name (**Domínguez**). Therefore, Eduardo's full name would be **Eduardo Martín Domínguez.** In most informal situations, though, Eduardo would use only his first last name, so he would call himself **Eduardo Martín.**

In most Hispanic countries, a woman usually retains the surname of her father upon marriage, while giving up her mother's surname. She takes her husband's last name, preceded by the preposition **de** (*of*). For example, when Eduardo's mother married his father, her name became **Rosario Domínguez de Martín.** Therefore, if a woman named **Carmen Torres López** married **Ricardo Colón Montoya,** her name would become **Carmen Torres de Colón.**

Preguntas

1. Hispanic last names may seem very long to you. Are there any equivalents in the United States or in other countries?
2. Can you think of any advantages to using both the mother's and the father's last names?

Fíjate

Below are some common Spanish first names and nicknames.

Hombres

Antonio	Toño, Toni
Francisco	Paco, Pancho, Cisco
Guillermo	Memo, Guillo, Guille
Jesús	Chu, Chuito, Chucho, Chus
José	Pepe
Manuel	Manolo, Mani
Ramón	Moncho, Monchi

Mujeres

Antonia	Toñín, Toña, Toñi(ta)
Concepción	Concha, Conchita
Guadalupe	Lupe, Lupita
María Soledad	Marisol
María Teresa	Maite, Marité, Maritere
Pilar	Pili
Rosario	Charo

GRAMÁTICA 2 El verbo *tener*

SAM 1-10 to 1-13
Guide 7, 11, 12, 15

In **Capítulo Preliminar A** you learned the present tense of **ser.** Another very common verb in Spanish is **tener** (*to have*). The present tense forms of the verb **tener** follow.

tener (*to have*)

Singular			Plural		
yo	**tengo**	*I have*	nosotros/as	**tenemos**	*we have*
tú	**tienes**	*you have*	vosotros/as	**tenéis**	*you have*
él, ella, Ud.	**tiene**	*he/she has, you have*	ellos/as, Uds.	**tienen**	*they have, you have*

1-6 ¿Quiénes tienen?

Take turns giving the correct form of the verb **tener** for each subject listed.

MODELO E1: la prima
E2: *tiene*

1. tú
2. los padres
3. nosotros
4. Pedro, Carmen y Rosario
5. yo
6. el tío

1-7 Practica conmigo

Take turns saying the following subject pronouns with the corresponding forms of **tener.** Practice in random order until you can say them quickly with no errors.

1. tú
2. Uds.
3. yo
4. nosotros
5. ella
6. ellas
7. él
8. ellos
9. Ud.
10. tú y yo

1-8 ¡Apúrate!

One person makes a ball out of a piece of paper, says a subject pronoun, and tosses the ball to someone in the group. That person catches it, gives the corresponding form of **tener**, then says another pronoun and tosses the ball to someone else. After finishing **tener**, repeat the game with **ser**.

MODELO E1: *yo*
E2: *tengo; ellas*
E3: *tienen; Ud.*
E4: *tiene; …*

Capítulo Preliminar A. El verbo *ser*, pág. 13.

1-9 La familia de José

Complete the paragraph with the correct forms of **tener.** Then share your answers with a partner. Finally, based on what you learned in the previous culture presentation regarding last names, what is José's father's last name? What is José's mother's maiden name?

José Olivo Peralta y su familia

Yo soy el primo de José. Él (1) ______ una familia grande. (2) ______ tres hermanos, Pepe, Alonso y Tina. Pepe está casado (*is married*) y (3) ______ dos hijos. También José y sus hermanos (4) ______ muchos tíos, siete en total. La madre de José (5) ______ tres hermanos y dos están casados. El padre de José (6) ______ una hermana y ella está casada con mi padre, ¡es mi madre! Nosotros (7) ______ una familia grande. ¿Y tú?, ¿(8) ______ una familia grande?

1-10 De tal palo, tal astilla

Create **three** sentences with **tener** based on the family tree that you sketched for actividad **1-5**, page 34. Tell them to your partner, who will then share what you said with another classmate.

MODELO E1 (ALICE): *Tengo un hermano, Scott. Tengo dos tíos, George y David. No tengo abuelos.*
E2 (JEFF): *Alice tiene un hermano, Scott. Tiene dos tíos, George y David. No tiene abuelos.*

Fíjate

The word *un* in the *modelo* for actividad **1-10** is the shortened form of the number *uno*. It is used before a masculine noun—a concept that will be explained later in this chapter.

El singular y el plural

1-14 to 1-16

2, 3

Raúl tiene dos primas y Jorge tiene una prima.

To pluralize singular nouns and adjectives in Spanish, follow these simple guidelines.

1. If the word ends in a vowel, add **-s.**

hermana	→	hermanas	abuelo	→	abuelos
día	→	días	mi	→	mis

2. If the word ends in a consonant, add **-es.**

mes	→	meses	ciudad	→	ciudades
televisión	→	televisiones	joven	→	jóvenes

3. If the word ends in a **-z**, change the **z** to **c**, and add **-es.**

lápiz	→	lápices	feliz	→	felices

Fíjate

Note that *televisión* loses its accent mark in the plural. Also note the plural of *joven* is *jóvenes*. You will learn about accent marks in *Capítulo 2*.

1•11 Te toca a ti

Take turns making the following singular nouns plural.

MODELO E1: primo
E2: *primos*

1. padre
2. tía
3. taxi
4. francés
5. nieto
6. alemán
7. abuela
8. sol
9. emoción
10. favor

1•12 De nuevo

Now take turns making the following plural nouns singular.

MODELO E1: primos
E2: *primo*

1. hijos
2. días
3. discusiones
4. madres
5. lápices
6. jóvenes

El masculino y el femenino

1-17 to 1-18

4

El abuelo y las tías.

In Spanish, all nouns (people, places, and things) have a gender; they are either masculine or feminine. Use the following rules to help you determine the gender of nouns. If a noun does not belong to any of the following categories, you must memorize the gender as you learn that noun.

1. Most words ending in -a are feminine.

   la hermana, la hija, la mamá, la tía

   *Some exceptions: **el día**, **el papá**, and words of Greek origin ending in -ma, such as **el problema** and **el programa.**

2. Most words ending in -o are masculine.

   el abuelo, el hermano, el hijo, el nieto

   *Some exceptions: **la foto** (*photo*), **la mano** (*hand*), **la moto** (*motorcycle*)

   *Note: **la foto** and **la moto** are shortened forms for **la fotografía** and **la motocicleta.**

3. Words ending in -ción and -sión are feminine.

   la discusión, la recepción, la televisión

   *Note: The suffix -ción is equivalent to the English *-tion.*

4. Words ending in -dad or -tad are feminine.

   la ciudad (*city*), **la libertad, la universidad**

   *Note: these suffixes are equivalent to the English *-ty.*

Estrategia

Making educated guesses about the meaning of unknown words will help to make you a successful Spanish learner!

As you learned in **Capítulo Preliminar A,** words that look alike and have the same meaning in both English and Spanish, such as **discusión** and **universidad,** are known as *cognates*. Use them to help you decipher meaning and to form words. For example, **prosperidad** looks like what English word? What is its gender?

1•13 ¿Recuerdas?

Take turns determining which of the following nouns are masculine (**M**) and which are feminine (**F**).
¡OJO! Some are exceptions!

1. ______ hijas
2. ______ discusión
3. ______ mapa
4. ______ nacionalidad
5. ______ hermano
6. ______ manos
7. ______ mamá
8. ______ abuelos

1•14 Para practicar

Take turns deciding whether these cognates are masculine or feminine. Can you guess their English equivalents?

1. guitarra
2. teléfono
3. computadora
4. drama
5. cafetería
6. educación

5 Los artículos definidos e indefinidos

1-19 to 1-22

1

Eduardo tiene una hermana. La hermana de Eduardo se llama Adriana.

Like English, Spanish has two kinds of articles, definite and indefinite. The definite article in English is *the*; the indefinite articles are *a*, *an*, and *some*.

In Spanish, articles and other adjectives mirror the gender (masculine or feminine) and number (singular or plural) of the nouns to which they refer. For example, an article referring to a singular masculine noun must also be singular and masculine. Note the forms of the articles in the following charts.

Fíjate

Note that *el* means "the," and *él* means "he."

Los artículos definidos

el hermano	*the brother*	los hermanos	*the brothers/the brothers and sisters*
la hermana	*the sister*	las hermanas	*the sisters*

Los artículos indefinidos

un hermano	*a/one brother*	unos hermanos	*some brothers/some brothers and sisters*
una hermana	*a/one sister*	unas hermanas	*some sisters*

1. ***Definite articles*** are used to refer to **the** person, place, or thing.
2. ***Indefinite articles*** are used to refer to **a** or **some** person, place, or thing.

Adriana es **la** hermana de Eduardo y **los** abuelos de él se llaman Carmen y Manuel. — *Adriana is Eduardo's sister, and his grandparents' names are Carmen and Manuel.*

Jorge tiene **una** tía y **unos** tíos. — *Jorge has an aunt and some uncles.*

1•15 Vamos a practicar

Complete these steps.

Paso 1 Take turns giving the correct form of the *definite* article for each of the following nouns.

MODELO E1: tías
E2: *las tías*

1. tío	3. mamá	5. hermanas	7. abuela
2. padres	4. papá	6. hijo	8. primo

Paso 2 This time provide the correct form of the *indefinite* article.

MODELO E1: tías
E2: *unas tías*

1•16 Una concordancia

Take turns matching the family members with the corresponding articles. Each family member will have **two** articles: one definite, one indefinite.

1. ______ hijo
2. ______ hermanas
3. ______ tía
4. ______ primas
5. ______ abuelos

a. el
b. la
c. los
d. las
e. un
f. una
g. unos
h. unas

1•17 ¿Quiénes son?

Fill in the blanks with the correct form of either the definite or indefinite article. Then take turns sharing your answers and explaining your choice. Use the family tree on page 32.

MODELO Adriana es <u>*la*</u> hermana de Eduardo.

(1) ________ abuelos se llaman Manuel y Carmen. Eduardo tiene (2) ________ tío. (3) ________ tío se llama Enrique. Eduardo tiene (4) ________ prima; se llama Sonia. (5) ________ hermano de Eduardo se llama Antonio.

Estrategia

To say "Eduardo's sister," or "Eduardo's grandparents," you add *de Eduardo* to each of your sentences: *Es la hermana de Eduardo. Son los abuelos de Eduardo.*

¿Cómo andas?

Each chapter has three places at which you will be asked to assess your progress. This first assessment comes as you have completed approximately one third of the chapter. How confident are you with your progress to date?

Having completed the first **Comunicación**, I now can...

	Feel Confident	Need to Review
• talk about my family using the verbs **ser** and **tener** (pp. 32, 35)	❑	❑
• pronounce the Spanish vowels correctly (p. 33)	❑	❑
• describe how Hispanic last names are formed (p. 34)	❑	❑
• pluralize singular words (p. 37)	❑	❑
• identify nouns as masculine or feminine (p. 38)	❑	❑
• say *the* and *a/an/some* in Spanish (p. 39)	❑	❑

Comunicación

- Describing yourself and others

Gente

1-23 to 1-25

Miguelito/Clarita

el niño/la niña

Daniel/Mariela

el chico, el muchacho/ la chica, la muchacha

Javier/Ana

el joven/la joven

Manolo/Pilar

el amigo/la amiga

Roberto/Pepita

el novio/la novia

Manuel/Manuela

el hombre/la mujer

el señor Martín/la señora Torres/la señorita Sánchez

el señor/la señora/ la señorita

El hombre and **la mujer** are terms for *man* and *woman*. **Señor, señora,** and **señorita** are often used as titles of address; in that case, they may also be abbreviated as **Sr., Sra.,** and **Srta.,** respectively.

—Buenos días, **señor** Martín. — *Good morning, Mr. Martín.*
—¿Cómo está Ud., **Sra.** Sánchez? — *How are you, Mrs. Sánchez?*

Fíjate

The abbreviations *Sr.*, *Sra.*, and *Srta.* are always capitalized, just like their equivalents in English.

1·18 Los opuestos

Take turns giving the gender opposites for the following words. Include the appropriate articles.

MODELO E1: el novio
E2: *la novia*

1. el chico
2. un hombre
3. la joven
4. un señor
5. una amiga
6. la niña

Take turns answering the following questions based on the drawings on page 41.

MODELO E1: ¿Cómo se llama el hombre?
E2: *El hombre se llama Manuel.*

1. ¿Cómo se llama la joven?
2. ¿Cómo se llama el niño?
3. ¿Cómo se llaman los novios?
4. ¿Cómo se llama la señora?

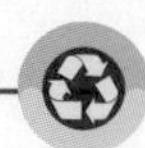

Capítulo Preliminar A. Saludos, despedidas y presentaciones pág. 4.

Los adjetivos posesivos

1-26 to 1-29

4, 17

You have already used the possessive adjective **mi** (*my*). Other forms of possessive adjectives are also useful in conversation.

Look at the following chart to see how to personalize talk about your family (*our* dad, *his* sister, *our* cousins, etc.) using possessive adjectives.

Fíjate

Vuestro/a/os/as is only used in Spain.

Los adjetivos posesivos

mi, mis	*my*	**nuestro/a/os/as**	*our*
tu, tus	*your*	**vuestro/a/os/as**	*your*
su, sus	*his, her, its, your*	**su, sus**	*their, your*

Fíjate

Note that *tu* means "your," and *tú* means "you."

Please note:

1. Possessive adjectives agree in form with the person, place, or thing possessed, *not with the possessor.*
2. Possessive adjectives agree in number (singular or plural), and in addition, **nuestro** and **vuestro** indicate gender (masculine or feminine).
3. The possessive adjectives **tu/tus** (*your*) refer to someone with whom you are familiar and/or on a first name basis. **Su/sus** (*your*) is used when you are referring to people whom you refer to with *Uds.*, that is, more formally and perhaps not on a first-name basis. **Su/sus** (*your* plural or *their*) is used when referring to individuals whom you are addressing with *Uds.*, or when expressing possession with *ellos* and *ellas.*

mi hermano	*my brother*	**mis** hermanos	*my brothers/siblings*
tu primo	*your cousin*	**tus** primos	*your cousins*
su tía	*her/his/your/their aunt*	**sus** tías	*her/his/your/their aunts*
nuestra familia	*our family*	**nuestras** familias	*our families*
vuestra mamá	*your mom*	**vuestras** mamás	*your moms*
su hija	*your/their daughter*	**sus** hijas	*your* (plural)/*their daughters*

Eduardo tiene una novia.	*Eduardo has a girlfriend.*
Su novia se llama Julia.	*His girlfriend's name is Julia.*
Nuestros padres tienen dos amigos.	*Our parents have two friends.*
Sus amigos son Jorge y Marta.	*Their friends are Jorge and Marta.*

1-20 ¿Quién pertenece a quién?

Take turns supplying the correct possessive adjectives for the family members listed.

MODELO E1: (*our*) papás
E2: *nuestros papás*

1. (*your*/familiar) novia
2. (*my*) hermanos
3. (*our*) mamá
4. (*your*/formal) tío
5. (*her*) amiga
6. (*his*) hermanas

1-21 Relaciones familiares

Take turns completing the paragraph about Eduardo's family relationships, from Sonia's point of view. You may want to refer to the family tree on page 32.

Yo soy Sonia. Eduardo es (1) ________ primo. Antonio y Adriana son (2) ________ primos también (*also*). (3) ________ padres, Pedro y Rosario, son (4) ________ tíos. (5) ________ padres se llaman Enrique y Francisca. (6) Además (*Furthermore*), ________ amiga Pilar es como (*like*) parte de (7) (*our*) ________ familia.

Estrategia

Using your own friends and family will help you remember the vocabulary. Write the names of your immediate family or your best friends. Then write a description of how those people are connected to each other. E.g., *Karen es la madre de Brian* or *Brian es el hijo de Karen.*

1-22 Tu familia

Using at least **three** different possessive adjectives, talk to a partner about your family. You may want to refer to the family tree you drew for actividad **1-5.**

MODELO *En mi familia somos cinco personas. Mi padre se llama John y mi madre es Marie. Sus amigos son Mary y Dennis. Tengo dos hermanos, Clark y Blake. Nuestros tíos son Alice y Ralph y nuestras primas se llaman Gina y Glynis.*

Los adjetivos descriptivos

1-30 to 1-35

3, 4

Descriptive adjectives are words that describe people and things. In English, adjectives usually come before the words they describe (e.g., ***red* car**), but in Spanish, they usually follow the word (e.g., **coche *rojo***).

1. Adjectives in Spanish agree with the noun they modify in number (singular or plural) and in gender (masculine or feminine).

Carlos es un **chico** simpático.	*Carlos is a nice boy.*
Adela es una **chica** simpática.	*Adela is a nice girl.*
Carlos y Adela son (unos) **chicos** simpáticos.	*Carlos and Adela are (some) nice children.*

2. A descriptive adjective can also follow the verb **ser** directly. When it does, it still agrees with the noun to which it refers, which is the subject in this case.

Carlos es simpático.	*Carlos is nice.*
Adela es simpática.	*Adela is nice.*
Carlos y Adela son simpáticos.	*Carlos and Adela are nice.*

> **Estrategia**
> Review *Los adjetivos de nacionalidad* in *Capítulo Preliminar A* in order to describe people in more detail.

Las características físicas, la personalidad y otros rasgos

alto alta bajo baja

guapo guapa

delgado delgada gordo gorda

débil fuerte

inteligente

joven mayor

pobre rico rica

La personalidad	Personality
aburrido/a	*boring*
antipático/a	*unpleasant*
bueno/a	*good*
cómico/a	*funny; comical*
interesante	*interesting*
malo/a	*bad*
paciente	*patient*
perezoso/a	*lazy*
responsable	*responsible*
simpático/a	*nice*
tonto/a	*silly; dumb*
trabajador/a	*hard-working*

Las características físicas	Physical characteristics
bonito/a	*pretty*
feo/a	*ugly*
grande	*big; large*
pequeño/a	*small*

Otras palabras útiles	Other useful words
muy	*very*
(un) poco	*(a) little*

1•23 ¿Cómo son?

Take turns describing the following people to a classmate.

MODELO E1: Jorge
E2: *Jorge es débil.*

Jorge

1. Juan

2. María

3. Lupe y Marco

4. Eduardo

5. Adela

6. yo

1•24 ¿Cómo los describes?

Circulate among your classmates, asking for descriptions of the people listed below. Write what each person says, along with his or her name.

MODELO E1: *¿Cómo es LeBron James?*
E2: *LeBron James es alto, fuerte, simpático, inteligente y muy rico.*
E1: *¿Cómo te llamas?*
E2: *Mi nombre es Rubén.*

PERSONA(S)	DESCRIPCIÓN	NOMBRE DEL ESTUDIANTE
LeBron James	*Es alto, fuerte, simpático, inteligente y muy rico.*	*Rubén*
1. Jennifer Aniston y Courteney Cox Arquette		
2. Kanye West		
3. Shakira		
4. tus padres		
5. tu mejor (*best*) amigo/a y tú		
6. David Letterman		
7. Dwayne "The Rock" Johnson		
8. Beyoncé		
9. Shaquille O'Neal		
10. yo		

1•25 Al contrario

Student 1 creates a sentence using the cues provided, and Student 2 expresses the opposite. Pay special attention to adjective agreement.

MODELO los hermanos González / guapo
E1: *Los hermanos González son guapos.*
E2: *¡Ay no, son muy feos!*

1. los abuelos / pobre
2. la señora López / muy antipático
3. Jaime / delgado
4. la tía Adela / mayor
5. Tomás y Antonia / alto
6. nosotros / perezoso

Capítulo Preliminar A. El verbo *ser*, pág. 13.

1•26 ¿Cómo eres?

Imagine you are applying to a dating service.

Paso 1 Describe yourself to your partner using at least **three** adjectives, and then describe your ideal date.

MODELO *Me llamo Julie. Soy joven, muy inteligente y alta.*
Mi hombre ideal es inteligente, paciente y cómico.

Paso 2 How similar are you and your partner's ideal mates?

MODELO *Rebeca y yo somos jóvenes, altas y muy inteligentes.*
Nuestros hombres ideales son cómicos y pacientes.

Soy inteligente, cómico y responsable. No soy muy rico pero soy trabajador. ¿Eres inteligente, simpática y cómica? Contacta con matchideal.com/chucho.

Estrategia

Being an "active listener" is an important skill in any language. *Active listening* means that you hear and understand what someone is saying. Being able to repeat what someone says helps you practice and perfect the skill of active listening.

1•27 ¿Es cierto o falso?

Describe **five** famous (or infamous!) people or characters. Your partner can react by saying **Es verdad** (*It's true*) or **No es verdad** (*It's not true*). If your partner disagrees with you, he/she must correct your statement.

MODELO
E1: *Garfield es gordo y un poco antipático.*
E2: *No es verdad. Sí, es gordo pero no es antipático. Es simpático.*

1•28 ¿Cuáles son sus cualidades?

Think of the qualities of your best friend and those of someone you do not particularly like (**una persona que no me gusta**). Using adjectives that you know in Spanish, write at least **three** sentences that describe each of these people. Share your list with a partner.

MODELO

MI MEJOR (*BEST*) AMIGO/A	UNA PERSONA QUE NO ME GUSTA
1. *Es trabajador/a.*	1. *Es antipático/a.*
2. *Es inteligente.*	2. *No es paciente.*
3. …	3. …

Capítulo Preliminar A. Los pronombres personales, pág. 11.

1•29 Describe una familia

Bring family photos (personal ones or some taken from the Internet or a magazine) to class and describe the family members to a classmate, using at least **five** sentences.

MODELO *Tengo dos hermanas, Kate y Ana. Ellas son simpáticas y bonitas. Mi papá no es aburrido y es muy trabajador. Tengo seis primos…*

1-36 to 1-37

El español, lengua diversa

Guagua, camión o autobús.

The title of this chapter, **¿Quiénes somos?**, suggests that we are all a varied combination of many factors, one of which is language. As you know, the English language is rich in state, regional, and national variations. For example, what word do you use when referring to soft drinks? Some people in the United States say *soda*, others say *pop*, and still others use *Coke* as a generic term for all brands and flavors of soft drinks.

The Spanish language also has many variations. For example, to describe someone as *funny* you could say **cómico/a** in many Latin American countries, but **divertido/a** or **gracioso/a** in Spain. Similarly, there are multiple ways to say the word *bus*: in Mexico, **camión;** in Puerto Rico and Cuba, **guagua;** in Spain, **autobús.** In ***¡Anda!,*** such variants will appear in **También se dice**..., Appendix 3.

The pronunciation of English also varies in different parts of the United States and throughout the rest of the English-speaking world, and so it is with Spanish across the Spanish-speaking world. Nevertheless, wherever you go you will find that Spanish is still Spanish, despite regional and national differences. You should have little trouble understanding native speakers from different countries or making yourself understood. You may have to attune your ears to local vocabulary or pronunciation, but that's part of the intrigue of communicating in another language.

Preguntas

1. What are some characteristics of the English spoken in other countries, such as Canada, Great Britain, Australia, and India?
2. What are some English words that are used where you live that are not necessarily used in other parts of the country?

Los números 31–100

1-38 to 1-41

The numbers 31–100 function in much the same way as the numbers 0–30. Consider how the numbers 30–39 are formed. This pattern will repeat itself up to 100.

31	**treinta y uno**	37	**treinta y siete**	51	**cincuenta y uno...**
32	**treinta y dos**	38	**treinta y ocho**	60	**sesenta**
33	**treinta y tres**	39	**treinta y nueve**	70	**setenta**
34	**treinta y cuatro**	40	**cuarenta**	80	**ochenta**
35	**treinta y cinco**	41	**cuarenta y uno...**	90	**noventa**
36	**treinta y seis**	50	**cincuenta**	100	**cien**

Estrategia

Practice the numbers in Spanish by reading and pronouncing any numbers you see in your daily routine (e.g., highway signs, prices on your shopping receipts, room numbers on campus, or phone numbers).

1•30 Examen de matemáticas

Are you ready to test your math skills? Take turns reading and solving the problems aloud. Then create your own math problems to test your partner.

Vocabulario útil

más	*plus*
menos	*minus*
son	*equals*
por	*times; by*
dividido por	*divided by*

MODELO E1: 97 − 53 =
E2: *Noventa y siete menos cincuenta y tres son cuarenta y cuatro.*

1. 81 + 13 =
2. 65 − 26 =
3. 24 + 76 =
4. 99 − 52 =
5. 12 × 8 =
6. 8 × 7 =
7. 65 ÷ 5 =
8. 100 ÷ 2 =

1•31 ¿Qué número es?

Look at the pages from the telephone book. Say **five** phone numbers and have your partner tell you whose numbers they are. Then switch roles.

MODELO E1: *Ochenta y ocho, sesenta y ocho, setenta y cinco*
E2: *Adelaida Santoyo*

SANTOS JAIME-SIERRA 12I 12 SM 3 CP 77500....**84-0661**
SANTOS JAVIER L1 Y 12 M10 SM43 PEDREGAL CP 77500........**80-5138**
SANTOS SEGOVIA FREDDY CALLE 45 NTE MANZ 34 LTE 3 COL 77528........**80-2242**
SANTOS SEGURA ALBA ROSA COL LEONA VICARIO M 8 L SM 74 77500........**80-0861**
SANTOS SOLIS FELIPE CALLE 20 OTE NO 181 SM 68 M 12 L 28 CP 77500........**80-1330**
SANTOS VELÁZQUEZ MARÍA JESÚS CALLE 3 NO 181 77537........**86-6949**
SANTOS VILLANUEVA ARMINDA CALLE 46 PTE MANZ 20 77510........**88-3999**
SANTOS JOSÉ E CALLE 33 OTE 171 L 14 M 25 CP 77500........**80-1175**
SANTOSCOY LAGUNES ELIZABETH CERRADA FLAMBOYANES 2 SM23........**87-6204**
SANTOYO ADELAIDA CALLE 75 NTE DEPTO 7 EDIF 2 SM 92 CP 77500........**88-6875**
SANTOYO BETANCOURT PEDRO ARIEL HDA NUM 12 NABZ 61 77517........**88-7941**
SANTOYO CORTEZ LIGIA EDIFICIO QUETZAL DEPTO C-1 SM 32 77500........**87-4676**
SANTOYO MARTÍN AIDA MARÍA NANCE DEP 4 MZA 12 NUM 13........**87-3799**

1•32 ¿Quiere dejar un recado?

Imagine that you work in a busy office. You take messages with the following phone numbers. Say the numbers to a partner who will write them down. Then switch roles, mixing the order of the numbers.

MODELO E1: 223-7256
E2: *dos, veintitrés, setenta y dos, cincuenta y seis*

1. 962-2136
2. 615-9563
3. 871-4954
4. 414-4415
5. 761-7920
6. 270-2325

1•33 Los hispanos en los EE.UU.

Use the information from the pie chart on page 53 to answer the following questions in Spanish. Round the answers to the nearest whole number.

Fíjate

In most of the Spanish-speaking world, commas are used where we use decimal points, and vice versa. For example, in English one says "six point four percent," in Spanish, *seis coma cuatro por ciento.*

Capítulo Preliminar A. Los números 0–30, pág. 16.

Vocabulario útil

por ciento *percent*

1. What percentage of U.S. Hispanics is from Cuba?
2. What percentage of U.S. Hispanics is from Puerto Rico?
3. What percentage of U.S. Hispanics is from Mexico?
4. What percentage of Hispanics comes from other Spanish-speaking countries?
5. What percentage of U.S. Hispanics comes from countries other than Mexico?

ESCUCHA

1-42 to 1-44

Alejandra

Aural comprehension is critical in learning to communicate in Spanish. You are working on developing your listening skills every time your instructor speaks or when you work in pairs or groups in class. You will also practice this skill when you watch the video episodes of **Ambiciones siniestras,** the mystery story that accompanies *¡Anda!*

In *¡Anda!* you will have the opportunity to learn and practice strategies to assist you in developing listening skills in Spanish. Let's begin with listening for words you know, including cognates.

ESTRATEGIA **Determining the topic and listening for words you know**

The first steps to becoming a successful listener are to determine the topic and then listen for words that you know. If you are in a social situation, you can determine the topic by looking for visual cues (body language, pictures, etc.) or by asking the speaker(s) for clarification. When listening to passages in ***¡Anda!,*** look at the activities or questions connected with the passage to help you determine the topic. Remember that words that you know include *cognates* which are words that look and sound like words in English.

1•34 **Antes de escuchar**

In the following segment, Alejandra, one of the characters from **Ambiciones siniestras,** introduces her family. Write down two things that you expect to hear.

1•35 **A escuchar**

CD 1
Track 18

Listen as Alejandra introduces her family. Use the following steps to help you.

a. First, look at the incomplete sentences in **c.** They will give you an idea about the topic of the passage.
b. Listen to the passage, concentrating on the words you know. Make a list of those words.
c. Listen one more time and complete these sentences.
   1. La familia de Alejandra es ________________.
   2. Los nombres de sus padres son ________________.
   3. Alejandra tiene ________________ hermanos y ________________ hermanas.

1•36 **Después de escuchar**

Take turns saying **three** sentences about you and your family to a partner. Your partner will tell you the words he/she knows.

SAM 1-45 to 1-46

1•37 **Antes de escribir**

Write down all the Spanish nouns and adjectives you can think of that describe you. Start by reviewing the vocabulary lists for **Capítulo 1** and **También se dice…**, Appendix 3.

1•38 **Un poema**

Complete the following steps in order to write your first poem in Spanish.

Paso 1 Using either your first, middle, or last name, match a noun or descriptive adjective with each letter of that name. For example:

*"Sarah": **S** = simpática, **a** = alta, **r** = responsable, **a** = amiga, **h** = hermana*

With these words, create what is known as an *acrostic* poem.

Paso 2 Now build phrases or sentences around your letters, using **tener, ser,** possessive adjectives, and numbers.

MODELO

***S**impática*	***SARAH***
***A**lta*	*es **S**impática*
***R**esponsable*	*no es baja; es **A**lta*
***A**miga*	*no es **R**esponsable*
***H**ermana*	*tiene cien **A**migos (¡es rica!)*
	*es mi **H**ermana.*

1•39 **Después de escribir**

Read your poem to a classmate.

¿Cómo andas?

This is your second self-assessment. You have now completed two thirds of the chapter. How confident are you with the following topics and concepts?

Having completed the second **Comunicación,** I now can…

	Feel Confident	Need to Review
• tell the difference between words like **niño** and **joven** as well as which titles (**Sr., Srta.,** etc.) to use when addressing someone (p. 41)	❑	❑
• use different types of adjectives: possessive (**mi, tus,** etc.) and descriptive (**inteligente, alto,** etc.) (p. 42, 44)	❑	❑
• describe myself and others in complete sentences (p. 44)	❑	❑
• state one fact about the diverse nature of the Spanish language (p. 48)	❑	❑
• count from 31 to 100 (p. 48)	❑	❑
• listen for words I know (p. 50)	❑	❑
• write a short poem (p. 51)	❑	❑

CULTURA

Los Estados Unidos

Alberto Martínez Vergara

CW eBook

CD 1
Track 19

SAM

1-47

Vistas culturales

Les presento mi país

Mi nombre es Alberto Martínez Vergara y soy de Paterson, Nueva Jersey. Soy bilingüe: hablo inglés y español. Soy estadounidense pero mi padre es de México y mi madre es de Puerto Rico. Hay muchos hispanohablantes (*Spanish speakers*) en los Estados Unidos. **¿Puedes** (*Can you*) **identificar otras cuatro o cinco ciudades en el mapa con grandes poblaciones hispanohablantes?** Hay hispanohablantes famosos de muchas carreras diferentes, como Jennifer López y Pedro Martínez. **¿Por qué son famosas estas personas?** También se nota la influencia hispana en los restaurantes y en los supermercados donde se ofrecen productos hispanos de compañías como Goya, Ortega, Corona, Marinela y Tecate. Mi restaurante favorito se llama *La Bodega*. **¿Cuál es tu restaurante favorito?**

Pedro Martínez es un beisbolista dominicano famoso.

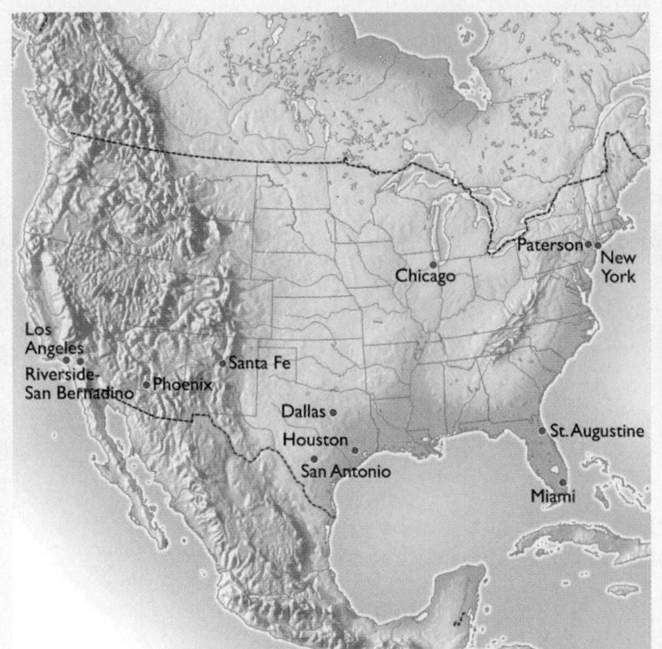

St. Augustine es la primera ciudad europea en los EE.UU., fundada en 1565 por los españoles.

Cristina Saralegui tiene un programa de televisión.

Celebrando la herencia puertorriqueña en Nueva York.

Los productos Goya se encuentran en muchos supermercados.

ALMANAQUE

Nombre oficial:	Estados Unidos de América
Gobierno:	República constitucional y federal
Población:	299.209.430 (est., 2006)
Población de origen hispano:	41,3 millones (est., 2006)
Moneda:	el dólar ($)

ESTADO

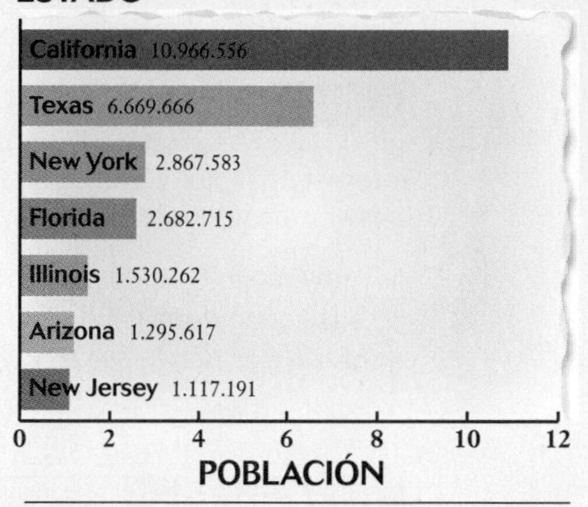

Source: Frank Hobbs and Nicole Stoops, U.S. Census Bureau, Special Reports, Series

PORCENTAJE DE POBLACIÓN HISPANA

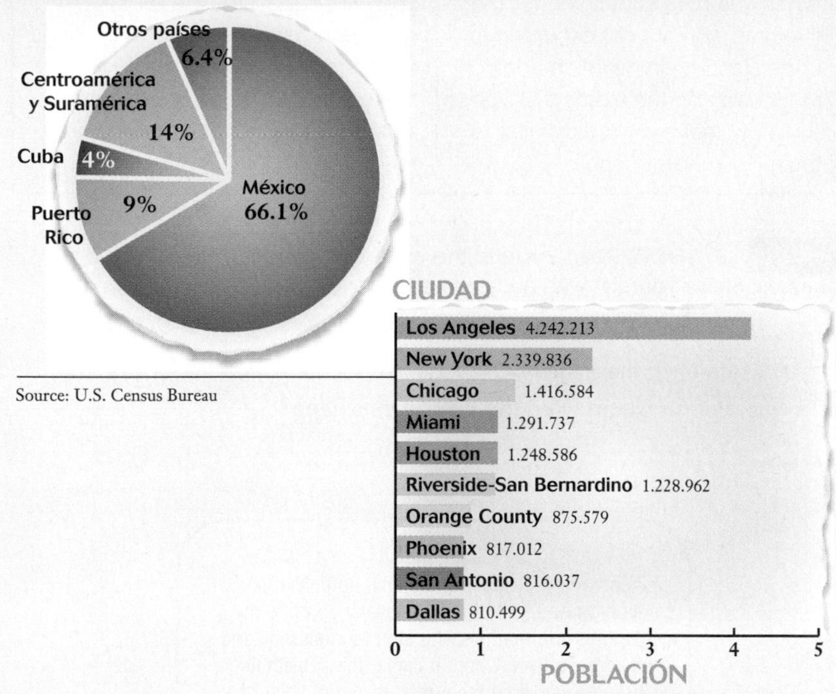

Source: U.S. Census Bureau

Source: Brookings Institution

AUMENTO *(Rise)* EN LA POBLACIÓN HISPANA EN LOS ÚLTIMOS 20 AÑOS

Ciudad	Población	Porcentaje
Raleigh, NC	72.580	1180%
Atlanta, GA	268.851	995%
Greensboro, NC	62.210	962%
Charlotte, NC	77.092	932%
Orlando, FL	271.627	859%
Las Vegas, NV	322.038	753%
Nashville, TN	40.139	630%
Fort Lauderdale, FL	271.652	578%
Sarasota, FL	38.682	538%

Source: Brookings Institution

¿Sabías que...?

- Para el año 2050, una de cada cuatro personas en los Estados Unidos va a ser de origen hispano.
- En los Estados Unidos se celebra el mes de la herencia hispana entre el 15 de septiembre y el 15 de octubre.

PREGUNTAS

1. ¿Qué importancia tiene St. Augustine, Florida?
2. ¿Qué estados tienen la mayor (*the largest*) población hispana?
3. ¿Quiénes son algunos (*some*) hispanos famosos en los EE.UU.? ¿Cuál es tu favorito?

En la Red
Learn more about Hispanics in the United States on your *¡Anda!* web site.

Ambiciones siniestras

EPISODIO 1

SAM 1-49

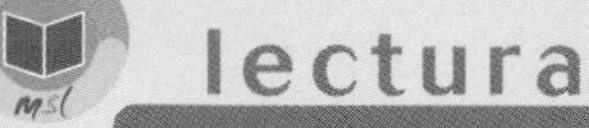

lectura

1-40 **Antes de leer.** You are about to discover what happens to a group of college students as they unwittingly become involved in a sinister international plot. Before you read the first episode of **Ambiciones siniestras,** answer these questions.

1. How much time do you spend on the computer composing, reading, and answering e-mails?
2. To whom do you write most frequently? For what purpose(s)?
3. With a partner, list as many reasons as you can for sending e-mails.

ESTRATEGIA **Recognizing Cognates**

When you read something for the first time, you are not expected to understand every word. In addition to focusing on the words that you *do* know, look for words similar to those you know in English, *cognates*. Cognates are an excellent way to help you understand what you are reading. Make sure that you complete the **Antes de leer** activities to practice this strategy.

Three students from different universities are writing e-mail messages to friends or family members. What can you learn about the three students from their e-mails? What can you learn about the person to whom or about whom each one is writing?

1-41 **A leer.** Read through the messages quickly, underlining all cognates. Share your list with a classmate. Then answer these questions.

1. How many messages are there?
2. Who wrote each message?
3. To whom or for whom were the messages written?

Estrategia

When writing or reading e-mails, note what parts are common to all of them. Usually you find the following information: who sent the message and the address from where it came, the subject line that indicates what the e-mail is about, a list of other people who might have received it, etc. Use your knowledge of writing and receiving e-mails in English to see if you can understand the additional information presented in *Ambiciones siniestras.*

CD 1
Track 20

Conexiones

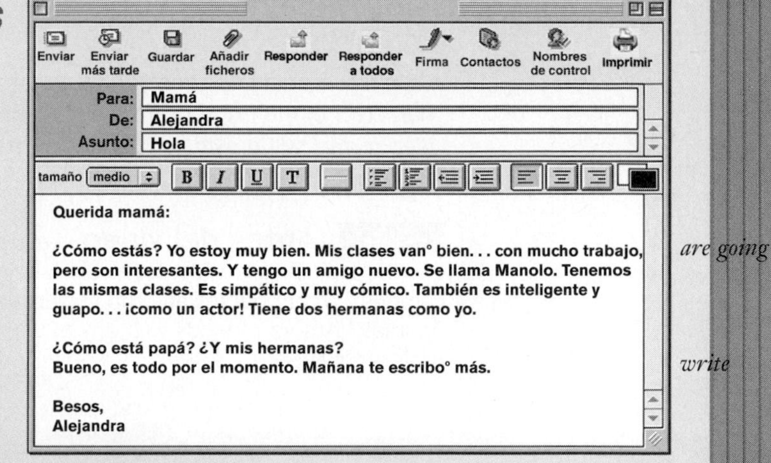

Enviar | Enviar más tarde | Guardar | Añadir ficheros | Responder | Responder a todos | Firma | Contactos | Nombres de control | Imprimir

Para: Mamá
De: Alejandra
Asunto: Hola

Querida mamá:

¿Cómo estás? Yo estoy muy bien. Mis clases van° bien. . . con mucho trabajo, pero son interesantes. Y tengo un amigo nuevo. Se llama Manolo. Tenemos las mismas clases. Es simpático y muy cómico. También es inteligente y guapo. . . ¡como un actor! Tiene dos hermanas como yo.

¿Cómo está papá? ¿Y mis hermanas?
Bueno, es todo por el momento. Mañana te escribo° más.

Besos,
Alejandra

are going
write

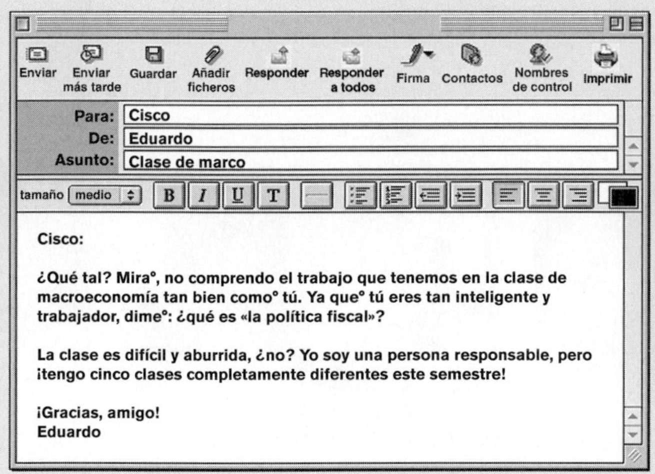

Enviar | Enviar más tarde | Guardar | Añadir ficheros | Responder | Responder a todos | Firma | Contactos | Nombres de control | Imprimir

Para: Cisco
De: Eduardo
Asunto: Clase de marco

Cisco:

¿Qué tal? Mira°, no comprendo el trabajo que tenemos en la clase de macroeconomía tan bien como° tú. Ya que° tú eres tan inteligente y trabajador, dime°: ¿qué es «la política fiscal»?

La clase es difícil y aburrida, ¿no? Yo soy una persona responsable, pero ¡tengo cinco clases completamente diferentes este semestre!

¡Gracias, amigo!
Eduardo

Look
as well as/Since
tell me

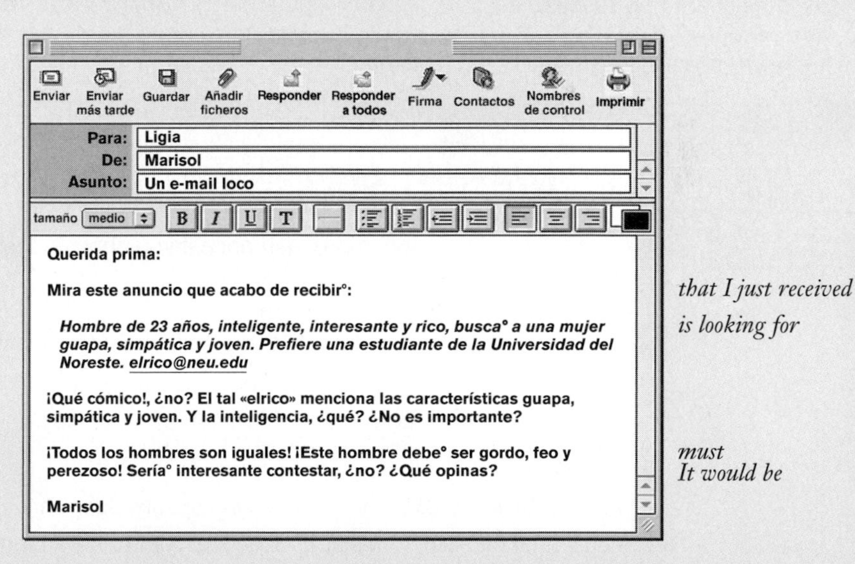

Enviar | Enviar más tarde | Guardar | Añadir ficheros | Responder | Responder a todos | Firma | Contactos | Nombres de control | Imprimir

Para: Ligia
De: Marisol
Asunto: Un e-mail loco

Querida prima:

Mira este anuncio que acabo de recibir°:

> ***Hombre de 23 años, inteligente, interesante y rico, busca° a una mujer guapa, simpática y joven. Prefiere una estudiante de la Universidad del Noreste. elrico@neu.edu***

¡Qué cómico!, ¿no? El tal «elrico» menciona las características guapa, simpática y joven. Y la inteligencia, ¿qué? ¿No es importante?

¡Todos los hombres son iguales! ¡Este hombre debe° ser gordo, feo y perezoso! Sería° interesante contestar, ¿no? ¿Qué opinas?

Marisol

that I just received
is looking for
must
It would be

1-42 **Después de leer.** Answer the following questions.

1. What was the purpose of each message? Was it friendly communication? Did the person need something from someone else?
2. Of the senders, recipients, and others mentioned in the messages, which person is most like you? Which one would you most like to meet? Why?

1-50 to 1-54

video

In the first reading episode you were introduced briefly to some of the characters of the mystery story **Ambiciones siniestras.** The next episode in video format will provide a further glimpse into the lives of the characters on their respective campuses.

1-43 Antes del video. Let's think about you and your campus experiences for a minute. Do you take classes on a traditional college campus? What courses are you currently taking? Are your classes large or small? Are you friends with any of your classmates? What are your professors like?

Cisco y Eduardo en su clase de macroeconomía.

La familia de Lupe es hispana y la familia de Marisol es hispana también.

Alejandra y Manolo en su clase de literatura española.

Episodio 1

¿Quiénes son?

Relax and watch the video, more than once if you choose, then complete the activity that follows.

1-44 Después del video. Identify the person(s) who fit(s) each description below.

Lupe Cisco Eduardo Marisol Manolo Alejandra

This character...

1. has grandparents who are Hispanic and speaks Spanish with siblings.
2. seems to like Phillip Jones and introduces him to her friend.
3. has a class every Tuesday and Thursday at 2 P.M.
4. helps Eduardo prepare for class.
5. is a student in a Spanish literature class.

Estrategia.

In this video episode, you get to place the names of the characters with their faces. Using the information in your textbook, focus on the specific items you will need to answer after watching the video. For actividad **1-44** (*Después del video*), you see the characters' names. While you are listening and watching, jot down the name of each character that fits the description.

Y por fin, ¿cómo andas?

Each chapter will end with a checklist like the one that follows. This is the third time in the chapter that you are given the opportunity to check your progress. Use the checklist to measure what you have learned in the chapter. Place a check in the *Feel confident* column of the topics you feel you know, and a check in the *Need to Review* column for the topics that you need to practice more.

Having completed this chapter, I now can…

	Feel Confident	Need to Review
Comunicación		
• talk about my family using the verbs **ser** and **tener** (pp. 32, 35)	❑	❑
• pronounce the Spanish vowels correctly (p. 33)	❑	❑
• pluralize singular words (p. 37)	❑	❑
• identify nouns as masculine or feminine (p. 38)	❑	❑
• use *the* and *a/an/some* appropriately in Spanish (p. 39)	❑	❑
• know the difference between words like **niño** and **joven** as well as which titles (**Sr., Srta.,** etc.) to use when addressing someone (p. 41)	❑	❑
• use different types of adjectives: possessive (**mi, tus,** etc.) and descriptive (**inteligente, alto,** etc.) (p. 42, 44)	❑	❑
• describe myself and others in complete sentences (p. 44)	❑	❑
• count from 31 to 100 (p. 48)	❑	❑
• listen for words I know (p. 50)	❑	❑
• write a short poem (p. 51)	❑	❑
Cultura		
• describe how Hispanic last names are formed (p. 34)	❑	❑
• state one fact about the diverse nature of the Spanish language (p. 48)	❑	❑
• state three facts about Hispanics in the United States (p. 52)	❑	❑
Ambiciones siniestras		
• recognize cognates when I read (p. 54)	❑	❑
• describe three of the protagonists in **Ambiciones siniestras** briefly (p. 56)	❑	❑

VOCABULARIO ACTIVO

CD 1
Tracks 21-28

La familia	Family
el/la abuelo/a	*grandfather/grandmother*
los abuelos	*grandparents*
el/la esposo/a	*husband/wife*
el/la hermano/a	*brother/sister*
los hermanos	*brothers and sisters; siblings*
el/la hijo/a	*son/daughter*
los hijos	*sons and daughters; children*
la madrastra	*stepmother*
la madre/la mamá	*mother/mom*
el padrastro	*stepfather*
el padre/el papá	*father/dad*
los padres	*parents*
el/la primo/a	*cousin*
los primos	*cousins*
el/la tío/a	*uncle/aunt*
los tíos	*aunts and uncles*

La gente	People
el/la amigo/a	*friend*
el/la chico/a	*boy/girl*
el hombre	*man*
el/la joven	*young man/young woman*
el/la muchacho/a	*boy/girl*
la mujer	*woman*
el/la niño/a	*little boy/little girl*
el/la novio/a	*boyfriend/girlfriend*
el señor (Sr.)	*man; gentleman; Mr.*
la señora (Sra.)	*woman; lady; Mrs.*
la señorita (Srta.)	*young woman; Miss*

Las características físicas	Physical characteristics
alto/a	*tall*
bajo/a	*short*
bonito/a	*pretty*
débil	*weak*
delgado/a	*thin*
feo/a	*ugly*
fuerte	*strong*
gordo/a	*fat*
grande	*big; large*
guapo/a	*handsome/pretty*
joven	*young*
mayor	*old*
pequeño/a	*small*

Los adjetivos	*Adjectives*
La personalidad y otros rasgos	*Personality and other characteristics*
aburrido/a	*boring*
antipático/a	*unpleasant*
bueno/a	*good*
cómico/a	*funny; comical*
inteligente	*intelligent*
interesante	*interesting*
malo/a	*bad*
paciente	*patient*
perezoso/a	*lazy*
pobre	*poor*
responsable	*responsible*
rico/a	*rich*
simpático/a	*nice*
tonto/a	*silly; dumb*
trabajador/a	*hard-working*

Los números 31–100	*Numbers 31–100*
treinta y uno	*thirty-one*
treinta y dos	*thirty-two*
treinta y tres	*thirty-three*
treinta y cuatro	*thirty-four*
treinta y cinco	*thirty-five*
treinta y seis	*thirty-six*
treinta y siete	*thirty-seven*
treinta y ocho	*thirty-eight*
treinta y nueve	*thirty-nine*
cuarenta	*forty*
cuarenta y uno	*forty-one*
cincuenta	*fifty*
cincuenta y uno	*fifty-one*
sesenta	*sixty*
setenta	*seventy*
ochenta	*eighty*
noventa	*ninety*
cien	*one hundred*

Los verbos	*Verbs*
tener	*to have*
Otras palabras útiles	*Other useful words*
muy	*very*
(un) poco	*(a) little*

Vocabulario útil	*Useful vocabulary*
más	*plus*
menos	*minus*
son	*equals*
por ciento	*percent*
por	*times; by*
dividido por	*divided by*

If you are interested in discovering additional vocabulary for the topics studied in each chapter, consult Appendix 3, **También se dice...**, for additional words. It contains expanded vocabulary that you may need for your own personal expression, including regionally used words and slang. Enjoy!

2

La vida universitaria

The majority of universities throughout the Spanish-speaking world tend to be public, charging minimal tuition, if any. Students must pass rigorous admission exams in order to attend. In many countries, the exams they take or the scores they receive determine the career they may choose. In their first year, college students begin to take courses in their major area. Public universities generally have vast numbers of students.

La biblioteca de la *Universidad Nacional Autónoma de México (UNAM)*

PREGUNTAS

1. How large is your college or university? What are the advantages of studying at a college or university of this size? Are there any disadvantages?
2. What are some possible advantages and disadvantages of the large universities of some Spanish-speaking countries?
3. Why do many colleges and universities require general education courses prior to entering courses for the major? Why do many colleges and universities have a language requirement?

Comunicación

- Talking about school

VOCABULARIO 1 Las materias y las especialidades

SAM 2-1 to 2-4

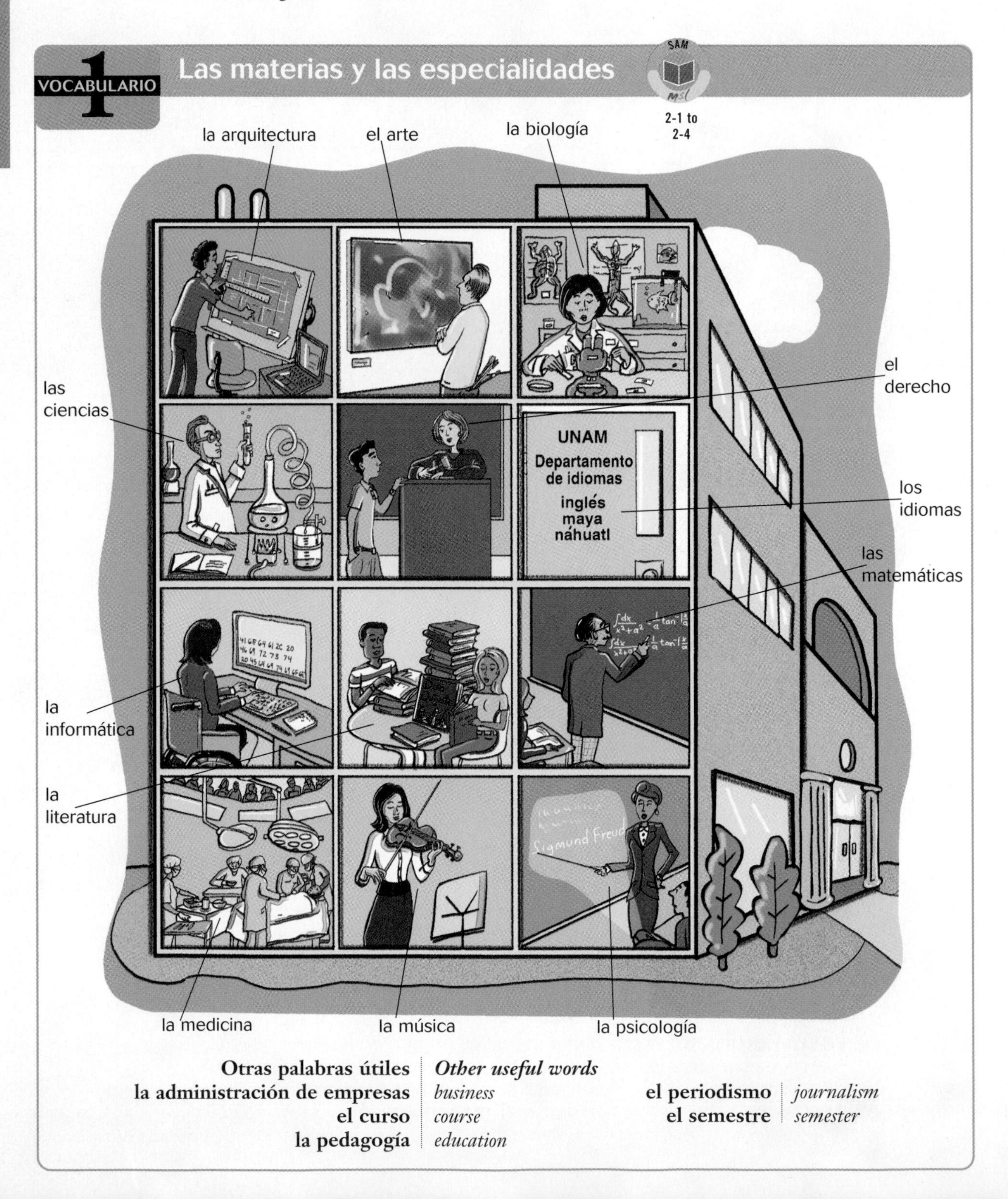

Otras palabras útiles	*Other useful words*
la administración de empresas	*business*
el curso	*course*
la pedagogía	*education*
el periodismo	*journalism*
el semestre	*semester*

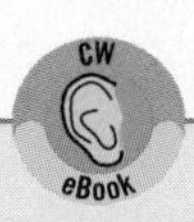

CD 1
Track 29

2-5 to
2-7

PRONUNCIACIÓN

Word stress and accent marks

In Spanish, written accents are used to distinguish word meaning, or when a word is "breaking" a pronunciation rule. Here are the basic rules of Spanish pronunciation and accentuation.

1. Words ending in a vowel, or in the consonants **n** or **s** are stressed on the *next-to-last syllable*. Listen to and then pronounce the following words.
   medicina, derecho, grande, tienen, abuelos, nosotros, arte
2. Words ending in consonants other than **n** or **s** are stressed on the *last syllable*. Listen to and then pronounce the following words.
   tener, usted, Rafael, ciudad, Gabriel, feliz, llegar
3. All words "breaking" rules **#1** and **#2** above need a written accent on the stressed syllable. Listen to and then pronounce the following words.
   televisión, biología, informática, fácil, Ramón, música
4. Written accents are used on all *interrogative* and *exclamatory* words. Listen to and then pronounce the following words.
   ¿Cómo?, ¿Qué?, ¿Cuándo?, ¿Quién?, ¿Cuántos?, ¿Dónde?, ¡Qué bueno!
5. Written accents are also used to *differentiate meaning* of certain one-syllable words that are written and pronounced alike. Listen to and then pronounce the following words.

él (*he*)	**el** (*the*)
mí (*me*)	**mi** (*my*)
sí (*yes*)	**si** (*if*)
tú (*you*)	**tu** (*your*)

Fíjate

Accent marks appear only over vowels.

2•1 **Las palabras**

Practice pronouncing the following words, focusing on the stress.

1. abuelos
2. medicina
3. ¿Dónde?
4. música
5. tener
6. arte
7. usted
8. derecho
9. nosotros
10. biología

2•2 **Las oraciones**

Practice pronouncing the following sentences and pay special attention to the stress.

1. Estudio medicina. ¿Qué estudias tú?
2. La música jazz es muy interesante.
3. Mi abuelo se llama Manuel Ramón Jiménez.

2•3 **Los dichos y refranes**

Now pronounce the following saying and focus on the stress.

Dime con quién andas y te diré quién eres.

2•4 ¿Cuál es su especialidad?

Complete the following steps.

Paso 1 Take turns matching the following famous people with the majors they may have studied in college.

1. ______ Pablo Picasso
2. ______ Maya Angelou
3. ______ Marie Curie
4. ______ Sigmund Freud
5. ______ el presidente de Coca-Cola
6. ______ former Supreme Court Justice Sandra Day O'Connor
7. ______ Shania Twain/Johann Sebastian Bach
8. ______ Bill Gates

a. música
b. arte
c. psicología
d. informática
e. literatura
f. ciencias
g. derecho
h. administración de empresas

Paso 2 Now, can you name the majors the following famous Hispanics may have studied in college?

Ellen Ochoa

Geraldo Rivera

Isabel Allende

Carlos Santana

2•5 ¿Qué clases tienes?

Complete the following chart, then share your schedule with a partner.

HORARIO DE CLASES

CLASES	DÍAS DE LA SEMANA	HORA
matemáticas	*martes y jueves*	*1:30*

Capítulo Preliminar A. La hora, pág. 18; Los días de la semana, pág. 20.

MODELO *Este semestre tengo cinco cursos. Tengo la clase de matemáticas los martes y jueves a la una y media… ¿Y tú?*

Estrategia

If the meaning of any of the vocabulary words is not clear, verify the definition in the *Vocabulario activo* at the end of this chapter.

2•6 Unos estereotipos

Do you think stereotypes exist just at your university? In your opinion, the following characteristics are stereotypically associated with students majoring in which fields? Share your responses with your group of three or four students, then report the group findings to the class.

Capítulo 1. El verbo *tener*, pág. 35; Los adjetivos descriptivos, pág. 44.

MODELO

E1: *Tengo "Los estudiantes de administración de empresas son ricos". ¿Qué tienes tú?*

E2: *También tengo "Los estudiantes de administración de empresas son ricos".*

E3: *Tengo "Los estudiantes de informática son ricos".*

GRUPO: *Tenemos "Los estudiantes de administración de empresas y los estudiantes de informática son ricos".*

Los estudiantes de…

1. ________________ son ricos.
2. ________________ son simpáticos.
3. ________________ son trabajadores.
4. ________________ son cómicos.
5. ________________ son responsables.
6. ________________ son pacientes.
7. ________________ son interesantes.
8. ________________ son muy inteligentes.

Estrategia

Go to Appendix 3, *También se dice…*, for an expanded list of college majors. *También se dice…* includes additional vocabulary and regional expressions for all chapters. Although not exhaustive, the list will give you an idea of the variety and richness of the Spanish language.

SAM 2-8

Los estereotipos

The first definition that the American Heritage Dictionary lists for *stereotype* is "a conventional, formulaic, and usually oversimplified conception, opinion, or belief." While we all make generalizations in fun about our world, e.g., "the absent-minded professor," perpetuating stereotypes can be hurtful and mean-spirited.

As we learn about the Spanish-speaking world, remember that it is comprised of a vast group of individuals united by the same language. Making generalizations about the Spanish-speaking world is as problematic as making generalizations about the English-speaking world.

Preguntas

1. What are some stereotypes that foreigners hold about people from the United States?
2. What confusion would using the phrase "I am an American" create at a meeting with people from Central and South America?

VOCABULARIO 2 La sala de clase

SAM 2-9 to 2-11

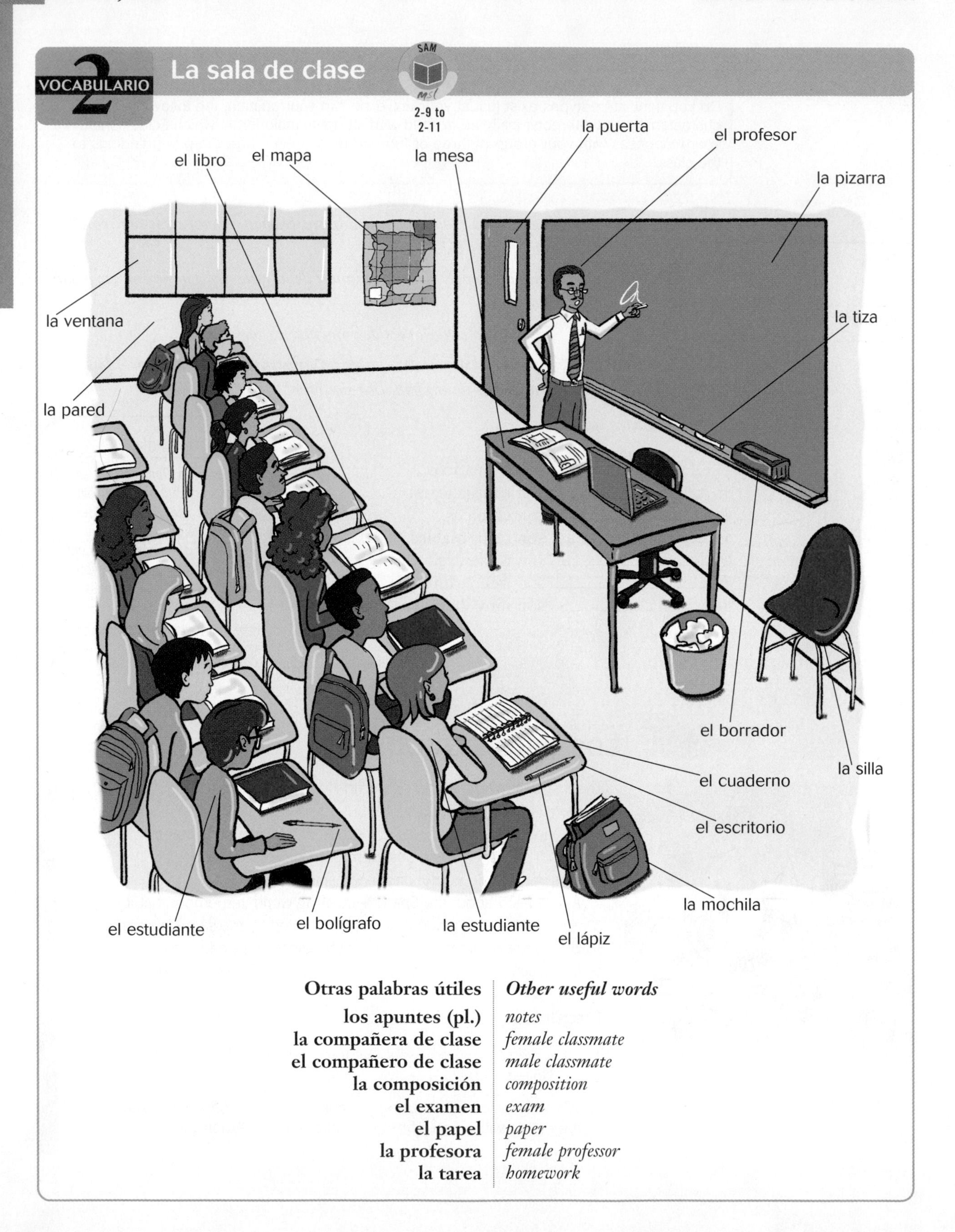

Otras palabras útiles	***Other useful words***
los apuntes (pl.)	*notes*
la compañera de clase	*female classmate*
el compañero de clase	*male classmate*
la composición	*composition*
el examen	*exam*
el papel	*paper*
la profesora	*female professor*
la tarea	*homework*

2•7 ¿Cómo es tu sala de clase?

Using the numbers 0–30, take turns indicating how many there are in your classroom of each of the items presented in **La sala de clase.** You and your partner should each create at least **five** sentences following the model.

Capítulo Preliminar A. Los números 0–30, pág. 16.

MODELO E1: *Hay veinticinco mochilas y tres ventanas.*
E2: *Sí, y también hay diecinueve cuadernos.*

Fíjate

Hay is a little word that carries a lot of meaning. It can be both singular and plural and it means both "there is" and "there are."

Vocabulario útil

hay	*there is; there are*
pero	*but*
también	*too; also*
y	*and*

2•8 ¿Qué tiene Chucho?

Chucho is running late for class again. He has remembered some things and forgotten others. Make a list of **five** things he possibly has and does not have for class, using the verb **tener.** Share your list with a classmate.

MODELO *Chucho tiene los apuntes pero no tiene el libro de matemáticas. También tiene…*

Fíjate

To make a negative statement, simply place the word *no* before the verb: *Chucho tiene los apuntes. Chucho **no** tiene los apuntes.*

2•9 ¿Qué tienen tus compañeros?

Randomly choose three students and complete the chart below. Then take turns having your partner identify the classmates as you state **five** things each one has or does not have for class.

Fíjate

As in English, when listing a series of things, the word *y* (*and*) is placed just before the last item. In Spanish, however, note that you do not place a comma before *y*.

MODELO E1: *La estudiante 1 tiene dos cuadernos, un libro, un bolígrafo y dos lápices. ¡No tiene la tarea!*

E2: *¿Es Sarah?*

E1: *Sí, es Sarah. / No, no es Sarah.*

ESTUDIANTE 1 _____	ESTUDIANTE 2 _____	ESTUDIANTE 3 _____
(NO) TIENE...	(NO) TIENE...	(NO) TIENE...
1.	1.	1.
2.	2.	2.
3.	3.	3.
4.	4.	4.
5.	5.	5.

GRAMÁTICA 3 Presente indicativo de verbos regulares

2-12 to 2-15

7, 11, 13, 14

Mario es un estudiante de derecho. ¿Qué hace (*does he do*) todos los días?

Llega a la clase a las nueve de la mañana.

Lee en la biblioteca.

Habla con sus compañeros.

Trabaja dos horas como tutor.

Come en la cafetería con amigos.

A las 6:30 **espera** el autobús y **regresa** a su apartamento.

Spanish has three groups of verbs which are categorized by the ending of the infinitive. Remember that an infinitive is expressed in English by the word *to: to have, to be*, and *to speak* are all infinitive forms of English verbs. Spanish infinitives end in **-ar, -er,** or **-ir.** Look at the following infinitives.

Verbos que terminan en *-ar*

comprar	*to buy*	**pregunt**ar	*to ask (a question)*
contestar	*to answer*	**prepar**ar	*to prepare; to get ready*
enseñar	*to teach; to show*	**regres**ar	*to return*
esperar	*to wait for; to hope*	**termin**ar	*to finish; to end*
estudiar	*to study*	**tom**ar	*to take; to drink*
hablar	*to speak*	**trabaj**ar	*to work*
llegar	*to arrive*	**us**ar	*to use*
necesitar	*to need*		

Verbos que terminan en *-er*

aprender	*to learn*	**corr**er	*to run*
comer	*to eat*	**cre**er	*to believe*
comprender	*to understand*	**le**er	*to read*

Verbos que terminan en *-ir*

abrir	*to open*	**recib**ir	*to receive*
escribir	*to write*	**viv**ir	*to live*

To talk about daily or ongoing activities or actions, you need to use the present tense. You can also use the present tense to express future events.

Mario **lee** en la biblioteca. — *Mario reads in the library.* / *Mario is reading in the library.*

Mario **lee** en la biblioteca mañana. — *Mario will read in the library tomorrow.*

To form the present indicative, drop the **-ar, -er,** or **-ir** endings from the infinitive, and add the appropriate ending. The endings are highlighted in the following chart. Follow this simple pattern with all regular verbs.

Estrategia

If you would like to review the difference between the formal "you" and the informal "you," return to the cultural reading *¿Tú o usted?* on page 12 of *Capítulo Preliminar A.*

	hablar (*to speak*)	**comer (*to eat*)**	**vivir (*to live*)**
yo	hablo	como	vivo
tú	hablas	comes	vives
él, ella, Ud.	habla	come	vive
nosotros/as	hablamos	comemos	vivimos
vosotros/as	habláis	coméis	vivís
ellos/as, Uds.	hablan	comen	viven

2•10 Vamos a practicar

Take ten small pieces of paper and write a different noun or pronoun (**yo, tú, él,** etc.) on each one. On another five small pieces of paper write five infinitives, one on each piece of paper. Take turns drawing a paper from each pile. Give the correct form of the verb you selected to match the noun or pronoun you picked from the pile. Each person should say at least **five** verbs in a row correctly.

MODELO INFINITIVE: *preguntar*
PRONOUN OR NOUN: *mi madre*
E1: *mi madre pregunta*

2•11 El *e-mail* de Carlos

Complete Carlos's e-mail message to his mother on a separate sheet of paper, using the correct form of the verbs.

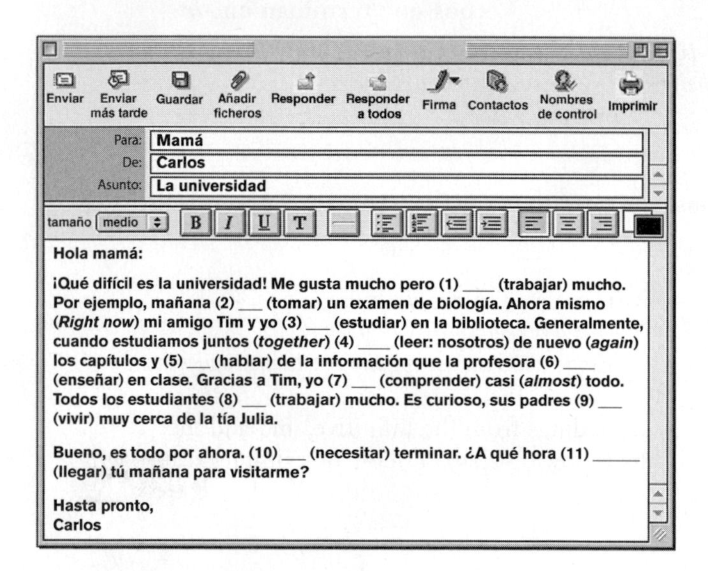

Enviar | Enviar más tarde | Guardar | Añadir ficheros | Responder | Responder a todos | Firma | Contactos | Nombres de control | Imprimir

Para: **Mamá**
De: **Carlos**
Asunto: **La universidad**

tamaño medio

Hola mamá:

¡Qué difícil es la universidad! Me gusta mucho pero (1) ____ (trabajar) mucho. Por ejemplo, mañana (2) ___ (tomar) un examen de biología. Ahora mismo (*Right now*) mi amigo Tim y yo (3) ___ (estudiar) en la biblioteca. Generalmente, cuando estudiamos juntos (*together*) (4) ____ (leer: nosotros) de nuevo (*again*) los capítulos y (5) ___ (hablar) de la información que la profesora (6) ____ (enseñar) en clase. Gracias a Tim, yo (7) ___ (comprender) casi (*almost*) todo. Todos los estudiantes (8) ___ (trabajar) mucho. Es curioso, sus padres (9) ___ (vivir) muy cerca de la tía Julia.

Bueno, es todo por ahora. (10) ___ (necesitar) terminar. ¿A qué hora (11) _____ (llegar) tú mañana para visitarme?

Hasta pronto,
Carlos

Carlos es estudiante de la UNAM. ¿Qué escribe?

2•12 Dime quién, dónde y cuándo

Look at the three columns below. With a pen, connect a pronoun to an activity and then to a class to create **five** sentences. Share your answers with a classmate.

MODELO E1: nosotros / usar un microscopio / clase de ciencias
E2: *Usamos un microscopio en la clase de ciencias.*

PRONOMBRE	ACTIVIDAD	CLASE
yo	preparar una presentación	matemáticas
nosotros/as	leer mucho	inglés
ellos/as	necesitar una calculadora	español
ella	estudiar leyes (*laws*)	periodismo
tú	escribir muchas composiciones	historia
Uds.	contestar muchas preguntas	derecho
él	aprender mucho	ciencias políticas

Fíjate

Remember that subject pronouns (*yo, tú, él, ella,* etc.) are used for emphasis or clarification, and therefore do not always need to be expressed.

2-13 ¿A quién conoces que...?

Who exhibits the following characteristics? Complete the questions below. Then take turns asking and answering in complete sentences to practice the new verbs.

MODELO ¿Quién _____ (hablar) mucho?

E1: *¿Quién habla mucho?*

E2: *Mi hermano Tom habla mucho. También mis hermanas hablan mucho.*

1. ¿Quién ______ (correr) mucho?
2. ¿Quién ______ (estudiar) muy poco (*very little*)?
3. ¿Quién ______ (escribir) muchos e-mails?
4. ¿Quién ______ (llegar) siempre tarde a la clase?
5. ¿Quién ______ (abrir) su mochila?
6. ¿Quién ______ (usar) los apuntes de sus amigos?
7. ¿Quién ______ (comprender) todo (*everything*) cuando el/la profesor/a habla español?
8. ¿Quién ______ (creer) en Santa Claus?

GRAMÁTICA 4 La formación de preguntas y las palabras interrogativas

SAM 2-16 to 2-19

Guide 8, 10

Asking yes/no questions

Yes/no questions in Spanish are formed in two different ways:

a. Adding question marks to the statement.

Antonio habla español.	→	¿Antonio habla español?
Antonio speaks Spanish.		*Does Antonio speak Spanish?* or *Antonio speaks Spanish?*

As in English, your voice goes up at the end of the sentence. Remember that written Spanish has an upside-down question mark at the beginning of a question.

b. Inverting the order of the subject and the verb.

Antonio habla español.	→	¿Habla Antonio español?
SUBJECT + VERB		VERB + SUBJECT
Antonio speaks Spanish.		*Does Antonio speak Spanish?*

Antonio: ¿Cuántos idiomas hablas?
Silvia: Hablo dos, español y francés. ¿Y tú?
Antonio: Sólo hablo español pero mi loro habla cinco idiomas.

Answering yes/no questions

Answering questions is also like English.

¿Habla Antonio español?	*Does Antonio speak Spanish?*
Sí, habla español.	*Yes, he speaks Spanish.*
No, no habla español.	*No, he does not speak Spanish.*

Notice that in the negative response to the question above, both English and Spanish have two negative words.

Information questions

Information questions begin with interrogative words. Study the list of question words below and remember, accents are used on all interrogative words and also on exclamatory words: **¡Qué bueno!** (*That's great!*).

Las palabras interrogativas

¿Adónde?	*To where?*	**¿Adónde** va Antonio?	*(To) Where is Antonio going?*
¿Cómo?	*How?*	**¿Cómo** está Antonio?	*How is Antonio?*
¿Cuál?	*Which (one)?*	**¿Cuál** es su clase favorita?	*Which is his favorite class?*
¿Cuáles?	*Which (ones)?*	**¿Cuáles** son sus clases favoritas?	*Which are his favorite classes?*
¿Cuándo?	*When?*	**¿Cuándo** es la clase?	*When is the class?*
¿Cuánto/a?	*How much?*	**¿Cuánto** estudia Antonio para la clase?	*How much does he study for the class?*
¿Cuántos/as?	*How many?*	**¿Cuántos** idiomas habla Antonio?	*How many languages does he speak?*
¿Dónde?	*Where?*	**¿Dónde** vive Antonio?	*Where does Antonio live?*
¿Por qué?	*Why?*	**¿Por qué** no trabaja Antonio?	*Why doesn't Antonio work?*
¿Qué?	*What?*	**¿Qué** idioma habla Antonio?	*What language does Antonio speak?*
¿Quién?	*Who?*	**¿Quién** habla cinco idomas?	*Who speaks five languages?*
¿Quiénes?	*Who?*	**¿Quiénes** hablan cinco idiomas?	*Who speaks five languages?*

Note that, although not always necessary, when the subject is included in the sentence it follows the verb.

2•14 ¿Sí o no?

Take turns asking and answering the following yes/no questions.

MODELO E1: ¿Estudias francés?
E2: *Sí, estudio francés. / No, no estudio francés.*

1. ¿Hablas español?
2. ¿Estudias mucho?
3. ¿Aprendes mucho?
4. ¿Escribes mucho en clase?
5. ¿Es tu profesor/a cubano/a?
6. ¿Trabajas?
7. ¿Vives con tus padres?
8. ¿Lees muchas novelas?

2•15 Preguntas, más preguntas

Determine with a partner which interrogative word would elicit the following responses and create a complete question that would elicit each statement.

MODELO E1: Estudio **matemáticas.**
E2: *¿Qué estudias?*

Fíjate

Porque written as one word and without an accent mark means "because."

1. Martín estudia **en la sala de clase.**
2. Estudiamos español **porque es interesante.**
3. **Susana y Julia** estudian.
4. Estudian **entre las 7:00 y las 10:00 de la noche.**
5. Leen **rápidamente.**
6. Leo **tres libros.**

2•16 ¿Y tú?

Interview your classmates using the following questions about Spanish class.

MODELO E1: ¿Cuántas sillas hay en la clase?
E2: *Hay veinte sillas.*

Vocabulario útil	
difícil	*difficult*
fácil	*easy*

1. ¿Quién enseña la clase?
2. ¿Dónde enseña la clase?
3. ¿Quiénes hablan en la clase generalmente?
4. ¿Cuántos estudiantes hay?
5. ¿Qué libro(s) usas en la clase?
6. ¿Tomas muchos apuntes en la clase?
7. ¿Es la clase fácil o difícil?
8. ¿Trabajas mucho en la clase de español?

2•17 ¿Y tu familia o amigos?

Write **five** questions you could ask classmates about their families or friends, then move around the room asking those questions of as many people as possible.

MODELO E1: *¿Cómo se llaman tus padres?*
¿Dónde viven tus abuelos?
E2: *¿Cuántos hermanos tienes? …*

Capítulo 1. La familia, pág. 32.

VOCABULARIO 5 Los números 100–1.000

2-20 to 2-22

100	**cien**	200	**doscientos**	600	**seiscientos**
101	**ciento uno**	201	**doscientos uno**	700	**setecientos**
102	**ciento dos**	300	**trescientos**	800	**ochocientos**
116	**ciento dieciséis**	400	**cuatrocientos**	900	**novecientos**
120	**ciento veinte**	500	**quinientos**	1.000	**mil**

1. The conjuction **y** is used to connect tens and ones only.
   32 = treinta **y** dos, 101 = ciento uno, 151 = ciento cincuenta **y** uno
2. **Ciento** is shortened to **cien** before any noun.
   cien hombres **cien** mujeres
3. Multiples of **cientos** agree in number and gender with nouns they modify.
   doscientos hombres **trescientas** mujeres
4. Note the use of a decimal instead of a comma in **1.000.**

2•18 ¡Dinero!

Take turns saying the following amounts of money aloud, in the currencies listed below.

MODELO E1: 325 USD
E2: *trescientos veinticinco dólares*

U.S. dollar (dólares) = USD

Euro (euros) = EUR

Mexican peso (pesos) = MXN

Peruvian Nuevo Sol (soles) = PEN

1. 110 USD
2. 415 MXN
3. 376 PEN
4. 822 EUR
5. 638 MXN
6. 544 USD
7. 763 PEN
8. 999 EUR

2•19 Vamos a adivinar

On a popular TV show, *The Price is Right,* contestants must guess the price of different items. Bring in **five** ads of items priced between $100 and $1,000 dollars and cover the prices. In groups of three or four, take turns guessing the prices in U.S. dollars. The person who comes closest without going over the price wins the item!

MODELO E1: *¿Cuesta* (It costs) *ciento cincuenta y cinco dólares?*
E2: *No.*
E1: *Cuesta ciento ochenta dólares.*
E2: *Sí.*

Fíjate

If the item you are pricing is plural, the verb form will be *cuestan*.

¿Cómo andas?

Having completed the first **Comunicación,** I now can...

	Feel Confident	Need to Review
• talk about school subjects and majors (p. 62)	❑	❑
• explain where the stress falls in Spanish words and when accents are used (p. 63)	❑	❑
• give an example of a stereotype (p. 65)	❑	❑
• describe a typical classroom (p. 66)	❑	❑
• form regular **-ar, -er,** and **-ir** verbs in the present tense, know their meanings, and use them in complete sentences (p. 68)	❑	❑
• create and answer questions (p. 71)	❑	❑
• use numbers 100–1,000 (p. 74)	❑	❑

Comunicación

- Describing student life, feelings, and where things are located

VOCABULARIO 6 En la universidad

SAM 2-23 to 2-26

Los lugares

Otras palabras útiles	*Other useful words*
el apartamento	*apartment*
el edificio	*building*
el laboratorio	*laboratory*
la tienda	*store*

La residencia

Fíjate

El radio is the radio, *la radio* is the broadcast.

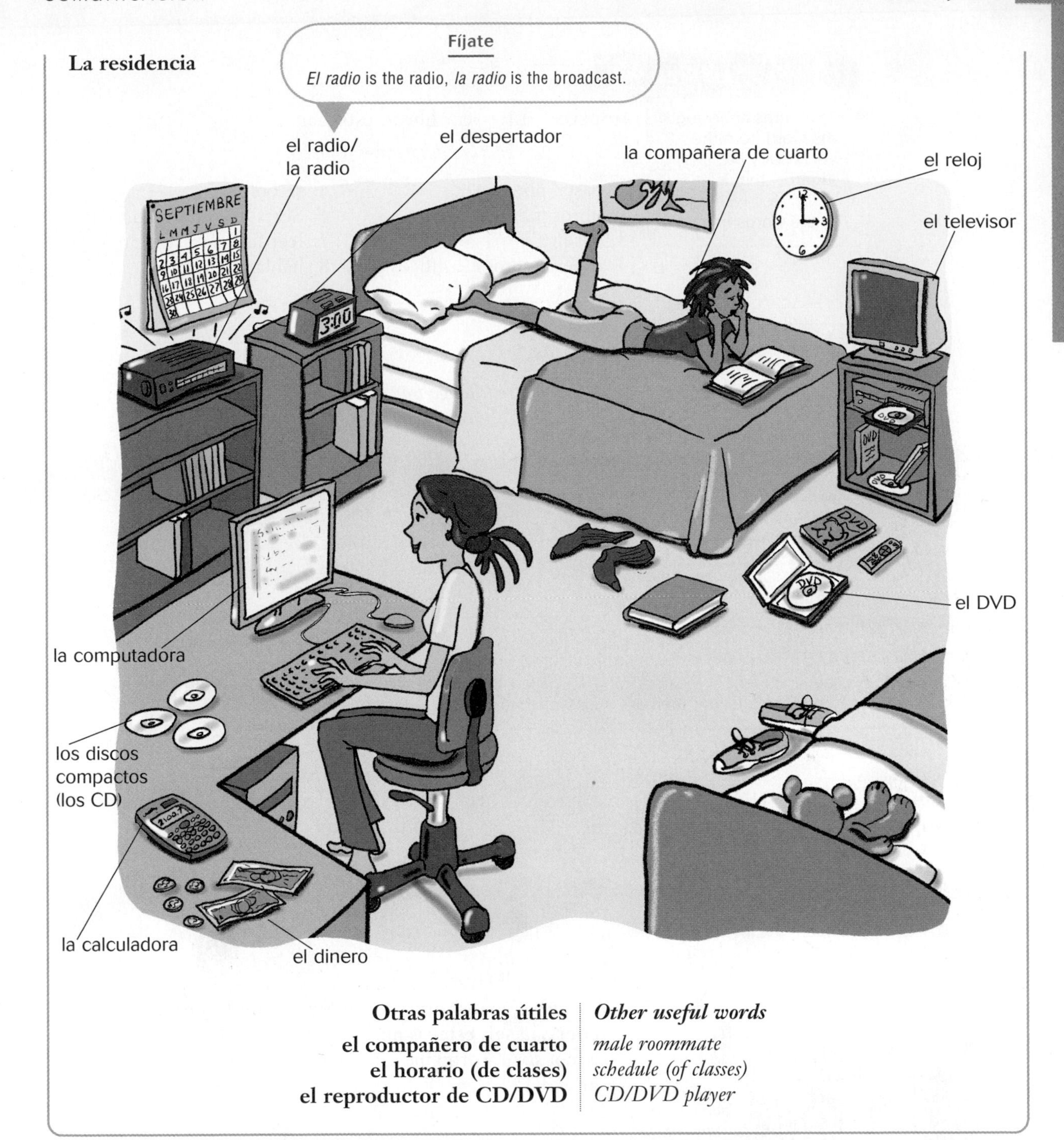

Otras palabras útiles	***Other useful words***
el compañero de cuarto	*male roommate*
el horario (de clases)	*schedule (of classes)*
el reproductor de CD/DVD	*CD/DVD player*

2•20 ¡Lo sé!

Take turns choosing the word from the vocabulary list, **Los lugares,** that is associated with each of the words below.

MODELO E1: leer libros, estudiar
E2: *la biblioteca*

1. pasta, pizza, café
2. libros para comprar
3. básquetbol
4. experimentos científicos
5. fútbol
6. Sears Tower, Chicago, IL
7. leer libros y estudiar
8. hablar con amigos

2•21 En mi cuarto...

Take turns telling your partner which items from the list **La residencia** you have in your room or where you live. Then say which items you do not have.

MODELO E1: *Tengo una calculadora, una computadora, un despertador...*
E2: *No tengo un radio, un reproductor de DVD...*

2•22 Datos personales

You are a foreign exchange student in Mexico, living with a family. Your Mexican little "brother" wants to know all about you! Answer his questions, which follow, then ask a classmate these same questions.

1. ¿De dónde eres?
2. ¿Qué estudias?
3. ¿Dónde estudias?
4. ¿Dónde comes?
5. ¿Dónde compras tus libros?
6. ¿Dónde vives?
7. ¿Qué necesitas para tu clase de español?
8. ¿Qué necesitas para una clase de matemáticas?
9. ¿Qué tienes en tu mochila?

El verbo *estar*

2-27 to 2-30

7, 11, 12, 15

Another verb that expresses *to be* in Spanish is **estar.** Like **tener** and **ser, estar** is not a regular verb; that is, you cannot simply drop the infinitive ending and add the usual **-ar** endings.

estar (*to be*)

Singular		Plural	
yo	**estoy**	nosotros/as	**estamos**
tú	**estás**	vosotros/as	**estáis**
él, ella, Ud.	**está**	ellos/as, Uds.	**están**

Ser and **estar** are not interchangeable because they are used differently. Two uses of **estar** are:

1. To describe the location of someone or something.

Manuel **está** en la sala de clase.	*Manuel is in the classroom.*
Nuestros padres **están** en México.	*Our parents are in Mexico.*

2. To describe how someone is feeling or to express a change from the norm.

Estoy bien. ¿Y tú?	*I'm fine. And you?*
Estamos tristes hoy.	*We are sad today. (Normally we are upbeat and happy.)*

2•23 ¿Cuál es la palabra?

Take turns giving the correct form of **estar** for each subject.

1. nosotras
2. el estudiante
3. tú
4. la pizarra
5. yo
6. los profesores

2•24 Busco...

You are on campus and you want to know where you can find the following. Take turns creating questions to determine the location of each person or thing. Your partner provides a response using the correct form of **estar** + **en** (*in, on,* or *at*).

Estrategia

You have noted that the majority of the classroom activities are with a partner. So that each person has equal opportunities, one of you should do the even numbered items in an activity, the other do the odd numbered items.

MODELO el mapa/libro

E1: *¿Dónde está el mapa?*

E2: *El mapa está en el libro.*

1. las calculadoras/la mochila
2. los apuntes/el cuaderno
3. tú/el laboratorio
4. el despertador/la mesa
5. yo/la residencia
6. mi amigo y yo/el centro estudiantil

2•25 ¡Ahora mismo!

Determine together what the following people may be doing, using the verbs listed below.

MODELO E1: Marta está en la sala de clase.

E2: *Toma apuntes.*

aprender	comprar	comer	escribir	estudiar
hablar	leer	preparar	tomar	trabajar

1. Juan y Pepa están en la biblioteca.
2. Mi hermana está en la librería.
3. El profesor está en su casa.
4. Los estudiantes están en la cafetería.
5. María está en su apartamento.
6. Patricia está en el centro estudiantil.
7. Tú estás en el laboratorio.
8. Mi amiga y yo estamos en la clase de español.

2•26 La clase de geografía

Take turns asking a partner in which countries the following capitals are located.

MODELO E1: *¿Dónde está Washington, D.C.?*
E2: *Washington, D.C. está en los Estados Unidos.*

Fíjate

Knowledge of geography is increasingly important in our global community. Actividad **2-26** presents an opportunity to review the countries and capitals of the Spanish-speaking world.

1. Madrid
2. México, D.F.
3. Lima
4. San Juan
5. La Paz
6. Buenos Aires
7. Santiago
8. Tegucigalpa
9. Santo Domingo
10. La Habana

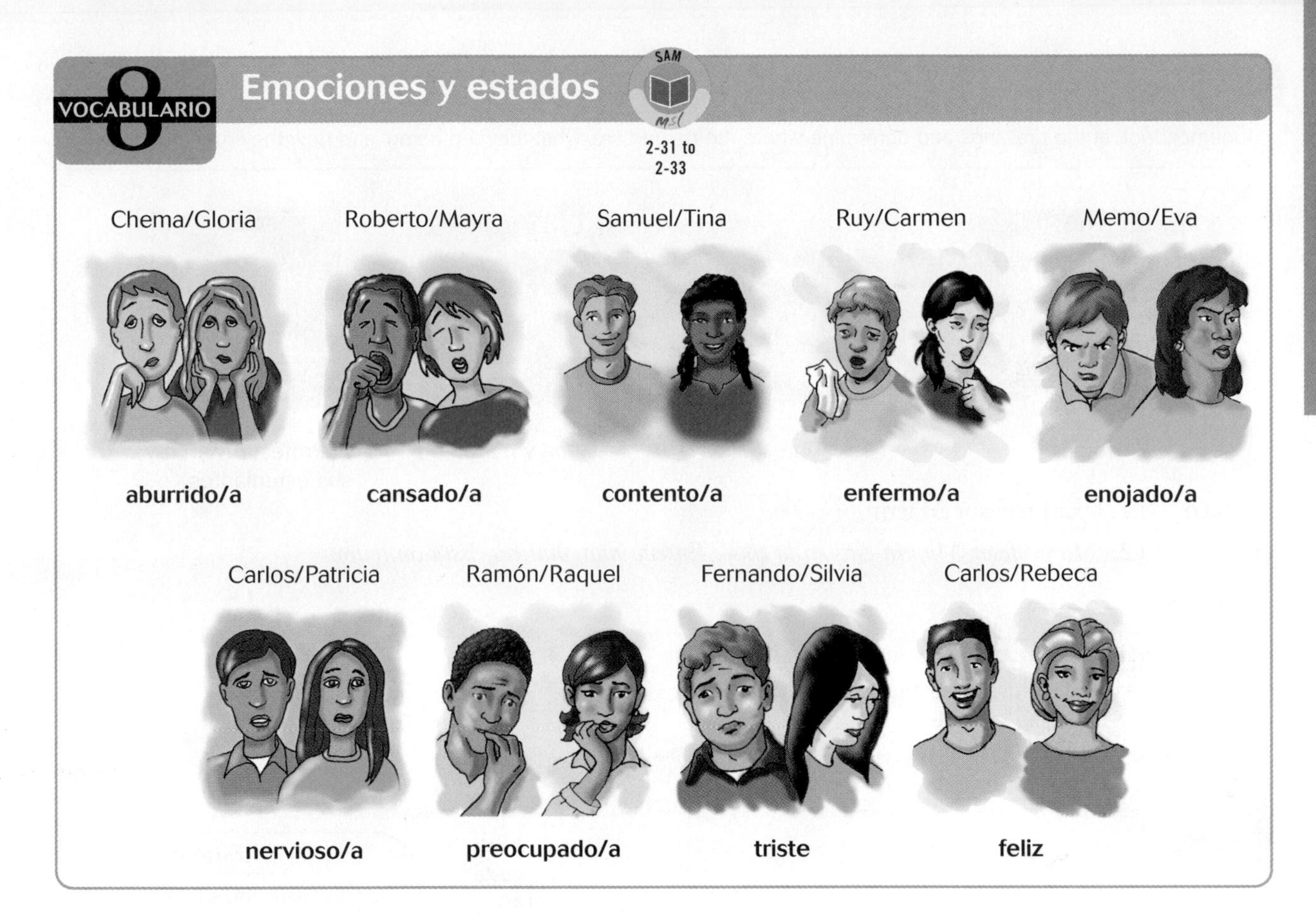

2•27 ¿Cómo están?

Look at the drawings above and take turns answering the following questions.

MODELO E1: ¿Cómo está Silvia?
E2: *Silvia está triste.*

1. ¿Cómo están Ruy y Carmen?
2. ¿Cómo está Roberto?
3. ¿Quién está preocupada?
4. ¿Quiénes están nerviosos?
5. ¿Cómo están Chema y Gloria?
6. ¿Cómo estás tú?

2•28 ¿Qué pasa?

Which adjectives from the drawings above best describe how you might feel in each situation? Share your responses with a partner.

MODELO E1: recibes $1.000
E2: *Estoy contento/a.*

1. Estás en el hospital.
2. Tienes un examen muy difícil hoy.
3. Corres quince millas (*miles*).
4. Tu profesor de historia lee un libro por (*for*) una hora y quince minutos.
5. Esperas y esperas pero tu amigo no llega (¡y no te llama por teléfono!).
6. Sacas una "A" en tu examen de español.

2•29 ¿Dónde y cómo?

Together, look at the drawings and determine where the people are, what they are doing, and how they might be feeling.

Tomás

Tina

Ana y Mirta

El Profesor Martín y sus estudiantes.

MODELO E1: El profesor Martín

E2: *El profesor Martín está en la clase. Enseña matemáticas. Está contento.*

1. Tomás
2. Tina
3. Ana y Mirta
4. Los estudiantes del profesor Martín

GRAMÁTICA 9 El verbo *gustar*

2-34 to 2-37

Fíjate

You can go back to page 25 in *Capítulo Preliminar A* for more information on *gustar*.

Estrategia

You may have noticed that there are two types of grammar presentations in *¡Anda!:*

1. You are given the grammar rule.
2. You are given guiding questions to help *you* construct the grammar rule, and to state the rule in your own words.

No matter which type of presentation, educational researchers have found it is *always* important for you to state the rules orally. Correctly stating the rules demonstrates that you are on the road to using the grammar concept(s) correctly in your speaking and writing.

To express likes and dislikes you say the following:

Me gusta la profesora.	*I like the professor.*
Me gustan las clases de idiomas.	*I like language classes.*
¿Te gustan las novelas de Sandra Cisneros?	*Do you like Sandra Cisneros's novels?*
Te gusta el arte abstracto.	*You like abstract art.*
No **le gusta** estudiar.	*He does not like to study.*

1. To say you like or dislike one thing, what form of **gustar** do you use?
2. To say you like or dislike more than one thing, what form of **gustar** do you use?
3. Which words in the examples mean *I? You? He/she?*
4. If a verb is needed after **gusta/gustan,** what form of the verb do you use?

To check your answers to the preceding questions, see Appendix 1.

2-30 ¿Qué te gusta?

Decide whether or not you like these items and share your opinions with a classmate.

MODELO E1: los lunes
E2: *(No) Me gustan los lunes.*

1. el centro estudiantil
2. los sábados
3. vivir en un apartamento
4. las matemáticas
5. aprender idiomas
6. la cafetería
7. correr
8. los libros de Harry Potter

2-31 Te toca a ti

Now change the cues from actividad **2-30** into questions, and ask a different classmate to answer.

MODELO E1: *¿Te gusta la informática?*
E2: *Sí, me gusta la informática.*
E1: *¿Te gustan los lunes?*
E2: *No, no me gustan los lunes.*

Estrategia

Remember, if you answer negatively, you will need to say *no* twice. If you need to review, check *La formación de preguntas* on page 71 of this chapter.

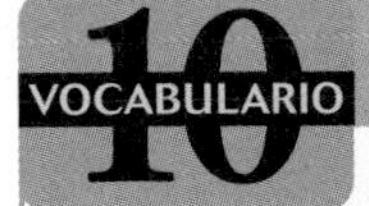

VOCABULARIO 10 Los deportes y los pasatiempos

2-38 to 2-42

The following are some sports and pastimes that Mexican students of the UNAM enjoy.

jugar al fútbol

ir de compras

hacer ejercicio

escuchar música

tomar el sol

jugar al tenis

Más deportes y pasatiempos	***More sports and pastimes***
bailar	*to dance*
caminar	*to walk*
jugar al básquetbol	*to play basketball*
jugar al béisbol	*to play baseball*
jugar al fútbol americano	*to play football*
jugar al golf	*to play golf*
montar en bicicleta	*to ride a bike*
nadar	*to swim*
patinar	*to skate*
tocar un instrumento	*to play an instrument*
ver la televisión	*to watch television*

Otras palabras útiles	***Other useful words***
el equipo	*team*
la pelota	*ball*

Capítulo Preliminar A. Los días, los meses y las estaciones, pág. 20.

2·32 ¿En qué mes te gusta...?

As a fan or a participant, sports can be seasonal.

Paso 1 Make a list of the top **three** sports or pastimes you enjoy in the months listed below.

enero mayo julio octubre

MODELO enero

1. patinar, 2. bailar, 3. tocar un instrumento

Paso 2 Circulate around the classroom and compare your preferences with those of your classmates. Do you see any trends?

MODELO E1: *¿Qué deportes y pasatiempos te gustan más en enero?*

E2: *Me gusta patinar, bailar y tocar un instrumento.*

2·33 ¿Cuánto te gusta?

What activities do you enjoy in your spare time? Write **ten** activities in the chart and rank the sports and pastimes by placing a mark in the column that best describes your feeling toward the sport or pastime. What do you suppose **¡Lo odio!** means? Share your answers, following the model.

MODELO E1: *Me gusta mucho bailar.*

E2: *No me gusta ver la televisión.*

	ME GUSTA MUCHO	ME GUSTA	NO ME GUSTA	¡LO ODIO!
1. el fútbol				
2. patinar				
3. ...				

Estrategia

Remember to use your reading strategy "*Recognizing cognates*" from *Capítulo 1* to assist you with this and all future reading passages.

2-43

Los deportes en el mundo hispano

Los Juegos Panamericanos ocurren cada cuatro años.

El fútbol es el deporte más popular en el mundo hispanohablante. Sin embargo (*Nevertheless*), los hispanos participan en una gran variedad de actividades físicas y deportivas como el béisbol, el boxeo, el básquetbol (o baloncesto), el tenis, el vóleibol y el atletismo (*track and field*). España y los países latinoamericanos participan en los Juegos Olímpicos. Además, los países latinoamericanos, juntos con Canadá y los Estados Unidos, participan en los Juegos Panamericanos que tienen lugar (*take place*) cada cuatro años, siempre un año antes de los Juegos Olímpicos.

Los deportes forman una parte importante de la vida universitaria, especialmente en la Universidad Nacional Autónoma de México (la UNAM). Además (*Furthermore*) de contar con el equipo de fútbol Club Universidad Nacional, ofrecen (*they offer*) unas treinta y nueve disciplinas deportivas que incluyen los deportes mencionados y también el fútbol americano, el judo, el karate, el ciclismo, la natación, la lucha libre (*wrestling*) y más. Hay gimnasios, dos estadios, siete piscinas y muchas otras áreas para practicar estos deportes.

Preguntas

1. What is the most important sport in the Spanish-speaking world?
2. Does your college/university offer the same sports as the UNAM? What are some differences?

2•34 ¿Eres activo/a?

Just how active are you? Complete the chart with activities that should, or do, occupy your time. Share your results with a partner. So… are you leading a well-balanced life?

Vocabulario útil

a menudo *often*
a veces *sometimes; from time to time*
nunca *never*

A MENUDO	A VECES	NUNCA	NECESITO HACERLO (*DO IT*) MÁS
1.	1.	1.	1.
2.	2.	2.	2.
3.	3.	3.	3.
4.	4.	4.	4.
5.	5.	5.	5.

2·35 Tus preferencias

Select your **three** favorite sports and/or pastimes (**que más me gustan**) and then select your **three** least favorite (**que menos me gustan**) from actividad **2-34.**

Paso 1 Write your choices in the chart. Then, create **two** sentences summarizing your choices.

LOS DEPORTES/PASATIEMPOS QUE MÁS ME GUSTAN	LOS DEPORTES/PASATIEMPOS QUE MENOS ME GUSTAN
1. *patinar*	1.
2. *bailar*	2.
3. *leer*	3.

MODELO *Los deportes o pasatiempos que más me gustan son patinar, bailar y leer.*
Los deportes o pasatiempos que menos me gustan son…

Paso 2 Circulate around the classroom to find classmates with the same likes and dislikes as you. Follow the model. When you find someone with the same likes or dislikes, write his/her name in the chart that follows.

MODELO E1: *¿Qué deporte o pasatiempo te gusta más?*
E2: *El deporte que me gusta más es jugar al tenis.*
E1: *¿Qué deporte o pasatiempo te gusta menos?*
E2: *El pasatiempo que me gusta menos es ir de compras.*

LOS/LAS COMPAÑEROS/AS	EL DEPORTE/PASATIEMPO QUE MÁS LES GUSTA
1.	
2.	
3.	
LOS/LAS COMPAÑEROS/AS	EL DEPORTE/PASATIEMPO QUE MENOS LES GUSTA
1.	
2.	
3.	

ESCUCHA

2-44 to 2-47

2•36 Antes de escuchar

In the following segment Eduardo, a university student and one of the characters from **Ambiciones siniestras,** is talking on the phone with his mother. Write a question you might possibly hear in their conversation.

ESTRATEGIA **Listening for the gist**

When *listening for the gist,* you listen for the main idea(s). You do not focus on each word, but rather on the overall meaning. When you listen for the gist, you should be able to summarize what you heard in several words or a sentence.

2•37 A escuchar

CD 1
Track 30

Listen as Eduardo and his mother converse.

1. The first time you listen, concentrate on the questions she asks. Also, jot down key words and ideas.
2. In the second listening, focus on Eduardo's answers. Jot down key words and ideas.
3. During the third listening determine if these sentences are true (**T**) or false (**F**).
   a. Eduardo's mother calls Eduardo to see how he is doing.
   b. Eduardo does not have classes on Tuesday.
   c. Eduardo's mother ends the conversation abruptly.
   d. Eduardo wants to ask his mother for something.
4. Now in one sentence, what is the gist of their conversation?

Eduardo habla con su madre.

2•38 Después de escuchar

With a partner, provide a different ending to the conversation. Then play the roles of Eduardo and his mother.

ESCRIBE

2•39 Antes de escribir

Have you ever tried to describe yourself to someone? Have you ever applied for a job for which describing yourself was a part of the application process? For some jobs it is important for the employer to know if you will indeed "fit in." Imagine that you are applying for a job on campus—either to work in the library, the student center, or the athletic department. Decide which department interests you most and determine the information you should share that would make you a viable applicant. Make a list of that information in Spanish.

MODELO (athletic department)

LISTA:

✓ *me gustan los deportes; nado y corro muy bien*
✓ *soy buena estudiante, inteligente, creativa, organizada y trabajadora*
✓ *me gustan las cosas nuevas/las personas nuevas*
✓ *no tengo clases después de las dos.*

2•40 Una descripción

Using your list, create a short personal description following the model below.

MODELO *Tengo veinte años y soy buena estudiante. Soy inteligente, creativa, organizada y trabajadora. Me gustan mucho los deportes. Me gusta aprender cosas nuevas y trabajar con personas diferentes. No tengo clases después de las dos de la tarde y tengo los fines de semana libres* (free) *también.*

2•41 Después de escribir

Your instructor will collect the descriptions and read some of them to the class. She/He may ask you to guess who wrote each one.

¿Cómo andas?

Having completed the second **Comunicación,** I now can…

	Feel Confident	Need to Review
• describe life at my college/university including the campus, things we need for school, etc. (pp. 76–77)	❑	❑
• use the verb **estar** to express location and feelings/emotions (p. 78, 81)	❑	❑
• say what I and others like and dislike (p. 82)	❑	❑
• talk about sports and pastimes (p. 83)	❑	❑
• list several sports and pastimes of the Hispanic world (p. 85)	❑	❑
• practice listening for the gist (p. 87)	❑	❑
• write a short personal description (p. 88)	❑	❑

Araceli Gabriela Campos Vega

México

Les presento mi país

CD 1 Track 31

2-50

Vistas culturales

Mi nombre es Araceli Campos y soy de Oaxaca, México. Soy una estudiante de la Universidad Nacional Autónoma de México (la UNAM) que está en la Ciudad de México. Vivo cerca de la universidad con la familia de mi tía porque normalmente hay pocas residencias estudiantiles en las universidades y muchos estudiantes viven con sus parientes (*relatives*). Con más de 270.000 estudiantes, la UNAM es la universidad más grande de México y de América Latina. **¿Cuántos estudiantes hay en tu universidad?** En la UNAM, tenemos un equipo de fútbol, los «Pumas». El fútbol es muy popular en mi país, es el pasatiempo nacional. **¿Qué deporte es muy popular en tu país?** Mi ciudad, Oaxaca, es un centro famoso de artesanía. En particular, hay hojalatería (*tin work*), cerámicas de barro negro (*black clay*), cestería (*basket making*), fabricación de textiles y de alebrijes (*painted wooden animals*) y mucho más. **¿Qué tipo de artesanía hay en tu región?**

El tianguis de Tepotzlán, Morelia.

ALMANAQUE

Nombre oficial:	Estados Unidos Mexicanos
Gobierno:	República federal
Población:	107.499.525 (est. 2006)
Idiomas:	español (oficial); maya, náhuatl
Moneda:	peso mexicano ($)

La biblioteca de la Universidad Nacional Autónoma de México. La fachada contiene un mosaico de la historia de México.

Frida Kahlo y Diego Rivera son pintores muy famosos: ella por sus autorretratos (*self-portraits*) psicológicos y él por sus pinturas y murales de temas históricos y sociales.

El fútbol es el pasatiempo nacional del país.

Oaxaca es un centro famoso de artesanía.

¿Sabías que...?

- El origen del chicle (*gum*) es el látex del chicozapote (*sapodilla tree* en inglés), un árbol tropical de la península de Yucatán. Los mayas, tribu antigua y muy importante del Yucatán, usaban (*used*) el látex como chicle.
- La planta, "cabeza de negro", del estado mexicano de Veracruz, forma la base del proceso para crear la cortisona y "la píldora", el contraceptivo oral.

PREGUNTAS

1. What is the most popular sport in Mexico?
2. What is a "tianguis"? What do we have in the United States that is similar?
3. What are the origins of cortisone and the birth control pill?
4. What are some of the handcrafted items from Mexico? What are similar handcrafted items made in your region?
5. What are some differences between the UNAM and your school?

En la Red
Amplía tus conocimientos sobre México en la página web de *¡Anda!*

Ambiciones siniestras

2-52

lectura

2-42 Antes de leer. In this episode you will discover more information about three of the university students who are among the six protagonists of the story, specifically Alejandra, Manolo, and Cisco. You will learn their complete names, where they are from, and some of their interests.

1. Note that there are a few key words in the reading passage you may not know. They are written below with their English equivalents and are listed in order of appearance. They are also boldfaced in the body of the reading.

la seguridad (-dad = -ty)	*security*
las solicitudes	*applications*
mientras	*while*
los ensayos	*essays*
el oeste	*west*
el noreste	*northeast*

   Based on this list of words, can you begin to guess what the context of the reading will be?

ESTRATEGIA Skimming

When you skim, or read quickly, you generally do so to capture the gist of the passage. Practice with skimming helps you learn to focus on main ideas in your reading.

2-43 A leer. To boost your comprehension, it is helpful to skim the passage for the first reading and then ask yourself what key information you have learned.

1. Skim the first two paragraphs of this episode, then answer the following questions.
   a. What is the person doing?
   b. Do you think what he is doing is part of his job?
   c. How many students has he located so far?
2. Now skim the remaining paragraphs and write down key points for each paragraph.
3. Then, reread the entire episode, this time more carefully, to add details to those main ideas. Do not forget to take advantage of cognates like **prestigiosa** and **paciencia** to boost your comprehension.

CD 1
Track 32

Las solicitudes

Un hombre joven está enfrente de° su computadora. Trabaja impacientemente y con rapidez. A su lado° tiene unos papeles con unos códigos misteriosos.

in front of
at his side

—A ver°. ¿Cómo paso por **la seguridad** de esta prestigiosa universidad? Ahhhh... sí. Paciencia. Ahora... para encontrar la lista de los estudiantes y sus **solicitudes**... Excelente. Es fácil dar con° jóvenes inteligentes, creativos e inocentes.—

Let's see
find

El hombre lee **los ensayos** de las solicitudes de varios estudiantes, dos de una universidad del oeste y uno de una universidad del noreste. **Mientras** lee, habla.

Fíjate

The dashes indicate dialogue or spoken words. In English we use quotation marks (" ").

—De la universidad del **oeste**:

Alejandra Sánchez Torres. Es de San Antonio, Texas; está lejos de su casa. Aquí habla mucho de su familia. Tiene muchos hermanos. Hmmm... le gusta pintar y escribir poesía. También le gusta viajar. ¡Perfecto! Y espera estudiar arte...

Manuel Rodríguez Ángulo. Manolo. Es de California, San Diego. Tiene cuatro hermanos... sus padres están divorciados. Le gustan todos los deportes, especialmente el fútbol americano. Es excelente estudiante también... desea especializarse en medicina.

De la universidad del **noreste**:

Francisco Quiroga Godoy, Cisco, es de familia hispana y vive en West Palm Beach. Cuando no estudia, trabaja en restaurantes, cafés y, ¡qué nombre°!, "El Golden Gal Day Spa". Con tantos° trabajos y tan° buenas notas debe ser un joven muy disciplinado. Especialidad: informática. Muy bien.—

what a name / so many
such

A este hombre tan sospechoso°... ¿por qué le interesan° estos estudiantes? ¿Qué quiere° de ellos?

suspicious / is he interested in
does he want

2-44 **Después de leer.** Answer the following questions.

1. How many applications does the man review in this episode? Who are the students about whom he reads?
2. Complete the following chart:

PERSONAJE	¿DE DÓNDE ES?	¿FAMILIA?	¿POSIBLE ESPECIALIDAD?	¿ACTIVIDADES?
Alejandra				
Manolo				
Cisco				

3. According to the information given, how might Manolo's family be different from those of the other two students? Do you notice any other major differences?

2-53 to 2-57

video

2-45 **Antes del video.** In **Las solicitudes**, a suspicious man is reading information off the computer about three of our protagonists. In the second part of this episode you will watch him in video format as he continues to discover information about our characters. Before watching the episode, think about the possible answers to these questions:

1. Who is this person and why is he interested in Lupe, Cisco, Eduardo, Marisol, Manolo, and Alejandra?
2. What information could this man discover on the Internet about you?
3. What sites could provide him with information about you?
4. What do you have in common with the characters so far?

Otras actividades: trabajar como voluntario en una organización de ayuda a los niños.

Especialidad: periodismo e historia. Aficiones: jugar al básquetbol, nadar y correr.

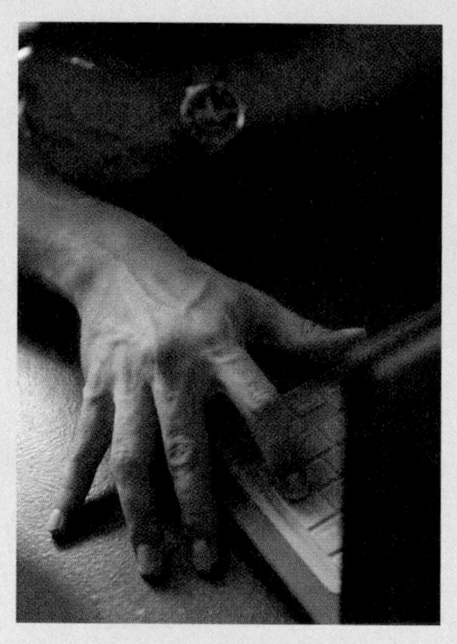

¡Aquí comienza la aventura!

Episodio 2

La aventura comienza

Relax and watch the video, more than once if you choose; then complete the activity below.

2-46 **Después del video.** Answer the following questions.

1. What Spanish adjectives best describe the man at the computer?
2. Where might he be? Is he alone?
3. Which characters is he investigating now? List two facts he discovers about each one.
4. What does he do with the information he gets?
5. What is he doing as the episode ends?

Y por fin, ¿cómo andas?

Having completed this chapter, I now can…

	Feel Confident	Need to Review
Comunicación		
• talk about my life as a university student (pp. 62, 76–77)	❑	❑
• explain where the stress falls in written words and when to use written accents (p. 63)	❑	❑
• describe my classroom (p. 66)	❑	❑
• use regular **-ar, -er,** and **-ir** verbs in the present tense (p. 68)	❑	❑
• formulate questions (p. 71)	❑	❑
• use numbers 100–1,000 (p. 74)	❑	❑
• use the verb **estar** (p. 78, 81)	❑	❑
• tell what I and others like and do not like, using **gustar** (p. 82)	❑	❑
• share information about my favorite and not-so-favorite pastimes and sports (p. 83)	❑	❑
• listen for the gist, or main idea, in a passage (p. 87)	❑	❑
• write a brief personal description for an application (p. 88)	❑	❑
Cultura		
• discuss diversity and stereotype issues (p. 65)	❑	❑
• list some sports and pastimes of the Hispanic world (p. 85)	❑	❑
• share three facts about Mexico that I find interesting (p. 90)	❑	❑
Ambiciones siniestras		
• skim the reading to get the main idea (p. 92)	❑	❑
• name and briefly describe two of your favorite characters from the mystery story (p. 94)	❑	❑

VOCABULARIO ACTIVO

CD 1
Tracks 33-42

Las materias y las especialidades	*Subjects and majors*
la administración de empresas	*business*
la arquitectura	*architecture*
el arte	*art*
la biología	*biology*
las ciencias (pl.)	*science*
el derecho	*law*
el idioma	*language*
los idiomas (pl.)	*languages*
la informática	*computer science*
la literatura	*literature*
las matemáticas (pl.)	*mathematics*
la medicina	*medicine*
la música	*music*
la pedagogía	*education*
el periodismo	*journalism*
la psicología	*psychology*

Los deportes y los pasatiempos	*Sports and pastimes*
bailar	*to dance*
caminar	*to walk*
escuchar música	*to listen to music*
hacer ejercicio	*to exercise*
ir de compras	*to go shopping*
jugar al básquetbol	*to play basketball*
jugar al béisbol	*to play baseball*
jugar al fútbol	*to play soccer*
jugar al fútbol americano	*to play football*
jugar al golf	*to play golf*
jugar al tenis	*to play tennis*
montar en bicicleta	*to ride a bike*
nadar	*to swim*
patinar	*to skate*
tocar un instrumento	*to play an instrument*
tomar el sol	*sunbathe*
ver la televisión	*to watch TV*

En la sala de clase	*In the classroom*
los apuntes (pl.)	*notes*
el bolígrafo	*ballpoint pen*
el borrador	*eraser*
el/la compañero/a de clase	*classmate*
la composición	*composition*
el cuaderno	*notebook*
el escritorio	*desk*
el/la estudiante	*student*
el examen	*exam*
el lápiz	*pencil*
el libro	*book*
el mapa	*map*
la mesa	*table*
la mochila	*book bag; knapsack*
el papel	*paper*
la pared	*wall*
la pizarra	*chalkboard*
el/la profesor/a	*professor*
la puerta	*door*
la sala de clase	*classroom*
la silla	*chair*
la tarea	*homework*
la tiza	*chalk*
la ventana	*window*

Emociones y estados	*Emotions and states of being*
aburrido/a	*bored (with* **estar***)*
cansado/a	*tired*
contento/a	*content; happy*
enfermo/a	*ill; sick*
enojado/a	*angry*
feliz	*happy*
nervioso/a	*upset; nervous*
preocupado/a	*worried*
triste	*sad*

Los números 100–1.000 — *Numbers 100–1,000*

See page 74.

Los verbos — *Verbs*

abrir	*to open*
aprender	*to learn*
comer	*to eat*
comprar	*to buy*
comprender	*to understand*
contestar	*to answer*
correr	*to run*
creer	*to believe*
enseñar	*to teach; to show*
escribir	*to write*
esperar	*to wait for; to hope*
estar	*to be*
estudiar	*to study*
hablar	*to speak*
leer	*to read*
llegar	*to arrive*
necesitar	*to need*
preguntar	*to ask (a question)*
preparar	*to prepare; to get ready*
recibir	*to receive*
regresar	*to return*
terminar	*to finish; to end*
tomar	*to take; to drink*
trabajar	*to work*
usar	*to use*
vivir	*to live*

Los lugares — *Places*

el apartamento	*apartment*
la biblioteca	*library*
la cafetería	*cafeteria*
el centro estudiantil	*student center; student union*
el cuarto	*room*
el edificio	*building*
el estadio	*stadium*
el gimnasio	*gymnasium*
el laboratorio	*laboratory*
la librería	*bookstore*
la residencia estudiantil	*dormitory*
la tienda	*store*

Las palabras interrogativas — *Interrogative words*

See page 71.

La residencia — *The dorm*

la calculadora	*calculator*
el/la compañero/a de cuarto	*roommate*
la computadora	*computer*
el despertador	*alarm clock*
el dinero	*money*
el disco compacto (el CD)	*compact disk*
el DVD	*DVD*
el horario (de clases)	*schedule (of classes)*
el radio/la radio	*radio*
el reloj	*clock; watch*
el reproductor de CD/DVD	*CD/DVD player*
el televisor	*TV set*

Otras palabras útiles — *Other useful words*

a menudo	*often*
a veces	*sometimes; from time to time*
ayer	*yesterday*
cerca (de)	*close; near*
con	*with*
el curso	*course*
difícil	*difficult*
el equipo	*team*
fácil	*easy*
hasta	*until*
hay	*there is; there are*
hoy	*today*
lejos (de)	*far; far away*
mañana	*tomorrow*
más	*more*
menos	*less*
mucho	*a lot*
nunca	*never*
la pelota	*ball*
pero	*but*
poco	*a little; few*
el semestre	*semester*
también	*too; also*
y	*and*

Estamos en casa

From the most modern of skyscrapers, to Spanish colonial styles, to the variety of homes of indigenous populations, Hispanic architecture is as varied as the people who speak Spanish. **En los países hispanohablantes** (*Spanish-speaking countries*), **hay de todo.**

Sevilla, España

PREGUNTAS

1. Why is Spanish architecture so prevalent throughout North, Central, and South America? Why can French influence be seen in Mexico?
2. How do geography and environment affect the design and construction of homes?
3. Is the style of your home found in any other region of the United States? Why or why not? Do you see any Spanish-inspired architecture in your region?

Comunicación

- Describing my house

VOCABULARIO 1 La casa

3-1 to 3-6

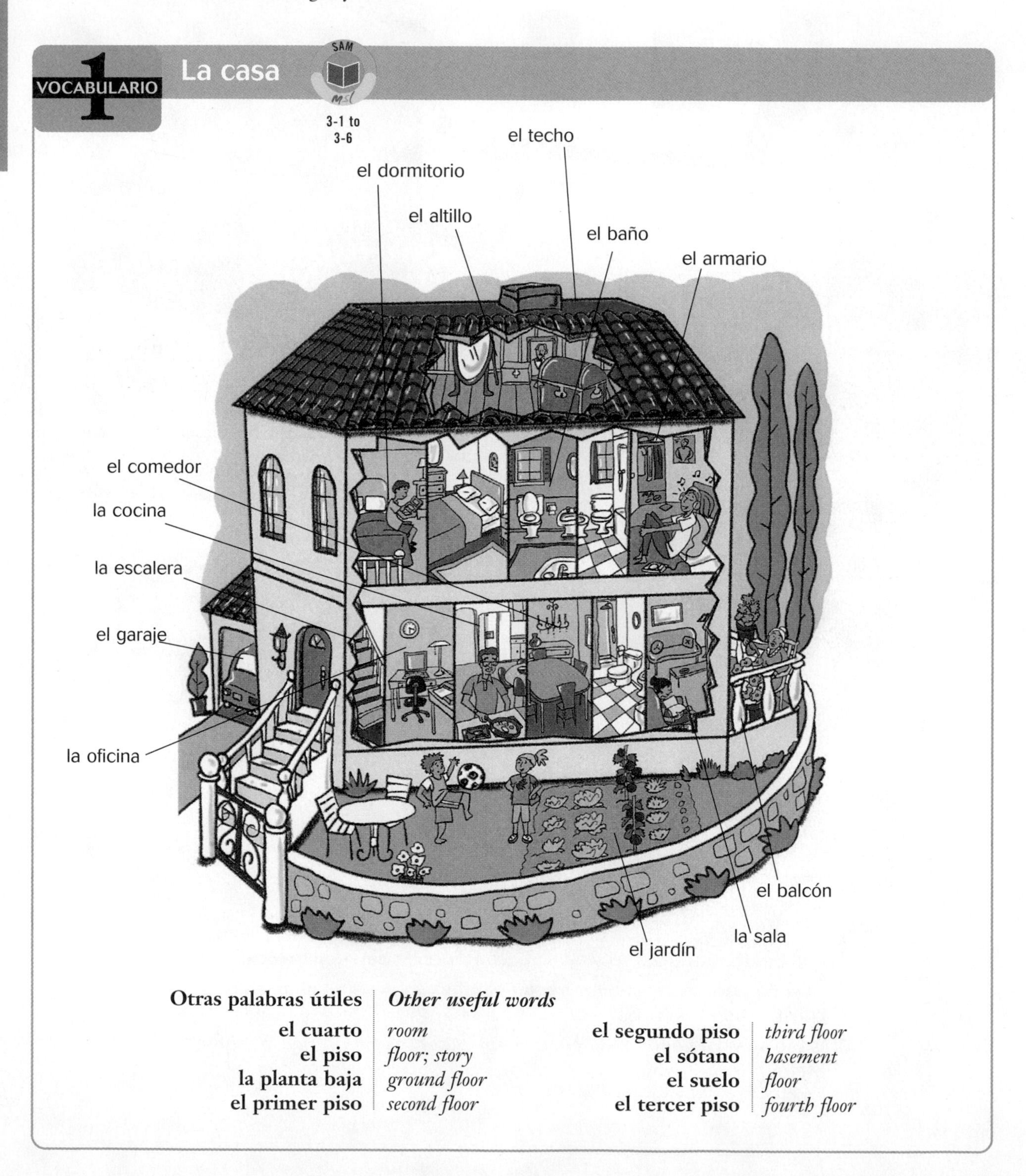

Otras palabras útiles	*Other useful words*		
el cuarto	*room*	**el segundo piso**	*third floor*
el piso	*floor; story*	**el sótano**	*basement*
la planta baja	*ground floor*	**el suelo**	*floor*
el primer piso	*second floor*	**el tercer piso**	*fourth floor*

CD 2
Track 1

PRONUNCIACIÓN

3-7 to 3-9

The letters *h, j,* and *g*

1. The Spanish **h** is always silent and never pronounced.
   hombre hola hay hora
2. The letter **j** is pronounced similar to the English *h* in *hot.*
   garaje jardín jueves baja
3. The letter **g** is pronounced similar to the English *g* in *goal,* except when followed by *e* or *i.*
   garaje globo guitarra gordo

   When **g** is followed by *e* or *i,* it is pronounced similar to the English *h* in *happy.*
   generalmente gitano agencia agitado

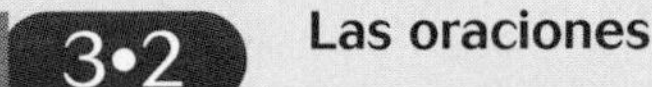

3•1 Las palabras

Pronounce the following words, paying special attention to the letters **h, j,** and **g.**

1. hay
2. jardín
3. garaje
4. hospital
5. pongo
6. baja
7. generoso
8. ahora
9. guardar

Estrategia

Listen to the audio portion of your textbook prior to coming to class to practice the *h, j,* and *g* sounds.

3•2 Las oraciones

Pronounce the following sentences, paying special attention to the letters **h, j,** and **g.**

1. Hola, Javier. ¿Qué hay?
2. Gloria, tu guitarra está en el garaje.
3. Generalmente, me gustan los jueves en julio.

3•3 Los dichos y refranes

Now pronounce the following sayings and focus on the letters h, j, and g.

1. A la larga, lo más dulce amarga.
2. El hábito no hace el monje.

Estrategia

In *Capítulo 3* many of the directions for the activities are written in Spanish. New words that appear in the directions will be translated for you the first time they are used. Keep a list of those words to refer to; it helps you increase your vocabulary.

Capítulo 2. El verbo *estar,* pág. 78.

3•4 ¿Dónde están?

Miren (*Look at*) el dibujo (*drawing*) de la casa en la página 100 y túrnense (*take turns*) para decir dónde están los siguientes (*following*) cuartos.

MODELO E1: el garaje
E2: *El garaje está en la planta baja.*

Fíjate

The first floor, or ground floor, is generally called *la planta baja; el primer piso* actually refers to the second floor. What is the third floor called?

	EN LA PLANTA BAJA	EN EL PRIMER PISO	EN EL SEGUNDO PISO
la sala			
el baño			
el dormitorio			
la cocina			
la oficina			
el altillo			

3•5 Las partes de la casa

Dile (*Tell*) a tu compañero/a en qué parte de la casa haces (*you do*) las siguientes actividades.

MODELO estudiar

E1: *Yo estudio en la oficina. ¿Y tú?*

E2: *Yo estudio en mi dormitorio.*

1. hablar por teléfono
2. leer un libro
3. ver la televisión
4. organizar papeles
5. preparar enchiladas
6. tocar un instrumento
7. escuchar música
8. tomar el sol

3•6 ¿Y tu casa...?

Fíjate

In the directions, words like *miren, túrnense, comparen,* and *usen* are plural—they refer to both of you.

Túrnense para describir sus casas (o la de un miembro de su familia o amigo) y compararlas con la casa de la página 100. Usen el modelo para crear por lo menos (*at least*) **cinco** oraciones (*sentences*).

MODELO *En la casa del dibujo, la sala está en la planta baja y mi sala está en la planta baja también. En la casa del dibujo, el dormitorio está en el segundo piso, pero mi dormitorio está en la planta baja. No tenemos un altillo…*

3•7 Es una casa interesante...

Look at the photos and together, create a short description of one of the houses. Imagine the inside and the person(s) who may live there. Share your description with the class.

MODELO *El apartamento está en Madrid en un edificio grande y tradicional. El apartamento es muy moderno. Tiene tres dormitorios, dos baños, una cocina pequeña, una sala grande y un balcón. Gastón y Patricia viven allí. No tienen hijos. Ellos trabajan en la ciudad.*

Vocabulario útil

antiguo/a	*old*	**humilde**	*humble*
la calle	*street*	**moderno/a**	*modern*
el campo	*country*	**nuevo/a**	*new*
la ciudad	*city*	**tradicional**	*traditional*
contemporáneo/a	*contemporary*	**viejo/a**	*old*

1.

2.

3.

4.

5.

6.

Algunos verbos irregulares

3-10 to 3-15

13, 14

Estrategia

Memorizing information is easier to do when the information is arranged in chunks. You will notice that some of the *yo* forms end in *-go*, such as *salgo, traigo,* and *pongo*. Learning the information as a chunk of "*go*" verbs may make it easier to remember.

Look at the present tense forms of the verbs below. Notice that they all follow the same patterns that you learned in **Capítulo 2** to form the present tense of regular verbs, *except* in the **yo** form.

	dar (*to give*)	**conocer** (*to be acquainted with*)	**hacer** (*to do; to make*)	**poner** (*to put; to place*)
yo	doy	conozco	hago	pongo
tú	das	conoces	haces	pones
él, ella, Ud.	da	conoce	hace	pone
nosotros/as	damos	conocemos	hacemos	ponemos
vosotros/as	dais	conocéis	hacéis	ponéis
ellos/as, Uds.	dan	conocen	hacen	ponen

Estrategia

Organize the new verbs you are learning in your notebook. Note whether the verb is regular or irregular, what it means in English, if any of the forms have accents, and if any other verbs follow this pattern. You might want to highlight or color code the verbs that follow a pattern.

	salir (*to leave; to go out*)	**traer** (*to bring*)	**ver** (*to see*)
yo	salgo	traigo	veo
tú	sales	traes	ves
él, ella, Ud.	sale	trae	ve
nosotros/as	salimos	traemos	vemos
vosotros/as	salís	traéis	veis
ellos/as, Uds.	salen	traen	ven

Capítulo 1. El verbo *tener*, pág. 35.

Two additional groups of very common irregular verbs follow. Note that **venir** is formed like **tener**.

	decir (*to say; to tell*)	**oír** (*to hear*)	**venir** (*to come*)
yo	digo	oigo	vengo
tú	dices	oyes	vienes
él, ella, Ud.	dice	oye	viene
nosotros/as	decimos	oímos	venimos
vosotros/as	decís	oís	venís
ellos/as, Uds.	dicen	oyen	vienen

	poder (*to be able to*)	**querer** (*to want; to love*)
yo	puedo	quiero
tú	puedes	quieres
él, ella, Ud.	puede	quiere
nosotros/as	podemos	queremos
vosotros/as	podéis	queréis
ellos/as, Uds.	pueden	quieren

3-8 La ruleta

How competitive are you? Listen as your instructor explains how to play this fast-paced game designed to practice the new verb forms. When you finish with this list, repeat the activity with different verbs and include **estar, ser,** and **tener**.

1. traer
2. hacer
3. oír
4. querer
5. conocer
6. dar
7. decir
8. venir
9. poder
10. poner
11. ver
12. salir

3-9 Combinaciones

Forma oraciones lógicas combinando los elementos de las dos columnas. Compara tus oraciones con las de tu compañero/a (*with those of your partner*).

1. _____ Hoy mis hermanos…
2. _____ Mis amigos y yo…
3. _____ Mi abuelo…
4. _____ Quiero…
5. _____ Mi perro (*dog*)…
6. _____ Mi profesor/a…
7. _____ Yo…
8. _____ Tú.…

a. pone sus recuerdos (*mementos*) en el altillo.
b. conoce bien la arquitectura de España.
c. oigo música en la sala.
d. hacemos fiestas en el jardín.
e. ves la televisión en tu dormitorio.
f. no pueden salir de casa.
g. una casa con dos pisos, tres baños y un garaje.
h. siempre viene a la cocina para comer.

3-10 Otras combinaciones

Completa los siguientes pasos.

Paso 1 Escribe una oración con cada (*each*) verbo, combinando elementos de las tres columnas.

MODELO (A) nosotros, (B) hacer, (C) la tarea en la oficina
Nosotros hacemos la tarea en la oficina.

Paso 2 En grupos de tres, lean las oraciones y corrijan (*correct*) los errores.

Paso 3 Escriban juntos (*together*) **dos** oraciones nuevas y compártanlas (*share them*) con la clase.

COLUMNA A	COLUMNA B	COLUMNA C
Uds.	(no) hacer	estudiar ciencias
mamá y papá	(no) ver	programas interesantes en la televisión los domingos
yo	(no) conocer	de Madrid mañana
tú	(no) oír	la tarea en el dormitorio
el profesor	(no) querer	mis libros a clase
nosotros/as	(no) salir	ruidos (*noises*) en el altillo por la noche
ellos/ellas	(no) traer	bien el arte de España

3•11 Confesiones

Time for true confessions! Take turns asking each other how often you do the following things.

siempre (*always*) a menudo (*often*) a veces (*sometimes*) nunca (*never*)

MODELO venir tarde (*late*) a la clase de español

E1: *¿Vienes tarde a la clase de español?*

E2: *Nunca vengo tarde a la clase de español. ¿Y tú?*

E1: *Yo vengo tarde a veces.*

Capítulo 2. La formación de preguntas y las palabras interrogativas, pág. 71.

1. querer estudiar
2. oír lo que (*what*) dice tu profesor/a
3. poder contestar las preguntas de tu profesor/a de español
4. escuchar música en la clase de español
5. hacer preguntas tontas en clase
6. traer tus libros a la clase
7. salir temprano (*early*) de tus clases
8. querer comer en la sala para ver la televisión

3•12 Firma aquí

Complete the following steps.

Paso 1 Circulate around the room asking your classmates appropriate questions using the cues provided. Ask those who answer **sí** to sign in the chart.

MODELO venir a clase todos los días

E1: *Roberto, ¿vienes a clase todos los días?*

E2: *No, no vengo a clase todos los días.*

E1: *Amanda, ¿vienes a clase todos los días?*

E3: *Sí, vengo a clase todos los días.*

E1: *Muy bien. Firma aquí, por favor.* ___Amanda___

Fíjate

Part of the enjoyment of learning another language is getting to know other people. Your instructor structures your class so that you have many opportunities to work with different classmates.

¿QUIÉN...?	
1. ver la televisión todas las noches	______
2. hacer la tarea siempre	______
3. salir con los amigos los jueves por la noche	______
4. estar enfermo/a hoy	______
5. conocer Madrid	______
6. poder estudiar con música fuerte (*loud*)	______
7. querer ser arquitecto	______
8. tener una nota muy buena en la clase de español	______

Paso 2 Report some of your information to the class.

MODELO *Joe ve la televisión todas las noches. Toni siempre hace la tarea. Chad está enfermo hoy.*

3-13 Entrevista

Complete the following steps.

Paso 1 Ask a classmate you do not know the following questions. Then change roles.

1. ¿Con quién(es) haces ejercicio? ¿Dónde?
2. ¿Cuándo ves la televisión? ¿Cuál es tu programa favorito?
3. ¿Con quiénes sales los fines de semana (*weekends*)? ¿Qué hacen Uds.?
4. ¿Qué días vienes a la clase de español? ¿A qué hora?
5. ¿Dónde pones tus libros? ¿Quién pone un examen en tu escritorio?
6. ¿Siempre dices la verdad?

Paso 2 Share a few of the things you have learned about your classmate with the class.

MODELO *Mi compañero sale los fines de semana con sus amigos y no hace ejercicio.*

3-16

¿Dónde viven los españoles?

En Madrid, la capital de España, al igual que en Barcelona, una ciudad cosmopolita en el noreste del país, la vida es tan rápida y vibrante como en la ciudad de Nueva York y otras grandes ciudades. Muchas personas viven en pisos (apartamentos) en edificios grandes, mientras que muchas otras viven ahora en las afueras (*outskirts*) en complejos (grupos) de casas llamados «urbanizaciones», y van a la ciudad para trabajar. Para muchas personas, el costo de vivir en los centros urbanos resulta demasiado caro. Para otras, es preferible vivir donde la vida es un poco más tranquila y tener algo de naturaleza (*nature*) cerca de su vivienda.

Sin embargo (*Nevertheless*), en los pueblos pequeños y en el campo la vida es diferente. Generalmente, las casas son bajas y algunas (*some*) tienen corrales con animales. Muchas personas se dedican a la agricultura y la vida es más lenta.

Preguntas

1. ¿Dónde viven generalmente las personas que residen en Barcelona y en Madrid? ¿Qué es una urbanización?
2. ¿Dónde prefieres vivir tú, en el campo o en la ciudad?

Los muebles y otros objetos de la casa

3-17 to 3-21

MUEBLES SÁNCHEZ

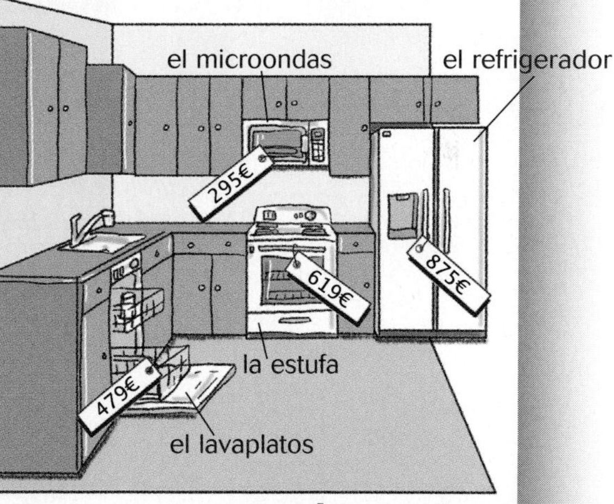

Otras palabras útiles	*Other useful words*
amueblado/a	*furnished*
el armario	*armoire; closet; cabinet*
la cosa	*thing*
el cuadro	*picture; painting*
el mueble	*piece of furniture*
los muebles	*furniture*
el objeto	*object*
la planta	*plant*

Capítulo 1. El verbo *tener*, pág. 35.

3•14 En mi casa

Túrnense para describir qué muebles y objetos tienen en sus casas.

MODELO E1: *Yo tengo una cama y dos sillas en mi dormitorio. ¿Qué tienes tú?*

E2: *Yo tengo una cama, un cuadro, una lámpara y un televisor. ¿Qué tienes en tu cocina?*

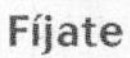

3•15 El dormitorio de Cecilia

Mira (*Look at*) la foto y con un/a compañero/a determina dónde está cada objeto.

Fíjate

The preposition *de* combines with the masculine definite article *el* to form the contraction *del*. The feminine article *la* does not contract. Note the following examples.

El tocador está a la derecha **de la** puerta.	*The dresser is to the right of the door.*
El tocador está a la derecha **del** armario.	*The dresser is to the right of the closet.*

MODELO E1: ¿Dónde está el cuadro?

E2: *El cuadro está en la pared a la derecha de la cama, al lado de la lámpara.*

Vocabulario útil

a la derecha (de)	*to the right (of)*
a la izquierda (de)	*to the left (of)*
al lado (de)	*beside*
encima (de)	*on top (of)*

¿Dónde está(n)...?

1. la cama
2. el armario
3. las lámparas
4. los sillones
5. la puerta
6. el estante

3•16 ¿Quieres una casa estupenda?

You have received a grant to study abroad in Sevilla, Spain! Now you need a place to live. Look at the three apartment ads below and select one of them. Give your partner at least **three** reasons for your choice. Use expressions like **Me gusta(n)... o Tiene un/una...** Be creative!

Capítulo 2. El verbo *gustar,* pág. 82.

MODELO *Me gusta el edificio nuevo y tiene muebles. No me gustan…*

Piso. Plaza de Cuba, Los Remedios. Edificio nuevo: dos dormitorios, baño, cocina, sala grande y balcón. Amueblado. 750€ al mes. Tel. 95 446 04 55.

Piso. Colonia San Luis. Sala, cocina, dormitorio y baño. Sin muebles. 400€ al mes. Tel. 95 448 85 32.

Alquilo piso de lujo en casa patio rehabilitada del siglo XVIII. Dos plantas, sala, cocina con zona de comedor, baño y dormitorio. Totalmente amueblado (junto a la Plaza Nueva, a dos minutos de la Catedral, Alcázar). Para más información por favor ponte en contacto con Teresa Rivas. Tel. 95 422 47 03.

¿Cómo andas?

Having completed the first **Comunicación,** I now can…

	Feel Confident	Need to Review
• describe my house and some of the items in it (p. 100)	❑	❑
• pronounce the letters **h, j,** and **g** properly in Spanish (p. 101)	❑	❑
• say and write the forms of the irregular **yo** verbs **dar, conocer, hacer, poner, salir, traer,** and **ver** and say what they mean (p. 104)	❑	❑
• create a simple sentence with each of the irregular **yo** verbs (p. 104)	❑	❑
• say and write the forms of the irregular verbs **decir, oír, venir, poder,** and **querer** (p. 105)	❑	❑
• create a simple sentence with the irregular verbs above (p. 105)	❑	❑
• describe some of the types of homes where Spaniards live (p. 108)	❑	❑

Comunicación

- Talking about household chores
- Describing places and certain feelings

VOCABULARIO 4 Los quehaceres de la casa

SAM 3-22 to 3-24

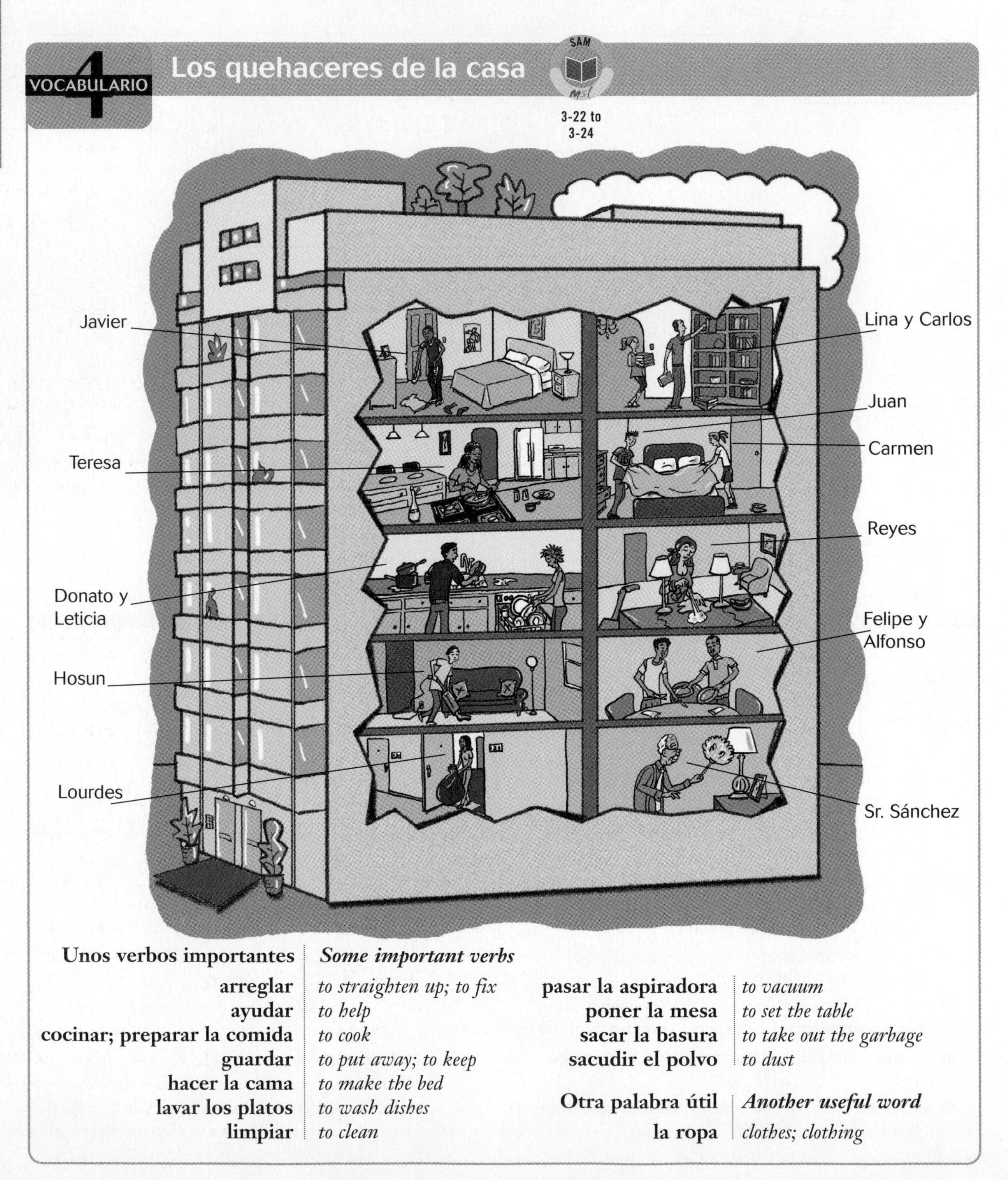

Unos verbos importantes	***Some important verbs***
arreglar	*to straighten up; to fix*
ayudar	*to help*
cocinar; preparar la comida	*to cook*
guardar	*to put away; to keep*
hacer la cama	*to make the bed*
lavar los platos	*to wash dishes*
limpiar	*to clean*
pasar la aspiradora	*to vacuum*
poner la mesa	*to set the table*
sacar la basura	*to take out the garbage*
sacudir el polvo	*to dust*

Otra palabra útil	***Another useful word***
la ropa	*clothes; clothing*

3•17 ¡Mucho trabajo!

Mira el dibujo en la página 112 y con un/a compañero/a determina qué hacen las personas de la lista.

MODELO E1: Carmen
E2: *Carmen hace la cama.*

1. El Sr. Sánchez
2. Hosun
3. Javier
4. Reyes
5. Donato y Leticia
6. Lourdes
7. Lina y Carlos
8. Teresa
9. Felipe y Alfonso
10. Juan y Carmen

3•18 Responsabilidades

¿Cuáles son tus responsabilidades? ¿Cuánto tiempo dedicas a (*do you devote to*) estas tareas? ¿Cuándo? Completa el cuadro y comparte (*share*) oralmente tu información con un/a compañero/a.

Fíjate

The expression *tener que* + infinitive means "to have to do" something *¿Qué tienes que hacer?* means "What do you have to do?" Later in this chapter you will learn more expressions with *tener.*

Vocabulario útil

desordenado/a	*messy*
limpio/a	*clean*
sucio/a	*dirty*
tener que + (*infinitive*)	*to have to (do something)*

MODELO *Tengo que limpiar y arreglar mi dormitorio los lunes. Dedico dos horas porque está muy sucio.*

LUGAR	¿QUÉ TIENES QUE HACER?	¿CUÁNDO?	¿CUÁNTO TIEMPO DEDICAS?
1. mi dormitorio	limpiar y arreglar	el lunes	dos horas
2. el baño			
3. la cocina			
4. la sala			
5. el garaje			
6. el comedor			

3-25 to
3-26

Las mujeres del mundo hispano

The roles of women in the Spanish-speaking world have changed dramatically in the past decades. Their quest for emancipation began somewhat later than in the United States. It has become more common for Hispanic women worldwide to work outside the home, own their own businesses, and have positions of responsibility, influence, and power. *El movimiento de las mujeres* is further along in the more industrialized Spanish-speaking countries.

These Hispanic women have achieved international recognition in different fields.

Verónica Michelle Bachelet Jeria (n. 1951), elegida presidenta de Chile en marzo de 2006.

Fue (*She was*) torturada y exiliada durante la dictadura del general Pinochet en Chile. Después de vivir en Australia y Alemania, vuelve a su país natal para trabajar como médica. Luego entra en el campo de la política. Habla español, francés, inglés y alemán. Es la primera mujer que sirve como presidenta en la historia del país.

Illy Nes (n. 1973), autora y periodista catalana.

Los temas de sus obras y de su trabajo como periodista y entrevistadora (*interviewer*) son el feminismo y la sexualidad. Ha recibido el premio (*She received the award*) Bigayles International dos veces: en 2000 por su novela *Morbo*, escrita a los quince años, y en 2004 por *Hijas de Adán: las mujeres también salen del armario*, una investigación de la homosexualidad dentro del mundo de las personas famosas.

Preguntas

1. ¿Por qué son importantes estas mujeres?
2. ¿Quiénes son otras mujeres hispanas famosas?

5 VOCABULARIO Los colores

SAM 3-27 to 3-29

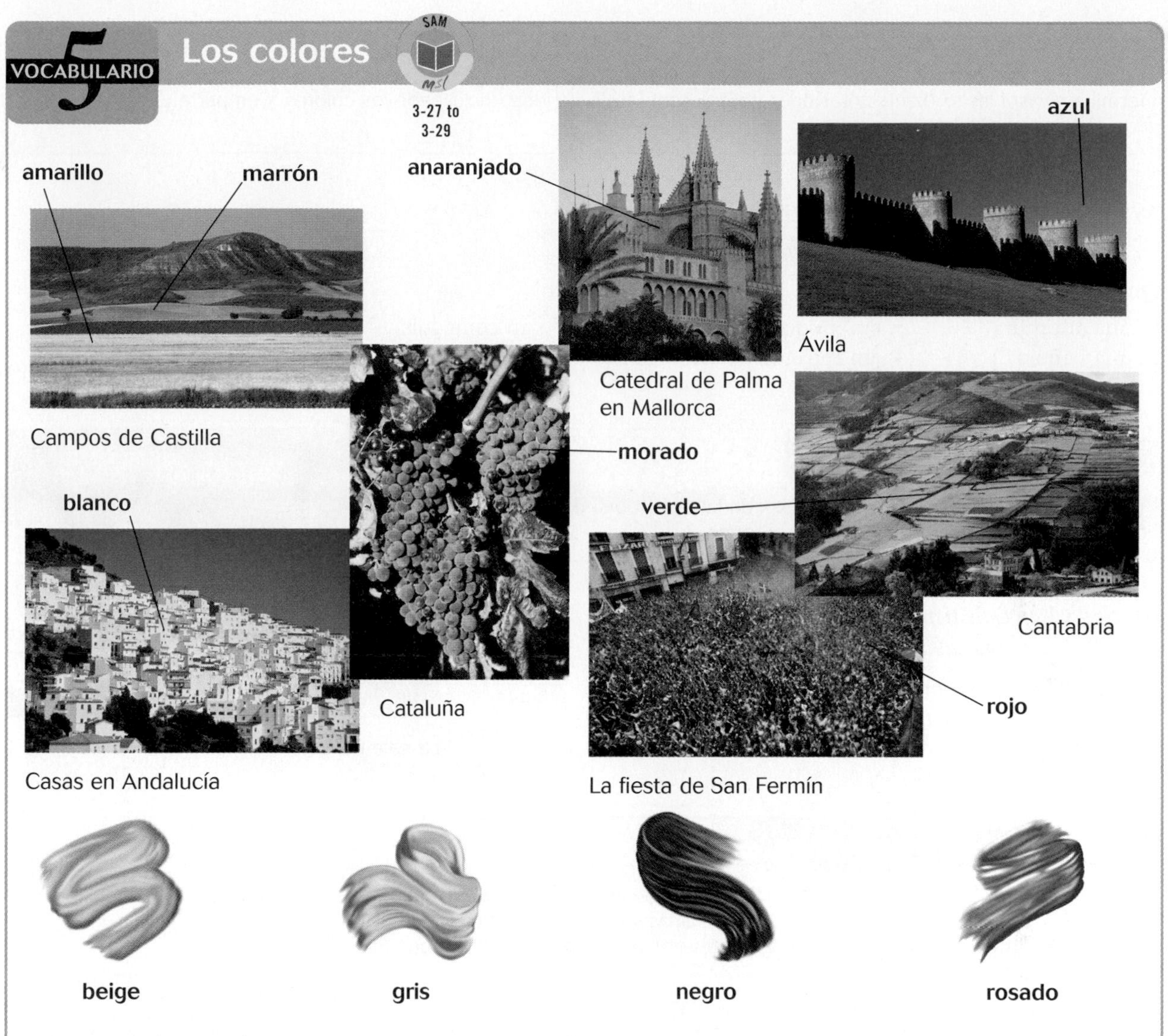

Campos de Castilla

Catedral de Palma en Mallorca

Ávila

Cataluña

Cantabria

Casas en Andalucía

La fiesta de San Fermín

beige **gris** **negro** **rosado**

¿De qué color es...? *What color is...?*

Colors are descriptive adjectives, and as such, they must agree with the noun they describe in number and gender.

- Adjectives ending in **-o** have four forms.

  roj**o** roj**a** roj**os** roj**as**

- Adjectives ending in a vowel other than **-o,** or in a consonant, have two forms.

  verd**e** verd**es**

  azul azul**es**

La cas**a** es blanc**a** y tiene un tech**o** roj**o**. *The house is white and has a red roof.*
Las cas**as** son blanc**as** y tienen tech**os** roj**os**. *The houses are white and have red roofs.*
Tengo un armari**o** marró**n**. *I have a brown armoire.*
Tengo una alfombr**a** marró**n**. *I have a brown rug.*
Tengo dos sillon**es** marron**es**. *I have two brown armchairs.*

How would you say "a black refrigerator," "a white sofa," "a green kitchen," and "some yellow chairs"?

3•19 La casa ideal

Termina (*Finish*) las siguientes oraciones para describir tu casa ideal, incluyendo los colores. Comparte tus respuestas con un/a compañero/a.

MODELO E1: Quiero una casa con... una cocina...
E2: *Quiero una casa con una cocina amarilla.*

Quiero una casa con...

1. una alfombra...
2. una bañera...
3. un inodoro y un lavabo...
4. un refrigerador...
5. un comedor...
6. unos sillones...
7. un techo
8. ¿?

3•20 ¿Cómo son?

Túrnense para comparar la sala de Luis con la tuya (*yours*) o la sala de un/a amigo/a. Usen los verbos **ser** y **tener.**

La sala de Luis

MODELO E1: *Luis tiene una sala grande pero yo tengo una sala pequeña.*
E2: *La sala de Luis es grande y mi sala es grande también.*

3•21 Buena memoria

Bring in colorful pictures of a house or rooms in a house. Select one picture and take a minute to study it carefully. Turn it over and relate to a partner as much detail as you can remember about the picture, especially pertaining to colors. Then listen to your partner talk about his or her picture. Who remembers more?

3•22 En la casa de Dalí

Go to your *¡Anda!* web site to take a virtual tour of the home of the famous Spanish artist Salvador Dalí, el Castillo Gala Dalí in Púbol, Spain. While you are exploring his house, answer the following questions. Then compare your answers with those of a classmate.

El Castillo Gala Dalí

1. ¿Qué ves en el jardín?
2. ¿Cuántas puertas tiene el salón de los escudos (*coats of arms*)?
3. ¿Qué ves a la izquierda de la puerta cerrada en el salón de escudos?
4. ¿Qué muebles ves en el salón del piano?
5. ¿Qué muebles ves en la biblioteca? ¿Cuántos cuadros ves?
6. ¿Cuáles son los colores principales que ves en la habitación de los invitados?
7. ¿Ves algo (*something*) diferente o extraño en el comedor?
8. ¿De qué color son las paredes de la casa?

Unas expresiones con *tener*

3-30 to 3-32

Susana

Rosario Alicia

Beatriz Julián

Pilar

Jorge Ramón Roberto

Carmen David

The verb **tener,** besides meaning *to have*, is used in a variety of expressions.

tener... años	*to be... years old*	**tener prisa**	*to be in a hurry*
tener calor	*to be hot*	**tener que + (*infinitive*)**	*to have to (do something)*
tener cuidado	*to be careful*	**tener razón**	*to be right*
tener éxito	*to be successful*	**tener sed**	*to be thirsty*
tener frío	*to be cold*	**tener sueño**	*to be sleepy*
tener ganas de + (*infinitive*)	*to feel like + (verb)*	**tener suerte**	*to be lucky*
tener hambre	*to be hungry*	**tener vergüenza**	*to be embarrassed*
tener miedo	*to be afraid*		

—Mamá, **tengo hambre.** ¿Cuándo comemos?
—**Tienes suerte,** hijo. Salimos para el restaurante Tío Tapas en diez minutos.

Mom, I'm hungry. When are we eating?
You are lucky, son. We are leaving for Tío Tapas Restaurant in ten minutes.

Fíjate

You have learned that some words in Spanish, like the color *amarillo*, have four forms (masculine singular, feminine singular, masculine plural, feminine plural). When you use the *tener* expressions like *tener frío* or *tener éxito*, you do not change the *o* of *frío* or *éxito* to make it feminine or plural.

3•23 ¿Qué pasa?

Mira los dibujos de la página 117 y, con un/a compañero/a, crea una oración para cada persona. Usa expresiones con **tener.**

MODELO *Beatriz tiene miedo.*

3•24 ¿Qué haces cuando...?

¿Qué haces en casa en las siguientes situaciones? Contesta combinando los elementos de las dos columnas de la forma más lógica. Compara tus respuestas con las de un/a compañero/a.

MODELO E1: tener ganas de descansar ver la televisión

E2: *Cuando tengo ganas de descansar, veo la televisión.*

Cuando...

1. _____ tener hambre	a. estar muy feliz
2. _____ tener suerte	b. preparar comida en la cocina
3. _____ tener miedo	c. hacer una limonada
4. _____ tener prisa	d. no tener que limpiar la casa
5. _____ tener frío	e. salir rápidamente en mi coche
6. _____ tener éxito	f. llamar a la policía
7. _____ tener sed	g. tomar el sol en el jardín

3•25 ¿Qué tengo yo?

Expresa cómo te sientes (*you feel*) en las siguientes ocasiones usando (*using*) expresiones con **tener.** Compara tus respuestas con las de un/a compañero/a.

MODELO E1: antes de comer

E2: *Antes de comer tengo hambre.*

1. temprano en la mañana
2. los viernes por la tarde
3. después de correr mucho
4. en el verano
5. en el invierno
6. cuando tienes tres minutos para llegar a clase
7. cuando sacas una "A" en un examen
8. cuando lees un libro de Stephen King o ves una película (*movie*) de terror

3-26 Pobre Pablo

Poor Pablo, our new friend from Madrid, is having one of those days! Together retell his story using **tener** expressions.

MODELO

El despertador de Pablo no funciona (*does not work*). Tiene una clase a las 8:00 y es tarde. Sale de casa a las 8:10.

Pablo tiene prisa.

1. Es invierno y Pablo no tiene abrigo (*coat*).

2. Pablo tiene un insuficiente (60% en EE.UU.) en un examen.

3. Pablo recibe una oferta (*offer*) de trabajo increíble.

4. Pablo ve que no tiene dinero para comer.

5. Pablo está en casa y quiere una botella de agua. En el refrigerador no hay ninguna (*none*).

3-27 Datos personales

Túrnense para hacerse esta entrevista (*interview*).

1. ¿Cuántos años tienes?
2. ¿Qué tienes que hacer hoy?
3. ¿Tienes ganas de hacer algo diferente? ¿Qué?
4. ¿En qué clase tienes sueño?
5. ¿En qué clase tienes mucha suerte?
6. ¿Siempre tienes razón?
7. ¿Cuándo tienes hambre?
8. ¿Cuándo tienes sueño?
9. Cuando tienes sed, ¿qué tomas?
10. ¿En qué tienes éxito?

Los números 1.000–100.000.000

3-33 to 3-37

1.000	**mil**	**100.000**	**cien mil**
1.001	**mil uno**	**400.000**	**cuatrocientos mil**
1.010	**mil diez**	**1.000.000**	**un millón**
2.000	**dos mil**	**2.000.000**	**dos millones**
30.000	**treinta mil**	**100.000.000**	**cien millones**

1. **Mil** is never used in the plural form when counting.

   mil dos mil tres mil

Fíjate

To express "a thousand," use *mil*, not *un mil*.

2. The plural of **millón** is **millones** and when followed by a noun, both take the preposition **de.**

   un millón de dólares cinco millones de personas

3. **Cien** is used before **mil** and **millones (de).**

   cien mil dólares cien millones de dólares

Fíjate

Note that *millón* has an accent in the singular form but loses the accent in the plural, *millones*.

4. Decimals are used instead of commas in some Hispanic countries to group three digits together, and commas are used to replace decimals.

   1.000.000 (un millón) $2.000,00 (dos mil dólares)

3-28 ¿Cuánto cuesta?

Look at the ads for houses in Spain. Take turns asking for the price and other details for each of the houses.

MODELO E1: *¿Cuánto cuesta la casa en Cullera?*
E2: *Cuesta seiscientos veinte mil euros.*
E1: *¿Cuántos dormitorios tiene?*
E2: *Tiene cuatro dormitorios.*

Chalet en venta

6 dormitorios
3 baños
calefacción
aire acondicionado
piscina

Dos Hermanas,

Sevilla, España.

Precio: 1.262.125€

Tel. 95 467 51 83

Chalet independiente en venta

4 dormitorios, 3 baños, cocina amueblada, terrazas, piscina.

Cullera, Valencia, España.
Precio: 620.000€
Tel. 96 264 79 51

Chalet independiente en venta

2 dormitorios, 1 baño, cocina amueblada, calefacción, terrazas, chimenea, jardín grande. Posibilidad de ampliación de dormitorios.

Fresno de la Vega, León, España.
Precio: 360.607€
Tel. 98 721 52 60

Casa independiente en venta

Casa señorial de dos plantas.
La construcción data de 1800. Muy buen estado de conservación.

5 dormitorios,
1 baño, chimenea, terrazas, jardín grande.

Toledo, España.
Precio: 420.000€
Tel. 92 592 72 23

3•29 ¿Cuál es su población?

Lee las poblaciones de estas ciudades de España mientras (*while*) tu compañero/a te escucha y corrige. Después, cambien de papel (*change roles*).

1. Madrid 5.423.384
2. Barcelona 4.805.927
3. Valencia 2.216.285
4. Sevilla 1.728.603
5. Granada 821.660

3•30 ¿Qué compras?

Your rich Spanish uncle left you an inheritance with the stipulation that you use the money to furnish your house. Refer to the pictures on page 109 to spend 3,500 € on your house. Make a list of what you want to buy, assigning prices to those items without tags. Then share your list with your partner, who will keep track of your spending. Did you overspend?

MODELO *Quiero comprar un televisor por* (for) *ochocientos noventa y nueve euros.*

Fíjate

The sentence in the model includes two verbs; the second verb is an infinitive (*-ar, -er, -ir*).

Quiero compr**ar** un televisor. — *I want to buy a TV set.*

GRAMÁTICA 8 Hay

3-38 to 3-41

In **Capítulo 2,** you became familiar with **hay** when you described your classroom. To say *there is* or *there are* in Spanish you use **hay.** The irregular form **hay** comes from the verb **haber,** which you will learn more about in a later chapter.

Hay un baño en mi casa. — *There is one bathroom in my house.*
Hay cuatro dormitorios también. — *There are also four bedrooms.*
—¿**Hay** tres baños en tu casa? — *Are there three bathrooms in your house?*
—No, no **hay** tres baños. — *No, there aren't three bathrooms.*

¿Qué hay en ese cuarto?

3-31 ¡Escucha bien!

Descríbele un cuarto de tu casa (real o imaginaria) a un/a compañero/a en **tres** oraciones. Él/Ella tiene que repetir las oraciones. Después, cambien de papel.

MODELO E1: *En mi dormitorio hay una cama, una lámpara y un tocador. También hay dos ventanas. No hay una alfombra.*

E2: *En tu dormitorio hay una cama, una lámpara y un tocador…*

3-32 ¿Qué hay en tu casa?

Descríbele tu casa a un compañero/a. Usen todas las palabras que puedan (*you can*) del vocabulario de *La casa*, p. 100, y *Los muebles y otros objetos de la casa*, p. 109.

MODELO E1: *En mi casa hay un garaje. ¿Hay un garaje en tu casa?*

E2: *No, en mi casa no hay un garaje.*

E2: *En mi baño hay una bañera y una ducha. ¿Qué hay en tu baño?*

E1: *Hay una ducha, un inodoro y un lavabo grande.*

3-33 ¿Cuántos hay?

Túrnense para preguntar y contestar cuántos objetos y personas hay en su clase aproximadamente.

Capítulo Preliminar A. Los números 0–30, pág. 16; Capítulo 2. La formación de preguntas y las palabras interrogativas, pág. 71.

MODELO libros de español

E1: *¿Cuántos libros de español hay?*

E2: *Hay treinta libros de español.*

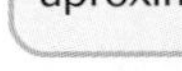

1. puertas
2. escritorios
3. mochilas azules
4. cuadernos negros
5. estudiantes contentos
6. estudiantes cansados
7. computadoras
8. estudiantes a quienes les gusta jugar al fútbol
9. estudiantes a quienes les gusta ir a fiestas
10. estudiantes a quienes les gusta estudiar

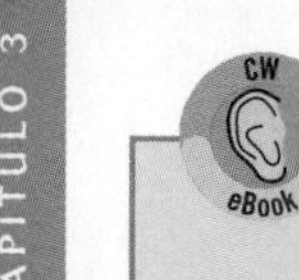

ESCUCHA

3-42 to 3-43

ESTRATEGIA **Listening for specific information**

To practice listening for specific information, first determine the context of the passage and then decide what information you need about that topic. For example, if you are listening to an ad about an apartment to rent, you may want to focus on size, location, and price. In ***¡Anda!*** the **Antes de escuchar** section will normally provide the context for each passage.

3•34 Antes de escuchar

A real estate agent is describing one of the homes she has listed to sell to the Jiménez family. Mr. Jiménez asks for a few details. Write a question Mr. Jiménez might ask the agent.

El Sr. Jiménez quiere comprar una casa.

3•35 A escuchar

CD 2 Track 2

Listen to the passage and complete the following list based on the information the agent provides. Listen a second time to verify your answers.

1. Number of floors: _____
2. Number of bedrooms: _____
3. Number of bathrooms: _____
4. Size of kitchen: _____
5. Size of living room: _____
6. Price: _____

3•36 Después de escuchar

In the role of Mr. Jiménez, describe the house to your partner using the information from **3-35**.

ESCRIBE

3-44 to 3-45

3•37 Antes de escribir

You have accepted a new job and you must sell your house and move to a different town (real or imagined). Before creating the flyer to sell your house, make a list as detailed as possible of the features you want to include.

3•38 Un anuncio (*flyer*)

Organize your list and create your flyer, making it as informative and attractive as possible. The flyer should include the following information:

- Location (city, country, street, etc.)
- Type of house or building
- Number and types of rooms
- Appliances in the kitchen
- Pieces of furniture included
- Colors
- Price and contact information
- Special features

3•39 Después de escribir

Circulate among your classmates, sharing flyers, and determine which house you would most like to buy.

¿Cómo andas?

Having completed the second **Comunicación,** I now can…

	Feel Confident	Need to Review
• describe what I and others do around the house (p. 112)	❑	❑
• state at least one interesting fact about the famous Hispanic women presented in the chapter (p. 114)	❑	❑
• describe my ideal house using colors (p. 115)	❑	❑
• discuss certain feelings using **tener** expressions (p. 117)	❑	❑
• count, quote prices, and give population figures using numbers 1,000–100,000,000 (p. 120)	❑	❑
• describe places using **hay** (p. 122)	❑	❑
• practice listening for specific information (p. 124)	❑	❑
• create a flyer (p. 125)	❑	❑

María Ángeles Solana Montoya

España

CW eBook CD 2 Track 3

SAM 3-46 to 3-47

DVD/VHS Vistas culturales

Les presento mi país

Mi nombre es María Ángeles Solana Montoya y soy de Madrid, la capital de España. Vivo con mis padres en un piso en el centro. **¿Dónde vives tú? ¿En una casa, en un apartamento o en una residencia estudiantil?** Me gusta la vida en la capital porque hay mucha actividad. A veces, me gusta salir con mis amigos por la tarde para comer tapas y tomar algo. La Plaza Mayor es uno de los lugares más típicos para ir de tapas. **¿Cuál es tu lugar favorito para conversar y pasar tiempo con tus amigos?** Frecuentemente, hablamos de los deportes, sobre todo el fútbol y los equipos españoles. ¡Cada uno tiene su favorito! **¿Cuál es tu deporte preferido? ¿Eres aficionado o jugador?**

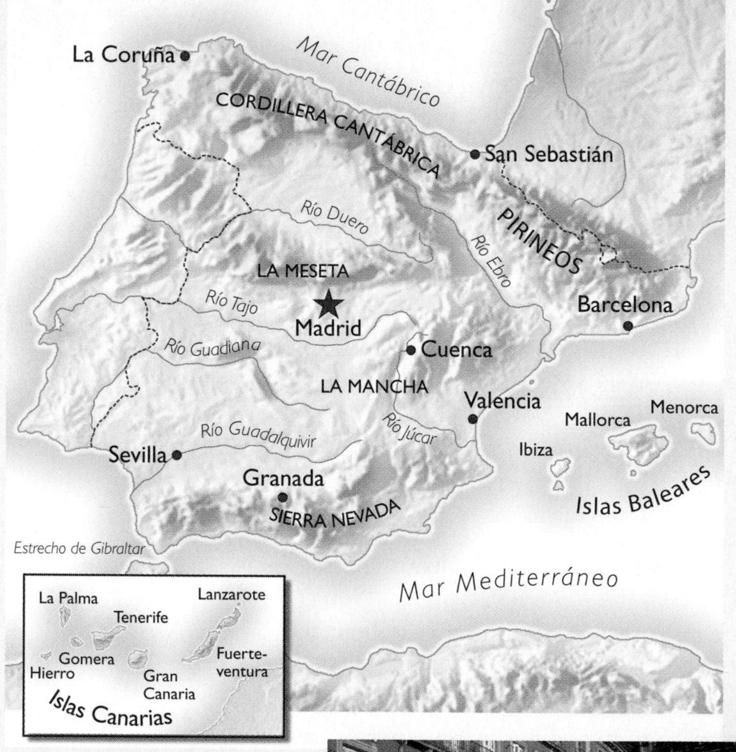

Don Quijote y Sancho Panza son personajes del autor Miguel de Cervantes Saavedra.
Picasso, Pablo (1881–1973), Don Quijote, 1955, Pen and Ink. Private Collection. Erich Lessing/Art Resource, NY. © 2004 Estate of Pablo Picasso/ Artists Rights Society (ARS), NY.

El fútbol es el deporte más importante del país.

La Plaza Mayor de Madrid es un lugar agradable para comer tapas, tomar una bebida y conversar con amigos.

ALMANAQUE

Nombre oficial:	Reino de España
Gobierno:	Monarquía parlamentaria
Población:	41.547.000 (est. 2006)
Idiomas oficiales:	español, catalán, gallego, eusquera (vasco)
Moneda:	euro (€)

La tortilla española es una tapa (un aperitivo) y un plato muy típico y popular.

Los *castells*—o castillos (*castles*) en español—son impresionantes construcciones humanas.

La Pedrera (la Casa Milà) en Barcelona es un ejemplo de la arquitectura creativa de Antonio Gaudí.

El patio de los leones de La Alhambra muestra la influencia árabe en Granada.

¿Sabías que...?

- La Organización Nacional de Ciegos Españoles, O.N.C.E., es una empresa que trabaja en beneficio de las personas ciegas (*blind*) y otros discapacitados.
- Los *castells* forman parte de una tradición empezada en Cataluña en el siglo (*century*) XVIII que consiste en competir por hacer la torre (*tower*) humana más alta. ¡Actualmente el récord es un castillo de nueve pisos!

PREGUNTAS

1. ¿Qué es una tapa?
2. ¿Qué evidencia hay de la presencia histórica de los árabes en España?
3. ¿Por qué son impresionantes los *castells*? Nombra una competencia famosa de tu país.
4. Describe la arquitectura de Antonio Gaudí. ¿Te gusta? ¿Por qué?
5. ¿Qué tienen en común México y España en cuanto a los deportes?

En la Red
Amplía tus conocimientos sobre España en la página web de *¡Anda!*

Ambiciones siniestras

EPISODIO 3

3-50

lectura

3-40 Antes de leer. In the third episode of **Ambiciones siniestras,** some of our protagonists receive an enticing e-mail message. You will discover the content of the mysterious message, as well as learn more about Alejandra's family. Before you read this episode, consider the following questions.

1. ¿Hablas sobre los miembros de tu familia con tus amigos? ¿Qué dices?
2. ¿Recibes mensajes curiosos que no vienen de amigos ni (*nor*) de personas de tu familia?
3. ¿Recibes mensajes sobre concursos (*contests*)?

ESTRATEGIA Scanning

To enhance comprehension, you can scan or search a reading passage for specific information. When skimming, you read quickly to get the gist of the passage, the main ideas. With scanning, you already know what you need to find out, so you concentrate on searching for that information.

3-41 A leer. Follow the steps below.

1. Scan the first two paragraphs of this episode, looking for the following specific information:
   a. the location of Alejandra and Manolo
   b. what they are doing there
   c. about whom Alejandra is talking
2. Now reread the second paragraph to determine why Alejandra is discussing this person. What is her concern?

Remember that successful reading in Spanish will require that you read the episodes more than once.

CD 2
Track 4

El concurso°

contest

Manolo y Alejandra están en el cibercafé NetEscape. Hablan mientras se toman un café y leen sus correos electrónicos.

message
to introduce him

Alejandra le dice a Manolo que quiere mirar su e-mail para ver si tiene un mensaje° de su hermana Pili. Alejandra explica que Pili tiene un novio nuevo y que quiere presentárselo° a sus padres esta noche. Su hermana está muy nerviosa. El novio, Peter, tiene veintinueve años y la hermana tiene solamente diecinueve. ¡Con razón tiene miedo! Alejandra dice que sus padres son muy estrictos y creen que ella es demasiado joven para tener novio.

Alejandra lee varios mensajes y exclama:

—Manolo, ¡mira!

—¿Qué pasa? ¿Tienes un mensaje de tu hermana? —le pregunta Manolo.

—No, pero tienes que leer esto°. ¡Es increíble!

this

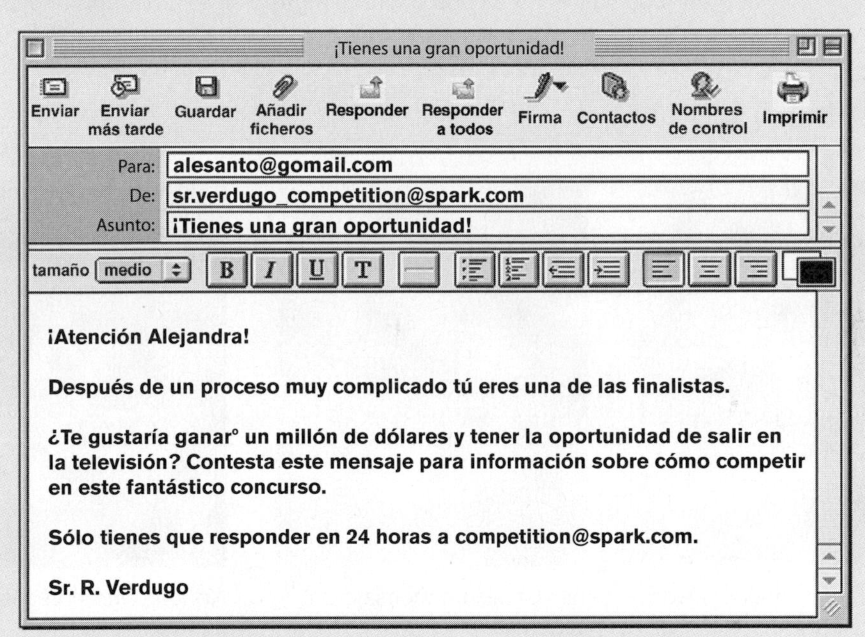

Para: alesanto@gomail.com

De: sr.verdugo_competition@spark.com

Asunto: ¡Tienes una gran oportunidad!

¡Atención Alejandra!

Después de un proceso muy complicado tú eres una de las finalistas.

¿Te gustaría ganar° un millón de dólares y tener la oportunidad de salir en la televisión? Contesta este mensaje para información sobre cómo competir en este fantástico concurso.

Sólo tienes que responder en 24 horas a competition@spark.com.

Sr. R. Verdugo

Would you like to win?

Entonces Manolo decide ver si él tiene el mismo mensaje.

—¡Mira! —exclama Manolo. —¡Aquí está! ¡Qué bueno! Pero, seguramente el país entero° tiene el mismo mensaje. ¿Es legítimo? Alejandra, ¿respondemos?

entire country

—No sé. —le contesta Alejandra. —Mis padres siempre me dicen que debo° tener cuidado con las ofertas. ¿Pero qué nos puede pasar si sólo contestamos que deseamos más información?

I must

—Sí. —le responde Manolo. —¿Qué nos puede pasar?

3-42 **Después de leer.** Contesta las siguientes preguntas.

1. ¿Cómo se llama la hermana de Alejandra? ¿Cuál es su problema?
2. ¿Qué recibe Alejandra?
3. ¿Qué puede ganar?
4. Según (*According to*) Manolo, ¿quiénes reciben la oferta?
5. En tu opinión, ¿qué crees que hacen?
6. Hagan los papeles (*roles*) de unas personas que acaban (*have just*) de recibir el mensaje. ¿Cómo reaccionan? ¿Qué dicen? ¿Qué hacen?

3-51 to 3-54

video

3-43 Antes del video. Take a minute to think back to the first time you visited a friend in his or her dorm room, apartment, or house. Were you interested in seeing what the new living space was like? Did he/she take time to show you around and elaborate on some of the furnishings? In this video episode you will see Lupe's apartment as well as Eduardo's and Cisco's families' homes. They are also checking e-mail. Listen for the phrase **Seguro que es una broma.** (*It's got to be a joke.*) Who says it? Also listen for **Tal vez** (*perhaps*) **sea un mensaje en cadena. Cadena** means "chain." Can you guess what the sentence means?

¡Es una gran oportunidad! ¿No crees?

Tal vez sea un mensaje en cadena.

No lo puedo creer. ¡Qué piscina! ¡Es impresionante!

Episodio 3

¡Tienes una gran oportunidad!

Relax and watch the video, more than once if you choose. Then answer the questions that follow.

3-44 Después del video. Contesta las siguientes preguntas.

1. ¿Cómo es el apartamento de Lupe?
2. ¿Qué mensaje recibe Marisol? ¿y Guadalupe?
3. ¿Dónde están Cisco y Eduardo? ¿Qué estudian?
4. ¿Cómo es la nueva habitación de Eduardo?
5. ¿Cómo es la casa de los padres de Cisco?
6. ¿Qué ocurre al final del episodio?

Y por fin, ¿cómo andas?

Having completed this chapter, I now can…

	Feel Confident	Need to Review
Comunicación		
• describe my house and the things in it (p. 100, 109)	❑	❑
• use new verbs that have irregular **yo** forms and that are stem-changing (p. 104)	❑	❑
• talk about what I do or should do around my house (p. 112)	❑	❑
• use colors to describe things (p. 115)	❑	❑
• use idiomatic expressions with the verb **tener** to express physical and emotional states (p. 117)	❑	❑
• use numbers 1,000–100,000,000 (p. 120)	❑	❑
• say what things there are in a place, or how many there are, using **hay** (p. 122)	❑	❑
Cultura		
• describe some of the types and styles of homes in the Spanish-speaking world (p. 108)	❑	❑
• discuss the changing roles of Hispanic women, and share facts about at least one Hispanic woman who has made an impact on society (p. 114)	❑	❑
• list at least three facts about **España** (p. 126)	❑	❑
Ambiciones siniestras		
• scan for specific information when I read (p. 128)	❑	❑
• explain what is contained in the e-mail message the protagonists receive (p. 129–130)	❑	❑

VOCABULARIO ACTIVO

CD 2
Tracks 5–16

La casa	The house
el altillo	*attic*
el balcón	*balcony*
el baño	*bathroom*
la cocina	*kitchen*
el comedor	*dining room*
el cuarto	*room*
el dormitorio	*bedroom*
la escalera	*staircase*
el garaje	*garage*
el jardín	*garden*
la oficina	*office*
el piso	*floor; story*
la planta baja	*ground floor*
el primer piso	*second floor*
la sala	*living room*
el segundo piso	*third floor*
el sótano	*basement*
el suelo	*floor*
el techo	*roof*
el tercer piso	*fourth floor*

Los verbos	Verbs
conocer	*to be aquainted with*
dar	*to give*
decir	*to say; to tell*
hacer	*to do; to make*
oír	*to hear*
poder	*to be able to*
poner	*to put; to place*
querer	*to want; to love*
salir	*to leave; to go out*
traer	*to bring*
venir	*to come*
ver	*to see*

Los muebles y otros objetos de la casa — *Furniture and other objects in the house*

La sala y el comedor	The living room and dining room
la alfombra	*rug; carpet*
el estante de libros	*bookcase*
la lámpara	*lamp*
el mueble	*piece of furniture*
los muebles	*furniture*
el sillón	*armchair*
el sofá	*sofa*

La cocina	The kitchen
la estufa	*stove*
el lavaplatos	*dishwasher*
el microondas	*microwave*
el refrigerador	*refrigerator*

El baño	The bathroom
la bañera	*bathtub*
el bidet	*bidet*
la ducha	*shower*
el inodoro	*toilet*
el lavabo	*sink*

El dormitorio	The bedroom
la almohada	*pillow*
el armario	*armoire; closet; cabinet*
la cama	*bed*
la colcha	*bedspread; comforter*
la manta	*blanket*
las sábanas	*sheets*
el tocador	*dresser*

Otras palabras útiles en la casa	Other useful words in the house
amueblado/a	*furnished*
la cosa	*thing*
el cuadro	*picture; painting*
el objeto	*object*
la planta	*plant*

Los quehaceres de la casa	Household chores
arreglar	*to straighten up; to fix*
ayudar	*to help*
cocinar, preparar la comida	*to cook*
guardar	*to put away; to keep*
hacer la cama	*to make the bed*
lavar los platos	*to wash dishes*
limpiar	*to clean*
pasar la aspiradora	*to vacuum*
poner la mesa	*to set the table*
sacar la basura	*to take out the garbage*
sacudir el polvo	*to dust*

Los colores	Colors
amarillo	*yellow*
anaranjado	*orange*
azul	*blue*
beige	*beige*
blanco	*white*
gris	*gray*
marrón	*brown*
morado	*purple*
negro	*black*
rojo	*red*
rosado	*pink*
verde	*green*

Expresiones con *tener*	Expressions with **tener**
tener … años	*to be… years old*
tener calor	*to be hot*
tener cuidado	*to be careful*
tener éxito	*to be successful*
tener frío	*to be cold*
tener ganas de + (*infinitive*)	*to feel like +* (*verb*)
tener hambre	*to be hungry*
tener miedo	*to be afraid*
tener prisa	*to be in a hurry*
tener que + (*infinitive*)	*to have to* (*do something*)
tener razón	*to be right*
tener sed	*to be thirsty*
tener sueño	*to be sleepy*
tener suerte	*to be lucky*
tener vergüenza	*to be embarrassed*

Los números 1.000–100.000.000	Numbers 1,000–100,000,000
See page 120	

Otras palabras útiles	Other useful words
a la derecha (de)	*to the right (of)*
a la izquierda (de)	*to the left (of)*
al lado (de)	*beside*
antiguo/a	*old*
la calle	*street*
el campo	*country*
la ciudad	*city*
contemporáneo/a	*contemporary*
desordenado/a	*messy*
encima (de)	*on top (of)*
humilde	*humble*
limpio/a	*clean*
moderno/a	*modern*
nuevo/a	*new*
la ropa	*clothes; clothing*
siempre	*always*
sucio/a	*dirty*
tener que + (*infinitive*)	*to have to +* (*verb*)
tradicional	*traditional*
viejo/a	*old*

4

Nuestra comunidad

No importa si vivimos en el campo (*countryside*), en un pueblo, en una ciudad o en otro país (*country*), tenemos mucho en común. Todos comemos, trabajamos, compramos, pasamos tiempo con la familia y los amigos y ayudamos a los demás (*others*). Nuestra vida en comunidad es similar.

	OBJETIVOS	CONTENIDOS	
Comunicación	• To relate information about your home and/or university town • To talk about whom and what you know or are acquainted with in your area • To share information about what will take place in the future • To discuss some service opportunities in your community • To paraphrase what you hear • To write a postcard about your town or city	1 Places 2 Two verbs that express *to know* (**saber/conocer**) 3 To have to do something (**tener** + **que** + *infinitive*) 4 Verbs with stem changes 5 The verb **ir** (*to go*) 6 The future expressed by **ir** + **a** + *infinitive* 7 Volunteerism 8 Affirmative and negative expressions 9 Review of **ser** and **estar** Pronunciación: The letters **c** and **z** Escucha: Estrategia: Paraphrasing what you hear Escribe: Writing a postcard	136 140 142 144 147 149 151 154 156 137 159 160
Cultura	• To compare your everyday, common tasks (such as shopping) with those of the Spanish-speaking world • To list ways of serving your community • To state three interesting facts about each of this chapter's feature countries: Honduras, Guatemala, and El Salvador	Daily activities Social conscience *Honduras*, *Guatemala*, and *El Salvador*	139 153 161–163
Ambiciones siniestras	• To practice the reading strategies of skimming and scanning • To learn more about Lupe and Marisol, and which of the characters have not been truthful.	Episodio 4 Lectura: *Las cosas no son siempre lo que parecen* Estrategia: Skimming and Scanning (II) Video: *¿Quiénes son en realidad?*	 164 166

La plaza de Chichicastenango en Guatemala

PREGUNTAS

1. Generalmente, ¿qué haces durante un día normal?
2. ¿Conoces a personas de otros países o culturas? ¿Cuáles son sus actividades típicas?
3. ¿Qué tienes en común con las personas de otros países?

Comunicación

- Identifying places
- Discussing what and whom you know
- Stating what you have to do

1 VOCABULARIO Los lugares

SAM 4-1 to 4-3

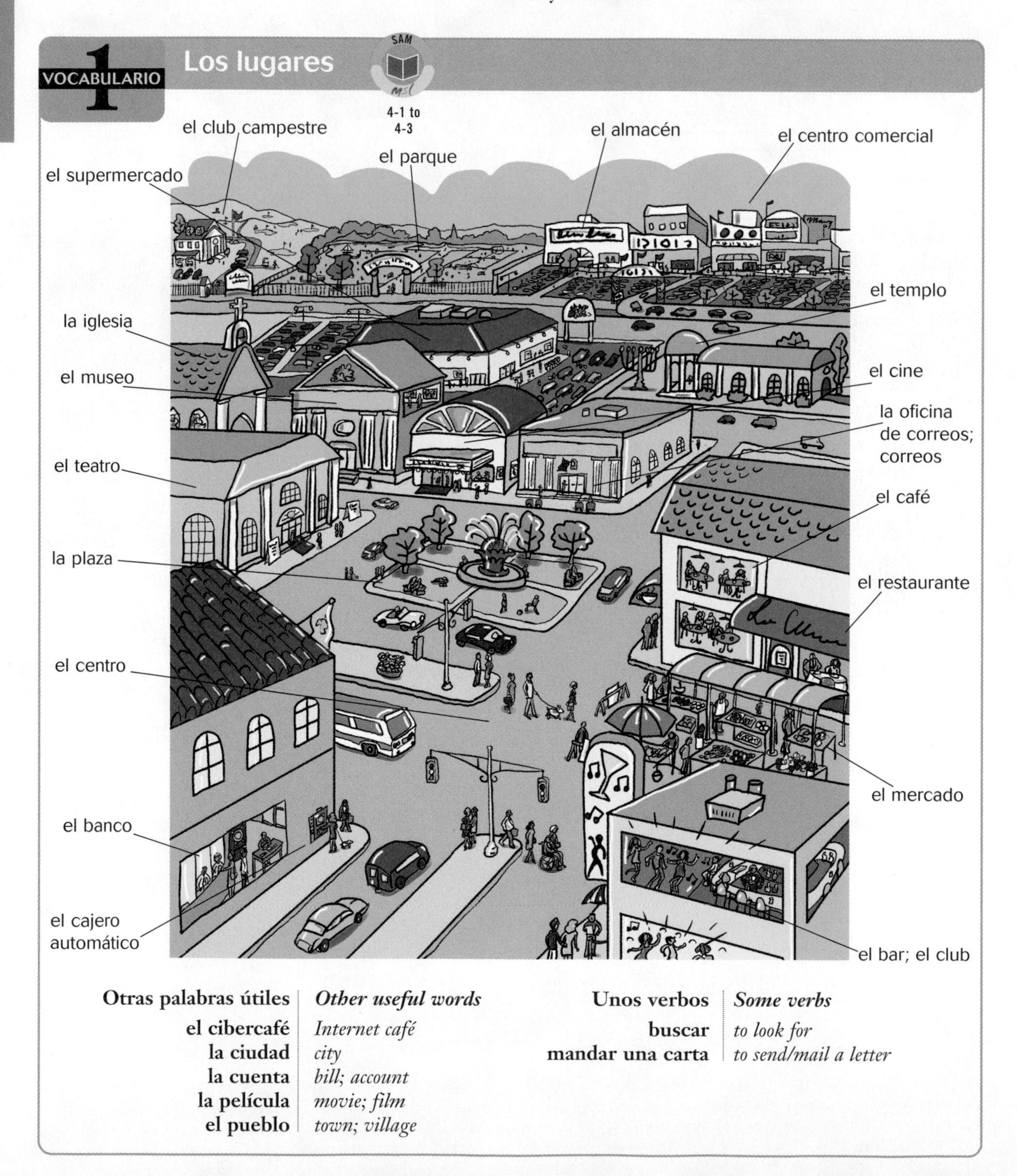

Otras palabras útiles	*Other useful words*
el cibercafé	*Internet café*
la ciudad	*city*
la cuenta	*bill; account*
la película	*movie; film*
el pueblo	*town; village*

Unos verbos	*Some verbs*
buscar	*to look for*
mandar una carta	*to send/mail a letter*

CD 2
Track 17

4-4 to
4-8

PRONUNCIACIÓN

The letters *c* and *z*

1. Before the vowels **a, o,** and **u,** and when followed by a consonant, the Spanish c is pronounced like the *c* in the English word *car.*
2. Before the vowels **e** and **i,** the Spanish c is pronounced like the *s* in the English word *seal.*
3. The Spanish z is pronounced like the *s* in the English word *seal.*

4•1 Las palabras

Practice pronouncing the following words, focusing on the letters **c** and **z.**

1. almacén
2. banco
3. club
4. cuidado
5. cibercafé
6. cajero
7. lápiz
8. plaza

4•2 Las oraciones

Pronounce the following sentences, paying special attention to the letters **c** and **z.**

1. ¿Cuánto cuesta el lápiz?
2. Cecilia cocina con cuidado en la cocina.
3. Carlos tiene que buscar a sus amigos en la plaza.

4•3 Los trabalenguas

Pronounce the following tongue twister (*trabalenguas*), focusing on the letters **c** and **z.**

El cerdo del centro corre con cuidado hacia Zaragoza con una cerveza.

Capítulo 2. El verbo *estar*, pág. 78.

4•4 ¿Dónde está?

Tu amigo está muy ocupado. Túrnate con un/a compañero/a para decir dónde está en este momento.

Fíjate

Notice that you use a form of *querer* + *infinitive* to express "to want to_____". For example:

Quiero mandar... = I want to send...

Queremos ver... = We want to see...

MODELO E1: Quiere mandar una carta.
E2: *Está en (la oficina de) correos.*

1. Quiere ver una película.
2. Necesita dinero para pagar una cuenta.
3. Quiere comer algo *(something)*.
4. Quiere ver una exposición de arte.
5. Quiere caminar y hacer ejercicio.
6. Tiene sed y quiere tomar algo.
7. Quiere jugar al golf.
8. Tiene que ir a una boda (*wedding*).

4•5 El mejor de los mejores

¿Cuáles son, en tu opinión, los mejores lugares?

Estrategia

Remember that you learned vocabulary in *Capítulos 2* and *3*, such as *a la derecha*, *a la izquierda*, and *al lado de* that you can also practice with your new vocabulary.

Vocabulario útil

detrás (de)	*behind*
enfrente (de)	*in front (of)*
estar de acuerdo	*to agree*
el/la mejor	*the best*
el/la peor	*the worst*

Paso 1 Haz (*Make*) una lista de los mejores lugares de tu pueblo o ciudad según las siguientes categorías.

MODELO E1: restaurante
E2: *El mejor restaurante es* The Lantern.

1. almacén
2. banco
3. centro comercial
4. cine
5. café
6. teatro
7. tienda
8. restaurante
9. supermercado

Paso 2 Compara tu lista con la lista de los otros estudiantes de la clase. ¿Están de acuerdo?

MODELO E1: *En mi opinión, el mejor restaurante es* The Lantern. *¿Estás de acuerdo?*
E2: *No, no estoy de acuerdo. El mejor restaurante es* The Cricket.

Paso 3 Túrnense para explicar dónde están los mejores lugares.

MODELO E1: *Busco el mejor restaurante.*
E2: *El mejor restaurante es* The Lantern.
E1: *¿Dónde está?*
E2: *Está al lado del Banco Nacional.*

Fíjate

A reminder from *Capítulo 3*: The preposition *de* combines with the masculine singular definite article *el* to form the contraction *del*. The feminine article *la* does not contract.

4•6 Chiquimula y mi ciudad...

Chiquimula es un pueblo de 24.000 personas que está en el este de Guatemala.

Paso 1 Túrnense para describir el centro del pueblo. Mencionen dónde están los edificios principales.

MODELO *El Hotel Victoria está al lado del Restaurante el Dorado…*

Paso 2 Ahora dibuja (*draw*) un mapa del centro de tu pueblo o ciudad. El dibujo debe incluir los edificios principales. Después, túrnense para describirlo oralmente.

Paso 3 Túrnense para describir sus dibujos mientras tu compañero/a dibuja lo que dices.

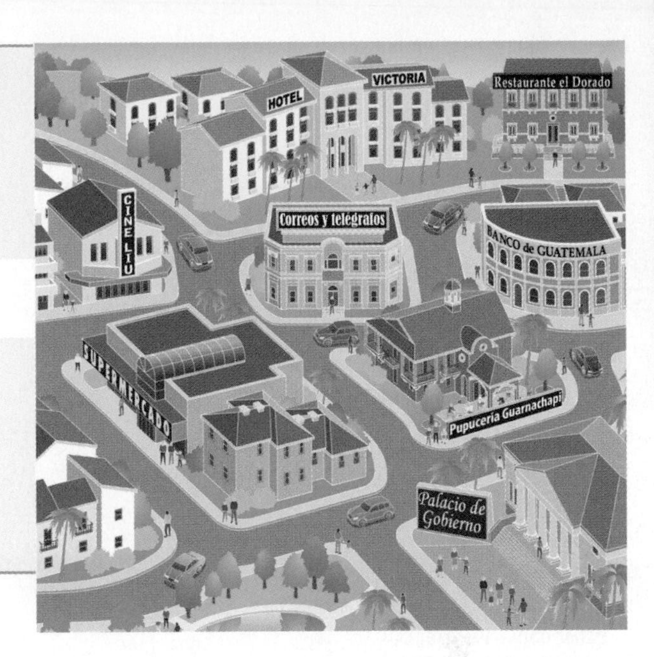

SAM 4-9 to 4-10

Actividades cotidianas: Las compras y el paseo

En los Estados Unidos, la gente hace gran parte de las compras en los centros comerciales. En los países hispanohablantes, también se hacen las compras en los centros comerciales, especialmente en las ciudades grandes. En Guatemala, Honduras y El Salvador algunos de los más conocidos son "Hiper Paiz", "Maxi Bodega" y "Despensa Familiar".

En los pueblos pequeños la gente va al centro de la ciudad. En el centro está el mercado y hay muchas tiendas además de la oficina de correos, el banco y los restaurantes. Se puede encontrar gente de todas las clases sociales y muchos vendedores ambulantes (*roving*).

Otro lugar importante en el centro de los pueblos es la plaza. Allí se encuentra la gente (*people meet*) para conversar, pasear, comprar o ir a la iglesia. Además, los lugareños (*locals*) pasean a diario por las calles principales y los parques del pueblo. En los pueblos hispanos siempre hay mucho bullicio (*hubbub*) y actividad, especialmente los fines de semana.

Preguntas

1. ¿Qué hay en las ciudades grandes? ¿Cómo son los pueblos pequeños? ¿Qué hace la gente todos los días?

Fíjate

Note that the word *gente*, unlike English, is singular: *La gente* ***va*** *al centro de la ciudad. Gente*, although made up of more than one person, is considered a collective noun like the singular nouns *la clase, el equipo,* or *la familia.*

2. ¿Dónde prefieres comprar, en las tiendas pequeñas o en los centros comerciales? ¿Por qué?

GRAMÁTICA 2 Saber y conocer

4-11 to 4-13

In **Capítulo 3** you learned that **conocer** means *to know*. Another verb, **saber,** also expresses *to know*.

> **Fíjate**
>
> Note that *conocer* and *saber* both have irregular *yo* forms: *conozco* and *sé* respectively.

saber (*to know*)

Singular		Plural	
yo	**sé**	nosotros/as	**sabemos**
tú	**sabes**	vosotros/as	**sabéis**
él, ella, Ud.	**sabe**	ellos/as, Uds.	**saben**

The verbs are not interchangeable. Note when to use each.

*Use **conocer** to express ***being familiar or acquainted with people, places, and things.***

Ellos **conocen** los mejores restaurantes de la ciudad. — *They know the best restaurants in the city.*

Sí, **conozco** a tu hermano, pero no muy bien. — *Yes, I know your brother, but not very well.*

Note:

1. When expressing that *a person* is known, you must use **"a."** For example, *Conozco **a** tu hermano…*
2. When **a** is followed by **el, a + el = al.** For example, **Conozco *al* señor (a + el señor)**…

*Use **saber** to express ***knowing facts, pieces of information,*** or ***how to do something.***

¿Qué **sabes** sobre la música de Guatemala? — *What do you know about Guatemalan music?*

Yo **sé** tocar la guitarra. — *I know how to play the guitar.*

> **Fíjate**
>
> A form of *saber + infinitive* expresses knowing how to do something. For example:
>
> *Sé nadar.* = I know how to swim.
>
> *Sabemos tocar la guitarra.* = We know how to play the guitar.

4-7 ¿Sabes o conoces?

Completa las siguientes preguntas usando **sabes** or **conoces.** Después, túrnate con un/a compañero/a para hacer y contestar las preguntas.

MODELO E1: ¿*Conoces* San Salvador?

E2: *Sí, conozco San Salvador. / No, no conozco San Salvador.*

1. ¿________ Tegucigalpa, Honduras?
2. ¿________ al presidente de la universidad?
3. ¿________ las películas de Alfred Hitchcock?
4. ¿________ cuál es el mejor café de esta ciudad?
5. ¿________ patinar?
6. ¿________ usar una computadora?
7. ¿________ el mejor restaurante mexicano?
8. ¿________ hacer tortillas?

4•8 ¿Qué sabemos de Honduras?

Completen juntos el diálogo con la forma correcta de **saber** o **conocer.**

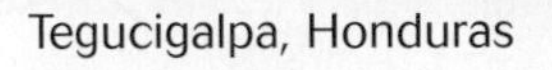
Tegucigalpa, Honduras

PROF. DOMÍNGUEZ: ¿Qué (1) ________ ustedes sobre Honduras?

DREW: Yo (2) ________ que la capital de Honduras es Tegucigalpa.

DREW Y TANYA: Nosotros (3) ________ mucho sobre el país.

PROF. DOMÍNGUEZ: ¿Y (4) ________ ustedes cómo se llaman las personas de Honduras?

TANYA: Sí, se llaman *hondureños.* (5) ________ la cultura hondureña bastante bien. Nuestra hermana, Gina, es una estudiante de intercambio allí este año y nos manda muchas fotos y cartas. Ella (6) ________ a mucha gente interesante, incluso al hijo del Presidente.

PROF. DOMÍNGUEZ: ¡No me digan! ¿Estudia allí su hermana? ¿(7) ________ ustedes que hay dos universidades muy buenas en Tegucigalpa?

TANYA: Sí, el novio de Gina estudia allí pero no (8) ________ en qué universidad. Él es salvadoreño y nuestros padres no lo (9)________ todavía. Gina dice que no quiere volver a los Estados Unidos. Yo (10) ________ que mis padres van a estar muy tristes si ella no vuelve.

PROF. DOMÍNGUEZ: Yo (11) ________ a tu hermana y (12) ________ que es una mujer inteligente. Va a pensarlo bien antes de tomar una decisión.

4•9 ¿Me puedes ayudar?

Sofía acaba de llegar a San Salvador y se siente un poco perdida (*she is feeling a little lost*). Túrnense para hacer y contestar sus preguntas de manera creativa. Luego, creen (*create*) y contesten **dos** preguntas más usando **saber** y **conocer**.

MODELO SOFÍA: *¿Sabes dónde hay una iglesia?*

TÚ: *Sí, sé que hay una iglesia en la plaza.*

1. ¿Conoces un buen restaurante típico?
2. ¿Sabes dónde está el restaurante?
3. ¿Sabes cuáles son los platos típicos del restaurante?
4. ¿Conoces al cocinero (*chef*)?
5. ¿?
6. ¿?

VOCABULARIO 3 ¿Qué tienen que hacer? ¿Qué pasa?

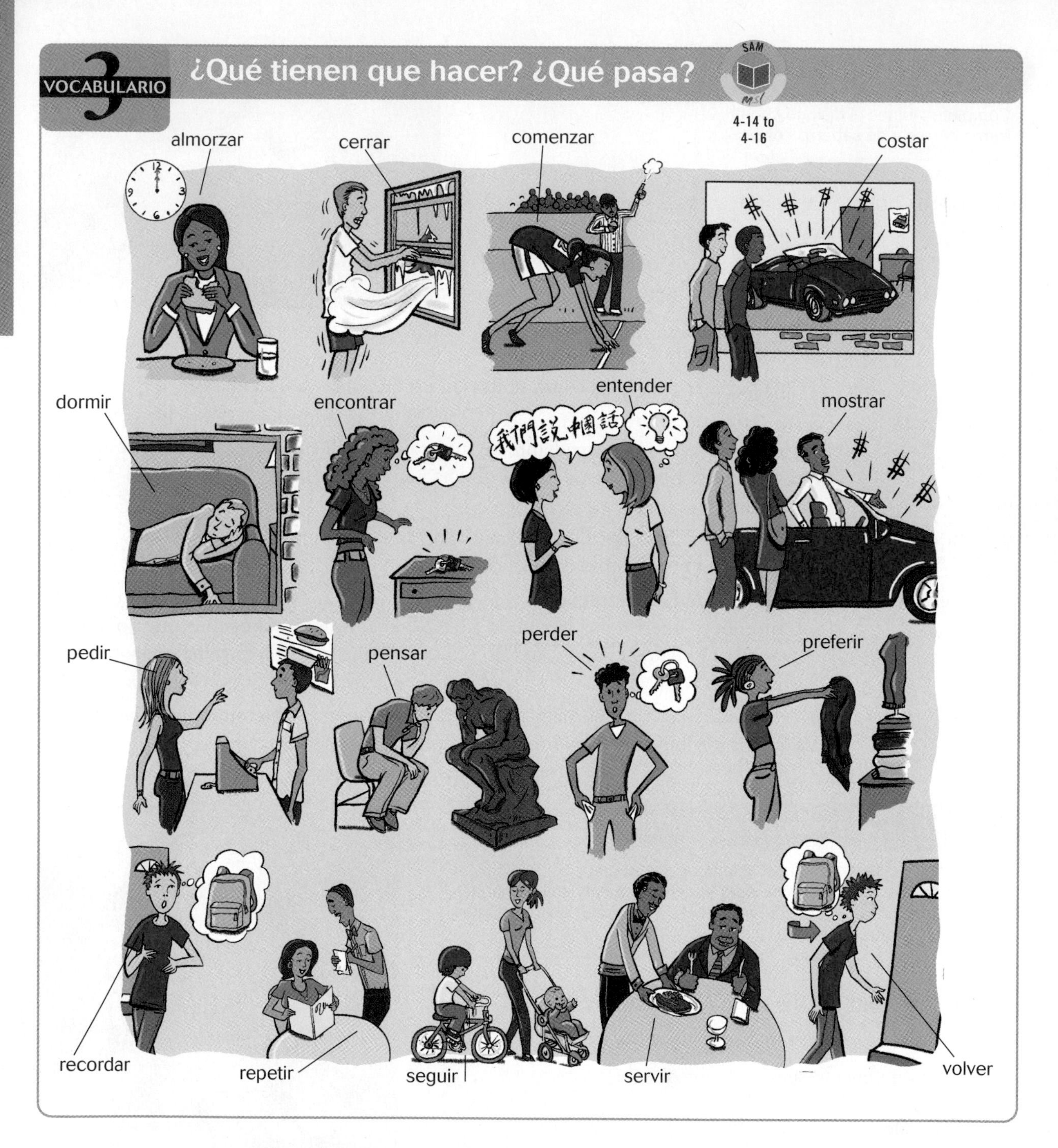

4•10 Tic-tac-toe

Escucha mientras tu instructor/a explica el juego del *tic-tac-toe*.

MODELO E1: *¿Tienes "volver"?*

E2: *Sí, tengo "volver". / No, no tengo "volver".*

4•11 ¿Y lo opuesto?

Decidan juntos qué verbo expresa lo opuesto (*opposite*) de las palabras o expresiones de la siguiente lista.

MODELO E1: no comer
E2: *almorzar*

repetir	encontrar	volver	entender	pedir
perder	comenzar	querer	cerrar	almorzar

1. salir
2. terminar
3. abrir
4. perder
5. decir una vez
6. dar
7. encontrar
8. no comprender

4•12 Los quehaceres

Túrnense para expresar qué tienen que hacer ustedes generalmente.

Estrategia

Make an attempt to work with a different partner in every class. This enables you to help and learn from a variety of your peers, an important and highly effective learning technique.

MODELO Tengo que comenzar...
E1: *Tengo que comenzar la tarea para mi clase de español.*
E2: *Tengo que comenzar la tarea para mi clase de inglés.*

1. Tengo que repetir...
2. Tengo que almorzar...
3. Tengo que recordar...
4. Tengo que dormir...

4•13 Entrevistas

Entrevista a tres compañeros para averiguar si (*to find out if*) hacen cosas similares. Después, comparte la información con la clase. ¿Qué tienen ustedes en común?

1. ¿Qué tienes que hacer para prepararte bien para las clases?
2. ¿Qué tienes que hacer durante la clase de español para sacar buenas notas?
3. Generalmente, ¿qué tienes que hacer cuando terminas con tus clases?

GRAMÁTICA 4 Los verbos con cambio de raíz

4-17 to 4-25

In **Capítulo 3,** you learned a variety of common verbs that are irregular. Two of those verbs were **querer** and **poder,** which are irregular due to some changes in their stems. Look at the following verb groups and answer the questions for each group.

Change e → ie

cerrar (*to close*)

Singular		Plural	
yo	cierro	nosotros/as	cerramos
tú	cierras	vosotros/as	cerráis
él, ella, Ud.	cierra	ellos/as, Uds.	cierran

1. Which verb forms look like the infinitive **cerrar**?
2. Which verb forms have a spelling change that differs from the infinitive **cerrar**?

Check your answers to the preceding questions in Appendix 1.

Other verbs like **cerrar** (**e → ie**) are:

comenzar	*to begin*	**mentir**	*to lie*	**preferir**	*to prefer*
empezar	*to begin*	**pensar**	*to think*	**recomendar**	*to recommend*
entender	*to understand*	**perder**	*to lose; to waste*		

Change e → i

pedir (*to ask for*)

Singular		Plural	
yo	pido	nosotros/as	pedimos
tú	pides	vosotros/as	pedís
él, ella, Ud.	pide	ellos/as, Uds.	piden

1. Which verb forms look like the infinitive **pedir**?
2. Which verb forms have a spelling change that differs from the infinitive **pedir**?

Check your answers to the preceding questions in Appendix 1.

Other verbs like **pedir** (**e → i**) are:

repetir *to repeat* **seguir*** *to follow; to continue (doing something)* **servir** *to serve*

*Note: The **yo** form of **seguir** is **sigo.**

Change o → ue

encontrar (*to find*)

Singular		Plural	
yo	encuentro	nosotros/as	encontramos
tú	encuentras	vosotros/as	encontráis
él, ella, Ud.	encuentra	ellos/as, Uds.	encuentran

1. Which verb forms look like the infinitive **encontrar**?
2. Which verb forms have a spelling change that differs from the infinitive **encontrar**?

Check your answers to the preceding questions in Appendix 1.

Other verbs like **encontrar** (**o → ue**) are:

almorzar	*to have lunch*	**dormir**	*to sleep*	**mostrar**	*to show*	**volver**	*to return*
costar	*to cost*	**morir**	*to die*	**recordar**	*to remember*		

Change u → ue

jugar (*to play*)

Singular		Plural	
yo	juego	nosotros/as	jugamos
tú	juegas	vosotros/as	jugáis
él, ella, Ud.	juega	ellos/as, Uds.	juegan

1. Which verb forms look like the infinitive **jugar**?
2. Which verb forms have a spelling change that differs from the infinitive **jugar**?
3. Why does **jugar** not belong with the verbs like **encontrar**?

Check your answers to the preceding questions in Appendix 1.

To summarize...

1. What rule can you make regarding all four groups of stem-changing verbs and their forms?
2. With what group of stem-changing verbs would you put **querer**?
3. With what group of stem-changing verbs would you put the following verbs?

demostrar	*to demonstrate*	**encerrar**	*to enclose*
devolver	*to return (an object)*	**perseguir**	*to chase*

Check your answers to the preceding questions in Appendix 1.

4-14 Categorías

Paso 1 With a partner, write the stem-changing verbs that were just presented on individual slips of paper. Next, make a chart with three categories: **e → ie, e → i, o → ue.**

Paso 2 Join another pair of students. When your instructor says **¡Empieza!**, place the verbs under the correct category (**e → ie, e → i,** or **o → ue**). Do several rounds of this activity, playing against different doubles partners.

4•15 Nuestras preferencias

Averigua cuáles son las preferencias de tu compañero/a. Comparte tus respuestas con la clase.

MODELO el café o la Coca-Cola
E1: *¿Qué prefieres, el café o la Coca-Cola?*
E2: *Prefiero el café.*

¿Qué prefieres,…?

1. las matemáticas o las ciencias
2. la primavera o el otoño
3. el frío o el calor
4. el béisbol o el básquetbol
5. un sofá o un sillón
6. pasar la aspiradora o sacar la basura

4•16 ¿Quién hace qué?

Túrnense para decir qué personas que ustedes conocen hacen las siguientes cosas.

MODELO E1: siempre perder la tarea
E2: *Mi hermano Tom siempre pierde la tarea.*

1. pensar ser profesor/a
2. almorzar en McDonald's a menudo
3. querer visitar Suramérica
4. siempre entender al/a la profesor/a de español
5. preferir dormir hasta el mediodía
6. volver tarde a casa a menudo
7. perder dinero
8. pensar que Santa Claus existe
9. nunca mentir
10. comenzar a hacer la tarea de noche

4•17 ¿Quién es?

Escribe las respuestas a las siguientes preguntas en forma de párrafos en una hoja de papel.

Primer párrafo

1. ¿Qué clases tienes este semestre?
2. ¿A qué hora empieza tu clase preferida? ¿Cuándo termina?
3. ¿Qué prefieres hacer si (*if*) tienes tiempo entre (*between*) tus clases?
4. ¿A qué hora vuelves a tu dormitorio/apartamento/casa?

Segundo párrafo

1. ¿Qué coche tienes (o quieres tener)? ¿Cuánto cuesta un coche nuevo?
2. ¿Cómo vienes a la universidad? (Por ejemplo, ¿vienes en coche?)
3. ¿Dónde prefieres vivir, en una residencia estudiantil, en un apartamento o en una casa?
4. ¿Dónde quieres vivir después de graduarte?

Tercer párrafo

1. ¿Qué deporte prefieres?
2. ¿Juegas a ese deporte? ¿Ves ese deporte en la televisión?
3. Normalmente, ¿cuándo y con quién(es) juegas?
4. ¿Qué otros deportes te gustan?

Capítulo Preliminar A. La hora, pág. 18; Capítulo 2. Las materias y las especialidades, pág. 62; Los deportes y los pasatiempos, pág. 83.

¿Cómo andas?

Having completed the first **Comunicación,** I now can…

	Feel Confident	Need to Review
• state where things are located around town and state what I could accomplish in each place (p. 136)	❑	❑
• pronounce the letters **c** and **z** correctly (p. 137)	❑	❑
• use **saber** and **conocer** appropriately (p. 140)	❑	❑
• list what I and others need to do using a form of **tener que…** (p. 142)	❑	❑
• use verbs that have stem changes correctly (p. 144)	❑	❑

Comunicación

- Describing what you will do
- Discussing volunteerism

GRAMÁTICA 5 El verbo *ir*

SAM 4-26 to 4-28

Another important verb in Spanish is **ir**. Note its irregular present tense forms below.

ir (*to go*)

Singular		Plural	
yo	voy	nosotros/as	vamos
tú	vas	vosotros/as	vais
él, ella, Ud.	va	ellos/as, Uds.	van

Voy al parque. ¿**Van** ustedes también? — *I'm going to the park. Are you all going too?*

No, no **vamos** ahora. Preferimos **ir** más tarde. — *No, we're not going now. We prefer to go later.*

4•18 ¿Adónde vas?

Túrnense para completar la conversación que tienen Memo y Esteban al salir de la clase de música. Usen las formas correctas del verbo **ir**.

MEMO: Hola, Esteban. ¿Adónde (1)________ ahora?

ESTEBAN: ¿Qué hay? Pues, (2)________ a la clase de física.

MEMO: Yo no. Mi compañero de cuarto y yo (3)________ al gimnasio. Tenemos un torneo (*tournament*) de tenis.

ESTEBAN: Buena suerte. Oye, ¿tú (4)________ a la fiesta de Isabel esta noche?

MEMO: No sé. ¿Quiénes (5)________? Creo que (yo) (6)________ al cine para ver la película nueva de Steven Spielberg.

ESTEBAN: ¿Por qué no (7)________ primero a la fiesta y después al cine?

MEMO: Buena idea. ¿(8)________ (tú y yo) juntos?

ESTEBAN: Muy bien. Mi amigo Roberto (9)________ también. Hablamos después del torneo.

MEMO: Bueno, hasta luego.

Fíjate

In *Capítulo 2* you learned two words for the question word "Where?" Use *¿Adónde?* with *ir*.

Fíjate

Remember that *a* + *el* = *al*.

4•19 Los "¿por qué?"

Esperanza tiene una sobrina que está en la etapa de los "¿por qué?", tiene muchas preguntas. Túrnense para darle las respuestas de Esperanza a Rosita.

MODELO ROSITA: ¿Por qué va mi papá al gimnasio?

ESPERANZA: *Tu papá va al gimnasio porque quiere hacer ejercicio.*

1. ¿Por qué va mi mamá al mercado?
2. ¿Por qué va mi hermana a la oficina de correos?
3. ¿Por qué van mis hermanos al parque?
4. ¿Por qué vas a la universidad?
5. ¿Por qué no vamos al cine ahora?

4-20 ¿Adónde van?

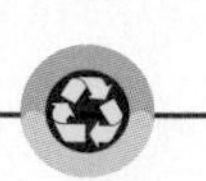

Capítulo Preliminar A. La hora, pág. 18.

Miren los horarios de las siguientes personas. Túrnense para decir adónde van, a qué hora y qué hacen en cada (*each*) lugar.

MODELO *A las diez mis padres van a la librería para buscar y comprar unos libros. Luego…*

Mis padres

Mi hermano

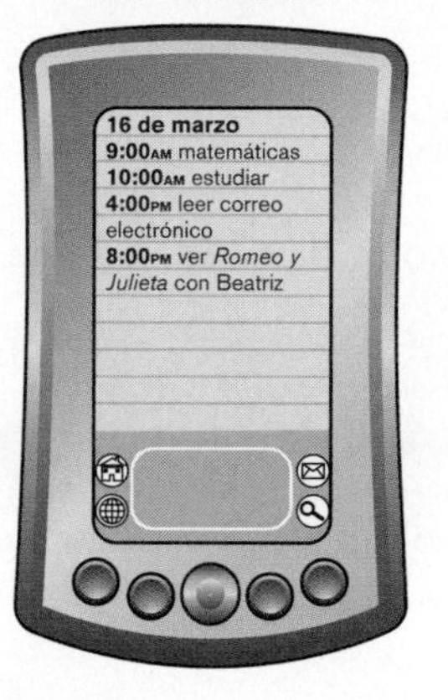

Yo

16 de marzo
8:00AM comprar comida
10:00AM mandar una carta
12:00PM ver la exposición de Picasso con mi clase de arte
2:00PM jugar al fútbol
8:00PM ir al cine a ver la película *Drácula* con amigos

GRAMÁTICA 6 *Ir + a +* infinitivo

4-29 to 4-31

¿Vamos a almorzar pronto? ¡Tengo hambre!

Sí. Voy a pedir comida salvadoreña.

Study the following sentences and then answer the questions that follow.

Voy a mandar esta carta. ¿Quieres ir conmigo?	*I'm going to mail this letter. Do you want to come with me?*
Sí. Luego, **¿vas a almorzar?**	*Yes. Then, are you going to have lunch?*
Sí, **vamos a comer** comida guatemalteca en el restaurante Tikal.	*Yes, we are going to eat Guatemalan food at Tikal Restaurant.*
¡Perfecto! Ya sé que **voy a pedir** unas empanadas.	*Perfect! I already know that I am going to order some empanadas.*
Muy bien. Pero, primero, tengo que ir al banco. **¡Vamos a necesitar** dinero!	*OK. But first I have to go to the bank. We are going to need money!*

1. When do the actions in the previous sentences take place: in the *past*, *present*, or *future*?
2. What is the first bold type verb you see in each sentence?
3. In what form is the second bolded verb?
4. What word comes between the two verbs? Does this word have an equivalent in English?
5. What is your rule, then, for expressing future actions or statements?

Check your answers to the preceding questions in Appendix 1.

4•21 ¿Y en el futuro?

Túrnense para contestar las siguientes preguntas sobre el futuro.

1. ¿Vas a dedicar más tiempo a tus estudios?
2. ¿Vas a vivir en una casa grande?
3. ¿Tu familia va a visitar Honduras?
4. ¿Los doctores van a encontrar la cura para el cáncer?
5. ¿Vamos a poder acabar con (*end*) el terrorismo?

Capítulo Preliminar A. Los días de la semana, los meses y las estaciones, pág. 20.

4•22 Mi agenda

¿Qué planes tienes para la semana que viene? Termina las frases sin (*without*) repetir los quehaceres.

MODELO E1: El lunes…
E2: *El lunes voy a lavar mi coche.*

1. El lunes…
2. El martes…
3. El miércoles…
4. El jueves…
5. El viernes…
6. El sábado…
7. El domingo…
8. El fin de semana…

4•23 Qué será, será…

¿Qué tiene el futuro para ti, tus amigos y tu familia? Escribe **cinco** predicciones de lo que va a ocurrir en el futuro.

MODELO *Mi primo va a ir a la Universidad Autónoma el año que viene. Mis padres van a limpiar el armario y el altillo. Yo voy a estudiar en Suramérica….*

VOCABULARIO 7 Trabajos y servicios voluntarios

SAM 4-32 to 4-34

Unos verbos	*Some verbs*	Otras palabras útiles	*Some useful words*
deber	*ought to; should*	**el deber**	*obligation; duty*
trabajar como voluntario/a	*to volunteer*	**el voluntariado**	*volunteerism*

4•24 Definiciones

Túrnense para leer las siguientes definiciones y decir cuál de las palabras o expresiones de la lista de **Trabajos y servicios voluntarios** corresponde a cada una.

MODELO E1: personas que tienen muchos años

E2: *las personas mayores*

1. un bote (*boat*) para una o dos personas
2. dar un documento a personas para obtener firmas (*signatures*)
3. una estructura portátil (no permanente) que se usa para dormir fuera de casa
4. acompañar a una persona a una cita (*appointment*) con el médico
5. una persona que trabaja con los niños en un campamento
6. servir a las personas sin recibir dinero a cambio (*in exchange*)
7. un tipo de arte que puedes crear con materiales diversos
8. un lugar donde van los niños, generalmente en el verano, para hacer muchas actividades diferentes
9. trabajar para un candidato político
10. un lugar donde viven las personas mayores

4•25 En tu opinión...

Termina las siguientes frases sobre el voluntariado. Después, comparte tus respuestas con un/a compañero/a.

MODELO *Yo soy una consejera perfecta porque me gustan los niños. También escucho muy bien....*

1. Yo (no) soy un/a consejero/a perfecto/a porque...
2. Dos trabajos voluntarios que me gustan son...
3. Hay muchas residencias de ancianos en los Estados Unidos porque...
4. Yo apoyo al candidato _____ porque...
5. Cuando repartes comidas, puedes...

4•26 Elaborando el tema

En grupos de tres o cuatro, discutan las siguientes preguntas.

1. ¿Cuáles son las actividades más interesantes en los campamentos de niños?
2. ¿Cuáles son las oportunidades de voluntariado que existen en tu universidad?
3. ¿Cuáles son los trabajos voluntarios que se asocian más con apoyar a un candidato?
4. ¿Crees que servir a la comunidad es un deber?

SAM 4-35 to 4-37

La conciencia social

Tanto en los Estados Unidos como en los países hispanohablantes, la gente se interesa cada día más en servir a la comunidad. Su conciencia social se puede manifestar tanto *(as much as)* en un trabajo remunerado *(job with a salary)* como en trabajos voluntarios, por ejemplo ser entrenadores de deportes, llevar a los ancianos a pasear por los centros comerciales, trabajar para los congresistas, etc. En los Estados Unidos muchos trabajos voluntarios tienen que ver con *(are related to)* las personas mayores o con los jóvenes.

En los países hispanohablantes, el voluntariado todavía no existe de la misma forma que conocemos en los Estados Unidos. Sin embargo *(Nevertheless)*, cuando la gente necesita ayuda, por ejemplo después de un desastre natural, los hispanos están allí para servir a su comunidad.

Preguntas

1. ¿Qué trabajos voluntarios hay en tu comunidad?
2. ¿Cómo sirves a tu comunidad?

Las expresiones afirmativas y negativas

In the previous chapters you have seen and used a number of the affirmative and negative expressions listed below. Study the list and learn the ones that are new to you.

Expresiones afirmativas		Expresiones negativas	
a veces	*sometimes*	**jamás**	*never; not ever* (emphatic)
algo	*something; anything*	**nada**	*nothing*
alguien	*someone*	**nadie**	*no one; nobody*
algún	*some; any*	**ningún**	*none*
alguno/a/os/as	*some; any*	**ninguno/a/os/as**	*none*
siempre	*always*	**nunca**	*never*
o... o	*either... or*	**ni... ni**	*neither... nor*

Look at the sentences below, paying special attention to the position of the negative words, and answer the questions that follow.

—¿Quién llama? — *Who is calling?*
—**Nadie** llama. (**No** llama **nadie.**) — *No one is calling.*

—¿Vas al gimnasio todos los días? — *Do you go to the gym every day?*
—No, **nunca** voy. (No, **no** voy **nunca.**) — *No, I never go.*

Fíjate

Unlike English, Spanish can have two or more negatives in the same sentence. A double negative is actually quite common. For example, *No tengo nada que hacer* is *I don't have anything to do.*

1. When you use a negative word (**nadie, nunca,** etc.) in a sentence, does it come before or after the verb?
2. When you use the word **no** and then a negative word in the same sentence, does **no** come before or after the verb? Where does the negative word come in these sentences?
3. Does the meaning change depending on where you put the negative word? (e.g., **Nadie llama** *versus* **No llama nadie**).

Check your answers to the preceding questions in Appendix 1.

Algún and *ningún*

1. Forms of **algún** and **ningún** need to agree in gender and number with the noun they modify.
2. Use **algún** and **ningún** when they are followed by *masculine, singular nouns.*
3. When no noun follows, use **alguno** or **ninguno** when referring to masculine, singular nouns, and **alguna** or **ninguna** when referring to feminine singular nouns.

Study the following sentences.

María: ¿Tienes **alguna** clase fácil este semestre?
Juan: No, no tengo **ninguna.** ¡Y **ningún** profesor es simpático!
María: Vaya, ¿y puedes hacer **algún** cambio?
Juan: No, no puedo hacer **ninguno.** (No, no puedo tomar **ningún** otro curso.)

4•27 ¿Con qué frecuencia?

Indica con una **X** con qué frecuencia tus compañeros/as de clase hacen las siguientes actividades. Escribe el nombre de tu compañero/a debajo de la **X** y comparte los resultados con la clase.

MODELO ir de excursión con niños
A veces Josefina va de excursión con niños.

	SIEMPRE	A VECES	NUNCA
1. ir de excursión con niños		*Josefina*	
2. trabajar en una campaña política			
3. hacer una hoguera			
4. circular una petición			
5. firmar una petición			
6. repartir comidas a los mayores			
7. visitar una residencia de ancianos			
8. trabajar en un campamento para niños			
9. trabajar como voluntario en un hospital o una clínica			
10. dormir en una tienda de campaña			

4•28 El/La profesor/a ideal

Túrnense para decir si las siguientes características son ciertas (*true*) o no en un/a profesor/a ideal.

MODELO E1: a veces duerme en su trabajo
E2: *No. Un profesor ideal nunca duerme en su trabajo.*
E1: jamás va a clase sin sus apuntes
E2: *Sí, un profesor ideal jamás va a clase sin sus apuntes.*

Un/a profesor/a ideal...

1. siempre está contento/a en su trabajo.
2. a veces llega a clase cinco minutos tarde.
3. prepara algo interesante para cada clase.
4. piensa que sabe más que nadie.
5. falta (*misses*) a unas clases.
6. nunca pone a los estudiantes en grupos.
7. jamás asigna tarea para la clase.
8. siempre prefiere leer sus apuntes.
9. no pierde nada (la tarea, los exámenes, etc.)
10. no habla con nadie después de la clase.

4•29 ¿Sí o no?

Túrnense para contestar las siguientes preguntas.

MODELO E1: *¿Siempre almuerzas a las cuatro de la tarde?*
E2: *No, nunca almuerzo a las cuatro de la tarde. / No, no almuerzo nunca/jamás a las cuatro de la tarde.*

1. ¿Pierdes algo cuando vas de vacaciones?
2. ¿Siempre encuentras las cosas que pierdes?
3. ¿A veces duermes más de diez horas?
4. ¿Haces algo para ayudar a los pobres?
5. ¿Siempre almuerzas en restaurantes caros (*expensive*)?
6. ¿Conoces a alguien de Guatemala?
7. ¿Siempre piensas en el amor?
8. ¿Hay algo más importante que el dinero?

4•30 No tienes razón

Tu amigo/a es muy idealista. Túrnense para decirle (*tell him/her*) que debe ser más realista, usando expresiones negativas.

MODELO

1. Tengo que buscar una profesión sin estrés.
2. Quiero el coche perfecto, un Lexus.
3. Voy a tener hijos perfectos.
4. Pienso que no voy a estudiar esta semana que viene.
5. Voy a encontrar unos muebles muy baratos y elegantes.

GRAMÁTICA 9 Un repaso de *ser* y *estar*

4-40 to 4-43

You have learned two Spanish verbs that mean ***to be*** in English. These verbs, **estar** and **ser,** are contrasted below.

***Estar** is used:

- **To describe physical or personality characteristics that can change, or to indicate a change in condition**

María **está** enferma hoy.	*María is sick today.*
Jorge y Julia **están** tristes.	*Jorge and Julia are sad.*
La cocina **está** sucia.	*The kitchen is dirty.*

- **To describe the location of people or places**

El museo **está** en la calle Quiroga.	*The museum is on Quiroga Street.*
Estamos en el centro comercial. ¿Dónde **estás** tú?	*We're at the mall. Where are you?*

***Ser** is used:

- **To describe physical or personality characteristics that remain relatively constant**

Gregorio **es** inteligente.	*Gregorio is intelligent.*
Yanina **es** guapa.	*Yanina is pretty.*
Su tienda de campaña **es** amarilla.	*Their tent is yellow.*
Las casas **son** grandes.	*The houses are large.*

- **To explain what or who someone or something is**

El Dr. Suárez **es** profesor de literatura.	*Dr. Suárez is a literature professor.*
Marisol **es** mi hermana.	*Marisol is my sister.*

- **To tell time, or to tell when or where an event takes place**

¿Qué hora **es**?	*What time is it?*
Son las ocho.	*It's eight o'clock.*
Mi clase de español **es** a las ocho y **es** en Peabody Hall.	*My Spanish class is at eight o'clock and is in Peabody Hall.*

- **To tell where someone is from and to express nationality**

Somos de Honduras.	*We are from Honduras.*
Somos hondureños.	*We are Honduran.*
Ellos **son** de Guatemala.	*They are from Guatemala.*
Son guatemaltecos.	*They are Guatemalan.*

Compare the following sentences and answer the questions below.

Su hermano **es** simpático.
Su hermano **está** enfermo.

1. Why do you use a form of **ser** in the first sentence?
2. Why do you use a form of **estar** in the second sentence?

Check your answers to the preceding questions in Appendix 1.

Estrategia

Review the forms of *ser* (p. 13) and *estar* (p. 78).

You will learn several more uses for **estar** and **ser** by the end of ***¡Anda!***

4•31 ¿Quién es Margarita?

Margarita es una estudiante de la Universidad Francisco Marroquín en la ciudad de Guatemala. Completen juntos el párrafo siguiente con las formas correctas de **ser** o **estar** para conocerla (*to know her*) mejor.

(1) ________________ las siete y media de la mañana. Margarita (2) ________________ cansada pero tiene que tener prisa porque su clase de física (3) ________________ a las ocho. ¿Me dices que no la conoces? Pues, Margarita (4) ________________ la hermana de mi amigo Roberto. (5) ________________ una mujer alta, inteligente y muy simpática. Le gusta estudiar. (6) ________________ de la ciudad de Antigua y sus padres viven allí (*there*) todavía (*still*). Ellos (7) ________________ muy contentos porque ella tiene muy buenas notas en todos sus cursos.

Bueno, casi (8) ________________ las ocho. ¿Dónde (9) ________________ Margarita ahora? Pues, como siempre, llega a tiempo a su clase; (10) ________________ muy puntual y no le gusta llegar tarde.

4•32 Así es

Expliquen por qué usaron (*you used*) **ser** o **estar** en la actividad **4-31**.

1. (*Son*) telling time

4•33 Nuestro conocimiento

¿Qué sabes de Guatemala, Honduras y El Salvador? Túrnense para hacerse y contestar las siguientes preguntas.

1. ¿Dónde están estos países, en Norteamérica, Centroamérica o Suramérica?
2. ¿Cuál está más cerca de México? ¿Cuál está más cerca de Panamá?
3. ¿Son países grandes o pequeños?
4. ¿Cuáles son sus capitales?

4•34 ¡A jugar!

Vamos a practicar **ser** y **estar.**

Paso 1 Draw two columns on a piece of paper. Label one column **ser** and the other **estar.** Your instructor will give you three minutes to write as many sentences with **ser** and **estar** as you can.

Paso 2 After you have finished writing, form groups of four to check your sentences and uses of the verbs. How many correct sentences do you have?

4·35 Somos iguales

Paso 1 Draw **three** circles, as per the model below, and ask each other questions to find out what things you have in common and what sets you apart. In the center circle write sentences using **ser** and **estar** about things you have in common, and in the side circles write sentences about things that set you apart.

MODELO
E1: *¿Cuál es tu color favorito?*
E2: *Mi color favorito es el negro.*
E1: *Mi color favorito es el negro también.*
(E1/E2 WRITE: *Nuestro color favorito es el negro.*)
E2: *Hoy estoy nerviosa. ¿Cómo estás tú?*
E1: *Yo estoy cansado.*
(E2 WRITES: *Hoy estoy nerviosa.*;
E1 WRITES: *Hoy estoy cansado.*)

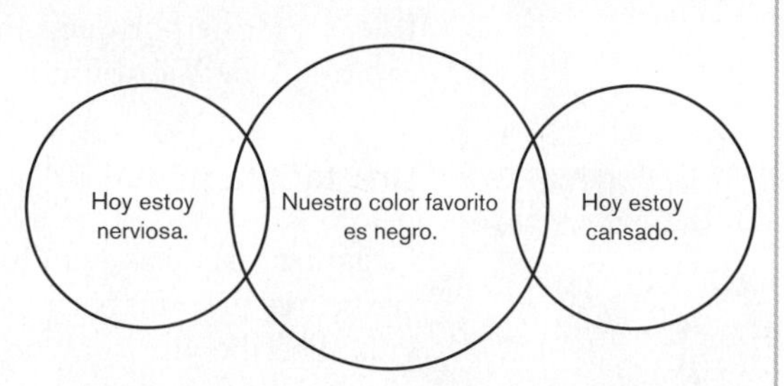

Paso 2 Share your drawings with the class. What are some of the things that all of your classmates have in common?

ESCUCHA

4-44

ESTRATEGIA **Paraphrasing what you hear**

When you know the context and listen carefully, you can repeat or paraphrase what you hear. Start by saying one or two words about what you hear, working up to complete sentences.

Marisol y Lupe conversan sobre el trabajo voluntario.

4•36 Antes de escuchar

Do you volunteer? What service opportunities exist in your city/town? You are going to hear a conversation between Marisol and Lupe, where Marisol shares her experiences with volunteering. Think of three Spanish words dealing with volunteering that you might hear.

4•37 A escuchar

CD 2
Track 18

After listening to Marisol and Lupe's conversation for the first time, jot down three main points, words, or topics. After listening to their conversation a second time, paraphrase their conversation with at least **three** complete sentences. You may use the following questions to guide your listening.

1. ¿Quién hace trabajo voluntario?
2. ¿Qué trabajo hace ella en la escuela? ¿Qué más quiere hacer?
3. ¿Adónde va a ir mañana? ¿Con quién?

4•38 Después de escuchar

Form *three* sentences about your volunteering experiences, or what you can do in your community, and tell them to your classmate. Your classmate will paraphrase what you have said.

ESCRIBE

SAM 4-45 to 4-46

4•39 Antes de escribir

Escribe una lista de los lugares importantes o interesantes de tu pueblo o ciudad. Luego escribe por qué son importantes o interesantes. Usa el vocabulario de este capítulo y de **También se dice...** Appendix 3.

4•40 Una tarjeta postal

Organiza tus ideas usando las siguientes preguntas como guía. Escribe por lo menos **cinco** oraciones completas. Si necesitas ayuda, puedes usar el modelo.

1. ¿Qué lugares hay en tu pueblo o ciudad?
2. ¿Por qué son importantes o interesantes?
3. Normalmente, ¿qué haces allí?
4. ¿Adónde vas los fines de semana?
5. ¿Qué te gusta de tu pueblo?

Querido/a__________:

Tienes que conocer mi pueblo, Roxborough. Hay _________. Me gusta(n) _________. Es interesante porque _______. Los fines de semana ___________. etc. . . .

Con cariño,
__(Tu nombre)__

4•41 Después de escribir

Tu profesor/a va a recoger las tarjetas y "mandárselas" (*mail them*) a otros miembros de la clase para leerlas.

¿Cómo andas?

Having completed the second **Comunicación,** I now can...

	Feel Confident	Need to Review
• express where I and others wish to go using the correct forms of **ir** (p. 147)	❏	❏
• talk about the future using **ir** + **a** + *infinitive* (p. 149)	❏	❏
• give examples of volunteer and service opportunities (p. 151)	❏	❏
• express concepts both affirmatively and negatively (p. 154)	❏	❏
• use **ser** and **estar** in the correct contexts (p. 156)	❏	❏
• paraphrase what I hear (p. 159)	❏	❏
• write a postcard (p. 160)	❏	❏

Alfonso Guillermo Rivera Zúñiga

CD 2 Track 19

4-47 to 4-49

Vistas culturales

Les presento mi país

Mi nombre es Alfonso Guillermo y soy de San Pedro Sula, Honduras. Mi país tiene un pasado cultural muy rico, ya que los mayas viven aquí desde la época precolombina. Las ruinas más importantes que tenemos están en Copán. **¿Hay ruinas importantes en tu pueblo?** Mi país es muy hermoso (*beautiful*) porque los bosques (*forests*) ocupan más del cincuenta por ciento del país, pero están en peligro (*danger*). **¿Te gustan los bosques? ¿Vives cerca de alguno?**

La Escalinata de Copán

La tala de bosques

ALMANAQUE

Nombre oficial:	República de Honduras
Gobierno:	República democrática constitucional
Población:	7.326.496 (2006)
Idiomas:	español (oficial); miskito, garífuna, otros dialectos amerindios
Moneda:	Lempira (L)

¿Sabías que...?

- El nombre original de esta región es *Higüeras,* que es el nombre de una planta nativa. Al llegar a la costa norteña, Cristóbal Colón renombra la región *Honduras* a causa de la profundidad del agua en la bahía.

PREGUNTAS

1. ¿Qué significa *Honduras*? ¿De dónde viene el nombre?
2. ¿Quiénes construyeron las ruinas de Copán?
3. ¿Qué semejanzas hay entre Honduras y México?

En la Red
Amplía tus conocimientos sobre Honduras en la página web de *¡Anda!*

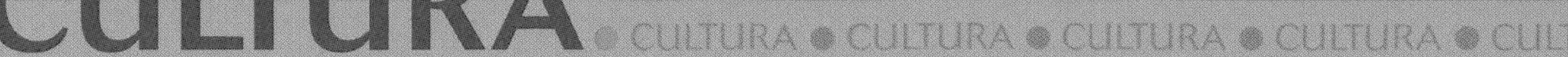

Itzel Fabiola Guerra Cruz

CD 2
Track 20

Vistas culturales

Guatemala

Les presento mi país

Mi nombre es Itzel Fabiola Guerra Cruz y soy de Quezaltenango, Guatemala. Soy maya y mi nombre, Itzel, significa "ella del arco iris (*rainbow*)". Muchas mujeres mayas llevan ropa tradicional de colores brillantes y diseños (*designs*) simbólicos. Mi país es montañoso (*mountainous*) con muchos volcanes, algunos de ellos muy activos. También hay ruinas mayas muy antiguas, como las de Tikal y algunas de nuestras pirámides son las más altas de las Américas. **¿En qué otros lugares encuentras pirámides?**

Tajumulco es el volcán más alto de Centroamérica y la montaña más alta de Guatemala.

Un templo muy alto de Tikal es El Gran Jaguar.

ALMANAQUE

Nombre oficial:	República de Guatemala
Gobierno:	República democrática constitucional
Población:	12.293.545 (2006)
Idiomas:	español (oficial); idiomas amerindios (23 reconocidos oficialmente)
Moneda:	Quetzal (Q)

¿Sabías que...?

- Los mayas tienen un calendario civil, *El Haab*. Consiste en 18 "meses" de 20 días cada uno. Los últimos cinco días del año, conocidos como *el Wayeb*, se consideran de muy mala suerte.

PREGUNTAS

1. Nombra dos cosas que sabes de la geografía guatemalteca.
2. ¿Cuántos idiomas se hablan en Guatemala?
3. ¿Qué otros países tienen herencia maya?

En la Red
Amplía tus conocimientos sobre Guatemala en la página web de *¡Anda!*

Alba Violeta Orellana Barrillas

El Salvador

CD 2 Track 21

Vistas culturales

Les presento mi país

Mi nombre es Alba Violeta Orellana Barrillas. Soy de un pueblo pequeño cerca de la playa El Sunzal, en la costa del Pacífico, donde mucha gente practica los deportes acuáticos. **¿Te gustan los deportes acuáticos?** El Salvador es el único país de Centroamérica que no tiene costa caribeña. En mi casa viven tres generaciones de mi familia y nos gusta mucho la comida salvadoreña, como las pupusas. **¿Cuál es tu comida favorita?**

La playa El Sunzal es un lugar excelente para el surfing, el snorkeling y el buceo.

Las pupusas son la comida nacional de El Salvador.

ALMANAQUE

Nombre oficial:	República de El Salvador
Gobierno:	República democrática constitucional
Población:	6.822.378 (2006)
Idiomas:	español (oficial)
Moneda:	Dólar estadounidense

¿Sabías que...?

- Durante la antigüedad, los mayas usaron (*used*) los granos de cacao como dinero.
- Algunos salvadoreños, sobre todo los que viven en las partes rurales del país, van a los curanderos (*folk healers*) para buscar ayuda médica.

PREGUNTAS

1. ¿Qué importancia tiene el cacao en la historia maya?
2. ¿Qué deportes practican en El Salvador?
3. ¿Qué cosas de El Salvador son únicas o diferentes a las de otros países hispanos?

En la Red
Amplía tus conocimientos sobre El Salvador en la página web de *¡Anda!*

Ambiciones siniestras

EPISODIO 4

SAM 4-54

4-42 Antes de leer. Ya (*Already*) sabemos que Manolo, Alejandra, Cisco, Eduardo, Lupe y Marisol son finalistas de un concurso misterioso. En este episodio Marisol y Lupe no lo pueden celebrar porque tienen que trabajar en un proyecto sobre (*about*) sus pueblos. Antes de leer contesta las siguientes preguntas.

1. ¿Cómo es tu pueblo? ¿Es un buen lugar donde vivir? ¿Por qué?
2. ¿De dónde son tus mejores amigos? ¿Sabes mucho sobre sus familias y sus pueblos?

ESTRATEGIA **Skimming and Scanning (II)**

Continue to practice focusing on main ideas and important information. Remember, when you *skim* a passage you read quickly to get the gist of the passage. When you *scan* a passage you already know what you need to find out, so you concentrate on searching for that particular information.

4-43 A leer. Complete the following steps.

1. *Skim* the first paragraph, looking for the answers to the following questions.
   a. About whom is this paragraph?
   b. Which statement best describes where they are?
      They are in sociology class.
      They are at a party.
      They are in an apartment.
2. Now *scan* the second paragraph, looking for the following information:
   a. Where is Lupe's parents' home—in the country or in the middle of town?
   b. Is her parents' home large or small?
   c. What city is next to Lupe's hometown?

This gives you a good start to discovering what happens next in **Ambiciones siniestras**.

CD 2
Track 22

Las cosas no son siempre lo que parecen°

seem

Alejandra, Manolo, Cisco, Eduardo, Marisol y Lupe —están emocionados al saber que son finalistas del concurso. Muchos van a celebrarlo, pero Marisol y Lupe no pueden. Están ahora en el apartamento de Lupe. Tienen que terminar un proyecto sobre sus pueblos para la clase de sociología.

Las fotos que tiene Lupe de la casa de sus padres y de su pueblo en general representan un lugar muy tranquilo en el campo°, con una casa pequeña y un jardín muy grande. Sin embargo°, Lupe nunca quiere hablar de su familia ni de su pueblo. Sólo dice que es de un pueblo de las afueras° de Akron, Ohio.

countryside
Nonetheless
outskirts

En cambio, a Marisol le encanta hablar de su familia y de su pueblo que está muy cerca de la ciudad de Nueva York. Marisol viene de una familia muy grande. Es hija única pero tiene muchos tíos y primos. Todos viven cerca de Nueva York.

Marisol está muy orgullosa° de su pueblo. Siempre le dice a Lupe que tiene de todo cerca de su casa. Por ejemplo, dice que hay un cine donde ponen quince películas diferentes a la vez. Ella vive en un apartamento y enfrente hay un supermercado pequeño, una librería y un restaurante que siempre recibe la distinción de ser el mejor restaurante chino del pueblo. Según ella, ¡no comprende cómo alguien puede vivir en otro lugar!

proud

Mientras Marisol trabaja de manera muy seria, escucha a Lupe reírse° y hacer comentarios casi inaudibles. De pronto Lupe le dice a Marisol que tiene que salir un momento para hacer una llamada por teléfono. Marisol, muy curiosa, decide mirar lo que Lupe escribe. Se acerca a su computadora y lee allí algo muy extraño° —Lupe no escribe sobre su pueblo en Ohio. ¡Escribe sobre Los Ángeles!

laugh
strange

4-44 **Después de leer.** Contesta las siguientes preguntas.

1. ¿Qué tipo de proyecto hacen Lupe y Marisol?
2. ¿Qué no quiere hacer Lupe?
3. ¿Cómo es la familia de Marisol?
4. ¿Dónde vive Marisol? ¿Cómo es su pueblo?
5. ¿Qué escribe Lupe en su computadora?

4-55 to 4-56

video

4-45 Antes del video. Do you volunteer your time with a group or organization? In the video episode of **Ambiciones siniestras** you will learn about Cisco's and Eduardo's volunteerism experiences (or the lack thereof!). Also listen for "**¡No toques** (*touch*) **mis cosas nunca más! ¿Me oyes?**" Why do you think the character says this? And finally, you will discover that either Cisco or Eduardo is not being totally honest! Who do you think it is? Why?

Trabajo como voluntario en una organización que ayuda a los niños.

¡No toques mis cosas nunca más! ¿Me oyes?

Cisco piensa que lo sabe todo…

¿Quiénes son en realidad?

Episodio 4

Relax and watch the video, more than once if you choose. Then complete the questions that follow.

4-46 Después del video. Contesta las siguientes preguntas.

1. ¿Adónde van Cisco y Eduardo?
2. ¿Qué hacen allí?
3. ¿Quién trabaja como voluntario? ¿A quiénes ayuda?
4. ¿Por qué está enojado Cisco?
5. ¿Qué hace Eduardo al final?

Y por fin, ¿cómo andas?

Having completed this chapter, I now can…

	Feel Confident	Need to Review
Comunicación		
• share information about places in my home and/or university town (p. 136)	❑	❑
• correctly pronounce **c** and **z** (p. 137)	❑	❑
• use **saber** and **conocer** correctly (p. 140)	❑	❑
• relate what I need to do (p. 142)	❑	❑
• use stem-changing verbs appropriately (p. 144)	❑	❑
• state where I and others are going with the verb **ir** (p. 147)	❑	❑
• talk about things that will happen using the construction **ir** + **a** + *infinitive* (p. 149)	❑	❑
• describe different types of community service (p. 151)	❑	❑
• use affirmative and negative expressions (p. 154)	❑	❑
• use **ser** and **estar** correctly (p. 156)	❑	❑
• paraphrase what I hear (p. 159)	❑	❑
• write a postcard about my hometown (p. 160)	❑	❑
Cultura		
• compare and contrast shopping and going out and about town in the United States with the Spanish-speaking world (p. 139)	❑	❑
• share ways that individuals demonstrate social consciousness (p. 153)	❑	❑
• state three facts about Honduras, Guatemala, and El Salvador (pp. 161–163)	❑	❑
Ambiciones siniestras		
• skim and scan for meaning (p. 164)	❑	❑
• state who are the finalists in the Internet contest of **Ambiciones siniestras** and which characters may not be telling the truth (p. 166)	❑	❑

VOCABULARIO ACTIVO

CD 2
Tracks 23-30

Los lugares	*Places*
el almacén	*department store*
el banco	*bank*
el bar; el club	*bar; club*
el café	*cafe*
el cajero automático	*ATM machine*
el centro	*downtown*
el centro comercial	*mall; business/shopping district*
el cibercafé	*Internet café*
el cine	*movie theater*
el club campestre	*country club*
la iglesia	*church*
el mercado	*market*
el museo	*museum*
la oficina de correos; correos	*post office*
el parque	*park*
la plaza	*town square*
el restaurante	*restaurant*
el supermercado	*supermarket*
el teatro	*theater*
el templo	*temple*

Unos verbos	*Some verbs*
buscar	*to look for*
estar de acuerdo	*to agree*
mandar una carta	*to send/mail a letter*

Otras palabras útiles	*Other useful words*
detrás (de)	*behind*
enfrente (de)	*in front (of)*
el/la mejor	*the best*
el/la peor	*the worst*
la ciudad	*city*
la cuenta	*bill; account*
la película	*movie; film*
el pueblo	*town; village*

Trabajos y servicios voluntarios	*Volunteerism opportunities*
apoyar a un/a candidato/a	*to support a candidate*
la artesanía	*arts and crafts*
el campamento de niños	*summer camp*
la campaña política	*political campaign*
la canoa	*canoe*
circular una petición	*to circulate a petition*
el/la consejero/a	*counselor*
deber	*ought to; should*
hacer una caminata	*to take a walk*
la hoguera	*campfire*
ir de excursión	*to take a short trip*
llevar a alguien al médico	*to take someone to the doctor*
trabajar como voluntario/a	*to volunteer*
organizar	*to organize*
las personas mayores, los mayores	*elderly people*
repartir comidas	*to hand out/deliver food*
la residencia de ancianos	*nursing home/assisted living facility*
la tienda de campaña	*tent*
trabajar como voluntario/a	*to volunteer*

¿Qué tienen que hacer?	*What do they have to do?*
(Verbos con cambio de raíz)	*(Stem-changing verbs)*
almorzar (ue)	*to have lunch*
cerrar (ie)	*to close*
comenzar (ie)	*to begin*
costar (ue)	*to cost*
demostrar (ue)	*to demonstrate*
devolver (ue)	*to return (an object)*
dormir (ue)	*to sleep*
empezar (ie)	*to begin*
encerrar (ie)	*to enclose*
encontrar (ue)	*to find*
entender (ie)	*to understand*
jugar (ue)	*to play*
mentir (ie)	*to lie*
morir (ue)	*to die*
mostrar (ue)	*to show*
pedir (i)	*to ask for*
pensar (ie)	*to think*
perder (ie)	*to lose; to waste*
perseguir (i)	*to chase*
preferir (ie)	*to prefer*
recomendar (ie)	*to recommend*
recordar (ue)	*to remember*
repetir (i)	*to repeat*
seguir (i)	*to follow; to continue (doing something)*
servir (i)	*to serve*
volver (ue)	*to return*

Otros verbos	*Other verbs*
ir	*to go*
saber	*to know*

Otras palabras útiles	*Other useful words*
el deber	*obligation; duty*
el voluntariado	*volunteerism*

Expresiones afirmativas y negativas	*Affirmative and negative expressions*
a veces	*sometimes*
algo	*something; anything*
alguien	*someone*
algún	*some; any*
alguno/a/os/as	*some; any*
jamás	*never; not ever* (emphatic)
nada	*nothing*
nadie	*no one; nobody*
ni…ni	*neither…nor*
ningún	*none*
ninguno/a/os/as	*none*
nunca	*never*
o…o	*either…or*
siempre	*always*

5

¡A divertirse! La música y el cine

En el mundo hispanohablante la gente trabaja pero también sabe divertirse (*enjoy themselves*). La música, el baile y el cine son formas de expresión y de distracción comunes. Estos pasatiempos, además de otros como los deportes o leer un buen libro, nos hacen la vida muy agradable. Sobre todo (*Above all*), es importante buscar maneras de relajarse y aliviar el estrés.

	OBJETIVOS	CONTENIDOS
Comunicación	• To discuss different types of music, including your personal preferences • To point out specific persons, places, things, and ideas • To state how or in what manner something is done • To express what is happening at the moment • To share information about your favorite movies and television programs • To rank people, places, and things • To state what needs to be accomplished • To listen with the goal of anticipating content • To write a movie review	1 The world of music 172 2 Demonstrative adjectives (*this, that, these, those*) 176 3 Demonstrative pronouns (*this one, that one, these, those*) 178 4 Adverbs (*-ly*) 180 5 Present progressive (*I am + -ing, You are + -ing,* etc.) 182 6 The world of cinema 185 7 Ordinal numbers (*first, second,* etc.) 188 8 **Hay que** (*It's necessary to…, one must…*) 189 9 Direct object pronouns and the personal *"a"* 190 Pronunciación: Diphthongs and linking 174 Escucha: 193 Estrategia: Anticipating content Escribe: Writing a movie review 194
Cultura	• To talk about Hispanic music in the United States • To begin exploring information regarding famous actors from the Spanish-speaking world • To create a list of at least three interesting facts about this chapter's featured countries: Nicaragua, Costa Rica, and Panama	Hispanic music in the United States 179 Hispanic influences in North American film 187 *Nicaragua, Costa Rica,* and *Panamá* 195–197
Ambiciones siniestras	• To learn to anticipate content • To discover what Cisco does in his search for Eduardo • To learn about the videoconference the characters have and find out who is the second student to disappear	Episodio 5 Lectura: *La búsqueda de Eduardo* 198 Estrategia: Anticipating content Video: *Se conocen* 200

Un concierto de Marc Anthony

PREGUNTAS

1. ¿Qué haces cuando no estudias?
2. ¿Qué hacen los miembros de tu familia para relajarse y aliviar el estrés?
3. Hay una expresión en español que dice: "Algunas personas viven para trabajar y otras trabajan para vivir". ¿Cuál es tu filosofía de la vida?

Comunicación

- Sharing thoughts about music
- Pointing out people and things
- State how or in what manner something is done
- Expressing what is happening at the moment

VOCABULARIO 1 El mundo de la música

SAM 5-1 to 5-7

Unos géneros musicales	*Some musical genres*
el jazz	*jazz*
la música clásica	*classical music*
la música popular	*pop music*
la ópera	*opera*
el rock	*rock*
la salsa	*salsa*

Unos verbos	*Some verbs*
dar un concierto	*to give/perform a concert*
ensayar	*to practice/rehearse*
grabar	*to record*
hacer una gira	*to tour*
sacar un CD	*to release a CD*
tocar	*to play (a musical instrument)*

Unas características	*Some characteristics*
apasionado/a	*passionate*
fino/a	*fine; delicate*
lento/a	*slow*
suave	*smooth*

Otras palabras útiles	*Other useful words*
el/la aficionado/a	*fan*
la fama	*fame*
el género	*genre*
la habilidad	*ability; skill*
la letra	*lyrics*
el ritmo	*rhythm*
el sabor	*flavor*
la voz	*voice*

5•1 Dibujemos

Escuchen mientras su instructor/a les da (*gives you*) las instrucciones de esta actividad.

5•2 Listas

Túrnate con un/a compañero/a para decir y escribir todas las palabras nuevas que recuerden (*you both remember*) de las tres categorías en el modelo. ¿Cuántas palabras son?

MODELO

TIPOS DE MÚSICA	INSTRUMENTOS	OTRAS PALABRAS
el jazz	*la trompeta*	*el conjunto*

CW eBook

CD 2 Track 31

SAM

5-8 to 5-13

PRONUNCIACIÓN

Diphthongs and linking

In Spanish, **a, e,** and **o** are what are known as *strong vowels.* The **i** and **u** are known as *weak vowels*. A **diphthong** is the combination of a strong and a weak vowel, or two weak vowels. Diphthongs are pronounced as a single syllable.

concierto empresaria grabaciones pianista

When pronouncing words in Spanish, *linking* occurs. Linking is what makes spoken Spanish appear to flow and be seamless. What follows is a summary of how words are linked.

1. A **consonant** at the *end* of one word is linked to a **vowel** at the *beginning* of the next word.

   el artista un aficionado ellos ensayan

2. A **vowel** at the *end* of one word is linked to a **vowel** at the *beginning* of the next word.

   su (h)abilidad tu orquesta nuestra ópera ella ensaya

3. **Identical consonants** (or consonant sounds) at the *end* of one word and at the *beginning* of the next word are linked.

   sus sabores con negro sabor rítmico voz suave

4. **Identical vowels** (or vowel sounds) at the *end* of one word and the *beginning* of the next word.

   la artista música apasionada la (h)abilidad la alfombra

Fíjate

Remember that the letter **h** in Spanish is silent and not pronounced.

5•3 Las palabras

Practice pronouncing the following words, focusing on the diphthongs and linking.

1. concierto
2. empresaria
3. grabaciones
4. pianista
5. el artista
6. un aficionado
7. ellos ensayan
8. tu orquesta
9. su (h)abilidad
10. nuestra ópera
11. ella ensaya
12. sus sabores
13. con negro
14. sabor rítmico
15. voz suave
16. la artista
17. música apasionada
18. la (h)abilidad

5•4 Las oraciones

Pronounce the following sentences, paying special attention to the diphthongs and linking.

1. La orquesta ensaya todos los días.
2. Toca con una habilidad impresionante.

5•5 Los dichos y refranes

Pronounce the following saying, focusing on diphthongs and linking.

Aquellos que tienen amigos son ricos.

5•6 A conocerte mejor

Hazle las siguientes preguntas a un/a compañero/a. Toma apuntes y luego comparte las respuestas con otros dos compañeros.

1. ¿Con qué frecuencia vas a conciertos?
2. ¿Qué género de música prefieres?
3. ¿Cuál es tu grupo favorito?
4. ¿Cuál es tu cantante favorito/a? ¿Cómo es su voz?
5. ¿Qué instrumento te gusta?
6. ¿Cuál es tu canción favorita?
7. ¿Sabes tocar un instrumento? ¿Cuál?
8. ¿Sabes cantar bien? ¿Te gusta cantar? ¿Cuándo y dónde cantas?
9. ¿En qué tienes mucha habilidad o talento?
10. ¿Conoces algún conjunto o cantante hispano? ¿Cuál?

Estrategia

When reporting your information, make complete sentences, and remember to use the *él* or *ella* form of the verb. Also, simply refer to your notes; do not read from them. This technique will help you to speak more fluidly and will help you speak in paragraphs, an important skill to perfect when learning a language.

Capítulo 2. La formación de preguntas y las palabras interrogativas, pág. 71.

5•7 Los famosos

Completa los siguientes pasos.

Paso 1 Como reportero/a de la revista *Rolling Stone* tienes la oportunidad de entrevistar a los hermanos Mejía, dos músicos populares de Nicaragua. Escribe por lo menos **cinco** preguntas que vas a hacerles.

Fíjate

Remember that if you are interviewing people whom you don't know, use the *usted/ustedes* form.

Ramón (Perrozompopo) Mejía

Luis Enrique Mejía

Paso 2 Ve a la página web de *¡Anda!* para ver si puedes descubrir las respuestas a tus preguntas y para escuchar la música de Luis y Ramón Mejía. Después, comparte tus resultados y tu opinión con la clase; díles (*tell them*) qué canción te gusta más y por qué.

Los adjetivos demostrativos

SAM 5-14 to 5-16 Guide 4, 21

When you want to point out a specific person, place, thing, or idea, you use a *demonstrative adjective*. In Spanish, they are:

DEMONSTRATIVE ADJECTIVES	MEANING	REFERRING TO...
este, esta, estos, estas	*this, these*	something nearby
ese, esa, esos, esas	*that, those over there*	something farther away
aquel, aquella, aquellos, aquellas	*that, those (way) over there*	something even farther away in distance and/or time... perhaps not even visible

Since forms of **este, ese,** and **aquel** are adjectives, they must agree in gender and number with the nouns they modify. Note the following examples.

Este conjunto es fantástico. — *This group is fantastic.*
Esta cantante es fenomenal. — *This singer is phenomenal.*
Estos conjuntos son fantásticos. — *These groups are fantastic.*
Estas cantantes son fenomenales. — *These singers are phenomenal.*

Ese conjunto es fantástico. — *That group is fantastic.*
Esa cantante es fenomenal. — *That singer is phenomenal.*
Esos conjuntos son fantásticos. — *Those groups are fantastic.*
Esas cantantes son fenomenales. — *Those singers are phenomenal.*

Aquel conjunto es fantástico. — *That group (over there) is fantastic.*
Aquella cantante es fenomenal. — *That singer (over there) is phenomenal.*
Aquellos conjuntos son fantásticos. — *Those groups (over there) are fantastic.*
Aquellas cantantes son fenomenales. — *Those singers (over there) are phenomenal.*

In summary:

1. When do you use **este, ese,** and **aquel**?
2. When do you use **esta, esa,** and **aquella**?
3. When do you use **estos, esos,** and **aquellos**?
4. When do you use **estas, esas,** and **aquellas**?

Check your answers to the preceding questions in Appendix 1.

5•8 Amiga, tienes razón

Tu amigo/a te da su opinión y tú respondes con una opinión similar. Cambia la forma de **este/a** a (*to*) **ese/a** y añade (*add*) la palabra "**también**".

MODELO TU AMIGO/A: Esta música es muy suave.
TÚ: *Sí, y esa música es suave también.*

1. Este grupo es fenomenal.
2. Estos cantantes son muy jóvenes.
3. Esta gira empieza en enero.
4. Este CD sale ahora.
5. Estas canciones son muy apasionadas.
6. Estos pianistas tocan muy bien.

5•9 En el centro estudiantil

Completen el diálogo de Lola y Tina con la forma correcta de **este, ese** y **aquel**.

LOLA: Tina, mira (1) ________ (*this*) grupo de estudiantes que acaba de entrar.

TINA: Sí, creo que conozco a (2) ________ (*this*) hombre alto. Es guitarrista del trío de jazz *Ritmos*.

LOLA: Tienes razón. Y (3) ________ (*this*) mujer rubia es pianista en la orquesta de la universidad.

TINA: ¿Quiénes son (4) ________ (*those*) dos mujeres morenas?

LOLA: Están en nuestra clase de química. ¿No las conoces? Y (5) ________ (*those over there*) dos hombres de las camisas rojas ¡son muy guapos!

5•10 ¿Qué opinas?

Miren el dibujo y expresen su opinión sobre las casas. Usen las formas apropiadas de **este, ese** y **aquel.**

Capítulo 2. El verbo *gustar*, pág. 82; Capítulo 4. Los verbos con cambios de raíz, pág. 144.

MODELO *Me gusta esta casa blanca pero prefiero esa casa beige. Pienso que aquella casa roja es fea. También creo que este jardín de la casa blanca es bonito.*

GRAMÁTICA 3 Los pronombres demostrativos

SAM 5-17 to 5-18 Guide 6, 22

Demonstrative pronouns take the place of nouns. They are identical in form and meaning to the demonstrative adjectives, with the exception of the ***accent mark***.

Masculino	Femenino	*Meaning*
éste	**ésta**	*this one*
éstos	**éstas**	*these*
ése	**ésa**	*that one*
ésos	**ésas**	*those*
aquél	**aquélla**	*that one (way over there/not visible)*
aquéllos	**aquéllas**	*those (way over there/not visible)*

A demonstrative pronoun must agree in gender and number with the noun it replaces. Observe how demonstrative adjectives and demonstrative pronouns are used in the following sentences.

Yo quiero comprar **este CD** pero mi hermana quiere comprar **ése.** — *I want to buy this CD but my sister wants to buy that one.*

—¿Te gusta **esa guitarra**? — *Do you like that guitar?*
—No, a mí me gusta **ésta.** — *No, I like this one.*

Estos instrumentos son interesantes, pero prefiero tocar **ésos.** — *These instruments are interesting, but I prefer to play those.*

En **esta** calle hay varios cines. ¿Quieres ir a **aquél**? — *There are several movie theaters on this street. Do you want to go to that one over there?*

5-11 Comparando cosas

Tu compañero/a te propone (*proposes*) una cosa pero tú siempre prefieres otra (*another one*). Responde a sus comentarios usando la forma correcta de **éste, ése** o **aquél.**

MODELO E1: ¿Quieres ir a este concierto?
E2: *No, quiero ir a ése/aquél.*

1. ¿Quieres escuchar estos músicos?
2. ¿Vamos a ir a ese teatro?
3. ¿Entiendes la letra de esta canción?
4. ¿Tus amigos tocan en aquel conjunto?
5. ¿Vas a comprar aquellas camisetas (*T-shirts*)?
6. ¿Piensas arreglar este cuarto para (*for*) la fiesta?

5•12 ¡Vamos a un concierto!

¡Qué suerte! Tienes dos entradas gratis (*free tickets*) para ir a un concierto.

Paso 1 Ve a la página web de *¡Anda!* para escuchar la música de El Gran Combo, Marc Anthony, Juan Luis Guerra y Los Tigres del Norte.

Paso 2 Tú compañero/a y tú tienen que decidir a qué concierto quieren ir. Túrnense para describir a quién prefieren escuchar y por qué. Usen **éste, ése** y **aquél** en sus descripciones.

MODELO *Prefiero ir al concierto de Marc Anthony. ¡Él canta muy bien! Pero es difícil decidir porque los músicos de Los Tigres del Norte son muy buenos también. Éstos saben tocar y cantar muy bien. Y aquéllos…*

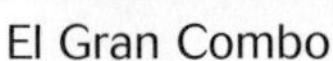
El Gran Combo

Marc Anthony

Juan Luis Guerra

Los Tigres del Norte

SAM
5-19 to 5-21

La música latina en los Estados Unidos

Néstor Torres

La música latina abarca (*encompasses*) muchos géneros, estilos e intérpretes (músicos, cantantes). Entre los géneros más populares en los Estados Unidos se encuentran la salsa, el merengue, el Tex-Mex o norteño y otros. Algunos intérpretes de estos tipos de música son El Gran Combo, Marc Anthony, Juan Luis Guerra y Los Tigres del Norte.

El rock y el jazz son influencias que están presentes en la música latina en los Estados Unidos, aunque ésta ha evolucionado (*has evolved*) y producido nuevos géneros como el merenhouse, el rock latino, el rap en español, el jazz latino, el reggaetón y otros.

La influencia de los países hispanohablantes del Caribe —Cuba, Puerto Rico y la República Dominicana— y su herencia africana forma parte de los ritmos, las melodías y la instrumentación de la música y los bailes latinos. También les dan vida (*they give life*) a géneros como la plena, la cumbia y la bachata.

Entre los artistas populares de hoy en día se encuentra Néstor Torres, flautista de música de jazz latino. Torres ganó un premio Grammy latino por su interpretación de "This Side of Paradise".

Preguntas

1. ¿Cuáles son cuatro de los géneros de la música latina? ¿Cuáles conoces tú?
2. ¿Quiénes son los artistas latinos más conocidos en este momento?

GRAMÁTICA 4 Los adverbios

5-22 to 5-24 45

Este baterista toca horriblemente.

Many Spanish adverbs end in **-mente,** which is equivalent to the English *-ly*. They describe the verb and usually answer the question *how*. These Spanish adverbs are formed as follows:

1. Add **-mente** to the *feminine singular* form of an *adjective*.

Adjetivos			Adverbios
Masculino	**Femenino**		
rápido →	*rápida* + -mente	→	**rápidamente**
lento →	*lenta* + -mente	→	**lentamente**
tranquilo →	*tranquila* + -mente	→	**tranquilamente**

2. If an *adjective* ends in a *consonant* or in **-e**, simply add **-mente.**

Adjetivos			Adverbios
Masculino	**Femenino**		
fácil →	*fácil* + -mente	→	**fácilmente**
suave →	*suave* + -mente	→	**suavemente**

*Note that if an adjective has a written accent, it is retained when **-mente** is added.

5-13 Lógicamente

Estrategia

Remember to first determine the *feminine singular* form of the adjective and then add *-mente.*

Túrnense para transformar en adverbios los siguientes adjetivos.

Capítulo 1. Los adjetivos descriptivos, pág. 44.

MODELO E1: normal
E2: *normalmente*

1. interesante
2. perezosos
3. feliz
4. nervioso
5. fuertes
6. claro
7. seguro
8. apasionadas
9. difícil
10. débil
11. rápida
12. pacientes

5•14 Para conocerte

Capítulo 2. Presente indicativo de verbos regulares, pág. 68; Capítulo 4. Los verbos con cambio de raíz, pág. 144.

Túrnense para hacerse y contestar las siguientes preguntas. Pueden usar los adjetivos de la lista.

alegre	constante	paciente	difícil	divino
fácil	horrible	perfecto	rápido	tranquilo

MODELO E1: ¿Cómo bailas? (divino)

E2: *Bailo divinamente.*

1. ¿Cómo cantas?
2. ¿Cómo duermes?
3. ¿Cómo hablas español?
4. ¿Cómo juegas al béisbol?
5. ¿Cómo tocas el piano?
6. ¿Cómo cocinas?
7. ¿Cómo lavas los platos?
8. ¿Cómo manejas (*drive*)?

5•15 Di la verdad

Estrategia

Answer in complete sentences when working with your partner. Even though it may seem mechanical at times, it leads to increased comfort speaking Spanish.

Hazle (*Ask*) a tu compañero/a las siguientes preguntas. Después, cambien de papel.

MODELO E1: ¿Qué haces diariamente (todos los días)?

E2: *Limpio mi dormitorio, voy a clase, estudio, como, hago ejercicio y duermo.*

1. ¿Qué haces perfectamente?
2. ¿Qué haces horriblemente?
3. ¿Qué haces fácilmente?
4. ¿Qué debes hacer rápidamente?
5. ¿Qué debes hacer lentamente?

GRAMÁTICA 5 El presente progresivo

5-25 to 5-27 31, 32

So far you have been learning and using the present tense to communicate ideas. If you want to emphasize that an action is occurring at the moment and is in progress, you can use the *present progressive* tense.

The English present progressive is made up of a form of the verb *to be* + *present participle* (*-ing*). Look at the following sentences and formulate a rule for creating the present progressive in Spanish. Use the questions below to guide you.

—¿Qué *estás* **haciendo**? — *What are you doing?*
—*Estoy* **estudiando.** — *I'm studying.*

—¿*Está* **escuchando** música tu hermano? — *Is your brother listening to music?*
—No, *está* **tocando** la guitarra. — *No, he is playing the guitar.*
—¿*Están* ustedes **viendo** la televisión? — *Are you watching television?*
—No, les *estamos* **escribiendo** una carta a nuestros padres. — *No, we are writing a letter to our parents.*

Fíjate

The present progressive is *not* used to express the future.

Present progressive: *Están ensayando.* They are rehearsing (right now).

Future: *Van a ensayar.* They are going to rehearse (in the future).

1. What is the infinitive of the first verb in each sentence that is in *italics*?
2. What are the infinitives of **haciendo, estudiando, escuchando, tocando, viendo,** and **escribiendo**?
3. How do you form the verb forms in **boldface**?
4. In this new tense, the *present progressive*, do any words come between the two parts of the verb?
5. Therefore, your formula for forming the *present progressive* is:
   a form of the verb _____ + a verb ending in _____ or _____

Check your answers to the preceding questions in Appendix 1.

*The following are some verbs that are irregular in this tense. Please note them below.

creer	creyendo	pedir	pidiendo	seguir	siguiendo
leer	leyendo	preferir	prefiriendo	servir	sirviendo
ir	yendo	perseguir	persiguiendo	dormir	durmiendo
decir	diciendo	repetir	repitiendo	morir	muriendo
mentir	mintiendo				

5•16 Progresando

Escuchen mientras su instructor/a les da (*gives you*) las instrucciones de esta actividad. ¡Diviértanse! (*Enjoy!*)

MODELO E1: *hablar, yo*

E2: *estoy hablando*

E2: *comer, nosotros*

E3: *estamos comiendo*

5•17 ¿Tienes telepatía?

Es sábado. Túrnense para decir qué está haciendo su profesor/a en varios momentos del día.

MODELO E1: Le gusta tomar café por la mañana. Son las siete y media.

E2: *Está tomando café en su terraza.*

1. Le gusta hacer ejercicio para comenzar su día.
2. Le gusta la música latina y está en una tienda.
3. Su coche está muy sucio y esta noche lleva a unos amigos a una gran fiesta.
4. Está trabajando en la computadora y resulta que tiene muchos mensajes de sus estudiantes.
5. Quiere comer algo ligero (*light*) antes de ir a la fiesta.
6. Está con sus amigos en la fiesta y los músicos están tocando.

5•18 ¿Qué está ocurriendo?

Túrnense para decir qué están haciendo estas personas.

MODELO E1: Felipe

E2: *Felipe está preparando su comida y está comiendo también.*

1. Manuel
2. Sofía
3. Raúl y Mari Carmen
4. José
5. Mercedes y Guillermo

5•19 ¡Qué creativo!

Creen juntos un diálogo de por lo menos **seis** oraciones usando los siguientes verbos. Usen el presente progresivo un mínimo de **tres** veces (*times*).

decir	dormir	repetir	creer	morir
mentir	leer	ir	seguir	servir

¿Cómo andas?

Having completed the first **Comunicación**, I now can…

	Feel Confident	Need to Review
• talk about the kinds of music that my friends and I like and dislike (p. 172)	❏	❏
• pronounce diphthongs correctly and use "linking" when speaking (p. 174)	❏	❏
• use demonstrative adjectives and pronouns (**este, ese,** and **aquel; éste, éste,** and **aquél**) in sentences (pp. 176, 178)	❏	❏
• state three facts about Latin music (p. 179)	❏	❏
• explain how something is done using adverbs (**-mente**) (p. 180)	❏	❏
• state what is happening right now using the present progressive (form of **estar** + **-ando, -iendo**) (p. 182)	❏	❏

Comunicación

- Sharing information and opinions about movies and actors
- Ranking items
- Stating what needs to be accomplished

VOCABULARIO 6 El mundo del cine

SAM 5-28 to 5-30

Otras palabras útiles	***Other Useful Words***
el estreno	*opening*
la película	*film; movie*
una película…	*a… movie*
aburrida	*boring*
animada	*animated*
conmovedora	*moving*
creativa	*creative*
emocionante	*moving*
entretenida	*entertaining*
épica	*epic*
espantosa	*scary*
estupenda	*stupendous*
imaginativa	*imaginative*
impresionante	*impressive*
pésima	*heavy; depressing*
sorprendente	*surprising*
trágica	*tragic*

Unos verbos	***Some verbs***
estrenar una película	*to release a film/movie*
presentar una película	*to show a film/movie*

5•20 ¿Cuál es el género?

Clasifiquen las siguientes películas según su género y usen el mayor (*the largest*) número de palabras posibles para describirlas.

MODELO E1: Jaws (*Tiburón*)

E2: *Tiburón es una película dramática, de acción. Es emocionante, entretenida, impresionante y trágica.*

1. Gone With the Wind (*Lo que el viento se llevó*)
2. Chicago
3. Titanic
4. Shrek II
5. Spiderman II (*El hombre araña II*)
6. Ben-Hur
7. Saving Private Ryan
8. Rush Hour (*Hora punta*)
9. The Exorcist (*El exorcista*)
10. ¿?

5•21 En mi opinión

Túrnense para completar las siguientes oraciones sobre las películas. ¿Están ustedes de acuerdo?

Capítulo Preliminar A. El verbo *ser*, pág. 13.

MODELO E1: La mejor película de terror…

E2: *La mejor película de terror es* Saw.

1. Las mejores películas de humor…
2. Una película épica pésima…
3. Mis actores favoritos de las películas de acción…
4. La película de misterio que más me gusta…
5. Unas películas animadas creativas…
6. La película más conmovedora…

5•22 Mis preferencias

Lee las reseñas (*reviews*) siguientes de unas películas. Después, túrnate con un/a compañero/a para describir la película que prefieren ver y por qué.

MODELO *Prefiero ver* ________________. *Es una película* ________ *y* ________. *Me gusta* ________. *También es* ________ …

En el cine

Cartas desde Iwo Jima (2006, EE.UU.)
Género: Película de guerra
Director: Clint Eastwood
Interpretación: Ken Watanabe, Kazunari Ninomiya...
Un tributo al rostro de la derrota en la célebre y decisiva batalla de Iwo Jima.

Dreamgirls (2006, EE.UU.)
Género: Película musical
Director: Bill Condon
Interpretación: Beyoncé Knowles, Jamie Foxx, Eddie Murphy...
Un festín bailable para los amantes del Motown y el Rhythm & Blues.

Invencible (2006, EE.UU)
Género: Película dramática
Director: Ericsson Core
Interpretación: Mark Wahlberg, Greg Kinnear...
La historia real de un ciudadano que se convirtió por sorpresa en estrella de la NFL.

el cine

5•23 En nuestra opinión...

Paso 1 Habla de algunas películas que conoces con un/a compañero/a, usando las preguntas siguientes como guía (*guide*).

1. ¿Cuáles son las películas que más te gustan? ¿Por qué?
2. ¿Quiénes son tus actores o actrices favoritos?
3. ¿Qué películas que van a estrenar pronto quieres ver?

Paso 2 Ahora hablen sobre unos programas de televisión.

5-31 to 5-32

La influencia hispana en el cine norteamericano

Antonio Banderas

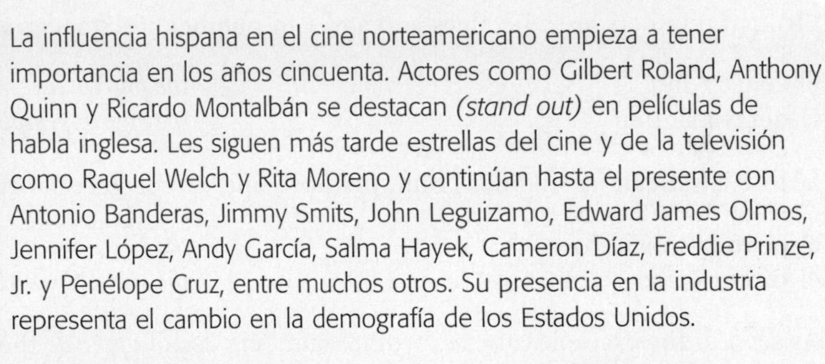

La influencia hispana en el cine norteamericano empieza a tener importancia en los años cincuenta. Actores como Gilbert Roland, Anthony Quinn y Ricardo Montalbán se destacan *(stand out)* en películas de habla inglesa. Les siguen más tarde estrellas del cine y de la televisión como Raquel Welch y Rita Moreno y continúan hasta el presente con Antonio Banderas, Jimmy Smits, John Leguizamo, Edward James Olmos, Jennifer López, Andy García, Salma Hayek, Cameron Díaz, Freddie Prinze, Jr. y Penélope Cruz, entre muchos otros. Su presencia en la industria representa el cambio en la demografía de los Estados Unidos.

Preguntas

1. De los actores mencionados, ¿a cuáles conoces? ¿Qué sabes de ellos?
2. ¿Quiénes son los actores hispanos más populares en este momento?

Salma Hayek

Cameron Díaz

Jennifer López

GRAMÁTICA 7 Los números ordinales

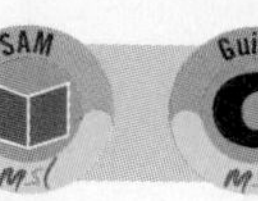

The first ten ordinal numbers in Spanish are listed below. They are the most commonly used.

primer, primero/a	*first*	**sexto/a**	*sixth*
segundo/a	*second*	**séptimo/a**	*seventh*
tercer, tercero/a	*third*	**octavo/a**	*eighth*
cuarto/a	*fourth*	**noveno/a**	*ninth*
quinto/a	*fifth*	**décimo/a**	*tenth*

1. Ordinal numbers are adjectives and agree in number and gender with the nouns they modify.

   el **cuarto** año — *the fourth year*
   la **octava** sinfonía — *the eighth symphony*

2. Before a masculine, singular noun, **primero** and **tercero** are shortened to **primer** and **tercer.**

   el **primer** concierto — *the first concert*
   el **tercer** curso de español — *the third Spanish course*

3. As seen in the examples above, ordinal numbers usually *precede* the noun.

5•24 Orden de preferencia

Asigna un orden de preferencia a las actividades de la lista: desde la más importante (primero) hasta la menos importante (octavo). Después, comparte tu lista con un/a compañero/a usando oraciones completas.

MODELO *Primero, me gusta ver una película con mi actor favorito, Tom Hanks. Segundo, quiero visitar a mis hermanos. Tercero, prefiero…*

1. ir a un concierto de tu conjunto favorito ____________
2. visitar a tus amigos ____________
3. ver una película con tu actor/actriz favorito/a ____________
4. leer una novela buena ____________
5. ir a un partido de fútbol americano ____________
6. estudiar para un examen ____________
7. visitar Costa Rica ____________
8. conocer al presidente de los Estados Unidos ____________

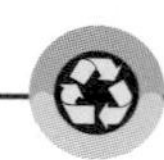

Capítulo Preliminar A. Los días, los meses y las estaciones, pág. 20.

5•25 Preguntas de trivia

Túrnense para hacerse y contestar las siguientes preguntas.

1. ¿En qué piso está esta sala de clase?
2. ¿A qué hora es tu primera clase los lunes? ¿y la segunda?
3. ¿Cuál es el tercer mes del año? ¿y el sexto?
4. ¿Cuál es el séptimo día de la semana?
5. ¿Cómo se llama el primer presidente de los Estados Unidos?
6. ¿Cómo se llama la cuarta persona de la tercera fila (*row*) en la clase de español?

Estrategia

Remember that when asked a question with *tu/tus*, you need to answer *mi/mis*.

5•26 La lista de los mejores

¿Cuáles son las mejores películas para los estudiantes de tu clase?

Paso 1 Entrevista a cinco estudiantes y pregúntales cuáles son sus tres películas favoritas. Usa las palabras **primera, segunda** y **tercera**.

Paso 2 Con el/la profesor/a, haz una lista de las **diez** películas más populares de la clase.

Paso 3 Organiza por orden de preferencia la lista de las películas más populares de la clase. Escribe el número ordinal apropiado para cada película.

PELÍCULAS FAVORITAS	ESTUDIANTE 1	ESTUDIANTE 2	ESTUDIANTE 3	ESTUDIANTE 4	ESTUDIANTE 5
Primera					
Segunda					
Tercera					

GRAMÁTICA 8 *Hay que* + infinitivo

5-36 to 5-37

Hay que trabajar. ¡No hay que ser perezoso!

So far when you have wanted to talk about what someone should do, needs to do, or has to do, you have used the expressions **debe, necesita,** or **tiene que.** The expression **hay que** + *infinitive* is another way to communicate responsibility, obligation, or the importance of something. **Hay que** + *infinitive* means:

It is necessary to…

You must…

One must/should…

Para ser un músico bueno **hay que** ensayar mucho. — *To be a good musician one must rehearse a lot.*

Hay que estudiar mucho para sacar buenas notas. — *It is necessary to study a lot to receive good grades.*

Hay que ver la nueva película de Almodóvar. — *You must see the new Almodóvar film.*

5•27 Para generalizar

Túrnense para sustituir **tener que** por **hay que.** Sigan el modelo.

MODELO E1: Tenemos que consultar al profesor para confirmar la información.

E2: *Hay que consultar al profesor para confirmar la información.*

1. Ustedes tienen que leer más si quieren sacar buenas notas en el examen.
2. Marisol, tú tienes que ser más paciente si quieres tener muchos amigos.
3. Mamá, tienes que comprar un carro nuevo. Tu carro es muy viejo.
4. Jorge y Catrina, ustedes tienen que preparar el almuerzo para sus padres.
5. Rafael, tienes que visitar a tu hermana porque está enferma.
6. Sara, tú tienes que terminar el proyecto antes del primero de diciembre.

5•28 ¿Obligaciones?

¿Qué hay que hacer para llegar a tener las siguientes características? Túrnense para completar las frases dando por lo menos **dos** ideas.

MODELO E1: Para ser un pintor excelente…
E2: *hay que pintar mucho y hay que ser muy creativo.*

Para ser…

1. un músico impresionante…
2. un político honesto…
3. un cantante estupendo…
4. un director de cine sorprendente…
5. una actriz conmovedora…
6. una novelista entretenida…

5•29 Y todos necesitamos…

¿Qué debemos hacer para tener un futuro mejor? Compartan sus ideas y comuniquen sus resultados a la clase usando **tres** oraciones completas.

MODELO E1: Hay que…
E2: *Hay que respetar las otras culturas.*

Vocabulario útil

el idioma/la lengua	*language*
la paz	*peace*
respetar	*to respect*

Los pronombres de complemento directo y la "a" personal

Direct objects receive the action of the verb and answer the questions *What?* or *Whom?* Note these examples.

A: I need to do *what?*
B: You need to pay *the bills* by Monday.
A: Yes, I do need to pay *them.*

A: I have to call *whom?*
B: You have to call *David.*
A: Yes, I do have to call *him.*

Note the following examples of *direct objects* in Spanish.

María toca **dos instrumentos** muy bien.	*María plays two instruments very well.*
Sacamos **un CD** el primero de septiembre.	*We are releasing a CD the first of September.*
¿Tienes **las entradas**?	*Do you have the tickets?*
No conozco a **Antonio Banderas.**	*I do not know Antonio Banderas.*
Siempre veo a **Shakira** en la televisión.	*I always watch Shakira on TV.*

Note: In *Capítulo 4*, you learned that to express knowing a person, you put "**a**" after the verb (*conocer* + *a* + person). Now that you have learned about direct objects, a more global way of stating the rule is: when direct objects refer to *people*, you must use the personal "**a.**" Review the following examples.

People	Things
¡Veo **a** *Cameron Díaz*!	¡Veo *el coche* de Cameron Díaz!
Hay que ver **a** *mis padres*.	Hay que ver *la película*.
¿**A** qué *actores* conoces?	¿Qué *ciudades* conoces?

As in English, we can replace direct objects nouns with *direct object pronouns.* Note the following examples.

María **los** toca muy bien.	*María plays them very well.*
Lo sacamos el primero de septiembre.	*We are releasing it the first of September.*
¿**Las** tienes?	*Do you have them?*
No **lo** conozco.	*I do not know him.*
Siempre **la** veo en la televisión.	*I always see her on TV.*

In Spanish, direct object pronouns *agree in gender and number with the nouns they replace.* The chart below lists the direct object pronouns.

Singular		Plural	
me	*me*	**nos**	*us*
te	*you*	**os**	*you all*
lo, la	*him, her, it, you*	**los, las**	*them, you all*

Placement of direct object pronouns

Direct object pronouns are:

1. Placed before the verb.
2. Attached to *infinitives* or to the *present participle* (**-ando, -iendo**).

¿Tienes los discos compactos?	→	Sí, **los** tengo.
Tengo que traer los instrumentos.	→	**Los** tengo que traer. / Tengo que traer**los.**
Tiene que llevar su guitarra.	→	**La** tiene que llevar. / Tiene que llevar**la.**

—¿Por qué estás preparando la comida para tu madre?
—**La** estoy preparando porque mi madre está enferma. /
Estoy preparándo**la** porque mi madre está enferma.

Capítulo 2. Presente indicativo de verbos regulares, pág. 68.

5•30 ¿Estás listo?

¿Estás preparado/a para el concierto de Perrozompopo? Túrnate con un/a compañero/a para revisar la lista, esta vez usando **lo, la, los** o **las.**

MODELO E1: confirmar *la hora* del concierto

E2: *La confirmo hoy.*

1. comprar *las entradas*
2. invitar *a mis amigos*
3. leer *el artículo* de *The New York Times* sobre Perrozompopo
4. compartir (*share*) *el artículo y los CD de Perrozompopo* con mis amigos
5. preparar *comida* para un pícnic
6. traer *la cámara*

5•31 ¿Hay deberes?

El concierto de Perrozompopo fue increíble, pero hay que volver al mundo real. Siempre hay trabajo, sobre todo en la casa. Túrnate con un/a compañero/a para hacer y contestar las siguientes preguntas.

Capítulo 3. Los quehaceres de la casa, pág. 112.

MODELO E1: ¿Lavas los pisos?

E2: *Sí, los lavo. / No, no/nunca los lavo.*

1. ¿Limpias la cocina?
2. ¿Arreglas tu cuarto?
3. ¿Lavas los platos?
4. ¿Guardas tus cosas?
5. ¿Sacudes los muebles?
6. ¿Haces las camas?
7. ¿Preparas la comida?
8. ¿Pones la mesa?
9. ¿Nos ayudas a arreglar el jardín?
10. ¿Me invitas a un concierto?

5•32 Una hora antes

Carlos Santana, como muchos músicos, es una persona muy organizada. Antes de cada concierto repasa con su ayudante (*assistant*) personal los preparativos. Aquí tienes las preguntas del ayudante. Contesta como si fueras (*as if you were*) Santana, usando **lo, la, los** o **las.**

Carlos Santana

MODELO E1: ¿Tienes tu anillo (*ring*) de la buena suerte?

E2: *Sí, lo tengo.*

1. Juan está enfermo. ¿Conoces al trompetista que toca esta noche con el conjunto?
2. ¿Traes tu guitarra nueva?
3. ¿Los cantantes saben la letra de la canción nueva?
4. ¿Traemos todos los trajes (*suits, outfits*)?
5. ¿Quieres unas botellas de agua (*water*)?
6. ¿Oyes al público? ¡Está listo para el concierto!
7. ¿Me van a necesitar después del concierto?
8. ¿El empresario te va a anunciar?

5•33 Mis preferencias

Túrnense para hacerse y contestar las siguientes preguntas usando el pronombre de complemento directo correcto.

MODELO E1: ¿Lees los poemas de Rubén Darío? ¿Por qué?
E2: *No, no los leo. No los leo porque no los conozco.*

1. ¿Escuchas música clásica? ¿Por qué?
2. ¿Tu amigo y tú tienen ganas de ver una película de acción de Antonio Banderas? ¿Por qué?
3. ¿Sus amigos limpian sus casas todos los días? ¿Por qué?
4. ¿Escuchas música jazz en tu iPod? ¿Por qué?
5. ¿Tocas un instrumento? ¿Por qué?

ESCUCHA

5-41 to 5-43

ESTRATEGIA **Anticipating content**

Use all clues available to you to anticipate what you are about to hear. That includes photos, captions, and body language if you are looking at the individual(s) speaking. If there are written synopses, they are important to read in advance. Finally, if you are doing a listening activity such as these, look ahead at the comprehension questions to give you an idea of the topic and important points.

5•34 Antes de escuchar

Mira la foto y contesta las siguientes preguntas.

1. ¿Quiénes están en la foto?
2. ¿De qué hablan Eduardo y Cisco?

Eduardo y Cisco

5•35 A escuchar

CD 2 Track 32

Escucha la conversación entre Eduardo y Cisco y averigua cuál es el tema (*topic*; *gist*). Después, escucha una vez más para contestar las siguientes preguntas.

1. ¿Quién va al concierto de Audioslave?
2. ¿Qué música prefiere Cisco?
3. Deciden no estudiar. ¿Adónde van a ir?

5•36 Después de escuchar

Describe una canción que te guste en **tres** oraciones y dibuja un cuadro (*picture*) que la represente. Preséntaselo a un/a compañero/a.

5•37 **Antes de escribir**

Piensa en una película que te guste mucho. Anota algunas ideas sobre los aspectos que te gustan más de esa película.

- ¿Qué tipo de película es?
- ¿Para qué grupo(s) es apropiada?
- ¿Cuál es el tema?
- ¿Tiene una lección para el público?

5•38 **Una reseña**

Organiza tus ideas y escribe una reseña (*review*), como una de las de la actividad **5-22**, de **cuatro** a **seis** oraciones. Puedes usar las siguientes preguntas para organizar tu reseña.

1. ¿Cómo se llama la película?
2. ¿De qué género es?
3. ¿Cómo la describes?
4. ¿A quiénes les va a gustar? ¿Por qué?
5. ¿La recomiendas? ¿Por qué?

5•39 **Después de escribir**

Tu profesor/a va a leer las reseñas. La clase tiene que adivinar cuáles son las películas.

¿Cómo andas?

Having completed the second **Comunicación,** I now can…

	Feel Confident	**Need to Review**
• talk about my favorite movies (p. 185)	❏	❏
• name at least three famous Hispanic actors (p. 187)	❏	❏
• rank things using ordinal numbers (p. 188)	❏	❏
• express things that need to be done by using **hay que…** (p. 189)	❏	❏
• replace direct objects with the direct object pronouns (**me, te, lo, la, nos, los, las**) in sentences (p. 190)	❏	❏
• explain the use of the personal "**a**" (p. 191)	❏	❏
• listen with the goal of anticipating content (p. 193)	❏	❏
• write a movie review (p. 194)	❏	❏

Mauricio Morales Prado

Nicaragua

CD 2
Track 33

5-45

Vistas culturales

Les presento mi país

Mi nombre es Mauricio Morales Prado y soy de Managua, Nicaragua. Mi país es conocido como la tierra de volcanes y lagos (*lakes*). Hay dos lagos principales y muchos volcanes. Siete están activos todavía. **¡Localiza estos lugares en el mapa!** Bluefields es la ciudad principal en la costa caribeña; allí se celebra la fiesta del Palo de Mayo. **¿Qué fiestas celebras en tu ciudad?** Mi familia y yo somos muy aficionados al béisbol. Vamos frecuentemente a los partidos en el Estadio Nacional en Managua.

El béisbol es muy popular en Nicaragua.

La fiesta del Palo de Mayo en Bluefields

ALMANAQUE

Nombre oficial:	República de Nicaragua
Gobierno:	República
Población:	5.570.129 (2006)
Idiomas:	español (oficial); miskito, otros idiomas indígenas
Moneda:	Córdoba (C$)

¿Sabías que...?

- El Lago de Nicaragua es el único lago de agua dulce (*fresh water*) del mundo donde se encuentran tiburones (*sharks*) y atunes.
- El 23 de diciembre de 1972, un terremoto (*earthquake*) desastroso de 6,5 en la escala Richter destruyó (*destroyed*) la ciudad de Managua.

PREGUNTAS

1. ¿Por qué se llama Nicaragua la tierra de lagos y volcanes?
2. ¿Qué tiene el Lago de Nicaragua de especial?
3. ¿Qué deporte es muy popular en Nicaragua? ¿En qué otros países hispanohablantes es popular?

En la Red
Amplía tus conocimientos sobre Nicaragua en la página web de *¡Anda!*

Alejandra Cecilia Montero Valverde

CD 2
Track 34

Vistas culturales

Costa Rica

Les presento mi país

Mi nombre es Alejandra Cecilia Montero Valverde y soy *tica*. *Ticos* es el apodo que tenemos todos los costarricenses. Soy de Sarchí, un pueblo famoso por su artesanía, sobre todo por la carreta, que es un símbolo nacional. **¿Cuáles son algunos símbolos de tu país y qué representan?** Si piensas visitar Costa Rica, te recomiendo una visita a los parques nacionales. Son bonitos y tienen flora y fauna únicas en el mundo. **¿Cuál es tu animal favorito?** ¡Costa Rica es pura vida!

Una carreta pintada de Sarchí

El ecoturismo es muy importante para la economía de Costa Rica.

El café, un producto principal de exportación.

ALMANAQUE

Nombre oficial:	República de Costa Rica
Gobierno:	República democrática
Población:	4.075.261 (2006)
Idiomas:	español (oficial); inglés
Moneda:	Colón (¢)

¿Sabías que...?

- El ejército (*army*) se abolió en Costa Rica en 1948. Los recursos monetarios desde aquel entonces apoyan (*support*) el sistema educativo. A causa de su dedicación a la paz (*peace*), la llaman “La Suiza de Centroamérica”.

PREGUNTAS

1. ¿Qué artesanía es un símbolo nacional costarricense?
2. ¿Cuál es uno de los productos de exportación importantes de Costa Rica? ¿Qué otros países exportan productos similares?
3. ¿Qué otra industria es importante para la economía de Costa Rica?

En la Red
Amplía tus conocimientos sobre Costa Rica en la página web de *¡Anda!*

Aída Elena Flores Solís

Panamá

CD 2
Track 35

Vistas culturales

Les presento mi país

Mi nombre es Aída Elena Flores Solís y soy de la ciudad de Panamá, la capital. Mi país es famoso por el canal. **¿Qué sabes tú de la historia del canal?** La economía de Panamá se basa principalmente en el sector de los servicios, la banca, el comercio y el turismo. Los turistas van al canal y también a las Islas San Blas. Allí pueden apreciar la artesanía de las mujeres indígenas. Los Kunas son un grupo de indígenas que viven en este lugar y las mujeres hacen *molas* como parte de su ropa tradicional.

Una mujer Kuna haciendo una mola, artesanía tradicional

El Canal de Panamá

ALMANAQUE

Nombre oficial:	República de Panamá
Gobierno:	Democracia constitucional
Población:	3.191.319 (2006)
Idiomas:	español (oficial); chibcha, inglés
Moneda:	Balboa (B/)

¿Sabías que...?

- Richard Halliburton nadó el canal en 1928 y la tarifa fue (*was*) 36 centavos. Hoy la tarifa promedio (*average*) por cruzar el canal es $40.00 U.S.
- Hay un palíndromo famoso en inglés asociado con el canal: *A man, a plan, a canal: ¡Panamá!*

PREGUNTAS

1. ¿Por qué es importante el canal?
2. Compara Panamá con Costa Rica y Nicaragua. ¿En qué son similares? ¿En qué son diferentes?
3. Compara Panamá, Costa Rica y Nicaragua con México. ¿En qué son similares? ¿En qué son diferentes?

En la Red
Amplía tus conocimientos sobre Panamá en la página web de *¡Anda!*

Ambiciones siniestras

EPISODIO 5

5-47

lectura

5-40 Antes de leer. En el **Episodio 4,** Marisol tiene sus dudas sobre Lupe. Cree que Lupe miente (*lies*) sobre su pueblo y posiblemente sobre otras cosas. En el **Episodio 4** del video, Cisco está enojado con Eduardo porque toca sus cosas. Luego, Eduardo se va misteriosamente. Teniendo esto en cuenta, contesta las siguientes preguntas.

- ¿Qué piensas? ¿De dónde es Lupe, de Akron, de Los Ángeles o de otro lugar?
- ¿Adónde va Eduardo?

ESTRATEGIA **Anticipating content**

You can often anticipate the content of a reading passage by paying attention to the title, to any available illustrations, and by quickly reading through the comprehension questions that may follow the passage.

5-41 A leer. Complete the following activities.

1. Take a look at the title of the episode, **La búsqueda de Eduardo,** and answer these questions.
   - What verb does **búsqueda** look like?
   - Who would be looking for Eduardo?
   - What might Cisco do to look for him?
2. Now read the **Después de leer** questions. What do you glean from the questions? Employ this new reading strategy along with the others you have been learning (identifying cognates, skimming, and scanning), and enjoy the episode!

CD 2
Track 36

La búsqueda de Eduardo

Cuando Cisco regresa a la sala, Eduardo no está. Pasa dos días haciendo llamadas y preguntándoles a otros amigos si saben algo de él. Nada. Nadie sabe nada. Cisco ya no° sabe qué hacer. ¿Debe llamar a la policía? ¿Debe avisar a los padres de Eduardo?

no longer

Por fin va a la computadora de Eduardo para ver si hay alguna pista°. Como Cisco es muy hábil con las computadoras, puede entrar en el correo electrónico de Eduardo. ¡Allí ve unos mensajes que le dan miedo!

clue

Lo piensa bien y finalmente decide mandarle un e-mail a su primo Manolo. Cisco admira y respeta mucho a su primo porque tiene mucha experiencia en la vida. Piensa que Manolo es muy responsable y casi siempre tiene respuestas para todo. Va a la computadora y empieza a escribir:

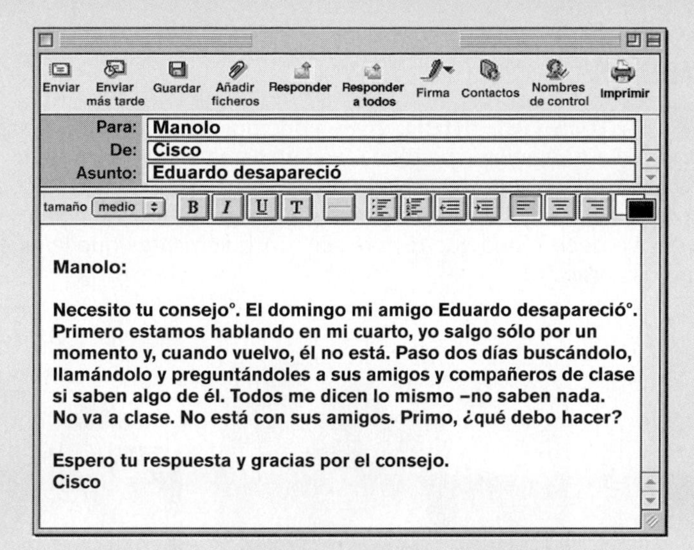

Para: Manolo
De: Cisco
Asunto: Eduardo desapareció

Manolo:

Necesito tu consejo°. El domingo mi amigo Eduardo desapareció°. Primero estamos hablando en mi cuarto, yo salgo sólo por un momento y, cuando vuelvo, él no está. Paso dos días buscándolo, llamándolo y preguntándoles a sus amigos y compañeros de clase si saben algo de él. Todos me dicen lo mismo –no saben nada. No va a clase. No está con sus amigos. Primo, ¿qué debo hacer?

Espero tu respuesta y gracias por el consejo.
Cisco

advice
disappeared

—Bueno, —piensa Cisco— necesito algo para distraerme°. Creo que voy al concierto.

entertain myself/get my mind off the situation

Su universidad siempre tiene buenos programas de música. Esta noche toca un grupo de fama internacional. Sus grabaciones son fenomenales y el cantante principal también tiene mucha habilidad como guitarrista. Cisco tiene todos sus CD.

—Sé quien va a estar sentada a mi lado—, piensa, —aquella chica guapísima de mi clase de economía compró su entrada al mismo tiempo que yo. ¡Ay! Las cosas se ven mucho mejor ahora.

Después de regresar del concierto, Cisco está de muy buen humor. Es muy tarde pero no quiere dormir. Quiere pensar en el concierto y en la chica. Decide ir a ver si tiene un mensaje de ella o de su primo. Al abrir su correo electrónico encuentra un mensaje de Eduardo con la fecha del mismo día de la «discusión»: ¡hace dos días!

¡Es increíble! Y algo igualmente increíble es que los destinatarios del mensaje sean Cisco y cuatro personas más: Alejandra Sánchez, María Soledad Valenzuela, Guadalupe Iriarte y Manolo Rodríguez. ¿Manolo? Su primo Manolo se llama *Rodríguez* también. ¿Puede ser el mismo?

5-42 Después de leer. Contesta las siguientes preguntas.

1. ¿Qué hace Cisco para buscar a Eduardo?
2. ¿A quién le escribe Cisco para pedirle consejo? ¿Por qué?
3. ¿Qué hace Cisco para distraerse? Describe el evento.
4. ¿De quién tiene Cisco un mensaje en su correo electrónico?
5. ¿Quiénes reciben el mismo mensaje?

5-48 to 5-50

video

5-43 **Antes del video.** ¿Qué podemos hacer cuando alguien desaparece? En tu opinión, ¿por qué Cisco no llama a la policía? En la segunda parte del episodio, vas a ver una videoconferencia entre todos los estudiantes menos Eduardo. ¿Qué piensas que van a decir? También, Alejandra va a decir, "Creo que te conozco". ¿A quién crees que le dice Alejandra esa oración?

¿Te gusta la música latina?

Creo que te conozco.

Debemos informar a la policía.

Episodio 5

Se conocen

Relájate y disfruta el video.

5-44 **Después del video.** Contesta las siguientes preguntas.

1. ¿Quién organiza la videoconferencia y por qué?
2. ¿De qué hablan Marisol y Lupe antes de la videoconferencia?
3. ¿Dónde están Alejandra y Manolo antes de la videoconferencia?
4. ¿Qué información comparten los estudiantes durante la videoconferencia?
5. Alejandra piensa que reconoce a alguien. ¿A quién? ¿Por qué?
6. ¿Quién desaparece al final de la videoconferencia?

Y por fin, ¿cómo andas?

Having completed this chapter, I now can…

	Feel Confident	Need to Review
Comunicación		
• share my likes and dislikes with regard to music (p. 172)	❑	❑
• pronounce diphthongs correctly and use "linking" when speaking (p. 174)	❑	❑
• point out specific persons, places, things, and ideas using demonstrative adjectives and pronouns (**este, ese, aquel** and **éste, ése, aquél**) (pp. 176, 178)	❑	❑
• state how or in what manner something is done using adverbs **(-mente)** (p. 180)	❑	❑
• state what is going on right now using the present progressive (form of **estar** + **-ando, -iendo**) (p. 182)	❑	❑
• discuss information regarding movies and television shows (p. 185)	❑	❑
• rank people, places, and things (p. 188)	❑	❑
• express the importance or necessity of doing something with **hay que** (p. 189)	❑	❑
• use direct object pronouns in complete sentences (p. 190)	❑	❑
• know when to use the personal "**a**" correctly when speaking and writing (p. 191)	❑	❑
• anticipate content when listening to someone (p. 193)	❑	❑
• write a brief movie review (p. 194)	❑	❑
Cultura		
• state two interesting things about Hispanic music and musicians (p. 179)	❑	❑
• share the names of two Hispanic actors that have influenced film and television (p. 187)	❑	❑
• give at least two interesting facts about each country: Nicaragua, Costa Rica, and Panama (pp. 195–197)	❑	❑
Ambiciones siniestras		
• anticipate content by looking for visual cues and other clues (p. 198)	❑	❑
• explain two things that Cisco does when he realizes Eduardo is missing (p. 198)	❑	❑
• share what happens when the contestants, minus Eduardo, have a videoconference (p. 200)	❑	❑

VOCABULARIO ACTIVO

CD 2
Tracks 37-46

El mundo de la música	The world of music
el/la artista	*artist*
la batería	*drums*
el/la baterista	*drummer*
el/la cantante	*singer*
el concierto	*concert*
el conjunto	*group; band*
el/la empresario/a	*agent; manager*
la gira	*tour*
las grabaciones	*recordings*
la guitarra	*guitar*
el/la guitarrista	*guitarist*
el/la músico/a	*musician*
la música	*music*
la orquesta	*orchestra*
el/la pianista	*pianist*
el piano	*piano*
el tambor	*drum*
el/la tamborista	*drummer*
la trompeta	*trumpet*
el/la trompetista	*trumpet player*

Unos géneros musicales	Some musical genres
el jazz	*jazz*
la música clásica	*classical*
la música popular	*pop music*
la ópera	*opera*
el rock	*rock*
la salsa	*salsa*

Unas características	Some characteristics
apasionado/a	*passionate*
cuidadoso/a	*careful*
fino/a	*fine; delicate*
lento/a	*slow*
suave	*smooth*

Unos verbos	Some verbs
dar un concierto	*to give/perform a concert*
ensayar	*to practice/rehearse*
grabar	*record*
hacer una gira	*to tour*
sacar un CD	*to release a CD*
tocar	*to play (a musical instrument)*

Otras palabras útiles	Some useful words
el/la aficionado/a	*fan*
la fama	*fame*
el género	*genre*
la habilidad	*ability; skill*
la letra	*lyrics*
el ritmo	*rhythm*
el sabor	*flavor*
la voz	*voice*

El mundo del cine	*The world of cinema*
el actor	*actor*
la actriz	*actress*
la entrada	*ticket*
la estrella	*star*
la pantalla	*screen*
una película...	*a... film; movie*
de acción	*action*
de ciencia ficción	*science fiction*
documental	*documentary*
dramática	*drama*
de guerra	*war*
de humor	*funny; comedy*
de misterio	*mystery*
musical	*musical*
romántica	*romantic*
de terror	*horror*

Otras palabras útiles	*Other useful words*
el estreno	*opening*
la película	*movie*
una película...	*a... movie*
aburrida	*boring*
animada	*animated*
conmovedora	*moving*
creativa	*creative*
emocionante	*moving*
entretenida	*entertaining*
épica	*epic*
espantosa	*scary*
estupenda	*stupendous*
imaginativa	*imaginative*
impresionante	*impressive*
pésima	*heavy; depressing*
sorprendente	*surprising*
trágica	*tragic*

Los números ordinales	*Ordinal numbers*
primer, primero/a	*first*
segundo/a	*second*
tercer, tercero/a	*third*
cuarto/a	*fourth*
quinto/a	*fifth*
sexto/a	*sixth*
séptimo/a	*seventh*
octavo/a	*eighth*
noveno/a	*ninth*
décimo/a	*tenth*

Unos verbos	*Some verbs*
estrenar una película	*to release a film/movie*
presentar una película	*to show a film/movie*

Vocabulario útil	*Useful vocabulary*
el idioma/la lengua	*language*
la paz	*peace*
respetar	*to respect*

6

¡Sí, lo sé!

OBJETIVOS

Comunicación

- To describe your family and other families
- To talk about your school and relate information about your university campus
- To share information about homes that you and your friends like and dislike
- To talk about what will take place in the future
- To share what you and others like to do and what you need to do
- To describe service opportunities in your community
- To discuss music and movies

Cultura

- To share information about Mexico, Spain, Honduras, Guatemala, El Salvador, Nicaragua, Costa Rica, and Panama, as well as about Hispanics in the United States
- To compare and contrast the countries you learned about in **Capítulos 1–5**

This chapter is a recycling chapter, designed for you to see just how much Spanish you have learned thus far. The *major points* of **Capítulos 1–5** are included in this chapter, providing you with the opportunity to "put it all together." You will be pleased to realize how much you are able to communicate in Spanish.

Since this is a recycling chapter, no new vocabulary is presented. The intention is that you review the vocabulary of **Capítulos 1–5** thoroughly, focusing on the words that you personally have difficulty remembering.

Everyone learns at a different pace. You and your classmates will vary in terms of how much of the material presented thus far you have mastered and what you still need to practice.

Remember, language learning is a process. Like any skill, learning Spanish requires practice, review, and then more practice!

6-1 to 6-29

Organizing Your Review

There are processes used by successful language learners for reviewing a world language. The following tips can help you organize your review. There is no one correct way, but these are some suggestions that will best utilize your time and energy.

1 Reviewing Strategies

1. Make a list of the *major* topics you have studied and need to review, dividing them into three categories: *vocabulary, grammar,* and *culture*. These are the topics where you need to focus the majority of your time and energy.

   Note: The two-page chapter openers can help you determine the *major* topics.
2. Allocate a minimum of an hour each day over a period of time to review. Budget the majority of your time for the major topics. After beginning with the most important grammar and vocabulary topics, review the secondary/supporting grammar topics and the culture. Cramming the night before a test is *not* an effective way to review and retain information.
3. Many educational researchers suggest that you start your review with the most recent chapter, or in this case, **Capítulo 5.** The most recent chapter is the freshest in your mind, so you tend to remember the concepts better, and you will experience quick success in your review.
4. Spend the most amount of time on concepts where you determine *you* need to improve. Revisit the self-assessment tools **Y por fin, ¿cómo andas?** in each chapter to see how you rated yourself. Those tools are designed to help you become good at self-assessing what you need to work on the most.

2 Reviewing Grammar

1. When reviewing grammar, begin with the *major* points, that is, begin with the *present tense* of regular, irregular, and stem-changing verbs. After feeling confident with using the major grammar points correctly, proceed to the additional grammar points and review them.
2. Good ways to review include redoing activities in your textbook, redoing activities in your **Student Activities Manual**, and (re)doing activities on your *¡Anda!* web site.

3 Reviewing Vocabulary

1. When studying vocabulary, it is usually most helpful to look at the English word, and then say or write the word in Spanish. Make a special list of words that are difficult for you to remember, writing them in a small notebook. Pull out the notebook every time you have a few minutes (in between classes, waiting in line at the grocery store, etc.) to review the words. The **Vocabulario activo** pages at the end of each chapter will help you organize the most important words of each chapter.
2. Saying vocabulary (which includes verbs) out loud helps you retain the words better.

4 Overall Review Technique

1. Get together with someone with whom you can practice speaking Spanish. If you need something to spark the conversation, take the composite art pictures from *¡Anda!* and say as many things as you can about each picture. Have a friendly challenge to see who can make more complete sentences or create the longest story about the pictures. This will help you build your confidence and practice stringing sentences together to speak in paragraphs.
2. Yes, it is important for you to know "mechanical" pieces of information such as verb endings, or how to take a sentence and replace the direct object with a pronoun. *But*, it is *much more important* that you are able to take those mechanical pieces of information and put them all together, creating meaningful and creative samples of your speaking and writing on the themes of the first five chapters.
3. You are well on the road to success if you can demonstrate that you can speak and write in paragraphs, using a wide variety of verbs and vocabulary words correctly. Keep up the good work!

Estrategia

Before beginning each activity, make sure that you have reviewed the identified recycled concepts carefully so that you are able to move through the activities seamlessly as you put it all together! *¡Sí, lo sabes!*

Estrategia

Being a good listener is an important life skill. Repeating what your classmate said gives you practice in demonstrating how well you listen.

Comunicación

Capítulos Preliminar A, 1 y 2

6-1 Nuestras familias

Completen los siguientes pasos en grupos de cuatro.

Paso 1 Con un/a compañero/a, túrnense para describir a varios miembros de sus familias usando por lo menos **diez** oraciones con un mínimo de **cinco** verbos diferentes. Incluyan *(Include)*: aspectos de personalidad, descripción física, qué hacen en su tiempo libre, cuántos años tienen, etc.

MODELO E1: *Mi familia no es muy grande. Mi madre es simpática, inteligente y trabajadora. Tiene cuarenta y cinco años…*

Paso 2 Ahora describe a la familia de tu compañero/a a otro miembro del grupo usando por lo menos **cinco** oraciones. Si no recuerdas bien los detalles o si necesitas clarificación, pregúntale *(ask him/her)*.

MODELO E2: *La familia de Adriana es pequeña. Su madre es simpática y trabajadora… Adriana, perdón, pero ¿cuántos años tiene tu madre? …*

Estrategia

With situations like those in actividad **6-1**, it is not essential that *all* details be remembered. Nor is it essential in this type of scenario to repeat *verbatim* what someone has said; it is totally acceptable to express the same idea in different words. When necessary ask him/her to repeat or clarify information.

6-2 ¿Cómo eres?

Conoces un poco a los estudiantes que estudiamos en *Les presento mi país* en los Capítulos **1–5**. ¿Qué más quieres saber de ellos? Escribe por lo menos **diez** preguntas que quieres hacerles. Sé *(Be)* creativo/a.

Estrategia

Pay attention to the particular grammar point you are practicing. If you are supposed to write sentences using *tener*, underline each form of *tener* that you use, and then check to make sure it agrees with the subject. Using strategies such as underlining can help you focus on important points.

MODELO
1. *¿Dónde estudias?*
2. *¿Te gusta leer libros de deportes?*
3. *¿Qué comes?*
4. …

Estrategia

Although these activities are focusing on *Capítulos Preliminar A, 1*, and *2*, feel free to use additional vocabulary from later chapters to create your questions. For example, in actividad **6-2**, you may want to use vocabulary from *Capítulo 5*.

Alberto Martínez Vergara

Araceli Gabriela Campos Vega

María Ángeles Solana Montoya

Alfonso Guillermo Rivera Zúñiga

Itzel Fabiola Guerra Cruz

Alba Violeta Orellana Barrillas

Mauricio Morales Prado

Alejandra Cecilia Montero Valverde

Aída Elena Flores Solís

6-3 Una gira

Trabajas en tu universidad como guía para los nuevos estudiantes. Crea una gira para ellos. Incluye por lo menos **cinco** lugares y **dos** deportes.

MODELO *Esta universidad tiene diez mil estudiantes. Ésta es la biblioteca. Los estudiantes estudian aquí y usan las computadoras. Allí está el gimnasio donde juegan al básquetbol. Tenemos las especialidades de matemáticas, español, …*

Vocabulario útil

aquí	*here*
allí	*there / over there*
allá	*over there (and potentially not visible)*

6-4 Mi casa favorita

Mira los dibujos y descríbele tu casa favorita a un/a compañero/a. Dile *(Tell)* por qué te gusta la casa y explícale por qué no te gustan las otras *(the other)* casas.

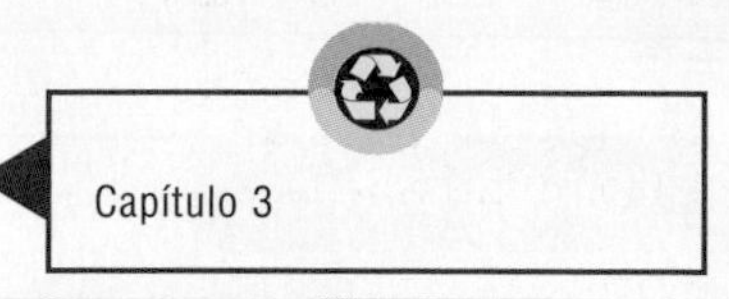

Estrategia

As you study vocabulary or grammar, it might be helpful to organize the information into a word web. Start with the concept you want to practice, such as *la casa*, write the word in the center of the page, and draw a circle around it. Then, as you brainstorm how your other vocabulary fits into *la casa*, you can create circles that branch off from your main idea, for example, *la cocina, la sala, el dormitorio*, etc. and list the furniture that belongs in each room.

6-5 Mi horario personal

Escribe tu horario (*schedule*) para una semana académica. Incluye por lo menos **siete** actividades usando **siete** verbos diferentes. Después comparte tu horario con un/a compañero/a.

Estrategia

When reviewing vocabulary, one strategy is to fold your paper lengthwise and have one column dedicated to the words in English and another column in Spanish. That way, you can fold the page over and look at the words, testing yourself to see if you really know the vocabulary.

6-6 Quiero saber...

Completa los siguientes pasos para entrevistar a un/a compañero/a.

Paso 1 Escribe tus preguntas usando los siguientes verbos.

hacer	oír	querer	salir	venir
poder	poner	saber	traer	conocer

MODELO E1: *¿Qué traes a tus clases todos los días?*

Paso 2 Entrevista a tu compañero/a.

MODELO E1: *¿Qué traes a tus clases todos los días?*
E2: *Traigo mi mochila a mis clases todos los días. …*

Paso 3 Comparte la información con tus compañeros de clase.

MODELO *Mi compañero Jake trae su mochila a sus clases. También,…*

6-7 ¿Qué tienen?

Túrnense para describir a las personas de los dibujos usando expresiones con **tener.**

MODELO *Jorge recibe una buena nota en su examen. Tiene éxito en su clase de periodismo.*

Julia

Susana Mirta

Beatriz Jorge

Guadalupe

Guillermo Miguel Beto

Adriana David

6-8 Lo conocemos y lo sabemos

Juntos hagan un diagrama de Venn sobre lo que conocen y saben, y sobre lo que no conocen o no saben. Escriban por lo menos **diez** oraciones.

Capítulo 4

MODELO

Janet
1. Mi familia y yo sabemos hablar español.
2. Mi amiga Julia y sus hermanos saben tocar el piano.

Nosotras
1. Sabemos patinar.
2. No sabemos hablar chino.
3. Conocemos a la profesora.

Audrey
1. Mi amiga Sally y su familia conocen al presidente de la universidad.

6-9 Un cuento divertido

Escriban en grupos un cuento creativo usando los siguientes verbos. Empiecen con la oración en el modelo. ¡Sean creativos!

almorzar (nosotros)	devolver (él)	mostrar (ella)	servir (ellos)
cerrar (ellas)	dormir (ellos)	pedir (tú)	volver (yo)
costar (los libros)	encontrar (nosotros)	seguir (yo)	comenzar (él)

MODELO

¡Qué día tan horrible! Primero pierdo la tarea para la clase de ________.

Vocabulario útil

entonces	*then*
después	*afterward*
finalmente	*finally*
luego	*then*
sin embargo	*nevertheless*

6-10 Mi comunidad ideal

Eres un/a arquitecto/a urbano/a y planeas tu ciudad ideal.

Paso 1 Dibuja el plano de tu ciudad con los lugares más necesarios (apartamentos, bancos, parques, etc.).

Paso 2 Descríbele tu ciudad a un/a compañero/a. Usa por lo menos **diez** oraciones con una variedad de verbos y vocabulario.

MODELO *Mi ciudad ideal se llama Ciudad Feliz. Hay una plaza en el centro. Tiene...*

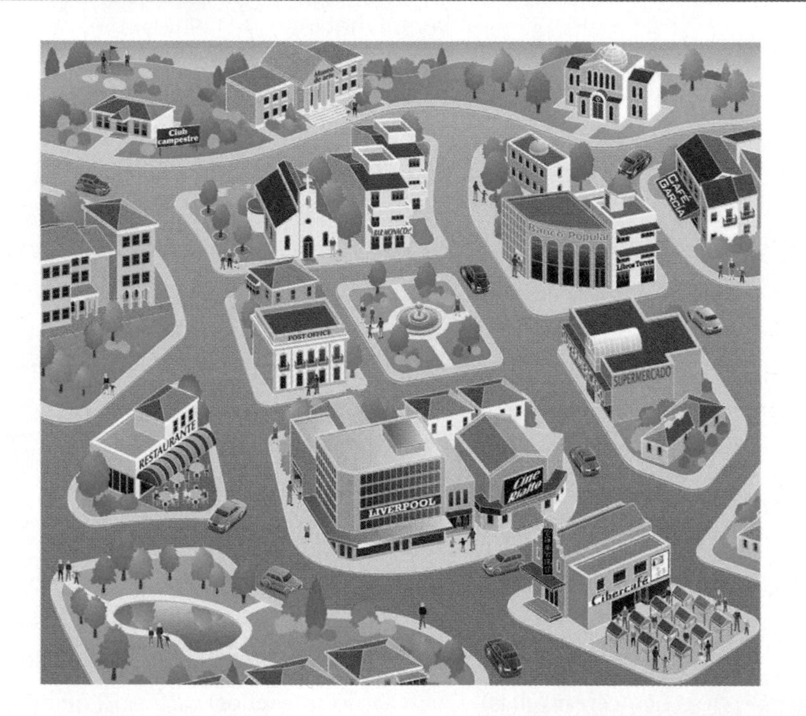

6-11 Querida familia:...

Trabajas como consejero/a en un campamento de niños. Un día ayudas a los niños a escribirles una carta a sus padres y piensas que es una buena idea escribirle a tu familia también. En tu carta, incluye oraciones que incorporen todos los usos que puedas (*all of the uses that you can*) de **ser** y **estar.**

MODELO

Querido José:

Estoy muy, muy cansada hoy. Tengo ganas de dormir pero ¡solamente son las 9!...

6-12 Mi tiempo libre

¡Tus compañeros y tú van a tener diez gloriosos días de vacaciones después de los exámenes! ¿Qué van a hacer? Túrnense **cinco** veces para decir oraciones usando **el futuro.** Después de decir tu oración, repite todo lo que dijeron (*you both said*) antes (*before*). Usen también diferentes pronombres (**yo, tú, ellos, nosotros,** etc.).

MODELO E1: *Voy a dormir diez horas cada día.*

E2: *Mis amigos van a ir a Cancún y tú vas a dormir diez horas cada día.*

E1: *Mi familia y yo vamos a nadar, tus amigos van a ir a Cancún, y voy a dormir diez horas cada día.*

E2: ...

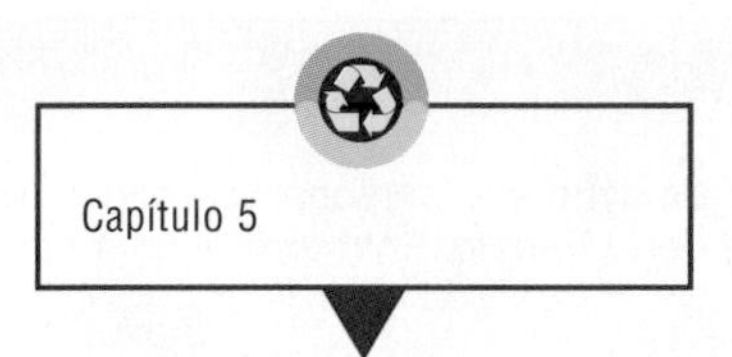

6-13 ¡El concierto del siglo!

Quieres ir al concierto de tu conjunto (*group*) o cantante favorito, pero tu compañero/a no quiere ir. Creen un diálogo sobre su situación y preséntenlo a la clase. Su diálogo debe incluir por lo menos **doce** oraciones. Usen: formas de **este, ese, aquel;** unos adverbios (**-mente**); **hay que...;** pronombres de objeto directo (**me, te, lo, la, nos, los, las**).

MODELO E1: *David, quiero ir al concierto de Marc Anthony. Es este sábado a las ocho. Las entradas no cuestan mucho. Te invito.*

E2: *No gracias, Mariela. No quiero ir. Realmente, no puedo ir. Tengo mucha tarea.*

E1: *Pero David,...*

6-14 ¡Bienvenido, estrella!

¡Tienes el trabajo ideal! Puedes entrevistar (*interview*) a tu actor o actriz favorito/a del cine. Escribe **diez** preguntas que vas a hacerle. Después, con un/a compañero/a de clase, hagan los papeles de (*play the roles of*) estrella y entrevistador/a para la clase.

Un poco de todo

6-15 ¡Ganaste la lotería!

Ganaste (*You won*) un millón de dólares en la lotería y te invitan a un programa de televisión para explicar qué vas a hacer con el dinero. Dile al/a la entrevistador/a (tu compañero/a) qué vas a hacer con el dinero en por lo menos **diez** oraciones. Después cambien de papel (*Take turns playing each role*).

6-16 Busco ayuda...

Con el dinero que ganaste en la lotería, decides buscar un ayudante personal (*personal assistant*) para ayudar con los quehaceres de la casa y con algunos asuntos (*matters*) de tu trabajo. Entrevista a un/a compañero/a que hace el papel de ayudante. Después cambien de papel.

MODELO E1: *Debe mandar mis cartas y escribir unos e-mails.*
E2: *Bueno, pero no limpio las ventanas.*
E1: *¿Cómo? ¿No las limpia? ¿Pasa la aspiradora?*
E2: …

6-17 Mi horario para la semana

Crea un horario para una semana durante el verano. Usa por lo menos **diez** verbos diferentes para explicar lo que tienes que hacer. Comparte tu horario con un/a compañero/a.

junio

L	M	M	J	V	S	D
	1	2	3	4	5	6
7	8	9	10	11	12	13
14	15	16	17	18	19	20
21	22	23	24	25	26	27
28	29	30				

julio

L	M	M	J	V	S	D
			1	2	3	4
5	6	7	8	9	10	11
12	13	14	15	16	17	18
19	20	21	22	23	24	25
26	27	28	29	30	31	

agosto

L	M	M	J	V	S	D
						1
2	3	4	5	6	7	8
9	10	11	12	13	14	15
16	17	18	19	20	21	22
23	24	25	26	27	28	29
30	31					

6-18 Mis planes para el verano

Escribe un e-mail a tus primos de **ocho** a **diez** oraciones sobre lo que vas a hacer este verano: **cuándo, dónde** y **con quién.**

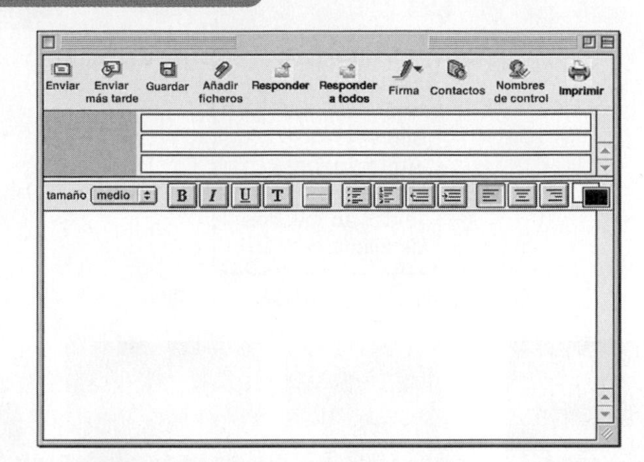

6-19 Para la comunidad

Escribe un poema en verso libre o una canción sobre el voluntariado y sus beneficios para los que dan y para los que reciben ayuda.

6-20 Mi comunidad

Túrnense para describir detalladamente su comunidad. Incluyan en su descripción oral detalles de su pueblo o ciudad (edificios, lugares para diversión, etc.), su casa y también las oportunidades que existen para hacer servicio voluntario.

Episodio 6

6•21 El juego de la narración

Túrnense para crear una narración oral sobre **Ambiciones siniestras.** ¡Incluyan muchos detalles!

MODELO E1: Ambiciones siniestras *es un misterio muy imaginativo.*
E2: *Hay seis estudiantes que se llaman…*
E1: …

Cisco

Eduardo

Manolo

Alejandra

Lupe

Marisol

Estrategia

The ability to retell information is an important language-learning strategy. Practice summarizing or retelling in your own words in Spanish the events from *Ambiciones siniestras*, chapter by chapter. Set a goal for yourself of saying or writing at least five important events in each episode that move the story along. Another technique is to recap as if you were retelling the story to another student who was absent.

6•22 ¿Me quiere?

Cisco, de **Ambiciones siniestras,** le escribe un correo electrónico a la chica que conoció *(he met)* en el concierto. En el e-mail habla de sus planes para el fin de semana y la invita a acompañarlo *(accompany him).* Escríbele ese mensaje para Cisco en **diez** oraciones.

MODELO

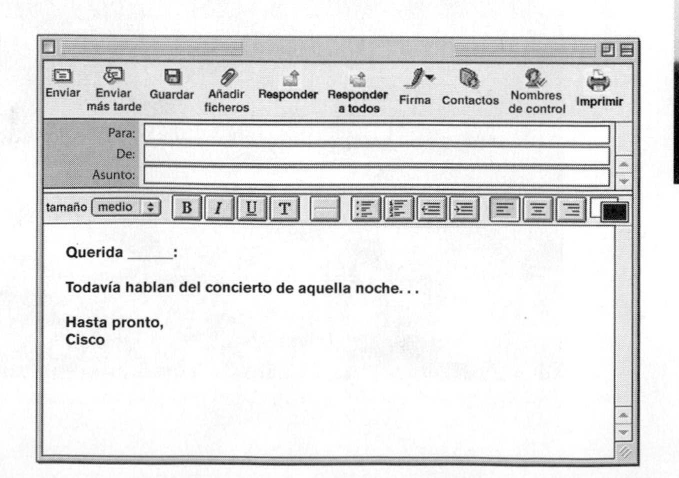
Enviar | Enviar más tarde | Guardar | Añadir ficheros | Responder | Responder a todos | Firma | Contactos | Nombres de control | Imprimir

Para:
De:
Asunto:

tamaño medio B I U T

Querida _____:

Todavía hablan del concierto de aquella noche…

Hasta pronto,
Cisco

6-23 Su versión

En la actividad **6-21,** narraron (*you narrated*) una versión del cuento **Ambiciones siniestras.** Ahora es su turno como escritores. Sean muy creativos y creen su propia (*own*) versión creativa. Su instructor les va a explicar cómo hacerlo. Empiecen con la oración del modelo. ¡Diviértanse!

MODELO *Hay seis estudiantes de tres universidades.*

6-24 Tu propia película

Eres cinematógrafo y puedes crear tu propia versión de **Ambiciones siniestras.** Primero, pon las fotos en el orden correcto y luego escribe el diálogo para la película. Luego, puedes filmar tu versión.

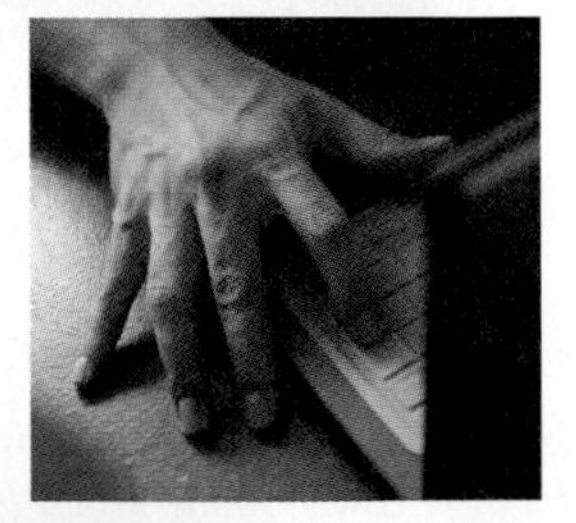

6-25 ¡A jugar!

En grupos de tres o cuatro, preparen las respuestas para las siguientes categorías de ***¿Lo sabes?,*** un juego como *Jeopardy!,* y después las preguntas correspondientes. Pueden usar valores de dólares, pesos, euros, etc. ¡Buena suerte!

CATEGORÍAS

VOCABULARIO
- la vida estudiantil
- las materias y las especialidades
- los deportes y los pasatiempos
- la casa y los muebles
- los quehaceres de la casa
- el cine
- la música
- el voluntariado

VERBOS
- verbos regulares
- verbos irregulares
- **saber** y **conocer**
- **ser** y **estar**
- **ir, ir** + **a** + infinitivo
- **estar** + **-ando, -iendo**

CULTURA
- los Estados Unidos
- México
- España
- Honduras
- Guatemala
- El Salvador
- Nicaragua
- Costa Rica
- Panamá

Estrategia

You have read numerous cultural notes throughout the first five chapters. To help you organize the material, make a chart of the most important information, or dedicate a separate page in your notebook for each country, recording the unique cultural items of that particular country.

MODELOS

CATEGORÍA: LA VIDA ESTUDIANTIL
Respuesta: en la residencia estudiantil
Pregunta: *¿Dónde viven los estudiantes?*

CATEGORÍA: LOS DEPORTES Y LOS PASATIEMPOS
Respuesta: Sammy Sosa
Pregunta: *¿Quién juega al béisbol muy bien?*

¿LO SABES? DOBLE

6•26 Los hispanos en los Estados Unidos

Escribe **cinco** influencias hispanas en los Estados Unidos.

MODELO 1. *St. Augustine fue fundada por los españoles.*

6•27 Aspectos interesantes

Escribe por lo menos **tres** cosas interesantes sobre cada uno de los siguientes países.

MÉXICO	ESPAÑA	HONDURAS	GUATEMALA

EL SALVADOR	NICARAGUA	COSTA RICA	PANAMÁ

6•28 Un agente de viajes

Durante el verano tienes la oportunidad de trabajar en una agencia de viajes (*travel agency*). Tienes unos clientes que quieren visitar un país hispanohablante. Escoge uno de los países que estudiamos y recomienda el país en por lo menos **seis** oraciones.

6•29 Mi país favorito

Describe tu país favorito entre los que hemos estudiado (*we have studied*). En por lo menos **ocho** oraciones explica por qué te gusta y lo que encuentras interesante e impresionante de ese país.

6•30 Compáralos

Escoge dos países que estudiamos y escribe las diferencias y semejanzas *(similarities)* entre los dos.

MODELO *México es un país grande en Norteamérica y Nicaragua es pequeño y está en Centroamérica.*

Y por fin, ¿cómo andas?

Having completed this chapter, I now can…

	Feel Confident	Need to Review
Comunicación		
• describe my family and other families	❑	❑
• talk about my school and relate information about my university campus	❑	❑
• state which homes I like and dislike	❑	❑
• tell what I and others need to do (**tener + que / hay que**)	❑	❑
• share information about what will take place in the future	❑	❑
• discuss some service opportunities in my community	❑	❑
Cultura		
• share information about Mexico, Spain, Honduras, Guatemala, El Salvador, Nicaragua, Costa Rica, and Panama, as well as Hispanics in the United States	❑	❑
• compare and contrast the countries I learned about in **Capítulos 1–5**	❑	❑

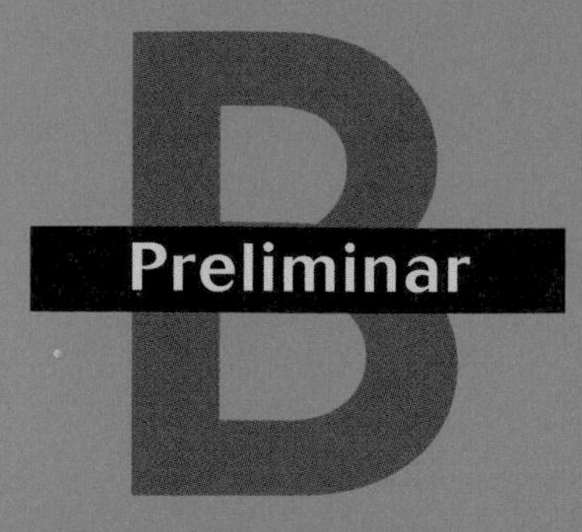

Introducciones y repasos

OBJETIVOS

Comunicación

- To greet, take leave of, and introduce others
- To describe yourself and others
- To talk about your school and your life as a student
- To share information about the sports and pastimes you and your friends like and dislike
- To describe your home and household chores
- To relate information about your home and/or university town
- To tell what you and others need to do
- To share information about what will take place in the future
- To discuss some service opportunities in your community
- To discuss different types of music, movies, and television programs, including your personal preferences

Ambiciones siniestras

- To describe what has happened thus far to the protagonists: Alejandra, Manolo, Cisco, Eduardo, Marisol, and Lupe
- To hypothesize about what you think will happen next

This chapter is a review of vocabulary and grammatical concepts that you are already familiar with in Spanish. Some of you are continuing with *¡Anda!* while others may be coming from a different program. As you begin the second half of *¡Anda!,* it is important for all students to feel confident about what they already know about the Spanish language as they continue to acquire knowledge and proficiency. This chapter will help you determine what you already know, and also help you focus on what you personally need to improve upon.

If you are new to *¡Anda!,* you will want to review not only the grammar concepts already introduced, but also familiarize yourself with the active vocabulary used in the textbook. *¡Anda!* recycles vocabulary and grammar concepts frequently to help you learn better, and this chapter will help you with what we consider to be the basics of the preceding chapters.

For all students, this chapter also reviews what has occurred to date in the thrilling episodic adventure, **Ambiciones siniestras.** Students who haven't seen the first episodes will have an

opportunity to do so. The episodes in the text and the video build upon each other, just like a **telenovela,** and starting in **Capítulo 7,** will continue from where the episode in **Capítulo 5** left off. **Capítulo 6** is a recycling chapter and no new episodes for **Ambiciones siniestras** were introduced.

Before you begin this chapter, you may wish to review the study and learning strategies on page 206 in **Capítulo 6.** These strategies are applicable to your other subjects as well. So on your mark, get set, let's review!

Comunicación

• Capítulo Preliminar A •

B-1

1. Para empezar. This chapter provided an introduction to Spanish via the following topics: greetings and farewells; classroom expressions; the alphabet; cognates; subject pronouns and the verb **ser**; adjectives of nationality; numbers 1–30; telling time; days and months; the weather; and the verb **gustar.** If you need to review any of these topics before proceeding, consult pages 4–25.

• Capítulo 1 •

B-2

2. La familia. Review the **La familia** vocabulary on page 32 and then do the following activities.

Estrategia

In **B-1**, you are directed to write at least five sentences. See how many more than five you can write in the time allotted.

B•1 Mi familia

Túrnense para describir a sus familias o a una de las familias de las fotos. Digan por lo menos **cinco** oraciones.

MODELO *George es mi tío. Mis primos son Stacy y Scott. …*

B-3

3. El verbo *tener*. Review the verb **tener** on page 35. What are all of the present tense forms of **tener**?

B•2 Y mis amigos...

Túrnense para hablar de sus familias y de la familia de uno de sus amigos usando el verbo **tener.** Digan por lo menos **ocho** oraciones.

MODELO *Tengo un hermano. Mi amigo, Joe, tiene dos hermanos. Mis amigas, Jennifer y Marty, no tienen abuelos. ...*

B-4

4. El singular y el plural. Review how to make singular nouns plural on page 37 and explain the rules to your partner. Then complete the following activity.

B•3 Te toca a ti

Digan el plural de estas palabras.

MODELO E1: primo
E2: *primos*

Fíjate

The rules for accents are listed in *Capítulo 2,* p. 63. Some words keep their accent marks in the plural while other words lose theirs in the plural.

1. madre
2. francés
3. taxi
4. nieto
5. abuela
6. joven

B-5

5. El masculino y el femenino. Review the differences between masculine and feminine nouns on page 38. State the rules to a partner, and then do the following activity.

B•4 ¿Recuerdas?

Digan si las siguientes palabras son masculinas o femeninas. **¡OJO!** Hay unas excepciones.

Fíjate

Some words that end in a consonant, like *profesor,* also have a feminine form, *profesora.* Pay attention to the form when making the noun plural, as in the case of *profesores* or *profesoras.*

MODELO E1: tía
E2: *femenina*

1. padrastros
2. televisión
3. foto
4. universidad
5. hermano
6. mano
7. tía
8. hijo

B-6

6. Los artículos definidos e indefinidos. How do you say *the* and *some* in Spanish? For a reminder, see page 39. Then do the following activity.

Túrnense para añadir el equivalente de *"the"* y *"a"* o *"some"* a estas palabras.

MODELO E1: tías

E2: *las tías/unas tías*

1. padrastro	3. madre	5. hijos	7. nieto
2. hermanas	4. tío	6. primas	8. padres

B-7 to B-8

7. Los adjetivos posesivos y descriptivos. How do you say *my, your, his, her, our,* and *their?* If you need help, see page 42. Also consult pages 44–45 to review words you may use to describe yourself and others. Then do the following activity.

B•6 Nuestras familias

Túrnense para hablar de y describir a su familia o a las familias de sus amigos. Digan por lo menos **ocho** oraciones.

MODELO *Mis padres son trabajadores. La mamá de mi amigo John es trabajadora. Nuestros primos son simpáticos. …*

Fíjate

When you see the (ii) by the activity number, you work with a partner. Words in the direction lines like *miren, túrnense, comparen,* and *usen* are plural—they refer to both of you.

• Capítulo 2 •

B-9 to B-10

8. Las materias y las especialidades. Review the **Las materias y las especialidades** vocabulary on page 62 of **Capítulo 2.** Then practice the vocabulary words with the following activity.

B•7 ¿Cuál es más fácil?

Expresa tu opinión sobre las materias y las especialidades. Comparte tus respuestas con un/a compañero/a. Puedes consultar **También se dice...** en el Apéndice 3.

MODELO *Las especialidades más difíciles son las matemáticas y los negocios. Las especialidades más fáciles son…*

Vocabulario útil

difícil	*difficult*
fácil	*easy*
aburrido/a	*boring*

Estrategia

For actividad **B-7** about *Las materias y las especialidades,* change partners and find someone whose major is different than yours. See if you have the same opinions.

LAS ESPECIALIDADES…				
MÁS DIFÍCILES	MÁS FÁCILES	MÁS CREATIVAS	MÁS INTERESANTES	MÁS ABURRIDAS
1.	1.	1.	1.	1.
2.	2.	2.	2.	2.

B-11

9. La sala de clase. Review the **La sala de clase** vocabulary on page 66 and then do the following activity.

B-8 ¿Qué tienen tus compañeros/as?

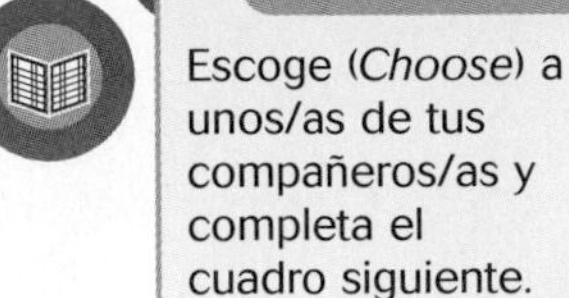

Escoge (*Choose*) a unos/as de tus compañeros/as y completa el cuadro siguiente.

MODELO ESTUDIANTE 1: *Sarah*

1. *Sarah tiene dos cuadernos, un libro, un bolígrafo y dos lápices.*
2. *¡Sarah no tiene la tarea!*
3. …

Estrategia

For actividad **B-8**, you and your partner may wish to ask other classmates questions such as: *¿Qué tienes en tu mochila? ¿Qué tienes en tu escritorio?*

ESTUDIANTE 1 *Sarah*	ESTUDIANTES 2 Y 3 _____	TÚ Y YO _____
(no) tiene	**(no) tienen**	**(no) tenemos**
1. *tiene dos cuadernos*	1.	1.
2. *tiene un libro*	2.	2.
3. *tiene un bolígrafo*	3.	3.
4. *tiene dos lápices*	4.	4.
5. *no tiene la tarea*	5.	5.

B-12 to B-13

10. Presente indicativo de verbos regulares. How do you form the *present tense* of *regular* **-ar, -er, -ir** *verbs*? If you need help, consult pages 68–69. Finally, before you complete the following activities, review the common verbs that are presented on the same page.

B-9 ¿A quién o quiénes conoces que…?

Túrnense para preguntarse y contestar para qué personas que ustedes conocen son ciertas (*true*) o falsas las siguientes afirmaciones.

Estrategia

You will notice that nearly all activities in *¡Anda!* are pair activities. You will be encouraged or required to change partners frequently, perhaps even daily. The purpose is for you to be able to practice Spanish with a wide array of speakers. Working with different classmates will help you to improve your spoken Spanish more quickly.

MODELO hablar poco

E1: *¿Quién habla poco?*

E2: *Mi hermano, Tom, habla poco.*

E2: *¿Quiénes hablan poco?*

E1: *Mis padres hablan poco. / Mis hermanos y yo hablamos poco.*

1. hablar demasiado
2. correr mucho
3. vivir lejos
4. escribir muchos e-mails
5. usar los apuntes de sus amigos
6. estudiar mucho
7. necesitar estudiar más
8. tomar un examen hoy
9. enseñar español

B-10 Dime quién, dónde y cuándo

Miren el dibujo y creen juntos una historia.

MODELO E1: *Josefina le escribe una carta a su novio.*
E2: *Ella escribe cartas todos los días.*
E1: *En otro apartamento Raúl y Mariela…*

Estrategia

¡Anda! encourages you to be creative when practicing and using Spanish. One way is to create mini-stories about photos or drawings that you see. Being creative includes giving individuals in drawings names and characteristics.

B-14 to B-15

11. La formación de preguntas y las palabras interrogativas. How do you form questions in Spanish? What are the question words in Spanish? To review this topic, consult pages 71–72 and then do the following activity.

Fíjate

Remember that all question words have accents. Also remember that when writing a question, there are two question marks, one at the beginning and one at the end of the question.

B-11 Preguntas y más preguntas

Túrnense para formar una pregunta con cada oración.

MODELO E1: Estudio **matemáticas.**
E2: *¿Qué estudias?*

1. Pilar estudia **en la biblioteca.**
2. **Guillermo y yo** estudiamos.
3. Comen **entre las 7:00 y las 8:00 de la noche.**
4. Aprendemos español **fácilmente.**
5. Leo **tres libros.**
6. Estudiamos español **porque nos gusta el profesor.**

B-16

12. Los números 1–1.000. Review the numbers 1–1,000, consulting pages 16, 48, and 74 if you need help. Then do the following activity.

Túrnense para decir los precios de los artículos en el catálogo.

MODELO E1: (325 €) *El precio es trescientos veinticinco euros.*
E2: (999 €) *El precio es…*

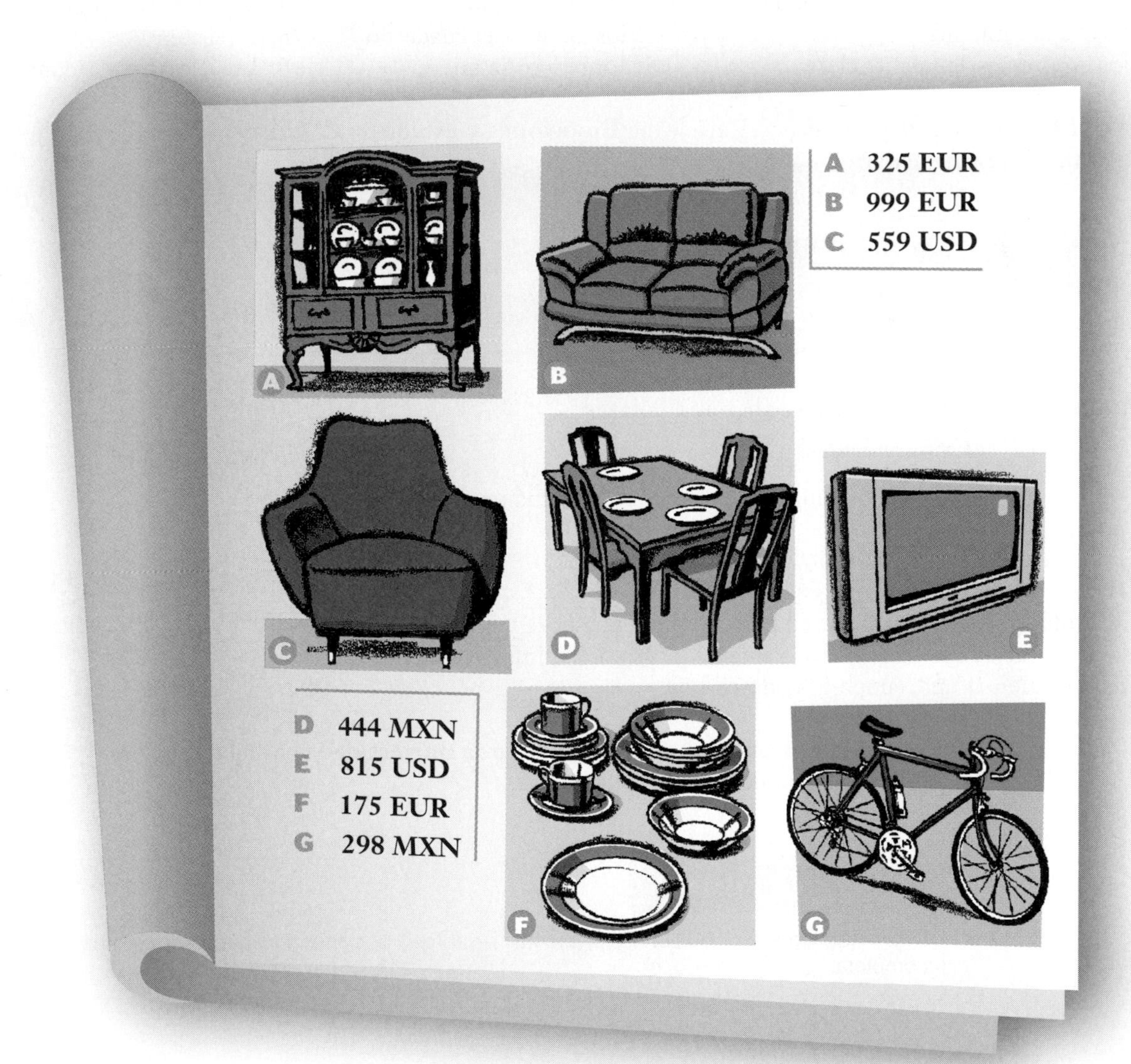

B-17

13. El verbo *estar*. What are the present tense forms of **estar**? When do you use **estar**? Check pages 78–79 if you need help before doing the following activity.

B•13 ¿Cómo se dice?

Túrnense para hacerse preguntas y responder usando **estar.**

MODELO el mapa/libro

E1: *¿Dónde está el mapa?*

E2: *El mapa está en el libro.*

Fíjate

Remember that four forms of *estar* have accents in the present tense: *estás, está, estáis,* and *están.*

1. mis amigos y yo/la clase de ciencias
2. tú/el apartamento
3. los escritorios/la sala de clase
4. el papel/la silla
5. los apuntes/el cuaderno
6. Jorge y tú/la puerta
7. los libros/la mochila
8. José/bien
9. Lupe y Mariela/contenta

B-18

14. Emociones y estados. Review the **Emociones y estados** vocabulary on page 81 and then do the following activity.

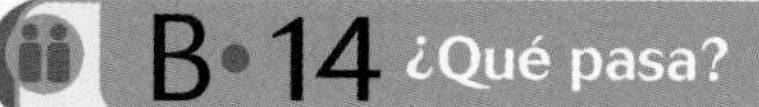

B•14 ¿Qué pasa?

Digan qué adjetivo describe las siguientes situaciones.

MODELO E1: Jorge y María reciben mil dólares.

E2: *Están contentos.*

1. Esperas y esperas pero tu amigo no llega (¡y no te llama por teléfono!).
2. Corres quince millas (*miles*).
3. Tus padres están en el hospital.
4. Tu novio/a está en Panamá y ¡no regresa!
5. El profesor de literatura lee sin parar durante una hora y quince minutos.
6. Ustedes sacan una "A" en sus exámenes de español e informática.
7. Ustedes tienen un examen muy difícil hoy.

Fíjate

In **B-14** you see *sus exámenes de español e informática.* The word ***y*** changes to ***e*** when the ***i*** sound appears immediately after the ***y,*** as in the case of the word *informática.*

B-19

15. En la universidad. Review the **En la universidad** vocabulary on page 76 and do the following activity.

B•15 ¡Lo sé!

Digan qué lugar asocian con las siguientes palabras y acciones. Después formen una oración completa.

MODELO estudiar

E1: *Voy a la biblioteca para estudiar.*

E2: *Estudio en mi apartamento.*

1. fútbol
2. comprar libros
3. hamburguesas, pizza, café, etc.
4. básquetbol
5. experimentos científicos
6. leer libros, estudiar, escribir composiciones, etc.

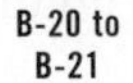

B-20 to B-21

16. El verbo *gustar*. How do you say *to like* in Spanish? Review page 82 and then do the following activity.

Estrategia

With actividad **B-16**, ask each other: *¿Qué materias te gustan? ¿Qué escritores te gustan? ¿Qué películas te gustan?*

B-16 Opiniones

Compara tu opinión con la de otros/as dos compañeros/as e informa después a la clase.

MODELO E1: *Las materias que más me gustan son las ciencias y las matemáticas. La escritora que más me gusta es J.K. Rowling…*

E2: *Las materias que más le gustan a David son las ciencias y las matemáticas. La escritora que más le gusta es J.K. Rowling…*

LAS MATERIAS…	LOS/AS ESCRITORES/AS…	LAS PELÍCULAS (*MOVIES*)…
que más me gustan son:	que más me gustan son:	que más me gustan son:
1.	1.	1.
que menos me gustan son:	que menos me gustan son:	que menos me gustan son:
1.	1.	1.

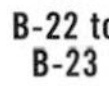

B-22 to B-23

17. Los deportes y los pasatiempos. Review the **Los deportes y los pasatiempos** vocabulary on pages 83–84 and then do the following activity.

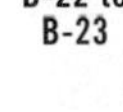

B-17 Tus preferencias

Selecciona los **tres** deportes o pasatiempos **que más te gustan** y luego los tres **que menos te gustan.** Después de completar el cuadro, comparte la información con un/a compañero/a, según el modelo.

MODELO *Los deportes o pasatiempos que más me gustan son patinar, bailar y leer. Los deportes o pasatiempos que menos me gustan son el fútbol, el fútbol americano y nadar.*

LOS DEPORTES Y PASATIEMPOS QUE MÁS ME GUSTAN	LOS DEPORTES Y PASATIEMPOS QUE MENOS ME GUSTAN
1.	1.
2.	2.
3.	3.

Capítulo 3

B-24 to B-25

18. La casa. Review the vocabulary about **La casa** on page 100 and do the following activities.

B•18 Las actividades

Túrnense para decir en qué parte o partes de la casa hacen estas actividades.

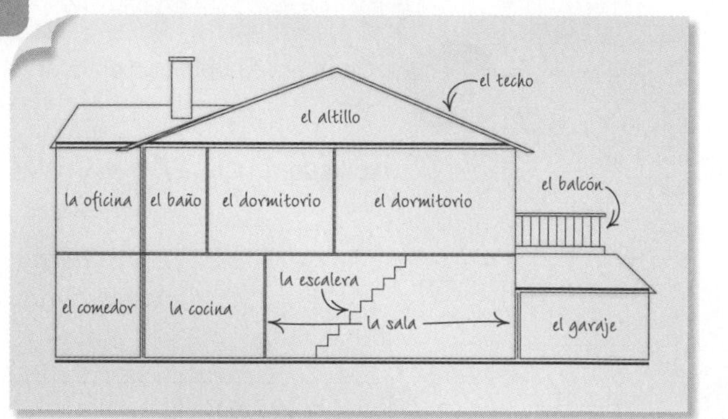

MODELO E1: estudiar
E2: *Estudio en la oficina y también en el dormitorio y en la cocina.*

1. escuchar música y ver la televisión
2. organizar papeles
3. echar una siesta (*take a nap*)
4. preparar tacos
5. tocar el piano
6. hablar por teléfono
7. tomar el sol
8. trabajar en la computadora

B•19 ¿Y tu casa...?

Descríbele tu casa o apartamento a un/a compañero/a. O si quieres, puedes describir tu casa ideal. Usa por lo menos **ocho** oraciones.

MODELO *Mi casa tiene dos pisos. Mi dormitorio está en la planta baja. No tenemos un altillo. Mi dormitorio está al lado del baño. La cocina es pequeña. ...*

B-26 to B-27

19. Algunos verbos irregulares. Review the irregular verbs on pages 104–105 and then practice them with the following activities.

B•20 Otras combinaciones

Túrnense para formar oraciones completas combinando elementos de las tres columnas. Formen una oración distinta con cada verbo de la columna B.

MODELO *Nosotros hacemos la tarea todos los días.*

COLUMNA A	COLUMNA B	COLUMNA C
Uds.	(no) hacer	estudiar ciencias
el profesor	(no) oír	a clase tarde
él, ella, Ud.	(no) querer	la tarea todos los días
nosotros/as	(no) salir	mis libros a clase
ellos/ellas	(no) traer	temprano de la universidad
yo	(no) venir	los viernes
tú		con mis abuelos los domingos
mamá y papá		ruidos (*noises*) por la noche

B•21 Entrevista

Túrnense para hacerse la siguiente entrevista.

1. ¿Practicas algún deporte?
2. ¿Haces ejercicio todos los días?
3. ¿Qué te dice tu mamá siempre? (Mi mamá me dice…)
4. ¿Siempre traes todo lo que necesitas a tus clases?
5. ¿Sales los fines de semana? ¿Con quién o quiénes sales?
6. ¿Qué quieres ser (o hacer) en el futuro?
7. ¿Conoces a una persona famosa?
8. ¿Qué pones en tu mochila los lunes? ¿Los martes?
9. ¿Vienes a la clase de español todos los días?
10. ¿A qué hora sales para la clase?

Estrategia

Getting to know your classmates helps you build confidence. It is much easier to interact with someone you know.

B-28

20. Hay. What does **hay** mean? Review page 122 if you need help. Then do the following activity.

B•22 ¿Qué hay en tu casa?

Descríbele tu casa a un/a compañero/a y averigua (*find out*) cómo es la suya (*his/hers*) usando **hay**.

Fíjate

Remember that you can form questions by adding question marks to the statement or inverting the order of the subject and the verb.

MODELO E1: *En mi casa hay un garaje. ¿Hay un garaje en tu casa?*
E2: *Sí, en mi casa hay un garaje. / No, en mi casa no hay un garaje.*
E1: *Mi casa tiene dos pisos. ¿Cuántos pisos hay en tu casa?*

B-29 to B-30

21. Los muebles y otros objetos de la casa. Review the **Los muebles y otros objetos de la casa** vocabulary on page 109. Then do the following activity.

B•23 En mi casa

¿Qué muebles y objetos tienes en casa? Descríbele los siguientes cuartos a un/a compañero/a y averigua qué tiene él/ella.

sala comedor cocina baño dormitorio garaje

MODELO E1: *Yo tengo una cama y dos sillas en mi dormitorio. ¿Qué tienes tú?*
E2: *Yo tengo un cuadro, una lámpara y un televisor.*

B-31 to B-33

22. Los quehaceres de la casa y los colores. Review the vocabulary dealing with **Los quehaceres de la casa** and **Los colores** on pages 112 and 115. Then, do the following activities.

B•24 Responsabilidades

¿Cuáles son tus responsabilidades? Túrnense para contestar las siguientes preguntas y explicar cuándo hacen estas tareas y cuánto tiempo dedican a hacerlas.

MODELO E1: mi dormitorio

E2: *Tengo que limpiar y arreglar mi dormitorio el lunes. Necesito dos horas porque está muy sucio.*

1. mi dormitorio
2. el baño
3. la cocina
4. la sala
5. el garaje
6. el comedor

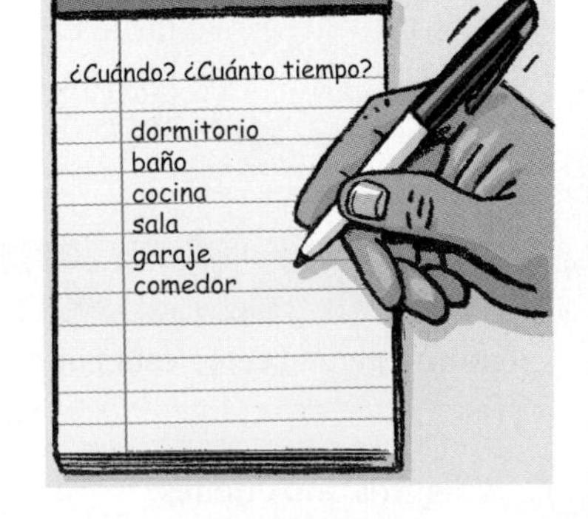

Estrategia

Group the rooms of the house with the verbs associated with each room. For example, match *comer* and *el comedor*, *bañarse* and *el baño*, *dormir* and *el dormitorio*, *cocinar* and *la cocina*.

¿QUÉ TIENES QUE HACER?	¿CUÁNDO?	¿CUÁNTO TIEMPO?
limpiar y arreglar mi dormitorio	*el lunes*	*dos horas*

B•25 La casa ideal

¿Cómo es tu casa ideal? ¿Y los colores? Descríbele tu casa ideal a un/a compañero/a usando las palabras siguientes en por lo menos **ocho** oraciones.

MODELO *Quiero una casa con una cocina amarilla. ...*

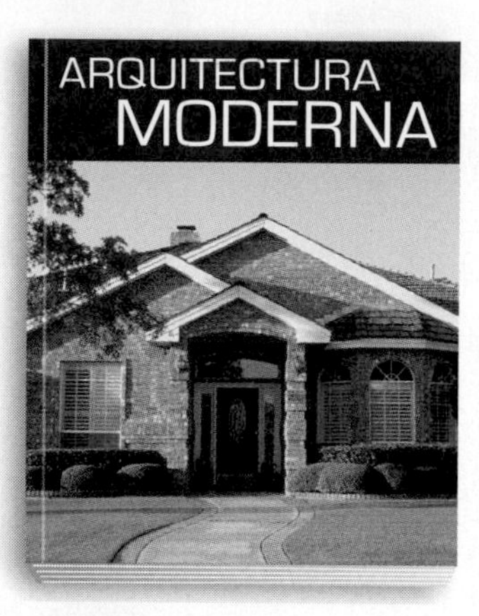

B-34

23. Unas expresiones con *tener*. Review the **tener** expressions on page 117 and then do the following activities.

B•26 ¿Qué tengo yo?

Túrnense para expresar cómo se sienten (*you feel*) en estas situaciones. Usen las expresiones con **tener.**

MODELO E1: antes de comer

E2: *Antes de comer tengo hambre.*

1. los lunes
2. los viernes
3. tarde en la noche
4. temprano en la mañana
5. antes de tener un examen
6. cuando ves una película de terror
7. en el verano
8. en el invierno
9. durante (*during*) la semana de los exámenes finales
10. cuando sacas una "A" en un examen

B•27 Datos personales

Túrnense para hacerse esta entrevista.

1. ¿Cuántos años tienes?
2. ¿Cuándo tienes hambre?
3. ¿Qué tienes que hacer hoy?
4. ¿Qué tienes ganas de hacer?
5. ¿En qué clase tienes sueño?
6. ¿En qué clase tienes mucha suerte?
7. ¿Siempre tienes razón?
8. ¿Cuándo tienes sueño?
9. Cuando tienes sed, ¿qué tomas?

B-35

24. Los números 1.000–100.000.000. Review the numbers on page 120 and then do the following activity.

B•28 ¿Cuál es su población?

Túrnense para leer las poblaciones de las siguientes capitales del mundo hispano en voz alta.

1. Buenos Aires, Argentina 12.000.000
2. La Paz, Bolivia 713.400
3. Bogotá, Colombia 1.945.488
4. La Habana, Cuba 2.241.000
5. San José, Costa Rica 315.909
6. México, D.F., México 18.731.000

• Capítulo 4 •

B-36

25. Los lugares. Review the **Los lugares** vocabulary on page 136 and then do the following activity.

B•29 ¿Dónde está?

Tus amigos y tú están muy ocupados. Túrnate con un/a compañero/a para decir dónde están.

MODELO E1: Uno de mis amigos quiere mandar una carta.

E2: *Está en la oficina de correos.*

1. Marta quiere leer y necesita comprar un libro.
2. Dos de mis amigos necesitan dinero.
3. Julio tiene hambre y quiere comer algo (*something*).
4. Queremos ver una exposición de arte.
5. Ustedes quieren ver una película.
6. Jorge tiene sed y quiere tomar algo.
7. Vamos a jugar al golf.
8. Tienen que ir a una boda (*wedding*).

B-37 to B-38

26. *Saber* y *conocer* and the personal *a*. Make a list of when you use **saber** and when you use **conocer.** You can review the uses on page 140. Then do the following activity.

B-30 ¿Lo sabes o lo conoces?

Completa las siguientes preguntas usando **sabes** o **conoces.** Después, túrnate con un/a compañero/a para hacerse y contestar las siguientes preguntas.

MODELO E1: *¿Conoces Buenos Aires?*
E2: *Sí, conozco Buenos Aires. / No, no conozco Buenos Aires.*

1. ¿__________ un buen lugar para comprar una televisión?
2. ¿__________ preparar tortillas?
3. ¿__________ cuál es el mejor café de esta ciudad?
4. ¿__________ San Juan, Puerto Rico?
5. ¿__________ jugar al ráquetbol?
6. ¿__________ dónde están tus amigos ahora?
7. ¿__________ usar una computadora?
8. ¿__________ al presidente de los Estados Unidos?
9. ¿__________ el mejor restaurante chino de nuestra ciudad?
10. ¿__________ las películas de Will Smith?

Fíjate

For more information about the personal **a**, consult *Capítulo 5*, page 191.

B-39 to B-40

27. ¿Qué tienen que hacer? What does **tener que + infinitivo** mean? Review page 142 if you have any questions before doing this activity.

B-31 Entrevistas

¿Hacen tus compañeros/as cosas similares?

Paso 1 Usando las siguientes preguntas, entrevista a tres compañeros/as.

1. ¿Cuáles son las cosas que haces para prepararte (*prepare yourself*) bien para tus clases?
2. Generalmente, ¿qué tienes que hacer después de terminar con tus clases?

Paso 2 Comparte la información con otros compañeros/as de la clase. ¿Qué tienen ustedes en común?

MODELO *Para prepararse bien para las clases Jack y Sally tienen que estudiar cinco horas cada día. Sally tiene que ir a la biblioteca. Jack tiene que organizar sus apuntes. Después de terminar nuestras clases, nosotros tenemos que limpiar nuestros apartamentos. …*

B-41 to B-42

28. Los verbos con cambio de raíz. Review the stem-changing verbs on page 144 and then practice with the following activities.

B•32 ¿Quién es?

Digan a cuales personas conocen que hacen las siguientes actividades.

MODELO siempre perder la tarea

E1: *Mi novia Adriana siempre pierde la tarea.*

E2: *Mis primos siempre pierden la tarea.*

1. almorzar en Burger King a menudo
2. siempre entender al/a la profesor/a de español
3. jugar al fútbol muy bien
4. preferir dormir hasta el mediodía
5. volver a casa tarde a menudo
6. nunca tener dinero y siempre tener que pedirlo
7. nunca encontrar sus cosas
8. querer visitar Centroamérica
9. pensar que Santa Claus existe
10. nunca mentir

B•33 Un poco de mi vida

Listen as your partner answers the following questions. Then repeat the information back to your partner. How good a listener are you? How much did you remember?

Estrategia

Being an "active listener" is an important skill in any language. *Active listening* means that you have heard and understood what someone is saying. Being able to repeat what someone says helps you practice and perfect the skill of active listening.

1. ¿Qué clases tienes este semestre?
2. ¿A qué hora empieza tu clase preferida?
3. ¿Qué prefieres hacer si tienes tiempo entre (*between*) las clases?
4. ¿A qué hora vuelves a tu residencia/apartamento/casa?
5. ¿Qué coche tienes (o quieres tener)?
6. ¿Cuánto cuesta el coche nuevo?
7. ¿Cómo vienes a la universidad? (Por ejemplo, ¿vienes en coche?)
8. ¿Dónde prefieres vivir, en una residencia estudiantil, en un apartamento o en una casa?
9. ¿Dónde quieres vivir después de graduarte?
10. ¿Qué deporte prefieres?

B-43 to B-45

29. El verbo *ir* e *ir* + a + infinitivo. What are the present tense forms of **ir**? How do you express the future with **ir**? Consult pages 147 and 149 if you need to do so and then do the following activities.

B-34 ¡Vámonos!

Completa las oraciones según el modelo. Túrnate después con un/a compañero/a para decir adónde van sus parientes y sus amigos en las siguientes situaciones.

Estrategia

When you write sentences that require more than one verb, as in **B-34**, make sure that your verbs match your subject throughout the sentence.

MODELO E1: Cuando tengo que estudiar…

E2: *Cuando tengo que estudiar voy a la biblioteca.*

1. Cuando quiere comer, mi compañero de cuarto…
2. Cuando queremos hacer ejercicio, nosotros…
3. Cuando tienes ganas de bailar, tú…
4. Para almorzar muy bien, mis amigos…
5. En la primavera me gusta…
6. Cuando mi hermana quiere comprar música, ella…
7. Para ver una película, tú…
8. Cuando llueve, yo…
9. Cuando hace frío, mis padres…
10. En el verano prefiero…

B-35 Nuestra agenda

¿Qué van a hacer la semana que viene? Termina las siguientes oraciones con planes diferentes. Compara tus respuestas con las de un/a compañero/a.

lunes ____________________

martes ____________________

miércoles ____________________

jueves ____________________

viernes ____________________

sábado ____________________

domingo ____________________

MODELO E1: El lunes, yo…

E2: *El lunes voy a lavar mi coche.*

1. El lunes, yo…
2. El martes, la profesora…
3. El miércoles, mis amigos…
4. El jueves, tú y yo…
5. El viernes, mis primos…
6. El sábado, tú…
7. El domingo, mi madre…

B•36 Qué será, será...

¿Qué tiene el futuro para ti, tus amigos y tu familia? Hagan **cinco** predicciones de lo que va a ocurrir en el futuro y compartan sus respuestas.

MODELO *Mi primo va a ir a la Universidad Autónoma el año que viene. Nosotros vamos a estudiar mucho para sacar buenas notas. Mis padres van a trabajar en Baltimore. ...*

B-46

30. Trabajos y servicios voluntarios. Review the vocabulary **Trabajos y servicios voluntarios** on page 151 and then do the following activity.

B•37 Definiciones

Túrnense para leer las siguientes definiciones y decir a qué palabra o expresión corresponde cada una.

MODELO E1: personas que tienen muchos años

E2: *Las personas que tienen muchos años son los mayores.*

1. servir a las personas sin (*without*) recibir dinero a cambio (*in exchange*)
2. un lugar donde viven las personas mayores
3. acompañar a una persona a una cita (*appointment*) con el médico
4. dar un documento a las personas para obtener firmas
5. trabajar para un candidato político sin recibir dinero a cambio (*in exchange*)
6. una persona que trabaja con los niños en un campamento
7. un bote (*boat*) para una o dos personas
8. un tipo de arte que puedes crear de muchos materiales
9. una estructura portátil (no permanente) que se usa para dormir fuera de casa
10. un lugar adonde van los niños, generalmente en el verano, para hacer muchas actividades diferentes

B-47 to B-48

31. Las expresiones afirmativas y negativas. Review the affirmative and negative expressions on page 154 and then do the following activity.

B•38 El/La profesor/a ideal

Túrnense para decir si las siguientes características son ciertas o falsas en un profesor ideal.

MODELO Un/a profesor/a ideal... siempre da buenas notas.

E1: *A veces un profesor ideal da buenas notas.*

E2: *No, el profesor ideal no siempre da buenas notas. A veces tiene que dar malas notas.*

Un/a profesor/a ideal...

1. nunca falta (*misses*) a una clase.
2. prepara algo interesante para cada clase.
3. siempre prefiere leer sus apuntes.
4. piensa que sabe más que nadie.
5. a veces organiza a sus estudiantes en grupos para discutir (*discuss*) ideas.
6. a veces llega a clase cinco minutos tarde.
7. jamás manda (da) tarea para la clase.
8. no pierde nada—por ejemplo la tarea, los exámenes, los trabajos escritos (*papers*), etc.
9. no habla con nadie después de la clase.
10. siempre está contento/a con su trabajo.

B-49

32. Un repaso de *ser* y *estar*. When do you use **ser** and **estar?** Write the reasons on a sheet of paper, and then check your list against the one on pages 156–157. Next, do the following activities.

B•39 ¿Qué tal?

Adriana le escribe un e-mail a su familia. Llenen los espacios en blanco con la forma correcta de **ser** o **estar** para conocerla (*to know her*) mejor.

Enviar | Enviar más tarde | Guardar | Añadir ficheros | Responder | Responder a todos | Firma | Contactos | Nombres de control | Imprimir

Para: Mamá
De: Adriana
Asunto: Saludos

tamaño medio

Querida familia:
¿Cómo (1) _____ todos? Yo (2) _____ muy bien, pero muy ocupada. La casa (3) _____ muy sucia y los niños (4) _____ enfermos. Raúl (5) _____ en Boston con su trabajo nuevo. Su oficina nueva (6) _____ en el centro. Yo (7) _____ muy orgullosa *(proud)* de él, pero ¿dónde (8) _____ cuando lo necesito? (9) _____ las dos de la tarde y (10) _____ cansada.

La próxima semana, los primos de Raúl van a venir a nuestra casa. Ellos (11) _____ de Los Ángeles. No los conozco pero Raúl me dice que (12) _____ simpáticos. Ahora ellos (13) _____ en Nueva York.

Bueno, ya (14) _____ tarde y me tengo que ir. Cuídense mucho *(Take care of yourselves)*.
Besos,
Adriana

B•40 Así es

Ahora expliquen por qué usaron (*you used*) **ser** o **estar** en la actividad **B-39.**

MODELO *están, physical condition*

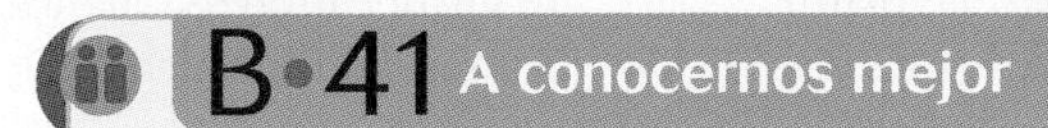

B•41 A conocernos mejor

Túrnense para hacerse y contestar las siguientes preguntas.

1. ¿De dónde eres?
2. ¿A qué hora son tus clases?
3. ¿Cómo es tu casa?
4. ¿Dónde está tu casa?
5. ¿Cómo es tu dormitorio?
6. ¿Dónde está tu dormitorio?
7. ¿De qué color es tu casa?
8. ¿Cuál es tu color favorito?
9. ¿Cómo es tu novio/a (esposo/a, amigo/a)?
10. ¿Dónde está él/ella ahora (*now*)?
11. ¿Cómo eres?
12. ¿Cómo estás hoy?

• Capítulo 5 •

B-50 to B-51

33. El mundo de la música. Review the **El mundo de la música** vocabulary on page 172 and then do the following activities.

B•42 ¿Qué quiere decir?

Lee las siguientes descripciones. Después, túrnate con un/a compañero/a para decir a qué palabra o expresión se refieren.

MODELO E1: dar conciertos en muchos lugares

E2: *Dar conciertos en muchos lugares es "hacer una gira".*

1. ser muy popular y conocido entre muchas personas
2. las palabras que cantas en una canción
3. la música de Mozart y Beethoven, por ejemplo
4. una persona que canta
5. lo que usas para cantar y hablar
6. un instrumento de percusión
7. sinónimo de grupo
8. hacer sonido bonito con un instrumento
9. cuando haces algo muy bien, dicen que tienes mucha _____

B•43 La música

Túrnense para hacerse esta entrevista.

1. ¿Cuál es tu grupo favorito?
2. ¿Cuál es tu cantante favorito?
3. ¿Cuál es tu instrumento favorito?
4. ¿Cuál es tu tipo de música favorito?
5. ¿Cuál es tu canción favorita?
6. ¿Sabes tocar un instrumento? ¿Cuál?
7. ¿Te gusta cantar? ¿Cuándo y dónde cantas?
8. ¿En qué tienes mucha habilidad o talento?

B-52

34. Los adjetivos y pronombres demostrativos. How do you say *this*, *that*, *these*, and *those* in Spanish? Review the demonstrative adjectives and pronouns on pages 176 and 178 and then do the following activities.

B•44 Comparando cosas

Tu mejor amigo/a te propone una cosa pero tú siempre prefieres otra. Túrnense para responder a sus comentarios usando una forma de **éste, ése** o **aquél.**

MODELO TU MEJOR AMIGO/A: ¿Quieres ir a este cine?
TÚ: *No, no quiero ir a éste. Quiero ir a aquél.*

1. ¿Vamos a ir a ese teatro?
2. ¿Tus hermanos tocan en aquel grupo?
3. ¿Quieres escuchar este CD?
3. ¿Piensan ustedes arreglar este cuarto para (*for*) la fiesta?
5. ¿Vas a comprar aquellas entradas?
6. ¿Entiendes la letra de esta canción?

B•45 En la universidad

Túrnense para hablar de lo que les gusta o no les gusta usando formas de **este, ese** y **aquel.** Hagan por lo menos **cinco** oraciones positivas y **cinco** oraciones negativas.

MODELO *Me gusta esta clase. Nuestro profesor de español es interesante, pero aquel profesor de sociología es un poco aburrido. Este libro es bueno pero ese libro de matemáticas es difícil. …*

B-53

35. Los adverbios. In Spanish, how do most adverbs end? How are they formed? Check page 180 to verify your answers. Then do the following activity.

B•46 ¿Qué ocurre en el concierto?

Vas a un concierto de varios conjuntos en el estadio de tu universidad. Para saber qué pasa, completa estas oraciones con los adverbios apropiados. Comparte tus respuestas con un/a compañero/a.

MODELO E1: Vamos al concierto (rápido, cuidadoso).

E2: *Vamos al concierto rápidamente.*

1. La gente espera a los conjuntos (paciente, lento).
2. El primer conjunto toca (triste, feliz).
3. Un grupo llega tarde y entra al estadio (seguro, nervioso).
4. Los otros músicos escuchan (cansado, atento).
5. De repente (*Suddenly*), empieza a llover (rápido, fuerte).
6. Terminan el concierto (inmediato, final).

B-54

36. El presente progresivo. How do you form the present progressive in Spanish (*I am _____ing, We are _____ing,* etc.)? Check your answer on page 182 and then do the following activity.

B•47 ¿Qué están haciendo?

Túrnense para decir qué están haciendo las siguientes personas.

MODELO E1: Son las siete y media de la mañana y mi papá está en su terraza.

E2: *Está tomando café.*

1. A mi hermano le gusta hacer ejercicio para comenzar su día.
2. A mi prima le gusta la música hispana y está en una tienda.
3. Esta noche mis abuelos llevan a unos amigos a una gran fiesta y su coche está muy sucio.
4. Nuestro/a profesor/a está en la computadora y resulta que tiene muchos mensajes de sus estudiantes.
5. Nuestros amigos quieren comer algo ligero (*light*) antes de ir a la fiesta.
6. Estamos con nuestros amigos en la fiesta y un grupo está tocando.

B-55

37. El mundo del cine. Review the **El mundo del cine** vocabulary on page 185 and practice it with the following activity.

B•48 En mi opinión

Termina las oraciones sobre las películas que tú has visto (*have seen*). Pueden ser películas viejas o nuevas, buenas o malas. Comparte tus respuestas con un/a compañero/a.

MODELO E1: La mejor película de terror...
E2: *La mejor película de terror es* Ring 2.

1. La mejor película de humor...
2. Una película épica pésima...
3. La película de misterio que más me gusta...
4. Mi actor/actriz favorito/a de las películas de acción...
5. La película animada más creativa...
6. La película más conmovedora...

B-56

38. Los números ordinales. How do you say *first, second, third,* etc. in Spanish? Check your answers on page 188 and then do the following activity.

B•49 Orden de preferencia

Asigna un orden de preferencia a las actividades de la lista: de la más importante (primero) a la menos importante (octavo). Luego compara tu lista con la de un/a compañero/a usando oraciones completas.

MODELO *Primero, me gusta ver una película de mi actor favorito Johnny Depp. Segundo, me gusta visitar a mis parientes...*

1. ir a un concierto de un grupo fabuloso ________
2. visitar a tus parientes ________
3. ver una película de tu actor/actriz favorito/a ________
4. leer una novela buena ________
5. ir a un partido de fútbol americano ________
6. estudiar para un examen ________
7. viajar a Venezuela ________
8. conocer al presidente de los Estados Unidos ________

B-57

39. ***Hay que* + infinitivo.** What does ***hay que*** **+ infinitivo** mean? Check your answer on page 189 and then do the following activity.

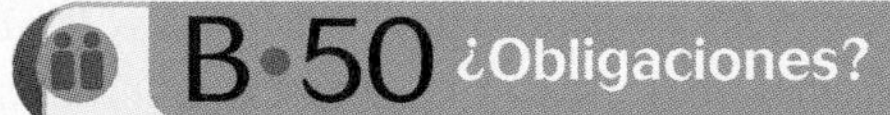

B•50 ¿Obligaciones?

Digan qué hay que hacer o cómo hay que ser para tener las siguientes profesiones.

MODELO un pintor
E1: *Hay que pintar mucho.*
E2: *Hay que ser muy creativo.*

1. novelista
2. cantante
3. músico/a
4. actriz
5. director/a de cine
6. político/a

B-58

40. Los pronombres de complemento directo. What is a *direct object*? What is a *direct object pronoun*? What are the direct object pronouns in Spanish? Where do you place direct object pronouns? Review pages 190–191 and then practice with the following activities.

B•51 ¿Estás listo/a?

¡Qué suerte! Vas al concierto del año en el anfiteatro Pine Park. Revisa la lista de preparativos con un/a compañero/a usando **lo, la, los** o **las.**

MODELO E1: ¿Tienes que comprar *las entradas* del concierto?
E2: *Sí, las tengo que comprar hoy. / Tengo que comprarlas hoy.*

1. ¿Vamos a preparar *una comida* (meal)?
2. ¿Vamos a invitar *a nuestros amigos*?
3. ¿Escuchan ellos *los CD del grupo*?
4. ¿Tengo que leer *la reseña* (review)?
5. ¿Vas a llevar *la cámara*?

B•52 ¿Hay deberes?

Siempre hay cosas que hacer. Usen **lo, la, los** o **las** para hablar de sus deberes.

MODELO ¿lavar los pisos todos los días?

E1: *Sí, tengo que lavarlos todos los días. /*

Sí, los tengo que lavar todos los días.

E2: *No, nunca los lavo. / No, los lavo los fines de semana.*

1. ¿sacudir los muebles?
2. ¿poner la mesa por la tarde?
3. ¿limpiar la cocina los sábados?
4. ¿preparar la comida todos los días?
5. ¿lavar los platos cada (*each*) día?
6. ¿hacer las camas por la mañana?
7. ¿guardar tus cosas?
8. ¿arreglar tu cuarto?

Episodio 6

B-59

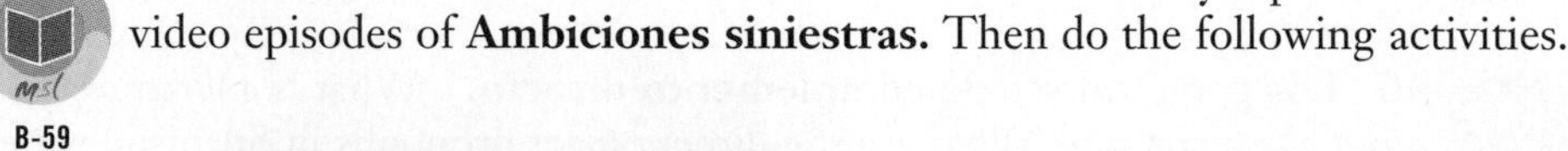

41. Ambiciones siniestras. Read and then view the synopsis of the first five text and video episodes of **Ambiciones siniestras.** Then do the following activities.

B•53 ¿Qué pasó?

Escribe un resumen de lo que ha pasado (*has happened*) en **Ambiciones siniestras.** Puedes describir a cada personaje o puedes escribir una síntesis de cada capítulo.

B•54 ¿Qué va a ocurrir?

Escribe un párrafo sobre lo que tú piensas que va a ocurrir en los próximos episodios de **Ambiciones siniestras.**

Estrategia

The *¿Cómo andas?* and *Y por fin, ¿cómo andas?* sections are designed to help you assess your understanding of specific concepts. In *Capítulo Preliminar B,* there is one opportunity for you to reflect on how well you understand the concepts. Beginning with *Capítulo 7* there will be three opportunities for you to stop and reflect on what you have learned. These checks help you become accountable for your own learning, and help you determine what you need to review. Also use the checklist as a way to communicate with your instructor about any concepts you still need to review. Additionally, you might also use your checklist as a way to study with a peer group or peer tutor. If you need to review a particular concept, more practice is available on your *¡Anda!* web site. There you will find quizzes online.

Y por fin, ¿cómo andas?

Having completed this chapter, I now can...

	Feel Confident	Need to Review
Comunicación		
• greet and take leave of others	❑	❑
• describe myself, my family, and my life as a student	❑	❑
• describe my house and jobs around the house	❑	❑
• talk about places in my community as well as community service opportunities	❑	❑
• relate my preferences for music and cinema	❑	❑
Ambiciones siniestras		
• narrate what has happened thus far to the protagonists in **Ambiciones siniestras** and hypothesize about what will happen in future episodes	❑	❑

Comer bien es un gran placer (*pleasure*). Dentro del mundo hispanohablante hay una tremenda variedad de comidas (*foods*) y la comida tiene una función social muy importante.

¡A comer!

	OBJETIVOS	CONTENIDOS
Comunicación	• To discuss your food preferences and compare them with those from the Spanish-speaking world • To talk and write about things you did and events that occurred in the past • To order some of your favorite foods in a restaurant • To combine listening strategies to maximize comprehension • To describe, in writing, a special day from your past	1 Food 252 2 Review of the direct object 257 3 The preterit tense 258 4 Food preparation 263 5 Irregular verbs in the preterit tense 266 6 In the restaurant 271 ☐ Pronunciación: The letters **r** and **rr** 253 ☐ Escucha: 274 Estrategia: Combining strategies ☐ Escribe: Relating a memory 275
Cultura	• To talk about eating habits and foods from different parts of the Hispanic world • To share important facts about this chapter's featured countries: Chile and Paraguay	☐ Meals in the Spanish-speaking world 256 ☐ Food in the Spanish-speaking world 265 ☐ *Chile* and *Paraguay* 276–277
Ambiciones siniestras	• To predict what will happen in a reading • To discover the voice-mail message that frightens Cisco • To determine who has received the riddle and what they have figured out so far	☐ Episodio 7 Lectura: *El rompecabezas* 278 Estrategia: Predicting Video: *¡Qué rico está el pisco!* 280

¡Buen provecho!

PREGUNTAS

1 ¿Cuáles son tus platos *(dishes)* favoritos?
2 ¿Hay alguna comida típica de la región donde vives tú? ¿Cuáles son algunas comidas típicas de los Estados Unidos?
3 ¿Qué platos de otras culturas te gustan?

Comunicación

- Talking about food
- Discussing past actions

VOCABULARIO 1 La comida

SAM 7-1 to 7-6

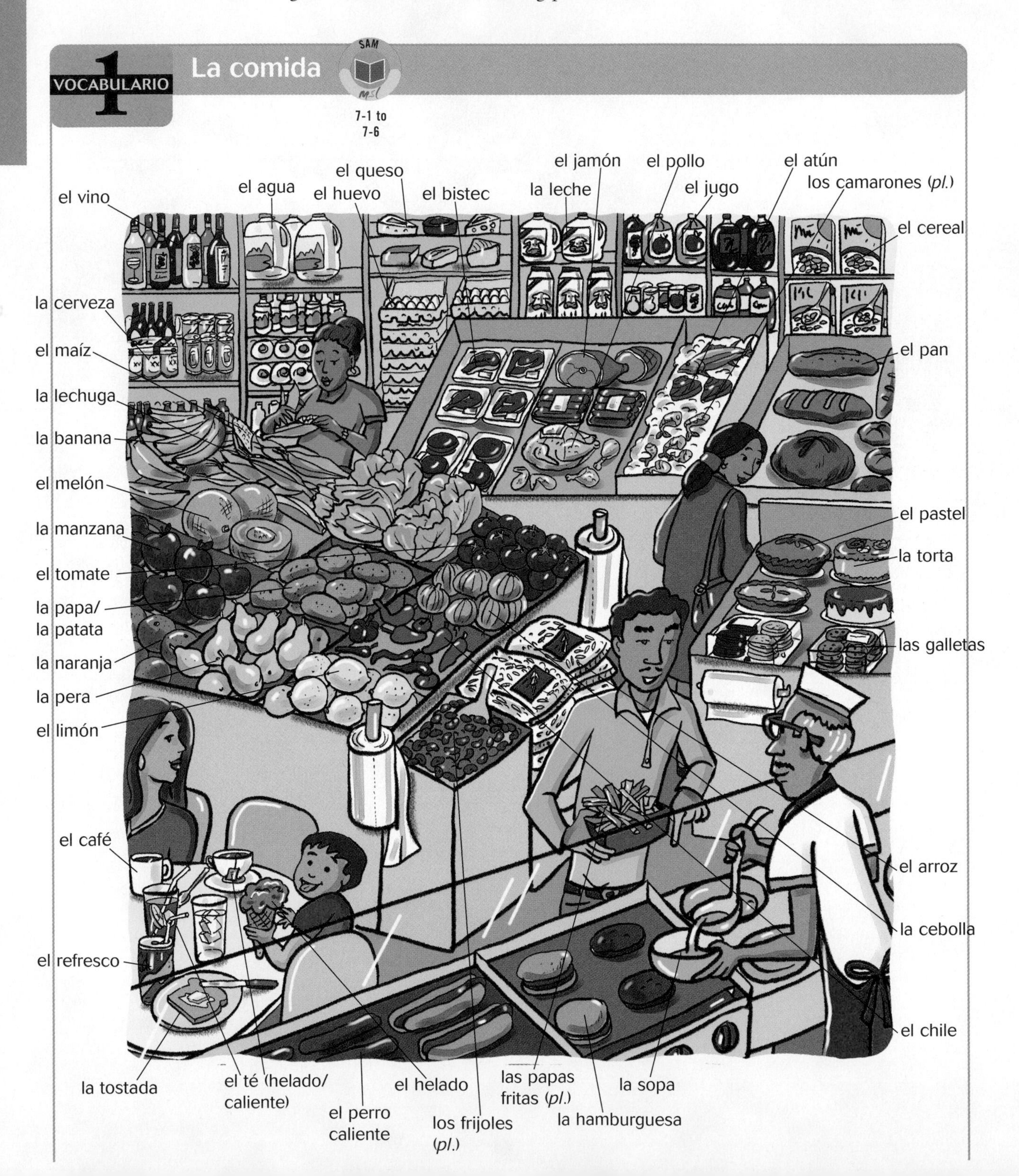

las aves	*poultry*
las bebidas	*beverages*
la carne	*meat*
la comida	*food; meal*
los dulces	*sweets*
la ensalada	*salad*
la fruta	*fruit*
el hielo	*ice*
los mariscos	*seafood*
el pescado	*fish*
el postre	*dessert*
la verdura	*vegetable*

Otras palabras útiles	*Other useful words*
el desayuno	*breakfast*
el almuerzo	*lunch*
la merienda	*snack*
la cena	*dinner*

Unos verbos	*Some verbs*
almorzar (ue)	*to have lunch*
beber	*to drink*
cenar	*to have dinner*
desayunar	*to have breakfast*
merendar (ie)	*to have a snack*

CD 3
Track 1

7-7 to
7-10

PRONUNCIACIÓN

The letters *r* and *rr*

1. In Spanish, the letter **r** at the beginning of a word, and the **rr** between vowels are *trilled* (or rolled). This sound is the equivalent to the trill in English when imitating a motor sound (*brrrrrr*).

   refresco   Rodríguez   arroz   perro caliente

2. All other **r** positions are pronounced with a *flap* of the tongue. The sound is similar to the English pronunciation of the *tt* in *Betty* or the *dd* in *ladder*.

   camarones   naranja   pera   torta

7•1 Las palabras

Pronounce the following words, paying special attention to the letters **r** and **rr.**

1. cerveza
2. merienda
3. frijoles
4. Ramón
5. rápidamente
6. refresco
7. guitarra
8. ritmo

7•2 Las oraciones

Pronounce the following sentences, paying special attention to the letters **r** and **rr.**

1. Rafael corre rápidamente.
2. Quiero arroz, camarones, un refresco y, de postre, una torta.
3. Me gustan las películas de guerra, humor, misterio y terror.

7•3 Dichos y trabalenguas

Now pronounce the following tongue twister and saying, focusing on the letters **r** and **rr.**

1. Erre con erre cigarro, erre con erre barril, rápido corre el ferrocarril.
2. Cuando una puerta se cierra dos mil se abren.

7•4 Concurso

Escoge **cinco** letras diferentes. Bajo cada letra escribe todas las palabras del vocabulario de **La comida** que recuerdes. Después, compara tu lista con la de un/a compañero/a.

MODELO

a	d	p
arroz	*desayuno*	*papas fritas*
agua	*dulce*	

Fíjate

Although *agua* and *ave* are feminine nouns, the masculine singular article *el* is used with them, as a way to separate and differentiate the similar stressed vowel sounds in each word (*la* and *a*). *Las* is used with the plurals of these words (*las aguas, las aves*). All adjectives describing these words are feminine.

7•5 ¡Ay, las calorías!

Túrnense para decir a qué comida corresponden las siguentes descripciones. Usen el cuadro de los valores nutritivos.

CUADRO DE LOS VALORES NUTRITIVOS

Comida	Calorías	Proteína	Grasa	Carbohidratos	Vitaminas
bistec	455	27	36	0	A, B
hamburguesa con queso	950	50	60	54	B
jugo de naranja	100	1	0	16	A, B, C
naranja	50	1	0	16	A, B, C
pan	150	6	2	38	B
papa	100	3	0	23	B, C
perro caliente	200	5	14	1	B, C
salmón	200	24	10	0	A, B
torta	455	4	13	76	A, B, C
lechuga	10	1	0	2	A, B, C

Capítulo Preliminar A. Los números 0–30, pág. 16; Capítulo 1. Los números 31–100, pág. 48; Capítulo 2. Los números 100–1.000, pág. 74.

Estrategia

¡Anda! has provided you with recycling references to help guide your continuous review of previously learned material. Make sure to consult the indicated pages if you need to refresh your memory about numbers.

MODELO E1: *Esta comida tiene mucha agua, es verde y tiene diez calorías.*

E2: *Es la lechuga.*

Esta comida tiene…

1. 60 gramos *(grams)* de grasa, 50 gramos de proteína y 950 calorías.
2. muchas proteínas, es un pescado y tiene 200 calorías.
3. vitamina C y 100 calorías. Es una verdura.
4. muchos carbohidratos y 150 calorías.
5. 27 gramos de proteína, es una carne y tiene 455 calorías.
6. 50 calorías y es una fruta.
7. 16 carbohidratos y es una bebida.
8. las vitaminas B y C, sólo un carbohidrato y 14 gramos de grasa.

7•6 La dieta de Nico

Paso 1 Nico es un estudiante universitario de Santiago de Chile. Mira lo que (*what*) come normalmente, a qué hora y compara la dieta de Nico con la tuya.

MODELO *Yo nunca tomo té para el desayuno. Generalmente desayuno más temprano que Nico.*

Vocabulario útil

más temprano que	*earlier than*
más tarde que	*later than*

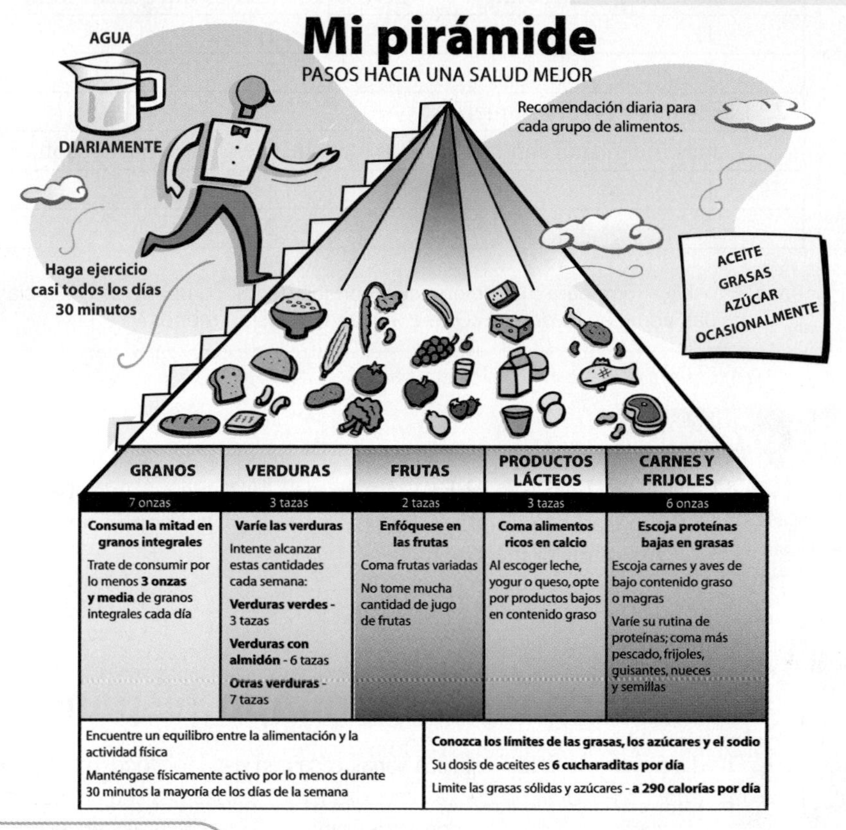

Fíjate

The word *galleta* means both *cookie* and *cracker*.

LA DIETA DE NICO

	DESAYUNO	ALMUERZO	MERIENDA	CENA
	8:30	12:00	5:30	8:00
DÍA 1:	té con galletas	ensalada, arroz con pollo, uvas	manzana	atún con una ensalada de lechuga con tomate y fruta
DÍA 2:	té y pan con mantequilla	sopa, tortilla de papas, flan	galletas	pan con mermelada

TU DIETA

	DESAYUNO	ALMUERZO	MERIENDA	CENA
DÍA 1:				
DÍA 2:				

Paso 2 Comparte tus conclusiones con un/a compañero/a.

Paso 3 Miren la pirámide de alimentación para determinar si todos los grupos están representados en sus dietas.

7•7 ¿Cuáles son tus preferencias?

Capítulo 2. El verbo *gustar*. pág. 82.

¿Qué comidas te gustan?

Paso 1 Completa el cuadro según tus preferencias.

Estrategia

You may want to talk about foods that are not included here. Refer to the *También se dice...* section in Appendix 3 for additional vocabulary.

1. Las carnes, las aves, el pescado y los mariscos que...	
a. más me gustan son...	b. menos me gustan son...
1.	1.
2.	2.
2. Las frutas y verduras que...	
a. más me gustan son...	b. menos me gustan son...
1.	1.
2.	2.

Paso 2 Ahora, compara tus preferencias con las de los compañeros de la clase: ¿cuáles son las comidas favoritas? ¿Qué comidas les gustan menos?

7•8 ¿Qué comes tú?

Entrevista a un/a compañero/a usando las siguientes preguntas.

1. ¿Comes bien o mal? Explica.
2. ¿Qué tipo de comida prefieres?
3. ¿Qué te gusta merendar?
4. ¿Qué comidas tienen vitaminas A y C?
5. ¿Qué comidas tienen mucha proteína?

SAM MSL 7-11 to 7-12

Las comidas en el mundo hispano

La palabra "comida" significa varias cosas en español: *food, meal* y *lunch (the main meal of the day).* Las comidas en los países hispanoamericanos son similares a las comidas norteamericanas pero también existen algunas diferencias. Por ejemplo, el desayuno en el mundo hispano normalmente consiste en café y pan o panes dulces. Generalmente es una comida ligera (*light*).

El almuerzo es normalmente la comida más grande y más fuerte del día. En lugares con una cultura más tradicional, el almuerzo puede empezar a eso de (*around*) las dos de la tarde. Los niños regresan de la escuela y el papá (y la mamá si trabaja fuera [*outside*] de la casa) comen juntos en casa. Entonces, hay tiempo para descansar (*to rest*) antes de volver al trabajo y a la escuela. En los países y las zonas con más industria y comercio puede haber un horario de almuerzo similar al horario de los Estados Unidos.

La cena generalmente es una comida más ligera. La gente en los países hispanohablantes cena más tarde que la mayoría de los norteamericanos. ¡Algunos no cenan hasta las diez o las once de la noche!

Preguntas

1. ¿Cómo es un desayuno típico en el mundo hispano? ¿un almuerzo? ¿una cena?
2. ¿Cuál es el horario de las comidas en los países hispanos?

Repaso del complemento directo

7-13 to 7-16 19, 20

In **Capítulo 5** you learned to use direct object pronouns in Spanish. Return to pages 190–191 for a quick review, then answer the following questions:

1. What are direct objects? What are direct object pronouns?
2. What are the pronouns (forms)? With what must they agree?
3. Where are direct object pronouns placed in a sentence?

Check your answers to the preceding questions in Appendix 1.

7•9 Las dietas

¿Piensas mucho en lo que *(what)* comes?

Paso 1 Subraya *(Underline)* los complementos directos en las siguientes preguntas. Compara tus respuestas con las de un/a compañero/a.

MODELO *¿Conoces la dieta Weight Watchers?*

Paso 2 Ahora contesten juntos las siguientes preguntas, usando los pronombres de complemento directo en sus respuestas.

MODELO E1: ¿Conoces la dieta Weight Watchers?
E2: *Sí, la conozco. / No, no la conozco.*

1. ¿Sigues la dieta South Beach?
2. ¿Prefieres los postres de chocolate?
3. ¿Sabes preparar bien el arroz?
4. ¿Comes muchas frutas diferentes?
5. ¿Preparas los huevos con queso?
6. ¿Lavas la lechuga bien antes de comerla?

7•10 Las buenas decisiones

Dile a tu compañero/a cómo te gusta tomar las siguientes comidas y bebidas y con qué frecuencia las tomas.

nunca algunas veces generalmente constantemente siempre

MODELO E1: la torta
E2: *La como con helado. La como algunas veces. / No la como nunca.*

1. el cereal
2. las tostadas
3. los tomates
4. las galletas
5. la cebolla
6. el café

El pretérito

7-17 to 7-23 35

Up to this point, you have been expressing ideas or actions that take place in the present and future. To talk about something you did or something that occurred in the past, you can use the **pretérito** (*preterit*). Below are the endings for regular verbs in the **pretérito.**

Los verbos regulares

Note the endings for regular verbs in the **pretérito** below and answer the questions that follow.

	-ar: comprar	**-er: comer**	**-ir: vivir**
yo	compré	comí	viví
tú	compraste	comiste	viviste
él, ella, Ud.	compró	comió	vivió
nosotros/as	compramos	comimos	vivimos
vosotros/as	comprasteis	comisteis	vivisteis
ellos/as, Uds.	compraron	comieron	vivieron

1. What do you notice about the endings for **-er** and **-ir** verbs?
2. Where are accent marks needed?

Check your answers to the preceding questions in Appendix 1.

Estrategia

Remember that there are two types of grammar presentations in *¡Anda!*:

1. You are given the grammar rule.
2. You are given guiding questions to help *you* construct the grammar rule, and state the rule in your own words.

—¿Dónde está el vino que **compré** ayer? *Where is the wine that I bought yesterday?*

—Mis primos se lo **bebieron** anoche. *My cousins drank it last night.*

—¿Ah, sí? ¿**Comieron** Uds. en casa? *Really? Did you all eat at home?*

—No, **comimos** en un restaurante chino. ¡**Terminaron** el vino antes de salir a cenar! *No, we ate at a Chinese restaurant. They finished the wine before we went out to dinner!*

Los verbos que terminan en *-car*, *-zar* y *-gar* y el verbo *leer*

Several verbs have small spelling changes in the preterit. Look at the charts below.

Fíjate

The *-ar* and *-er* stem-changing verbs in the present tense do not have stem changes in the preterit. There may be spelling changes, however, as with *empezar* and *jugar*.

tocar (c → qu)

yo	toqué
tú	tocaste
él, ella, Ud.	tocó
nosotros/as	tocamos
vosotros/as	tocasteis
ellos/as, Uds.	tocaron

* (**sacar** and **buscar** have the same spelling change)

empezar (z → c)

yo	empecé
tú	empezaste
él, ella, Ud.	empezó
nosotros/as	empezamos
vosotros/as	empezasteis
ellos/as, Uds.	empezaron

* (**comenzar** and **organizar** have the same spelling change)

jugar (g → gu)

yo	jugué
tú	jugaste
él, ella, Ud.	jugó
nosotros/as	jugamos
vosotros/as	jugasteis
ellos/as, Uds.	jugaron

* (**llegar** has the same spelling change)

leer (i → y)

yo	leí
tú	leíste
él, ella, Ud.	leyó
nosotros/as	leímos
vosotros/as	leísteis
ellos/as, Uds.	leyeron

* (**creer** and **oír** have the same spelling change)

—**Toqué** la trompeta por seis horas ayer porque tengo un concierto esta noche. *I played the trumpet for six hours yesterday because I have a concert tonight.*

—¿A qué hora **empezaste**? *At what time did you begin?*

—**Empecé** a las nueve. *I began at nine.*

—¿**Jugaron** tus hermanos al béisbol hoy? *Did your brothers play baseball today?*

—No, **leyeron** una novela para la clase de inglés. *No, they read a novel for English class.*

Some things to remember:

1. With verbs that end in **-car,** the **c** changes to **qu** in the **yo** form to preserve the sound of the hard **c** of the infinitive.
2. With verbs that end in **-zar,** the **z** changes to **c** before **e.**
3. With verbs that end in **-gar,** the **g** changes to **gu** to preserve the sound of the hard **g** (**g** before **e** or **i** sounds like the **j** sound in Spanish).
4. For **leer, creer,** and **oír,** change the **i** to **y** in the third-person singular and plural.

7•11 De la teoría a la práctica

Write six different infinitives on six small pieces of paper. Next, on six different small pieces of paper, write six different subject pronouns. Take turns selecting a paper from each pile and give the correct **pretérito** form of the verb. After several rounds, write six different verbs.

7•12 Creaciones

Paso 1 Combinen elementos de las tres columnas para escribir **ocho** oraciones que describan lo que hicieron estas personas.

MODELO Yolanda comprar un coche nuevo.
Yolanda compró un coche nuevo.

Yolanda	beber	el piano durante la cena
Ud.	limpiar	cuatro botellas de agua
los estudiantes	preparar	un coche nuevo
yo	buscar	dos hamburguesas con queso
mi mejor amigo y yo	leer	la cocina después del almuerzo
tú	tocar	una cena deliciosa
mis primos	comprar	el restaurante La Frontera
el/la profesor/a	comer	sobre el gran cocinero Emeril Lagasse

Paso 2 Túrnense para preguntarse cuándo occurrió cada actividad mencionada en **Paso 1.**

E1: *¿Cuándo compró Yolanda un coche nuevo?*
E2: *Compró un coche nuevo el año pasado./Lo compró el año pasado.*

Vocabulario útil

anoche	*last night*
anteayer	*the day before yesterday*
ayer	*yesterday*
el año pasado	*last year*
el fin de semana pasado	*last weekend*
el martes/viernes/domingo, etc. pasado	*last Tuesday/Friday/Sunday, etc.*
la semana pasada	*last week*

Fíjate

In the list of *Vocabulario útil*, note that for the words “last weekend” (*el fin de semana pasado*), the adjective *pasado* agrees with the masculine noun *el fin* and not *semana.* In contrast, for “last week” (*la semana pasada*), the word “last” agrees with the feminine noun *semana.*

7 • 13 Cocinero/a

Tu compañero/a y tú van a preparar un almuerzo especial para sus amigos. Para saber si todo está listo, túrnense para contestar las siguientes preguntas usando el pretérito y un pronombre de complemento directo (**lo, la, los, las**).

MODELO E1: ¿Compraste la carne?
E2: *Sí, la compré.*

1. ¿Compraste los refrescos?
2. ¿Buscaste las recetas (*recipes*) de tu abuela?
3. ¿Cocinaste tus platos (*dishes*) favoritos?
4. ¿Encontraste fruta muy fresca para la ensalada?
5. ¿Preparaste una mesa bonita?
6. ¿Limpiaste el comedor?
7. ¿Mandaste las invitaciones?

Capítulo 3. Los quehaceres de la casa, pág. 112.

7 • 14 Los quehaceres de Inés

Paso 1 Escribe una oración para cada quehacer que terminó Inés. Después, compara tus oraciones con las de un/a compañero/a.

MODELO E1: el suelo
E2: *Inés barrió el suelo.*

1. la ropa
2. la aspiradora
3. el baño
4. los muebles
5. la basura
6. el armario

Paso 2 Túrnense para decir qué hizo Inés en el centro después de terminar sus quehaceres. Sigan el modelo.

MODELO E1: el correo
E2: *Compró sellos.*

1. la librería
2. el cine
3. el banco
4. el cibercafé
5. la biblioteca
6. el café
7. el supermercado
8. la tienda

7 • 15 ¿Y cuándo...?

Entrevista a un/a compañero/a para saber cuándo ocurrieron las siguientes cosas.

MODELO ¿Cuándo... (tú) comprar esta lechuga?
E1: *¿Cuándo compraste esta lechuga?*
E2: *La compré el sábado pasado.*

¿Cuándo...?

1. (tú) tocar un instrumento
2. (tus amigos) visitar a sus padres
3. (tú) comprar un CD nuevo
4. (tus amigos y tú) comer en un restaurante muy bueno
5. (tú) empezar tus estudios universitarios
6. (tu profesor/a) leer una novela de Dan Brown
7. (tus amigos y tú) bailar
8. (Uds.) invitar a un amigo a ir a una fiesta

7·16 ¿Te puedo hacer una pregunta?

Entrevista a cinco estudiantes diferentes y anota sus respuestas (**sí** o **no**). Después, compara tus respuestas con las de los otros estudiantes de la clase. ¿Cuáles son las tendencias?

MODELO arreglar el cuarto hoy

TÚ: *¿Arreglaste tu cuarto hoy?*
E1: *Sí, lo arreglé.*
E2: *No, no lo arreglé.*
E3: *Sí, arreglé mi cuarto.*
E4: *No, no arreglé mi cuarto.*
E5: *No, yo no lo arreglé, pero mi compañero lo arregló.*

	E1	E2	E3	E4	E5
1. arreglar el cuarto hoy					
2. comer en un restaurante el sábado pasado					
3. estudiar anoche					
4. lavar los platos ayer					
5. hablar por teléfono con los padres anteayer					
6. jugar al golf el verano pasado					
7. escribir un ensayo para la clase de inglés la semana pasada					
8. terminar la tarea para la clase de español anoche					

¿Cómo andas?

Having completed the first **Comunicación,** I now can…

	Feel Confident	Need to Review
• talk about food that I like and dislike (p. 252)	❑	❑
• pronounce the letters **r** and **rr** properly in Spanish (p. 253)	❑	❑
• talk about past actions using direct object pronouns (p. 257)	❑	❑
• correctly use verbs that are regular in the preterit (p. 258)	❑	❑
• talk about past actions and events (p. 258)	❑	❑
• use verbs that end in **-car, -zar,** and **-gar** and the verb **leer** in the preterit correctly (p. 259)	❑	❑

Comunicación

- Describing food preparation and restaurant activity
- Describing past actions

VOCABULARIO 4 La preparación de las comidas

SAM 7-24 to 7-26

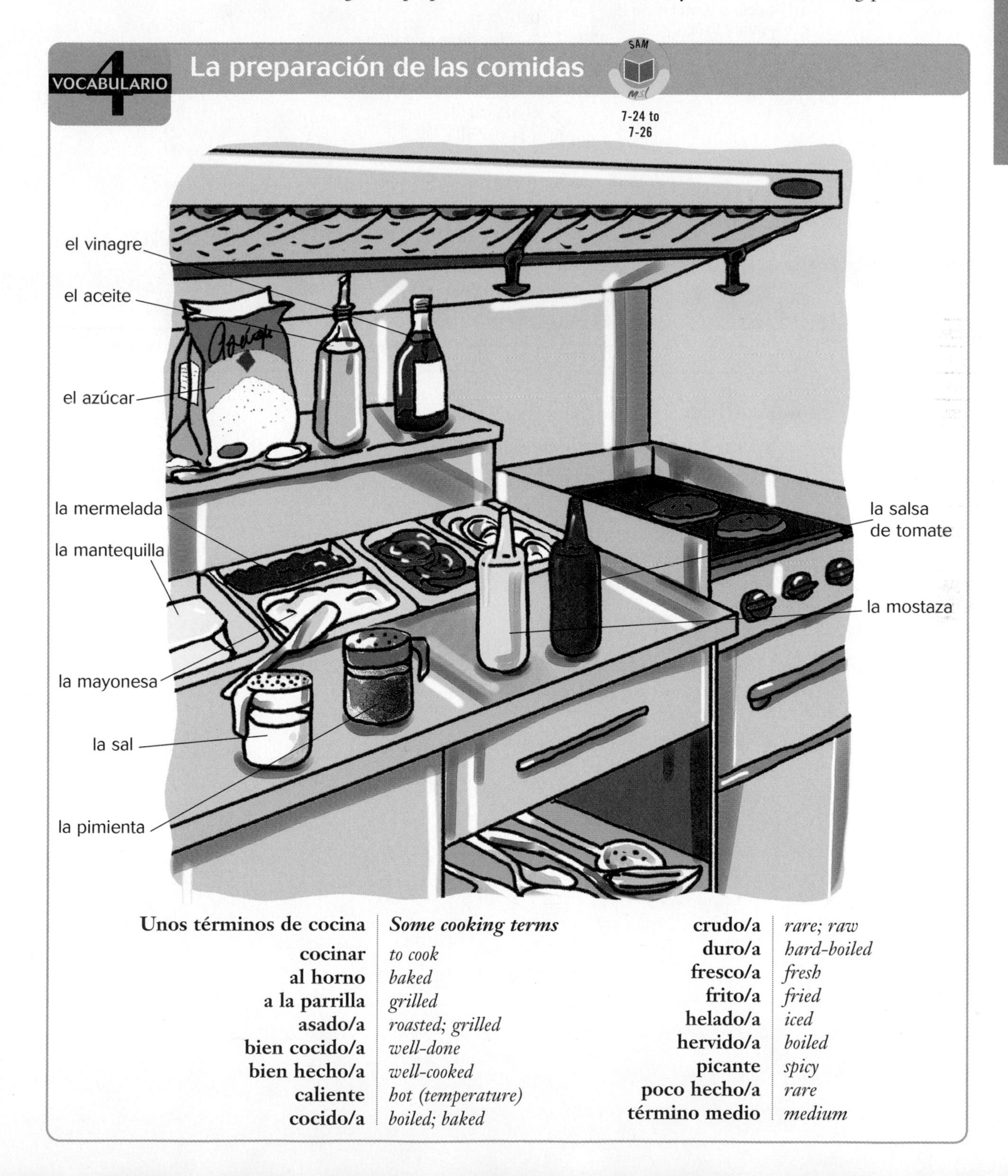

Unos términos de cocina	*Some cooking terms*
cocinar	*to cook*
al horno	*baked*
a la parrilla	*grilled*
asado/a	*roasted; grilled*
bien cocido/a	*well-done*
bien hecho/a	*well-cooked*
caliente	*hot (temperature)*
cocido/a	*boiled; baked*
crudo/a	*rare; raw*
duro/a	*hard-boiled*
fresco/a	*fresh*
frito/a	*fried*
helado/a	*iced*
hervido/a	*boiled*
picante	*spicy*
poco hecho/a	*rare*
término medio	*medium*

7•17 La asociación

Digan una palabra o expresión que asocian con cada condimento, especia o término de la siguiente lista.

MODELO E1: picante
E2: *salsa*

1. frito/a
2. la salsa de tomate
3. crudo/a
4. la mayonesa
5. el azúcar
6. a la parrilla
7. fresco/a
8. al horno
9. la mostaza
10. la mantequilla

Capítulo 4. Los verbos con cambio de raíz, pág. 144.

7•18 ¿Cómo lo prefieres?

Entrevista a un/a compañero/a para conocer sus preferencias. Después cambien de papel.

MODELO E1: ¿Cómo quieres tu hamburguesa?
E2: *La quiero término medio.*

1. ¿Cómo quieres tu bistec?
2. ¿Con qué condimento(s) lo quieres?
3. ¿Cómo quieres tu ensalada?
4. ¿Cómo prefieres el pescado?
5. ¿Cómo quieres tu refresco, con o sin hielo?
6. ¿Cómo te gustan los huevos?
7. ¿Cómo prefieres la pizza?
8. ¿Cómo te gusta el té, helado o caliente?
9. ¿Cómo pides la sopa, con mucha o poca sal?
10. ¿Cómo tomas el café?

7-27 to 7-28

La comida hispana

La parrillada

La comida hispana es muy variada. En España se comen muchos pescados y mariscos, pero cada región tiene sus platos típicos. Por ejemplo, en Asturias tienen la fabada (*bean stew*), en Valencia la paella y en Andalucía el gazpacho. La parte central de España es conocida por su carne asada.

La comida mexicana se define por sus técnicas y por los ingredientes propios del país. Las diferentes formas de preparar el maíz y los chiles son exclusivas a la cocina mexicana; también se destacan (*they distinguish themselves*) en la manera de cocinar verduras, carnes, mariscos, huevos, salsas, sopas y aves. Desde Baja California hasta la península de Yucatán, se encuentran platos típicos mexicanos de cada región.

Las islas del Caribe tienen en común la herencia de las culturas española, indígena y africana combinadas con la cultura nativa. Las comidas de estos países llevan una gran variedad de condimentos (*seasonings*) como la bija (*annatto*) o el achiote, el orégano, la cebolla, el ajo, el cilantro y muchos más. El arroz es indispensable en la dieta caribeña, también los plátanos, los mariscos y los frijoles (o habichuelas). El arroz es muy importante también en la dieta centroamericana, igual que el maíz, los frijoles, las tortillas, las enchiladas, las verduras, el pollo, los tamales y las frutas.

En los países de Suramérica comen mucho arroz, frijoles, pollo, carne, frutas y mariscos. En Paraguay y Uruguay se comen muchas sopas, verduras, pan de maíz con queso y carne de cerdo (*pork*). En Chile, igual que en Argentina, las parrilladas (*mixed grills*) son muy populares. Las empanadas o empanadillas (un *turnover* de carne de res, legumbres, queso, mariscos o pollo) son famosas en toda la América Latina, desde Cuba hasta Argentina.

Preguntas

1. ¿Cuáles de los platos típicos (o ingredientes) mencionados te gustan?
2. ¿Cómo se compara la comida del Caribe con la comida de otras partes del mundo hispanohablante?

Unos verbos irregulares en el préterito

7-29 to 7-33

In the first **Comunicación** you learned about verbs that are regular in the **pretérito** and others that have spelling changes. The following verbs are *irregular* in the **pretérito;** they follow a pattern of their own. Study the verb charts to determine the similarities and differences among the forms.

Ayer anduvimos diez millas.

	andar (*to walk*)	**estar**	**tener**
yo	anduve	estuve	tuve
tú	anduviste	estuviste	tuviste
él, ella, Ud.	anduvo	estuvo	tuvo
nosotros/as	anduvimos	estuvimos	tuvimos
vosotros/as	anduvisteis	estuvisteis	tuvisteis
ellos/as, Uds.	anduvieron	estuvieron	tuvieron

El verano pasado **anduvimos** mucho por la playa. *Last summer we walked along the beach a lot.*
¿En qué bar **estuvieron** Uds.? *In which bar were you all?*
Juan **tuvo** muy buena suerte. ¡Ganó la lotería! *Juan was really lucky. He won the lottery!*

	conducir (*to drive*)	**traer**	**decir**
yo	conduje	traje	dije
tú	condujiste	trajiste	dijiste
él, ella, Ud.	condujo	trajo	dijo
nosotros/as	condujimos	trajimos	dijimos
vosotros/as	condujisteis	trajisteis	dijisteis
ellos/as, Uds.	condujeron	trajeron	dijeron

Fíjate

Note that the third-person plural ending of *conducir, decir,* and *traer* is *-eron.*

Conduje el coche nuevo de mi padre anoche. *I drove my father's new car last night.*
Rubén **trajo** a su madre a la fiesta. *Rubén brought his mother to the party.*
¿**Dijeron** la verdad sobre el accidente? *Did they tell the truth about the accident?*

	ir	**ser**
yo	fui	fui
tú	fuiste	fuiste
él, ella, Ud.	fue	fue
nosotros/as	fuimos	fuimos
vosotros/as	fuisteis	fuisteis
ellos/as, Uds.	fueron	fueron

Fíjate

Note that *ser* and *ir* have the same forms in the preterit. You must rely on the context of the sentence or conversation to determine the meaning.

Ayer cené con Ana. *I had dinner with Ana yesterday.*
La cena **fue** deliciosa. *The dinner was delicious.*
Fuimos al mercado para comprar mariscos. *We went to the market to buy seafood.*
La gente del mercado **fue** muy amable. *The people at the market were very kind.*

	dar	ver	venir
yo	di	vi	vine
tú	diste	viste	viniste
él, ella, Ud.	dio	vio	vino
nosotros/as	dimos	vimos	vinimos
vosotros/as	disteis	visteis	vinisteis
ellos/as, Uds.	dieron	vieron	vinieron

	hacer	querer
yo	hice	quise
tú	hiciste	quisiste
él, ella, Ud.	hizo	quiso
nosotros/as	hicimos	quisimos
vosotros/as	hicisteis	quisisteis
ellos/as, Uds.	hicieron	quisieron

	poder	poner	saber
yo	pude	puse	supe
tú	pudiste	pusiste	supiste
él, ella, Ud.	pudo	puso	supo
nosotros/as	pudimos	pusimos	supimos
vosotros/as	pudisteis	pusisteis	supisteis
ellos/as, Uds.	pudieron	pusieron	supieron

—**Vimos** a mucha gente en tu fiesta. *We saw a lot of people at your party.*
—Sí, ¡y todos me **dieron** un regalo! *Yes, and everyone gave me a gift!*
—¿**Vinieron** tus tíos también? *Did your aunt and uncle come as well?*
—No, no **pudieron** venir por sus trabajos. *They couldn't come because of their jobs.*
—¡Que lástima! ¿Qué **hiciste** después de la fiesta? *What a shame! What did you do after the party?*

Verbos con cambio de raíz

The next group of verbs also follows its own pattern. In these stem-changing verbs, the first letters next to the infinitives, listed in parentheses, represent the present tense spelling changes; the last letter indicates the spelling change in the **él** and **ellos** forms of the **pretérito.**

Fíjate

The *-ir* stem-changing verbs are irregular in the third person singular and plural forms only.

	dormir (o → ue → u)	pedir (e → i → i)	preferir (e → ie → i)
yo	dormí	pedí	preferí
tú	dormiste	pediste	preferiste
él, ella, Ud.	durmió	pidió	prefirió
nosotros/as	dormimos	pedimos	preferimos
vosotros/as	dormisteis	pedisteis	preferisteis
ellos/as, Uds.	durmieron	pidieron	prefirieron

¿Qué comida **pidieron** Sara y Manolo? *What food did Sara and Manolo order?*
Mis abuelos **prefirieron** la carne de res. *My grandparents preferred the beef.*
Después de comer, los niños se **durmieron.** *After eating, the children fell asleep.*

7•19 Más práctica

Repite el juego de verbos de la actividad **7-11**, esta vez usando los nuevos verbos irregulares.

7•20 El mercado

El año pasado, Amanda fue estudiante de intercambio y vivió con una familia en Asunción. Completa el siguiente párrafo sobre su primera visita al mercado y después compártelo con un/a compañero/a.

andar	traer	decidir	ir
pedir	poder	poner	tener

Ayer mis nuevas "hermanas", Patricia y Gloria, y yo (1) _______________ al mercado por primera vez. Como perdimos el autobús, (2) _______________ que ir caminando. (3) ¡Nosotras _______________ por más de media hora! Por fin llegamos y (4) _______________ tomar un café antes de entrar en el mercado. Yo pedí un café doble con leche y ellas (5) _______________ café con leche y tostada. Cuando el señor nos (6) _______________ los cafés, Patricia (7) _______________ seis cucharadas (*spoonfuls*) de azúcar en el suyo (*hers*). (Yo) No lo (8) _______________ creer, ¡demasiado dulce para mí!

comprar	decir	estar	poner
ser	tomar	ver	volver

Al entrar en el mercado, yo (9) _______________ un montón de verduras y frutas de muchos colores brillantes. (10) _______________ impresionante. Después yo les (11) _______________ varias fotos a las chicas. Primero compramos una lechuga, dos cebollas, ajo, medio kilo de zanahorias y un pimiento verde. Hablamos unos cinco minutos con la vendedora sobre su sobrina. Ella (12) _______________ seis meses en los Estados Unidos como estudiante de intercambio. Después miramos las frutas y por fin escogimos dos melones y medio kilo de peras. Las chicas (13) _______________ las verduras en el bolso grande y la fruta en el bolso más pequeño. Entonces pasamos a la parte del pescado donde nosotras (14) _______________ atún. La señora lo envolvió (*wrapped*) en papel antes de ponerlo en una bolsa de plástico. Hicimos las compras en menos de media hora. A las nueve y cuarto les (15) _______________ adiós a todos y (16)_______________ a casa …esta vez en autobús.

Fíjate

Amanda refers to a *medio kilo de zanahorias*. Remember that in most parts of the world the metric system is the preferred system of measurement.

7•21 ¿Hay rutina en tu semana?

¿Cuántas veces hiciste estas cosas la semana pasada?

Paso 1 Escribe las respuestas a las siguientes preguntas, según el modelo.

Estrategia

Remember that *una vez* means *once* and *veces* means *times*: *Yo fui al restaurante una vez pero tú fuiste tres veces. = I went to the restaurant once but you went three times.*

MODELO E1: La semana pasada, ¿cuántas veces viste una película en la televisión?
E2: *Vi una película en la televisión una vez (dos veces, tres veces, etc.).*

La semana pasada, ¿cuántas veces…?

1. hiciste tu tarea
2. diste la respuesta correcta en clase
3. no viniste a la clase de español
4. condujiste a la universidad
5. dormiste ocho horas
6. anduviste por el centro
7. fuiste al cine
8. jugaste a un deporte
9. viste un partido en la televisión
10. comiste comida rápida

Paso 2 Pídele a tu compañero/a que advine (*guess*) cuántas veces hiciste las actividades anteriores. Sigue el modelo.

MODELOS E1: *La semana pasada, ¿cuántas veces piensas que (yo) hice la tarea?*
E2: *Pienso que la hiciste una vez.*
E1: *Sí, tienes razón. ¡La hice una vez!*
(o)
E1: *¿Cuántas veces piensas que fui al cine?*
E2: *Pienso que no fuiste.*
E1: *No, no tienes razón. Fui una vez.*

7•22 ¿Adónde fui?

Hazle a tu compañero/a las siguientes preguntas para averiguar adónde fue de vacaciones. Después, cambien de papel. (**¡OJO!** *Before asking the last question, try to guess where he or she went.*)

MODELO E1: ¿Fuiste en verano?
E2: *No, fui en otoño. / Sí, fui en verano.*

1. ¿Fuiste a la playa?
2. ¿Visitaste un museo?
3. ¿Viste un partido de béisbol?
4. ¿Montaste en bicicleta?
5. ¿Qué compraste?
6. ¿Comiste mariscos?
7. ¿Tomaste el sol?
8. ¿Jugaste al golf?
9. ¿Nadaste?
10. ¿Dormiste en un hotel?
11. ¿Jugaste al tenis?
12. ¿Fuiste a un parque?
13. ¿Qué más hiciste?
14. ¿Adónde fuiste?

7•23 Chismes (*Gossip*)

Imagina que eres el/la editor/a de la columna de chismes de un periódico. Escribe en el cuadro tus respuestas a las siguientes preguntas. Después, entrevista a tres compañeros/as y anota sus respuestas. ¿Están de acuerdo?

1. ¿Qué película tuvo mucho éxito el año pasado?
2. ¿Qué actor salió en una película que **no** tuvo éxito?
3. ¿Qué miembro del gobierno (*member of the government*) dijo algo tonto?
4. ¿Quién hizo un CD recientemente?
5. ¿Cuál de tus amigos estuvo en la playa recientemente?
6. ¿Quién vino tarde a la clase una vez?
7. ¿Quién no trajo sus libros a clase?
8. ¿Quién les dio un examen muy difícil la semana pasada?

YO	ESTUDIANTE 1	ESTUDIANTE 2	ESTUDIANTE 3
1.			
2.			
3.			

7•24 ¿Qué dijo?

Form groups of at least six students and sit in a circle. **Estudiante 1** starts by saying his/her name and something that he/she did yesterday, last week, or last year. **Estudiante 2** gives his/her name, says something he/she did, and then tells what the preceding person (**Estudiante 1**) did. **Estudiante 3** tells his/her name, says what he/she did, and then tells what **Estudiante 2** and **Estudiante 1** did (in that order). Follow the model.

MODELO E1: *Soy Fran y ayer fui a la playa.*

E2: *Soy Tom y ayer jugué al tenis. Fran fue a la playa.*

E3: *Soy Chris y ayer tuve que llamar a mis padres. Tom jugó al tenis y Fran fue a la playa.*

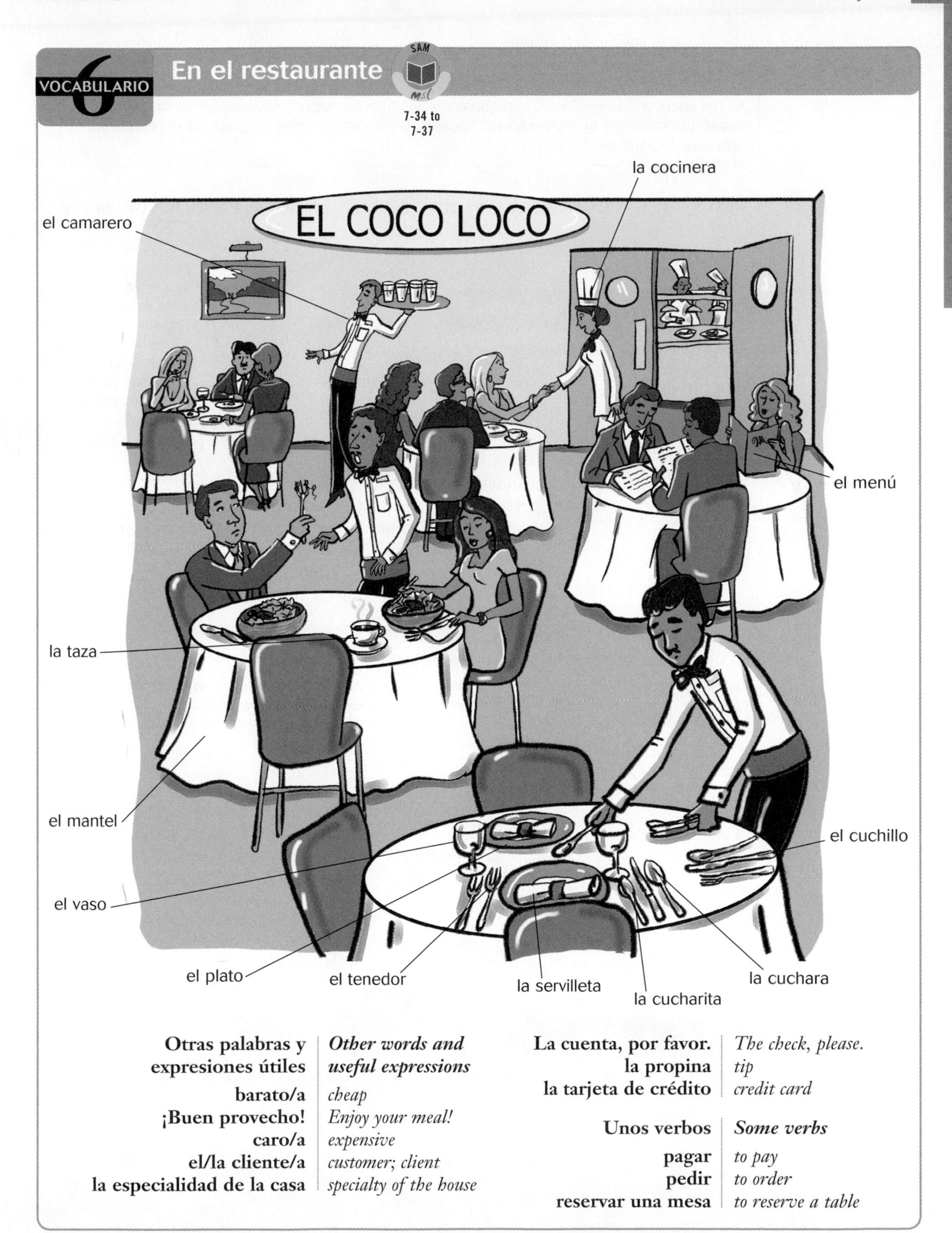

VOCABULARIO 6 En el restaurante

Otras palabras y expresiones útiles	*Other words and useful expressions*
barato/a	*cheap*
¡Buen provecho!	*Enjoy your meal!*
caro/a	*expensive*
el/la cliente/a	*customer; client*
la especialidad de la casa	*specialty of the house*
La cuenta, por favor.	*The check, please.*
la propina	*tip*
la tarjeta de crédito	*credit card*

Unos verbos	*Some verbs*
pagar	*to pay*
pedir	*to order*
reservar una mesa	*to reserve a table*

7•25 La organización es clave

Juntos escriban las siguientes categorías en una hoja de papel: **cosas en la mesa, pedir y pagar, personas en el restaurante.** Después, organicen el vocabulario de **En el restaurante** bajo esas categorías.

MODELO

COSAS EN LA MESA	PEDIR Y PAGAR	PERSONAS EN EL RESTAURANTE
el cuchillo	*la propina*	*el camarero*

Estrategia

As you acquire more Spanish in each chapter, try to write definitions in Spanish of your new vocabulary words like in the model. Learning new vocabulary will become easier the more you practice. Also, it will help you use your new vocabulary in sentences.

7•26 ¿Cómo se dice?

Túrnense para decir qué palabra o frase corresponde a las siguientes descripciones.

MODELO E1: el "Gran Especial"
E2: *la especialidad de la casa*

1. persona que sirve la comida
2. dinero que das por buen servicio
3. lista de comidas y bebidas
4. necesario para limpiar las manos
5. persona que prepara la comida en un restaurante
6. necesario para comer *Frosted Flakes*
7. necesario para beber café
8. persona que come en el restaurante

7•27 Una mesa bien puesta

Dibuja la mesa de tu familia o de la familia de un/a buen/a amigo/a para una cena especial con todo bien puesto (*well set*). Ahora, sin mostrar tu dibujo, descríbeselo a un/a compañero/a mientras él/ella lo dibuja. ¿Lo dibujó bien? Luego cambien de papeles.

Vocabulario útil

al lado (de)	*beside; next to*
a la izquierda (de)	*to the left (of)*
a la derecha (de)	*to the right (of)*
cerca (de)	*near*
debajo (de)	*under; underneath*
encima (de)	*on top of; above*

7•28 ¿Qué pasó?

Miren el dibujo en la página 271 y digan por lo menos **cinco** oraciones acerca de lo que pasó anoche en el restaurante El Coco Loco.

7•29 ¿Me puede servir...?

Vas con dos amigos/as al restaurante más popular de Asunción para cenar.

Paso 1 Miren el menú y determinen qué van a pedir sabiendo que tienen 60.000 guaraníes para pagar.

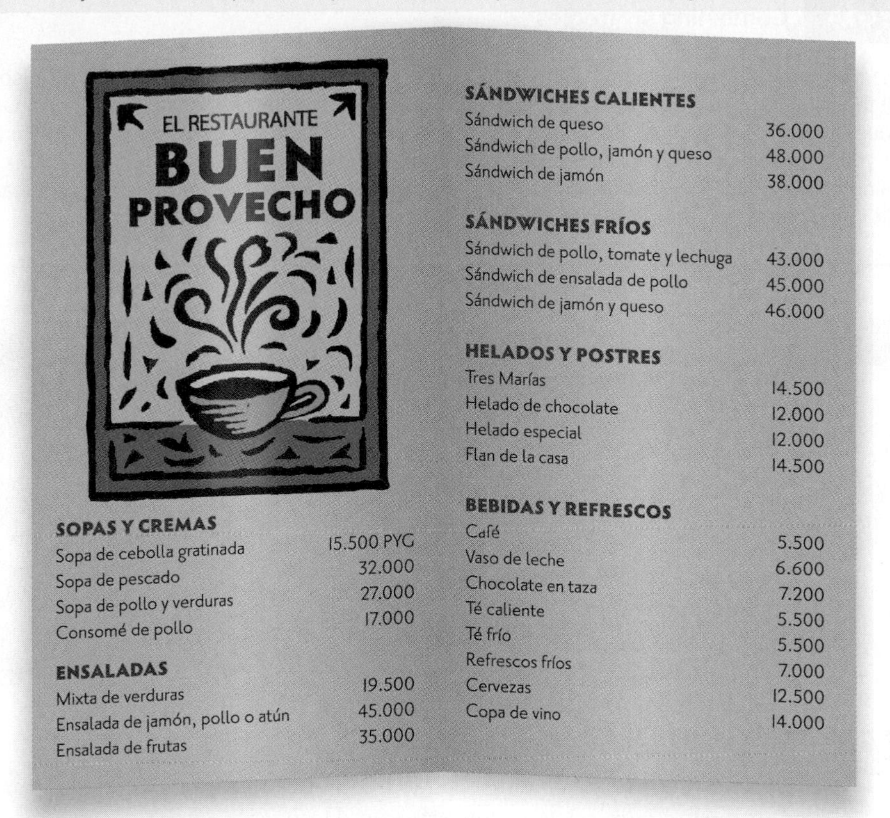

Paso 2 Ahora, utilizando esa información, realicen *(act out)* una escena en un restaurante para la clase. Una persona debe ser el/la camarero/a y las otras dos personas deben ser los clientes.

Capítulo 2. Presente indicativo de verbos regulares, pág. 68.

7•30 De compras en el mercado

Algunos estudiantes van a hacer el papel de vendedores y otros de clientes. Tu profesor/a te va a dar una lista de los productos que tienes para vender o de los que necesitas comprar. Los vendedores deben ganar cincuenta mil guaraníes y los clientes sólo pueden gastar cincuenta mil guaraníes. Va a haber competencia entre los vendedores y sí, ¡puedes regatear (*bargain; negotiate the price*)!

ESCUCHA

7-38 to 7-39

ESTRATEGIA **Combining strategies**

To begin the new term it is useful to review and combine all the listening strategies you have practiced thus far. Remember to use all clues available to you to anticipate what you are about to hear, including photos, captions, and pre-listening synopses or questions. If you are performing a listening activity like the one to follow, also look ahead at the comprehension questions. Once you have an idea of the context, consider what you already know about it. Taking time to think about and practice these specific strategies will enhance your ability to listen effectively.

7•31 **Antes de escuchar**

Contesta las siguientes preguntas.

1. Mira la foto. ¿Dónde está la mujer? ¿Qué hace?
2. ¿Haces las compras (*Do you shop*) en un mercado como éste, donde hay muchos vendedores en un solo lugar, o en un supermercado?
3. ¿Qué tipo de vocabulario necesitas saber para poder hacer las compras en un mercado?

La madre de Alejandra

7•32 **A escuchar**

CD 3 Track 2

Escucha la conversación entre la madre de Alejandra y un vendedor para averiguar el propósito (*purpose*) de la conversación. Después, escucha una vez más para contestar las siguientes preguntas.

1. ¿Qué compra? Pon una tacha (✓) delante de los ingredientes o condimentos que ella compra.

______ mantequilla	______ vinagre
______ azúcar	______ huevos
______ queso	______ pan
______ mayonesa	______ leche

2. Determina si las siguientes oraciones son verdaderas (**V**) o falsas (**F**).
   a. La madre necesita ingredientes para preparar un plato nuevo.
   b. El Sr. Gómez tiene todo lo que la madre necesita comprar.

7•33 **Después de escuchar**

Realiza (*Act out*) con un/a compañero/a la escena entre la madre y el Sr. Gómez.

ESCRIBE

7•34 Antes de escribir

Piensa en el mejor día festivo que pasaste de niño. Haz una lista de los siguientes detalles:

- las personas con quienes celebraste o las que fueron a la fiesta
- lo que comieron y bebieron
- las cosas que hicieron
- los regalos que dieron y recibieron

7•35 Un recuerdo (*memory*)

Ahora, usando los detalles de la lista, escribe un párrafo bien desarrollado (*well developed*) sobre ese día, con introducción y conclusión.

7•36 Después de escribir

En grupos de cuatro o cinco estudiantes, lean los párrafos de la actividad **7-35.** Ofrezcan (*Offer*) ideas a sus compañeros para mejorar su trabajo. Después, escriban la versión final para entregársela (*turn it in*) a su profesor/a.

¿Cómo andas?

Having completed the second **Comunicación,** I now can…

	Feel Confident	Need to Review
• discuss foods that I like and dislike and say how I like them prepared (p. 263)	❏	❏
• describe actions in the past using a variety of regular and irregular verbs (p. 266)	❏	❏
• describe how to set a table (p. 271)	❏	❏
• order food in a restaurant (p. 271)	❏	❏
• buy food in a market (p. 273)	❏	❏
• combine listening strategies (p. 274)	❏	❏
• write about a special day from my past (p. 275)	❏	❏

Gino Breschi Arteaga

Chile

CW eBook
CD 3 Track 3

SAM 7-42

DVD/VHS Vistas culturales

Les presento mi país

Mi nombre es Gino Breschi Arteaga y soy de Viña del Mar, Chile. Viña del Mar es una ciudad turística en la costa y tiene una playa hermosa. El país es muy largo y estrecho, con un promedio (*average*) de 180 kilómetros de ancho (*wide*) y aproximadamente 4.300 kilómetros de largo. Al oeste, tenemos el océano Pacífico y al este, la cordillera majestuosa de los Andes. **¿Prefieres vivir cerca del océano o de las montañas?** Al norte, está el desierto de Atacama, el más árido del mundo. Al sur, hay una serie de glaciares en parques nacionales. Soy soltero (*bachelor*) así que todavía vivo con mis padres, como la mayoría de los chilenos antes de casarse (*to marry*). Así puedo comer el pastel de choclo que mi madre me hace con frecuencia. ¡Qué rico!

El glaciar San Rafael, Patagonia

El pastel de choclo es un plato favorito de los chilenos.

La playa en Viña del Mar

ALMANAQUE

Nombre oficial:	República de Chile
Gobierno:	República
Población:	16.134.219 (2006)
Idiomas:	español
Moneda:	Peso chileno ($)

¿Sabías que...?

- Además del (*In addition to*) desayuno, el almuerzo y la cena, los chilenos toman una merienda llamada "las onces", que comen entre las 4:00 y las 7:00 de la tarde.
- El baile nacional de Chile es la cueca. Este baile se inspira en el rito de cortejo (*courting*) del gallo (*rooster*) y la gallina (*hen*).

PREGUNTAS

1. ¿Qué extremos geográficos y climatológicos se mencionan? ¿Hay algo parecido en los Estados Unidos?
2. Generalmente, ¿cuándo salen de casa los jóvenes chilenos para vivir por su cuenta (*on their own*)? ¿Cuál es la costumbre en los Estados Unidos?
3. Describe el baile nacional. En tu opinión, ¿cuál debe ser el baile nacional de los Estados Unidos? ¿Por qué?

En la Red
Amplía tus conocimientos sobre Chile en la página web de *¡Anda!*

Mirta Beatriz Chávez Villalba

CD 3
Track 4

Vistas culturales

Paraguay

Les presento mi país

Mi nombre es Mirta Beatriz Chávez Villalba y vivo en Asunción, Paraguay. Como un gran porcentaje de los paraguayos, soy bilingüe: hablo español y guaraní. **¿En qué otros países hay una población bilingüe?** El guaraní es el idioma hablado por los indígenas originales del país: los guaraníes. Hoy día, el noventa por ciento de los paraguayos somos **mestizos,** una mezcla (*mixture*) de los indígenas y los conquistadores españoles. Los indígenas cultivaron la mandioca (*yucca*), la batata (*yam*), el maíz y la yerba mate entre otras cosechas (*crops*). Estas comidas se usan hoy día en nuestros platos y bebidas principales. Durante el día, se ve a los paraguayos tomando su **tereré,** una infusión fría de yerba mate. **¿Qué refresco te gusta tomar?**

El tereré, una infusión fría de yerba mate, es la bebida preferida en Paraguay.

El ñandú es una especie de ave nativa y amenazada (*endangered*) de El Chaco.

La Represa Hidroeléctrica de Itaipú, en la frontera entre Paraguay y Brasil.

ALMANAQUE

Nombre oficial:	República del Paraguay
Gobierno:	República constitucional
Población:	6.506.464 (2006)
Idiomas:	español (oficial); guaraní (oficial)
Moneda:	Guaraní (G)

¿Sabías que...?

- Muchos paraguayos son aficionados a los remedios caseros (*home-made remedies*).
- El Chaco cubre el 60% de la superficie de Paraguay pero contiene solamente un 2% de la población del país.

PREGUNTAS

1. ¿Qué comidas se comen en Paraguay?
2. ¿Por qué un gran porcentaje de los paraguayos son bilingües?
3. ¿En qué aspectos son Chile y Paraguay diferentes y similares? ¿Cómo se comparan con los otros países que hemos estudiado?

En la Red
Amplía tus conocimientos sobre Paraguay en la página web de *¡Anda!*

Ambiciones siniestras

7-46 to 7-47

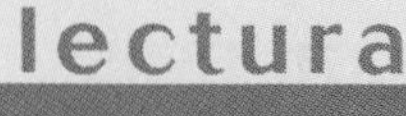

7-37 Antes de leer. En el **Episodio 5,** Eduardo desaparece. Cisco no sabe qué hacer y le pide consejo a su primo, Manolo. Después, todos los estudiantes menos Eduardo y Alejandra tienen una videoconferencia. Antes de continuar con el siguiente episodio contesta estas preguntas.

1. Mira el título. ¿Cuál es un ejemplo de un rompecabezas? ¿Qué experiencia tienes con los rompecabezas?
2. ¿Quién está en la foto? ¿Qué hace?

ESTRATEGIA **Predicting**

To predict what a reading passage is about, first anticipate the content by considering the title, visual cues (illustrations, photos), and comprehension questions. Once you have a general idea of what the passage is about, connect any personal knowledge or experience you have with it. Then, quickly skim the reading for the main idea(s). At that point you can predict what will happen in the reading.

7-38 A leer. Completa los siguientes pasos.

1. Lee superficialmente (*skim*) el episodio para averiguar cuáles son los personajes y dónde están.
2. Escribe **dos** predicciones de lo que crees que va a ocurrir en el episodio.
3. Lee el episodio y determina si las predicciones que hiciste son correctas.

CD 3 Track 5

El rompecabezas°

riddle

Cisco está muy preocupado por Alejandra. Por eso después de la videoconferencia llamó a Manolo y le preguntó por ella. Manolo le dijo que Alejandra no respondió al último correo electrónico. Tampoco° estuvo en la clase de literatura. Manolo le dijo a Cisco que la esperó por media hora después de la clase y no vino. No sabe nada de ella.

Nor

Ellos dos están muy preocupados acerca de lo que está pasando. ¿Por qué fueron escogidos°? ¿Qué pasó con Eduardo? ¿Dónde está Eduardo? ¿Y dónde está Alejandra?

selected

Con los nervios y la preocupación, Cisco tenía mucha hambre así que decidió ir a su restaurante favorito, Mamá Mía. Ahí siempre puede comer algo y pensar en todo lo que está pasando. Pidió lo que su madre llama *comfort food*: pollo frito, papas, maíz y frijoles. Durante la comida, conversó con sus amigos que trabajan allí. Cuando pagó, le sonó el teléfono celular. Cisco contestó y oyó una voz de hombre: —*Cisco Quiroga. Tiene cuatro pistas° para resolver este rompecabezas o Eduardo va a morir. Aquí están:*

Conocido por su longitud

Por la razón o la fuerza

Qué rico está el pisco

Para quien baile la cueca

Recuerde, tiene dos días para resolver el rompecabezas o Eduardo va a morir. No vaya a la policía.—

CLIC…

Cisco se quedó sin palabras, le temblaron las manos. Tomó el teléfono y llamó a Manolo. La línea estaba ocupada. —Vamos Manolo, cuelga° el teléfono, —pensó Cisco— necesito hablar contigo.— Por fin, después de llamar varias veces, Manolo contestó con voz de pánico.

—¿Quién es? —contestó Manolo.

—Soy yo, Cisco —respondió Cisco. —Mira…
(Manolo interrumpe)

—Cisco, recibí una llamada antes de la tuya°…

—¿De un hombre con una voz muy rara? —le preguntó Cisco.

—Así que te llamó a ti también —respondió Manolo. —Cisco, tenemos que llamar a los demás. Yo llamo a Lupe y a Alejandra y tú llamas a Marisol, ¿está bien?

—De acuerdo. Muy bien. —dijo Cisco.

Manolo llamó a Alejandra pero no consiguió hablar con ella. La voz del contestador automático era la de un hombre… *«Lo sentimos, no estamos en casa en estos momentos. Pueden dejar un mensaje.»* Intentó llamar de nuevo. Otra vez el contestador. ¿Dónde está Alejandra? Cree que conoce la voz del hombre del contestador.

De repente°, Manolo, pensando en voz alta y horrorizado, gritó: —¡Por favor no… No puede ser…!—

clues · (colgar) *hang up* · *yours* · *Suddenly*

7-39 Después de leer. Contesta las siguientes preguntas.

1. ¿Qué dijo Manolo de Alejandra?
2. ¿Dónde estaba *(was)* Cisco cuando recibió la llamada misteriosa?
3. ¿Qué acababa *(had just done)* de hacer cuando recibió la llamada?
4. ¿De qué se trató la llamada?
5. ¿Por qué estaba *(was)* Cisco asustado *(frightened)*?
6. ¿Qué hizo Cisco después de colgar el teléfono?
7. ¿Qué ocurrió cuando Manolo llamó a Alejandra?

7-48 to 7-50

video

7-40 **Antes del video.** ¿Dónde puede estar Alejandra? ¿De quién es la voz en su contestador automático? ¿Quién más recibió el rompecabezas? En la segunda parte del episodio, vas a ver a Lupe trabajando en su computadora. ¿Qué piensas que está haciendo? También Manolo, Cisco, Marisol y Lupe van a tener otra videoconferencia. ¿De qué necesitan hablar ahora?

¿Qué lees?

Esto es muy peligroso.

¡No tengo nada que ver con la desaparición de Eduardo!

Episodio 7

¡Qué rico está el pisco!

Relájate y disfruta el video.

7-41 **Después del video.** Contesta las siguientes preguntas.

1. ¿Dónde estaba Lupe? ¿Qué hizo?
2. ¿Dónde estaba Cisco? ¿Qué hizo?
3. ¿Cuál es la mentira (*lie*) de Lupe?
4. ¿Qué **no** les va a mencionar Cisco a los otros?
5. ¿De qué le "acusó" Manolo a Lupe?
6. ¿Por qué le respondió Cisco a Manolo de una manera defensiva?
7. ¿Qué descubrió Cisco al final del episodio?

Y por fin, ¿cómo andas?

Having completed this chapter, I now can...

	Feel Confident	Need to Review
Comunicación		
• discuss my food preferences (p. 252)	❑	❑
• pronounce **r** and **rr** correctly, distinguishing between the two (p. 253)	❑	❑
• talk and write about things I did and events that occurred in the past (p. 258)	❑	❑
• explain how I like my food prepared (p. 263)	❑	❑
• order food in a restaurant (p. 271)	❑	❑
• buy food in a market or supermarket (p. 273)	❑	❑
• combine strategies to better understand when listening (p. 274)	❑	❑
• write about a childhood memory (p. 275)	❑	❑
Cultura		
• discuss meals of the Spanish-speaking world and when they are eaten (p. 256)	❑	❑
• give examples of the variety of foods in the Spanish-speaking world (p. 265)	❑	❑
• give at least two interesting facts about Chile and Paraguay (pp. 276–277)	❑	❑
Ambiciones siniestras		
• predict what will happen in a reading (p. 278)	❑	❑
• share the content of the latest message the students have received (p. 280)	❑	❑

VOCABULARIO ACTIVO

CD 3
Tracks 6-19

Las carnes y las aves	*Meat and poultry*
las aves	*poultry*
el bistec	*steak*
la carne	*meat*
la hamburguesa	*hamburger*
el jamón	*ham*
el perro caliente	*hot dog*
el pollo	*chicken*

El pescado y los mariscos	*Fish and seafood*
el atún	*tuna*
los camarones (*pl.*)	*shrimp*
el pescado	*fish*

Las frutas	*Fruit*
la banana/el plátano	*banana*
el limón	*lemon*
la manzana	*apple*
el melón	*melon*
la naranja	*orange*
la pera	*pear*
el tomate	*tomato*

Las verduras	*Vegetables*
la cebolla	*onion*
el chile	*chili pepper*
la ensalada	*salad*
los frijoles (*pl.*)	*beans*
la lechuga	*lettuce*
el maíz	*corn*
la papa /la patata	*potato*
las papas fritas (*pl.*)	*french fries; potato chips*
la verdura	*vegetable*

Los postres	*Desserts*
los dulces	*candy; sweets*
las galletas	*cookies; crackers*
el helado	*ice cream*
el pastel	*pastry; pie*
el postre	*dessert*
la torta	*cake*

Las bebidas	*Beverages*
el agua (con hielo)	*water (with ice)*
el café	*coffee*
la cerveza	*beer*
el jugo	*juice*
la leche	*milk*
el refresco	*soft drink*
el té (helado/caliente)	*tea (iced/hot)*
el vino	*wine*

Más comidas	*More foods*
el arroz	*rice*
el cereal	*cereal*
el huevo	*egg*
el pan	*bread*
el queso	*cheese*
la sopa	*soup*
la tostada	*toast*

Las comidas	*Meals*
el almuerzo	*lunch*
la cena	*dinner*
la comida	*food; meal*
el desayuno	*breakfast*
la merienda	*snack*

Verbos	*Verbs*
almorzar (ue)	*to have lunch*
andar	*to walk*
beber	*to drink*
cocinar	*to cook*
conducir	*to drive*
cenar	*to have dinner*
desayunar	*to have breakfast*
merendar	*to have a snack*

Los condimentos y las especias	*Condiments and spices*
el aceite	*oil*
el azúcar	*sugar*
la mantequilla	*butter*
la mayonesa	*mayonnaise*
la mermelada	*jam; marmalade*
la mostaza	*mustard*
la pimienta	*pepper*
la sal	*salt*
la salsa de tomate	*ketchup*
el vinagre	*vinegar*

Unos términos de cocina	*Cooking terms*
a la parrilla	*grilled*
al horna	*baked*
asado/a	*roasted; grilled*
bien cocido/a	*well done*
bien hecho/a	*well cooked*
caliente	*hot (temperature)*
cocido/a	*boiled; baked*
crudo/a	*rare; raw*
duro/a	*hard-boiled*
fresco/a	*fresh*
frito/a	*fried*
helado/a	*iced*
hervido/a	*boiled*
picante	*spicy*
poco hecho/a	*rare*
término medio	*medium*

En el restaurante	*In the restaurant*
el/la camarero/a	*waiter/waitress*
el/la cliente/a	*customer; client*
el/la cocinero/a	*cook*
la cuchara	*soup spoon; tablespoon*
la cucharita	*teaspoon*
el cuchillo	*knife*
la especialidad de la casa	*specialty of the house*
el mantel	*tablecloth*
el menú	*menu*
el plato	*plate; dish*
la propina	*tip*
la servilleta	*napkin*
la tarjeta de crédito	*credit card*
la taza	*cup*
el tenedor	*fork*
el vaso	*glass*

Verbos	*Verbs*
pagar	*to pay*
pedir	*to order*
reservar una mesa	*to reserve a table*

Otras palabras útiles	*Other useful words*
anoche	*last night*
anteayer	*the day before yesterday*
el año pasado	*last year*
ayer	*yesterday*
barato/a	*cheap*
¡Buen provecho!	*Enjoy your meal!*
caro/a	*expensive*
cerca (de)	*near*
debajo (de)	*under; underneath*
encima (de)	*on top (of); above*
el fin de semana pasado	*last weekend*
el… (jueves) pasado	*last… (Thursday)*
La cuenta, por favor.	*The check, please.*
la semana pasada	*last week*
más tarde que	*later than*
más temprano que	*earlier than*

¿Qué te pones?

En los países hispanohablantes la gente lleva (*wears*) ropa (*clothing*) muy similar a la que llevan por todo el mundo pero también se usa ropa más tradicional. Por ejemplo, en México se encuentran sarapes, ponchos y huaraches y en Colombia usan rebozos (ponchos) y alpargatas (*espadrilles*).

	OBJETIVOS	CONTENIDOS
Comunicación	● To describe what you and others are wearing as well as your clothing preferences ● To talk about to whom and for whom things are done ● To discuss what delights, fascinates, bothers, matters, and is needed by you and others ● To describe your typical day and compare it to that of a classmate ● To describe situations in the past and share how things used to be ● To guess the meaning of unfamiliar words, when listening, from the context ● To write an e-mail about your childhood	1 Clothing 286 2 Indirect object pronouns 292 3 **Gustar** and similar verbs 294 4 Direct and indirect object pronouns used together 298 5 Reflexive verbs 302 6 The imperfect tense 306 ☐ Pronunciación: The letters **ll** and **ñ** 287 ☐ Escucha: 310 Estrategia: Guessing meaning from context ☐ Escribe: Writing a paragraph about childhood 311
Cultura	● To talk about a Spanish clothing company ● To discuss shopping in the Spanish-speaking world ● To share important facts about this chapter's featured countries: Argentina and Uruguay	☐ Zara: la moda internacional 291 ☐ Los centros comerciales en Latinoamérica 306 ☐ *Argentina* and *Uruguay* 312–313
Ambiciones siniestras	● To guess the meaning of unfamiliar words in a reading passage ● To explain the significance of the latest e-mail from el Sr. Verdugo ● To reveal some secrets regarding Lupe	☐ Episodio 8 Lectura: *¿Quién fue?* 314 Estrategia: Guessing meaning from context Video: *El misterio crece* 316

Óscar de la Renta: diseñador dominicano

PREGUNTAS

1. ¿Qué tipo de ropa te gusta? ¿Prefieres la ropa formal o la ropa informal?
2. ¿Te interesa la moda *(fashion)*? ¿Te interesan distintos tipos de ropa? Explica.
3. ¿Qué semejanzas hay entre la ropa de la gente joven y la gente mayor en los Estados Unidos? ¿Qué diferencias hay?

Comunicación

- Discussing clothing
- Talking about to whom and for whom something is done
- Expressing likes and dislikes

1 VOCABULARIO La ropa

SAM 8-1 to 8-8

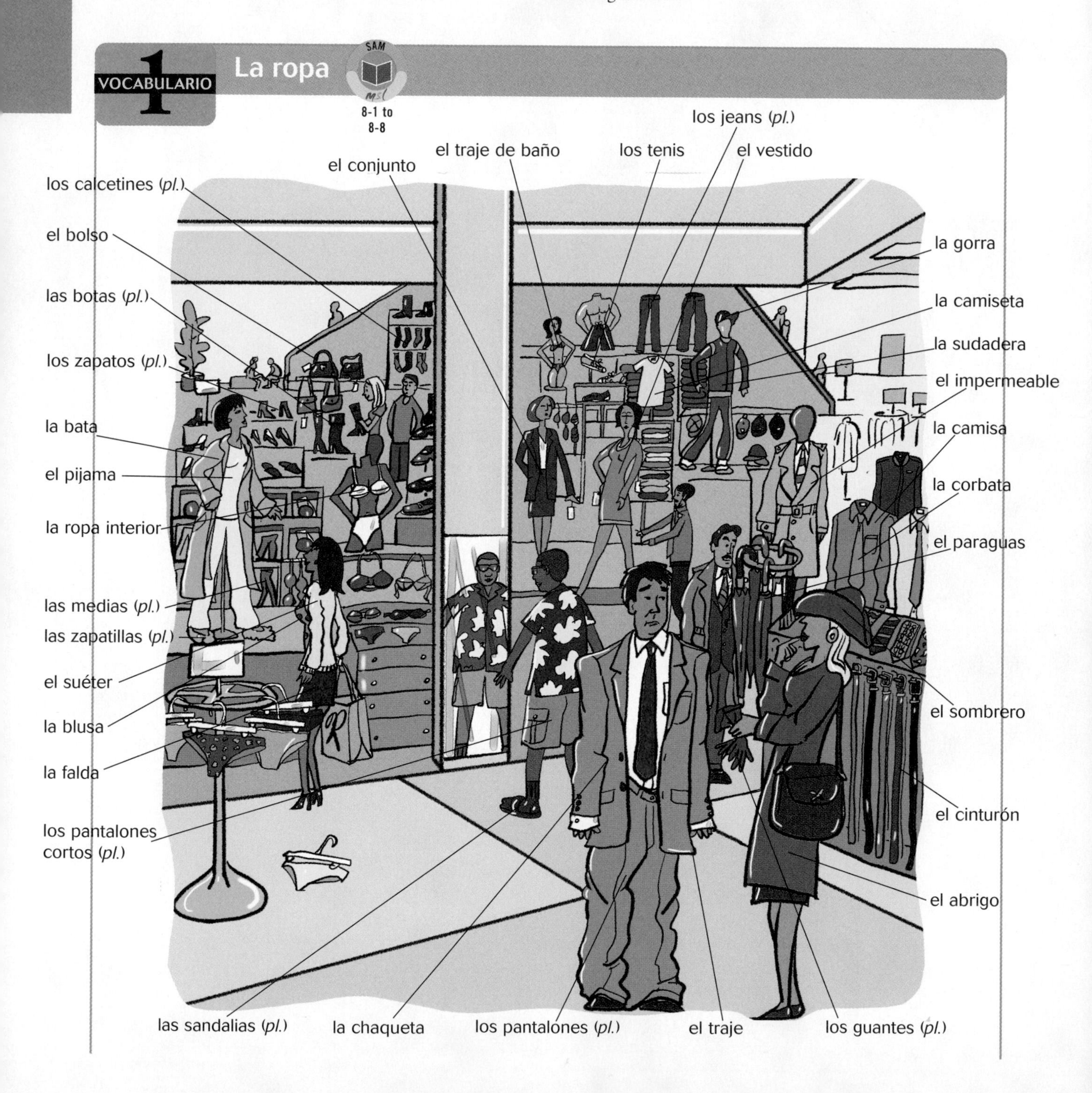

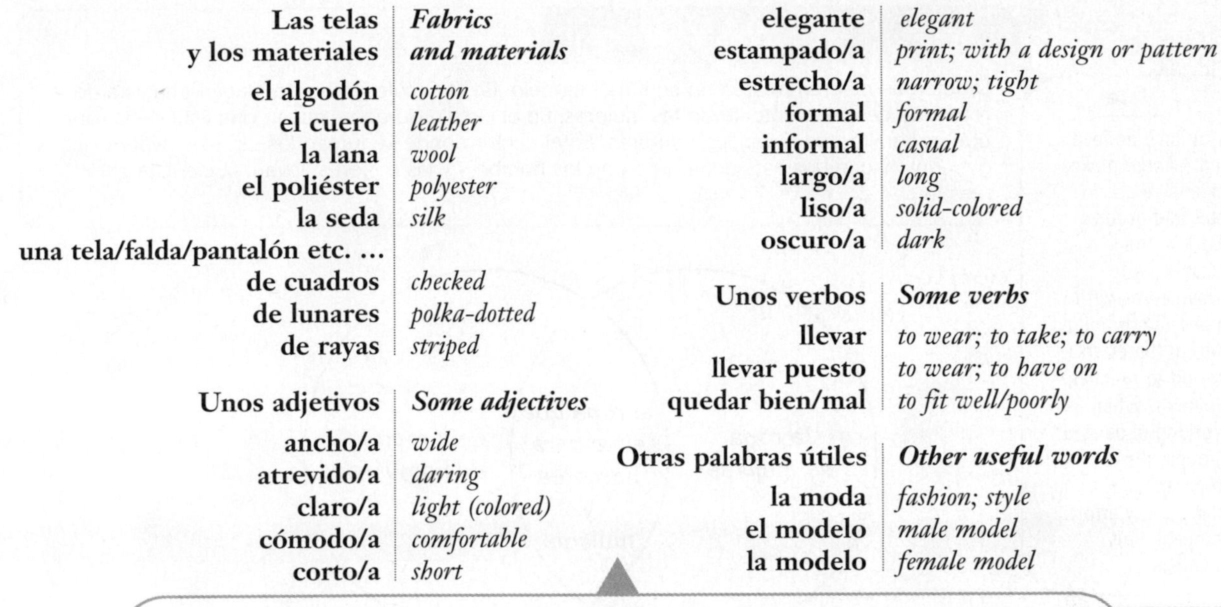

Las telas y los materiales	***Fabrics and materials***
el algodón	*cotton*
el cuero	*leather*
la lana	*wool*
el poliéster	*polyester*
la seda	*silk*
una tela/falda/pantalón etc. ...	
de cuadros	*checked*
de lunares	*polka-dotted*
de rayas	*striped*
Unos adjetivos	***Some adjectives***
ancho/a	*wide*
atrevido/a	*daring*
claro/a	*light (colored)*
cómodo/a	*comfortable*
corto/a	*short*
elegante	*elegant*
estampado/a	*print; with a design or pattern*
estrecho/a	*narrow; tight*
formal	*formal*
informal	*casual*
largo/a	*long*
liso/a	*solid-colored*
oscuro/a	*dark*
Unos verbos	***Some verbs***
llevar	*to wear; to take; to carry*
llevar puesto	*to wear; to have on*
quedar bien/mal	*to fit well/poorly*
Otras palabras útiles	***Other useful words***
la moda	*fashion; style*
el modelo	*male model*
la modelo	*female model*

Fíjate

In your vocabulary list you see the letters (*pl.*) beside words such as *las medias* or *los jeans* to indicate that they are plural in Spanish. You will also notice (*pl.*) beside *los calcetines.* Each sock is a *calcetín.*

CD 3
Track 20

SAM
8-9 to
8-11

PRONUNCIACIÓN

The letters *ll* and *ñ*

1. The **ll** is pronounced by most Spanish speakers like the *y* in the English word *yellow.*

   zapatilla llevar cuchillo servilleta

2. The **ñ** is pronounced like the *ny* in the English word *canyon.*

   año mañana campaña bañera

8•1 Las palabras

Pronounce the following words, paying special attention to the letters **ll** and **ñ.**

1. llamo
2. llegamos
3. millón
4. ella
5. señores
6. niños
7. enseñamos
8. pequeñas
9. años

8•2 Las oraciones

Pronounce the following sentences, paying special attention to the letters **ll** and **ñ.**

1. ¿Llevas las zapatillas amarillas?
2. Enseño a niños pequeños.

8•3 Los dichos y refranes

Now pronounce the following sayings and focus on the letters **ll** and **ñ.**

1. El que busca, halla.
2. Donde hay gana hay maña.

8•4 ¡Señoras y señores!

Dibujen un diagrama de Venn según el modelo. En el círculo izquierdo, hagan una lista de la ropa que generalmente llevan las mujeres. En el círculo derecho, hagan una lista de la ropa que generalmente llevan los hombres. En el centro donde se juntan los círculos (*where circles overlap*), hagan una lista de la ropa que los hombres y las mujeres llevan. ¿Que lista es más larga?

Fíjate

You have noticed that *¡Anda!* makes extensive use of pair and group work in the classroom to provide you with many opportunities during the class period to practice Spanish. When working in pairs or groups, it's imperative that you make every effort to speak only Spanish.

MODELO

8•5 ¿Cómo se visten?

Túrnense para describir qué ropa llevan las personas en las fotos.

MODELO: *Los hombres llevan pantalones blancos.*

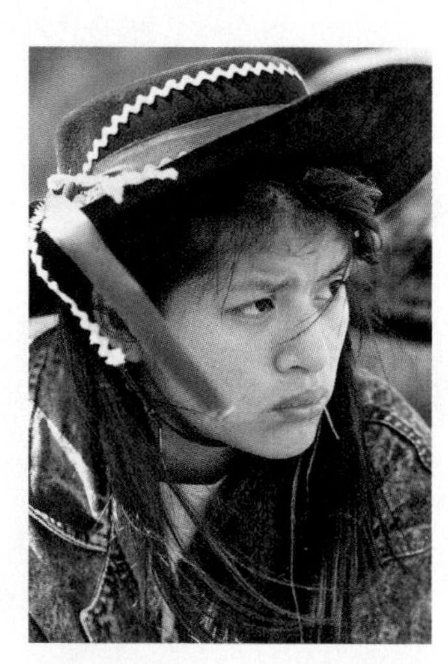

Estrategia

Remember that adjectives describe nouns and agree in number (singular/plural) and gender (masculine/feminine) with the nouns they are describing.

Fíjate

Notice that *ropa* is a singular noun. All verb forms and adjectives used with it should be singular. Think *clothing* instead of *clothes*.

8-6 ¿Qué está de moda?

Trae a la clase tres o cuatro fotos de modelos (pueden ser de una revista (*magazine*), un catálogo o del Internet). Túrnate con un/a compañero/a para describir en por lo menos **tres** frases lo que los modelos llevan puesto. Digan qué ropa les gusta más y qué ropa les gusta menos. ¿Están de acuerdo?

Capítulo Preliminar A. Los días, los meses y las estaciones, pág. 20.

8-7 Señora, ¿qué debo llevar?

Trabajas para una agencia de viajes y, para ayudar a tus clientes, tienes que preparar una lista de la ropa que deben llevar a cada destino (*destination*). Compara tu lista con la de un/a compañero/a.

Fíjate

Remember that the seasons south of the equator are the opposite of those in the northern hemisphere, e.g., when it is summer in the northern hemisphere it is winter in the southern hemisphere.

1. Argentina en julio
2. Costa Rica en junio
3. México en septiembre
4. Cuba en diciembre
5. Uruguay en marzo
6. España en febrero

8•8 El juego del viaje (*travel*)

¿Te gusta viajar? Formen un círculo de cinco estudiantes o más. Primero, decidan dónde quieren ir de viaje. Después, túrnense para decir sus nombres y un artículo de ropa que quieren llevar. Cada estudiante tiene que repetir lo que dijeron los estudiantes anteriores. **¡OJO!** Si no recuerdan (*If you don't remember*), tienen que preguntar: **¿Qué dijiste, por favor?** o **¿Puedes repetir, por favor?**

MODELO Vamos a Cancún.

E1: *Soy Beverly y voy a llevar un traje de baño.*

E2: *Soy Tim y voy a llevar una camiseta blanca.*
Beverly va a llevar un traje de baño.

E3: *Soy Kelly y voy a llevar una chaqueta.*
Tim va a llevar una camiseta blanca.
Beverly va a llevar un traje de baño.

E4: ...

Estrategia

It is important to be supportive of your fellow classmates during these activities, which includes making suggestions and helpful comments and corrections. Because you will be learning from each other, it is good to know the following expressions to help you interact with each other:

(No) Estoy de acuerdo.	*I agree./I don't agree.*
Yo pienso que es...	*I think it's...*
¿No debería ser...?	*Shouldn't it be...?*

Capítulo 4. Ir + a + infinitivo, pág. 149;
Capítulo 5. Los pronombres de complemento directo, pág. 190;
Capítulo 7. El pretérito, pág. 258.

8•9 ¿Tienes un presupuesto (*budget*)?

Completa el siguiente cuadro con las prendas que acabas de comprar (*have just bought*) y con las que necesitas comprar. Después, comparte tus respuestas con un/a compañero/a.

Fíjate

The expression *acabar de + infinitive* means *to have just done something.* Use this expression in the present tense when you want to refer to the very recent past. As in the *modelo*, this expression is useful for establishing a context for the use of the preterit.

MODELO *Acabo de comprar una blusa. La compré en J.C. Penney la semana pasada. Pagué quince dólares. Necesito comprar una falda.*

ACABO DE COMPRAR...	LO(S)/LA(S) COMPRÉ...	PAGUÉ...	VOY A/NECESITO COMPRAR...
1. *una blusa*	*en J.C. Penney*	*$15*	*una falda*
2.			
3.			

8•10 ¿Quién puede ser?

Escoge a una persona de tu clase y piensa en la ropa que lleva incluyendo el estilo (*style*), el color y la tela. Describe **cuatro** de sus prendas a tu compañero/a, quien tiene que adivinar a quién describes. Túrnense para describir a **tres** compañeros de clase.

MODELO E1: *Esta persona lleva unos pantalones largos de rayas blancas, una camiseta oscura, una chaqueta informal y unos zapatos de tenis blancos.*

E2: *Es Mayra.*

8-12 to 8-13

Zara: la moda internacional

En España, uno de los negocios más florecientes (*flourishing*) es la empresa de ropa Zara. El fundador, Amancio Ortega Gaona, empezó el negocio (*business*) en La Coruña, en el norte de España, con unas 5.000 pesetas ($83.00 US). Ahora el Sr. Ortega es uno de los hombres más ricos de este país.

Fíjate

In 2002, Spain converted to the *euro*. Previously, its currency was the *peseta*.

Una de las razones del gran éxito del negocio es que continuamente ofrece lo que la gente quiere. Su filosofía es vender ropa "barata y de buena calidad". Tiene unos doscientos diseñadores (*designers*) que son los responsables de crear la moda Zara. Las diferentes líneas creadas por los diseñadores proporcionan un *look* completo para hombres y mujeres.

La mayoría de la ropa se hace en una fábrica (*factory*) muy moderna en La Coruña. Desde el momento que surge la idea hasta que la prenda llega a la tienda, sólo pasan unas tres semanas. Dos o tres veces por semana llegan productos nuevos a las tiendas y así se renueva más del cuarenta por ciento del inventario.

Ahora se puede comprar la moda Zara en más de 626 tiendas en 46 países, por catálogo y por el Internet. Para conocer la moda internacional del momento, hay que conocer Zara.

Preguntas

1. ¿Quién empezó el negocio Zara y dónde? ¿Cuánto le costó?
2. ¿Por qué tiene tanto éxito el negocio?

Los pronombres de complemento indirecto

8-14 to 8-16

33, 34

The indirect object indicates *to whom* or *for whom* an action is done. Note these examples:

A: My mom bought this dress *for whom*?

B: She bought this dress *for you*.

A: Yes, she bought *me* this dress.

Review the chart of the indirect object pronouns and their English equivalents:

Los pronombres de complemento indirecto

me	*to/for me*
te	*to/for you*
le	*to/for him, her, you* (Ud.)
nos	*to/for us*
os	*to/for you all* (vosotros)
les	*to/for them, you all* (Uds.)

Now study the sentences in the following box and answer the questions that follow.

Mi madre	**me**	compra mucha ropa.
Mi madre	**te**	compra mucha ropa.
Mi madre	**le**	compra mucha ropa a mi hermano.
Mi madre	**nos**	compra mucha ropa.
Mi madre	**os**	compra mucha ropa.
Mi madre	**les**	compra mucha ropa a mis hermanos.

In each of the above sentences:

1. Who is *buying* the clothing?
2. Who is *receiving* the clothing?

Check your answers to the preceding questions in Appendix 1.

Now, look at the following examples. Can you identify the direct objects along with the indirect object pronouns?

¿Me traes la falda de rayas?	*Will you bring me the striped skirt?*
Su novio le regaló la chaqueta de cuero.	*Her boyfriend gave her the leather jacket.*
Mi hermana me compró la blusa de seda.	*My sister bought me the silk blouse.*
Nuestra compañera de cuarto nos lavó la ropa.	*Our roommate washed our clothes for us.*

Some things to remember:

1. Like direct object pronouns, indirect object pronouns *precede* the verb and can also be *attached to infinitives and present participles* (**-ando, -iendo**).

¿**Me** quieres dar el dinero? ¿Quieres dar**me** el dinero?	*Do you want to give me the money?*
¿**Me** vas a dar el dinero? ¿Vas a dar**me** el dinero?	*Are you going to give me the money?*
¿**Me** estás dando el dinero? ¿Estás dándo**me** el dinero?	*Are you giving me the money?*
Manolo **te** puede comprar la gorra en la tienda. Manolo puede comprar**te** la gorra en la tienda.	*Manolo can buy you the hat at the store.*
Su hermano **le** va a regalar una camiseta. Su hermano va a regalar**le** una camiseta.	*Her brother is going to give her a T-shirt.*

2. To clarify or emphasize the indirect object, a prepositional phrase (**a** + *prepositional pronoun*) can be added, as in the following sentences. Clarification of **le** and **les** is especially important since they can refer to different people (*him, her, you, them, you all*).

Le presto el abrigo **a él** pero no **le** presto nada **a ella.**	*I'm loaning him my coat but I'm not loaning her anything.* (clarification)
¿**Me** preguntas **a mí**?	*Are you asking me?* (emphasis)

3. As you have seen, indirect object pronouns are used without the indirect object noun when the person to/for whom the action is being done is known.

8•11 Amigos perfectos

Cuando sus mejores amigos celebran sus cumpleaños, tu pareja y tú siempre organizan las fiestas. Juntos escriban frases sobre las cosas que hacen, usando **me, te, nos, le** y **les.**

MODELO E1: yo/preparar/las fiestas de cumpleaños/para mis amigos

E2: *Yo preparo las fiestas de cumpleaños para mis amigos. / Les preparo las fiestas.*

1. yo/preparar/una fiesta de sorpresa/para él o ella
2. yo/mandar/invitaciones/a todos nuestros amigos
3. mis otros amigos y yo/comprar/unos regalos cómicos/para él o ella
4. yo/hacer/una torta/para mi amigo
5. nosotros/dar/unas flores bonitas/a nuestra amiga
6. nosotros/cantar/a nuestro amigo/una canción especial

8•12 ¿Qué me recomienda?

Una persona hace el papel de consejero/a y la otra de estudiante de primer año (*freshman*). Deben hacer y contestar las siguientes preguntas según el modelo. Al terminar, cambien de papel.

MODELO E1: ¿Me recomienda la clase de Conversación 101?

E2: *No, no le recomiendo esa clase. Le recomiendo la clase de civilización española.*

1. ¿Me está pidiendo Ud. información sobre mi familia?
2. ¿Me recomienda Ud. algunas clases fáciles?
3. ¿Me ayuda Ud. con mis estudios?
4. ¿Me recomienda Ud. jugar algún deporte?
5. ¿Me recomienda Ud. hablar con mis profesores fuera de clase?
6. ¿Me recomienda Ud. la cafetería?

Capítulo 3. Los quehaceres de la casa, pág. 112; Capítulo 7. El pretérito, pág. 258.

8•13 ¡Qué suerte!

Haz una lista de por lo menos **cuatro** cosas que tú hiciste por tu compañero/a de cuarto o tu familia la semana pasada. Después, haz otra lista de tres o cuatro cosas que esa persona hizo por ti. Compara tu lista con la de un/a compañero/a.

MODELO E1: *A mi compañero de cuarto le arreglé la sala y le contesté el teléfono.*

E2: *Mi compañera de cuarto me lavó la ropa. Me preparó la comida…*

Capítulo 7. El pretérito, pág. 258.

8•14 Los regalos

¿Te regalaron muchas cosas este año? ¿Regalaste muchas cosas tú? Escribe una lista de **cuatro** regalos que te dieron y de **cuatro** cosas que tú les regalaste. Después comparte tu lista con un/a compañero/a según el modelo. ¡Hay que ser creativos!

MODELO E1: *Le di una corbata a mi padre.*

E2: *¿Ah sí? ¿De qué color? ¿Le gustó a tu padre?*

E1: *Sí, le gustó mucho la corbata azul. Y mis padres me regalaron una bicicleta.*

E2: *¡Qué suerte! ¿Te gusta andar en bicicleta?*

Fíjate

As in English, there are word "families." *El regalo* (noun) means "gift" and *regalar* (verb) means "to give a gift."

GRAMÁTICA 3 *Gustar* y verbos como *gustar*

SAM 8-17 to 8-20

Guide 11, 12, 15, 19

As you already know, the verb **gustar** is used to express likes and dislikes. **Gustar** functions differently from other verbs you have studied so far.

- The person, thing, or idea that is liked is the *subject* (S) of the sentence.
- The person who likes the other person, thing, or idea is the *indirect object* (IO).

Consider the chart below:

(A mí) **me** gusta el traje.	*I like the suit.*	(A nosotros/as) **nos** gusta el traje.	*We like the suit.*
(A ti) **te** gusta el traje.	*You like the suit.*	(A vosotros/as) **os** gusta el traje.	*You (all) like the suit.*
(A él) **le** gusta el traje.	*He likes the suit.*	(A ellos/as) **les** gusta el traje.	*They like the suit.*
(A ella) **le** gusta el traje.	*She likes the suit.*	(A Uds.) **les** gusta el traje.	*You (all) like the suit.*
(A Ud.) **le** gusta el traje.	*You like the suit.*		

Note the following:

1. The construction **a** + *pronoun* (**a mí, a ti, a él,** etc.) or **a** + *noun* is optional most of the time. It is used for clarification or emphasis. Clarification of **le gusta** and **les gusta** is especially important since the indirect object pronouns **le** and **les** can refer to different people (*him, her, you, them, you all*).

A él le gusta llevar ropa cómoda. (clarification)	*He likes to wear comfortable clothes.*
A Ana le gusta llevar ropa cómoda. (clarification)	*Ana likes to wear comfortable clothes.*
Me gustan esos pantalones de lunares.	*I like those pants with the polka dots.*
A mí me gustan más ésos de rayas (emphasis).	*I like those striped ones even more.*

2. Use the plural form **gustan** when what is liked (the subject of the sentence) is plural.

Me gusta **el traje.**	→	Me gusta**n los trajes.**
I like the suit.		*I like the suits.*

3. To express the idea that one likes *to do* something, **gustar** is followed by an infinitive. In that case you always use the singular **gusta,** even when you use more than one infinitive in the sentence:

Me gusta ir de compras por la mañana.	*I like to go shopping in the morning.*
A Pepe **le gusta leer** revistas de moda y **llevar** ropa atrevida.	*Pepe likes to read fashion magazines and wear daring clothing.*
Nos gusta hacer ejercicio y **andar** antes de ir a clase.	*We like to exercise and walk before going to class.*

The verbs listed below function like **gustar:**

encantar	*to love; delight*	**importar**	*to matter; to be important*
fascinar	*to fascinate*	**molestar**	*to bother*
hacer falta	*to need; to be lacking*		

Me encanta ir de compras.	*I love to go shopping. (Shopping delights me.)*
A Doug y a David **les fascina** la tienda de ropa Rugby.	*The Rugby clothing store fascinates (is fascinating to) Doug and David.*
¿**Te hace falta** dinero para comprar el vestido?	*Do you need (are you lacking) money to buy the dress?*
A Juan **le importa** el precio de la ropa, no la moda.	*The price of the clothing, not the style, matters (is important) to Juan.*
Nos molestan las personas que llevan sandalias en invierno.	*People who wear sandals in the winter bother us.*

Capítulo 5. El mundo de la música, pág. 172.

8•15 Hablando de la música...

A Jaime y a Celia les gusta mucho la música. Completa las oraciones para descubrir sus preferencias. Después, comparte tu párrafo con un/a compañero/a.

MODELO A nosotros *nos fascina* (fascinar) la música rap.

A nosotros (1) ______ ________________ (encantar) la música rock. A mí (2) ______ ________________ (gustar) los grupos como Aerosmith y Tool. Mi cantante favorito es Dave Matthews y (3) ______ ________________ (gustar) su grupo también. A Celia (4) ______ ________________ (fascinar) el grupo No Doubt. Celia tiene casi todos los CD pero (5) ______ ________________ ________________ (hacer falta) uno que se llama *Running*. A nuestros compañeros (6) ______ ________________ (molestar) tener que escuchar nuestra música favorita. Ellos prefieren la música jazz. A Celia y a mí no (7) ______ ________________ (importar) su opinión, ¡somos amigos pero no nos tienen que gustar las mismas cosas siempre!

8•16 ¿Qué opinas?

Da tu opinión sobre estas personas famosas poniendo una equis (**X**) en la columna apropiada. Después, comparte tu opinión con un/a compañero/a.

MODELO E1: *¿Te fascinan los diseños de Óscar de la Renta y Narciso Rodríguez?*

E2: *Sí, me fascinan. / No, no me importan mucho. / No sé, no los conozco.*

Salvador Dalí

Gloria Estefan

Antonio Banderas

Isabel Allende

Diego Rivera

Carlos Santana

Salma Hayek

Pablo Neruda

	ME FASCINA(N)	ME ENCANTA(N)	NO ME IMPORTA(N) MUCHO	NO LO(S)/LA(S) CONOZCO
1. las pinturas de Salvador Dalí				
2. las canciones de Gloria Estefan				
3. las películas de Antonio Banderas				
4. las novelas de Isabel Allende				
5. los murales de Diego Rivera				
6. la música de Carlos Santana				
7. las películas de Salma Hayek				
8. los poemas de Pablo Neruda				

8-17 En mi opinión...

¿Qué te gusta y no te gusta de tu universidad?

Paso 1 Completa el siguiente cuadro según tu opinión.

ME MOLESTA(N)...	ME ENCANTA(N)...	NOS HACE(N) FALTA...
1.	1.	1.
2.	2.	2.
3.	3.	3.

Paso 2 Ahora, circula por la clase para pedirles a tres compañeros su opinión.

MODELO E1 (TÚ): *¿Qué te molesta?*

E2: *Me molesta la comida de la cafetería.*

A _____ LE MOLESTA(N)...	A _____ LE ENCANTA(N)...	NOS HACE(N) FALTA...
1.	1.	1.
2.	2.	2.
3.	3.	3.

4 GRAMÁTICA Los pronombres de complemento directo e indirecto usados juntos

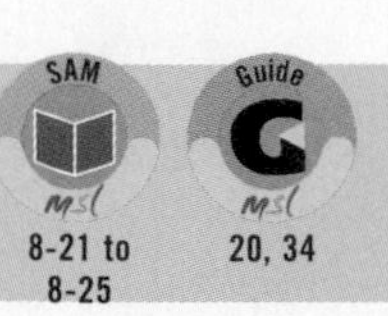

You have worked with two types of object pronouns, direct and indirect. Now note how they are used together in the same sentence.

La profesora nos está devolviendo **los exámenes**. → La profesora nos **los** está devolviendo.
The professor is giving us back the exams. *The professor is giving them back to us.*
¡Ella no nos regala **las notas**! → ¡Ella no nos **las** regala!
She does not give away grades! *She does not give them to us!*
Tatiana me pide **dinero** ahora. → Tatiana me **lo** pide ahora.
Tatiana is asking me for money now. *Tatiana is asking me for it now.*
Mi novio me trae **la comida**. → Mi novio me **la** trae.
My boyfriend brings me food. *My boyfriend brings it to me.*

1. You know that direct and indirect objects come after the verb. Where do you find the direct and indirect object pronouns?
2. Reading from left to right, which pronoun comes first (direct or indirect)? Which pronoun comes second?

Check your answers for the preceding questions in Appendix 1.

¡OJO! A change occurs when you use **le** or **les** along with a direct object pronoun that begins with **l: (lo, la, los, las)**: **le** or **les** changes to **se.**

le → se

Tatiana le pide **un favor** a él. → Tatiana se **lo** pide a él.
Memo le lleva **comida** a su novia. → Memo se **la** lleva a su novia.
La profesora no le regala **la nota** al estudiante. → La profesora no se **la** regala al estudiante.

les → se

La profesora les devuelve **los exámenes** a ellos. → La profesora se **los** devuelve a ellos.
Ella les da **buenas notas** a todos los estudiantes. → Ella se **las** da a todos los estudiantes.
Yo no le pido **un favor** al profesor. → Yo no se **lo** pido al profesor.

Direct and indirect object pronouns may also be attached to infinitives and present participles. Note that when attached, an accent is placed over the final vowel of the infinitive and the next-to-last vowel of the participle.

¿Aquel abrigo? Mi madre **me lo** va a comprar.
¿Aquel abrigo? Mi madre va a comprár**melo.** } *That coat over there? My mother is going to buy it for me.*

Me lo está comprando ahora.
Está comprándo**melo** ahora. } *She is buying it for me now.*

Capítulo 7. El pretérito, pág. 258; Unos verbos irregulares en el pretérito, pág. 266.

8-18 Combinaciones

Escribe oraciones completas sobre Pablo y su hermano Antonio usando los pronombres de complemento directo e indirecto. Comparte tus frases con un/a compañero/a.

MODELO Mi hermano Antonio/prestar/(a mí)/sus libros favoritos/ayer

E1: *Mi hermano Antonio* ***me*** *prestó* ***sus libros favoritos*** *ayer.*

E2: *Mi hermano Antonio* ***me los*** *prestó ayer.*

1. Yo/dar/(a Antonio)/unos CD/la semana pasada
2. Mis padres/regalar/(a Antonio)/un coche nuevo/el año pasado
3. Yo/lavar/la ropa/(a Antonio)/anteayer
4. Antonio/cantar/una canción/(a mí)/anoche
5. Antonio y yo/decir/la verdad sobre el accidente/(a nuestros padres)/ayer

8-19 Antonio, ¿me prestas...?

Ahora Pablo va a una fiesta y quiere usar la ropa de su hermano Antonio. Túrnense para hacer los papeles de Pablo y Antonio usando los pronombres de complemento directo e indirecto.

MODELO prestar/un abrigo

E1: (Pablo): *¿Me prestas el abrigo?*

E2: (Antonio): *Sí, te lo presto. / No, no te lo presto.*

1. prestar/los zapatos negros
2. prestar/la corbata de rayas azules
3. prestar/una camiseta blanca y una camisa azul de manga larga (*long sleeved*)
4. prestar/el cinturón de cuero negro
5. prestar/tu coche nuevo

8•20 Mis recomendaciones

¿Qué recomiendas? Lee la lista y pon una equis (**X**) en la columna apropiada. Después, comparte tus opiniones con un/a compañero/a según el modelo.

MODELO los libros de Tom Clancy (a tus primas)

E1: *¿Les recomiendas los libros de Tom Clancy a tus primas?*

E2: *No, no se los recomiendo.*

	SÍ	NO
1. las novelas de Stephen King (a tus tíos)		
2. la música de Eminem (a tu compañero/a de cuarto)		
3. el restaurante Taco Bell (a nosotros)		
4. el hotel Hilton (a tu amiga que no tiene mucho dinero)		
5. la película *Drácula* (a tus primos de cinco años)		
6. Disney World (a tu hermano)		
7. el Museo de Arte Moderno (a tu profesor/a)		
8. la clase de español (a tu mejor amigo/a)		

8•21 ¿En qué puedo servirle?

Acabas de empezar un trabajo en prácticas (*internship*). En vez de (*Instead of*) tareas productivas asociadas con la profesión, te dan el trabajo de ayudante de una de las vice presidentas. Túrnense para contestar sus preguntas.

MODELO E1: ¿Me puede comprar un periódico?

E2: *Sí, se lo puedo comprar. / Sí, puedo comprárselo.*

1. ¿Me puede traer un café?
2. ¿Me puede comprar los boletos (*tickets*) para un viaje a Nueva York?
3. ¿Me puede arreglar los apuntes y los papeles para la reunión de esta tarde?
4. ¿Me puede buscar un artículo en el periódico?
5. ¿Me puede reservar una mesa en un restaurante elegante para esta noche?
6. ¿Me puede comprar unas rosas para la recepcionista? Es su cumpleaños hoy.

Estrategia

Remember that when addressing an employer, you would use *Usted*, not *tú*. Also, be sure to practice both ways of structuring the sentence with two object pronouns, as in the *modelo*.

¿Cómo andas?

Having completed the first **Comunicación**, I now can…

	Feel Confident	Need to Review
• describe clothing (p. 286)	❑	❑
• pronounce the letters **ll** and **ñ** properly in Spanish (p. 287)	❑	❑
• talk about a Spanish clothing company (p. 291)	❑	❑
• talk about to whom and for whom things are done (p. 292)	❑	❑
• talk about clothing I like and dislike (p. 294)	❑	❑
• share what delights, fascinates, bothers, and matters to me and others, as well as what I and others need using the verbs **encantar, fascinar, hacer falta, importar,** and **molestar** (p. 295)	❑	❑
• use **me, te, le, nos, les** (indirect object pronouns) correctly in sentences as well as in combination with **me, te, lo, la, nos, los, las** (direct object pronouns) in the same sentence (p. 298)	❑	❑

Comunicación

- Discussing daily routines
- Describing situations in the past

Las construcciones reflexivas

8-26 to 8-31

25, 26

Study the captions for the drawings below.

In each drawing:

- Who is performing/doing the action?
- Who or what is receiving the action?

When the subject both performs and receives the action of the verb, a reflexive verb and pronoun are used.

- Which of the drawings and captions demonstrate reflexive verbs?

Look at the chart that follows; the reflexive pronouns are highlighted.

La fiesta **los** despierta.

Alberto **la** acuesta.

Beatriz **lo** lava.

Raúl y Gloria **se** despiertan.

Alberto **se** acuesta.

Beatriz **se** lava la cara.

Reflexive pronouns

Siempre	**me**	divierto	en las fiestas.
Siempre	**te**	diviertes	en las fiestas.
Siempre	**se**	divierte	en las fiestas.
Siempre	**nos**	divertimos	en las fiestas.
Siempre	**os**	divertís	en las fiestas.
Siempre	**se**	divierten	en las fiestas.

Reflexive pronouns follow the same rules for position as other object pronouns. Reflexive pronouns:

1. precede a conjugated verb.
2. can be attached to *infinitives* and *present participles* (**-ando, -iendo**).

Te vas a dormir. Vas a dormir**te**.	*You are falling asleep.*
¿**Se** van a dormir esta noche? ¿Van a dormir**se** esta noche?	*Are they going to fall asleep tonight?*
¿**Se** están durmiendo? ¿Están durmiéndo**se**?	*Are you all falling asleep?*

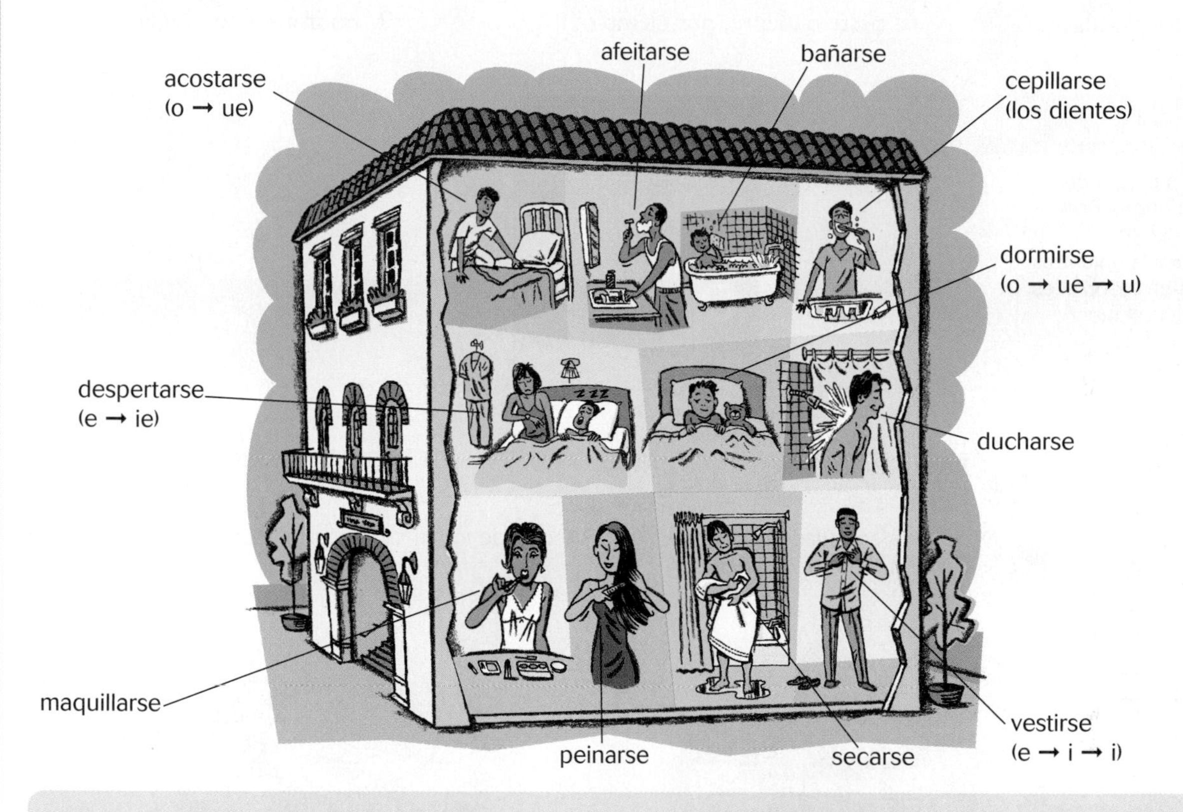

Unos verbos reflexivos

acordarse de (o → ue)	*to remember*	**ponerse (la ropa)**	*to put on (one's clothes)*
arreglarse	*to get ready*	**ponerse (nervioso/a)**	*to get (nervous)*
callarse	*to get/keep quiet*	**quedarse**	*to stay; to remain*
divertirse (e → ie → i)	*to enjoy oneself; to have fun*	**quitarse (la ropa)**	*to take off (one's clothes)*
irse	*to go away; to leave*	**reunirse**	*to get together; to meet*
lavarse	*to wash oneself*	**secarse**	*to dry off*
levantarse	*to get up; to stand up*	**sentarse (e → ie)**	*to sit down*
llamarse	*to be called*	**sentirse (e → ie → i)**	*to feel*

Note: To identify all of the previous verbs as *reflexive*, the infinitive ends in **-se.**

Estrategia

When a new infinitive is presented, if it is a stem-changing verb, the irregularities will be given in parentheses. For example, if you see *divertirse* (*e → ie → i*) you know that this infinitive is an *-ir* stem-changing verb, that the first "e" in the infinitive changes to "ie" in the present indicative, and that the "e" changes to "i" in the 3rd person singular and plural of the preterit.

Fíjate

Some verbs change their meaning slightly between non-reflexive and reflexive verbs, for example: *dormir* (to sleep) and *dormirse* (to fall asleep); *ir* (to go) and *irse* (to leave).

8•22 El juego de la asociación

Juntos decidan qué verbos reflexivos asocian con las siguientes palabras y expresiones.

1. no decir nada
2. una silla
3. recordar algo
4. tener sueño
5. no recordar algo
6. triste o alegre, por ejemplo
7. un sombrero
8. estar sucio
9. no ir a ningún lugar

8•23 ¡Batalla!

Van a jugar con un/a compañero/a a *tic-tac-toe*. Escuchen mientras el/la profesor/a les explica el juego.

Capítulo 7. El pretérito, pág. 258. Unos verbos irregulares en el pretérito, pág. 266.

8•24 Un día en la vida

Ordena las actividades diarias de María y Tomás de forma cronológica. Después, compara tu lista con la de un/a compañero/a.

El día de María

1. Antes de irse a la universidad, se acordó de la tarea que no hizo para su clase de historia.
2. Se duchó.
3. Se maquilló.
4. Llegó a la clase de historia y se quitó el abrigo.
5. Se vistió.
6. Se secó.
7. Se levantó.

El día de Tomás

1. Se acostó tarde.
2. Se levantó rápidamente a las ocho.
3. Se despertó tarde.
4. No se durmió inmediatamente.
5. Se divirtió con sus amigos.
6. Después de las clases se fue con los amigos para pasar el fin de semana en la playa.
7. Se fue para la clase de química.

8•25 Un día normal

Capítulo Preliminar A. La hora, pág. 18.

Escribe por lo menos **cinco** actividades que haces normalmente y a qué hora las haces. Usa verbos reflexivos. Después, comparte tu lista con un/a compañero/a.

8•26 A conocerte más aún

Túrnense para hacerse esta entrevista y conocer mejor sus hábitos.

MODELO E1: ¿Qué te pones para ir al cine?

E2: *Me pongo pantalones vaqueros con una camiseta. ¿Y tú? ¿Qué te pones?*

E1: *Generalmente me pongo pantalones con una blusa o un suéter.*

E2: ¿Qué…?

1. ¿Qué te pones cuando sales con esa "persona especial"?
2. Cuando estás durmiéndote, ¿te acuerdas de las cosas que no hiciste durante el día?
3. ¿Cómo te diviertes?
4. Si tienes tiempo, ¿con quién(es) te reúnes?
5. ¿Cuándo te pones nervioso/a?
6. ¿Cuándo te sientes feliz?

8•27 Mímica

Hagan mímica (*charades*) en grupos de cuatro. Túrnense para escoger un verbo reflexivo para representar al grupo. El grupo tiene que adivinar qué verbo es. Sigan jugando hasta que cada estudiante represente **cuatro** verbos diferentes.

8•28 ¿Conoces bien a tus compañeros?

Trabaja en grupos de cuatro para hacer esta actividad.

Paso 1 Un/a compañero/a debe salir de la sala de clase por un momento. Los otros estudiantes escriben **cinco** preguntas sobre la vida diaria del/de la compañero/a, usando los verbos reflexivos.

MODELO *¿A qué hora te despiertas?*

¿Te duchas todos los días?

Paso 2 Antes de entrar el/la compañero/a, el grupo de estudiantes debe adivinar cuáles van a ser las respuestas a esas preguntas.

MODELO *Me despierto a las siete.*

Sí, me ducho todos los días.

Paso 3 Entra el/la compañero/a y los otros le hacen las preguntas.

Paso 4 Comparen las respuestas del grupo con las del/de la compañero/a. ¿Tenían razón? Pueden repetir la actividad con los otros miembros del grupo.

8-32 to 8-33

Los centros comerciales en Latinoamérica

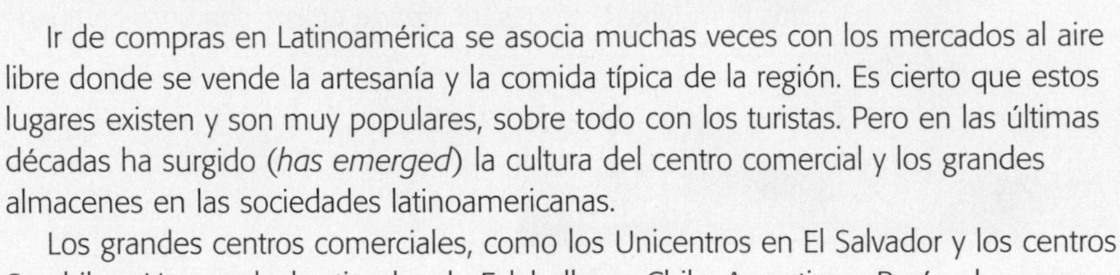

Ir de compras en Latinoamérica se asocia muchas veces con los mercados al aire libre donde se vende la artesanía y la comida típica de la región. Es cierto que estos lugares existen y son muy populares, sobre todo con los turistas. Pero en las últimas décadas ha surgido (*has emerged*) la cultura del centro comercial y los grandes almacenes en las sociedades latinoamericanas.

Los grandes centros comerciales, como los Unicentros en El Salvador y los centros Sambil en Venezuela, las tiendas de Falabella en Chile, Argentina y Perú, y los almacenes Liverpool en México son buenos ejemplos de mercados modernos que atraen a la población latina de varias clases económicas. Estas tiendas son modernas y ofrecen de todo a los clientes que buscan una gran variedad de productos como, por ejemplo, ropa, artículos y aparatos domésticos y muebles.

La gente va a los centros comerciales para pasear, mirar y entretenerse (*to entertain oneself*). En muchos hay hipermercados donde se puede comprar comida y artículos diversos para el hogar. Los centros comerciales son lugares para citas, para pasar el tiempo, para ir al cine, para reunirse con amigos, para observar a la gente, para ojear las vitrinas (*window shop*) y para enterarse de las últimas tendencias de la moda. Verdaderamente, estos centros han cambiado (*have changed*) mucho el estilo de vida de la gente hoy en día.

Preguntas

1. Antes de leer "Los centros comerciales en Latinoamérica", ¿qué entendías tú (*did you understand*) por "mercado latinoamericano"? ¿Qué imagen tenías (*did you used to have*)?
2. ¿Qué hace la gente en los centros comerciales latinoamericanos? ¿Cómo se comparan estas actividades con las de los centros comerciales estadounidenses?

El imperfecto

8-34 to 8-38

36, 41

In **Capítulo 7** you learned how to express certain ideas and notions that happened in the past with the preterit. Spanish has another past tense, **el imperfecto,** that *expresses habitual or ongoing past actions, provides descriptions,* or *describes conditions.*

Cuando Pepe vivía en la playa, nadaba en el mar todas las mañanas.

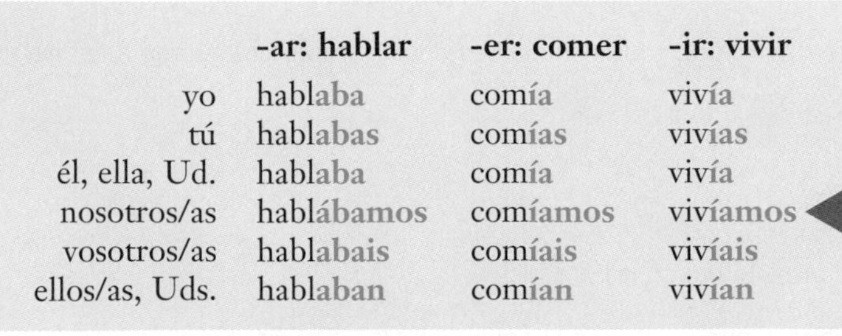

	-ar: hablar	**-er: comer**	**-ir: vivir**
yo	hablaba	comía	vivía
tú	hablabas	comías	vivías
él, ella, Ud.	hablaba	comía	vivía
nosotros/as	hablábamos	comíamos	vivíamos
vosotros/as	hablabais	comíais	vivíais
ellos/as, Uds.	hablaban	comían	vivían

Estrategia

Focus on the forms and when to use the *imperfecto.* Note that the *-er* and *-ir* forms are exactly the same, and that they have accents in every form. Also note that in the *-ar* verbs the *nosotros/nosotras* form has an accent.

There are only *three irregular verbs* in the imperfect: **ir, ser,** and **ver.**

	ir	**ser**	**ver**
yo	iba	era	veía
tú	ibas	eras	veías
él, ella, Ud.	iba	era	veía
nosotros/as	íbamos	éramos	veíamos
vosotros/as	ibais	erais	veíais
ellos/as, Uds.	iban	eran	veían

The imperfect is used to:

1. provide background information, set the stage, or express a condition that existed

Llovía mucho. — *It was raining a lot.*

Era una noche oscura y nublada. — *It was a dark and cloudy night.*

Estábamos en el segundo año de la universidad. — *We were in our second year of college.*

Adriana **estaba** enferma y no **quería** levantarse. — *Adriana was ill and didn't want to get up/get out of bed.*

Fíjate

Repeated actions are usually expressed in English with *used to...* or *would...*

2. describe habitual or often repeated actions

Íbamos al cine todos los viernes. Nos **divertíamos** mucho. — *We went (used to go) to the movies every Friday. We had a lot of fun.*

Cuando **era** pequeño, Lebron **jugaba** al básquetbol por lo menos dos horas al día. — *When he was little Lebron played (used to play) basketball for at least two hours a day.*

Mis padres siempre **se levantaban** a las seis de la mañana. — *My parents always got up (used to get up) at 6:00 A.M.*

Some words or expressions for describing habitual and repeated actions are:

a menudo	*often*	**muchas veces**	*many times*
casi siempre	*almost always*	**mucho**	*a lot*
frecuentemente	*frequently*	**normalmente**	*normally*
generalmente	*generally*	**siempre**	*always*
mientras	*while*	**todos los días**	*every day*

3. express *was* or *were* + *-ing*

¿**Dormías**? — *Were you sleeping?*

Me duchaba cuando Juan llamó. — *I was showering when Juan called.*

Alberto **leía** mientras Alicia **escuchaba** música. — *Alberto was reading while Alicia was listening to music.*

4. tell time in the past

Era la una y yo todavía **estudiaba.** — *It was 1:00 and I was still studying.*

Eran las siete y media y los niños **se dormían.** — *It was 7:30 and the children were falling asleep.*

8-29 La práctica

Repitan el juego de la actividad **7-11** en la página 260, esta vez para practicar el imperfecto.

8-30 Cuando era joven

Completa el párrafo sobre Eva Perón para saber cómo pudo ser su vida cuando era joven. Después, compara tus respuestas con las de un/a compañero/a.

ayudar	encantar	gustar	poder	querer
preferir	sentirse	ser	tener	trabajar

María Eva Duarte, como primero se llamaba, nació en una provincia de Buenos Aires en 1919. Cuando (1) ______________ seis o siete años su padre murió. Eva y sus cuatro hermanos (2) ______________ muy tristes y para ellos la vida (3) ______________ muy difícil porque les faltaban dinero y comida. La madre (4) ______________ como costurera (*seamstress*) y los niños le (5) ______________ en la casa. Imaginamos que a Eva le (6) ______________ el verano cuando (7) ______________ estar en casa con sus hermanos. No le (8) ______________ las muñecas y (9) ______________ inventar juegos o imaginar situaciones diferentes. Parece que desde el principio (*from the start*) Eva (10) ______________ ser actriz.

8-31 En el colegio...

¿Qué hacías cuando estabas en el colegio? ¿Con qué frecuencia? Escribe una equis (**X**) en la columna apropiada. Luego, compara tus respuestas con las de un/a compañero/a.

Fíjate

In actividad **8-31**, you see the word *el colegio*. Remember that *colegio* is a false cognate in Spanish; it can mean *school* or *high school*.

MODELO E1: *¿Escuchabas música de Frank Sinatra?*

E2: *No, nunca escuchaba música de Frank Sinatra. / Sí, a veces escuchaba música de Frank Sinatra.*

	TODOS LOS DÍAS	MUCHAS VECES	A VECES	NUNCA
1. escuchar música de Frank Sinatra				
2. nadar en la playa				
3. leer obras de Shakespeare				
4. bañarse				
5. acostarse temprano				
6. dormirse en las clases				
7. ponerse nervioso/a antes de un examen				
8. reunirse con los amigos				
9. vestirse como querías				
10. querer ir a la escuela				
11. levantarse muy tarde				
12. no hacer nada por la noche				

Capítulo 3. La casa, pág. 100.

8-32 Mi primera casa

¿Cómo era tu primera casa o la casa de tu amigo/a? Descríbesela a un/a compañero/a dándole por lo menos **cinco** detalles. Después, cambien de papel.

MODELO *Mi primera casa estaba en una ciudad pequeña. Tenía dos dormitorios. La cocina era amarilla. El comedor y la sala eran pequeños. Tenía solamente* (only) *un baño.*

8-33 Cómo ha cambiado la vida

Miren el dibujo y escriban **siete** oraciones que contesten la pregunta "¿cómo era la vida en los años setenta?". Usen verbos como **tener, estar, ser, haber, ayudar, limpiar** y **jugar.** Sean creativos.

8-34 Preguntas personales

Cuando tenían dieciséis años, ¿qué hacían tus compañeros/as de clase? Circula por la clase para preguntárselo.

MODELO E1: ¿Jugabas al fútbol con los amigos?
E2: *Sí, jugaba todos los días después de salir del colegio.*
E3: *Sí, jugaba con el equipo del colegio.*
E4: *No, nunca jugaba al fútbol. No me gustaba.*

	ESTUDIANTE 1:	ESTUDIANTE 2:	ESTUDIANTE 3:
1. ¿Te quedabas en casa los fines de semana?			
2. ¿Qué hacías los fines de semana?			
3. ¿Manejabas?			
4. ¿Tenías coche?			
5. ¿Trabajabas?			
6. ¿Qué hacías cuando hacía mal tiempo?			
7. ¿Qué hacías cuando hacía buen tiempo?			
8. ¿Qué hacías cuando tenías dinero?			
9. ¿Qué hacías cuando no tenías dinero?			
10. ¿Qué hacías para divertirte?			

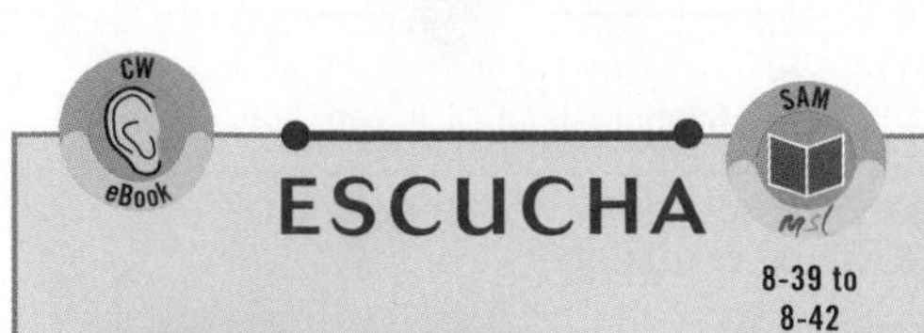

8-39 to
8-42

ESTRATEGIA **Guessing meaning from context**

You do not need to know every word to understand a listening passage or to get the gist of a conversation. Think about the overall message, then use the surrounding words or sentences to guess at meaning.

8•35 Antes de escuchar

Beatriz, la prima de Marisol, es estudiante de intercambio en Buenos Aires. Va de compras con su "hermana" argentina, Luz. Están en la tienda Zara, comprando ropa.

1. ¿Cómo es la tienda Zara?
2. ¿Piensas que ir de compras en Zara en Buenos Aires es igual que ir de compras en Zara en Nueva York (o en cualquier otra ciudad)?

Beatriz y Luz van de compras.

8•36 A escuchar

CD 3
Track 21

Completa las siguientes actividades.

1. Escucha la conversación entre Beatriz y Luz y después selecciona la opción que mejor conteste la pregunta. ¿De qué se trata (*What is the gist of*) la conversación?
   _____ a. A Beatriz no le gustan las blusas de la tienda y tampoco la tienda. Jamás va de compras allí.
   _____ b. A Beatriz le encanta el dependiente. Vive cerca de Luz.
   _____ c. A Luz le gustan los perros negros. Alguien tiene un perro que se llama Toro o posiblemente Goro.
2. Escucha una vez más y termina las siguientes frases.
   a. Marisol y Beatriz visitaron una de las tiendas Zara… (dónde y cuándo)
   b. Marisol y Beatriz no compraron nada porque…
   c. Luz no quiere comprar la blusa de seda o la falda de lana porque…
   d. Beatriz reconoce (*recognizes*) al dependiente porque…
3. ¿Qué significa "dependiente"?

8•37 Después de escuchar

En grupos de tres, realicen (*act out*) la escena entre Beatriz, Luz y el dependiente.

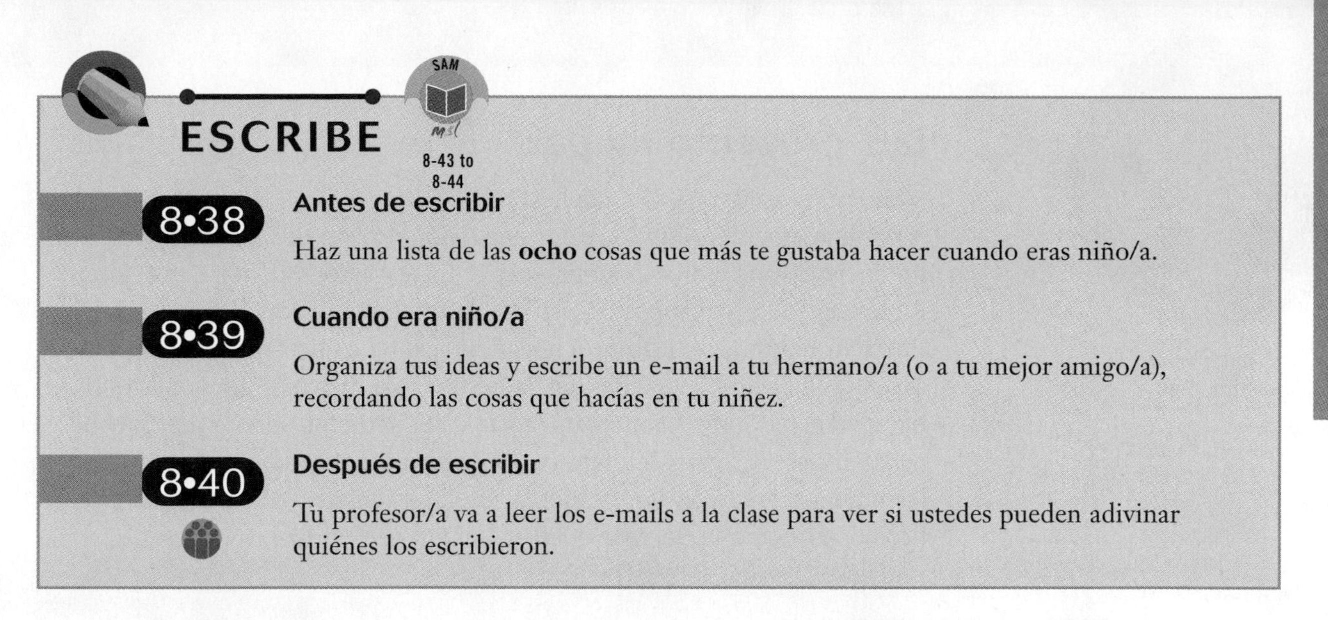

ESCRIBE

SAM 8-43 to 8-44

8•38 **Antes de escribir**

Haz una lista de las **ocho** cosas que más te gustaba hacer cuando eras niño/a.

8•39 **Cuando era niño/a**

Organiza tus ideas y escribe un e-mail a tu hermano/a (o a tu mejor amigo/a), recordando las cosas que hacías en tu niñez.

8•40 **Después de escribir**

Tu profesor/a va a leer los e-mails a la clase para ver si ustedes pueden adivinar quiénes los escribieron.

¿Cómo andas?

Having completed the second **Comunicación,** I now can…

	Feel Confident	**Need to Review**
• describe my daily routine (p. 302)	❑	❑
• talk about shopping in a department store in a Spanish-speaking country (p. 306)	❑	❑
• use regular and irregular verbs in the imperfect tense correctly (p. 306)	❑	❑
• talk about how things were in the past and what I used to do (p. 307)	❑	❑
• glean meaning from context when listening (p. 310)	❑	❑
• write an e-mail about my childhood (p. 311)	❑	❑

Argentina

Marina Claudia Luschini Ojeda

CW eBook

CD 3 Track 22

SAM 8-45 to 8-46

DVD/VHS Vistas culturales

Les presento mi país

Mi nombre es Marina Claudia Luschini Ojeda y vivo en la capital de Argentina, Buenos Aires. Soy porteña *(una persona de Buenos Aires)* y de herencia italiana, como puedes ver por mi apellido. Muchos argentinos tienen apellidos italianos a causa de la gran inmigración europea a fines del siglo diecinueve. **¿De qué herencia sos vos, che?** Mi país es grande y la geografía es muy variada: desde la montaña más alta del hemisferio occidental, el Cerro Aconcagua, hasta la ciudad más sureña *(del sur)* del mundo, Ushuaia. También tenemos lugares naturales como los glaciares, las pampas, la región de Patagonia, las cataratas del Iguazú y unas playas hermosas, como la del Mar del Plata. **¿Qué regiones y riquezas naturales hay en tu país?**

Las Cataratas del Iguazú en la frontera con Brasil y Paraguay

El tango en San Telmo, un antiguo barrio en la capital.

Las Galerías Pacífico en la calle Florida

ALMANAQUE

Nombre oficial:	República de Argentina
Gobierno:	República
Población:	39.921.833 (2006)
Idioma:	español
Moneda:	Peso argentino ($)

¿Sabías que...?

- El **lunfardo** es un dialecto o jerga que tuvo su origen en los barrios de Buenos Aires a finales del siglo XIX. Es la lengua del tango y también de la jerga de las prisiones a principios del siglo XX. Se forman palabras diciendo las sílabas al revés (*reversing the syllables*): "tango" en lunfardo es *gotan*.

PREGUNTAS

1. ¿Cuáles son tres de las distintas regiones geográficas del país? Cuando es verano en Argentina, ¿en qué estación estamos aquí? ¿Por qué?
2. ¿Dónde puedes ir de compras en Buenos Aires?
3. ¿Qué tienen en común Argentina y Chile?

En la Red
Amplía tus conocimientos sobre Argentina en la página web de *¡Anda!*

Francisco Tomás Bacigalupe Bustamante

Uruguay

CD 3
Track 23

DVD/VHS
Vistas culturales

Les presento mi país

Mi nombre es Francisco Tomás Bacigalupe Bustamante, aunque de pequeño me llamaban Paquito. Soy de Montevideo, la capital de Uruguay. Mi país es pequeño pero tranquilo y bonito, y la mayoría de la población, el ochenta por ciento, vive en los centros urbanos. El clima es templado (no hace mucho calor ni mucho frío) y perfecto para nuestras playas increíbles. Cuando era niño las playas eran nuestro destino favorito para ir de vacaciones. **¿Dónde ibas tú de vacaciones?** Tenemos mucho en común con nuestros vecinos los argentinos: el tango, la yerba mate, los gauchos y una dieta que contiene mucha carne. También comemos mucha pizza y pasta, debido a nuestra herencia italiana. **¿Qué comida de otros países te gusta comer?**

La Rambla de Montevideo

Punta del Este es un balneario (*resort*) muy turístico.

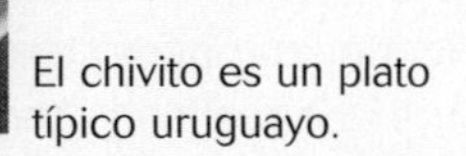

El chivito es un plato típico uruguayo.

Nombre oficial:	República Oriental del Uruguay
Gobierno:	República democrática
Población:	3.431.932 (2006)
Idiomas:	español (oficial); portuñol/brazilero
Moneda:	Peso uruguayo ($U)

¿Sabías que...?

- Debido al índice de alfabetización (*literacy*), el clima agradable y templado, la belleza del paisaje y la hospitalidad de la gente, Uruguay se le conoce como "la Suiza de América".

PREGUNTAS

1. ¿Dónde vive la mayoría de los uruguayos?
2. Muchos uruguayos son de herencia italiana. ¿En qué se ve esta herencia?
3. ¿Qué tiene en común Uruguay con su país vecino Argentina?

En la Red
Amplía tus conocimientos sobre Uruguay en la página web de *¡Anda!*

Ambiciones siniestras

EPISODIO 8

8-50 to 8-51

lectura

8-41 Antes de leer. En el **Episodio 7,** los protagonistas seguían preocupados por Eduardo y tampoco sabían dónde estaba Alejandra. Cuando Manolo intentó llamarla, salió la voz de un hombre en su contestador automático. Tuvieron otra videoconferencia para hablar de Eduardo, Alejandra y el rompecabezas que recibieron. Para prepararte bien para el **Episodio 8,** contesta las siguientes preguntas basadas en el **Episodio 7.**

1. ¿Cómo se sentía Marisol? ¿Manolo? Explica.
2. ¿Por qué era importante resolver el rompecabezas?
3. ¿Cuáles eran las dudas que tenían?

ESTRATEGIA Guessing meaning from context

Before consulting a dictionary, always try to guess the meaning of an unfamiliar word from the context of the reading. In other words, looking closely at the surrounding words and sentences can help you determine the meaning. Even if you cannot come up with an exact translation, you can get the general idea of what the word means.

Estrategia

The new strategy *guessing meaning from context* is especially useful to beginning language students. It is much easier to focus on what you can understand and make logical guesses about the new information instead of trying to focus on what you cannot understand and attempting to look up every word. Only look up a word if it interferes with your ability to comprehend the sentence, question, or the main idea.

8-42 A leer. Completa las siguientes actividades.

1. Al empezar el episodio, sabemos que Marisol estaba "preocupada" y "no tenía ganas" de hacer nada ni de comer nada (primer párrafo). En el segundo párrafo, cuando ella fue a su computadora *"Tenía varios mensajes, pero inmediatamente vio uno del hombre del concurso. Empezó a temblar sin saber por qué."*

   ¿Qué significa la palabra "temblar"? ¿Cómo podía sentirse Marisol al recibir otro mensaje del hombre del concurso? ¿feliz? ¿contenta? ¿asustada? Si leemos el mensaje podemos imaginar la reacción de ella. Creemos que Marisol se puso nerviosa al leerlo, entonces "temblar" es más una reacción de miedo que de felicidad, ¿no? En realidad, "temblar" significa *"to tremble."*
2. Lee superficialmente el episodio y subraya (*underline*) las palabras que no conoces. Intenta adivinar el significado de cada una, según el contexto. (Sigue el proceso indicado en el apartado 1.) Después, compara tus palabras subrayadas y sus posibles significados con las de tu compañero/a.
3. Lee el episodio una vez más, revisando los posibles significados cuando sea necesario (*as needed*). Al terminar, comparte tus resultados con el/la profesor/a.

CD 3
Track 24

¿Quién fue?

Eran las ocho y Marisol estaba en la cama, preocupada y confusa. No quería levantarse. No tenía ganas de arreglarse… no podía comer porque no tenía hambre ni para sus dulces favoritos.

Sonó el teléfono pero Marisol decidió no contestarlo. Prefería escuchar un mensaje que hablar con alguien en estos momentos. Nada: nadie dejó un mensaje. Decidió levantarse e ir a la computadora para leer su correo electrónico. Tenía varios mensajes, pero inmediatamente vio uno del hombre del concurso. Empezó a temblar sin saber por qué. Por fin lo abrió y leyó:

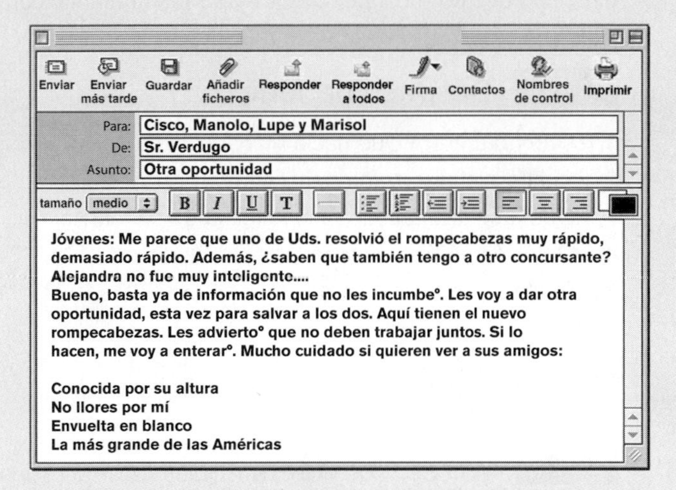

Jóvenes: Me parece que uno de Uds. resolvió el rompecabezas muy rápido, demasiado rápido. Además, ¿saben que también tengo a otro concursante? Alejandra no fue muy inteligente....
Bueno, basta ya de información que no les incumbe°. Les voy a dar otra oportunidad, esta vez para salvar a los dos. Aquí tienen el nuevo rompecabezas. Les advierto° que no deben trabajar juntos. Si lo hacen, me voy a enterar°. Mucho cuidado si quieren ver a sus amigos:

Conocida por su altura
No llores por mí
Envuelta en blanco
La más grande de las Américas

incumbe: you do not need to know
advierto: warn
enterar: find out

Marisol no podía creerlo. ¡Qué pesadilla°! ¿Quién resolvió el primer rompecabezas? Ella no tuvo nada que ver con eso°. ¿Y qué pasó con Lupe en estos últimos días? Estaba portándose° muy rara y misteriosamente. Dijo que las cosas no eran importantes, pero sí, lo son. Parecía que escondía° algo. ¡Podía ser que este último mensaje fuera° de ella! En ese momento sonó el teléfono.

pesadilla: nightmare
no tuvo nada que ver con eso: She had nothing to do with that
portándose: behaving
escondía: was hiding
fuera: was

—Marisol, soy Manolo. Encontré tu número en el Internet.

—Manolo, gracias por llamar —respondió Marisol —Tengo que hablar contigo. Tengo mucho miedo. ¿Recibiste el nuevo rompecabezas? ¿Fuiste tú quien solucionó el primer rompecabezas? —le preguntó.

—Sí, —explicó Manolo, —recibí el nuevo pero no, no fui yo quien solucionó el primero —explicó Manolo.

—¿Sabes qué? —empezó a decir Marisol. —Creo que es Lupe quien nos manda los e-mails. Creo que ella es el «Sr. Verdugo», —le dijo muy convencida.

—¿Sí? —respondió Manolo —y yo creía que era Cisco. Él tiene mucho talento con las computadoras. Me da mucho miedo. Creo que Cisco sí sabe lo que pasa con Eduardo y no nos dice nada. Temo que él sea el culpable°.

Temo que él sea el culpable: I'm afraid he may be the guilty one

—No sé—le refutó Marisol—. No lo sé. Hay cosas muy misteriosas con Lupe también. Siempre está en el Internet y cuando me acerco° a ella, cierra su computadora y me dice que no está haciendo nada. ¿Qué hacemos? —le preguntó. *approach*

Manolo se quedó pensando.

—Tal vez debemos llamar a la policía—contestó Manolo—, pero ¿qué decimos? No sabemos nada en concreto ni de Eduardo ni de Alejandra. Vamos a pensarlo bien. ¿Y si es una broma° de mal gusto? Te llamo pronto. *joke*

—Bueno. —respondió Marisol angustiada—. Adiós.

Marisol, temblando de nuevo, volvió a sus mensajes. Miró la lista y vio una dirección que no reconoció: muchasuerte@comando.com. Abrió el mensaje y gritó°. *screamed*

8-43 Después de leer

1. ¿Qué hora era? ¿Qué hacía Marisol al empezar el episodio?
2. ¿Cuál era el nuevo rompecabezas?
3. ¿Qué amenaza (*threat*) había al final de su mensaje?
4. ¿Quién llamó por teléfono?
5. ¿Cuáles eran las dudas de Manolo? ¿y de Marisol?

8-52 to 8-53

video

8-44 Antes del video. ¿Quién resolvió el primer rompecabezas? ¿Por qué gritó Alejandra? En la segunda parte del episodio vas a saber quién resolvió el rompecabezas, pero al mismo tiempo vas a tener más dudas sobre algunos de los protagonistas. También, Manolo va a hablar de algo peligroso (*dangerous*). Y finalmente, ¿quién tiene una pistola?

Eso es todo lo que necesito.

Cisco, te lo digo en serio, esto puede ser muy peligroso.

Oye, Manolo. Perdón pero tengo que irme.

Episodio 8

«El misterio crece»

Relájate y disfruta el video.

8-45 Después del video. Contesta las siguientes preguntas.

1. ¿Qué hacía Lupe mientras hablaba con Manolo?
2. ¿Quién resolvió el primer rompecabezas? ¿Cuál era la respuesta?
3. Según Lupe, ¿quién debía saber algo sobre Eduardo?
4. ¿Qué ocurrió justo antes de colgar los teléfonos?
5. ¿Por qué se puso nervioso Manolo al final del episodio?
6. ¿A quién vimos al final del episodio?

Y por fin, ¿cómo andas?

Having completed this chapter, I now can…

	Feel Confident	Need to Review
Comunicación		
• describe clothing (p. 286)	❏	❏
• pronounce **ll** and **ñ** correctly (p. 287)	❏	❏
• talk about to whom and for whom things are done (p. 292)	❏	❏
• discuss likes and dislikes, what is and is not important, what is bothersome, and what is lacking or needed (p. 294)	❏	❏
• describe my daily routine (p. 302)	❏	❏
• talk and write about the past, describing situations and telling how things used to be (p. 306)	❏	❏
• guess the meaning of unfamiliar words using contextual clues when listening (p. 310)	❏	❏
• write an e-mail about my childhood (p. 311)	❏	❏
Cultura		
• talk about a Spanish clothing company (p. 291)	❏	❏
• talk about shopping in a department store in a Spanish-speaking country (p. 306)	❏	❏
• share at least two interesting facts about each country: Argentina and Uruguay (pp. 312–313)	❏	❏
Ambiciones siniestras		
• guess the meaning of unfamiliar words from context in a reading passage (p. 314)	❏	❏
• tell who solved the first riddle (p. 316)	❏	❏
• list doubts that Marisol and Manolo have about Lupe and Cisco (p. 316)	❏	❏

VOCABULARIO ACTIVO

CD 3
Tracks 25-31

La ropa	*Clothing*
el abrigo	*overcoat*
la bata	*robe*
la blusa	*blouse*
el bolso	*purse*
las botas (*pl.*)	*boots*
los calcetines (*pl.*)	*socks*
la camisa	*shirt*
la camiseta	*T-shirt*
la chaqueta	*jacket*
el cinturón	*belt*
el conjunto	*outfit*
la corbata	*tie*
la falda	*skirt*
la gorra	*cap*
los guantes	*gloves*
el impermeable	*raincoat*
los jeans (*pl.*)	*jeans*
las medias (*pl.*)	*stockings; hose*
los pantalones (*pl.*)	*pants*
los pantalones cortos (*pl.*)	*shorts*
el paraguas	*umbrella*
el pijama	*pajamas*
la ropa interior	*underwear*
las sandalias (*pl.*)	*sandals*
el sombrero	*hat*
la sudadera	*sweatshirt*
el suéter	*sweater*
los tenis (*pl.*)	*tennis shoes*
el traje	*suit*
el traje de baño	*swimsuit; bathing suit*
el vestido	*dress*
las zapatillas (*pl.*)	*slippers*
los zapatos (*pl.*)	*shoes*

Las telas y los materiales	*Fabrics and materials*
el algodón	*cotton*
el cuero	*leather*
la lana	*wool*
el poliéster	*polyester*
la seda	*silk*
la tela	*fabric*

Unos adjetivos	*Some adjectives*
ancho/a	*wide*
atrevido/a	*daring*
claro/a	*light (colored)*
cómodo/a	*comfortable*
corto/a	*short*
de cuadros	*checked*
de lunares	*polka-dotted*
de rayas	*striped*
elegante	*elegant*
estampado/a	*print; with a design or pattern*
estrecho/a	*narrow; tight*
formal	*formal*
informal	*casual*
largo/a	*long*
liso/a	*solid-colored*
oscuro/a	*dark*

Unos verbos	Some verbs
llevar	*to wear; to take; to carry*
llevar puesto	*to wear; to have on*
quedar bien/mal	*to fit well/poorly*

Otras palabras útiles	Other useful words
la moda	*fashion; style*
el/la modelo	*model*

Unos verbos como *gustar*	Verbs similar to **gustar**
encantar	*to love; delight*
fascinar	*to fascinate*
hacer falta	*to need; to be lacking*
importar	*to matter; to be important*
molestar	*to bother*

Unos verbos reflexivos	Some reflexive verbs
acordarse de (o → ue)	*to remember*
acostarse (o → ue)	*to go to bed*
afeitarse	*to shave*
arreglarse	*to get ready*
bañarse	*to bathe*
callarse	*to get/keep quiet*
cepillarse (el pelo, los dientes)	*to brush (one's hair, teeth)*
despertarse (e → ie)	*to wake up; to awaken*
divertirse (e → ie → i)	*to enjoy oneself; to have fun*
dormirse (o → ue → u)	*to fall asleep*
ducharse	*to shower*
irse	*to go away; to leave*
lavarse	*to wash oneself*
levantarse	*to get up; to stand up*
llamarse	*to be called*
maquillarse	*to put on make up*
peinarse	*to comb one's hair*
ponerse (la ropa)	*to put on (one's clothes)*
ponerse (nervioso/a)	*to get (nervous)*
quedarse	*to stay; to remain*
quitarse (la ropa)	*to take off (one's clothes)*
reunirse	*to get together; to meet*
secarse	*to dry off*
sentarse (e → ie)	*to sit down*
sentirse (e → ie → i)	*to feel*
vestirse (e → i → i)	*to get dressed*

Estamos en forma

Todos queremos tener una buena calidad de vida y prolongarla lo más posible. No podemos cambiar nuestra herencia genética transmitida de padres a hijos, pero sí tenemos control sobre decisiones que pueden afectar nuestro estilo de vida: el ejercicio, la dieta, la prevención de accidentes y el uso de sustancias adictivas como el tabaco.

	OBJETIVOS	CONTENIDOS	
Comunicación	• To describe parts of the human body • To avoid repetition of previously mentioned people and things • To describe what one does to himself/herself • To explain what ails you and suggest treatments for certain ailments • To make exclamatory or emphatic statements • To narrate in the past • To talk about how long something has been going on and how long ago something occurred • To ask yourself questions when listening to a passage to help organize and summarize what you heard • To write a summary using the past tenses	1 The human body 2 Review of direct and indirect object pronouns and reflexive pronouns 3 Some illnesses and medical treatments 4 The exclamations **¡qué!** and **¡cuánto!** 5 The preterit and imperfect 6 Expressions with **hacer** (*hace* + time, etc.) ☐ Pronunciación: The letters **d** and **t** ☐ Escucha: Estrategia: Asking yourself questions ☐ Escribe: Writing a summary using the past tenses	322 325 328 332 334 341 323 343 344
Cultura	• To discuss the importance of water in maintaining good health • To talk about pharmacies in Latin America and how they differ from those in the United States • To talk about this chapter's featured countries: Peru, Bolivia, and Ecuador	☐ Water and good health ☐ Pharmacies in the Spanish-speaking world ☐ *Perú, Bolivia,* and *Ecuador*	331 340 345–347
Ambiciones siniestras	• To create check questions to facilitate comprehension when reading • To discuss the contents of the new e-mail message • To talk about the progress the characters are making in deciphering the new riddle	☐ Episodio 9 Lectura: *¡Qué mentira!* Estrategia: Asking yourself questions Video: *No llores por mí*	 348 350

¡A ponerse en forma!

PREGUNTAS

1 ¿Vives una vida sana (*healthy*)? ¿Qué haces (o no haces) para tener una vida más sana?

2 ¿Qué tipo de ejercicio te gusta hacer?

3 ¿Crees que es más fácil vivir una vida sana a ciertas edades? ¿Por qué?

Comunicación

- Describing the human body
- Avoiding repetition of previously mentioned people and things
- Describing what one does to oneself
- Making exclamations

1 VOCABULARIO El cuerpo humano

SAM 9-1 to 9-6

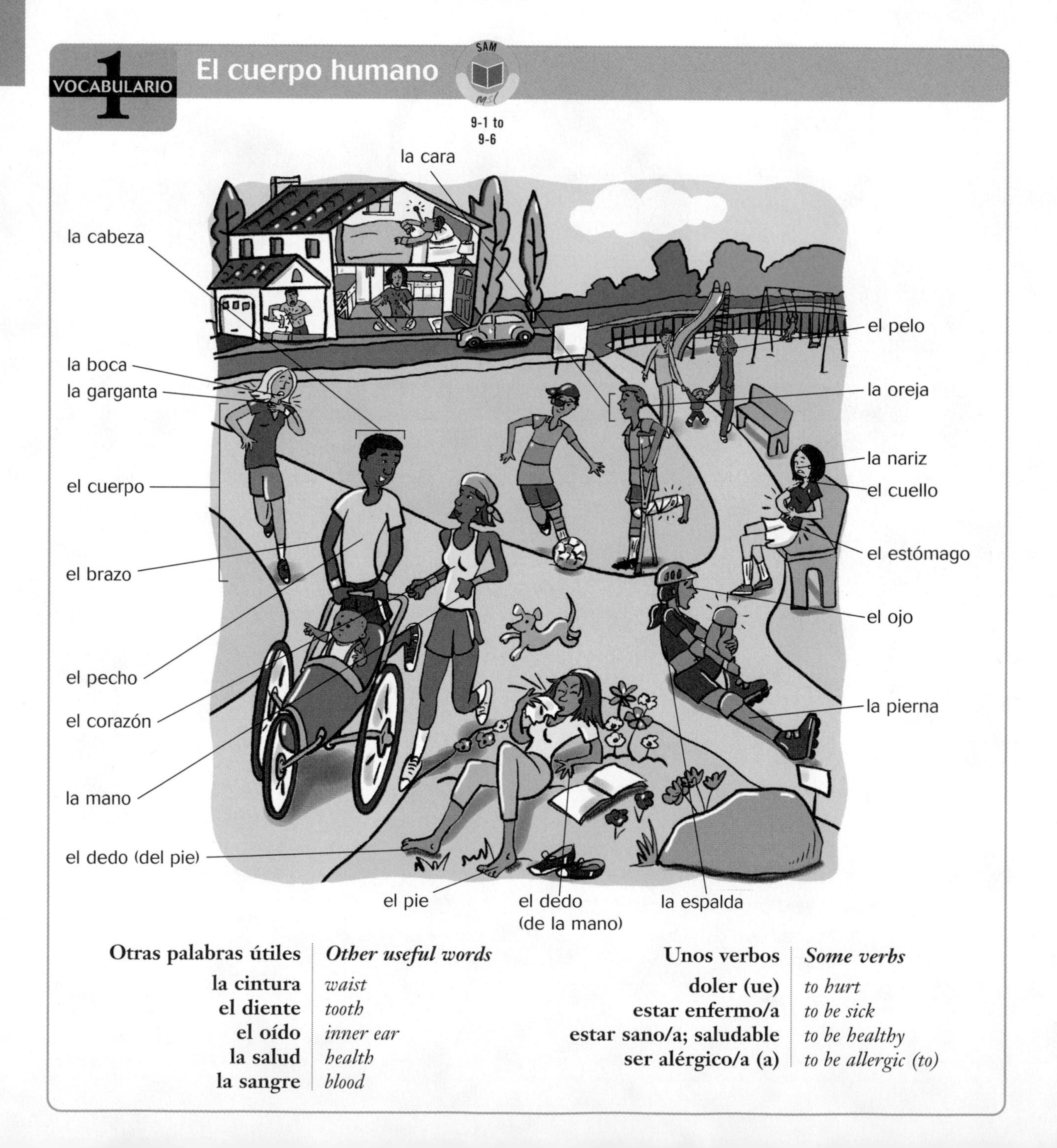

Otras palabras útiles	*Other useful words*
la cintura	*waist*
el diente	*tooth*
el oído	*inner ear*
la salud	*health*
la sangre	*blood*

Unos verbos	*Some verbs*
doler (ue)	*to hurt*
estar enfermo/a	*to be sick*
estar sano/a; saludable	*to be healthy*
ser alérgico/a (a)	*to be allergic (to)*

CD 4
Track 1

9-7 to
9-10

PRONUNCIACIÓN

The letters *d* and *t*

1. The Spanish **d** is pronounced with a hard sound when it appears at the beginning of a sentence or phrase, or after the letters **n** or **l**. The sound is similar to the *d* in the English word *dog*.
   doctor   Daniel   espalda   dónde
2. In all other cases, the Spanish **d** is pronounced like the *th* in the English words *they* or *father*.
   oído   quedarse   antiácido   algodón
3. When pronouncing the Spanish **t**, the tongue touches the back of the upper teeth. It sounds like the *t* in the English word *star*.
   diente   garganta   estómago   quitarse

9•1 Las palabras

Pronounce the following words, paying special attention to the letters **d** and **t**.

1. dedo
2. doctora
3. despertarse
4. David
5. vestido
6. diente
7. frecuentemente
8. todos
9. tenedor

9•2 Las oraciones

Pronounce the following sentences, paying special attention to the letters **d** and **t**.

1. A David le duelen los dientes y la garganta.
2. Estas sandalias y esa sudadera son cómodas. ¿Te gustan?
3. Deseo algo dulce como un helado u otro postre.

9•3 Los dichos y refranes

Now pronounce the following sayings and focus on the letters **d** and **t**.

1. Aunque la mona se vista de seda, mona se queda.
2. Del dicho al hecho hay mucho trecho.

9•4 ¿Cómo nos vestimos?

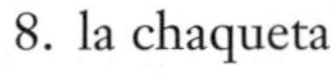
Capítulo 8. La ropa, pág. 286.

Túrnense para decir qué partes del cuerpo asocian con la siguiente lista de ropa.

MODELO E1: los zapatos
E2: *los pies*

1. las botas
2. los guantes
3. los pantalones
4. la gorra
5. la corbata
6. la camiseta
7. los calcetines
8. la chaqueta

Capítulo 3. *Hay*, pág. 122.

9•5 Una obra de arte

Miren el cuadro y descríbenlo usando las siguientes preguntas como guía.

1. ¿Cuántas personas hay en la pintura?
2. ¿Cuántas caras hay?
3. ¿Cuántas manos pueden ver?
4. ¿Cuántos ojos pueden ver?
5. ¿Cuántas narices hay?
6. ¿Qué otras cosas ven en la pintura?
7. Estas personas son…
8. La pintura representa…

Fíjate

Note that *la mano* is irregular; it ends in *o* but the word is feminine.

Estrategia

Being an "active listener" is an important skill in any language; it means that you have heard and understood what someone is saying. Being able to demonstrate that you have understood correctly, as in reproducing this drawing of the monster, helps you practice and perfect the skill of active listening.

9•6 ¿Es un monstruo o una obra de arte?

Su instructor va a dibujar un monstruo. En parejas, un estudiante va a describir lo que ve y el otro estudiante va a dibujar lo que su compañero le describe. Al terminar, cambien de papel.

El monstruo tiene…

a la derecha	a la izquierda	encima de	debajo de

SAM 9-11 to 9-15 | Guide 20, 26, 34

GRAMÁTICA 2 Un resumen de los pronombres de complemento directo, indirecto y reflexivos

Let's review the forms, functions, and positioning of the *direct* and *indirect object pronouns*, as well as the *reflexive pronouns*:

LOS PRONOMBRES DE COMPLEMENTO **DIRECTO**

Direct object pronouns tell *what* or *who* receives the action of the verb. They replace direct object nouns and are used to avoid repetition.

me	*me*
te	*you*
lo, la	*him/her/you/it*
nos	*us*
os	*you (all)*
los, las	*them/you*

Compré el coche ayer. **Lo** compré por diez mil euros. Quiero regalárse**lo** a mi hijo.

I bought the car yesterday. I bought it for ten thousand euros. I want to give it to my son.

LOS PRONOMBRES DE COMPLEMENTO **INDIRECTO**

Indirect object pronouns tell *to whom* or *for whom* something is done or given.

me	*to/for me*
te	*to/for you*
le (se)	*to/for him/her/you*
nos	*to/for us*
os	*to/for you (all)*
les (se)	*to/for them/you*

Le compré el coche ayer. **Le** voy a regalar el coche para su cumpleaños.

I bought him the car yesterday. I am going to give him the car for his birthday.

LOS PRONOMBRES **REFLEXIVOS**

Reflexive pronouns indicate that the *subject* of a sentence or clause *receives the action of the verb.*

me	*myself*
te	*yourself*
se	*himself/herself/yourself*
nos	*ourselves*
os	*yourselves*
se	*themselves/yourselves*

Me cepillo los dientes tres veces al día.

I brush my teeth three times a day.

Remember the following guidelines on position and sequence:

Position

- Object pronouns and reflexive pronouns come **before** the verb.

Mi asistente **le** mandó la carta. — *My assistant sent him the letter.*
Después **se** sintió aliviado. — *Then he felt relieved.*

- Object pronouns and reflexive pronouns can also be placed before or be attached to the end of:
  a. **infinitives**

El señor Rodríguez **me** va a contestar rápidamente.
El señor Rodríguez va a contestar**me** rápidamente. } *Mr. Rodríguez will respond to me quickly.*

Después **se** va a reunir con los gerentes.
Después va a reunir**se** con los gerentes. } *Then he will meet with the managers.*

b. **present participles (*-ando*, *-endo* and *-iendo*)**

La está leyendo ahora.
Está leyéndo**la** ahora. } *He is reading it now.*

Se está poniendo nervioso.
Está poniéndo**se** nervioso. } *He is getting nervous.*

Sequence

- When a direct (DO) and indirect object (IO) pronoun are used together, ***the indirect object precedes the direct object.***
- If both the direct and the indirect object pronoun begin with the letter "*l*" the indirect object pronoun changes from **le** or **les** to **se,** as in the example below.

Quiero mandar la carta al director ahora. *I want to send the letter to the director now.*

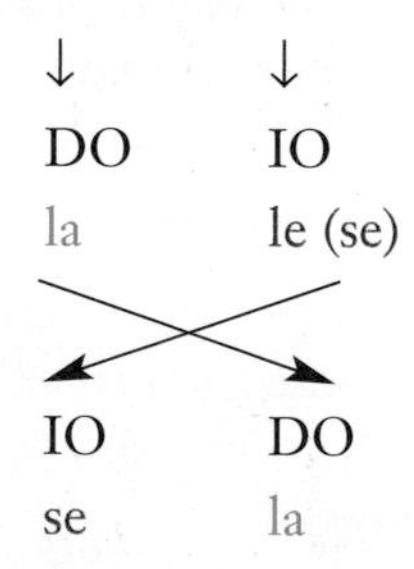

DO IO (*letter*, *director*)

Se la quiero mandar ahora mismo.
Quiero mandár**se**la ahora mismo. } *I want to send it to him right now.*

9•7 Un animal muy extraño

Juntos respondan a las oraciones exclamativas con el pronombre de complemento directo apropiado y un adjetivo.

MODELO E1: ¡Mira la nariz!
E2: *Sí, la tiene muy grande (pequeña/fea/bonita...).*

Fíjate

In Spanish, an animal's legs are referred to as *patas. Pierna(s)* is only used for people.

1. ¡Mira la boca!
2. ¡Mira las orejas!
3. ¡Mira los dientes!
4. ¡Mira las patas!
5. ¡Mira la cabeza!
6. ¡Mira el estómago!
7. ¡Mira la cara!
8. ¡Mira el cuello!

Capítulo 8. *Gustar* y verbos como *gustar*, pág. 294.

9•8 Las preferencias

Escribe oraciones completas usando siempre los pronombres de complemento indirecto. Después compara tus oraciones con las de un/a compañero/a.

MODELO A Betty / gustar despertarse temprano
A Betty le gusta despertarse temprano.

1. A mis padres / importar el dinero
2. A mí / molestar las personas irresponsables
3. A Manolo / encantar las novelas de Rushdie
4. A nosotros / hacer falta estudiar mucho más
5. A nuestro/a profesor/a / fascinar el cine japonés

9•9 En el restaurante

¿Qué les ocurrió ayer a Paco y a Pati en el Restaurante Boca Grande?

Paso 1 Completa las oraciones con los pronombres de complemento directo, indirecto o reflexivo apropiados. Después, compara tus respuestas con las de un/a compañero/a.

Paco y Pati se conocieron en el gimnasio. Decidieron cenar juntos y llegaron al restaurante con mucha hambre. (1) ________ sentaron en una mesa grande al lado de las ventanas. Primero pidieron el menú. El camarero (2) ________ (3) ________ trajo en seguida (inmediatamente). Después, (4) ________ recomendó unos platos muy ricos. Paco pidió un bistec para él y a Pati (5) ________ pidió pollo asado con ajo. ¡Pati no (6) ________ podía creer! ¡Paco ni (7) ________ preguntó qué quería! Ella (8) ________ sentía muy incómoda—ningún hombre, excepto su padre, (9) ________ había tratado (*had treated*) así antes. Pati (10) ________ calló mientras Paco hablaba de su día, su trabajo y su familia. Cuando por fin el camarero (11) ________ sirvió la comida, Pati miró su plato y (12) ________ levantó gritando. ¡Su plato era del «Menú para niños»!

Paso 2 Digan qué tipo de pronombre es cada uno que usaron.

9•10 ¿Quién...?

Jacobo está enfermo y no puede levantarse de la cama. Es un poco exigente *(demanding)* y quiere saber quiénes lo van a atender *(wait on him)*. Contesta sus preguntas y después comparte tus respuestas con un/a compañero/a.

MODELO ¿Quién va a traerme la tarea? (hermano)
Tu hermano te la va a traer. / Tu hermano va a traértela.

1. ¿Quién va a traerme los libros que pedí? (Patricia)
2. ¿Quién está comprándome la medicina que necesito? (Paco)
3. ¿Quién me va a limpiar el cuarto? (Guadalupe y Lina)
4. ¿Quién me está lavando la ropa? (tu madre)
5. ¿Quién está preparándome la comida? (Tina y Luisa)
6. ¿Quién me va a hacer la tarea? (nadie)

VOCABULARIO 3 Unas enfermedades y tratamientos médicos

SAM 9-16 to 9-21

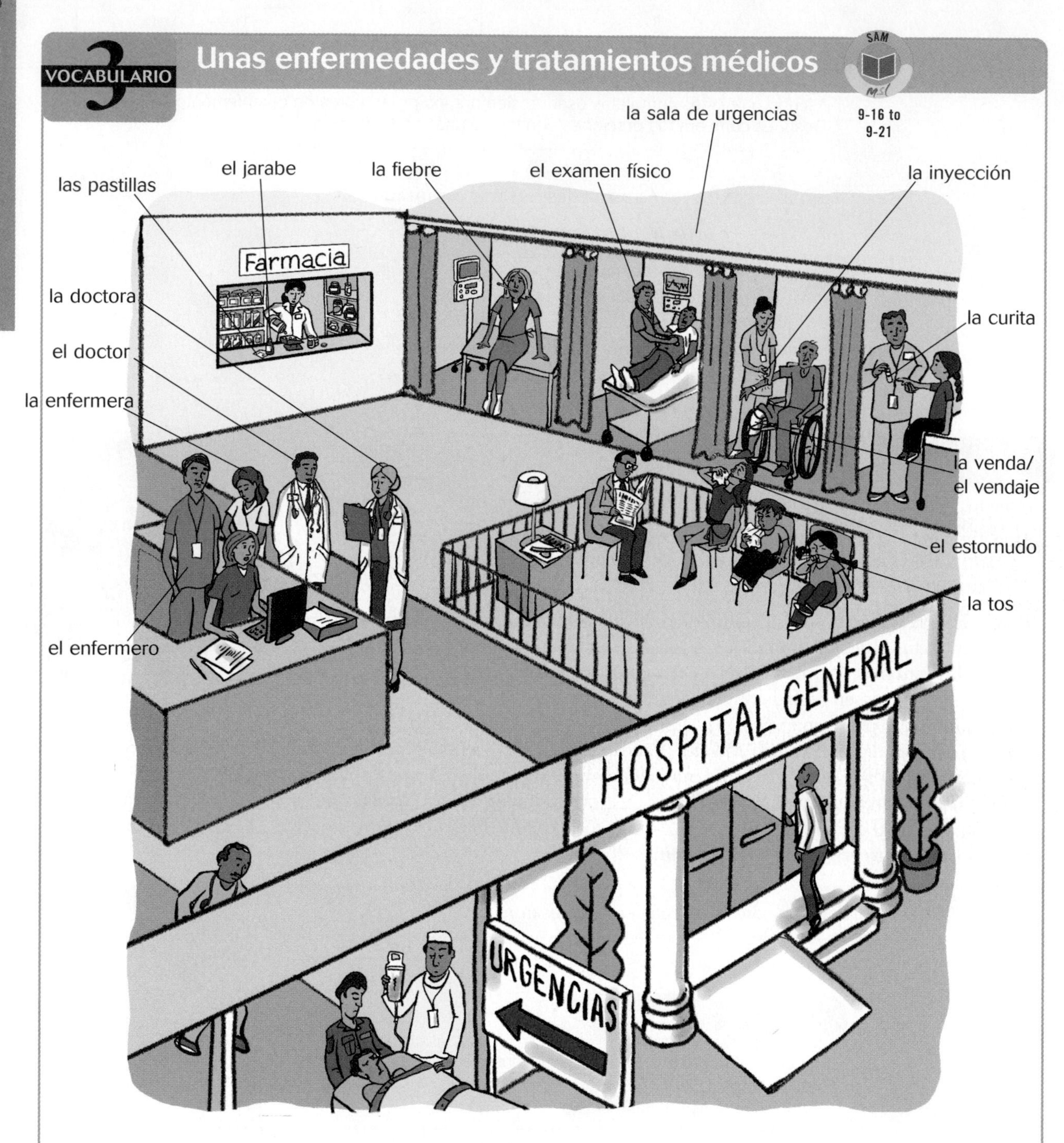

Otras palabras útiles	***Other useful words***
el médico	*male doctor*
la médica	*female doctor*
Los síntomas y las enfermedades	***Symptoms and illnesses***
el dolor	*pain*
la gripe	*flu*
la herida	*wound; injury*
la náusea	*nausea*
Los tratamientos	***Treatments***
el antiácido	*antacid*
el antibiótico	*antibiotic*
la aspirina	*aspirin*
la receta	*prescription*

Unos verbos	***Some verbs***
acabar de + infinitivo	*to have just finished + (something)*
cortar(se)	*to cut (oneself)*
curar(se)	*to cure; to be cured*
enfermar(se)	*to get sick*
estornudar	*to sneeze*
evitar	*to avoid*
guardar cama	*to stay in bed*
lastimar(se)	*to get hurt*
mejorar(se)	*to improve; to get better*
ocurrir	*to occur*
quemar(se)	*to burn; to get burned*
romper(se)	*to break*
tener...	
alergia (a)	*to be allergic (to)*
(un) catarro, resfriado	*to have a cold*
(la/una) gripe	*to have the flu*
una infección	*to have an infection*
tos	*to have a cough*
un virus	*to have a virus*
tener dolor de...	
cabeza	*to have a headache*
espalda	*to have a backache*
estómago	*to have a stomachache*
garganta	*to have a sore throat*
toser	*to cough*
tratar de	*to try to*
vendar(se)	*to bandage (oneself); to dress (a wound)*

Fíjate

A verb with **se** in parentheses indicates that it can be also used as a reflexive verb.

quemar(se): Ayer me quemé. (reflexive) — *Yesterday I burned myself.*
Ayer quemé los papeles viejos. — *Yesterday I burned the old papers.*

9-11 Unos tratamientos

¿Adónde tienes que ir para poder curarte o buscar tratamiento para las siguientes condiciones? Pon una equis (**X**) en la columna apropiada. Después, túrnate con un/a compañero/a para decir adónde van.

MODELO un brazo roto (*broken*)

E1: *Si tengo un brazo roto, voy a la sala de urgencias.*

CONDICIÓN	A LA CAMA	A LA FARMACIA	AL CONSULTORIO DEL MÉDICO	AL HOSPITAL	A LA SALA DE URGENCIAS
1. tos					
2. náusea					
3. (la) gripe					
4. (un) dolor de garganta					
5. una infección de la sangre					
6. una herida en la pierna					
7. (un) catarro					
8. fiebre					

Fíjate

Body parts are usually referred to with an article, not a possessive adjective.

Me duele **la** mano. — ***My** hand hurts.*

9•12 El soroche

El verano pasado Nina fue a Bolivia como voluntaria para ayudar a construir una escuela en el altiplano (*high plateau*).

Paso 1 Juntos terminen la conversación entre Nina y su padre con las palabras de la lista.

corazón	enfermedad	evitar	me duele
mejorar	náusea	pastillas	estómago

NINA: Hola, Papá.

PAPÁ: ¡Ay, Nina! ¿Cómo estás, hija? ¿Llegaste bien?

NINA: Sí. Ayer llegamos bien pero hoy me siento enferma. (1) ________ la cabeza. No me duele mucho el (2) ________ pero tengo (3) ________ cuando pienso en la comida—me entran ganas *(I get the urge)* de vomitar.

PAPÁ: Pobrecita. ¿Qué te pasa? ¿Comiste ayer?

NINA: Sí, un poco. Pero desde que *(since)* llegamos no tengo mucha hambre.

PAPÁ: ¿Tienes otros síntomas?

NINA: Sí. El (4) ________ me late (*is beating*) rápidamente y no puedo respirar (*breathe*) muy bien. ¿Crees que tengo alguna (5) ________?

PAPÁ: Nina, me parece que tienes soroche.

NINA: ¿Soroche? ¿Qué es eso?

PAPÁ: Es el mal de altura (*altitude sickness*). Debes empezar a sentirte mejor (*better*) en un par de días. Mientras tanto, necesitas intentar relajarte, tomar mucha agua y (6) ________ el alcohol y el tabaco. También puedes tomar unas (7) ________ de ibuprofén y beber un té medicinal hecho de (*made from*) hojas de coca (*coca leaves*).

NINA: Gracias, Papá. Ya que entiendo qué me ocurre, creo que me voy a (8) ________ pronto.

Paso 2 Ahora, contesten las siguientes preguntas.

1. ¿Qué es el soroche?
2. ¿Cuáles son los síntomas?
3. ¿Qué tratamiento le recomienda su papá?

9•13 Para evitar lo inevitable

¿Cómo tratan de evitar tus compañeros las siguientes enfermedades y condiciones? Circula por la clase para hacerles estas preguntas. Necesitas **tres** respuestas para cada pregunta.

MODELO TÚ: ¿Cómo tratas de evitar el dolor de garganta?
E1: *Bebo mucho jugo de naranja.*
E2: *Llevo una bufanda* (scarf) *en el cuello.*
E3: *Tomo mucha vitamina C.*

1. ¿Cómo tratas de evitar el dolor de cabeza? E1: ____ E2: ____ E3: ____	4. ¿Cómo evitas enfermarte? E1: ____ E2: ____ E3: ____
2. ¿Cómo tratas de evitar el dolor de estómago? E1: ____ E2: ____ E3: ____	5. ¿Cómo evitas cortarte? E1: ____ E2: ____ E3: ____
3. ¿Cómo tratas de evitar el dolor de espalda? E1: ____ E2: ____ E3: ____	6. ¿Cómo tratas de evitar la depresión? E1: ____ E2: ____ E3: ____

9-22 to 9-23

El agua y la buena salud

¿Sabías que tres cuartas partes de tu peso corporal son de agua? Tu vida empezó en un mar de líquido amniótico y ahora, como adulto, alrededor del ochenta y cinco por ciento de la sangre, el setenta por ciento de los músculos y el veintidós por ciento de tu cerebro consiste en agua.

Para mantener la buena salud se debe beber por lo menos dos litros (seis a ocho vasos) de agua al día. El cuerpo elimina de unos quinientos a setecientos centímetros cúbicos diarios de agua al sudar (*sweat*) y es muy importante reponer esa cantidad y más.

Los alimentos son una fuente importante de agua para el cuerpo, sobre todo las frutas y las verduras. También cuentan otras bebidas además del agua, pero hay que considerar que algunas tienen el efecto contrario. El café y las bebidas alcohólicas deshidratan. Para compensar esta deshidratación hay que beber agua. Por ejemplo, por cada vaso de cerveza se debe tomar otro vaso de agua.

Preguntas

1. ¿Por qué es importante beber tanta (*so much*) agua? ¿Cuántos vasos de agua bebes al día?
2. ¿Qué otros beneficios tiene beber suficiente agua al día?

¡Qué! y ¡cuánto!

9-24 to 9-26

So far you have used **qué** and **cuánto** as interrogative words, but these words can also be used in exclamatory sentences.

—Felipe, ¡**qué** anillo!	*Felipe, what a ring!*
—María, ¡**cuánto** te quiero!	*María, I love you so much!*
—Mi cabeza, ¡**qué** dolor!	*My head—what pain!*
—**Cuánto** lo siento.	*I'm so sorry. (How sorry I am.)*
—¡**Qué** susto! ¡Se cortó el dedo!	*What a scare! He cut his finger!*
—Se ve muy mal. ¡**Qué** feo!	*It looks really bad. How awful! (It looks awful/ugly.)*
—¡**Qué** doctor! Le salvó la vida.	*What a doctor! He saved his life.*
—**Cuánto** se lo agradezco.	*I'm so thankful. (How grateful I am.)*

*Note that in the examples above, **cuánto** accompanies *verbs* and is masculine and singular. When **cuánto** accompanies *nouns* it must agree with them in gender and number:

—¡**Cuántas** recetas y todavía estoy tosiendo!	*So many prescriptions and I am still coughing!*
—Sí, y ¡**cuántos** estudiantes con la misma cosa!	*Yes, and so many students with the same thing.*

9-14 ¿Cómo respondes?

Elige la respuesta apropiada para cada comentario. Después, comparte tus respuestas con un/a compañero/a.

1. ______ ¡Ay, el estómago!
2. ______ Su novia se graduó con honores.
3. ______ Pepe me compró veinticuatro rosas rojas.
4. ______ Esta comida es deliciosa.
5. ______ Este doctor es el novio de aquella enfermera.
6. ______ Mi madre preparó tapas para cincuenta personas.
7. ______ Tiene la cara de un monstruo.
8. ______ Tengo que leer dos libros para mi clase de historia y preparar un informe.

a. ¡Qué feo!
b. ¡Cuánto trabajo!
c. ¡Qué inteligente!
d. ¡Cuánto me duele!
e. ¡Cuánto me gusta!
f. ¡Qué interesante!
g. ¡Cuánta comida!
h. ¡Qué romántico!

9•15 ¿Qué tiene?

¿Cómo responden Uds. a las siguientes situaciones?

MODELO E1: Tito está muy mal porque tiene un dolor terrible de estómago.

E2: *¡Cuánto le duele!*

E1: Yo no puedo hablar porque estoy tosiendo mucho.

E2: *¡Qué tos tengo!*

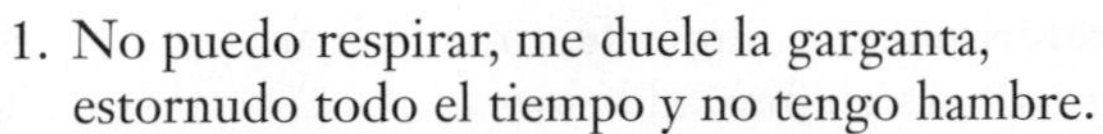

1. No puedo respirar, me duele la garganta, estornudo todo el tiempo y no tengo hambre.
2. A mi hermano siempre le ocurre algo malo: un accidente, se rompe algo…
3. ¡Ay! Necesito un antiácido ahora mismo, por favor.
4. Mi abuelo acaba de salir del hospital después de pasar mucho tiempo allí. No tiene seguro médico (*insurance*).
5. Tú tienes mucha fiebre y te duele el cuerpo.

¿Cómo andas?

Having completed the first **Comunicación,** I now can…

	Feel Confident	Need to Review
• describe the human body (p. 322)	❑	❑
• pronounce the letters **d** and **t** correctly (p. 323)	❑	❑
• identify and use direct object, indirect object, and reflexive pronouns with more confidence (p. 325)	❑	❑
• explain what ails me and understand others when they say where "it" hurts (p. 328)	❑	❑
• suggest treatments for various ailments (p. 328)	❑	❑
• explain the importance of water in maintaining good health (p. 331)	❑	❑
• use the exclamations **¡qué!** and **¡cuánto!** (p. 332)	❑	❑

Comunicación

- Talking about the past
- Narrating in the past
- Explaining how long something has been going on
- Telling how long ago something happened

El pretérito y el imperfecto

9-27 to 9-34

35, 36, 41

In **Capítulos 7** and **8** you learned about two aspects of the past tense in Spanish, **el pretérito** and **el imperfecto,** which are not interchangeable. Their uses are contrasted below.

Fuimos a Cuzco y subimos a Machu Picchu. Hacía buen tiempo.

THE **PRETERIT** IS USED:	THE **IMPERFECT** IS USED:
1. To relate an event or occurrence that refers to *one specific time in the past* • **Fuimos** a Cuzco el año pasado. *We went to Cuzco last year.* • **Comimos** en el restaurante El Sol y **nos gustó** mucho. *We ate at El Sol restaurant and liked it a lot.*	**1.** To express *habitual* or often *repeated actions* • **Íbamos** a Cuzco todos los veranos. *We used to go to Cuzco every summer.* • **Comíamos** en el restaurante El Sol todos los lunes. *We used to eat at El Sol Restaurant every Monday.*
2. To relate an act *begun or completed in the past* • **Empezó** a llover. *It started to rain.* • **Comenzaron** los juegos. *The games began.* • La gira **terminó.** *The tour ended.*	**2.** To express *was/were + -ing* • **Llovía** sin parar. *It rained without stopping.* • **Comenzaban** los juegos cuando llegamos. *The games were beginning when we arrived.* • La gira **transcurría** sin ningún problema. *The tour continued without any problems.*
3. To relate a *sequence of events,* each completed and moving the narrative along toward its conclusion • **Llegamos** en avión, **recogimos** las maletas y **fuimos** al hotel. *We arrived by plane, picked up our luggage, and went to the hotel.* • Al día siguiente **decidimos** ir a Machu Picchu. *The next day we decided to go to Machu Picchu.* • **Vimos** muchos ejemplos de la magnífica arquitectura incaica. Después **anduvimos** un poco por el camino de los incas. **Nos divertimos** mucho. *We saw many examples of the magnificent Incan architecture. Afterward we walked a bit on the Incan road. We had a great time.*	**3.** To provide *background* information, set the stage, or express a pre-existing condition • **Era** un día oscuro. **Llovía** de vez en cuando. *It was a dark day and it rained once in a while.* • Los turistas **llevaban** pantalones cortos y lentes de sol. *The tourists were wearing shorts and sunglasses.* • El camino **era** estrecho y **había** muchos turistas. *The path was narrow and there were many tourists.*

4. To relate an action that took place within a specified or *specific amount* (segment) *of time.* **Caminé** (por) dos horas. *I walked for two hours.* **Hablamos** (por) cinco minutos. *We talked for five minutes.* **Contemplaron** el templo un rato. *They contemplated the temple for a while.* **Viví** en Ecuador (por) seis años. *I lived in Ecuador for six years.*	4. To *tell time* in the past **Era** la una. *It was 1:00.* **Eran** las tres y media. *It was 3:30.* **Era** muy tarde. *It was very late.* **Era** la medianoche. *It was midnight.*

Fíjate

The use of *por* is optional in these cases.

WORDS AND EXPRESSIONS THAT COMMONLY SIGNAL:

PRETERIT	IMPERFECT
anoche anteayer ayer de repente (*suddenly*) el fin de semana pasado el mes pasado el lunes pasado/el martes pasado, etc. esta mañana una vez, dos veces, etc. siempre (when an end point is obvious)	a menudo cada semana/mes/año con frecuencia de vez en cuando (*once in a while*) mientras muchas veces frecuentemente todos los lunes/martes, etc. todas las semanas todos los días/meses/años siempre (when an event is repeated with no particular end point)

***Please note:** The **pretérito** and the **imperfecto** can be used in the same sentence.

Miraban la tele cuando **sonó** el teléfono. — *They were watching TV when the phone rang.*

In the preceding sentence, an action was going on **(miraban)** when it was interrupted by another action **(sonó el teléfono).**

9-16 Una (muy) breve historia de los incas

¿Qué sabes sobre los incas? Lee el siguiente fragmento y completa las actividades que siguen con un/a compañero/a.

Machu Picchu, la ciudad perdida de los incas.

El imperio de los incas.

El imperio de los incas fue uno de los imperios más importantes de las civilizaciones precolombinas. Se encontraba (*It was located*) en lo que es hoy Perú, Bolivia, el norte de Chile y parte de Ecuador. El imperio se dividía en tres partes iguales: una tercera parte pertenecía (*pertained to*) a los indígenas y pasaba de padre a hijo; otra tercera parte era del Inca, o sea, del Gobierno; la otra tercera parte pertenecía a la Iglesia.

Los incas adoraban al hijo del Sol. Según la leyenda (*legend*), el hijo cayó (*fell*) en algún lugar cerca del lago Titicaca. Con él llegó su hermana y según la leyenda, ellos eran los padres de todos los incas. Esta civilización practicaba sacrificios de animales y algunas veces sacrificios humanos. También le ofrecían objetos preciosos y joyas (*jewels*) al sol. El último cacique (o jefe político) famoso de los incas fue Atahualpa.

1. Subrayen los verbos.
2. Digan cuáles son pretéritos y cuáles son imperfectos.
3. Expliquen por qué usaron cada uno de estos tiempos verbales.

9-17 Un cuento de hadas

En grupos de tres o cuatro personas, pongan las siguientes oraciones en orden cronológico para terminar el cuento de Ricitos de Oro (*Goldilocks*). Después, analicen los usos del pretérito y el imperfecto dentro del cuento como lo hicieron en la actividad **9-16.**

Había una vez una niña muy curiosa. Un día, mientras caminaba por el bosque, encontró una casa muy bonita. En la casa vivían tres osos. Mientras los osos no estaban, …

______ Los osos la asustaron *(scared her)*.
______ Entró en el dormitorio de los osos.
______ Mientras ella dormía entraron los osos.
______ La niña se levantó y salió corriendo de la casa.
______ Tenía sueño.
______ Buscó una cama.
______ La niña entró en la casa.
______ Vio que una cama era muy grande, otra era muy pequeña y la otra tenía el tamaño perfecto.
______ Encontraron a la niña dormida en la cama.
______ Se acostó.

9-18 En el consultorio

Capítulo 8. Las construcciones reflexivas, pág. 302.

Completa el siguiente pasaje con la forma correcta del pretérito o el imperfecto de cada verbo. Después, comparte las respuestas con un/a compañero/a y explícale por qué usaste el pretérito o el imperfecto.

Ayer en el consultorio del Dr. Fuentes (1. haber) ________ mucha actividad. Muchos pacientes (2. esperar) ________ al médico y yo no (3. encontrar) ________ dónde sentarme. Dos horas (4. pasar) ________ lentamente. (5. Ser) ________ las once cuando por fin la recepcionista me (6. llamar) ________ y la enfermera (7. salir) ________ para buscarme. Juntas (8. entrar) ________ al cuarto donde (9. estar) ________ el médico. El Dr. Fuentes (10. levantarse) ________ y me (11. mirar) ________ con mucha curiosidad. (12. Empezar) ________ a examinarme y a hacerme preguntas.

Yo (13. ponerse) ________ nerviosa y (14. callarse) ________. Sólo (15. esperar) ________ un examen anual típico pero las preguntas (16. ser) ________ demasiadas específicas. Por ejemplo, me (17. preguntar) ________ si (18. sentirse) ________ mareada (*faint*) por la mañana y si (19. comer) ________ bien cuando (20. tener) ________ hambre.

Por fin (21. darse cuenta [*to realize*]: yo) ________ de lo que (22. ocurrir) ________. ¡El Dr. Fuentes (23. pensar) ________ que yo (24. estar) ________ embarazada (*pregnant*)! Por lo visto la enfermera (25. equivocarse [*to be mistaken*]) ________ y ¡le (26. dar) ________ al médico la información de otra paciente!

9-19 En el pasado

Termina las siguientes oraciones. Después, compártelas con un/a compañero/a.

MODELO Cuando era niño/a…

E1: *Cuando era niño me gustaba subirme a los árboles.*

1. Cuando era niño/a…
2. Cuando tenía entre catorce y dieciséis años, frecuentemente…
3. Una vez el verano pasado…
4. Ayer tenía ganas de _____ pero…
5. Anoche…
6. Cuando vivía con mis padres, todas las semanas…

9•20 Nuestro cuento

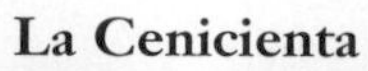

En grupos de tres, van a contar una historia (en el pasado) basada en los dibujos. Al terminar van a compartir su historia con los otros miembros de la clase.

Estrategia

In this variation of "Cinderella," remember to use the *imperfect* for *description* and *background* information. Use the *preterit* for *sequences of actions.*

La Cenicienta

9•21 Y en el hospital

Imagina que trabajas como enfermero/a en la sala de urgencias de un hospital. Un día entra un joven de unos veinte años con unos síntomas raros.

Paso 1 Llena el siguiente formulario médico para el joven enfermo como si fueras un/a enfermero/a.

FORMULARIO MÉDICO

Por favor complete este formulario con la mayor precisión posible. Toda la infomación en este formulario es confidencial y será utilizada en caso de emergencia. Por favor escriba legiblemente.

HISTORIA MÉDICA

Nombre ____________________
Dirección ____________________
Ciudad y estado ____________________
Código postal ____________________
Número de teléfono ____________________
Edad ____________________
Fecha de nacimiento ____________________
Sexo ______ Peso ______ Altura ______
Grupo sanguíneo ____________________

1. ¿Está bajo tratamiento por alguna enfermedad? Explique.____________________
2. ¿Toma algún tipo de medicamento? ____________________
3. ¿Tiene algún tipo de alergia?____________________
4. ¿Ha tenido cirugía alguna vez?____________________

CONDICIONES MÉDICAS

Por favor marque cualquier enfermedad que haya tenido en el pasado y la fecha en que comenzó.

_____artritis	_____asma	_____dolor de espalda
_____mareos	_____tos crónica	_____dolor de pecho
_____diabetes	_____epilepsia	_____fracturas
_____dolor de cabeza	_____hernia	_____presión alta

¿Ha tenido otra condición que no hemos mencionado?____________________

Paso 2 Crea seis preguntas para determinar cuál es su problema, según el modelo.

MODELO E1: ¿Dar / todos sus datos / en recepción?
E2: *¿Dio todos sus datos en recepción?*

1. ¿Cuándo / llegar / la sala de urgencias?
2. ¿Cuándo / le empezar / a doler?
3. ¿Qué / hacer / cuando / le empezar / a doler?
4. ¿Quién / estar / con Ud.?
5. ¿Cómo / sentirse / cuando / acostarse / anoche?
6. ¿Qué / hacer / para causar el dolor?

Paso 3 Crea un diálogo con un/a compañero/a entre el joven y el/la enfermero/a usando las preguntas que escribiste.

9•22 La última vez que me enfermé

Túrnense para describir la última vez que se enfermaron. Incluyan esta información.

- ¿Cuándo fue?
- ¿Cómo te sentías?
- ¿Cuáles fueron los síntomas?
- Si fuiste al médico, ¿qué te hizo? ¿Qué te dijo?
- ¿Te recetó (recetar = *to prescribe*) algo? ¿Cuánto pagaste por la visita? Si no fuiste al médico, ¿qué hiciste para curarte?
- ¿Cuánto tiempo duró (durar = *to last*) la enfermedad?

Fíjate

Use the term *médico* when referring to the profession of a doctor. Use *doctor* for the title of the person.

El Doctor Ramírez es un médico excelente.

Fíjate

When the preterit and imperfect are used together in narratives in which events are retold, you will notice that the *imperfect* provides the background information such as the time, weather, and location. The *preterit* relates the specific events that occurred.

9•23 ¿Y ayer?

Descríbele a un/a compañero/a tu día de ayer en por lo menos **cinco** oraciones.

MODELO *Ayer hacía mal tiempo cuando me desperté. No quería levantarme, pero por fin salí de la cama. Fui a mi clase de español. El profesor nos dio mucha tarea. Luego fui a la bilioteca. Estudiaba cuando llegó mi mejor amigo Jeff.*

9•24 Luces, cámara, acción

Capítulo 5. El mundo del cine, pág. 185.

¿Te gustan las películas? ¿Vas al cine a menudo? Cuéntale (*Narrate*) a un/a compañero/a una película que hayas visto (*you have seen*) últimamente. Usa por lo menos **siete** oraciones. ¡Recuerda! Generalmente el imperfecto se usa para la descripción y el pretérito para la acción.

SAM 9-35

Las farmacias en el mundo hispanohablante

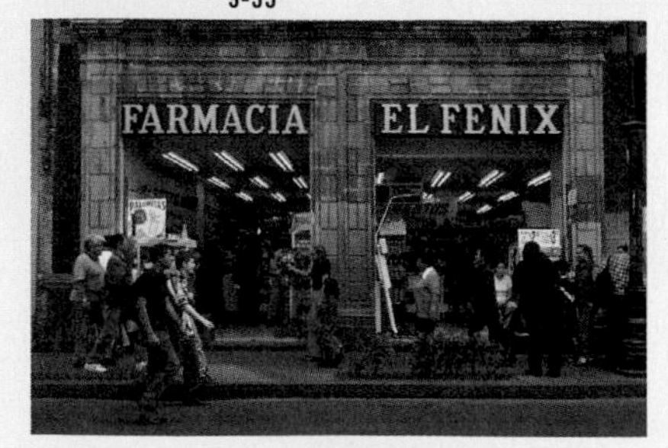

En Latinoamérica, las farmacias son, por la mayor parte, dispensarios de medicina únicamente. El farmacéutico (*pharmacist*) muchas veces ofrece consejos sobre los medicamentos (medicinas). Es fácil conseguir muchos tipos de medicina sin receta en las farmacias. Por ejemplo, puedes ir a la farmacia, describir los síntomas (como tos y fiebre) y pedir que te den unos antibióticos. Todo ello sin consultar al médico. Muchos países tienen *farmacias de turno* o *de guardia* que atienden al público las veinticuatro horas al día.

En algunos países (como Argentina, Chile y Perú) hay un nuevo tipo de farmacia al estilo estadounidense, que vende de todo. Estas farmacias pertenecen a grandes cadenas (Farmacity en Argentina, FASA en Chile, Inka Farma en Perú) que atraen a los consumidores con una gran variedad de productos, aparte de los medicamentos.

Preguntas

1. ¿Qué es una *farmacia de turno* o *farmacia de guardia*? ¿Existe este sistema en los Estados Unidos?
2. ¿Qué diferencias hay entre las farmacias hispanas tradicionales y las de los Estados Unidos?

Expresiones con *hacer*

9-36 to 9-39

The verb **hacer** means *to do* or *to make*. You have also used **hacer** in idiomatic expressions dealing with weather. There are some additional special constructions with **hacer** that deal with time. **Hace** is used:

1. to discuss an action that began in the past but is still going on in the present.

hace + *period of time* + **que** + *verb in the present tense*

Hace cuatro meses **que** estudio español.	*I've been studying Spanish for four months.*
Hace dos años **que** vivo aquí.	*I've been living here for two years.*

2. to ask how long something has been going on.

cuánto (tiempo) + **hace** + **que** + *verb in present tense*

¿Cuántos meses **hace que** estudias español?	*How many months have you been studying Spanish?*
¿Cuánto tiempo **hace que** estudias español?	*How long have you been studying Spanish?*
¿Cuántas semanas **hace que** vives aquí?	*How many weeks have you been living here?*

3. in the preterit to tell how long ago something happened.

hace + *period of time* + **que** + *verb in the preterit*

Hace cuatro meses **que** empecé a estudiar español.	*I began to study Spanish four months ago.*
Hace dos años **que** me mudé aquí.	*I moved here two years ago.*

or

verb in the preterit + **hace** + *period of time*

Empecé a estudiar español **hace** cuatro meses.	*I began to study Spanish four months ago.*
Me mudé aquí **hace** dos años.	*I moved here two years ago.*

*Note that in this construction **hace** can either precede or follow the rest of the sentence. When it follows, **que** is not used.

4. to ask how long ago something happened.

cuánto (tiempo) + **hace** + **que** + *verb in preterit*

¿Cuánto tiempo **hace que** empezaste a estudiar español?	*How long ago did you begin to study Spanish?*
¿Cuánto tiempo **hace que** te enfermaste?	*How long ago did you get sick?*

9-25 ¿Qué pasa?

Juntos completen el diálogo entre Julián, Pati y su mamá con las palabras apropiadas.

Julián, ¡ese sofá es horrible!

MAMÁ: Julián (1) ¿ ________ tiempo hace (2) ________ vives en esta casa?

JULIÁN: Bueno, creo que (3) ________ unos dos años que vivo aquí.

MAMÁ: Y (4) ¿ ________ ________ ________ que tienes ese sofá? Está muy sucio.

JULIÁN: No sé, mamá. Fue un regalo de un amigo. Lo tenía en su apartamento.

MAMÁ: Creo que (5) ________ por lo menos diez años (6) ________ tiene esas manchas (*stains*) negras. ¡Es horrible!

JULIÁN: Mamá, (7) ________ media hora (8) ________ criticas mi casa y…

PATI: ¡Mamá! (9) ¡ ________ cinco minutos (10) ________ te estoy llamando! ¡Tráeme agua!

Fíjate

Note that *cuánto* agrees with the amount of time: cuánto tiempo cuántas semanas/horas; cuántos años/días

9-26 Firma aquí

Circula por la clase hasta encontrar a un estudiante que pueda contestar afirmativamente tu pregunta.

MODELO empezar a estudiar español hace menos de (*less than*) un año

E1: *¿Empezaste a estudiar español hace menos de un año?*

E2: *No, empecé a estudiar español hace dos años.*

E1: (a otro estudiante) *¿Empezaste a estudiar español hace menos de un año?*

E3: *Sí, empecé a estudiar español hace seis meses.*

E1: *Muy bien. Firma* (Sign) *aquí por favor.*

________________ Janet ________________

1. empezar a estudiar español hace menos de un año	________
2. graduarse de la escuela secundaria (*high school*) hace dos años	________
3. conocer a su mejor amigo/a hace muchos años	________
4. ver una película de terror hace dos o tres semanas	________
5. ir a un concierto hace uno o dos meses	________
6. tomar café hace una hora	________
7. comer en un restaurante elegante hace unos (*some*) días	________
8. hacer ejercicio hace unas horas	________
9. hablar con alguien de su familia hace una semana	________
10. enfermarse hace una semana	________

9-27 Conversando

Habla con varios compañeros de clase utilizando las siguientes preguntas para guiar la conversación.

1. ¿Cuánto tiempo hace que vives en este estado (*state*)? ¿Dónde vivías antes?
2. ¿Cuánto tiempo hace que estudias en esta universidad? ¿En qué año te gradúas?
3. ¿Cuánto tiempo hace que conoces a tu mejor amigo/a? ¿Dónde lo/la conociste?
4. ¿Cuánto tiempo hace que viste a tus padres? ¿Volviste a casa o te visitaron?
5. ¿Cuánto tiempo hace que fuiste al médico? ¿Qué te recomendó?

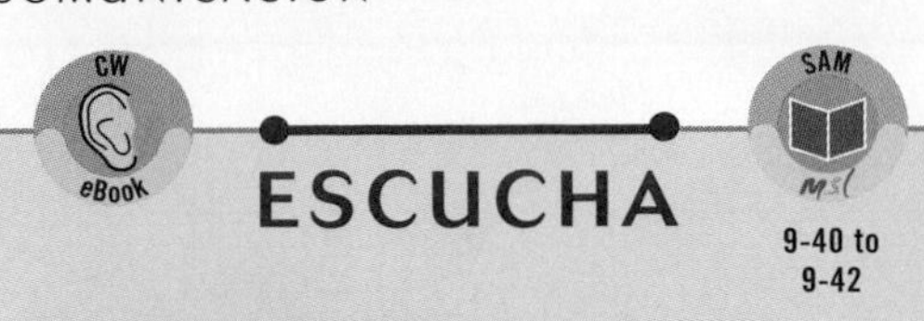

ESTRATEGIA **Asking yourself questions**

A useful tool for boosting comprehension is asking yourself check questions to help you organize information and summarize what you have heard.

To practice this strategy be sure to complete the **Antes de escuchar** section.

9•28 Antes de escuchar

Marisol no se siente bien y llama a su madre para pedirle consejo. Cuando tú no te sientes bien, ¿qué haces generalmente: llamas al médico, hablas con un/a amigo/a, llamas a tu madre u otro pariente o te cuidas solo/a (*take care of yourself*)?

Marisol llama a su madre.

9•29 A escuchar

CD 4 Track 2

Completen las siguientes actividades.

1. La conversación entre Marisol y su madre se divide en tres partes. Escucha la primera parte y después escoge la pregunta que mejor resuma (*summarizes*) lo que escuchaste. Repite el proceso con cada parte.

   Primera parte
   a. ¿Por qué llama Marisol a su madre?
   b. ¿Cuáles son los síntomas de Marisol?
   c. ¿Qué hizo Marisol cuando se levantó?

   Segunda parte
   a. ¿Con quiénes salió Marisol anoche?
   b. ¿A Marisol le gustan las galletas?
   c. ¿Qué comió Marisol anoche?

   Tercera parte
   a. ¿Debe ir a clase?
   b. ¿Debe comer mucho hoy?
   c. ¿Qué puede hacer Marisol para sentirse mejor?

2. Escucha una vez más para averiguar si escogiste las preguntas apropiadas. Compáralas con las de un/a compañero/a. Expliquen por qué son las mejores preguntas.
3. Ahora escucha la conversación por última vez para contestar las siguientes preguntas.
   a. ¿Por qué llama Marisol a su madre?
   b. ¿Cuáles son sus síntomas?
   c. ¿Qué comió Marisol anoche?
   d. ¿Cuál es el consejo de su mamá?

9•30 Después de escuchar

Realicen la escena entre Marisol y su madre.

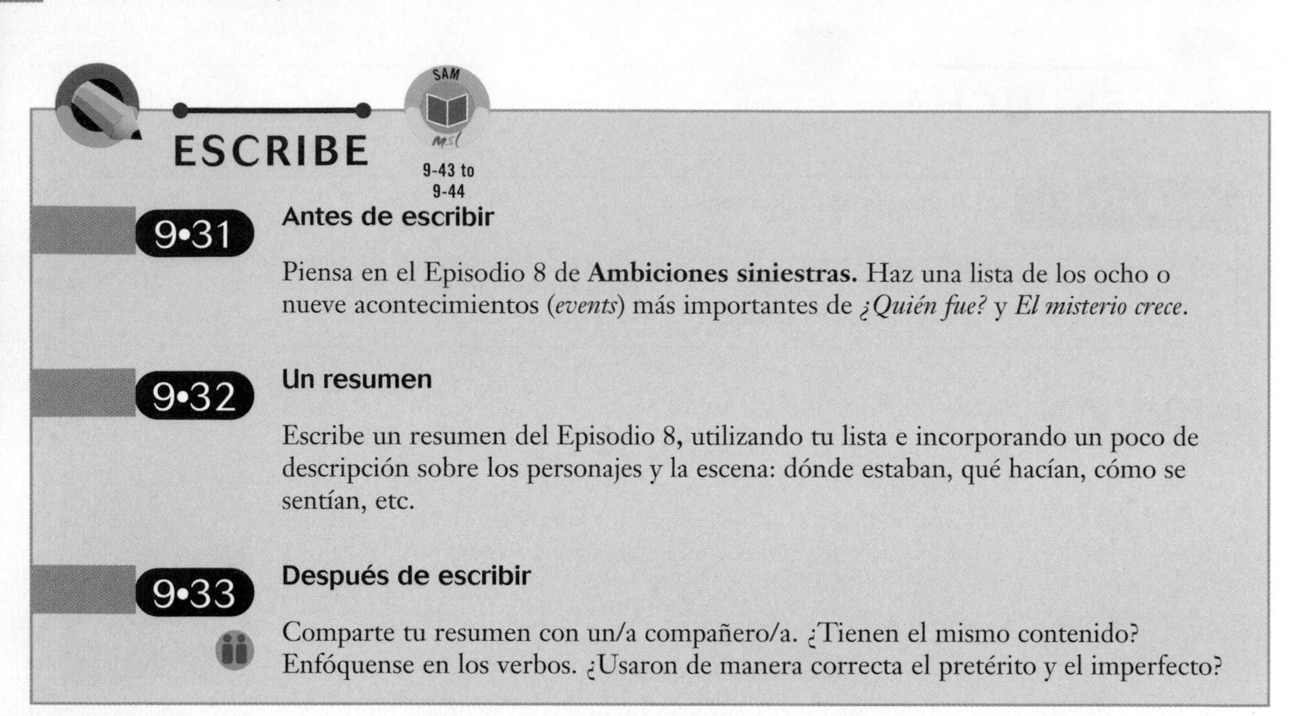

ESCRIBE

SAM 9-43 to 9-44

9•31 Antes de escribir

Piensa en el Episodio 8 de **Ambiciones siniestras.** Haz una lista de los ocho o nueve acontecimientos (*events*) más importantes de *¿Quién fue?* y *El misterio crece*.

9•32 Un resumen

Escribe un resumen del Episodio 8, utilizando tu lista e incorporando un poco de descripción sobre los personajes y la escena: dónde estaban, qué hacían, cómo se sentían, etc.

9•33 Después de escribir

Comparte tu resumen con un/a compañero/a. ¿Tienen el mismo contenido? Enfóquense en los verbos. ¿Usaron de manera correcta el pretérito y el imperfecto?

¿Cómo andas?

Having completed the second **Comunicación,** I now can...

	Feel Confident	**Need to Review**
● talk about how things used to be and narrate events in the past (p. 334)	❑	❑
● talk about how long something has been going on (p. 335)	❑	❑
● talk about pharmacies in Latin America and how they differ from those in the United States (p. 340)	❑	❑
● talk about how long ago something occurred (p. 341)	❑	❑
● ask myself questions when listening to a passage to help organize and summarize what I hear (p. 343)	❑	❑
● write a summary of a story using the preterit and imperfect (p. 344)	❑	❑

Milagros Alejandra Romero Zárate

Perú

CD 4
Track 3

9-45

Vistas culturales

Les presento mi país

Mi nombre es Milagros Alejandra Romero Zárate y soy de Arequipa, Perú. Soy estudiante de arqueología en la Universidad Nacional Mayor de San Marcos en Lima. Mientras estudio, vivo con unos parientes en Miraflores, un barrio de la capital. Quiero ser arqueóloga porque me fascina la historia del país; hay muchas ruinas de la civilización incaica en Perú. **¿Qué sabes de la historia de tu país y sus pueblos antiguos?** Perú es un país de extremos geográficos: tenemos la costa, al nivel del mar, los Andes, montañas impresionantes, cañones profundos, la selva y los principios del río Amazonas. ¡Puedes mantenerte en forma caminando por estas regiones!

Miraflores, en las afueras de Lima, Perú

Las líneas de Nazca

ALMANAQUE

Nombre oficial:	República del Perú
Gobierno:	República constitucional
Población:	28.302.603 (2006)
Idiomas:	español (oficial); quechua (oficial); idiomas indígenas
Moneda:	Nuevo sol (S/)

¿Sabías que...?

- Las líneas de Nazca, que se encuentran en un desierto del sur del país, son un enigma. Consisten en una serie de dibujos de diferentes animales, plantas y flores, y figuras geométricas que se reconocen solamente desde el aire.
- Hay casi 3,5 millones de llamas en los Andes.

PREGUNTAS

1. ¿Por qué Milagros quiere ser arqueóloga?
2. ¿Por qué se dice que Perú es un país de geografía muy variada?
3. ¿Qué otros países comparten algunas de las características geográficas de Perú?

En la Red
Amplía tus conocimientos sobre Perú en la página web de *¡Anda!*

Raúl Eduardo Loza Arce

Bolivia

CD 4
Track 4

DVD/VHS

Vistas culturales

Les presento mi país

Mi nombre es Raúl Eduardo Loza Arce y soy de La Paz, la capital administrativa de Bolivia. Hay otra capital, Sucre, que es la sede (*headquarters*) constitucional; allí se mantiene el Tribunal Supremo del país. La Paz es la capital más alta del mundo, a unos 3.650 m.s.n.m. en los Andes. **¿A qué altura está tu ciudad?** La gente indígena constituye más del cincuenta por ciento de la población del país, y muchos viven en el altiplano, un área cerca del lago Titicaca, que es el lago navegable más alto del mundo. En el altiplano se encuentran las ruinas de una civilización antigua preincaica, anterior a los aymara, que pueblan la región hoy en día.

Fíjate

The abbreviation *m.s.n.m.* means *metros sobre nivel del mar*, or meters above sea level.

Una mujer aymara con ropa tradicional

En las islas flotantes del lago Titicaca viven algunos indígenas.

ALMANAQUE

Nombre oficial:	República de Bolivia
Gobierno:	República
Población:	8.989.046 (2006)
Idiomas:	español (oficial); quechua (oficial); aymara (oficial)
Moneda:	Boliviano (Bs)

¿Sabías que...?

- La papa, nativa de Suramérica, es un alimento básico en Bolivia. Se cultivan más de doscientos tipos de papa en el país.
- Aunque no tiene salida al mar, Bolivia tiene una fuerza marina: la Armada Boliviana.

PREGUNTAS

1. ¿Por qué crees que Bolivia tiene tres idiomas oficiales?
2. ¿Qué distinción tiene La Paz como capital?
3. ¿Qué riesgo para la salud (*health risk*) comparten Bolivia y Perú?

En la Red
Amplía tus conocimientos sobre Bolivia en la página web de *¡Anda!*

María Yolanda Palacios Mena

Ecuador

CD 4 Track 5

Vistas culturales

Les presento mi país

Mi nombre es María Yolanda Palacios Mena y soy de Santo Domingo de los Colorados. Ecuador tiene tres diferentes tipos de geografía: la costa, la sierra y el oriente o la selva. La población, principalmente mestiza e indígena, se concentra en la sierra y la costa. **¿Dónde vive la mayoría de la población en tu país?** Uno de los grupos indígenas de Ecuador son los tsáchilas, también llamados "los colorados", debido a la costumbre de los hombres de pintarse (*dye*) el pelo de color rojo. Los chamanes (*shamans*) de esta tribu tienen gran conocimiento de las plantas medicinales y, por lo tanto, tienen mucho poder en la comunidad.

Un sombrero Panamá

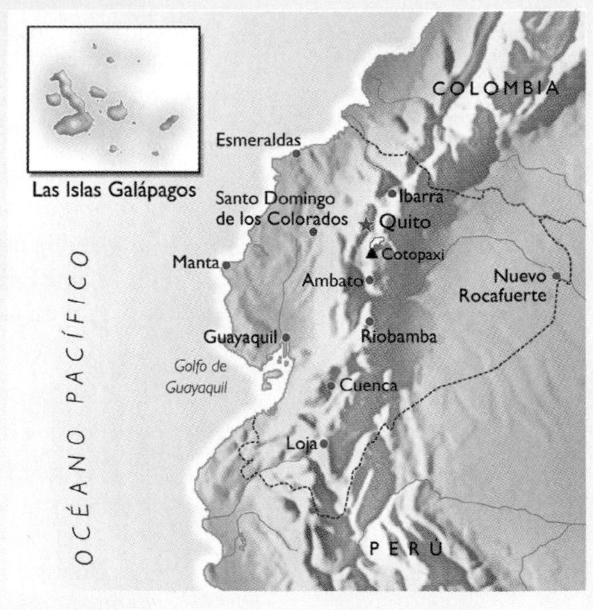

Un tsáchila de Santo Domingo de los Colorados

ALMANAQUE

Nombre oficial:	República del Ecuador
Gobierno:	República
Población:	13.547.510 (2006)
Idiomas:	español (oficial); quechua y otros idiomas indígenas
Moneda:	El dólar estadounidense ($)

¿Sabías que...?

- El famoso sombrero panamá es en realidad de Ecuador.
- El volcán Cotopaxi se considera el volcán activo más alto del mundo.

PREGUNTAS

1. ¿Cuál es una costumbre de los tsáchilas?
2. ¿Qué tiene Ecuador en común geográficamente con Perú y Bolivia?
3. ¿En qué otros países se encuentra un gran porcentaje de mestizos e indígenas?

En la Red
Amplía tus conocimientos sobre Ecuador en la página web de *¡Anda!*

Ambiciones siniestras

EPISODIO 9

lectura

9-48

9-34 **Antes de leer.** En el **Episodio 8** Marisol y Manolo hablan de las dudas que tienen sobre Lupe y Cisco. Teniendo esto en cuenta, contesta las siguientes preguntas.

- ¿Es posible que Lupe sea (*is*) el Sr. Verdugo?
- ¿Por qué actúa Cisco de manera tan misteriosa?
- Si resuelven el nuevo rompecabezas, ¿van a poder salvar (*save*) a Alejandra y a Eduardo?

ESTRATEGIA **Asking yourself questions**

Just as with listening, it is helpful to learn to ask yourself check questions as you read, which help you summarize and organize information.

9-35 **A leer.** Completa las siguientes actividades.

1. Lee el primer párrafo y elige la pregunta que mejor lo resuma (*summarizes it*).
   a. ¿Dónde están los protagonistas?
   b. ¿Cómo están Eduardo y Alejandra?
   c. ¿Qué saben Manolo, Cisco, Marisol y Lupe de Eduardo y Alejandra?
2. Ahora lee el segundo párrafo y elige la pregunta que mejor lo resuma.
   a. ¿Por qué tienen miedo Manolo, Cisco, Marisol y Lupe?
   b. ¿Por qué Manolo, Cisco, Marisol y Lupe participaron en el concurso?
   c. ¿Por qué se desaparecieron Eduardo y Alejandra?
3. Continúa leyendo el episodio pero ahora, en vez de elegir la mejor pregunta, tú vas a escribir una pregunta para cada sección indicada (secciones de 3 a 9). Al terminar, compara tus preguntas con las de tus compañeros.

CD 4
Track 6

¡Qué mentira!

[1] En distintas partes del país hay cuatro estudiantes universitarios muy preocupados. Todavía no saben ni dónde ni cómo están Eduardo y Alejandra. Sólo saben que desaparecieron y que un tal Verdugo tiene algo que ver con todo eso°.

° *has something to do with it*

[2] El concurso —¡Qué mentira°!— ¿Cómo pudieron creerlo? Este tipo de cosas tan increíbles generalmente terminan siendo falsas. Para Manolo, Cisco, Marisol y Lupe es mucho más serio. Hay dos desaparecidos° ya y los otros con el miedo de no saber si les va a pasar lo mismo a ellos. El Sr. Verdugo les dijo que no hablaran° con nadie —especialmente con la policía— o les haría daño a todos°. Así que todos los días se levantan y se acuestan con miedo.

lie
missing
not to talk
would hurt all of them

[3] Hoy Manolo se despertó asustado° y se levantó inmediatamente. Durmió mal anoche y ahora le duele todo el cuerpo. Decidió tomar tres aspirinas y volvió a acostarse. Pocos minutos después, sonó el teléfono celular. Era Cisco.

scared

[4]—¿Manolo? ¿Estás levantado?

—Sí —respondió Manolo— hace media hora. ¿Qué pasa?

—Acabamos de recibir otro mensaje. Este hombre está loco —explicó Cisco.

—Voy a leer el mensaje y te llamo más tarde —le dijo Manolo.

[5] Colgaron°. Otra llamada. Esta vez fue Marisol.

They hung up

—¿Manolo? Tienes que leer el último mensaje. No sé qué hacer…

—Mira Marisol, voy a leerlo ahora mismo. Ya me llamó Cisco hace unos minutos. Llama tú a Lupe y dentro de diez minutos te llamo. ¿Está bien? ¿Estás en tu teléfono celular?

—Sí. Bueno, te espero.

[6] Manolo encendió° la computadora y leyó:

turned on

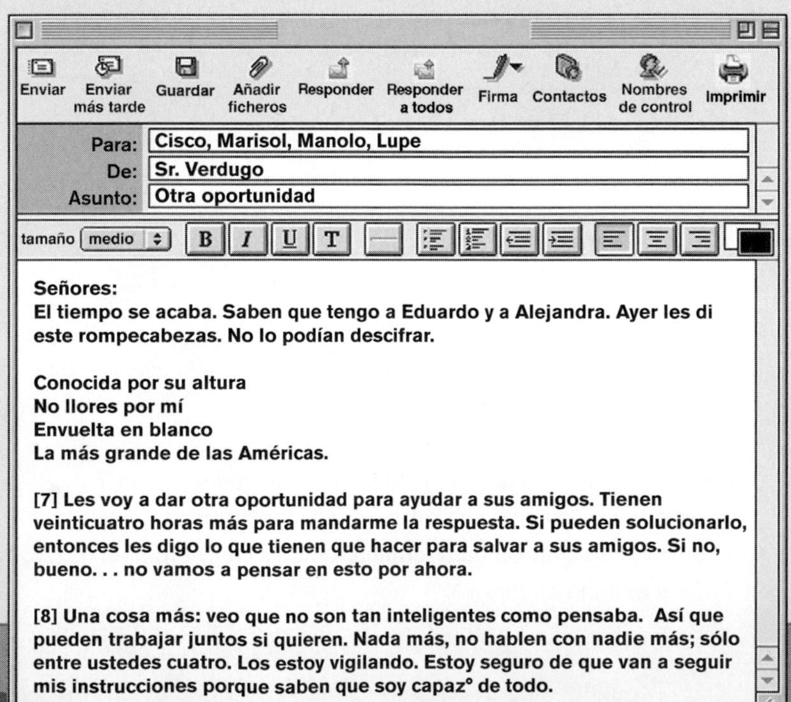

Para: Cisco, Marisol, Manolo, Lupe
De: Sr. Verdugo
Asunto: Otra oportunidad

Señores:
El tiempo se acaba. Saben que tengo a Eduardo y a Alejandra. Ayer les di este rompecabezas. No lo podían descifrar.

Conocida por su altura
No llores por mí
Envuelta en blanco
La más grande de las Américas.

[7] Les voy a dar otra oportunidad para ayudar a sus amigos. Tienen veinticuatro horas más para mandarme la respuesta. Si pueden solucionarlo, entonces les digo lo que tienen que hacer para salvar a sus amigos. Si no, bueno. . . no vamos a pensar en esto por ahora.

[8] Una cosa más: veo que no son tan inteligentes como pensaba. Así que pueden trabajar juntos si quieren. Nada más, no hablen con nadie más; sólo entre ustedes cuatro. Los estoy vigilando. Estoy seguro de que van a seguir mis instrucciones porque saben que soy capaz° de todo.

capable

[9] Con un gran suspiro, Manolo buscó su teléfono y empezó a marcar°... De pronto dejó de marcar, se quedó mirando el teléfono un momento y lo tiró° con fuerza contra la pared...

dial
threw it

9-36 **Después de leer.** Contesta las siguientes preguntas.

1. ¿Por qué se levantan y se acuestan con miedo nuestros protagonistas?
2. ¿Cómo se sentía Manolo cuando se levantó?
3. ¿Quiénes llamaron a Manolo? ¿Por qué?
4. Además de un rompecabezas, ¿qué información nueva contiene el mensaje?
5. En tu opinión, ¿qué fue lo más aterrador (*frightening*) de todo lo que dijo el mensaje?

9-49 to 9-50

video

9-37 **Antes del video.** ¿Por qué crees que Manolo tiró el teléfono contra la pared? ¿Los protagonistas van a poder descifrar ese nuevo rompecabezas? ¿Van a trabajar juntos esta vez? ¿Van a poder salvar a Eduardo y a Alejandra?

Sin embargo, creo que ya tenemos una pista (*clue*).

Todo este lío (*mess*) con los rompecabezas me tiene bastante nerviosa.

Tengo que confesar algo.

Episodio 9

«No llores por mí»

Relájate y disfruta el video.

9-38 **Después del video.** Contesta las siguientes preguntas.

1. ¿Dónde estaban Marisol y Lupe?
2. ¿Qué hacían ellas?
3. ¿Qué información tenía Marisol que creía que podía ayudar con la primera pista?
4. ¿Cómo respondió Lupe a su idea?
5. ¿Por qué decidieron ellas llamar a Cisco y a Manolo?
6. ¿Qué dijo Cisco sobre la segunda pista, "No llores por mí"?
7. ¿Qué propuso Manolo sobre las dos últimas pistas?
8. ¿Cuántas horas tenían para terminar de descifrar el rompecabezas?
9. ¿Cómo terminó el episodio?

Y por fin, ¿cómo andas?

Having completed this chapter, I now can...

	Feel Confident	Need to Review
Comunicación		
• describe the human body (p. 322)	❑	❑
• pronounce **d** and **t** correctly (p. 323)	❑	❑
• identify and use the direct and indirect object pronouns and reflexive pronouns with more confidence (p. 325)	❑	❑
• talk about what ails me and understand when others tell me where "it" hurts (p. 328)	❑	❑
• discuss certain ailments and treatments (p. 328)	❑	❑
• make exclamatory and emphatic statements using **¡qué!** and **¡cuánto!** (p. 332)	❑	❑
• explain when to use the preterit and the imperfect (p. 334)	❑	❑
• narrate in the past (p. 334)	❑	❑
• talk about how long something has been going on and how long ago something occurred (pp. 335, 341)	❑	❑
• organize and summarize a listening passage by asking myself check questions (p. 343)	❑	❑
• write a summary of a story using past tenses (p. 344)	❑	❑
Cultura		
• discuss the importance of water in maintaining good health (p. 331)	❑	❑
• talk about pharmacies in the Spanish-speaking world (p. 340)	❑	❑
• share at least two interesting facts about each country: Peru, Bolivia, and Ecuador (pp. 345–347)	❑	❑
Ambiciones siniestras		
• create check questions to facilitate comprehension when reading (p. 348)	❑	❑
• discuss the contents of the new e-mail message (p. 349)	❑	❑
• talk about the progress the characters are making in deciphering the new riddle (p. 350)	❑	❑

VOCABULARIO ACTIVO

CD 4
Tracks 7-11

El cuerpo humano	The human body
la boca	*mouth*
el brazo	*arm*
la cabeza	*head*
la cara	*face*
la cintura	*waist*
el corazón	*heart*
el cuello	*neck*
el cuerpo	*body*
el dedo (de la mano)	*finger*
el dedo (del pie)	*toe*
el diente	*tooth*
la espalda	*back*
el estómago	*stomach*
la garganta	*throat*
la mano	*hand*
la nariz	*nose*
el oído	*inner ear*
el ojo	*eye*
la oreja	*ear*
el pecho	*chest*
el pelo	*hair*
el pie	*foot*
la pierna	*leg*

Unos verbos	Some verbs
doler (ue)	*to hurt*
estar enfermo/a	*to be sick*
estar sano/a; saludable	*to be healthy*
ser alérgico/a (a)	*to be allergic (to)*

Otras palabras útiles	Other useful words
la salud	*health*
la sangre	*blood*

Unas enfermedades y tratamientos médicos	Illnesses and medical treatments
el antiácido	*antacid*
el antibiótico	*antibiotic*
la aspirina	*aspirin*
el catarro/el resfriado	*cold*
la curita	*adhesive bandage*
el/la doctor/a	*doctor*
el dolor	*pain*
el/la enfermero/a	*nurse*
el estornudo	*sneeze*
el examen físico	*physical exam*
la farmacia	*pharmacy*
la fiebre	*fever*
la gripe	*flu*
la herida	*wound; injury*
el hospital	*hospital*
la inyección	*shot*
el jarabe	*cough syrup*
el/la médico/a	*doctor*
la náusea	*nausea*
las pastillas	*pills*
la receta	*prescription*
la sala de urgencias	*emergency room*
la tos	*cough*
la venda/el vendaje	*bandage*

Unos verbos	*Some verbs*
acabar de + infinitivo	*to have just finished + (something)*
cortar(se)	*to cut (oneself)*
curar(se)	*to cure; to be cured*
enfermar(se)	*to get sick*
estornudar	*to sneeze*
evitar	*to avoid*
guardar cama	*to stay in bed*
lastimar(se)	*to get hurt*
mejorar(se)	*to improve; to get better*
ocurrir	*to occur*
quemar(se)	*to burn; to get burned*
romper(se)	*to break*
tener…	
alergia (a)	*to be allergic (to)*
(un) catarro, resfriado	*to have a cold*
(la/una) gripe	*to have the flu*
una infección	*to have an infection*
tos	*to have a cough*
un virus	*to have a virus*
tener dolor de…	*to have a…*
cabeza	*headache*
espalda	*backache*
estómago	*stomachache*
garganta	*sore throat*
toser	*to cough*
tratar de	*to try to*
vendar(se)	*to bandage(oneself); to dress (a wound)*

10

¡Viajemos!

¿Vas a viajar al extranjero (*abroad*)? Debes averiguar (*find out*) todo lo que puedas acerca del sitio que piensas visitar, pensar en tus gastos (*expenses*) y hacer un presupuesto (*budget*) y poner tu información personal afuera de cada maleta (*suitcase*). Y ahora… ¡viajemos!

	OBJETIVOS	CONTENIDOS
Comunicación	• To discuss travel and different modes of transportation • To list the various parts of a car in Spanish • To influence others by using commands • To discuss what belongs to you and others • To compare people, places, and things • To focus on linguistic cues when listening to a passage to enhance comprehension • To write and present a report about an interesting tourist spot in Colombia or Venezuela	
Cultura	• To list some public transportation options and discuss procedures for getting a driver's license in Hispanic countries • To discuss travel/tourism opportunities in Venezuela • To share important facts about this chapter's featured countries: Colombia and Venezuela	
Ambiciones siniestras	• To determine when it is appropriate to skip unfamiliar words and still comprehend when reading a passage • To discover the truth about what Cisco knows • To confirm that Lupe is not what she appears to be	

¡Buen viaje!

PREGUNTAS

1 Cuando viajas, ¿adónde vas generalmente?
2 Antes de viajar, ¿qué haces normalmente?
3 ¿Qué precauciones tomas?

Comunicación

- Discussing different modes of transportation
- Naming the parts of a car
- Telling people what to do and what not to do

VOCABULARIO 1 Los medios de transporte

SAM MSL 10-1 to 10-7

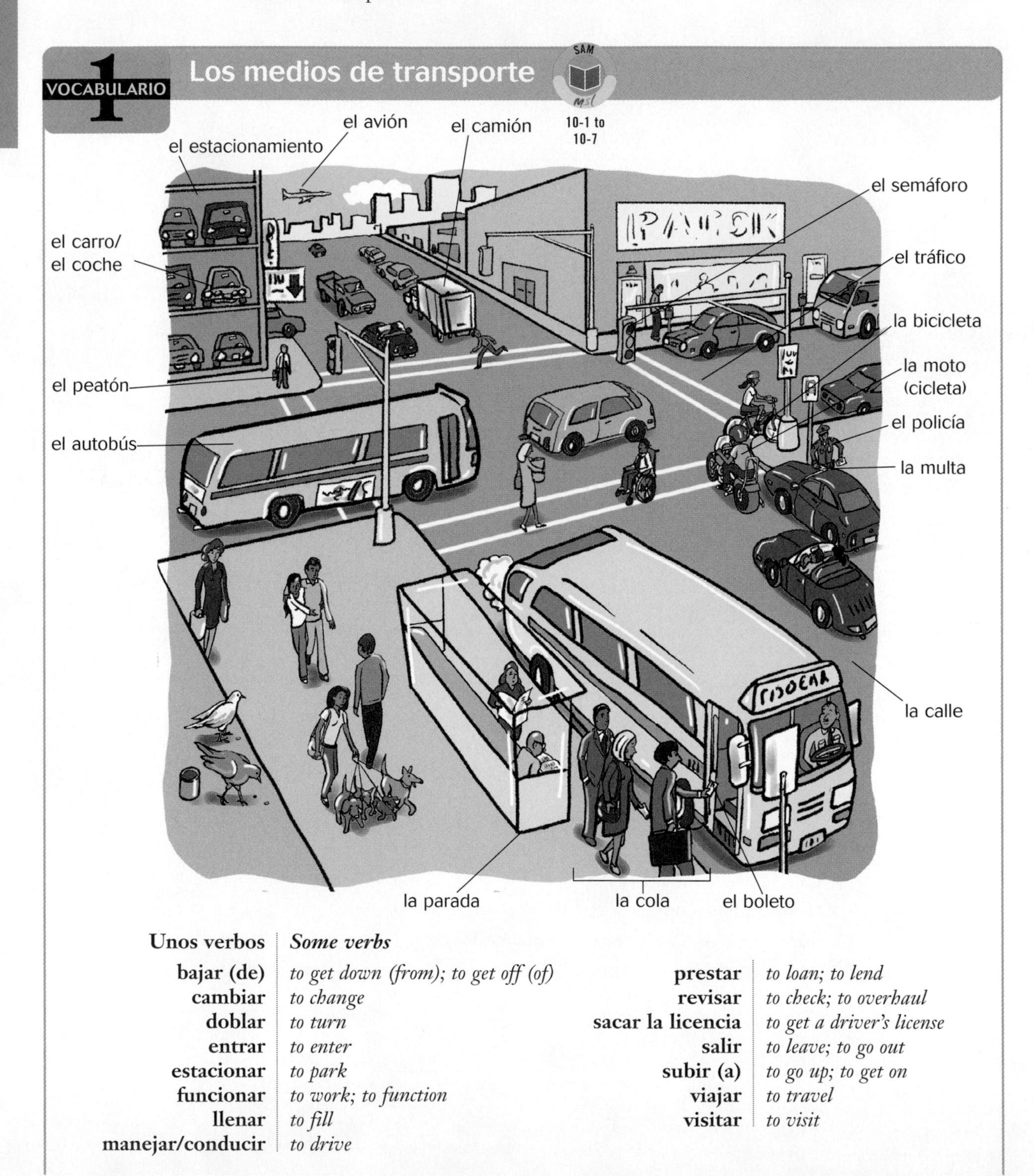

Unos verbos	*Some verbs*
bajar (de)	*to get down (from); to get off (of)*
cambiar	*to change*
doblar	*to turn*
entrar	*to enter*
estacionar	*to park*
funcionar	*to work; to function*
llenar	*to fill*
manejar/conducir	*to drive*
prestar	*to loan; to lend*
revisar	*to check; to overhaul*
sacar la licencia	*to get a driver's license*
salir	*to leave; to go out*
subir (a)	*to go up; to get on*
viajar	*to travel*
visitar	*to visit*

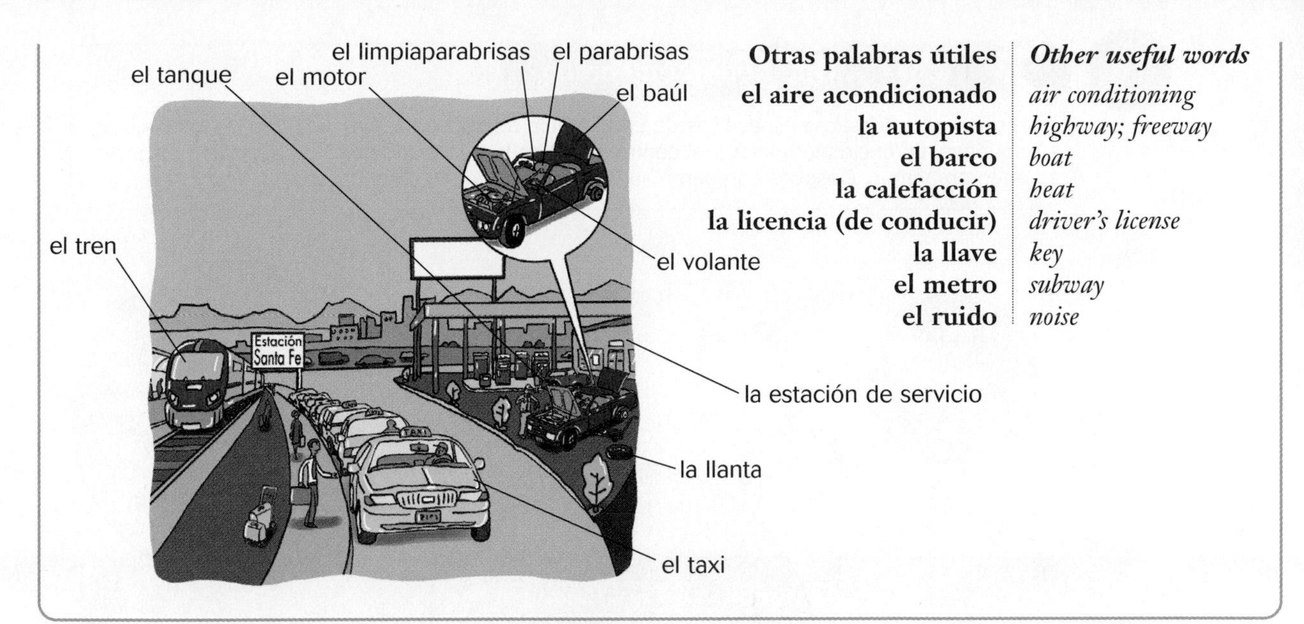

Otras palabras útiles	Other useful words
el aire acondicionado	*air conditioning*
la autopista	*highway; freeway*
el barco	*boat*
la calefacción	*heat*
la licencia (de conducir)	*driver's license*
la llave	*key*
el metro	*subway*
el ruido	*noise*

CD 4
Track 12

10-8 to
10-11

PRONUNCIACIÓN

The letters *b* and *v*

1. In Spanish, the letters b and v are pronounced alike. When each letter comes at the beginning of a word or phrase, or after the letters **m** or **n**, they are both pronounced like the b in the English word *bat.*
   vaso boleto también invierno
2. In all other instances, the Spanish b and v have an identical, soft pronunciation. There is no equivalent in English. The lips come together but do not close so some air may pass between the lips.
   parabrisas revisar avión autobús

10•1 Las palabras

Pronounce the following words, paying special attention to the letters **b** and **v**.

1. barco
2. boleto
3. baúl
4. cambiar
5. viajar
6. servicio
7. limpiaparabrisas
8. doblar
9. volar

10•2 Las oraciones

Pronounce the following sentences, paying special attention to the letters **b** and **v**.

1. Beto y Verónica viajaron a Barcelona en avión para visitar a sus abuelos.
2. Esperábamos el autobús cuando hubo un accidente de bicicletas.
3. El boleto para viajar en barco costaba menos que el boleto para volar.

10•3 Los dichos y refranes

Now pronounce the following sayings and focus on the letters **b** and **v**.

1. No hay mal que por bien no venga.
2. Vale más tarde que nunca.

10•4 ¿Qué tienen en común?

Escriban características específicas de cada medio de transporte en cada uno de los círculos pequeños. En el círculo grande del centro, escriban lo que todos estos medios de transporte tienen en común. Después comparen su diagrama con otros compañeros.

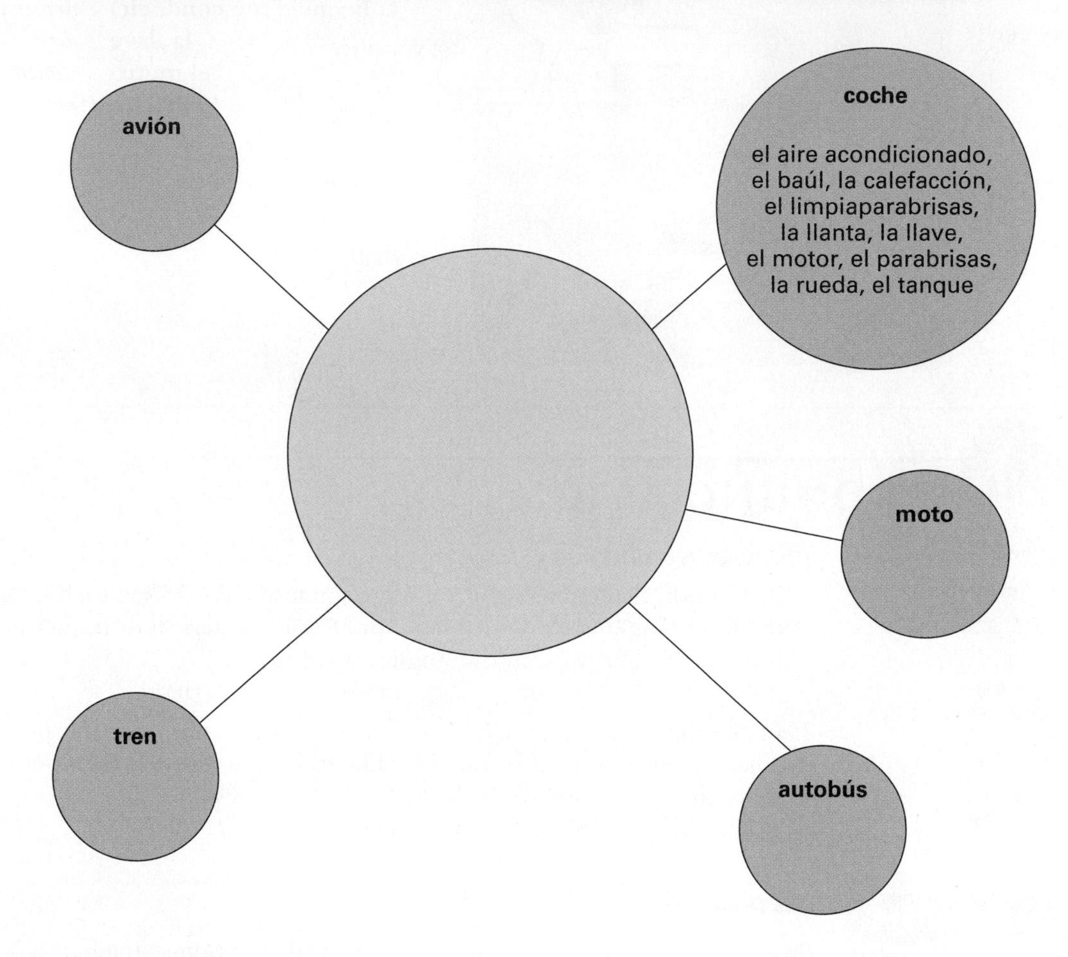

10•5 ¿Es verdad?

Decide si estas frases son ciertas o falsas. Si son falsas, corrígelas *(correct them)*. Compara tus respuestas con las de un/a compañero/a.

MODELO Un carro tiene seis llantas.
Un carro tiene cuatro llantas.

> **Estrategia**
>
> When correcting true/false statements, instead of simply adding a negative word, correct the word that is false to make the statement true.

1. Hay semáforos en las autopistas.
2. Para llegar a la universidad yo puedo tomar el autobús o ir a pie.
3. Ir en avión es más rápido que ir en tren.
4. Un coche no puede funcionar sin limpiaparabrisas.
5. Hay que cambiar el aceite de un coche cada 100.000 millas.
6. Puedes llenar el tanque con gasolina en la estación de servicio.
7. Usamos la calefacción en el verano.
8. Si manejamos muy rápido el policía nos puede dar una llave.

10·6 Cinco preguntas

En grupos de tres o cuatro estudiantes, escriban **cinco** preguntas interesantes relacionadas con el vocabulario nuevo. Después, para cada pregunta, deben escoger a una persona de otro grupo para contestarla.

MODELO

GRUPO 1: *¿Cambiaste el aceite del coche la semana pasada?*
GRUPO 2 (PHILIP): *No, no cambié el aceite la semana pasada pero tengo que cambiarlo pronto.*
GRUPO 1: *¿Viajaste a México el verano pasado?*
GRUPO 2 (GENA): *Sí, fui a Cancún con mi familia.*

10·7 Firma aquí

Estrategia

When performing a signature search (or *Firma aquí*) activity, remember to circulate around the classroom, speaking to many different classmates. You should try to have a different student's signature for each item.

Circula por la clase hasta encontrar a un estudiante que pueda contestar afirmativamente a tu pregunta. **¡OJO!** Debes usar **el pretérito** en muchas de las preguntas.

MODELO manejar un camión

E1: *¿Manejas un camión?*
E2: *Sí, manejo un camión.*
E1: *Pues, firma aquí.*

Rosario
____

manejar un camión _______________	ir a una gasolinera esta mañana _______________	saber manejar un barco _______________
tener más de tres llaves contigo _______________	llegar a la universidad por autopista _______________	tener un coche sin calefacción _______________
perder sus llaves alguna vez _______________	viajar a algún lugar exótico durante las últimas vacaciones _______________	recibir una multa el año pasado _______________
tener un accidente en la autopista en los últimos dos años _______________	llevar su coche al mecánico el mes pasado _______________	viajar en tren el año pasado _______________

Los mandatos informales

10-12 to 10-16

52

When you need to give instructions, advise, or ask people to do something, you use commands. If you are addressing a friend or someone you normally address as **tú,** you use informal commands. You have been responding to **tú** commands since the beginning of ***¡Anda!*****: escucha, escribe, abre tu libro en la página...,** etc.

1. **The affirmative *tú* command form is the same as the *él, ella, Ud.* form of the present tense of the verb:**

Infinitive		Present tense	Affirmative *tú* command
llen**ar**	él, ella, Ud.	llen**a**	llena
le**er**	él, ella, Ud.	le**e**	lee
ped**ir**	él, ella, Ud.	pid**e**	pide

Llen**a** el tanque.	*Fill the tank.*
Dobl**a** a la derecha.	*Turn to the right.*
Conduc**e** con cuidado.	*Drive carefully.*
Pid**e** permiso.	*Ask permission.*

There are eight common verbs that have irregular affirmative *tú* commands:

decir	**di**	ir	**ve**	salir	**sal**	tener	**ten**
hacer	**haz**	poner	**pon**	ser	**sé**	venir	**ven**

Sé respetuoso con los peatones.	*Be respectful of pedestrians.*
Ten cuidado al conducir.	*Be careful when driving.*
Ven al aeropuerto con tu pasaporte.	*Come to the airport with your passport.*
Pon las llaves en la mesa.	*Put the keys on the table.*

2. **To form the negative *tú* commands:**
   1. Take the **yo** form of the present tense of the verb.
   2. Drop the **-o** ending.
   3. Add ***-es*** for **-ar** verbs, and add ***-as*** for **-er** and **-ir** verbs.

Infinitive	Present tense		Negative *tú* command
llen**ar**	yo llen**ø**	+ es	no llenes
le**er**	yo le**ø**	+ as	no leas
ped**ir**	yo pid**ø**	+ as	no pidas

No llen**es** el tanque. — *Don't fill the tank.*

No dobl**es** a la derecha. — *Don't turn to the right.*

No conduzc**as** muy rápido. — *Don't drive very fast.*

No pid**as** permiso. — *Don't ask permission.*

Verbs ending in **-car, -gar,** and **-zar** have a spelling change in the negative **tú** command. These spelling changes are needed to preserve the sound of the infinitive ending.

Infinitive	Present tense		Negative *tú* command
sa**car**	yo sa**co**	**c → qu**	no saques
lle**gar**	yo lle**go**	**g → gu**	no llegues
empe**zar**	yo empiezo	**z → c**	no empieces

3. Object and reflexive pronouns are used with *tú* commands in the following ways.

a. They are *attached* to the end of *affirmative* commands. When the command is made up of more than two syllables after the pronoun(s) is/are attached, a written accent mark is placed over the stressed vowel.

Se pinchó una llanta. **¡Cámbiamela!** — *I got a flat tire. Change it for me!*

Tu bicicleta no funciona. **Revísala.** — *Your bike does not work. Check it.*

Me gusta tu coche. **Préstamelo.** — *I like your car. Loan it to me.*

Llegamos tarde. ¡**Estaciónate,** por favor! — *We are late. Park, please!*

b. They are placed *before negative* **tú** commands.

No se nos pinchó una llanta. — *We don't have a flat tire.*
¡No **me la** cambies! — *Don't change it for me!*

Tu bicicleta funciona. — *Your bicycle works.*
No **la** vendas. — *Don't sell it.*

No me gusta ese coche. — *I don't like that car.*
No **me lo** compres. — *Don't buy it for me.*

Llegamos tarde. — *We are late.*
No **te** estaciones aquí, por favor. — *Do not park here, please.*

10-8 ¿Qué diría el profesor?

Túrnense para decir cuál de los dos mandatos diría (*would say*) un/a profesor/a de una escuela de conducir.

MODELO a. Toma apuntes mientras hablo.
b. No tomes apuntes mientras hablo.
E1: *Toma apuntes mientras hablo.*

1. a. Estudia las reglas.
   b. No estudies las reglas.
2. a. Ven tarde a la clase.
   b. No vengas tarde a la clase.
3. a. Lee el manual con cuidado.
   b. No leas el manual con cuidado.
4. a. Practica fuera de la clase.
   b. No practiques fuera de la clase.
5. a. Ponte nervioso/a.
   b. No te pongas nervioso/a.
6. a. Conduce con cuidado.
   b. No conduzcas con cuidado.
7. a. Sal de la clase antes de tiempo.
   b. No salgas de la clase antes de tiempo.
8. a. Trae tu manual a clase.
   b. No traigas tu manual a clase.

Capítulo 5. Los pronombres de complemento directo, pág. 190.

10-9 Hazlo, por favor

Estrategia

For activities like **10-9** you can take turns by having one student do the even-numbered items while the other does the odd-numbered ones. Or, one can give the affirmative commands while the other gives the negatives, then switch roles.

Túrnense para expresar mandatos afirmativos y negativos usando los pronombres de complemento directo.

MODELO esperar el autobús
E1: *¡Espéralo!*
E2: *¡No lo esperes!*

1. tomar el autobús
2. prestarme las llaves
3. conducir el carro
4. usar la calefacción
5. hacer un ruido
6. limpiar el parabrisas
7. subir la ventana
8. estacionar el coche en el garaje
9. buscar un estacionamiento

10•10 ¡Ayúdame!

¡Tu compañero/a de apartamento te vuelve loco/a!

Paso 1 Usa los verbos siguientes para decirle lo que debe y no debe hacer y compara tus respuestas con las de un/a compañero/a.

MODELO no poner tus libros en mi cama
No pongas tus libros en mi cama.

1. no dormirse en el sofá
2. sacar la basura
3. no comer en la sala
4. no beber de mi vaso
5. decirme la verdad siempre
6. no vestirse en la cocina
7. tener más paciencia con mi gato (*cat*)
8. no invitar siempre a tus amigos después de las once de la noche

Paso 2 Para cada mandato negativo que dieron juntos, den otra alternativa.

MODELO E1: *No pongas tus libros en mi cama.*
E2: *Ponlos en la mesa.*

10•11 ¡Una fiesta!

Uds. organizan una fiesta para sus amigos. Tienen mucho que hacer: limpiar el apartamento, organizar la música, comprar y preparar la comida, vestirse, etc. Un amigo se ofrece a ayudarles. Hagan una lista de las cosas que él puede hacer.

MODELO *1. Organiza los CD.*

Los mandatos formales

10-17 to 10-20

52

When you need to influence others by making a request, giving advice, or giving orders to people you normally treat as **Ud.** or **Uds.,** you are going to use a different set of commands: **Ud.** and **Uds.** commands. The forms of these commands are similar to the negative **tú** command forms.

1. **To form the *Ud.* and *Uds.* commands:**
   1. Take the **yo** form of the present tense of the verb.
   2. Drop the **-o** ending.
   3. Add ***-e(n)*** for **-ar** verbs, and add ***-a(n)*** for **-er** and **-ir** verbs.

Infinitive	Present tense		*Ud.* commands	*Uds.* commands
limpi**ar**	yo limpi**ø**	+ e(n)	(no) limpie	(no) limpien
le**er**	yo le**ø**	+ a(n)	(no) lea	(no) lean
ped**ir**	yo pid**ø**	+ a(n)	(no) pida	(no) pidan

Llene el tanque. **Llénelo.** — *Fill up the tank. Fill it.*
No limpie el parabrisas. **No lo limpie.** — *Don't clean the windshield. Don't clean it.*
Conduzca el camión para su tío. **Condúzcalo.** — *Drive the truck for your uncle. Drive it.*
No ponga esa gasolina cara en el coche. — *Don't put that expensive gasoline in the car.*
No la ponga en el coche. — *Don't put it in the car.*
Traiga su licencia. **Tráigala.** — *Bring your license. Bring it.*
No busquen sus llaves. **No las busquen.** — *Don't look for your keys. Don't look for them.*

1. Where do the object pronouns appear in affirmative commands? In negative commands? In what order?
2. Why are there written accents on some of the commands and not on others?

Check your answers to the preceding questions in Appendix 1.

2. **Verbs ending in *-car*, *-gar*, and *-zar* have a spelling change in the *Ud.* and *Uds.* commands. These spelling changes are needed to preserve the sound of the infinitive ending.**

Infinitive	Present tense		*Ud. /Uds.* commands
sac**ar**	yo saco	**c → qu**	saque(n)
lleg**ar**	yo llego	**g → gu**	llegue(n)
empez**ar**	yo empiezo	**z → c**	empiece(n)

3. **These verbs also have irregular forms for the *Ud./Uds.* commands:**

dar	**dé(n)**	ir	**vaya(n)**	ser	**sea(n)**
estar	**esté(n)**	saber	**sepa(n)**		

4. Finally, compare the forms of the *tú* and *Ud./Uds.* commands:

	Tú commands		*Ud./Uds.* commands	
	affirmative	negative	affirmative	negative
hablar	habla	no hables	hable(n)	no hable(n)
comer	come	no comas	coma(n)	no coma(n)
pedir	pide	no pidas	pida(n)	no pida(n)

10•12 Consejos

Capítulo 8. Las construcciones reflexivas, pág. 302.

Dos estudiantes de intercambio (*exchange students*) van a llegar a tu universidad y necesitan tu ayuda con lo que deben y no deben hacer antes de llegar a los Estados Unidos. Comparte la lista con un/a compañero/a.

MODELO E1: acostarse temprano la noche antes de viajar

E2: *Acuéstense temprano la noche antes de viajar.*

1. levantarse temprano el día del viaje
2. preparar el equipaje (*luggage*) el día anterior
3. ponerse ropa cómoda
4. no ponerse nervioso/a
5. evitar el alcohol
6. tener su pasaporte a mano (*on hand*)
7. sentarse en el asiento correcto
8. dormirse durante el vuelo

10•13 La multa

Capítulo 9. Un resumen de los pronombres de complemento directo, indirecto y reflexivos, pág. 325.

Termina el diálogo entre Mayra y el policía. Después realicen la escena con un/a compañero/a.

MAYRA: Buenas noches. ¿Iba muy rápido, señor policía?

POLICÍA: Sí, señorita. (1) _______________ (mostrarme) su licencia, por favor.

MAYRA: Aquí la tiene (*here you go*), señor. Sé que la foto es muy mala.

POLICÍA: No (2) _______________ (preocuparse). Ahora, (3) _______________ (contarme), señorita. ¿A qué velocidad (*speed*) iba?

MAYRA: Pues… la verdad es que no estoy segura. (4) _______________ (decírmelo) usted.

POLICÍA: Iba a ochenta kilómetros por hora y el límite aquí es sesenta y cinco.

MAYRA: ¡Ay! ¡Mi padre me va a matar! Por favor, no (5) _______________ (darme) una multa. Lo siento. Le aseguro que voy a manejar mucho más lento ahora.

POLICÍA: No es mi decisión. Es la ley (*law*).

MAYRA: Entonces, por lo menos no (6) _______________ (escribir) ochenta kilómetros por hora en la multa. (7) _______________ (poner) setenta, por favor.

POLICÍA: No puedo hacer eso. Bueno, (8) _______________ (tomarla).

MAYRA: *(silencio)*

POLICÍA: Y no (9) _______________ (manejar) tan rápidamente en el futuro. (10) _______________ (tener) más cuidado.

10•14 El transporte rápido

El Transmilenio es un sistema de transporte masivo de pasajeros (*passengers*) en autobús que permite llegar rápidamente a cualquier (*any*) lugar de la ciudad de Bogotá. Lee las siguientes reglas del Transmilenio y completa la lista con mandatos formales. Luego, compártela con un/a compañero/a.

entrar	llevar	pagar	pararse (*to stand*)
permitir	respetar	evitar	transitar (*to enter/exit*)

MODELO Siempre evite correr.

- Instrucciones para el uso adecuado (*suitable*) del sistema:

1. Cuando espere al autobús, ______ detrás de la línea amarilla de seguridad.
2. Antes de entrar, ______ que salgan los pasajeros.
3. ______ con su tarjeta al entrar.
4. Al usar las rampas, túneles o plataformas, ______ por la derecha.
5. No ______ paquetes (*packages*) grandes ni mascotas (*pets*).
6. No ______ en el autobús bebiendo o fumando ni en estado de embriaguez (*intoxication*).
7. ______ las sillas azules que son para personas con discapacidad, mujeres embarazadas, niños de brazos y adultos mayores.

10-21

¿Cómo nos movemos?

El saber conducir o manejar un auto no suele ser tan importante en los países hispanohablantes como en los Estados Unidos. Por lo general, la gente camina más y usa el transporte público, ya sea el autobús, el metro o el taxi. Las personas que sí quieren conducir, generalmente tienen que tomar un curso en una escuela privada de conducir.

En Colombia, por ejemplo, para obtener (*get*) una licencia de conducir es necesario:

- tener 16 años.
- saber leer y escribir.
- aprobar un examen teórico o presentar un certificado de aptitud en conducción (*driving*) emitido por una escuela aprobada (*approved*) por el Ministerio de Educación Nacional en coordinación con el Ministerio de Transporte.
- presentar un certificado de aptitud física y mental expedido por (*completed by*) un médico.

Una de las escuelas de conducir más conocidas en Colombia es ConducirColombia. Los cursos y los precios varían según la experiencia previa del estudiante. Hay cursos básicos de diez clases por unos ciento cincuenta y nueve dólares hasta cursos avanzados de catorce clases por unos doscientos dólares.

Preguntas

1. ¿Sabes conducir? ¿Cuándo aprendiste? ¿Quién te enseñó? ¿Cuándo sacaste la licencia de conducir?
2. Según esta lectura, ¿crees que es generalmente más fácil o más difícil obtener una licencia en Colombia que en los Estados Unidos? Explica.

10•15 La estación de servicio

Acabas de llegar a una gasolinera. Dile a la persona responsable lo que necesitas.

MODELO No puedo abrir el baúl.
Ábrame el baúl, por favor. / *Ábramelo, por favor.*

1. Necesito gasolina.
2. El parabrisas está sucio.
3. El limpiaparabrisas no funciona.
4. El motor tiene un ruido extraño.
5. Las llantas necesitan aire.
6. El aceite está sucio.

Capítulo 8. Los pronombres de complemento indirecto, pág. 292; Los pronombres de complemento directo e indirecto usados juntos, pág. 298.

10•16 ¡A su servicio!

Capítulo 3. La casa, pág. 100; Los muebles y otros objetos de la casa, pág. 109; Los quehaceres de la casa, pág. 112.

Uds. son compañeros/as de apartamento y acaban de ganar el concurso ¡A su servicio! Reciben como premio la ayuda de Jaime, un mayordomo (*butler*), por una semana. Díganle **ocho** cosas que quieren que haga (*you want him to do*) para ayudarles hoy con los quehaceres. Después, díganle **tres** cosas que no debe hacer.

MODELO *Jaime, saque la basura, por favor.*

¿Cómo andas?

Having completed the first **Comunicación**, I now can…

	Feel Confident	Need to Review
• discuss different modes of transportation (p. 356)	❑	❑
• name the various parts of a car (p. 357)	❑	❑
• pronounce **b** and **v** properly in Spanish (p. 357)	❑	❑
• influence others by using commands (pp. 360, 364)	❑	❑
• list some public transportation options and discuss procedures for getting a driver's license in Hispanic countries (p. 366)	❑	❑

Comunicación

- Discussing travel
- Describing a past trip
- Discussing to whom things belong
- Comparing people, places, and things

VOCABULARIO 4 El viaje

SAM 10-22 to 10-27

Otras palabras útiles	*Other useful words*
la agencia de viajes	*travel agency*
la estación de tren	*train station*
el extranjero	*abroad*
la recepción	*front desk*
la reserva	*reservation*
el sello	*postage stamp*
la tarjeta postal	*postcard*
las vacaciones	*vacation*
los viajeros	*travelers*
el vuelo	*flight*

Unos verbos útiles	*Some useful verbs*
caminar, ir a pie	*to walk; to go on foot*
dejar	*to leave*
ir de vacaciones	*to go on vacation*
ir de viaje	*to go on a trip*
irse del hotel	*to leave the hotel; to check out*
registrarse (en el hotel)	*to check in*
volar (o → ue)	*to fly; to fly away*

10•17 Categorías

Tienes tres minutos para escribir todas las palabras que pertenecen (*pertain*) a las siguientes categorías. No debes repetir palabras. Después, compara tus listas con las de un/a compañero/a. Date un punto por cada palabra que tienes que tu compañero/a no tiene.

EL AEROPUERTO	EL HOTEL	LAS VACACIONES

10•18 ¿Quiénes lo hacen?

Circula por la clase hasta encontrar a un/a estudiante que pueda contestar afirmativamente a tu pregunta. **¡OJO!** Debes usar el pretérito en **dos** de las preguntas.

MODELO ¿Quién…?

siempre dejar una buena propina cuando va a un restaurante

TIFFANY: *¿Siempre dejas una buena propina cuando vas a un restaurante?*

ROB: *Sí, siempre dejo una buena propina.*

TIFFANY: *Pues, firma aquí.*

Rob
____

¿QUIÉN…?		
siempre dejar una buena propina cuando va a un restaurante ______	nunca ir a un parque de atracciones ______	viajar al extranjero ______
ir a la playa el verano pasado ______	nunca volar en avión ______	coleccionar tarjetas postales ______
quedarse en un hotel elegante una vez ______	vivir en las montañas ______	tener más de tres maletas ______

10•19 Antes de ir

Tu amigo tiene que ir a Venezuela para una reunión (*meeting*) de negocios. Dale **cinco** consejos sobre lo que debe o no debe hacer para prepararse para el viaje y compara tu lista con la de tu compañero.

MODELO 1. *Busca tu pasaporte.*

10•20 Las mejores vacaciones

Piensa en tus mejores vacaciones al contestar las siguientes preguntas. Después, circula por la clase para entrevistar a tus compañeros/as.

Capítulo 7. El pretérito, pág. 258; Unos verbos irregulares en el pretérito, pág. 266.

1. ¿Adónde fuiste?
2. ¿Cómo viajaste?
3. ¿Dónde te quedaste?
4. ¿Cuánto tiempo estuviste allí?
5. ¿Qué hiciste durante aquellas vacaciones especiales?
6. ¿A quién le mandaste una tarjeta postal? ¿una tarjeta electrónica?

Venezuela, país de aventuras

Venezuela, país de aventuras

¿Es Ud. aventurero/a? En Venezuela tenemos muchas oportunidades para conocer nuestro país a base de la aventura. Le proponemos *(propose)* una excursión de dos días en el Canaima. El primer día le ofrecemos un paseo en barco por la Laguna Ucaima y una visita al Salto Ucaima. La excursión del segundo día le permite conocer el Salto Ángel, donde podemos nadar al pie de la cascada *(waterfall)*.

Si le gusta hacer trekking, puede disfrutar de una excursión a los tepuyes (una palabra

indígena que significa "montaña"). Se puede subir el Pico Humboldt; a unos 4.942 m.s.n.m. es el segundo pico del país. Una excursión de este tipo está dentro de los considerados "deportes extremos" que se pueden practicar.

Si quiere combinar la aventura con una estancia en un hotel de lujo *(luxury)*, debe considerar La Isla de Margarita. Está situada al norte de Caracas a sólo treinta y cinco minutos en avión o a un par de horas en ferry. Allí puede disfrutar de todos los deportes de agua, pescar, jugar al golf y explorar las numerosas y variadas playas. Por la noche hay restaurantes, clubes de baile, bares y casinos. Para informarse mejor, póngase en contacto hoy con su agencia de viajes preferida.

Preguntas

1. ¿Qué puedes hacer durante la excursión en el Canaima? ¿en la excursión a los tepuyes? ¿en la Isla de Margarita?
2. De las "aventuras" que ofrece Venezuela, ¿cuál prefieres? ¿Por qué?
3. ¿Eres aventurero/a? ¿Cuál es la aventura más atrevida que has tenido (*you have had*)?

Otras formas del posesivo

10-28 to 10-29 17, 61

In **Capítulo 1** you learned how to say *my*, *your*, *his*, *ours*, etc. (**mi/s, tu/s, su/s, nuestro/a/os/as, vuestro/a/os/as, su/s**). In Spanish you can also show possession with the long (or stressed) forms, the equivalent of the English *of mine*, *of yours*, *of his*, *of hers*, *of ours*, and *of theirs*.

Singular		Plural		
Masculine	**Feminine**	**Masculine**	**Feminine**	
mío	**mía**	**míos**	**mías**	*mine*
tuyo	**tuya**	**tuyos**	**tuyas**	*yours* (fam.)
suyo	**suya**	**suyos**	**suyas**	*his, hers, yours, theirs* (form.)
nuestro	**nuestra**	**nuestros**	**nuestras**	*ours*
vuestro	**vuestra**	**vuestros**	**vuestras**	*yours* (fam.)

Study the following examples.

Mi coche funciona bien.	**El coche mío** funciona bien.	**El mío** funciona bien.
Nuestros boletos cuestan mucho.	**Los boletos nuestros** cuestan mucho.	**Los nuestros** cuestan mucho.
¿Dónde están **tus** llaves?	¿Dónde están **las llaves tuyas**?	¿Dónde están **las tuyas**?
Su multa es de $100.	**La multa suya** es de $100.	**La suya** es de $100.

Compare the possessives in the above sentences.

1. What is the position of each possessive in the left-hand column? the middle column?
2. How do the possessive adjectives and pronouns agree?
3. What do the sentences mean in the column on the right? What have you removed from the previous sentence?

Check your answers to the preceding questions in Appendix 1.

*Note that the third person forms (**suyo/a/os/as**) can have more than one meaning. To avoid confusion, you can use:

article + *noun* + de + *subject pronoun:*

el coche suyo {
- el coche de él/ella
- el coche de Ud.
- el coche de ellos/ellas
- el coche de Uds.

10•21 Entre hermanos

Cambia todos los posesivos a la forma nueva (larga) en la conversación entre Marco y Mari. Después compara los cambios con los de un/a compañero/a.

MODELO El problema que tienes con tu coche es serio.
El problema que tienes con el coche tuyo es serio.

MARCO: Mari, parece que tu llanta pierde aire.
MARI: Ah ¿sí? Tampoco funciona bien mi coche.
MARCO: Pues, mi mecánico es muy bueno.
MARI: Gracias, pero pienso llevar el coche a nuestro mecánico. Hace muchos años que Tom y yo lo conocemos.
MARCO: ¿Él tiene su negocio en la calle Bolívar?
MARI: Sí, y trabaja con uno de sus hermanos.
MARCO: ¿Puedes usar uno de sus coches mientras arregla el tuyo?
MARI: Sí, pero prefiero sacar tu BMW del garaje. Nunca lo manejas.
MARCO: Escucha, hermana. Ese BMW es un tesoro (*treasure*) y nadie lo maneja.

10•22 ¡Problemas!

Capítulo 8. La ropa, pág. 286.

Están de viaje con algunos de sus mejores amigos. El hotel les lavó la ropa pero ahora Uds. no saben de quiénes son las prendas. Túrnense para hacer y contestar las preguntas de Ana, quien está intentando organizar la ropa.

MODELO E1 (ANA): Los calcetines rojos, ¿son los tuyos? (de Felipe)
E2: *No, son de Felipe. Los calcetines son suyos.*

1. Los pantalones cortos azules, ¿son los tuyos? (de Tina)
2. La camisa de rayas, ¿es la mía? (de Susana)
3. Los calcetines estampados, ¿son los tuyos? (mío)
4. La chaqueta negra, ¿es la tuya? (de Felipe)
5. El suéter de algodón, ¿es el tuyo? (mío)
6. Las camisetas blancas, ¿son las tuyas? (de Tina)

10•23 Personalmente...

Termina las siguientes oraciones sobre tu mejor amigo/a y tú y después compártelas con un/a compañero/a.

1. El mejor amigo mío…
2. La casa suya…
3. La especialidad mía…
4. La materia favorita suya…
5. El restaurante favorito nuestro…
6. A los otros amigos nuestros les encanta(n)…

El comparativo y el superlativo

El comparativo

1. The formula for comparing unequal things follows the same pattern as in English:

más + *adjective/adverb/noun* + **que**
menos + *adjective/adverb/noun* + **que**

El Hotel Hilton es **más** caro **que** el Motel 6.	*The Hilton is **more** expensive **than** Motel 6.*
El Motel 6 hace reservas **más** rápidamente **que** el Hotel Hilton.	*Motel 6 makes reservations **faster than** the Hilton.*
En esta ciudad hay **menos** hoteles **que** moteles.	*In this city there are **fewer** hotels **than** motels.*

- When comparing numbers, **de** is used instead of **que:**

El Hilton de Bogotá tiene **más de** doscientas habitaciones.	*The Bogotá Hilton has **more than** two hundred rooms.*

2. The formula for comparing two or more *equal* things also follows the same pattern as in English:

tan + *adjective/adverb* + **como**	*as... as*
tanto(a/os/as) + *noun* + **como**	*as much/many... as*

La agencia de viajes Mundotur es **tan** conocida **como** Meliá.	*The Mundotur travel agency is **as** well known **as** Meliá.*
Estos vuelos son **tan** caros **como** ésos.	*These flights are **as** expensive **as** those.*
Mi coche va **tan** rápido **como** un Ferrari.	*My car is **as** fast **as** a Ferrari.*
No tengo **tantas** maletas **como** tú.	*I don't have **as many** suitcases **as** you (do).*
No hay **tanto** tráfico **como** ayer.	*There isn't **as much** traffic **as** yesterday.*

El superlativo

1. To compare three or more people or things, use the superlative. The formula for expressing the superlative is:

el, la, los, las *(noun)* + **más/menos** + *adjective* (+ **de**)

La agencia de viajes Viking es **la** agencia **más** popular **de** nuestro pueblo. *The Viking Travel Agency is the most popular (travel) agency in our town.*

—¿Es el aeropuerto Hartsfield de Atlanta **el** aeropuerto **más** concurrido **de** los Estados Unidos? *Is Atlanta's Hartsfield Airport the busiest airport in the United States?*

—Sí, ¡y el aeropuerto de mi ciudad es **el menos** concurrido! *Yes, and my city's airport is the least busy!*

2. The adjectives *bueno/a*, *malo/a*, *grande*, and *pequeño/a* are irregular in the comparative and the superlative.

		Comparative		Superlative	
bueno/a	*good*	**mejor**	*better*	**el/la mejor**	*the best*
malo/a	*bad*	**peor**	*worse*	**el/la peor**	*the worst*
grande	*big*	**mayor**	*bigger*	**el/la mayor**	*the biggest*
pequeño/a	*small*	**menor**	*smaller*	**el/la menor**	*the smallest*

Comparative:

Mi clase de español es **mejor que** mis otras clases. *My Spanish class is better than my other classes.*

Superlative:

Mi clase de español es **la mejor de** mis clases. *My Spanish class is the best (one) of my classes.*

10•24 ¿Cierto o falso?

¿Qué sabes de la geografía? Indica si las siguientes oraciones son ciertas o falsas; si son falsas, corrígelas. Comparte tus oraciones con las de un/a compañero/a siguiendo el modelo.

MODELO México es más grande que Uruguay.

E1: *¿Es México más grande que Uruguay?*

E2: *Sí. México es mucho más grande que Uruguay. ¿Es Chile tan grande como Argentina?*

E1: *No. Chile es más pequeño que Argentina, pero creo que es tan grande como Venezuela.*

1. México es más pequeño que Colombia.
2. Colombia es tan grande como Venezuela.
3. Panamá es más grande que Venezuela.
4. De estos países, Panamá es el más pequeño.
5. Bogotá se encuentra a mayor altura sobre el nivel del mar (es más alta) que Lima.
6. Colombia es más grande que los Estados Unidos.
7. Caracas es tan grande como México, D.F.
8. La Paz es la capital situada a la mayor altitud (es la más alta).

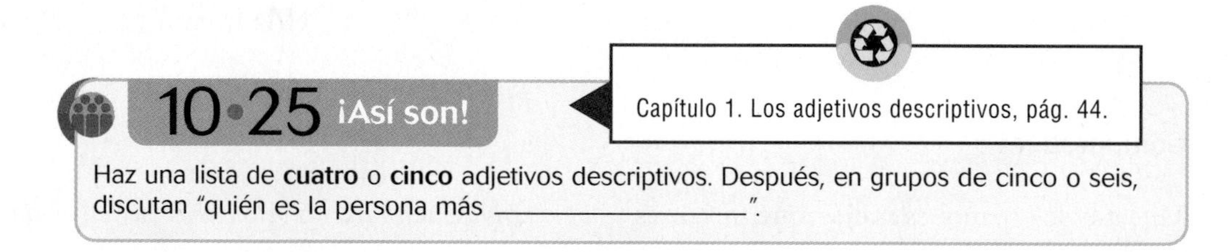

10•25 ¡Así son!

Capítulo 1. Los adjetivos descriptivos, pág. 44.

Haz una lista de **cuatro** o **cinco** adjetivos descriptivos. Después, en grupos de cinco o seis, discutan "quién es la persona más ________________".

MODELO de la clase (alta)

E1: *¿Quién es la persona más alta de la clase?*

E2: *La persona más alta de la clase es Catalina.*

1. de la televisión
2. del cine
3. del mundo de los deportes
4. de la música
5. de la universidad
6. de la política

10•26 ¿El mejor o el peor?

Circula por la clase para averiguar qué opinan los estudiantes sobre "los mejores" y "los peores". Necesita al menos **dos** opiniones para cada categoría.

Estrategia

You can also use the following expressions to express your opinions: *Pienso que..., Creo que..., Estoy de acuerdo, No estoy de acuerdo,* and *En mi opinión...*

MODELO E1: *¿Cuál es el mejor supermercado?*
E2: *En mi opinión, Whole Foods es el mejor supermercado. Y tú, ¿qué piensas?*
E1: *Creo que el mejor supermercado es Kroger.*

	ESTUDIANTE 1	ESTUDIANTE 2
1. el mejor supermercado		
el peor supermercado		
2. el mejor almacén		
el peor almacén		
3. el mejor restaurante		
el peor restaurante		
4. el mejor aeropuerto		
el peor aeropuerto		
5. el mejor hotel		
el peor hotel		
6. el mejor parque de atracciones		
el peor parque de atracciones		
7. la mejor playa		
la peor playa		
8. el mejor lugar para la luna de miel (*honeymoon*)		
el peor lugar para la luna de miel		
9. la mejor aerolínea (*airline*)		
la peor aerolínea		
10. el mejor coche		
el peor coche		

10•27 Adivina, adivinanza

Estrategia

One way to approach actividad **10-27** is to arrange your clues from most general to most specific.

Trae un objeto personal a la clase y escribe **cuatro** o **cinco** frases sobre él, usando las formas comparativas. No digas el nombre de tu objeto. Lee las frases en grupos de cuatro o cinco estudiantes para ver si los compañeros pueden adivinar (*guess*) lo que es.

MODELO un bolígrafo

E1: *1. Es más grande que un anillo.*

2. Es tan importante como un libro.

3. Es menos largo que mi zapato.

4. Seguramente Uds. lo usan tanto como yo.

5. Es tan útil como un lápiz.

E2: *¡Es un bolígrafo!*

10•28 El transporte

Habla con un/a compañero/a de todos los medios de transporte que usan o han usado (*have used*) y compárenlos, pensando en los aspectos positivos y negativos de cada uno.

MODELO E1: *Uso el coche más que el metro pero el metro es más rápido que el coche.*

E2: *Nunca voy en metro porque no hay metro en mi ciudad. Voy mucho en autobús porque es más barato que un taxi y es más rápido que mi bicicleta.*

10•29 Los mejores regalos (*gifts*)

Escoge uno de los siguientes temas y descríbele la situación a un/a compañero/a. Debes mencionar cuándo y dónde ocurrió, quiénes estaban contigo y qué pasó. Túrnense.

1. el mejor regalo que recibí
2. el mejor regalo que regalé (*gave*)
3. el mejor día de mi vida
4. el peor día de mi vida
5. las mejores vacaciones que tomé
6. las peores vacaciones que tomé

Capítulo 7. El pretérito, pág. 258. Unos verbos irregulares en el pretérito, pág. 266; Capítulo 8. El imperfecto, pág. 306; Capítulo 9. El pretérito y el imperfecto, pág. 334.

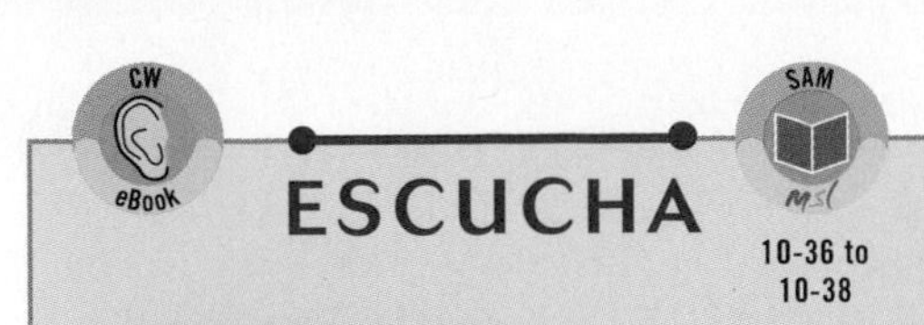

ESCUCHA

ESTRATEGIA **Listening for linguistic cues**

You can enhance comprehension by listening for linguistic cues. For example, verb endings can tell you who is participating and whether the incident is taking place now, already took place in the past, or will take place in the future.

10•30 Antes de escuchar

Los amigos de Manolo están en una fiesta. Oyen por casualidad una conversación entre varias personas sobre el viaje y específicamente de algunos viajes que ya tomaron o que quieren tomar en el futuro.

1. ¿Cuáles fueron tus viajes más memorables?
2. ¿Hay un viaje en particular que le puedes recomendar a un/a amigo/a?
3. ¿A dónde quieres ir en tu próximo viaje?

Memo, Cristina, Rosa y sus amigos hablan de unos viajes interesantes.

10•31 A escuchar

CW eBook CD 4 Track 13

Paso 1 Escucha la conversación entre Memo, Cristina y Rosa para tener una idea general de lo que dicen.

Paso 2 Cristina habla de Venezuela. Escucha otra vez y apunta todos los verbos que puedas que ella usa. ¿Cuál es el tiempo verbal que usa más? Entonces, es un viaje que…

a. hizo ya.
b. va a hacer.
c. quiere hacer.

Paso 3 Escucha una vez más para poder completar la siguiente actividad.

1. ¿Quién sale mañana para Colombia? Escribe los verbos que usa esta persona para hablar de su viaje.
2. ¿Habla Rosa de un viaje que hizo ya, va a hacer o quiere hacer? ¿Cómo lo sabes?

10•32 Después de escuchar

En grupos de tres o cuatro hablen de dos o tres lugares turísticos diferentes que conozcan (*you know*).

ESCRIBE

10•33 Antes de escribir

Escoge un lugar turístico de Colombia o Venezuela y búscalo en la Red. Toma apuntes sobre los aspectos que encuentres más interesantes del lugar.

10•34 Un reportaje de un lugar turístico

Organiza tus ideas y escribe un reportaje para una revista turística que incluya como mínimo la siguiente información:

1. dónde está
2. cómo llegar allí
3. qué actividades se pueden hacer
4. dónde uno puede quedarse (hotel de lujo, etc.)
5. el precio del viaje
6. este lugar es más interesante que…
7. este lugar es más/menos barato que…
8. este lugar es el más _____ porque…

10•35 Después de escribir

Presenta tu reportaje a los compañeros de clase. Después de todas las presentaciones deben votar para elegir los **tres** lugares que les gustan más.

¿Cómo andas?

Having completed the second **Comunicación,** I now can…

	Feel Confident	Need to Review
• plan a trip (p. 368)	❑	❑
• describe a past trip (p. 368)	❑	❑
• discuss to whom things belong (p. 372)	❑	❑
• compare people, places, and things (p. 374)	❑	❑
• listen for linguistic cues (p. 379)	❑	❑
• write and present a report on a tourist destination (p. 380)	❑	❑

Rosa María Gutiérrez Murcia

Colombia

CD 4 Track 14

10-41 to 10-42

Vistas culturales

Les presento mi país

Mi nombre es Rosa María Gutiérrez Murcia y soy de Medellín, la segunda ciudad de Colombia. El setenta y cinco por ciento de la población colombiana se concentra en los centros urbanos y las regiones montañosas del país. En Medellín disfrutamos del único sistema de metro del país que proporciona transporte a la gente que vive en las afueras de la ciudad. **¿Qué tipos de transporte público hay en tu pueblo o ciudad?** Bogotá tiene el sistema más extenso de ciclorrutas (caminos para bicicletas) del país; gracias a él, la gente puede circular y disfrutar de los espacios públicos y verdes de la capital. Mi país es muy bello y tiene muchas atracciones para los turistas. Además, es el único país de Suramérica que tiene costa en el Océano Pacífico y en el Mar Caribe.

La catedral de sal de Zipaquirá

El Museo del Oro en Bogotá

ALMANAQUE

Nombre oficial:	República de Colombia
Gobierno:	República
Población:	43.593.035 (2006 est.)
Idiomas:	español
Moneda:	Peso colombiano (COP/$)

¿Sabías que...?

- En Zipaquirá Colombia hay una catedral única. ¡La catedral está situada a 600 pies adentro de una montaña de sal! Es impresionante.
- Simón Bolívar es conocido por ser *El Libertador*. Se considera un héroe en Colombia, Venezuela, Ecuador, Perú, Panamá y Bolivia, entre otros países hispanoamericanos.

PREGUNTAS

1. ¿Qué tiene Colombia que no tiene ningún otro país del continente?
2. ¿Cómo se comparan los medios de transporte de Medellín y Bogotá con los de tu área?
3. ¿Qué tienen en común Colombia, Perú y Chile?

En la Red
Amplía tus conocimientos sobre Colombia en la página web de *¡Anda!*

Víctor Luis González Martínez

Venezuela

CD 4 Track 15

Vistas culturales

Les presento mi país

Mi nombre es Víctor Luis González Martínez y soy de Mérida, Venezuela. Actualmente vivo en la capital, Caracas, porque estoy estudiando en la Universidad Central de Venezuela. Mientras estudio, vivo con mis parientes en el centro. Mi tío es ingeniero y trabaja en la industria petrolera. Venezuela es miembro de la Organización de Países Exportadores de Petróleo, conocida como la OPEP. **¿Qué papel tiene Venezuela en la OPEP?** Me encanta vivir con mis tíos, pues mi tía es la mejor cocinera de Venezuela; así disfruto de las comidas tradicionales venezolanas como las arepas, las hallacas y el pabellón criollo. ¡Qué ricos! Vivir en la capital, es decir, en la costa, es muy agradable, porque hay mucho que hacer, tanto para nosotros como para los turistas.

La industria petrolera es muy importante para la economía venezolana.

Caracas tiene cuatro millones de habitantes.

ALMANAQUE

Nombre oficial:	República Bolivariana de Venezuela
Gobierno:	República federal
Población:	25.730.435 (2006)
Idiomas:	español (oficial); lenguas indígenas
Moneda:	Bolívar (Bs)

¿Sabías que...?

- El Salto Ángel, a unos 978 metros de altura, es la catarata más alta del mundo. El agua cae desde la cima del Auyantepuy, que está en el Parque Nacional Canaima, en el sureste del país.
- En Mérida hay una heladería que ha figurado en el libro Mundial de Récords Guinness por el mayor número de helados: tienen más de 600 sabores. Por costumbre hay 110 sabores disponibles diariamente.

PREGUNTAS

1. ¿Dónde vive Victor? ¿Le gusta? Explica.
2. ¿Cuál es la base principal de la economía venezolana actualmente?
3. La bandera de Venezuela es muy parecida a la de Colombia y a la de Ecuador. ¿Por qué piensas que es así? ¿En qué se diferencian las banderas y a qué se deben estas diferencias?

En la Red
Amplía tus conocimientos sobre Venezuela en la página web de *¡Anda!*

lectura

10-46 to 10-47

10-36 **Antes de leer.** En preparación para el **Episodio 10,** contesta las siguientes preguntas basadas en el **Episodio 9.**

1. ¿Crees que Manolo, Cisco, Lupe y Marisol van a poder solucionar el nuevo rompecabezas?
2. ¿Crees que van a poder salvar a Eduardo y Alejandra si lo solucionan?
3. ¿Qué le pasa a Marisol? ¿Está enferma?
4. En tu opinión, ¿qué tiene que confesar Cisco?

ESTRATEGIA **Skipping words**

If you have attempted to guess the meaning of unfamiliar words from context and are still having problems understanding, you may want to skip the word(s) and follow these steps:

1. Identify the subject and main verb of each sentence.
2. Find descriptions of the subject in the sentence(s).
3. Identify words and phrases that indicate time and place.
4. Look for words that indicate cause and effect.
5. Ignore words set off by commas.
6. Summarize the content of each paragraph and look for information to fill in gaps or to answer any questions you may have.

10-37 **A leer.** Completa las siguientes actividades.

1. Lee superficialmente el episodio y subraya las palabras que no conoces.
2. A continuación hay unas frases de la lectura con posibles palabras problemáticas subrayadas. Léelas y responde.
   a. *Cisco estaba destrozado. —Me siento responsable por todo— les dijo. —Me pregunto por qué no fui a la policía en seguida. ¡Soy el hombre más tonto del mundo!—*
   - El sujeto de la primera frase es ______ y el verbo es ______. La palabra destrozado describe a ______.
   - Por las tres oraciones que siguen sabemos que Cisco se siente:
     1. muy bien
     2. muy mal
     3. regular

   b. *En medio de su remordimiento Manolo lo interrumpió.*

Si dividimos esa oración en dos partes, *«En medio de su remordimiento»* y *«Manolo lo interrumpió»*:

- ¿cuál es la parte más importante para la comprensión de la lectura?

c. *"Cisco, ¿no te dijo nada?" implorό Manolo.*

- ¿Por qué *no* es crítico saber lo que significa "imploró" en esta frase?

d. *Aquí les mando como documento adjunto el resto de lo que encontré en la computadora de Eduardo el día que desapareció.*

- La palabra "adjunto" es:
  1. un sustantivo (*noun*).
  2. un verbo.
  3. un adjetivo.
- Si ignoras la palabra, ¿puedes entender la frase?

3. Lee el episodio otra vez, empleando esa estrategia con cualquier otra palabra que no comprendas (*you do not understand*).

¿Qué sabía?

CD 4
Track 16

Cisco les confesó todo a Manolo, Marisol y Lupe en la videoconferencia. Les dijo que sabía más del caso de lo que les había dicho°. Les mandó el e-mail de Eduardo el cual descubrió el día que éste desapareció.

° *had told them*

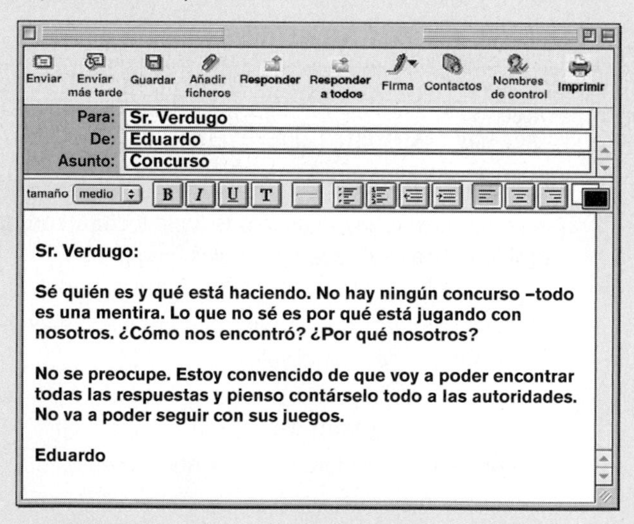

Enviar | Enviar más tarde | Guardar | Añadir ficheros | Responder | Responder a todos | Firma | Contactos | Nombres de control | Imprimir

Para: Sr. Verdugo
De: Eduardo
Asunto: Concurso

tamaño medio

Sr. Verdugo:

Sé quién es y qué está haciendo. No hay ningún concurso –todo es una mentira. Lo que no sé es por qué está jugando con nosotros. ¿Cómo nos encontró? ¿Por qué nosotros?

No se preocupe. Estoy convencido de que voy a poder encontrar todas las respuestas y pienso contárselo todo a las autoridades. No va a poder seguir con sus juegos.

Eduardo

Cisco estaba destrozado.

—Me siento responsable por todo— les dijo. Me pregunto por qué no fui a la policía en seguida. ¡Soy el hombre más tonto del mundo!

En medio de su remordimiento Manolo lo interrumpió.

—¿Qué sabía Eduardo? Era obvio por su mensaje que sabía que el concurso era fraudulento, pero me pregunto cómo se enteró°. ¿Cómo y dónde descubrió esa información? ¿Cuándo empezó a tener dudas? Cisco, ¿no te dijo nada?— imploró Manolo.

how he found out

Cisco se quedó mirando la pantalla por varios minutos antes de responder:

—Aquí les mando como documento adjunto el resto de lo que encontré en la computadora de Eduardo el día que desapareció. Les tengo que confesar que yo también tuve dudas e investigué varias ideas que tenía sobre el concurso. Descubrí que era una conspiración Ponzi para estafar° a la gente. El Sr. Verdugo buscaba jóvenes inteligentes que le ayudaran con su malvado° plan. Eduardo encontró los papeles con mis apuntes que tenía al lado de mi computadora y desapareció con ellos. Yo iba a contactar a las autoridades pero cuando Eduardo se fue con toda mi información, yo tenía que reproducirlo todo. Sin las pruebas°, ¿quién me iba a creer? Lo siento mucho, perdónenme...

to defraud
evil
proof

Manolo, Marisol y Lupe escucharon atentamente y recibieron el documento adjunto de Cisco casi al mismo tiempo en sus computadoras y lo leyeron. Marisol fue la primera en responder:

—Me pregunto si Eduardo pudo hablar con las autoridades antes de desaparecer. ¿Se fue en su coche en busca del Sr. Verdugo? ¿Sabía adónde tenía que ir? ¿Qué piensan?

Manolo les respondió:

—Eso es precisamente lo que yo estaba pensando. Y algo más: ¿qué tenía que ver Alejandra con todo esto? No podemos olvidarnos de ella.

La única persona que no respondió fue Lupe. Ella también recibió los mensajes y seguía la teleconferencia entre ellos sin participar. De repente abrió otra ventana en su pantalla y empezó a escribir algo muy detallado. Al mismo tiempo, tomó su teléfono celular y empezó a marcar°...

dial

10-38 Después de leer.

1. Por fin ¿qué les confesó Cisco a Marisol, Manolo y Lupe?
2. Si no había (*If there wasn't*) ningún concurso, ¿en qué consistía "el juego" del Sr. Verdugo?
3. ¿Cuáles eran las preguntas que tenían Manolo y Marisol ahora?
4. ¿Quién no dijo nada?
5. ¿Qué hacía Lupe al final del episodio?

10-48 to
10-50

video

10-39 Antes del video. ¿Qué habrá hecho Eduardo (*What must Eduardo have done*) con la información sobre la conspiración Ponzi? ¿Qué escribe Lupe en la computadora y a quién llama? En la segunda parte del episodio vas a saber quién resuelve el rompecabezas y vas a ver una confrontación entre Marisol y Lupe.

¡Marisol, no salgas de tu casa! ¡Estás en peligro!

Chicos, tenemos buenas noticias.

Hace mucho tiempo que descubrí que tú no eres la persona que dices ser.

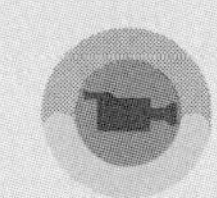

Episodio 10

«Falsas apariencias»

Relájate y disfruta el video.

10-40 Después del video. Contesta las siguientes preguntas.

1. ¿Quién resuelve el rompecabezas?
2. ¿Cómo responde Lupe cuando Marisol le dice que va a ir a su casa?
3. ¿Por qué tiene miedo Marisol?
4. ¿Qué hacen Lupe y Marisol con la respuesta del rompecabezas?
5. ¿Qué quiere hacer Cisco?
6. ¿Qué prueba (*proof*) tiene Marisol de que Lupe no es quien dice ser?
7. ¿Cómo termina el episodio?

Y por fin, ¿cómo andas?

Having completed this chapter, I now can…

	Feel Confident	Need to Review
Comunicación		
• talk about modes of transportation (p. 356)	❑	❑
• name the parts of a car (p. 357)	❑	❑
• correctly pronounce **b** and **v** (p. 357)	❑	❑
• influence others by using commands (pp. 360, 364)	❑	❑
• talk about travel (p. 368)	❑	❑
• discuss to whom things belong (p. 372)	❑	❑
• compare people, places, and things (p. 374)	❑	❑
• listen for cues (p. 379)	❑	❑
• write and present a report about a tourist spot (p. 380)	❑	❑
Cultura		
• discuss modes of transportation in the Hispanic world (p. 366)	❑	❑
• discuss travel opportunities in Venezuela (p. 371)	❑	❑
• state three facts about Venezuela and Colombia (pp. 381–382)	❑	❑
Ambiciones siniestras		
• skip words that hinder comprehension (p. 383)	❑	❑
• state what Cisco knows about the contest, provide the answer to the riddle, and give reasons that Lupe may not be what she appears to be (p. 386)	❑	❑

VOCABULARIO ACTIVO

CD 4
Tracks 17-23

El transporte	*Transportation*
el autobús	*bus*
el avión	*airplane*
la bicicleta	*bicycle*
el camión	*truck*
el carro/el coche	*car*
el metro	*subway*
la moto(cicleta)	*motorcycle*
el taxi	*taxi*
el tren	*train*

Unas partes de un vehículo	*Parts of a vehicle*
el aire acondicionado	*air conditioning*
el baúl	*trunk*
la calefacción	*heat*
el limpiaparabrisas	*windshield wiper*
la llanta	*tire*
la llave	*key*
el motor	*motor; engine*
el parabrisas	*windshield*
el tanque	*gas tank*
el volante	*steering wheel*

Otras palabras útiles	*Other useful words*
la autopista	*highway; freeway*
el boleto	*ticket*
la calle	*street*
la cola	*line (of people)*
la estación de servicio	*gas station*
el estacionamiento	*parking*
la licencia (de conducir)	*driver's license*
la multa	*traffic ticket; fine*
la parada	*bus stop*
el peatón	*pedestrian*
el policía	*policeman*
el ruido	*noise*
el semáforo	*traffic light*
el tráfico	*traffic*

Unos verbos útiles	*Some useful verbs*
arreglar/hacer la maleta	*to pack a suitcase*
bajar (de)	*to get down (from); to get off (of)*
cambiar	*to change*
caminar, ir a pie	*to walk; to go on foot*
dejar	*to leave*
doblar	*to turn*
entrar	*to enter*
estacionar	*to park*
funcionar	*to work; to function*
ir de vacaciones	*to go on vacation*
ir de viaje	*to go on a trip*
irse del hotel	*to leave the hotel; to check out*
llenar	*to fill*
manejar/conducir	*to drive*
prestar	*to loan; to lend*
registrarse (en el hotel)	*to check in*
revisar	*to check; to overhaul*
sacar la licencia	*to get a driver's license*
salir	*to leave; to go out*
subir (a)	*to go up; to get on*
viajar	*to travel*
visitar	*to visit*
volar (o → ue)	*to fly; to fly away*

El viaje	*The trip*
el aeropuerto	*airport*
la agencia de viajes	*travel agency*
el/la agente de viajes	*travel agent*
el barco	*boat*
el boleto de ida y vuelta	*round-trip ticket*
la estación (de tren, de autobús)	*(train, bus) station*
el extranjero	*abroad*
la maleta	*suitcase*
el pasaporte	*passport*
la reserva	*reservation*
el sello	*postage stamp*
la tarjeta postal	*postcard*
las vacaciones	*vacation*
los viajeros	*travelers*
el vuelo	*flight*

El hotel	*The hotel*
el botones	*bellman*
el cuarto doble	*double room*
el cuarto individual	*single room*
la recepción	*front desk*

Unos lugares	*Some places*
el lago	*lake*
las montañas	*mountains*
el parque de atracciones	*theme park*
la playa	*beach*

11

El mundo actual

¿Qué peligros existen hoy en día para el medio ambiente (*environment*)? Hay más de 5.000 especies de animales en peligro (*danger*) de extinción, 70% del aire en las ciudades está contaminado y las selvas (*jungles*), las cuales contienen más del 50% de todas las especies de plantas y animales existentes, se reducen drásticamente cada año.

	OBJETIVOS	CONTENIDOS
Comunicación	• To give your opinion on environmental issues in the United States and in the Spanish-speaking world • To express what is important or necessary for you and others to do • To comment on what is possible, probable, and improbable • To comment on government and current affairs • To use visual organizers when listening • To write a public announcement	1 Animals 392 2 The environment 396 3 The subjunctive 398 4 Politics 405 5 **Por** and **para** 408 6 Prepositions and pronouns that follow them 410 7 Infinitives that follow prepositions 414 ☐ Pronunciación: Review of word stress and accent marks 393 ☐ Escucha: 415 Estrategia: Using visual organizers ☐ Escribe: Writing a public announcement 416
Cultura	• To describe El Yunque, the rain forest of Puerto Rico • To list specific facts about politics in the Spanish-speaking world • To state two interesting facts about this chapter's featured countries: Cuba, Puerto Rico, and the Dominican Republic	☐ El Yunque: tesoro tropical 398 ☐ Politics in the Hispanic world 407 ☐ *Cuba, Puerto Rico,* and *La República Dominicana* 417–419
Ambiciones siniestras	• To use visual organizers when reading • To explain who Lupe really is • To relate what happened to Eduardo and Alejandra	☐ Episodio 11 Lectura: *Celia* 420 Estrategia: Using visual organizers Video: *El desenlace* 422

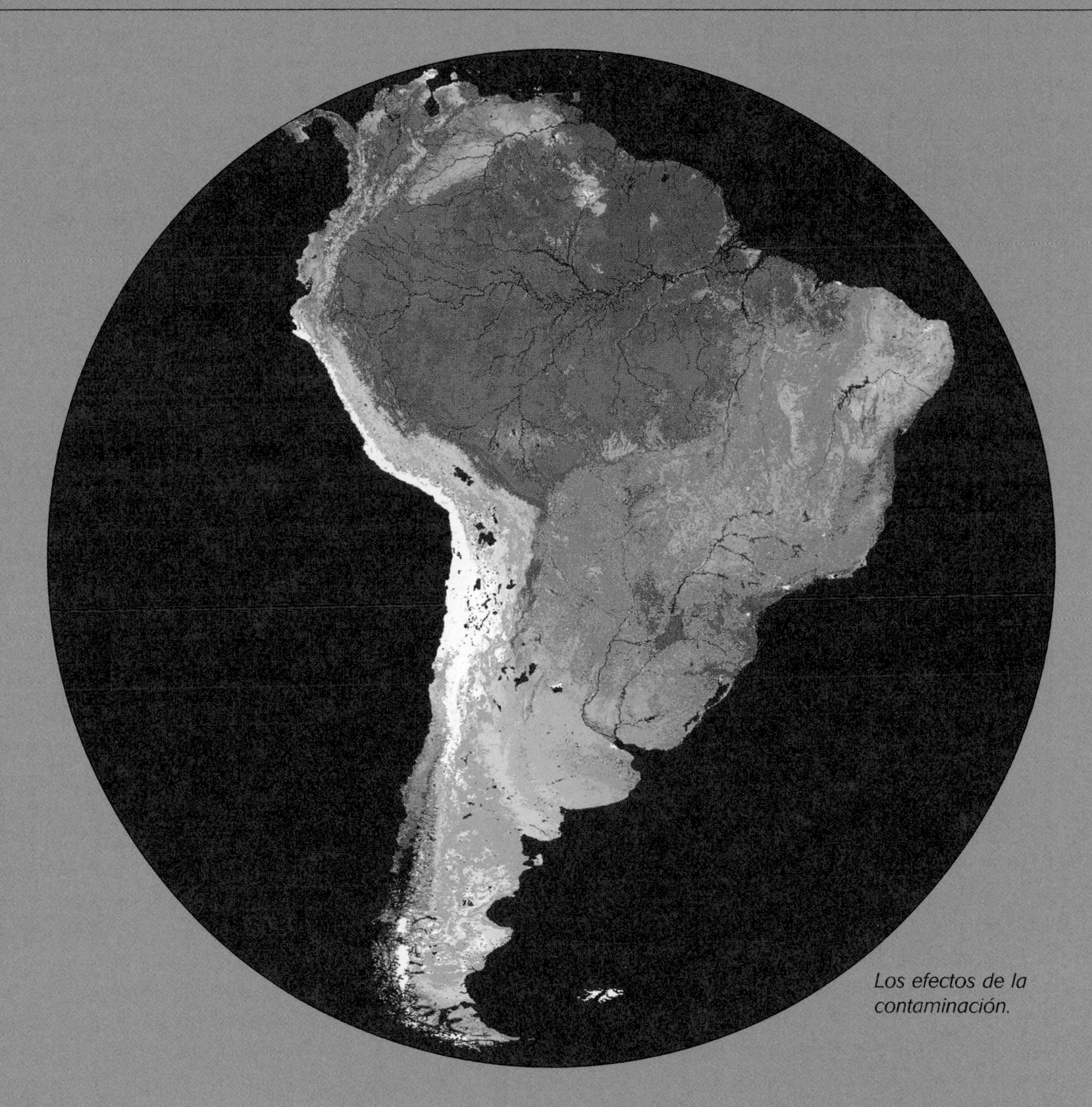

Los efectos de la contaminación.

PREGUNTAS

1 ¿Dónde hay selvas tropicales?
2 ¿Cuántos animales están en peligro de extinción?
3 ¿Dónde está contaminado el aire en los Estados Unidos?

Comunicación

- Talking about animals
- Discussing environmental issues
- Talking about what is important, probable, and necessary

VOCABULARIO 1 Los animales

SAM MSL 11-1 to 11-5

Los animales de la granja

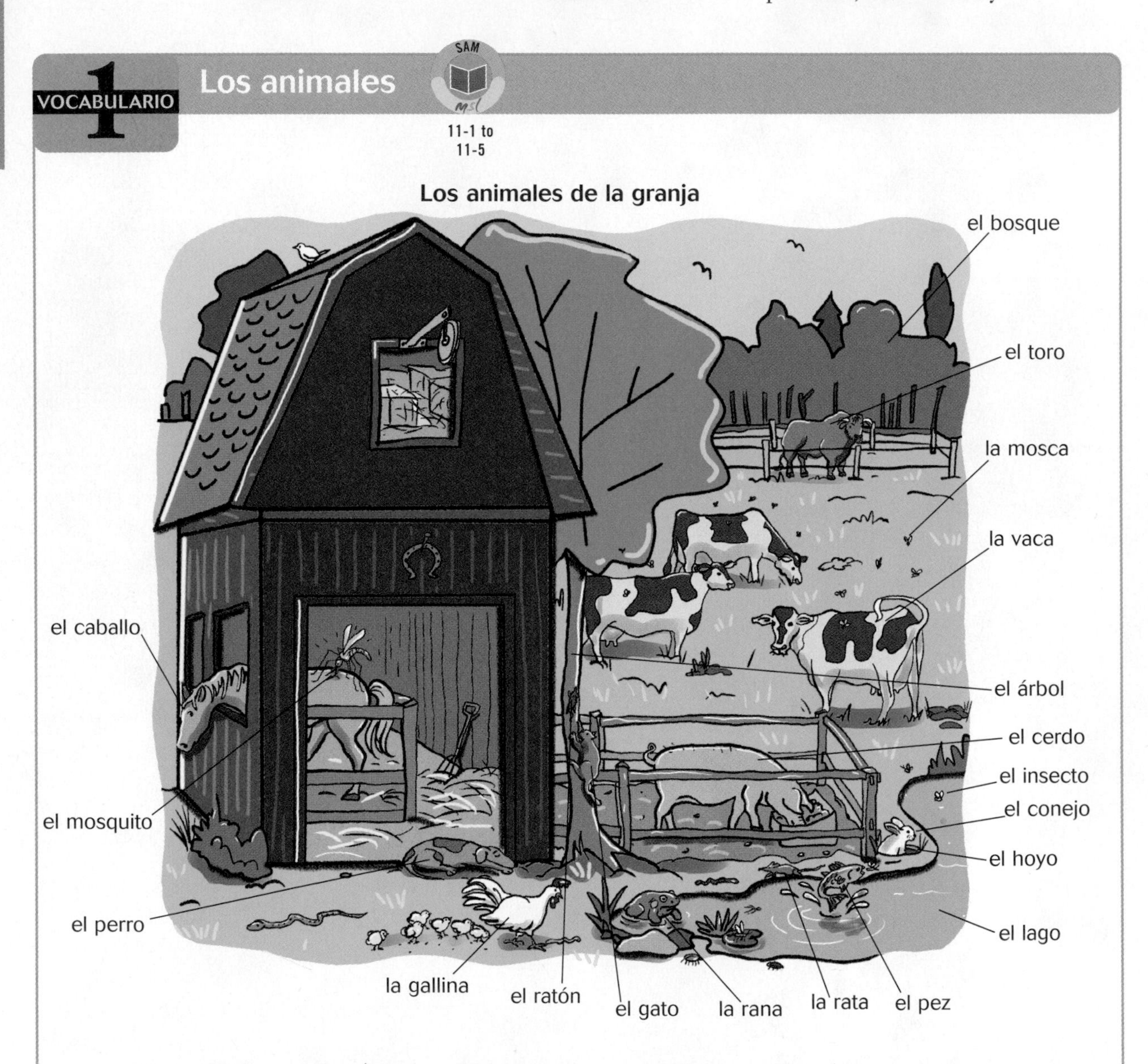

Otras palabras útiles	*Other useful words*
los animales de la granja	*farm animals*
un animal doméstico	*domesticated animal; pet*
la granja/la finca	*farm*

Unos verbos	*Some verbs*
cuidar	*to take care of*
montar a caballo	*to ride a horse*
preocuparse por	*to worry about; to concern oneself with*

Los animales salvajes

Otras palabras útiles	*Other useful words*
los animales salvajes	*wild animals*
un animal en peligro de extinción	*an endangered species*
el bosque	*forest*
el océano	*ocean*
peligroso/a	*dangerous*
la selva	*jungle*

CD 4
Track 24

PRONUNCIACIÓN

11-6 to
11-10

Review of Word Stress and Accent Marks

In **Capítulo 2,** the rules on Spanish word stress and written accent marks were presented. Please review page 63 and complete the following activities.

11•1 Las palabras

Practice pronouncing the following words, focusing on the stress.

1. cerdo
2. conejo
3. árbol
4. preocuparse
5. río
6. montaña
7. bosque
8. cuevas

11•2 Las oraciones

Practice pronouncing the following sentences and pay special attention to the stress.

1. Me preocupo por los animales en peligro de extinción.
2. Mis niños quieren un perro pero sé que no van a cuidarlo.

11•3 Los trabalenguas

Now pronounce the following tongue twister and focus on the stress.

En el campo hay una cabra (*goat*), ética, perlética, pelapelambrética, pelúa, pelapelambrúa.

Tiene los hijitos éticos, perléticos, pelapelambréticos, pelúos, pelapelambrúos.

11•4 La fauna

Organiza los animales del vocabulario con un/a compañero/a según las siguientes categorías: **insecto, reptil, mamífero, ave** y **anfibio.**

INSECTO	REPTIL	MAMÍFERO	AVE	ANFIBIO

11•5 ¿Dónde viven?

Digan en qué lugar viven los siguientes animales.

1. ______ el conejo
2. ______ el león
3. ______ el pájaro
4. ______ el oso
5. ______ el pez
6. ______ la gallina

a. la selva
b. un lago
c. una granja
d. el bosque
e. un hoyo
f. un árbol

Capítulo 8. *Gustar* y verbos como gustar, pág. 294.

11•6 Las preferencias

Completa los siguientes pasos.

Paso 1 Escribe los nombres de los **tres** animales que más te gustan y de los **tres** que menos te gustan y explica por qué. Usa verbos como **gustar, fascinar, encantar, hacer falta** y **molestar.** Después, comparte tus respuestas con un/a compañero/a.

MODELO *El animal que más me gusta es el caballo porque es muy fuerte y me encanta montar a caballo. También me gustan los gatos y los perros porque puedo tenerlos en casa. Los tres animales que menos me gustan son… porque…*

Paso 2 Presenten sus respuestas a los compañeros de la clase. ¿Cuál es el animal que más les gusta? ¿El que menos les gusta?

11•7 ¿Qué opinas?

Circula por la clase para hacerles las siguientes preguntas a tres compañeros diferentes. Si alguien contesta afirmativamente, recoge su firma.

Capítulo 7. El préterito, pág. 258; Unos verbos irregulares en el pretérito pág. 266.

Estrategia

Remember that when completing signature search activities like **11-7,** it is important to move quickly around the room, trying to get as many different signatures as possible, while asking and answering all questions in Spanish.

MODELO ¿Quién… se sacó un conejo de la manga?

E1: *¿Te sacaste un conejo de la manga?*

E2: *Sí, me saqué un conejo de la manga en una fiesta.*

E1: *Pues, firma aquí.*

Roberto

¿QUIÉN…?		
corrió delante de los toros en los Sanfermines E1: ____ E2: ____ E3: ____	puso una rana en la silla del profesor E1: ____ E2: ____ E3: ____	imitó una vez el ruido del cerdo E1: ____ E2: ____ E3: ____
es alérgico a la picadura de los mosquitos E1: ____ E2: ____ E3: ____	fue de safari y estuvo cerca de un león E1: ____ E2: ____ E3: ____	se sentó encima de un hormiguero *(anthill)* E1: ____ E2: ____ E3: ____

El medio ambiente

11-11 to 11-17

Los desastres

El reciclaje

El planeta	***The planet***
el cielo	*sky; heaven*
la naturaleza	*nature*
el recurso natural	*natural resource*
la selva (tropical)	*jungle; (tropical) rain forest*
la tierra	*land; soil*
la Tierra	*Earth*
Los desastres	***Disasters***
la destrucción	*destruction*
el efecto invernadero	*global warming*
la lluvia ácida	*acid rain*
la tragedia	*tragedy*
Otras palabras útiles	***Other useful words***
el aire	*air*
la basura	*garbage*
la calidad	*quality*
la ecología	*ecology*
puro/a	*pure*
el vertedero	*dump*
vivo/a	*alive; living*
Unos verbos	***Some verbs***
botar	*to throw away*
contaminar	*to pollute*
evitar	*to avoid*
hacer daño	*to (do) damage; to harm*
matar	*to kill*
proteger	*to protect*
reciclar	*to recycle*
reforestar	*to reforest*
rehusar	*to refuse*

11•8 ¿Qué es...?

Aquí tienen las definiciones. ¿Cuáles son las palabras?

MODELO E1: lo opuesto de contaminado

E2: *puro*

Fíjate

Note that *la Tierra* (Earth) is capitalized in Spanish but *la tierra* (land, soil) is not.

1. plantar árboles donde antes los había
2. el estudio de la protección del medio ambiente
3. un lugar designado donde botamos la basura
4. responder de manera negativa a una petición (*request*)
5. estas plantas grandes protegen la Tierra de la potencia del sol
6. ensuciar el agua o el aire, por ejemplo
7. lo opuesto de muerto
8. el posible resultado de la contaminación del aire

11•9 El reportaje

¿Cómo podemos proteger el medio ambiente?

Paso 1 Escribe un párrafo de **seis** a **ocho** oraciones sobre qué podemos hacer en el futuro para proteger el medio ambiente. Puedes usar la lista de abajo para más ideas.

- sembrar muchas plantas
- reciclar el plástico, el vidrio, el papel y el cartón
- usar carros eléctricos
- proteger los animales en peligro de extinción
- apoyar las instituciones de conservación de los recursos naturales
- proteger la selva tropical
- reforestar los bosques
- usar el carro lo menos posible
- usar energía solar
- no prender (*turn on*) a menudo el aire acondicionado

MODELO *Para evitar la destrucción de los bosques y la selva tropical, no debemos cortar más árboles. En el futuro, debemos plantar más árboles para reforestar el bosque…*

Paso 2 Después, en grupos pequeños, comparen sus oraciones y juntos escriban un reportaje corto con recomendaciones para proteger el medio ambiente.

11-18 to 11-19

El Yunque: tesoro tropical

El Bosque Nacional del Caribe también se conoce como El Bosque Lluvioso de El Yunque, en honor al dios bondadoso (*kind*) indígena Yuquiyú. El Yunque es el único bosque lluvioso tropical que pertenece al Sistema de Bosques Nacionales de los Estados Unidos. Más de 100 billones de galones de agua de lluvia caen anualmente en el bosque sobre el monte El Toro (a 1.076 metros).

El Yunque es el bosque nacional más viejo y pequeño de las Américas. Sin embargo, cuenta con la mayor diversidad de flora. Hay más de 240 especies de árboles en un área de poco más de 11.760 hectáreas (28,000 acres). Además, sirve de refugio a muchas especies de pájaros incluyendo la cotorra o loro (*parrot*) puertorriqueño, el cual está en peligro de extinción. Después del huracán Hugo en 1989 quedaron sólo 20 loros. En esos momentos se empezó un programa para salvarlos y hoy en día existen unos 85. La ranita (rana pequeña) llamada *coquí* es original de Puerto Rico y hay muchas clases diferentes de coquíes en el Yunque.

El Bosque Nacional del Caribe es el lugar de Puerto Rico más frecuentado por los turistas. También lo frecuentan mucho las familias puertorriqueñas durante los fines de semana para pasar el día.

Preguntas

1. ¿Por qué es tan importante El Yunque?
2. ¿Cuáles son algunas de las características del Yunque que lo hacen tan especial?

El subjuntivo

11-20 to 11-24 46, 51

In Spanish, *tenses* such as the present, past, and future are grouped under two different moods, the **indicative** mood and the **subjunctive** mood.

Indicative mood	Subjunctive mood
Present	Present
Past	Past
Future	Future

Es una lástima que no quieran reciclar el plástico, el vidrio, el aluminio y el papel.

Up to this point you have studied tenses grouped under the *indicative* mood (with the exception of commands) to report what happened, is happening, or will happen. The *subjunctive* mood, on the other hand, is used to express doubt, insecurity, influence, opinion, feelings, hope, wishes, or desires that can be happening now, have happened in the past, or will happen in the future. In this chapter you will learn the present tense of the *subjunctive mood*.

Fíjate

You are already somewhat familiar with the subjunctive forms from your practice with *Ud.* (*¡Estudie!*) and negative *tú* (*¡No hables!*) commands.

Present subjunctive

To form the subjunctive, take the **yo** form of the present indicative, drop the final **-o,** and add the following endings.

Present indicative	*yo* form		Present subjunctive
estudiar	estudiø	+ e	**estudie**
comer	comø	+ a	**coma**
vivir	vivø	+ a	**viva**

	estudiar	comer	vivir
yo	estudie	coma	viva
tú	estudies	comas	vivas
él, ella, Ud.	estudie	coma	viva
nosotros/as	estudiemos	comamos	vivamos
vosotros/as	estudiéis	comáis	viváis
ellos/as, Uds.	estudien	coman	vivan

Irregular forms

- Verbs with irregular **yo** forms mantain this irregularity in all forms of the present subjunctive. Note the following examples.

	conocer	hacer	poner	venir
yo	conozca	haga	ponga	venga
tú	conozcas	hagas	pongas	vengas
él, ella, Ud.	conozca	haga	ponga	venga
nosotros/as	conozcamos	hagamos	pongamos	vengamos
vosotros/as	conozcáis	hagáis	pongáis	vengáis
ellos/as, Uds.	conozcan	hagan	pongan	vengan

- Verbs ending in **-car, -gar,** and **-zar** have a spelling change in all present subjunctive forms, in order to maintain the sound of the infinitive.

		Present indicative	Present subjunctive
buscar	**c → qu**	**yo** busco	busque
pagar	**g → gu**	**yo** pago	pague
empezar	**z → c**	**yo** empiezo	empiece

	buscar	pagar	empezar
yo	busque	pague	empiece
tú	busques	pagues	empieces
él, ella, Ud.	busque	pague	empiece
nosotros/as	busquemos	paguemos	empecemos
vosotros/as	busquéis	paguéis	empecéis
ellos/as, Uds.	busquen	paguen	empiecen

Stem-changing verbs

In the present subjunctive, stem-changing **-ar** and **-er** verbs make the same vowel change that they do in the present indicative: **e → ie** and **o → ue**.

	pensar (e → ie)	poder (o → ue)
yo	piense	pueda
tú	pienses	puedas
él, ella, Ud.	piense	pueda
nosotros/as	pensemos	podamos
vosotros/as	penséis	podáis
ellos/as, Uds.	piensen	puedan

The pattern is different with the **-ir** stem-changing verbs. In addition to their usual changes of **e → ie, e → i,** and **o → ue,** in the **nosotros** and **vosotros** forms the stem vowels change **ie → i** and **ue → u.**

	sentir (e → ie, i)	dormir (o → ue, u)
yo	sienta	duerma
tú	sientas	duermas
él, ella, Ud.	sienta	duerma
nosotros/as	sintamos	durmamos
vosotros/as	sintáis	durmáis
ellos/as, Uds.	sientan	duerman

The **e → i** stem-changing verbs keep the change in all forms.

	pedir (e → i, i)
yo	pida
tú	pidas
él, ella, Ud.	pida
nosotros/as	pidamos
vosotros/as	pidáis
ellos/as, Uds.	pidan

Irregular verbs in the present subjunctive

- The following verbs are irregular in the subjunctive.

	dar	estar	saber	ser	ir
yo	dé	esté	sepa	sea	vaya
tú	des	estés	sepas	seas	vayas
él, ella, Ud.	dé	esté	sepa	sea	vaya
nosotros/as	demos	estemos	sepamos	seamos	vayamos
vosotros/as	deis	estéis	sepáis	seáis	vayáis
ellos/as, Uds.	den	estén	sepan	sean	vayan

Dar has a written accent on the first- and third-person singular forms **(dé)** to distinguish it from the preposition **de.** All forms of **estar,** except the **nosotros** form, have a written accent in the present subjunctive.

¡Es increíble que este capítulo sea el último!

Using the subjunctive

One of the uses of the subjunctive is with fixed expressions that communicate opinion, doubt, probability, and wishes. They are always followed by the subjunctive.

Opinion

Es bueno/malo/mejor que... — *It's good/bad/better that...*

Es importante que... — *It's important that...*

Es increíble que... — *It's incredible that...*

Es una lástima que... — *It's a pity that...*

Es necesario que... — *It's necessary that...*

Es preferible que... — *It's preferable that...*

Es raro que... — *It's rare that...*

Doubt and probability

Es dudoso que... — *It's doubtful that...*

Es imposible que... — *It's impossible that...*

Es improbable que... — *It's unlikely that...*

Es posible que... — *It's possible that...*

Es probable que... — *It's likely that...*

Wishes and hopes

Ojalá (que)... — *Let's hope that.../Hopefully...*

> **Fíjate**
>
> The expression *Ojalá* (*que*) comes from the Arabic expression meaning *May it be Allah's will.* The conjunction *que* is optional in this expression.

Es necesario que protejamos los animales en peligro de extinción. — *It's necessary that we protect endangered animals.*

Es una lástima que algunas personas no quieran reciclar el plástico, el vidrio, el aluminio y el papel. — *It's a shame that some people don't want to recycle plastic, glass, aluminum, and paper.*

Ojalá (que) haya menos destrucción del medio ambiente en el futuro. — *Let's hope that there is less destruction of the environment in the future.*

> **Fíjate**
>
> The subjunctive of *hay* is *haya.*

1. What is the difference between the subjunctive and the indicative moods?
2. What other verb forms look like the subjunctive?
3. Where does the subjunctive verb come in relation to the word **que?**

Check your answers to the preceding questions in Appendix 1.

11•10 ¡Corre!

Escuchen mientras su profesor/a les explica cómo jugar con las formas de los verbos en el subjuntivo.

11•11 Opciones

Túrnense para crear oraciones completas usando los sujetos indicados en cada frase.

MODELO Es preferible que ella/nosotros/tú (reciclar el vidrio)

E1: *Es preferible que ella recicle el vidrio.*

E2: *Es preferible que nosotros reciclemos el vidrio.*

E3: *Es preferible que tú recicles el vidrio.*

1. Es dudoso que tú/Marta y yo/ella (rehusar reciclar el aluminio)
2. Es necesario que el gobierno/ellos/Uds. (reforestar los bosques)
3. Ojalá que ellos/él/nosotros (conservar las selvas tropicales)
4. Es posible que yo/tú/Uds. (poder evitar la lluvia ácida)
5. Es importante que mi país/los jóvenes/nosotros (respetar la naturaleza)
6. Es una lástima que papá/tú/tus hermanos (botar basura por las calles)

11•12 El cocodrilo

Completa el siguiente párrafo con la forma correcta del verbo apropiado en el subjuntivo. Después, comparte tus respuestas con un/a compañero/a.

El cocodrilo cubano

Fíjate

The *yo* form of the present tense (indicative mode) of *proteger* is *protejo*. Therefore the subjunctive of *proteger* is *proteja*, *protejas*, etc.

estar	proteger	haber	matar
poder	existir	ser	vivir

Es raro que los cocodrilos (1) ________________ en el hemisferio occidental. ¡Siempre pienso en el continente de África como hábitat para este animal! Es una lástima que el cocodrilo americano y el cocodrilo cubano (2) ________________ en peligro de extinción. Es bueno que el cocodrilo americano (3) ________________ en varias partes del hemisferio (Florida, algunas islas del Caribe y varias zonas costeras del Golfo de México y el Océano Pacífico), porque así tiene menos peligro de extinción que el cocodrilo cubano, el cual (*which*) existe solamente en el sureste de Cuba. Es posible que el cocodrilo americano (4) ________________ peligroso para los humanos. Son tan grandes que pueden atacar y comer animales de gran tamaño cuando se acercan a beber agua. Es improbable que el cocodrilo cubano (5) ________________ a una persona porque es mucho más pequeño y prefiere las aves, pequeños mamíferos, peces y otros animales acuáticos. Es increíble que el cocodrilo americano (6) ________________ galopar distancias cortas, lo que significa que puede matar fuera del agua también. Es necesario que nosotros (7) ________________ estos reptiles y ojalá que (8) ________________ muchos más en el futuro.

11-13 Mis mejores consejos (*advice*)...

Completa el cuadro con tus mejores consejos. Después, comparte tu información con un/a compañero/a.

PARA PROTEGER LOS RÍOS Y OCÉANOS	PARA EVITAR LA CONTAMINACIÓN DEL AIRE	PARA MANTENER LAS CALLES LIMPIAS
1. *Es importante que no botemos la basura en los ríos.*	1.	1.
2.	2.	2.
3.	3.	3.
4.	4.	4.
5.	5.	5.

11-14 ¿Para quién es necesario que...?

Túrnense para hacer y contestar las preguntas sobre las siguientes situaciones usando una de las expresiones de la pág. 401.

MODELO estudiar esta noche

E1: *Es probable que estudie esta noche. ¿Y tú?*

E2: *Tengo que estudiar pero es posible que vaya al cine.*

1. estudiar este fin de semana
2. comer menos comida rápida
3. arreglar su cuarto
4. gastar menos dinero
5. buscar un nuevo compañero de cuarto
6. dormir más
7. sacar mejores notas
8. comprar un coche nuevo
9. reciclar más

11-15 Posibles determinaciones

¿Cuáles pueden ser tus determinaciones (*resolutions*) para el próximo año? Descríbelas y después compártelas con un/a compañero/a.

Estrategia

Take advantage of activities like **11-15** to challenge yourself to go beyond a simple answer, providing as much pertinent information as you can.

MODELO *Es mejor que no coma tanto chocolate el próximo año pero es dudoso que pueda evitarlo. ¡Me fascina el chocolate! Es importante que haga más ejercicio. Es una lástima que no me guste hacerlo.*

11·16 Es importante que...

Juntos escojan una de las siguientes situaciones para desarrollar en forma de diálogo. Usando las expresiones que acaban de (*have just*) aprender, den consejos según la situación escogida (*chosen*). Después, presenten el diálogo a los compañeros de clase.

Situación A:

La doctora Pérez es especialista en nutrición. María Cecilia es una joven universitaria de dieciocho años que va a hacerle una consulta a la doctora sobre cómo mejorar el cutis *(complexion)*.

Situación B:

Bruno quiere comprar un carro usado y le pide a su amigo Manolo, quien trabaja en una agencia de carros, que le ayude.

Situación C:

El sargento López está enamorado de la linda Carolina, pero es tan tímido que nunca la invita a salir con él. Su amiga Carmen trata de ayudarlo.

Situación D:

Patricio se mata estudiando para el examen de matemáticas. Un día antes del examen se da cuenta *(he notices)* de que no tenía un examen de matemáticas, ¡sino de español! Va a su consejero para ver qué le aconseja.

¿Cómo andas?

Having completed the first **Comunicación,** I now can...

	Feel Confident	**Need to Review**
• talk about certain animals and their habitats (pp. 392–393)	❑	❑
• pronounce words applying appropriate word stress, and know when written accent marks are needed (p. 393)	❑	❑
• discuss the environment and ways to protect it (p. 396)	❑	❑
• form the present subjunctive (p. 398)	❑	❑
• use the subjunctive correctly with fixed expressions to communicate opinion, doubt, probability, and wishes (p. 401)	❑	❑

Comunicación

- Talking about politics
- Specifying location and information using prepositions and prepositional phrases

VOCABULARIO 4 La política

SAM 11-25 to 11-28

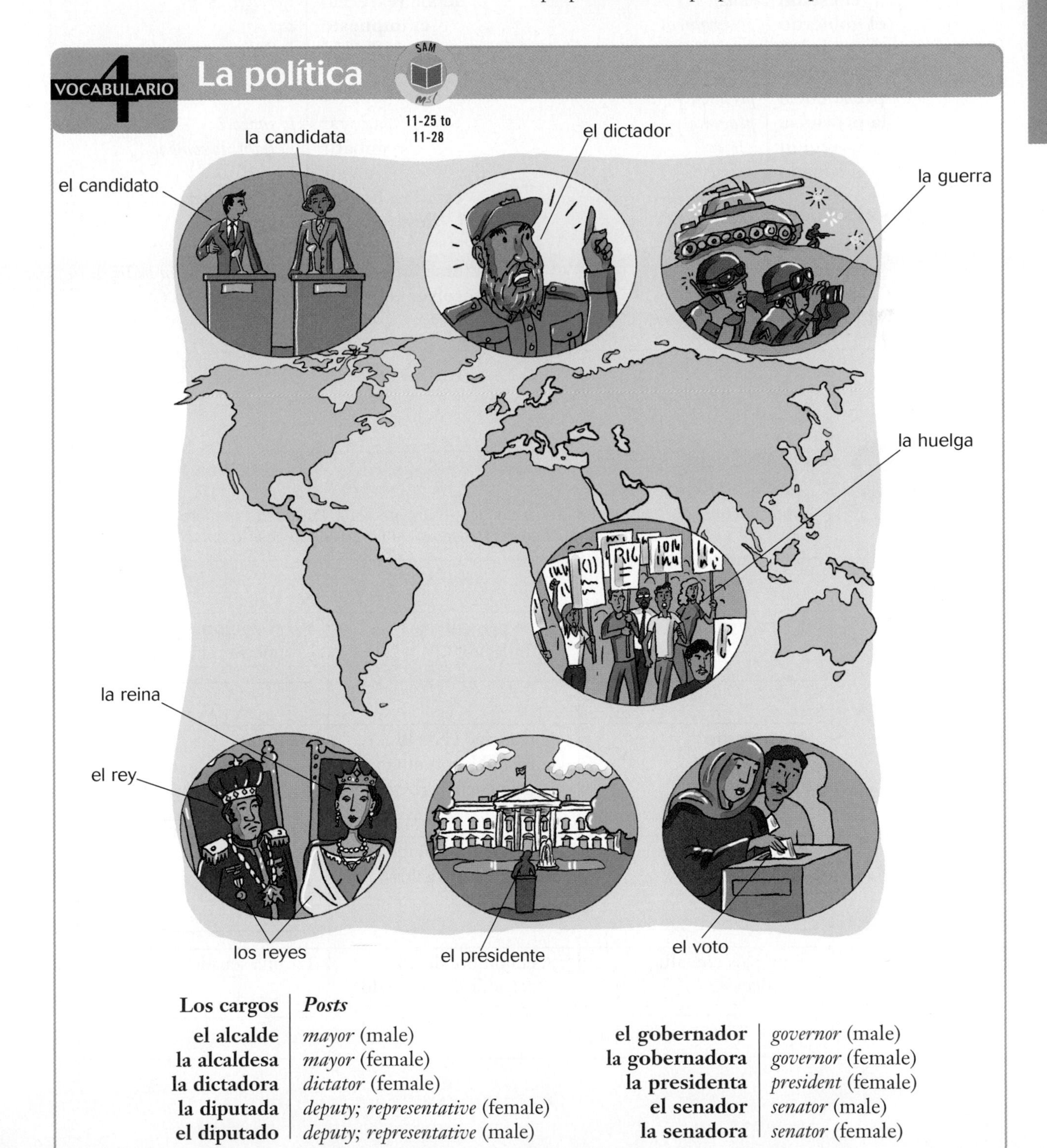

Los cargos	Posts
el alcalde	*mayor* (male)
la alcaldesa	*mayor* (female)
la dictadora	*dictator* (female)
la diputada	*deputy; representative* (female)
el diputado	*deputy; representative* (male)
el gobernador	*governor* (male)
la gobernadora	*governor* (female)
la presidenta	*president* (female)
el senador	*senator* (male)
la senadora	*senator* (female)

Las administraciones y los regímenes	***Administrations and regimes***
el congreso	*congress*
la democracia	*democracy*
la dictadura	*dictatorship*
el estado	*state*
el gobierno	*government*
la ley	*law*
la monarquía	*monarchy*
la presidencia	*presidency*
la provincia	*province*
la región	*region*
el senado	*senate*

Las elecciones	***Elections***
la campaña	*campaign*
el discurso	*speech*
la encuesta	*survey; poll*
el partido político	*political party*

Las cuestiones políticas	***Political matters***
el bienestar	*well-being; welfare*
la defensa	*defense*
la delincuencia	*crime*
el desempleo	*unemployment*
la deuda (externa)	*(foreign) debt*
el impuesto	*tax*
la inflación	*inflation*

Unos verbos	***Some verbs***
apoyar	*to support*
combatir	*to fight; to combat*
elegir	*to elect*
estar en huelga	*to be on strike*
llevar a cabo	*to carry out*
luchar	*to fight; to combat*
meterse en política	*to get involved in politics*
resolver (o → ue)	*to resolve*
votar	*to vote*

11•17 Batalla

Completa el cuadro con el nombre de un lugar o una persona. Después, compara tus respuestas con las de un/a compañero/a. Dense un punto por cada acierto (*match*).

1. una reina ____________	5. un país con baja inflación ____________	9. el nombre de una guerra muy larga ____________
2. un estado ____________	6. una ciudad de los EE.UU. con mucha delincuencia (*crime*) ____________	10. un rey ____________
3. un país con monarquía ____________	7. el nombre del mejor presidente de los EE.UU. ____________	11. un alcalde ____________
4. un país con alta inflación ____________	8. el nombre de un senador de tu estado ____________	12. una senadora ____________

11-29

La política en el mundo hispano

Evo Morales, elegido en diciembre de 2005, es el primer presidente indígena de Bolivia.

La historia política de Latinoamérica es la historia de la lucha dramática del ser humano contra fuerzas destructivas como la colonización, el imperialismo, la esclavitud y el genocidio en siglos anteriores y, en épocas más recientes, la pobreza, la corrupción, el nepotismo, la división rígida de clases y el militarismo. Muchos países hispanohablantes han sufrido severas dictaduras o democracias débiles e ineficaces. Esta lucha ahora se traduce en la búsqueda de una relación más justa con el mundo desarrollado y en particular con los Estados Unidos.

En décadas recientes, España ha surgido como un país moderno y avanzado, con un rey progresista y amante de la democracia. América Latina, a su vez, experimentó un periodo de paz y esperanza en la segunda mitad del siglo XX. La guerra que azotó (*whipped*) a Centroamérica en la década de los ochenta acabó y, aunque sus efectos aún se sienten y la recuperación es lenta en algunos países, el estándar de vida en Centroamérica ha aumentado (*has grown*), así como el comercio y el deseo de fortalecer las instituciones democráticas.

Preguntas

1. ¿Cuáles fueron algunos de los problemas en la historia política de los países hispanos?
2. ¿Qué cambios han experimentado (*have they experienced*) muchos de los países hispanos en los últimos quince o veinte años?

11·18 ¿Qué sabes de...?

Juntos contesten las siguientes preguntas para mostrar sus conocimientos políticos.

1. ¿Cuándo fue la última campaña para la presidencia de los EE.UU.?
2. ¿Cómo se llama el/la gobernador/a de tu estado?
3. ¿Quién fue un/a dictador/a infame? ¿De qué país? ¿Cuándo fue dictador/a?
4. ¿Qué países tiene un rey o una reina? ¿Cómo se llama(n)?
5. ¿Cuántos senadores hay en el senado de los EE.UU.?

11·19 El futuro político

Escribe algunas ideas sobre lo que debe pasar en el futuro en tu ciudad, estado, país o en el mundo. Después, en grupos de tres, escriban un párrafo colectivo para la clase. Usen las expresiones que requieren subjuntivo cuando sea posible.

MODELO *Es necesario que los partidos políticos no combatan tanto entre sí* (among themselves). *También es importante que el presidente resuelva problemas económicos como la inflación. Es dudoso que podamos bajar la deuda nacional porque todos quieren dinero para sus programas.*

11•20 Los partidos políticos

En grupos de cinco o seis estudiantes van a crear un partido político nuevo. Tienen que determinar el nombre del partido y el programa (*platform*). Después, presenten sus partidos a los otros grupos y juntos decidan cuál(es) de los partidos mejor representa(n) las opiniones de la clase.

GRAMÁTICA 5 Por y para

SAM 11-30 to 11-33

¿Por cuánto tiempo ocupa el presidente la presidencia?

As you have seen, Spanish has two main words to express *for*: **por** and **para.** They have distinct uses and are not interchangeable.

POR is used to express:

1. Duration of time (*during, for*)

El presidente ocupa la presidencia (**por**) cuatro años consecutivos.

The president holds the presidency for four consecutive years.

El alcalde habló (**por**) más de media hora.

The mayor spoke for more than a half hour.

2. Movement or location (*through, along, past, around*)

Los candidatos van **por** la calle hablando con la gente.

The candidates are going through the streets talking with the people.

El rey saluda **por** la ventana.

The king is waving through the window.

PARA is used to express:

1. Point in time or a deadline (*for, by*)

Es dudoso que todos los problemas se solucionen **para** el final de su presidencia.

It is doubtful that all problems will be solved by the end of her presidency.

Es importante que bajemos los impuestos **para** el próximo año.

It is important that we lower taxes by next year.

2. Destination (*for*)

La reina sale hoy **para** Puerto Rico.

The queen leaves for Puerto Rico today.

Los diputados se fueron **para** el Capitolio.

The representatives left for the Capitol.

3. Motive (*on account of, because of, for*)
Decidimos meternos en política **por** nuestros hijos. Queremos asegurarles un futuro mejor.
We decided to get involved in politics because of our children. We want to assure them a better future.
En resumen, nos dijeron que hay que reciclar **por** el futuro de nuestro planeta.
In short, they told us that we must recycle for the future of our planet.

4. Exchange (*in exchange for*)
Gracias **por** su ayuda, señora Presidenta.
Thank you for your help, Madam President.
Limpiaron el vertedero **por** diez mil dólares.
They cleaned the dump for ten thousand dollars.

5. Means (*by*)
Los diputados discutieron los resultados de las elecciones **por** teléfono.
The representatives argued about the election results over the phone.
¿Los reyes van a viajar **por** barco o **por** avión?
Are the king and queen going to travel by ship or by plane?

3. Recipients or intended person or persons (*for*)
Mi hermano escribe discursos **para** la gobernadora.
My brother writes speeches for the governor.
Necesitamos un avión **para** el dictador.
We need a plane for the dictator.

4. Comparison (*for*)
Para un hombre que sabe tanto de la política, no tiene ni idea sobre la delincuencia de nuestras calles.
For a man who knows so much about politics, he has no idea about the crime on our streets.
La taza de desempleo es bastante bajo **para** un país en desarrollo.
The unemployment rate is quite low for a developing country.

5. Purpose or goal (*to, in order to*)
Para recibir más votos, la candidata necesita proponer soluciones **para** los problemas con la deuda externa.
(In order) to receive more votes, the candidate needs to propose solutions for the problems with foreign debt.
Hay que luchar contra la contaminacón **para** proteger el medio ambiente.
One needs to fight pollution to protect the environment.

11•21 Mi hermana Leonor

Mi hermana Leonor me dio una gran sorpresa para mi cumpleaños.

Paso 1 Para saber qué pasó, completa el siguiente párrafo con **por** o **para**.

Paso 2 Comparte tus respuestas con un/a compañero/a y explícale por qué usaste **por** o **para**.

Leonor, mi hermana, estuvo en mi casa (1) ________ un mes el verano pasado. Vino (2) ________ mi cumpleaños. Leonor llegó con tres maletas y una enorme caja misteriosa. El día de mi cumpleaños me dijo que (yo) tenía que estar lista (3) ________ las cinco de la tarde. Efectivamente, a las cinco en punto estaba sentada en la sala cuando vi (4) ________ la ventana a un grupo de amigos. Venían con un trío de guitarras. ¡Era una serenata (5) ________ mí! ¡Qué emoción tan grande! La serenata comenzó y Leonor bajó (6) ________ la escalera (*staircase*) con una caja. —Es (7) ________ ti —me dijo. La abrí y ¡qué sorpresa! Era una hamaca de yute (*jute hammock*) de la República Dominicana, donde Leonor había vivido (*had been*) (8) ________ varios meses. —¡Una hamaca (9) ________ el patio— exclamé— (10) ________ leer y dormir al sol! ¡Qué delicia! Y en seguida pregunté: —Pero, Leonor, ¿cómo trajiste esta hamaca desde Santo Domingo? ¿La trajiste (11) ________ avión o la mandaste (12) ________ correo? Leonor se rió y me contestó: — (13) ________ ti, querida hermana, soy capaz de hacer muchas cosas. Me la traje en avión. (14) ________ ser una caja tan grande la verdad es que no me causó tantos problemas. ¡Feliz cumpleaños!

11•22 Preguntas personales

Túrnense para contestar las siguientes preguntas.

1. ¿Por cuánto tiempo miraste las noticias en la televisión anoche?
2. ¿Por cuánto tiempo estudiaste anoche?
3. ¿Qué ves por la ventana de tu cuarto?
4. ¿Viniste a esta universidad por tus padres o por ti?
5. ¿Para quién votaste la primera vez que pudiste votar?
6. ¿Qué puede hacer un estudiante universitario para ser más activo en la política?
7. ¿Sabes si hay un centro de reciclaje por aquí? ¿Por dónde voy para llegar a él?
8. ¿Qué necesitamos hacer para evitar la contaminación?

GRAMÁTICA 6 Las preposiciones y los pronombres preposicionales

Besides the prepositions **por** and **para,** there is a variety of useful prepositions and prepositional phrases, many of which you have already been using throughout ***¡Anda!*** Study the following list to review the ones you already know and to acquaint yourself with those that may be new to you.

a	*to; at*	**después de**	*after*
a la derecha de	*to the right of*	**detrás de**	*behind*
a la izquierda de	*to the left of*	**en**	*in*
acerca de	*about*	**encima de**	*on top of*
(a)fuera de	*outside of*	**enfrente de**	*across from; facing*
al lado de	*next to*	**entre**	*among; between*
antes de	*before (time/space)*	**hasta**	*until*
cerca de	*near*	**lejos de**	*far from*
con	*with*	**para**	*for; in order to*
de	*of; from; about*	**por**	*for; through; by; because of*
debajo de	*under; underneath*	**según**	*according to*
delante de	*in front of*	**sin**	*without*
dentro de	*inside of*	**sobre**	*over; about*
desde	*from*		

El centro de reciclaje está **a la derecha del** supermercado. *The recycling center is to the right of the supermarket.*

La alcadesa va a hablar **acerca de** los problemas que tenemos con la protección del cocodrilo cubano. *The mayor is going to speak about the problems we are having with the protection of the Cuban crocodile.*

Vimos un montón de plástico **encima del** papel. *We saw a mountain of plastic on top of the paper.*

Quieren sembrar flores **enfrente del** vertedero. *They want to plant flowers in front of the dump.*

El proyecto no puede tener éxito **sin** el apoyo del gobierno local. *The project cannot be successful without the support of the local government.*

Los pronombres preposicionales

Study the list of pronouns that are used following prepositions.

Fíjate

The list of pronouns that follow prepositions is the same as the list of subject pronouns, except for the first two (*mí* is used instead of *yo*, and *ti* instead of *tú*).

mí	*me*	**nosotros/as**	*us*
ti	*you*	**vosotros/as**	*you*
él	*him*	**ellos**	*them*
ella	*her*	**ellas**	*them*
usted	*you*	**ustedes**	*you*

Para mí, es muy importante resolver el problema de la lluvia ácida. *For me, it's really important to solve the problem of acid rain.*

¿Qué candidato está sentado **enfrente de ti**? *Which candidate is seated in front of you?*

Se fueron de la huelga **sin nosotros.** *They left the strike without us.*

Trabajamos **con ellos** para proteger el medio ambiente. *We work with them to protect the environment.*

* Note that **con** has two special forms:

1. con + mí = **conmigo** *with me*
2. con + ti = **contigo** *with you*

—¿Vienes **conmigo** al discurso? *Are you coming with me to listen to the speech?*

—Sí, voy **contigo.** *Yes, I'm going with you.*

11-23 Hablando del candidato

Termina la conversación entre Celia y Manolo sobre el candidato Carlos Arroyo con los pronombres preposicionales apropiados y después comparte tu trabajo con un/a compañero/a.

CELIA: Manolo, ¿qué opinas tú de (1) ________?

MANOLO: Pues, te digo que para (2) ________ está muy claro. El señor Arroyo no piensa en (3) ________ ni en nuestros problemas.

CELIA: Sí, siempre está con las personas ricas e influyentes (*influential*), tratando de conseguir dinero de (4) ________ para su campaña.

MANOLO: También creo que vive parte del año aquí y parte en la costa. Para (5) ________ eso significa que quiere ser nuestro líder pero no quiere vivir con (6) ________. ¿Y para (7) ________, Celia?

CELIA: Creo que tienes razón. Me gusta hablar con (8) ________ porque me haces pensar en las cosas que no son tan obvias.

11•24 Descríbemelo

Juntos describan el dibujo usando por lo menos **ocho** preposiciones diferentes.

MODELO *El gato está al lado del árbol.*

1. al lado de
2. a la derecha de
3. a la izquierda de
4. cerca de
5. debajo de
6. delante de
7. detrás de
8. lejos de

11•25 Una política joven

Completa el párrafo sobre Martina, una candidata nueva en el mundo político, con las preposiciones de la lista. Después compara tu párrafo con el de un compañero.

a	antes de	con (2 veces)	de
después de	entre	sobre	sin

(1) ________________ meterse en la política Martina compartió sus ideas (2) ________________ mucha gente. (3) ________________ otras personas se reunió (4) ________________ políticos importantes y, (5) ________________ ellos, aprendió mucho (6) ________________ el bienestar, el desempleo y la inflación. (7) ________________ escuchar todo lo que tenían que decir, ella volvió (8) ________________ su casa y empezó a convertir sus ideas en discursos. El próximo paso fue buscar apoyo y dinero. Sabía perfectamente que (9) ________________ ese apoyo no iba a ser posible ganar las elecciones.

11•26 ¿Dónde están?

Juntos expliquen dónde están los siguientes lugares en El Viejo San Juan, usando siempre las preposiciones apropiadas.

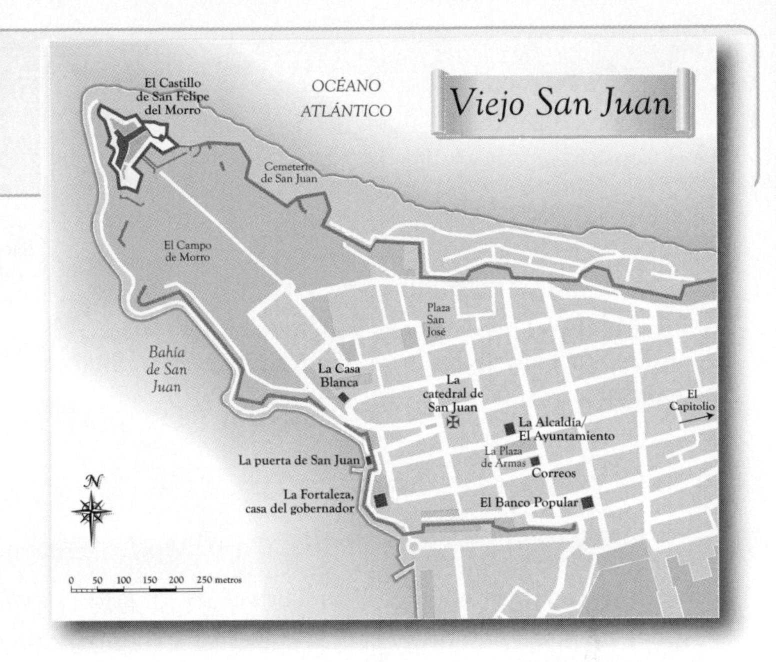

1. La Fortaleza, casa del gobernador
2. El Capitolio, edificio de las oficinas de los senadores y los representantes
3. La Plaza de Armas
4. El Castillo de San Felipe del Morro
5. La Casa Blanca, casa de la familia de Juan Ponce de León
6. La Alcaldía/El Ayuntamiento, edificio donde el alcalde tiene sus oficinas
7. Correos
8. El Banco Popular
9. La puerta de San Juan
10. La catedral de San Juan

Capítulo 3. La casa, pág. 100.

11•27 Mi casa

Descríbele a un/a compañero/a tu casa (o la casa de tus padres o de un amigo) utilizando las preposiciones apropiadas. Tu compañero/a tiene que dibujar lo que describes. Después, cambien de papel.

Estrategia

Creating visual representations of words and phrases can be a powerful learning tool.

MODELO *Mi casa tiene cinco habitaciones. Al lado de la puerta principal hay una sala. Detrás de la sala está la cocina. La cocina está a la derecha del comedor…*

11•28 ¿Con quién…?

Decide quién hace estas actividades contigo y después comparte las respuestas con un/a compañero/a.

MODELO
E1: ¿Quién… habla contigo por teléfono todos los días?
E2: *Mi madre habla conmigo por teléfono todos los días.*

¿Quién…?
1. viene a clase contigo
2. se sienta contigo en la sala de clase
3. hace las actividades de clase contigo
4. estudia contigo fuera de clase
5. almuerza o cena contigo
6. sale contigo por la tarde (para ir al cine/bar/club de baile, etc.)

El infinitivo después de preposiciones

11-37 to 11-39

In Spanish, if you need to use a verb immediately after a preposition, it must always be in the **infinitive** form. Study the following examples:

Antes de reciclar las latas debes limpiarlas.	*Before recycling the cans, you should clean them.*
Después de pisar la hormiga la niña empezó a llorar.	*After stepping on the ant, the little girl began to cry.*
Es fácil decidir **entre reciclar** y **botar.**	*It is easy to decide between recycling and throwing away.*
Necesitamos trabajar con personas de todos los países **para proteger** mejor la Tierra.	*We need to work with people from all countries in order to better protect the Earth.*
Ganaste el premio **por estar** tan interesado en el medio ambiente.	*You won the prize for being so interested in the environment.*
No podemos vivir **sin trabajar** juntos.	*We cannot live without working together.*

11•29 De viaje

Forma oraciones lógicas usando **antes de** o **después de.** Después, compártelas con un/a compañero/a.

Capítulo 10. El viaje, pág. 368.

MODELO

E1: salir/hacer la maleta

E2: *Antes de salir, necesito hacer la maleta. / Antes de salir, tengo que hacer la maleta.*

1. comprar el boleto/ir al banco
2. pasar por recepción/subir a la habitación
3. llegar al aeropuerto/mostrar el pasaporte
4. hacer la maleta/lavar la ropa
5. ir de vacaciones/dejar el gato con mis padres

Fíjate

The sentences for **11-29** can be written two ways. Start the sentence with *antes de + infinitive* or *después de + infinitive* and finish the sentence, as in *Antes de salir necesito hacer la maleta.* Or end the sentence with the prepositional phrase, e.g., *Necesito hacer la maleta antes de salir.*

11•30 Mis decisiones

Termina estas oraciones y después compártelas con un/a compañero/a.

MODELO E1: No me voy de aquí sin…

E2: *No me voy de aquí sin terminar la tarea.*

1. Necesito pensar en el futuro antes de…
2. Quiero hablar con mis padres/mi mejor amigo sobre…
3. Voy a buscar un trabajo después de…
4. Tengo que escoger entre…
5. Me quedo en este lugar hasta…
6. Después pienso ir a _____ para…

ESCUCHA

11-40 to 11-42

ESTRATEGIA **Using visual organizers**

Once you know the topic or gist of a passage, it may be helpful to mentally organize what you are about to hear. Determine if a list, chart, or diagram could be useful in helping you keep track of the information.

11•31 Antes de escuchar

Sonia Quiñones tiene un anuncio político en la radio.

1. ¿Qué es un anuncio político?
2. ¿Escuchaste alguna vez un anuncio político de un candidato en la radio o viste uno de estos anuncios en la televisión?
3. ¿Qué información contiene generalmente un anuncio de este tipo?

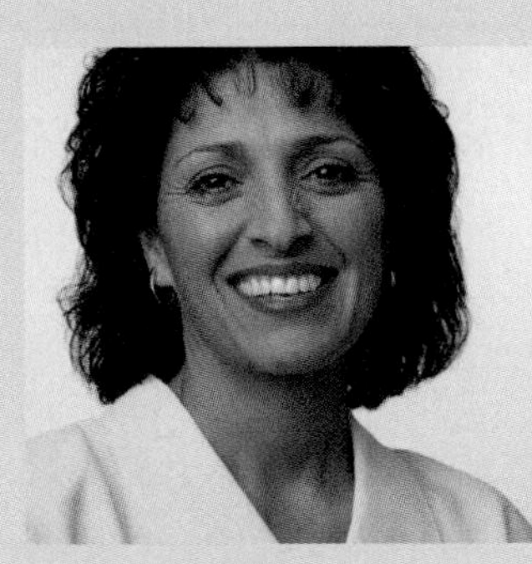

Sonia Quiñones, candidata

11•32 Al escuchar

CD 4 Track 25

Completa las siguientes actividades.

1. Escucha el anuncio para sacar la idea general.
2. Decide de qué forma quieres organizar la información (*list*, *chart*, *diagram*, etc.).
3. Escucha otra vez para completar tu diagrama o lista con la información esencial.
4. Escucha una vez más para añadir algunos detalles.

11•33 Después de escuchar

En grupos de tres o cuatro, compartan su información y juntos decidan si la Dra. Quiñones sería (*would be*) una buena alcaldesa. Expliquen.

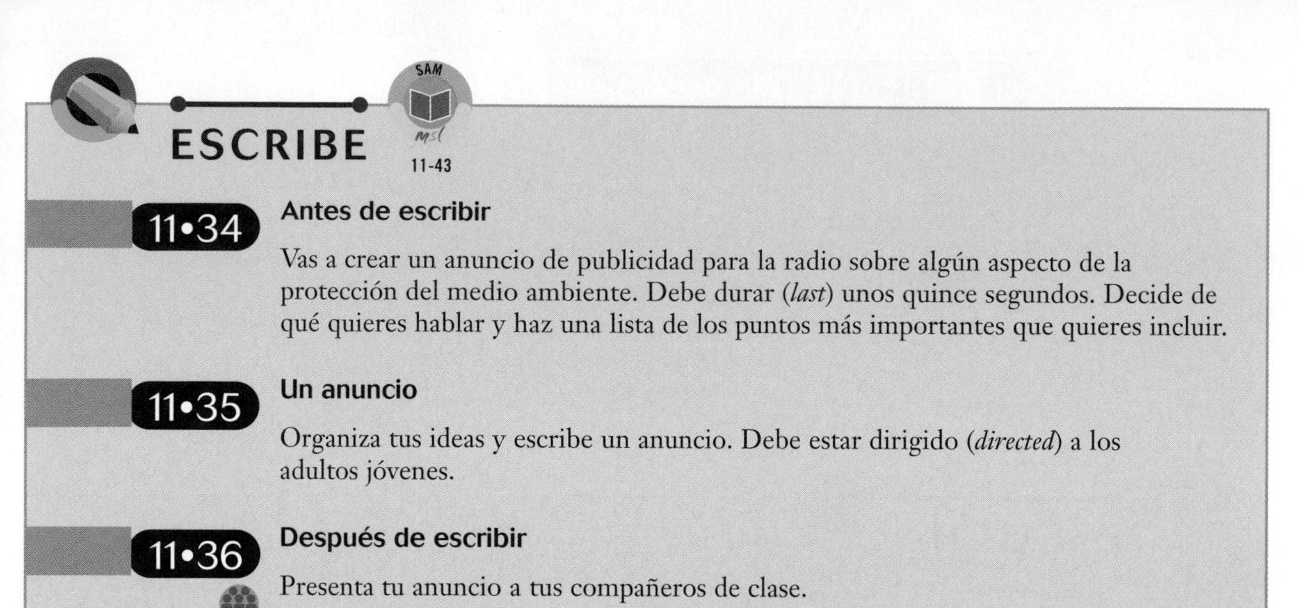

ESCRIBE

SAM 11-43

11•34 Antes de escribir

Vas a crear un anuncio de publicidad para la radio sobre algún aspecto de la protección del medio ambiente. Debe durar (*last*) unos quince segundos. Decide de qué quieres hablar y haz una lista de los puntos más importantes que quieres incluir.

11•35 Un anuncio

Organiza tus ideas y escribe un anuncio. Debe estar dirigido (*directed*) a los adultos jóvenes.

11•36 Después de escribir

Presenta tu anuncio a tus compañeros de clase.

¿Cómo andas?

Having completed the second **Comunicación,** I now can…

	Feel Confident	Need to Review
• talk about politics (p. 405)	❑	❑
• use **por, para,** and other prepositions correctly (p. 408)	❑	❑
• use the pronouns that follow prepositions correctly (p. 410)	❑	❑
• use infinitives when a verb is needed immediately after prepositions (p. 414)	❑	❑
• use visual organizers when listening (p. 415)	❑	❑
• write an ad about protecting the environment (p. 416)	❑	❑

Alicia Ortega Mujica

Cuba

CD 4
Track 26

11-44

Vistas culturales

Les presento mi país

Mi nombre es Alicia Ortega Mujica y soy de La Habana, la capital de Cuba. La mayoría de los cubanos tenemos herencia española, africana o una mezcla (*mixture*) de las dos. La influencia africana se nota sobre todo en la música cubana, especialmente en la salsa. Celia Cruz, "la reina de la salsa", siempre alababa estas raíces africanas en sus canciones. **¿Qué influencia africana se siente en la música de tu país?** Antes, la economía cubana dependía mayormente de la producción de azúcar, pero ahora el turismo es muy importante y el gobierno invierte recursos para desarrollar esa infraestructura a fin de (*in order to*) atraer más visitantes al país.

El Gran Teatro de La Habana y El Ballet Nacional de Cuba

La Plaza de la Revolución

El ajiaco, un plato típico cubano

● ALMANAQUE ●

Nombre oficial:	República de Cuba
Gobierno:	Estado/Régimen comunista
Población:	11.382.820 (2006 est.)
Idiomas:	español
Moneda:	Peso cubano (CUP) y Peso convertible (CUC)

¿Sabías que...?

- El zunzuncito, el ave más pequeño del mundo, es endémico (*common*) de Cuba. Mide menos de 6 centímetros y pesa menos de 2 gramos. Es una especie de colibrí (*hummingbird*).

PREGUNTAS

1. ¿Cuál es la composición étnica de la población cubana?
2. ¿Cuáles son las bases principales de la economía cubana?
3. ¿Qué tipo de música es popular en Cuba? ¿Es popular en otras partes del mundo?

En la Red
Amplía tus conocimientos sobre Cuba en la página web de *¡Anda!*

Víctor Manuel Báez Montalvo

CD 4 Track 27

Vistas culturales

Puerto Rico

Les presento mi país

Mi nombre es Víctor Manuel Baéz Montalvo y soy de San Juan, Puerto Rico. Soy estudiante del Recinto Universitario de Mayagüez, donde han asistido estudiantes muy distinguidos, entre ellos algunos ingenieros de NASA. El Observatorio de Arecibo, sitio del radiotelescopio de un solo plato más grande del mundo, no queda muy lejos. También se puede estudiar una naturaleza muy diversa en la isla: desde un área de cuevas del norte hasta El Yunque, bosque lluvioso del este. Puerto Rico es territorio de los Estados Unidos pero la cuestión de la independencia y la estadidad (*statehood*) se sigue debatiendo. **¿Qué opinas tú de esta cuestión?**

Vista de San Juan, la capital

El coquí, el famoso símbolo de Puerto Rico

El radiotelescopio del Observatorio de Arecibo

ALMANAQUE

Nombre oficial:	Estado Libre Asociado de Puerto Rico
Gobierno:	Territorio de los EE.UU.; Estado Libre Asociado
Población:	3.927.188 (2006 est.)
Idiomas:	español e inglés
Moneda:	Dólar estadounidense ($)

¿Sabías que...?

- Puerto Rico tiene tres bahías fosforescentes habitadas por millones de microorganismos (dinoflagelados) que emanan (*emanate*) luz cuando son alborotados (*stirred up*). Se puede observar este fenómeno por la noche. ¡Qué maravilla!

PREGUNTAS

1. ¿Qué evidencia del desarrollo avanzado de las ciencias hay en Puerto Rico?
2. Describe la variedad natural de la isla.
3. ¿Hay otros países de Centroamérica que tienen bosques lluviosos?

En la Red
Amplía tus conocimientos sobre Puerto Rico en la página web de *¡Anda!*

La República Dominicana

María Carmen Alcántara Rojas

CW eBook

CD 4 Track 28

Vistas culturales

Les presento mi país

Mi nombre es María Carmen Alcántara Rojas pero mi familia y mis amigos me llaman Mari Carmen. Soy de la República Dominicana, país que ocupa los dos tercios orientales de la isla de La Española. El país es muy montañoso y áspero (*rough*) con cuatro sistemas principales de cordilleras (*mountain ranges*). Un plato típico es *la bandera dominicana*, que consiste en arroz, habichuelas rojas, carne, ensalada y tostones (*plantain chips*)... Si nos visitas, vas a escuchar el merengue y la bachata con sus ritmos contagiosos. Otras aficiones del país son los deportes acuáticos y el béisbol. **¿Sabes qué jugadores dominicanos juegan para equipos estadounidenses?**

El merengue, el baile nacional

Vista de Santo Domingo, la capital

El Pico Duarte, en la Cordillera Central, es el pico más alto de las Antillas a unos 3.175 m.s.n.m. (10.417 pies).

ALMANAQUE

Nombre oficial:	La República Dominicana
Gobierno:	Democracia representativa
Población:	9.183.984 (2006 est.)
Idiomas:	español (oficial)
Moneda:	Peso dominicano ($RD)

¿Sabías que...?

- Cristóbal Colón descubrió la isla en su primer viaje y la nombró La Española. Santo Domingo fue la primera ciudad europea fundada en el Nuevo Mundo y hoy en día casi la mitad de la población vive ahí, en la capital.
- La mayoría de los beisbolistas hispanos en las Grandes Ligas son dominicanos.

PREGUNTAS

1. ¿Cómo es la geografía dominicana y qué tiene de especial?
2. ¿Qué es "la bandera dominicana"?
3. ¿Qué tienen en común la República Dominicana y los otros países del Caribe que hemos estudiado?

En la Red
Amplía tus conocimientos sobre la República Dominicana en la página web de *¡Anda!*

Ambiciones siniestras

11-48

11-37 Antes de leer. En el **Episodio 10** tuvimos una confesión de Cisco y surgieron más dudas sobre Lupe. Parece que tiene secretos.

Teniendo esto en cuenta, contesta las siguientes preguntas.

1. ¿Quién es Lupe?
2. ¿Cuáles pueden ser sus secretos?
3. ¿Está en peligro Marisol?

ESTRATEGIA Using visual organizers

After you have read a text, it may be useful to create a visual organizer for the information contained therein. In *¡Anda!* you have already worked with timelines, semantic maps (or web diagrams), charts, and Venn diagrams in completing activities. Try these organizers as you read.

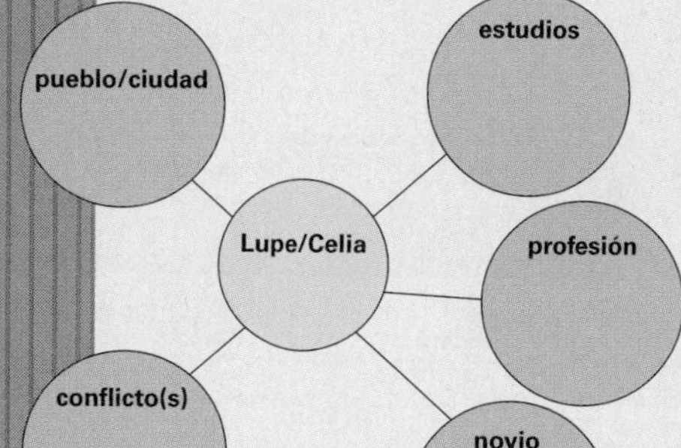

11-38 A leer. Complete the following steps.

1. Skim the episode and think about which visual organizer(s) would best summarize what you learn about Lupe.
2. Create the visual organizer(s), then read the passage carefully to gather all the information you can to complete your organizer. Finally, share it with your classmates. Did you all create the same type of visual organizer? Which one(s) proved to be most beneficial?

Celia

CD 4 Track 29

Marisol tenía una cara de terror. Lupe se quedó° mirando la pistola que tenía en la mano. Por fin la puso en la mesa y suspiró° lentamente.

stayed there
sighed

—Bueno, —dijo Lupe. —Veo que es necesario que te lo cuente todo ahora. Pensaba hacerlo, pero no en este momento. Creía que te protegía… No quise hacerle daño° a nadie, Marisol. Me mandaron aquí para ayudar.

hurt

—¿Protegerme? ¿Ayudarme? —respondió Marisol. —No sé qué creer. No sé quién eres. No sé qué quieres de mí… de nosotros.

—Marisol, no soy estudiante. Soy agente del FBI.

—¿Cómo? ¿Cómo que eres una agente? No lo comprendo —dijo Marisol. —Te ves tan joven.

—Yo sé que no he sido° honesta —respondió Lupe. —No estoy nada orgullosa de las falsas apariencias y de tantas mentiras°. A veces tengo la sensación de que mi vida es una mentira… pero después pienso en las personas a las que estoy ayudando.

I haven't been
lies

—¿A quiénes estás ayudando? —preguntó Marisol. —Estoy desilusionada… muy desilusionada.

—Escuche —imploró Lupe.

—¿Escuche? —preguntó Marisol, incrédula. —¿Ahora me tratas de «usted»? ¡Éramos amigas! Confiaba en ti.

—Bueno, Marisol. *Te* lo cuento todo pero tienes que dejarme hablar —dijo Lupe.

—Te escucho… ojalá que sea la verdad —respondió Marisol con voz desesperada.

Entonces se sentaron juntas y Lupe empezó a explicárselo todo:

—Mi nombre verdadero es Celia Cortez y soy de Los Ángeles. Me gradué hace ocho años de la Universidad de Georgetown con una especialidad en ciencias políticas. Mientras estaba en el último año, conocí a un hombre increíble y me enamoré de él en seguida. Era el hombre más inteligente, más atractivo, más interesante que había conocido jamás°. Tenía un trabajo muy bueno con el gobierno federal. Era mi mejor amigo… Decidimos casarnos en cuanto me graduara°. Una noche dábamos un paseo por el centro de Washington cuando me dijo que tenía que contarme algo muy importante, que no había sido° totalmente honesto conmigo. Me dijo entonces que trabajaba para el FBI, no para el Departamento del Estado como yo pensaba. Le pregunté por qué decidió contármelo todo aquella noche y me respondió que era porque estaba involucrado° en un trabajo que requería que saliera° de Washington por varias semanas. Me explicó que no iba a poder estar en contacto conmigo mientras tanto. Sin preguntar, imaginaba que iba encubierto°. Nunca pensé en el peligro que le podía esperar. Yo era muy joven y realmente no sabía nada de su trabajo. Dos semanas después recibí la llamada que cambió mi vida por completo— mi amor estaba muerto. Lo mataron. Yo estaba perdida…

that I had ever met
as soon as I graduated
he had not been
involved
required that he leave
undercover

—Ay Lupe… perdón, Celia —respondió Marisol. —Lo siento. ¿Qué hiciste entonces?

—Me gradué y fui a trabajar para la misma agencia para conocer mejor quién era él, para poder saber más de su vida y para sentirme más unida a él. Eso fue, como te dije, hace ocho años.

Sonó el teléfono celular de Celia. Contestó y se quedó escuchando sin decir nada. Cortó y le dijo a Marisol:

—Perdona. Es muy importante que hable con esta persona. Tengo que salir ahora pero después, vuelvo para contestar tus preguntas. Y no te preocupes por Eduardo y Alejandra. Todo eso fue una mentira también.

11-39 **Después de leer.** Contesta las preguntas.

1. ¿Cómo se llama Lupe en realidad?
2. ¿De dónde es?
3. ¿Dónde estudió y cuál era su especialidad?
4. ¿Cuál es su trabajo ahora?
5. ¿Cuándo y dónde conoció a su novio?
6. ¿Qué le pasó al novio?
7. ¿Qué hizo ella después?
8. ¿Cómo termina la lectura?

11-49 to 11-50

video

11-40 **Antes del video.** ¿Qué crees que sabe Celia del Sr. Verdugo? ¿De Eduardo y Alejandra? ¿Quién llama a Celia? ¿Adónde va ella? En la segunda parte del episodio vas a encontrar todas las respuestas, y más.

Buenas tardes. Soy la agente Celia Cortez.

Llegamos demasiado tarde. Todos se fueron.

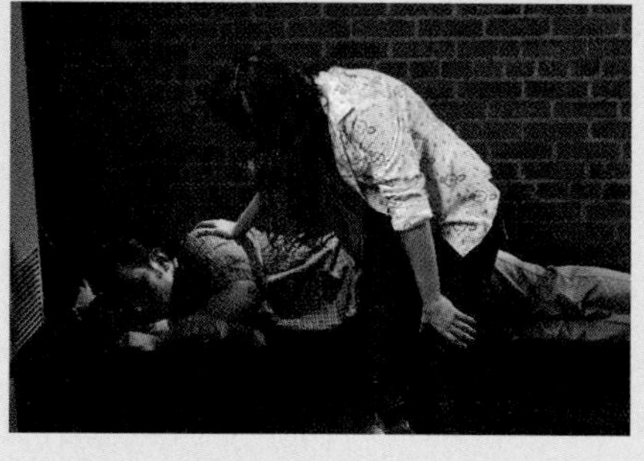

Eduardo, ¿estás bien?

Episodio 11

«El desenlace»

Relájate y disfruta el video.

11-41 **Después del video.** Contesta las preguntas.

1. ¿Dónde estaba Celia cuando empezó el episodio del video?
2. ¿Adónde fueron?
3. ¿A quién(es) encontraron allí?
4. ¿Qué les pasó a Eduardo y Alejandra cuando desaparecieron?
5. ¿Quién escribió los rompecabezas? ¿Por qué?
6. ¿Cómo termina **Ambiciones siniestras?**

Y por fin, ¿cómo andas?

Having completed this chapter, I now can…

	Feel Confident	Need to review
Comunicación		
• talk about animals and their habitats (pp. 392–393)	❑	❑
• pronounce words applying appropriate word stress and know when written accents are needed (p. 393)	❑	❑
• discuss matters related to the environment (p. 396)	❑	❑
• use the subjunctive correctly with fixed expressions to communicate opinion, doubt, probability, and wishes (p. 398)	❑	❑
• talk about politics (p. 405)	❑	❑
• use **por** and **para** with more accuracy (p. 408)	❑	❑
• speak and write using a variety of prepositions (p. 410)	❑	❑
• use visual organizers when listening (p. 415)	❑	❑
• write an ad about protecting the environment (p. 416)	❑	❑
Cultura		
• talk about El Yunque (p. 398)	❑	❑
• talk about some aspects of political history and current politics in the Hispanic world (p. 407)	❑	❑
• share at least two interesting facts about each country: Cuba, Puerto Rico, and the Dominican Republic (pp. 417–419)	❑	❑
Ambiciones siniestras		
• use visual organizers to aid in comprehension of a reading passage (p. 420)	❑	❑
• explain the truth about Lupe (p. 420)	❑	❑
• explain what happened to Eduardo and Alejandra and why (p. 422)	❑	❑

VOCABULARIO ACTIVO

CD 4
Tracks 30–40

Unos animales	*Some animals*
el caballo	*horse*
el cerdo	*pig*
el conejo	*rabbit*
el elefante	*elephant*
la gallina	*chicken, hen*
el gato	*cat*
la hormiga	*ant*
el insecto	*insect*
el león	*lion*
la mosca	*fly*
el mosquito	*mosquito*
el oso	*bear*
el pájaro	*bird*
el perro	*dog*
el pez (*pl.*, los peces)	*fish*
la rana	*frog*
la rata	*rat*
el ratón	*mouse*
la serpiente	*snake*
el toro	*bull*
la vaca	*cow*

Unos verbos	*Some verbs*
cuidar	*to take care of*
montar (a caballo)	*to ride a horse*
preocuparse por	*to worry about; to concern oneself with*

Las cuestiones políticas	*Political issues*
el bienestar	*well-being; welfare*
la defensa	*defense*
la delincuencia	*crime*
el desempleo	*unemployment*
la deuda (externa)	*(foreign) debt*
el impuesto	*tax*
la inflación	*inflation*

Otras palabras útiles	*Other useful words*
un animal doméstico	*a domesticated animal; pet*
un animal en peligro de extinción	*an endangered species*
un animal salvaje	*a wild animal*
el árbol	*tree*
el bosque	*forest*
la cueva	*cave*
la finca	*farm*
la granja	*farm*
el hoyo	*hole*
el lago	*lake*
la montaña	*mountain*
el océano	*ocean*
peligroso/a	*dangerous*
el río	*river*
la selva	*jungle*

El medio ambiente	*The environment*
el aluminio	*aluminum*
la botella	*bottle*
la caja (de cartón)	*(cardboard) box*
la contaminación	*pollution*
el derrame de petróleo	*oil spill*
el huracán	*hurricane*
el incendio	*fire*
la inundación	*flood*
la lata	*can*
el papel	*paper*
el periódico	*newspaper*
el plástico	*plastic*
el sunami	*tsunami*
el terremoto	*earthquake*
la tormenta	*storm*
el tornado	*tornado*
el vidrio	*glass*

Unos verbos *Some verbs*

apoyar	*to support*
botar	*to throw away*
combatir	*to fight; to combat*
contaminar	*to pollute*
cuidar	*to take care of*
elegir	*to elect*
estar en huelga	*to be on strike*
evitar	*to avoid*
hacer daño	*to (do) damage; to harm*
llevar a cabo	*to carry out*
luchar	*to fight; to combat*
matar	*to kill*
meterse en política	*to get involved in politics*
plantar	*to plant*
preocuparse por	*to worry about; to concern oneself with*
proteger	*to protect*
reciclar	*to recycle*
reforestar	*to reforest*
rehusar	*to refuse*
resolver (o → ue)	*to resolve*
sembrar (e → ie)	*to sow*
volver	*to return*
votar	*to vote*

La política *Politics*

el alcalde/la alcaldesa	*mayor*
el/la candidato/a	*candidate*
el/la dictador/a	*dictator*
el/la diputado/a	*deputy; representative*
el/la gobernador/a	*governor*
la guerra	*war*
la huelga	*strike*
el/la presidente/a	*president*
el rey/la reina	*king/queen*
el/la senador/a	*senator*

Las preposiciones *Prepositions*

See page 410.

Las administraciones y los regímenes *Administrations and regimes*

el congreso	*congress*
la democracia	*democracy*
la dictadura	*dictatorship*
el estado	*state*
el gobierno	*government*
la ley	*law*
la monarquía	*monarchy*
la presidencia	*presidency*
la provincia	*province*
la región	*region*
el senado	*senate*

Las elecciones *Elections*

la campaña	*campaign*
el discurso	*speech*
la encuesta	*survey; poll*
el partido político	*political party*
el voto	*vote*

Otras palabras útiles *Other useful words*

el aire	*air*
la basura	*garbage*
la calidad	*quality*
la capa de ozono	*ozone layer*
el cielo	*sky; heaven*
el desastre	*disaster*
la destrucción	*destruction*
la ecología	*ecology*
el efecto invernadero	*global warming*
la lluvia ácida	*acid rain*
la naturaleza	*nature*
el planeta	*planet*
puro/a	*pure*
el recurso natural	*natural resource*
la selva tropical	*jungle; (tropical) rain forest*
la Tierra	*Earth*
la tierra	*land; soil*
la tragedia	*tragedy*
el vertedero	*dump*
vivo/a	*alive; living*

12

Y por fin, ¡lo sé!

OBJETIVOS

Comunicación	• To convey ideas about past experiences and your daily routine • To share preferences regarding food, clothing, and other topics • To make requests and give advice using commands • To express desires and opinions on a variety of topics • To describe your travel experiences • To express ideas on topics such as health, animals, the environment, and politics
Cultura	• To share information about Chile, Paraguay, Argentina, Uruguay, Perú, Bolivia, Ecuador, Venezuela, Colombia, Cuba, Puerto Rico, and La República Dominicana • To compare and contrast the countries you learned about in **Capítulos 7–11**
Ambiciones siniestras	• To go behind the scenes of **Ambiciones siniestras**

This final chapter is designed for you to see just how much Spanish you have acquired thus far. The *major points* of **Capítulos 7–11** are recycled in this chapter. No new vocabulary is presented.

All learners are different in terms of what they have mastered and what they still need to practice. Take the time with this chapter to determine what you feel confident with, and what you personally need to work on. And remember, language learning is a process. Like any skill, learning Spanish requires practice, review of the basics, and then more practice!

Before we begin revisiting the important grammar concepts, go to the end of each chapter, to the **Vocabulario activo** summary sections, and review the vocabulary that you have learned. Doing so now will help you successfully and creatively complete the following recycling activities. Consult the **Vocabulario activo** pages as needed as you progress through this chapter.

Organizing Your Review

12-1 to 12-41

There are processes used by successful language learners for reviewing a world language. What follows are tips that can help you organize your review. There is no one correct way, but these are some suggestions that will best utilize your time and energy.

1 Reviewing Strategies

1. Make a list of the *major* topics you have studied and need to review, dividing them into categories: *vocabulary, grammar,* and *culture.* These are the topics where you need to focus the majority of your time and energy.

   Note: The two-page chapter openers can help you determine the *major* topics.
2. Allocate a minimum of an hour each day over a period of days to review. Budget the majority of your time with the major topics. After beginning with the major grammar and vocabulary topics, review the secondary/supporting grammar topics and the culture. Cramming the night before a test is *not* an effective way to review and retain information.
3. Many educational researchers suggest that you start your review with the most recent chapter, or for this review, **Capítulo 11.** The most recent chapter is the freshest in your mind, you tend to remember the concepts better, and you will experience quick success in your review.
4. Spend the most amount of time on concepts where you determine *you* need to improve. Revisit the self-assessment tools from **Y por fin, ¿cómo andas?** in each chapter to see how you rated yourself. Those tools are designed to help you become good at self-assessing what *you* need to work on the most.

2 Reviewing Grammar

1. When reviewing grammar, begin with the **major** points, that is, begin with the *preterit, imperfect, pronouns (direct, indirect, and reflexive), commands,* and the *subjunctive*. After feeling confident using the major grammar points correctly, then proceed with the additional grammar points and review them.
2. Good ways to review include redoing activities in your textbook, redoing activities in your **Student Activities Manual**, and (re)doing activities on your *¡Anda!* web site.

3 Reviewing Vocabulary

1. When studying vocabulary, it is usually most helpful to look at the English word, and then say or write the word in Spanish. Make a special list of words that are difficult for you to remember, writing them in a small notebook. Pull out the notebook every time you have a few minutes (in between classes, waiting in line at the grocery store, etc.) to review the words. The **Vocabulario activo** pages at the end of each chapter will help you organize the most important words of each chapter.
2. Saying vocabulary (which includes verbs) out loud helps you retain the words better and incorporate them into your personal active vocabulary.

4 Overall Review Technique

1. Get together with someone with whom you can practice speaking Spanish. It is always good to structure the oral practice. One way of doing this is to utilize the composite art pictures from *¡Anda!* and say as many things as you can about each picture. Have a friendly challenge to see who can make more complete sentences or create the longest story about the pictures. You can also structure the practice by speaking solely in the past, for example, or practicing using object pronouns as you speak. This will help you build your confidence and practice stringing sentences together to speak in paragraphs.
2. Yes, it is important for you to know "mechanical" pieces of information such as verb endings, or how to take a sentence and replace the direct object with a pronoun. *But,* it is *much more important* for you to be able to take those mechanical pieces of information and put them all together, creating meaningful and creative samples of your speaking and writing on the themes of **Capítulos 7–11.** Also remember that **Capítulos 7–11** are built upon previous knowledge that you acquired in the beginning chapters of *¡Anda!*
3. You are on the road to success if you can demonstrate that you can speak and write in paragraphs that express the present, past, and future tenses. Along with expressing ideas in the three major time frames, it is important to demonstrate your richness of language, employing a wide variety of verbs and other words. Keep up the good work!

Comunicación

Estrategia

Before beginning each activity, make sure that you have reviewed carefully the concepts in each given chapter so that you are able to move through the activities seamlessly as you put it all together.

12-1 ¡Fiesta!

Capítulo 7

Decidieron tener una fiesta y tienen que trabajar mucho para prepararlo todo. Organícense siguiendo el modelo.

MODELO

¿Comprar / tú / las bebidas?

E1: *¿Compraste las bebidas?*

E2: *Sí, las compré ayer.*

1. ¿Pedir / Uds. / los mariscos?
2. ¿Preparar / tu compañero / los perros calientes?
3. ¿Comprar / tu amigo / el pastel?
4. ¿Limpiar / tú / la sala?
5. ¿Lavar / Uds. / los manteles (*tablecloths*)?
6. ¿Encontrar / Manuel y Manuela / las servilletas?
7. ¿Organizar / Jorge / los CD?
8. ¿Invitar / tú / al profesor?

12-2 Después de la fiesta

¡La fiesta de la actividad **12-1** fue un éxito! Describan lo que pasó en la fiesta y qué hicieron cuando se fueron los invitados. Sean creativos y usen por lo menos **siete** oraciones.

MODELO *¡Nuestra fiesta fue un éxito! Vinieron muchos invitados. La gente bailó, comió y se divirtió mucho. Escuchamos música latina y rock. Después, tuvimos que pasar la aspiradora…*

12-3 La semana pasada

Túrnense para describir qué hicieron y adónde fueron la semana pasada, usando por lo menos **siete** oraciones en el pretérito con verbos diferentes.

l	m	m	j	v	s	d
estudiar, ver una película	ir al médico	ir al concierto de Juanes			ir al café Chulo	

MODELO *La semana pasada hice muchas cosas. Por ejemplo, vi una película en la televisión. Estudié mucho también. Conduje a la universidad el martes en vez de tomar el autobús porque tuve que ir al médico por la tarde. El miércoles por la noche mi amigo y yo fuimos al concierto de Juanes. Dormí muy poco toda la semana…*

12-4 La boda del siglo

Capítulo 8

David y Adriana se casan. Tu compañero/a y tú están invitados y están planeando cómo vestirse. Túrnense para hablar del evento siguiendo el modelo.

MODELO tú / prestar / a mí / pantalones / amarillo

E1: *¿Me prestas tus pantalones amarillos?*

E2: *Sí, te los presto. / No, no te los presto.*

1. tú / ponerse / zapatos / negro
2. tú / prestar / a Julieta / blusa / azul / seda
3. ellas / prestar / a Mariela / falda / corto / atrevido
4. Raúl y Rafa / prestar / a Jorge / el cinturón / de cuero / negro
5. Ud. / prestar / a Jaime / coche / nuevo

12-5 La recomendación fue...

¿Cuáles fueron sus recomendaciones? Túrnense para formar preguntas y contestar según el modelo.

MODELO tú / las blusas de Donna Karan (a tus primas)

E1: *¿Les recomendaste las blusas de Donna Karan a tus primas?*

E2: *No, no se las recomendé.*

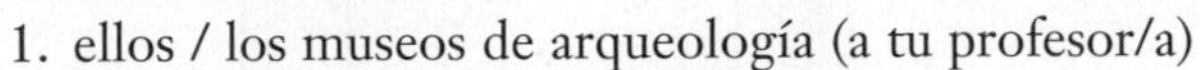

1. ellos / los museos de arqueología (a tu profesor/a)
2. tú / el café Starbucks (a tus padres)
3. tu hermano / el hotel Ritz (a su amiga que no tiene dinero)
4. nosotros / la música de Shakira (a unos compañeros)
5. yo / la película *Shrek* (a mis primos de cinco años)
6. Uds. / las novelas de Gabriel García Márquez (a sus tíos)
7. tú / la clase de español (a tu mejor amigo/a)

Estrategia

You can elaborate on your answers as to why you recommended or did not recommend something by adding ***porque*** and a short explanation. In the model, you could say *No, no se las recomendé porque son muy caras.*

12-6 Una encuesta

Usa las siguientes expresiones para crear una encuesta (*survey*) de **diez** preguntas. Hazles las preguntas a diez personas diferentes y comparte tus resultados con la clase.

PREGUNTA	ME ENCANTA(N)	ME MOLESTA(N)	ME IMPORTA(N)	ME HACE(N) FALTA	ME FASCINA(N)
¿Te gustan los animales salvajes? ¿Cuáles?					*Erika: Me fascinan los tigres.*
¿Te gusta la ropa elegante?		*Alex: Prefiero la ropa informal.*			

12-7 ¿Qué hiciste ayer?

Escribe un párrafo sobre lo que hiciste ayer. Incluye por lo menos **diez** actividades usando un mínimo de **siete** verbos reflexivos. Después, léeselo a un/a compañero/a.

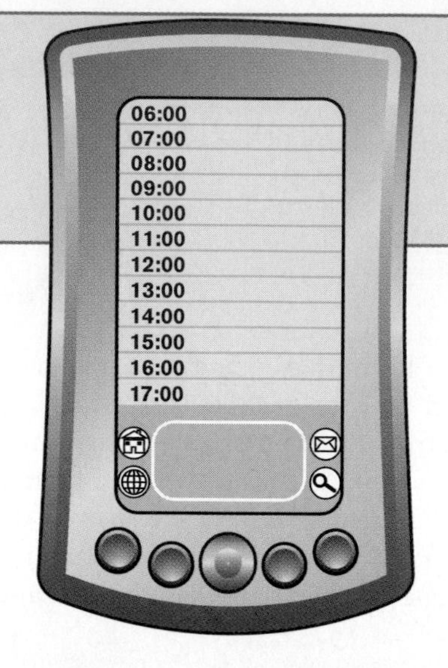

MODELO *Ayer me levanté a las seis de la mañana. Me duché en tres minutos. Me puse los pantalones rojos con rayas blancas…*

12-8 A conocerte más aún

Cuando tenías quince años, ¿qué hacías en las siguientes situaciones?

Paso 1 Contesta las preguntas.

MODELO E1: ¿Qué hacías por las tardes, después de salir del colegio?
E2: *Yo jugaba al tenis. ¿Qué hacías tú?*
E1: *Hacía la tarea y ayudaba a mi madre con los quehaceres de la casa.*

1. ¿Qué te ponías cuando salías con esa "persona especial"?
2. Antes de dormirte, ¿pensabas en tu día?
3. ¿Tenías un perro?
4. ¿Cómo te divertías?
5. ¿Siempre te acordabas de hacer toda la tarea?
6. Si tenías tiempo, ¿con quién(es) te reunías?
7. ¿Dónde te gustaba sentarte en el cine, adelante o atrás?
8. ¿Qué querías ser de mayor?
9. ¿En qué situaciones te ponías nervioso/a?
10. ¿Cuándo te sentías feliz?

Estrategia

Being a good listener is an important life skill. Repeating what your classmate said gives you practice in demonstrating how well you listened.

Paso 2 Escucha las respuestas de tu compañero/a. ¿Cuántas preguntas contestaron Uds. de manera similar? ¿De manera diferente?

12-9 Mi primera casa

¿Cómo era tu primera casa o la de un/a amigo/a de tu infancia? Descríbesela a un/a compañero/a en por lo menos **diez** oraciones incluyendo todos los detalles posibles (muebles, colores, etc.).

MODELO *Mi primera casa estaba en una ciudad pequeña. Tenía dos dormitorios. La cocina era amarilla. El comedor y la sala eran pequeños. Tenía solamente* (only) *un baño…*

Capítulo 9

12-10 Un diálogo

Imaginen que trabajan como voluntarios con un médico. Creen un diálogo entre el médico y el paciente con respecto a sus síntomas y su tratamiento. Escriban por lo menos **catorce** oraciones.

MODELO
E1 (MÉDICO): *¿Cómo está? ¿Qué le duele?*
E2 (PACIENTE): *Creo que tengo catarro o un virus. Me duele todo.*
E1: *¿Tiene fiebre? ¿Tose? ¿Estornuda?*
E2: *No, no tengo fiebre pero sí tengo tos. Y sí, estornudo mucho. ¡También me quemé!*
E1: *¿Se quemó? ¿Cómo?*
E2: …

12-11 ¡Me enfermé!

¿Cuándo fue la última vez que se enfermaron? ¿Qué hicieron? ¿Qué pasó?

Paso 1 Descríbele a un/a compañero/a tu última enfermedad en por lo menos **diez** oraciones.

MODELO *Hace dos semanas que me enfermé. Tuve la gripe y guardé cama por una semana. Mi madre me llevó al médico porque me dolía el cuerpo y tenía una fiebre…*

Paso 2 Describe en tus propias (*own*) palabras la enfermedad de tu compañero/a de clase.

Estrategia

It is rare when people remember *everything* that they hear! It is important that you feel comfortable asking someone to repeat information or asking for clarification.

12•12 Los días de vacaciones

Capítulo 10

¿Qué hiciste durante las últimas vacaciones? Descríbele a tu compañero/a, en por lo menos **diez** oraciones y usando una variedad de verbos y vocabulario, tus últimas vacaciones. Incluye las siguientes palabras:

todos los días	todas las noches	generalmente	normalmente
un día	una vez	una mañana	nunca

MODELO *Durante las últimas vacaciones nosotros fuimos a Punta Cana. Fue la primera vez que visitamos la República Dominicana. Todos los días íbamos a la playa. Allí nadábamos…*

12•13 Mis vacaciones favoritas

¿Adónde fuiste y cómo fueron tus vacaciones favoritas? Descríbeselas a un/a compañero/a en por lo menos **siete** oraciones usando el pretérito y una variedad de verbos.

MODELO *Mis vacaciones en Argentina fueron mis mejores vacaciones. Fuimos a la playa, donde mi familia y yo anduvimos muchas horas. Nadé en el océano…*

12•14 Y también...

Imagina que tienes un hijo y que, por primera vez, él va a salir solo con sus amigos y se va a llevar el coche. ¿Qué le aconsejas? Haz mandatos familiares con los siguientes verbos.

MODELO E1: leer / el manual

E2: *Lee el manual.*

1. conducir/con cuidado
2. llevar/el permiso
3. tener cuidado/los peatones
4. llenar el tanque/gasolina
5. limpiar/parabrisas
6. no perder/llaves
7. no abrir/ventanas/si llueve
8. no estacionarse/lugares prohibidos
9. no doblar a la izquierda/sin mirar
10. no comer ni beber/en el coche

12•15 ¡Me molestas!

¿En tu vida hay alguien que te está volviendo loco/a (*is driving you crazy*)? Dile lo que debe y no debe hacer. Puedes usar las palabras y expresiones de la lista y otras también. ¡Sé creativo!

MODELO *Raúl, por favor, ¡me estás volviendo loca! Primero, guarda tu comida en el refrigerador, no la pongas en el sofá. Segundo, ¡no estornudes encima de la comida! Ponte el abrigo porque hace frío. Cuídate, por favor...*

Estrategia

Organize your thoughts in chronological order, and use transitions in your paragraphs. Consider words like *primero, segundo, tercero, próximo, después*, and *finalmente*.

guardar tu comida	tener más paciencia
no dejar la ropa sucia en el piso	no estornudar
lavar los platos	mejorarte
sacar la basura	cuidarte
no invitar siempre a tus amigos	no ponerte mi ropa

12•16 Estación de servicio

Están en una gasolinera. Túrnense para decirle al empleado (*attendant*) lo que necesitan.

MODELO *Ponga aire en las llantas, por favor. También, abra el baúl, por favor. Yo no puedo abrirlo...*

12•17 ¡Por fin!

¡Éste es el momento que esperabas! ¡Por fin ustedes son los profesores de español! Túrnense para decirles a sus estudiantes por lo menos **ocho** cosas que deben o no deben hacer. ¡Sean creativos!

MODELO *Hagan la tarea para mañana. También, hablen en español durante toda la clase…*

12•18 Comparando

Estás planeando unas vacaciones. Dile a tu compañero/a cuáles son, en tu opinión, los mejores y los peores servicios y destinos. Usa comparaciones y superlativos. Crea por lo menos **diez** oraciones.

MODELO *El aeropuerto de Austin es más pequeño que el aeropuerto de Dallas pero en mi opinión es mejor porque no es muy grande. Para mí, la agencia Travel Experts es la mejor porque saben preparar unos viajes estupendos. Por ejemplo, la playa de Ixtapa en México es tan bonita como la playa de Cancún, y los hoteles no cuestan tanto como los hoteles de Cancún…*

Capítulo 11

12•19 Mis deberes

Siempre hay algo que podemos hacer para mejorarnos. Di por lo menos **diez** cosas que debes hacer ahora o que te propones (*you intend*) hacer en el futuro. Usa el subjuntivo cuando sea necesario.

MODELO *Primero, es necesario que estudie más en el futuro. También es importante que no coma tanto chocolate pero es dudoso que pueda evitarlo. Entonces, es importante que compre cosas saludables. Pero, ¡qué lástima! ¡Me fascina el chocolate! Pues, como me gusta tanto, es importante que haga más ejercicio. ¡Es una lástima que no me guste hacerlo!*

12·20 Mi casa ideal

¿Cómo esperas que sea tu casa en diez años?

Paso 1 Descríbesela a un/a compañero/a con todo detalle (cuartos, muebles, colores, etc.). Incluye por lo menos **cinco** preposiciones diferentes en la descripción.

MODELO *Espero que mi casa tenga cinco habitaciones. Al lado de la puerta quiero que haya una sala y una cocina detrás de la sala. ¡Ojalá que tenga una cocina muy grande!*

Estrategia

You may want to draw the floor plan of your house and label the rooms. That way, it will be easier to talk about where each room is located in relation to other rooms. When working with a partner, you might want to draw your partner's house as you hear it described, taking note of the prepositions he/she has mentioned.

Paso 2 Repite lo que tu compañero/a te dijo. Es importante que uses y practiques las preposiciones.

Un poco de todo

12·21 Nuestro medio ambiente y más aún

Creen juntos un reportaje (*report*) para la televisión sobre uno de los siguientes temas.

TEMAS

1. el medio ambiente
2. la política y cuestiones políticas
3. el tiempo
4. el arte, los deportes y otros eventos

12-22 ¿Cómo eres?

Conoces un poco a los estudiantes de los países que estudiamos en los capítulos anteriores. ¿Qué más quieres saber de ellos? Escribe por lo menos **diez** preguntas que quieres hacerles. Usa el pretérito, el imperfecto y el subjuntivo.

Gino Breschi Arteaga

Mirta Beatriz Chávez Villalba

Marina Claudia Luschini Ojeda

Francisco Tomás Bacigalupe Bustamente

Milagros Alejandra Romero Zárate

Raúl Eduardo Loza Arce

María Yolanda Palacios Mena

Rosa María Gutiérrez Murcia

Victor Luis González Martínez

Alicia Ortega Mujica

Victor Manuel Báez Montalvo

María Carmen Alcántara Rojas

MODELO
1. *¿Qué estudiaste el semestre pasado?*
2. *¿Adónde fuiste el verano pasado?*
3. *¿Es posible que viajes este verano?*
4. ...

12·23 ¿Sabías que...?

Completa estas actividades.

Paso 1 Escribe una o dos cosas interesantes que no sabías antes pero que aprendiste sobre cada uno de los siguientes países.

CHILE	PARAGUAY	ARGENTINA	URUGUAY
1.	1.	1.	1.
2.	2.	2.	2.

PERÚ	BOLIVIA	ECUADOR	COLOMBIA
1.	1.	1.	1.
2.	2.	2.	2.

VENEZUELA	CUBA	LA REPÚBLICA DOMINICANA	PUERTO RICO
1.	1.	1.	1.
2.	2.	2.	2.

Paso 2 Compara la información con el lugar donde tú vives, el estado o el país. ¿Qué cosas son similares? ¿Qué diferencias hay?

12•24 ¿Y de postre?

Vas a preparar una cena latina para tus amigos con platos representativos de varios países. Selecciona por lo menos **tres** platos y algo para beber. Indica el país de origen de cada plato y los ingredientes. Si varios países comparten el plato, menciónalos también.

Ropa vieja de Cuba

Una parrillada argentina

12•25 Los símbolos nacionales

Escoge **tres** países distintos y un símbolo para cada uno de ellos. Describe estos símbolos nacionales y habla de cómo y por qué son representativos del país. Después, haz una comparación entre los países y sus símbolos.

12•26 ¿El ecoturismo o una expedición científica?

¡Qué suerte! Recibiste la distinción de ser el/la mejor estudiante de español y puedes elegir entre un viaje de ecoturismo o una expedición antropológica. Piensa en lo que aprendiste de cada país y decide adónde quieres ir para divertirte e investigar más. Después, describe el lugar específico que vas a visitar y di por qué, cómo, cuándo, etc. Si hay dos países con lugares similares, compáralos e indica por qué seleccionaste uno en particular.

Episodio 12

12•27 Tus propias ambiciones siniestras

¡Ahora te toca a ti! Puedes seleccionar entre las siguientes actividades basadas en **Ambiciones siniestras.**

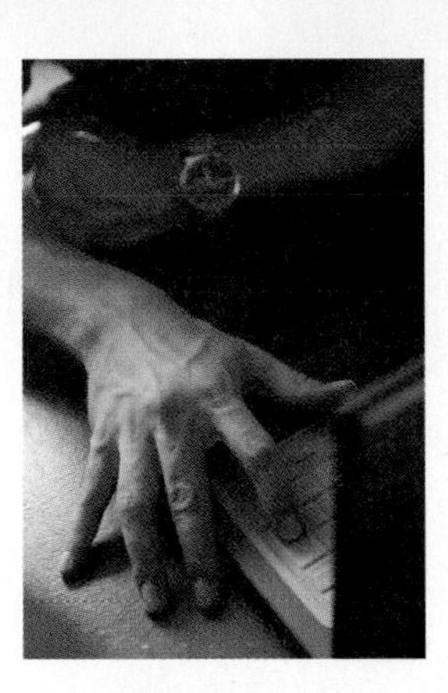

1. Imagina que eres Oprah o Cristina y que tienes la oportunidad de entrevistar a los actores de **Ambiciones siniestras.** Prepara la entrevista con un/a compañero/a.

2. Escribe tu propia versión reducida de **Ambiciones siniestras.** ¿Termina igual que el original? Compara tu versión con la de un/a compañero/a.

3. Escribe y filma **Ambiciones siniestras II.** Al final, ¿qué pasa con el Sr. Verdugo? Preséntale tu película a la clase.

Y por fin, ¿cómo andas?

Having completed this chapter, I now can…

	Feel Confident	Need to Review
Comunicación		
• convey ideas about past experiences and my daily routine	❑	❑
• share my preferences regarding food, clothing, and other topics	❑	❑
• make requests and give advice using commands	❑	❑
• express desires and opinions on a variety of topics	❑	❑
• describe my travels and the trips of others	❑	❑
• express ideas on topics such as health, animals, the environment, and politics	❑	❑
Cultura		
• share information about Chile, Paraguay, Argentina, Uruguay, Perú, Bolivia, Ecuador, Venezuela, Colombia, Cuba, Puerto Rico, and La República Dominicana	❑	❑
• compare and contrast many characteristics of the countries I learned about in **Capítulos 7–11**	❑	❑

APPENDIX 1

CAPÍTULO PRELIMINAR A

12. Gustar

1. To say you like or dislike one thing, what form of **gustar** do you use?
   gusta
2. To say you like or dislike more than one thing, what form of **gustar** do you use?
   gustan

CAPÍTULO 2

9. El verbo *gustar*

1. To say you like or dislike one thing, what form of **gustar** do you use?
   gusta
2. To say you like or dislike more than one thing, what form of **gustar** do you use?
   gustan
3. Which words in the examples mean *I?* **(Me)** *You?* **(Te)** *He/she?* **(le)**
4. If a verb is needed after gusta/gustan, what form of the verb do you use?
   the infinitive form of the verb

CAPÍTULO 4

4. Los verbos con cambio de raíz

1. Which verb forms look like the infinitive **cerrar**?
   nosotros, vosotros
2. Which verb forms have a spelling change that differs from the infinitive **cerrar**?
   yo, tú, él, ella, usted, ellos, ellas, ustedes.

1. Which verb forms look like the infinitive **pedir**?
   nosotros, vosotros
2. Which verb forms have a spelling change that differs from the infinitive **pedir**?
   yo, tú, él, ella, usted, ellos, ellas, ustedes.

1. Which verb forms look like the infinitive **encontrar**?
   nosotros, vosotros
2. Which verb forms have a spelling change that differs from the infinitive **encontrar**?
   yo, tú, él, ella, usted, ellos, ellas, ustedes.

1. Which verb forms look like the infinitive **jugar**?
   nosotros, vosotros
2. Which verb forms have a spelling change that differs from the infinitive **jugar**?
   yo, tú, él, ella, usted, ellos, ellas, ustedes.
3. Why does **jugar** not belong with the verbs like **encontrar**?
   because the change is *u* → *ue*, not *o* → *ue* like *encontrar*.

To summarize…

1. What is a rule that you can make regarding all four groups (**e → ie, e → i, o → ue,** and **u → ue**) of stem-changing verbs and their forms?
   ***Nosotros/vosotros* look like the infinitive. All the other forms have the spelling change.**
2. With what group of stem-changing verbs would you put **querer**?
   e → ie
3. With what group of stem-changing verbs would you put the following verbs:
   demostrar *to demonstrate* **o → ue**
   devolver *to return (an object)* **o → ue**
   encerrar *to enclose* **e → ie**
   perseguir *to chase* **e → i**

6. *Ir* + *a* + infinitivo

1. When do the actions in these sentences take place: in the past, present, or future?
   future
2. What is the first bold type verb you see in each sentence?
   a form of *ir*
3. In what form is the second bolded verb?
   infinitive
4. What word comes between the two verbs?
   a
   Does this word have an equivalent in English?
   no
5. What is your rule, then, for expressing future actions?
   use a form of *ir* + *a* + infinitive

8. Las expresiones afirmativas y negativas

1. When you use a negative word (**nadie, nunca,** etc.) in a sentence, does it come before or after the verb?
   The negative word can go before or after the verb.

2. When you use the word **no** and then a negative word in the same sentence, does **no** come before or after the verb? Where does the negative word come in these sentences?

   ***No* comes before the verb. The negative word can go before or after the verb.**

3. Does the meaning change depending on where you put the negative word? (E.g., **Nadie llama** *versus* **No llama nadie.)**

   No, the meaning stays the same.

9. Un repaso de *ser* y *estar*

1. Why do you use a form of **ser** in the first sentence?

   because it is a characteristic that remains relatively constant

2. Why do you use a form of **estar** in the second sentence?

   because it describes a physical or personality characteristic that can change, or a change in condition

CAPÍTULO 5

2. Los adjetivos demostrativos

1. When do you use **este, ese,** and **aquel**?

   when you want to point out *one* masculine person or object

2. When do you use **esta, esa,** and **aquella**?

   when you want to point out *one* feminine person or object

3. When do you use **estos, esos,** and **aquellos**?

   when you want to point out *two or more* masculine persons or objects, or a mix of masculine and feminine persons or objects

4. When do you use **estas, esas,** and **aquellas**?

   when you want to point out *two or more* feminine persons or objects

5. El presente progresivo

1. What is the infinitive of the first verb in each sentence that is in *italics*?

   estar

2. What are the infinitives of **haciendo, estudiando, escuchando, tocando, viendo,** and **escribiendo**?

   hacer, estudiar, escuchar, tocar, ver, escribir

3. How do you form the verb forms in **boldface**?

   Take the infinitive, drop the *-ar*, *-er*, or *-ir*, and add *-ando* or *-iendo*.

4. In this new tense, the *present progressive*, do any words come between the two parts of the verb?

   no

5. Therefore, your formula for forming the present progressive is:

   a form of the verb *estar* + a verb ending in *-ando* or *-iendo*

CAPÍTULO 6

Major grammar points to be reviewed

1. Present tense of:
   Regular **ar, er, ir** verbs
   Irregular verbs
   Stem changing verbs **e → ie, e → i, o → ue, u → ue**
2. Future tense *ir + a + infinitive*
3. Use of direct object pronouns
4. Correctly using *ser* and *estar*
5. Correctly using *gustar*

Major vocabulary to be reviewed

1. The *Vocabulario activo* at the end of each chapter

Major cultural information to be reviewed

1. At least two facts about each of the feature countries
2. At least one point about each of the two culture presentations in each chapter

CAPÍTULO 7

2. Repaso del complemento directo

1. What are direct objects? What are direct object pronouns?

   Direct objects receive the action of the verb, answering the questions *what* or *whom*. Direct object pronouns replace direct objects.

2. What are the pronouns (forms)? With what must they agree?

   The pronoun forms are *me, te, lo, la, nos, los, las*. They must agree with the direct object.

3. Where are direct object pronouns placed in a sentence?

   They are placed either before the verb or attached to the infinitive or *-ando* or *-iendo*.

3. El pretérito

1. What do you notice about the endings for **-er** and **-ir** verbs?

   they are the same

2. Where are accent marks needed?

   The accent marks are needed on the *yo* and *él/ella/usted* forms.

CAPÍTULO 8

2. Los pronombres de complemento indirecto

1. Who is buying the clothing?
   Mi madre.

2. Who is receiving the clothing?

   Mi madre **me** compra mucha ropa.
   I am receiving the clothes.
   Mi madre **te** compra mucha ropa.

You are receiving the clothes.
Mi madre **le** compra mucha ropa a mi hermano.
My brother is receiving the clothes.
Mi madre **nos** compra mucha ropa.
We are receiving the clothes.
Mi madre **os** compra mucha ropa.
You all are receiving the clothes.
Mi madre **les** compra mucha ropa a mis hermanos.
My brothers are receiving the clothes.

¿Me (i.o.) traes la falda de rayas (d.o.)?	*Will you bring me the striped skirt?*
Su novio le (i.o.) regaló la chaqueta de cuero (d.o.).	*Her boyfriend gave her the leather jacket.*
Mi hermana me (i.o.) compró la blusa de seda (d.o.).	*My sister bought me the silk blouse.*
Nuestra compañera de cuarto nos (i.o.) lavó la ropa (d.o.).	*Our roommate washed our clothes for us.*

4. Los pronombres de complemento directo e indirecto usados juntos

1. You know that direct and indirect objects come after the verb. Where do you find the direct and indirect object pronouns?
   before the verb or attached to infinitives or present participles
2. Reading from left to right, which pronoun comes first (direct or indirect)? Which pronoun comes second?
   The indirect object pronoun comes first, and the direct object pronoun comes second.

5. Las construcciones reflexivas

In each drawing:

Who is performing/doing the action?

a. ***La fiesta*** **d.** ***Raúl y Gloria***
b. ***Alberto*** **e.** ***Alberto***
c. ***Beatriz*** **f.** ***Beatriz***

Who or what is receiving the action?

a. ***neighbors*** **d.** ***Raúl and Gloria***
b. ***daughter*** **e.** ***Alberto***
c. ***car*** **f.** ***Beatriz***

Which of the drawings and captions demonstrate reflexive verbs?

d, e, f (the bottom row.)

CAPÍTULO 10

3. Los mandatos formales

1. Where do the object pronouns appear in affirmative commands? In negative commands? In what order?
   attached to the command; before the command and not attached; IO / DO
2. Why are there written accents on some of the commands and not on others?
   because some commands would change pronunciation without the accent mark

5. Otras formas del posesivo

1. What is the position of each possessive in the left-hand column? in the middle column?
   before the noun; after the noun
2. How do the possessive adjectives and pronouns agree?
   They agree in number and gender with the nouns they describe or replace.
3. What do the sentences mean in the column on the right? What have you removed from the previous sentence?
   Mine works fine; Ours cost a lot; Where are yours? His/hers/yours is $100; the noun

CAPÍTULO 11

3. El subjuntivo

1. What is the difference between the subjunctive and the indicative moods?
   The subjunctive expresses concepts such as doubts, emotions, wishes, and desires. The indicative reports events and happenings.
2. What other verb forms look like the subjunctive?
   The *Usted* and *Ustedes* commands.
3. Where does the subjunctive verb come in relation to the word **que?**
   after the word *que*

CAPÍTULO 12

Major grammar points to be reviewed

1. Past tenses:
   Regular and irregular preterit
   Regular and irregular imperfect
   Uses of the preterit and imperfect
2. Pronouns:
   Direct object
   Indirect object
   Reflexive
   Placement of pronouns
3. Commands:
   Familiar affirmative and negative
   Formal affirmative and negative
4. Subjunctive:
   Formation
   Usage

Major vocabulary to be reviewed

1. The **Vocabulario activo** at the end of each chapter

Major cultural information to be reviewed

1. At least two facts about each of the feature countries
2. At least one point about each of the two culture presentations in each chapter

APPENDIX 2

Regular Verbs: Simple Tenses

Infinitive Present Participle Past Participle	Indicative					Subjunctive		Imperative
	Present	Imperfect	Preterit	Future	Conditional	Present	Imperfect	
hablar hablando hablado	hablo hablas habla hablamos habláis hablan	hablaba hablabas hablaba hablábamos hablabais hablaban	hablé hablaste habló hablamos hablasteis hablaron	hablaré hablarás hablará hablaremos hablaréis hablarán	hablaría hablarías hablaría hablaríamos hablaríais hablarían	hable hables hable hablemos habléis hablen	hablara hablaras hablara habláramos hablarais hablaran	habla (tú), no hables hable (usted) hablemos hablen (Uds.)
comer comiendo comido	como comes come comemos coméis comen	comía comías comía comíamos comíais comían	comí comiste comió comimos comisteis comieron	comeré comerás comerá comeremos comeréis comerán	comería comerías comería comeríamos comeríais comerían	coma comas coma comamos comáis coman	comiera comieras comiera comiéramos comierais comieran	come (tú), no comas coma (usted) comamos coman (Uds.)
vivir viviendo vivido	vivo vives vive vivimos vivís viven	vivía vivías vivía vivíamos vivíais vivían	viví viviste vivió vivimos vivisteis vivieron	viviré vivirás vivirá viviremos viviréis vivirán	viviría vivirías viviría viviríamos viviríais vivirían	viva vivas viva vivamos viváis vivan	viviera vivieras viviera viviéramos vivierais vivieran	vive (tú), no vivas viva (usted) vivamos vivan (Uds.)

Vosotros Commands					
hablar	hablad, no habléis	comer	comed, no comáis	vivir	vivid, no viváis

Regular Verbs: Perfect Tenses

Indicative										Subjunctive			
Present Perfect		Past Perfect		Preterit Perfect		Future Perfect		Conditional Perfect		Present Perfect		Past Perfect	
he has ha hemos habéis han	hablado comido vivido	había habías había habíamos habíais habían	hablado comido vivido	hube hubiste hubo hubimos hubisteis hubieron	hablado comido vivido	habré habrás habrá habremos habréis habrán	hablado comido vivido	habría habrías habría habríamos habríais habrían	hablado comido vivido	haya hayas haya hayamos hayáis hayan	hablado comido vivido	hubiera hubieras hubiera hubiéramos hubierais hubieran	hablado comido vivido

Irregular Verbs

Infinitive Present Participle Past Participle	Indicative					Subjunctive		Imperative
	Present	Imperfect	Preterit	Future	Conditional	Present	Imperfect	
andar andando andado	ando andas anda andamos andáis andan	andaba andabas andaba andábamos andabais andaban	anduve anduviste anduvo anduvimos anduvisteis anduvieron	andaré andarás andará andaremos andaréis andarán	andaría andarías andaría andaríamos andaríais andarían	ande andes ande andemos andéis anden	anduviera anduvieras anduviera anduviéramos anduvierais anduvieran	anda (tú), no andes ande (usted) andemos anden (Uds.)
caer cayendo caído	caigo caes cae caemos caéis caen	caía caías caía caíamos caíais caían	caí caíste cayó caímos caísteis cayeron	caeré caerás caerá caeremos caeréis caerán	caería caerías caería caeríamos caeríais caerían	caiga caigas caiga caigamos caigáis caigan	cayera cayeras cayera cayéramos cayerais cayeran	cae (tú), no caigas caiga (usted) caigamos caigan (Uds.)
dar dando dado	doy das da damos dais dan	daba dabas daba dábamos dabais daban	di diste dio dimos disteis dieron	daré darás dará daremos daréis darán	daría darías daría daríamos daríais darían	dé des dé demos deis den	diera dieras diera diéramos dierais dieran	da (tú), no des dé (usted) demos den (Uds.)

Irregular Verbs (continued)

Infinitive Present Participle Past Participle	Indicative					Subjunctive		Imperative
	Present	Imperfect	Preterit	Future	Conditional	Present	Imperfect	
decir diciendo dicho	digo dices dice decimos decís dicen	decía decías decía decíamos decíais decían	dije dijiste dijo dijimos dijisteis dijeron	diré dirás dirá diremos diréis dirán	diría dirías diría diríamos diríais dirían	diga digas diga digamos digáis digan	dijera dijeras dijera dijéramos dijerais dijeran	di (tú), no digas diga (usted) digamos decid (vosotros), no digáis digan (Uds.)
estar estando estado	estoy estás está estamos estáis están	estaba estabas estaba estábamos estabais estaban	estuve estuviste estuvo estuvimos estuvisteis estuvieron	estaré estarás estará estaremos estaréis estarán	estaría estarías estaría estaríamos estaríais estarían	esté estés esté estemos estéis estén	estuviera estuvieras estuviera estuviéramos estuvierais estuvieran	está (tú), no estés esté (usted) estemos estad (vosotros), no estéis estén (Uds.)
haber habiendo habido	he has ha hemos habéis han	había habías había habíamos habíais habían	hube hubiste hubo hubimos hubisteis hubieron	habré habrás habrá habremos habréis habrán	habría habrías habría habríamos habríais habrían	haya hayas haya hayamos hayáis hayan	hubiera hubieras hubiera hubiéramos hubierais hubieran	
hacer haciendo hecho	hago haces hace hacemos hacéis hacen	hacía hacías hacía hacíamos hacíais hacían	hice hiciste hizo hicimos hicisteis hicieron	haré harás hará haremos haréis harán	haría harías haría haríamos haríais harían	haga hagas haga hagamos hagáis hagan	hiciera hicieras hiciera hiciéramos hicierais hicieran	haz (tú), no hagas haga (usted) hagamos haced (vosotros), no hagáis hagan (Uds.)
ir yendo ido	voy vas va vamos vais van	iba ibas iba íbamos ibais iban	fui fuiste fue fuimos fuisteis fueron	iré irás irá iremos iréis irán	iría irías iría iríamos iríais irían	vaya vayas vaya vayamos vayáis vayan	fuera fueras fuera fuéramos fuerais fueran	ve (tú), no vayas vaya (usted) vamos, no vayamos id (vosotros), no vayáis vayan (Uds.)

Irregular Verbs (continued)

Infinitive Present Participle Past Participle	Indicative					Subjunctive		Imperative
	Present	Imperfect	Preterit	Future	Conditional	Present	Imperfect	
oír oyendo oído	oigo oyes oye oímos oís oyen	oía oías oía oíamos oíais oían	oí oíste oyó oímos oístes oyeron	oiré oirás oirá oiremos oiréis oirán	oiría oirías oiría oiríamos oiríais oirían	oiga oigas oiga oigamos oigáis oigan	oyera oyeras oyera oyéramos oyerais oyeran	oye (tú), no oigas oiga (usted) oigamos oigan (Uds.)
poder pudiendo podido	puedo puedes puede podemos podéis pueden	podía podías podía podíamos podíais podían	pude pudiste pudo pudimos pudisteis pudieron	podré podrás podrá podremos podréis podrán	podría podrías podría podríamos podríais podrían	pueda puedas pueda podamos podáis puedan	pudiera pudieras pudiera pudiéramos pudierais pudieran	
poner poniendo puesto	pongo pones pone ponemos ponéis ponen	ponía ponías ponía poníamos poníais ponían	puse pusiste puso pusimos pusisteis pusieron	pondré pondrás pondrá pondremos pondréis pondrán	pondría pondrías pondría pondríamos pondríais pondrían	ponga pongas ponga pongamos pongáis pongan	pusiera pusieras pusiera pusiéramos pusierais pusieran	pon (tú), no pongas ponga (usted) pongamos pongan (Uds.)
querer queriendo querido	quiero quieres quiere queremos queréis quieren	quería querías quería queríamos queríais querían	quise quisiste quiso quisimos quisisteis quisieron	querré querrás querrá querremos querréis querrán	querría querrías querría querríamos querríais querrían	quiera quieras quiera queramos queráis quieran	quisiera quisieras quisiera quisiéramos quisiérais quisieran	quiere (tú), no quieras quiera (usted) queramos quieran (Uds.)
saber sabiendo sabido	sé sabes sabe sabemos sabéis saben	sabía sabías sabía sabíamos sabíais sabían	supe supiste supo supimos supisteis supieron	sabré sabrás sabrá sabremos sabréis sabrán	sabría sabrías sabría sabríamos sabríais sabrían	sepa sepas sepa sepamos sepáis sepan	supiera supieras supiera supiéramos supiérais supieran	sabe (tú), no sepas sepa (usted) sepamos sepan (Uds.)

Irregular Verbs (continued)

Infinitive Present Participle Past Participle	Indicative					Subjunctive		Imperative
	Present	Imperfect	Preterit	Future	Conditional	Present	Imperfect	
salir saliendo salido	salgo sales sale salimos salís salen	salía salías salía salíamos salíais salían	salí saliste salió salimos salisteis salieron	saldré saldrás saldrá saldremos saldréis saldrán	saldría saldrías saldría saldríamos saldríais saldrían	salga salgas salga salgamos salgáis salgan	saliera salieras saliera saliéramos salierais salieran	sal (tú), no salgas salga (usted) salgamos salgan (Uds.)
ser siendo sido	soy eres es somos sois son	era eras era éramos erais eran	fui fuiste fue fuimos fuisteis fueron	seré serás será seremos seréis serán	sería serías sería seríamos seríais serían	sea seas sea seamos seáis sean	fuera fueras fuera fuéramos fuerais fueran	sé (tú), no seas sea (usted) seamos sed (vosotros), no seáis sean (Uds.)
tener teniendo tenido	tengo tienes tiene tenemos tenéis tienen	tenía tenías tenía teníamos teníais tenían	tuve tuviste tuvo tuvimos tuvisteis tuvieron	tendré tendrás tendrá tendremos tendréis tendrán	tendría tendrías tendría tendríamos tendríais tendrían	tenga tengas tenga tengamos tengáis tengan	tuviera tuvieras tuviera tuviéramos tuvierais tuvieran	ten (tú), no tengas tenga (usted) tengamos tened (vosotros), no tengáis tengan (Uds.)
traer trayendo traído	traigo traes trae traemos traéis traen	traía traías traía traíamos traíais traían	traje trajiste trajo trajimos trajisteis trajeron	traeré traerás traerá traeremos traeréis traerán	traería traerías traería traeríamos traeríais traerían	traiga traigas traiga traigamos traigáis traigan	trajera trajeras trajera trajéramos trajerais trajeran	trae (tú), no traigas traiga (usted) traigamos traed (vosotros), no traigáis traigan (Uds.)
venir viniendo venido	vengo vienes viene venimos venís vienen	venía venías venía veníamos veníais venían	vine viniste vino vinimos vinisteis vinieron	vendré vendrás vendrá vendremos vendréis vendrán	vendría vendrías vendría vendríamos vendríais vendrían	venga vengas venga vengamos vengáis vengan	viniera vinieras viniera viniéramos vinierais vinieran	ven (tú), no vengas venga (usted) vengamos venid (vosotros), no vengáis vengan (Uds.)

Irregular Verbs (continued)

Infinitive Present Participle Past Participle	Indicative					Subjunctive		Imperative
	Present	Imperfect	Preterit	Future	Conditional	Present	Imperfect	
ver viendo visto	veo ves ve vemos véis ven	veía veías veía veíamos veíais veían	vi viste vio vimos visteis vieron	veré verás verá veremos veréis verán	vería verías vería veríamos veríais verían	vea veas vea veamos veáis vean	viera vieras viera viéramos vierais vieran	ve (tú), no veas vea (usted) veamos ved (vosotros), no veáis vean (Uds.)

Stem-Changing and Orthographic-Changing Verbs

Infinitive Present Participle Past Participle	Indicative					Subjunctive		Imperative
	Present	Imperfect	Preterit	Future	Conditional	Present	Imperfect	
almorzar (z, c) almorzando almorzado	almuerzo almuerzas almuerza almorzamos almorzáis almuerzan	almorzaba almorzabas almorzaba almorzábamos almorzabais almorzaban	almorcé almorzaste almorzó almorzamos almorzasteis almorzaron	almorzaré almorzarás almorzará almorzaremos almorzaréis almorzarán	almorzaría almorzarías almorzaría almorzaríamos almorzaríais almorzarían	almuerce almuerces almuerce almorcemos almorcéis almuercen	almorzara almorzaras almorzaras almorzáramos almorzarais almorzaran	almuerza (tú) no almuerces almuerce (usted) almorcemos almorzad (vosotros) no almorcéis almuercen (Uds.)
buscar (c, qu) buscando buscado	busco buscas busca buscamos buscáis buscan	buscaba buscabas buscaba buscábamos buscabais buscaban	busqué buscaste buscó buscamos buscasteis buscaron	buscaré buscarás buscará buscaremos buscaréis buscarán	buscaría buscarías buscaría buscaríamos buscaríais buscarían	busque busques busque busquemos busquéis busquen	buscara buscaras buscara buscáramos buscarais buscaran	busca (tú) no busques busque (usted) busquemos buscad (vosotros) no busquéis busquen (Uds.)

Stem-Changing and Orthographic-Changing Verbs (continued)

Infinitive Present Participle Past Participle	Indicative					Subjunctive		Imperative
	Present	Imperfect	Preterit	Future	Conditional	Present	Imperfect	
corregir (g, j) corrigiendo corregido	corrijo corriges corrige corregimos corregís corrigen	corregía corregías corregía corregíamos corregíais corregían	corregí corregiste corrigió corregimos corregisteis corrigieron	corregiré corregirás corregirá corregiremos corregiréis corregirán	corregiría corregirías corregiría corregiríamos corregiríais corregirían	corrija corrijas corrija corrijamos corrijáis corrijan	corrigiera corrigieras corrigiera corrigiéramos corrigierais corrigieran	corrige (tú) no corrijas corrija (usted) corrijamos corregid (vosotros) no corrijáis corrijan (Uds.)
dormir (ue, u) durmiendo dormido	duermo duermes duerme dormimos dormís duermen	dormía dormías dormía dormíamos dormíais dormían	dormí dormiste durmió dormimos dormisteis durmieron	dormiré dormirás dormirá dormiremos dormiréis dormirán	dormiría dormirías dormiría dormiríamos dormiríais dormirían	duerma duermas duerma durmamos durmáis duerman	durmiera durmieras durmiera durmiéramos durmierais durmieran	duerme (tú), no duermas duerma (usted) durmamos dormid (vosotros), no dormáis duerman (Uds.)
incluir (y) incluyendo incluido	incluyo incluyes incluye incluimos incluís incluyen	incluía incluías incluía incluíamos incluíais incluían	incluí incluiste incluyó incluimos incluisteis incluyeron	incluiré incluirás incluirá incluiremos incluiréis incluirán	incluiría incluirías incluiría incluiríamos incluiríais incluirían	incluya incluyas incluya incluyamos incluyáis incluyan	incluyera incluyeras incluyera incluyéramos incluyerais incluyeran	incluye (tú), no incluyas incluya (usted) incluyamos incluid (vosotros), no incluyáis incluyan (Uds.)
llegar (g, gu) llegando llegado	llego llegas llega llegamos llegáis llegan	llegaba llegabas llegaba llegábamos llegabais llegaban	llegué llegaste llegó llegamos llegasteis llegaron	llegaré llegarás llegará llegaremos llegaréis llegarán	llegaría llegarías llegaría llegaríamos llegaríais llegarían	llegue llegues llegue lleguemos lleguéis lleguen	llegara llegaras llegara llegáramos llegareis llegaran	llega (tú) no llegues llegue (usted) lleguemos llegad (vosotros) no lleguéis lleguen (Uds.)
pedir (i, i) pidiendo pedido	pido pides pide pedimos pedís piden	pedía pedías pedía pedíamos pedíais pedían	pedí pediste pidió pedimos pedisteis pidieron	pediré pedirás pedirá pediremos pediréis pedirán	pediría pedirías pediría pediríamos pediríais pedirían	pida pidas pida pidamos pidáis pidan	pidiera pidieras pidiera pidiéramos pidierais pidieran	pide (tú), no pidas pida (usted) pidamos pedid (vosotros), no pidáis pidan (Uds.)

Stem-Changing and Orthographic-Changing Verbs (continued)

Infinitive Present Participle Past Participle	Indicative					Subjunctive		Imperative
	Present	Imperfect	Preterit	Future	Conditional	Present	Imperfect	
pensar (ie) pensando pensado	pienso piensas piensa pensamos pensáis piensan	pensaba pensabas pensaba pensábamos pensabais pensaban	pensé pensaste pensó pensamos pensasteis pensaron	pensaré pensarás pensará pensaremos pensaréis pensarán	pensaría pensarías pensaría pensaríamos pensaríais pensarían	piense pienses piense pensemos penséis piensen	pensara pensaras pensara pensáramos pensarais pensaran	piensa (tú), no pienses piense (usted) pensemos pensad (vosotros), no penséis piensen (Uds.)
producir (zc) produciendo producido	produzco produces produce producimos producís producen	producía producías producía producíamos producíais producían	produje produjiste produjo produjimos produjisteis produjeron	produciré producirás producirá produciremos produciréis producirán	produciría producirías produciría produciríamos produciríais producirían	produzca produzcas produzca produzcamos produzcáis produzcan	produjera produjeras produjera produjéramos produjerais produjeran	produce (tú), no produzcas produzca (usted) produzcamos pruducid (vosotros), no produzcáis produzcan (Uds.)
reír (i, i) riendo reído	río ríes ríe reímos reís ríen	reía reías reía reíamos reíais reían	reí reíste rio reímos reísteis rieron	reiré reirás reirá reiremos reiréis reirán	reiría reirías reiría reiríamos reiríais reirían	ría rías ría riamos riáis rían	riera rieras riera riéramos rierais rieran	ríe (tú), no rías ría (usted) riamos reíd (vosotros), no riáis rían (Uds.)
seguir (i, i) (ga) siguiendo seguido	sigo sigues sigue seguimos seguís siguen	seguía seguías seguía seguíamos seguíais seguían	seguí seguiste siguió seguimos seguisteis siguieron	seguiré seguirás seguirá seguiremos seguiréis seguirán	seguiría seguirías seguiría seguiríamos seguiríais seguirían	siga sigas siga sigamos sigáis sigan	siguiera siguieras siguiera siguiéramos siguierais siguieran	sigue (tú), no sigas siga (usted) sigamos seguid (vosotros), no sigáis sigan (Uds.)
sentir (ie, i) sintiendo sentido	siento sientes siente sentimos sentís sienten	sentía sentías sentía sentíamos sentíais sentían	sentí sentiste sintió sentimos sentisteis sintieron	sentiré sentirás sentirá sentiremos sentiréis sentirán	sentiría sentirías sentiría sentiríamos sentiríais sentirían	sienta sientas sienta sintamos sintáis sientan	sintiera sintieras sintiera sintiéramos sintierais sintieran	siente (tú), no sientas sienta (usted) sintamos sentid (vosotros), no sintáis sientan (Uds.)

Stem-Changing and Orthographic-Changing Verbs (continued)

Infinitive Present Participle Past Participle	Indicative					Subjunctive		Imperative
	Present	Imperfect	Preterit	Future	Conditional	Present	Imperfect	
volver (ue) volviendo vuelto	vuelvo vuelves vuelve volvemos volvéis vuelven	volvía volvías volvía volvíamos volvíais volvían	volví volviste volvió volvimos volvisteis volvieron	volveré volverás volverá volveremos volveréis volverán	volvería volverías volvería volveríamos volveríais volverían	vuelva vuelvas vuelva volvamos volváis vuelvan	volviera volvieras volviera volviéramos volvierais volvieran	vuelve (tú), no vuelvas vuelva (usted) volvamos volved (vosotros), no volváis vuelvan (Uds.)

APPENDIX 3

CAPÍTULO PRELIMINAR A

Los saludos/*Greetings*

¿Cómo andas? *How are you doing?*
¿Cómo vas? *How are you doing?*
El gusto es mío. *Pleased to meet you; The pleasure is all mine.*
Hasta entonces. *Until then.*
¿Qué hubo? *How's it going? What's happening? What's new?*
¿Qué pasa? *How's it going? What's happening? What's new?*
¿Qué pasó? *How's it going? What's happening? What's new?*

Las despedidas/*Farewells*

Nos vemos. *See you.*
Que te vaya bien. *Hope everything goes well.*
Que tenga(s) un buen día. *Have a nice day.*
Vaya con Dios. *Go with God.*

Las presentaciones/*Introductions*

Me gustaría presentarle a... *I would like to introduce you to... (formal)*
Me gustaría presentarte a... *I would like to introduce you to... (familiar)*

Expresiones útiles para la clase/*Useful classroom expressions*

Preguntas y respuestas/*Questions and answers*

(No) entiendo. *I (don't) understand.*
¿Puede repetir, por favor? *Could you repeat, please?*

Expresiones de cortesía/*Polite expressions*

Muchas gracias. *Thank you very much.*
No hay de qué. *Not at all.*

Mandatos para la clase/*Instructions for class*

Saque(n) un bolígrafo/papel/lápiz. *Take out a pen/a piece of paper/pencil.*

Las nacionalidades/*Nationalities*

argentino/a *Argentinian*
boliviano/a *Bolivian*
chileno/a *Chilean*
colombiano/a *Colombian*
costarricense *Costa Rican*
dominicano/a *Dominican*
ecuatoriano/a *Ecuadorian*
guatemalteco/a *Guatemalan*
hondureño/a *Honduran*
nicaragüense *Nicaraguan*
panameño/a *Panamanian*
peruano/a *Peruvian*
uruguayo/a *Uruguayan*
venezolano/a *Venezuelan*

Expresiones del tiempo/*Weather expressions*

el arco iris *rainbow*
el chirimiri *drizzle (Spain)*
Está despejado. *It's clear.*
Hace fresco. *It's cool.*
Hay neblina/niebla. *It's foggy.*
la humedad *humidity*
los copos de nieve *snowflakes*
las gotas de lluvia *raindrops*
el granizo *hail*
el hielo *ice*
el huracán *hurricane*
la llovizna *drizzle*
el pronóstico *weather forecast*
el/los rayo/s, el relámpago *lightning*
la tormenta *storm*
el tornado *tornado*
el/los trueno/s *thunder*

CAPÍTULO 1

La familia/*Family*

el/la ahijado/a *godchild*
el bisabuelo *great-grandfather*
la bisabuela *great-grandmother*
el/la cuñado/a *brother-in-law/sister-in-law*
la familia política *in-laws*
el/la hermanastro/a *stepbrother/stepsister*
el/la hijastro/a *stepson/stepdaughter*
el/la hijo/a único/a *only child*
la madrina *godmother*
el/la medio/a hermano/a *half brother/half sister*
los medios hermanos *half brothers and sisters*
la mami *Mommy; Mom (Latin America)*
el marido *husband*
la mujer *wife*
el/la nieto/a *grandson/granddaughter*
los nietos *grandchildren*
la nuera *daughter-in-law*
el padrino *godfather*
el papi *Daddy; Dad (Latin America)*
el pariente *relative*
el/la prometido/a *fiancé(e)*
los sobrinos *nieces and nephews*
el/la suegro/a *father-in-law/mother-in-law*
los suegros *in-laws*
la tatarabuela *great-great-grandmother*
el tatarabuelo *great-great-grandfather*
la tía abuela *great-aunt*
el tío abuelo *great-uncle*
el/la viudo/a *widower/widow*
el yerno *son-in-law*

Otra palabra útil/*Another useful word*

divorciado/a *divorced*

La gente/*People*

el bato *friend; guy (in SE USA slang)*
el/la chaval/a *young man/young woman (Spain)*
el chamaco *young man (Cuba, Honduras, Mexico, El Salvador)*
el/la fulano/a *unknown man/woman*

Los adjetivos/*Adjectives*

La personalidad y otros rasgos/*Personality and other characteristics*

amable *nice; kind*
bobo/a *stupid; silly*
el/la bromista *person who likes to play jokes*
cariñoso/a *loving; affectionate*
chistoso/a *funny*
cursi *pretentious; affected*
divertido/a *funny*
educado/a *well-mannered; polite*
elegante *elegant*
empollón/ona *bookworm; nerd*
encantador/a *charming; lovely*
espabilado/a *smart; vivacious; alert (Latin America)*
frustrado/a *frustrated*
gracioso/a *funny*
grosero/a *unpleasant*
histérico/a *crazed*
impaciente *impatient*
indiferente *indifferent*
irresponsable *irresponsible*
malvado/a *evil; wicked*
majo/a *pretty; nice (Spain)*
mono/a *pretty; nice (Spain, Caribbean)*
odioso/a *unpleasant*
pesado/a *annoying person*
pijo/a *posh; snooty (Spain)*
progre *liberal; progressive (Spain)*
sabelotodo/a *know-it-all*
viejo/a *old*

Las características físicas/*Physical characteristics*

atlético/a *athletic*
bello/a *beautiful (Latin America)*
blando/a *soft*
esbelto/a *slender*
flaco/a *thin*
frágil *fragile*
hermoso/a *beautiful; lovely*
musculoso/a *muscular*
robusto/a *sturdy*

Otras palabras útiles/*Other useful words*

demasiado/a *too much*
suficiente *enough*

CAPÍTULO 2

Las materias y las especialidades/*Subjects and majors*

la agronomía *agriculture*
la antropología *anthropology*
el cálculo *calculus*
las ciencias políticas *political sciences*
las comunicaciones *communications*
la contabilidad *accounting*
la economía *economics*
la educación física *physical education*
la enfermería *nursing*
la filosofía *philosophy*
la física *physics*
la geografía *geography*
la geología *geology*
la historia *history*
la ingeniería *engineering*
la literatura comparada *comparative literature*
el mercadeo *marketing (Latin America)*
la mercadotecnia (el márketing) *marketing (Spain)*
la medicina del deporte *sports medicine*
la química *chemistry*
los servicios sociales *social work*
la sociología *sociology*
la terapia física *physical therapy*

En la sala de clase/*In the classroom*

el aula *classroom*
el/la alumno/a *student*
la bombilla *light bulb*
la cámara proyectora *overhead camera*
el cielorraso *ceiling*
el enchufe *wall socket*
el interruptor *light switch*
las luces *lights*
el ordenador *computer (Spain)*
la pantalla *screen*
el proyector *projector*
la prueba *test*
el pupitre *student desk*
el rotulador *marker*
el sacapuntas *pencil sharpener*
el suelo *floor*
la tarima *dais; platform*

Los verbos/*Verbs*

apuntar *to point*
asistir a clase *to attend class*
beber *to drink*
entrar *to enter*
entregar *to hand in*
mirar *to look; observe*
prestar atención *to pay attention*
repasar *to review*
responder *to answer*
sacar *to take out*
sacar buenas/malas notas *to get good/bad grades*
tomar apuntes *to take notes*

Las palabras interrogativas/*Interrogative words*

¿Con cuánto/a/os/as? *With how many…?*
¿Con qué? *With what…?*
¿Con quién? *With whom…?*
¿De dónde? *From where…?*
¿De qué? *About what…?*
¿De quién? *Of whom…?*

Emociones y estados/*Emotions and states of being*

agotado/a *exhausted*
agradable *nice*
alegre *happy*
asombrado/a *amazed; astonished*

asqueado/a *disgusted*
asustado/a *scared*
deprimido/a *depressed*
desanimado/a *discouraged; disheartened*
disgustado/a *upset*
dormido/a *sleepy*
emocionado/a *moved; touched*
entusiasmado/a *delighted*
fastidiado/a *annoyed; bothered*
ilusionado/a *thrilled*
optimista *optimistic*
pesimista *pessimistic*
retrasado/a *late*
sonriente *smiling*
soñoliento/a *sleepy (Spain)*

Los lugares/*Places*

el apartamento estudiantil *student apartment*
el campo de fútbol *football field*
el campus *campus*
la cancha de tenis/baloncesto *tennis/basketball court*
la/s casa/s de hermandad/es *fraternity and sorority housing*
el centro comercial *mall*
el comedor estudiantil *student dining hall*
la habitación *room*
la matrícula *registration*
el museo *museum*
la oficina de consejeros *guidance/advising office*
el supermercado *supermarket*
el teatro *theater*

La residencia/*The dorm*

los bafles *speakers (Spain)*
el calendario *calendar*
la cama *bed*
el iPod *iPod*
el Internet *Web*
las literas *bunkbeds*
la llave *memory stick*
la mesita de noche *nightstand*
el móvil *cell phone (Spain)*
la redacción/la composición *essay*
la tarjeta de crédito *credit card*
la tarjeta de identidad; el carnet *ID card*
los videojuegos *video games*

Los deportes y los pasatiempos/*Sports and pastimes*

cazar *to hunt*
conversar con amigos *to talk with friends*
escalar *to go mountain climbing*
esquiar *to ski*
estar en forma *to be in shape*
hablar por teléfono *to talk on the phone*
hacer alpinismo *to go hiking*
hacer el footing *to go jogging (Spain)*
hacer gimnasia *to exercise*
hacer senderismo *to hike*
hacer yoga *to do yoga*
ir al centro comercial *to go the mall; to go downtown*
ir a fiestas *to go to parties*
ir a un partido de... *to go to a ... (game)*
jugar al ajedrez *to play chess*
jugar al boliche *to bowl*
jugar al ráquetbol *to play racquetball*
jugar juegos electrónicos *to play video games*
levantar pesas *to lift weights*
mirar videos *to watch videos*
montar a caballo *to go horseback riding*
pasear *to go out for a ride; to take a walk*
pasear en barco *to sail*
ir a navegar *to sail*
pescar *to fish*
practicar boxeo *to box*
practicar ciclismo *to cycle*
practicar lucha libre *to wrestle*
practicar las artes marciales *to do martial arts*
salir a cenar/comer *to go out to dinner/eat*
tirar un platillo volador *to throw a Frisbee*

Palabras asociadas con los deportes y los pasatiempos/*Words associated with sports and pastimes*

el/la aficionado/a *fan*
el bate *bat*
el campo *field*
los libros de...
acción *action books*
aventura *adventure books*
cuentos cortos *short stories*
ficción (ciencia-ficción) *fiction (science fiction)*
horror *horror books*
misterio *mystery books*
romance *romance books*
espías *spy books*
el palo de golf *golf club*
la pista *track*
la pista y el campo *track and field (Spain)*
la raqueta *racket*

CAPÍTULO 3

La casa/*The house*

la alcoba *bedroom*
el armario empotrado *closet (Spain)*
el ático *attic*
la bodega *cellar*
la buhardilla *attic*
el clóset *closet (Latin America)*
el corredor *hall*
el cuarto *bedroom*
el despacho *office*
el desván *attic*
el pasillo *hallway*
el patio *patio; yard*
el placar *closet (Argentina)*
el portal *porch*
el porche *porch*
la recámara *bedroom (Mexico)*
el salón *salon; lounge; living room*
el tejado *roof*
la terraza *terrace; porch*
el vestíbulo *entrance hall*

En la sala y el comedor/*In the living room and dining room*

la banqueta/el banquillo *small seating stool*
la estantería *bookcase*
la mecedora *rocking chair*
la moqueta *carpet (Spain)*

En la cocina/*In the kitchen*

el congelador *deep freezer*
el friegaplatos *diswasher*
el frigorífico *refrigerator (Spain)*
el horno *oven*
el lavavajillas *dishwasher (Spain)*
el taburete *bar stool*

Otras palabras/*Other words*

el aparato eléctrico *electric appliance*
la chimenea *chimney*
la cómoda *dresser*
las cortinas *curtains*
el espejo *mirror*
el fregadero *sink*
los gabinetes *cabinets*
la lavadora *washer*
la secadora *dryer*
el librero *bookcase (Mexico)*
la nevera *refrigerator*
las persianas *shutters; window blinds*

En el baño/*In the bathroom*

la cisterna *toilet water tank*
el espejo *mirror*
los grifos *faucets*
la jabonera *soap dish*
el toallero *towel rack*

En el dormitorio/*In the bedroom*

el edredón *comforter*
la frazada *blanket (Latin America)*

Los quehaceres de la casa/*Household chores*

barrer *to sweep*
cortar el césped *to cut the grass*
fregar los platos *to wash the dishes*
fregar los suelos *to clean the floors*
guardar la ropa *to put away clothes*
lavar la ropa *to do laundry*
ordenar *to put in order*
planchar la ropa *to iron*
recoger *to clean up in general*
recoger la mesa *to clean up after a meal*
regar las plantas *to water the plants*
sacudir las alfombras *to shake out the rugs*

Expresiones con *tener*/*Expressions with* tener

tener celos *to be jealous*
tener novio/a *to have a boyfriend/girlfriend*

Los colores/*Colors*

púrpura *purple (Spain)*
azul/verde claro *light blue/green*
azul/verde oscuro *dark blue/green*
rosa *pink (Spain)*

CAPÍTULO 4

Lugares en una ciudad o pueblo/*Places in a city or town*

la alberca *swimming pool—sports complex (Mexico)*
el ambulatorio *medical center—(not a hospital) (Spain)*
el aseo *public restroom*
la catedral *cathedral*
el campo de golf *golf course*
la capilla *chapel*
la clínica *clinic*
el consultorio *doctor's office*
el convento *convent*
la cuadra *block (Latin America)*
la ferretería *hardware store*
la fogata *bonfire*
la frutería *fruit store*
la fuente *fountain*
la gasolinera *gas station*
la heladería *ice cream shop*
la manzana *block (Spain)*
el mercadillo *open-air market*
la mezquita *mosque*
la papelería *stationary store*
la panadería *bread store*
la pastelería *pastry shop*
la pescadería *fish shop; fishmonger*
la piscina *pool*
el polideportivo *sports center*
el quiosco *newsstand*
los servicios *public restrooms*
la sinagoga *synagogue*
la tienda de juguetes *toy store*
la tienda de ropa *clothing store*
el zócalo *plaza (Mexico)*

CAPÍTULO 5

El mundo de la música/*The world of music*

la musica…alternativa *alternative*
…bluegrass *bluegrass*
el coro *the choir*
el cuarteto *quartet*
el equipo de cámara/sonido *camera/sound crew*
el/la mánager *manager*
el merengue *merengue*
la música popular *popular music*
el/la organista *organist*
la pandilla *gang; posse*
los seguidores *groupies*
el teclado *keyboard*

El mundo del cine/*The world of film*

Gente/*People*

el/la cinematógrafo/a *cinematographer*
el/la director/a *director*
el/la guionista *scriptwriter*

Las películas/*Movies*

el cortometraje *short (film)*
los dibujos animados *cartoons*
el guión *script*
el montaje *montage*

CAPÍTULO 7

Las carnes y las aves/*Meats and poultry*

las aves de corral *poultry*
la carne de cerdo *pork*
la carne de cordero *lamb*
la carne de res *beef*
la carne molida *ground beef*
la carne picada *ground beef (Spain)*
el chorizo *highly seasoned pork sausage*
la chuleta *chop*
el chuletón *T-bone (Spain)*
el jamón serrano *prosciutto ham (Spain)*
el pavo *turkey*
la salchicha *sausage; hot dog*
el salchichón *spiced sausage (Spain)*
la ternera *veal*
el tocino *bacon*

El pescado y los mariscos/*Fish and seafood*

las almejas *clams*
las anchoas *anchovies*
los calamares *squid*
el cangrejo *crab*
el chillo *red snapper (Puerto Rico)*
las gambas *shrimp*
el huachinango *red snapper (Mexico)*
la langosta *lobster*
el lenguado *flounder*
la ostra *oyster*
el pulpo *octopus*
la sardina *sardines*

Las frutas/*Fruits*

el aguacate *avocado*
el albaricoque *apricot*
el ananá *pineapple (Latin America)*
el banano *banana; banana tree*
la cereza *cherry*
la china *orange (Puerto Rico)*
la ciruela *plum*
el durazno *peach*
la fresa *strawberry*
el melocotón *peach*
la papaya *papaya*
la piña *pineapple*
el pomelo *grapefruit*
la sandía *watermelon*
la toronja *grapefruit*

Las verduras/*Vegetables*

la aceituna *olive*
la alcaparra *caper*
el apio *celery*
la berza *cabbage (Spain)*
el calabacín *zucchini*
la calabaza *squash; pumpkin*
los champiñones *mushrooms*
la col *cabbage*
la coliflor *cauliflower*
los espárragos *asparagus*
las espinacas *spinach*
los guisantes *peas*
las habichuelas *kidney beans (Puerto Rico)*
los hongos *mushrooms (Latin America)*
la judías verdes *green beans*
el pepinillo *pickle*
el pepino *cucumber*
el pimiento *pepper*
el repollo *cabbage*
la salsa *sauce*
las setas *wild mushrooms (Spain)*
la zanahoria *carrot*

Los postres/*Desserts*

el arroz con leche *rice pudding*
la batida *milkshake*
el batido *milkshake (Spain)*
los bocaditos *bite-size sandwiches*
los bollos *sweet bread*
el bombón *sweets; candy*
el caramelo *sweets; candy*
los chocolates *chocolates*
los chuches *candies in general (Spain)*
la dona *donut*
el dónut *donut (Spain)*
el flan *caramel custard*
la natilla *custard*
los pastelitos *turnover, pastry, finger cakes*
la tarta *cake*

Las bebidas/*Beverages*

el champán *champagne*
la sidra *cider*
el zumo *juice (Spain)*

Más comidas/*More foods*

el ajo *garlic*
la avena *oatmeal*
el caldo *broth*
el consomé *clear soup*
los fideos *noodles (in soup)*
la harina *flour*
la jalea *jelly; marmalade (Spain, Puerto Rico)*
la mantequilla *butter*
la margarina *margarine*
la miel *honey*
el pan dulce *sweet roll*

el panqueque *pancake*
las tortas americanas *pancakes (Spain)*

Las comidas/*Meals*

el aperitivo *appetizer*
las tapas *hors d'oeuvres*

Los condimentos y las especias/*Condiments and spices*

el aderezo *seasoning; dressing*
el aliño *seasoning; dressing (Spain)*

Unos términos de la cocina/*Some cooking terms*

agregar *to add*
asar *to roast; broil*
aumentar libras/kilos *to gain weight*
batir *to beat*
calentar *to heat*
derretir *to melt*
espesarse *to thicken*
freír *to fry*
mezclar *to mix*
revolver *to stir*
servir *to serve*
unir *to combine*
verter *to pour*

Otras palabras/*Other words*

aclararse *to thin*
añadir *to add*
el batidor *beater*
la batidora *hand-held mixer*
la cacerola *saucepan*
cocer *to cook*
la copa *goblet; wine glass*
el cuenco *bowl; mixing bowl*
echar (algo) *to add*
el fuego (lento, mediano, alto) *(low, medium, high) heat*
la fuente *serving platter/dish*
el ingrediente *ingredient*
el kilogramo *kilogram (or 2.2 pounds)*
el nivel *level*
la olla *pot*
el pedazo *piece*
el platillo *saucer*
el plato hondo *bowl*
el plato sopero *soup bowl*
la receta *recipe*
recalentar *to reheat*
remover *to stir (Spain)*
la sartén *frying pan*
el/la sopero/a *soup serving bowl*

En el restaurante/*In the restaurant*

la cucharilla *teaspoon (Spain)*
el friegaplatos *dishwasher (person)*
el/la mesero/a *waiter/waitress (Latin America)*
el/la pinche *kitchen assistant*

CAPÍTULO 8

La ropa y la joyería/*Clothing and jewelry*

el albornoz *bathrobe (Spain)*
las alpargatas *espadrille shoes (Spain)*
el anorak *rain-proof coat*
los aretes *earrings*
la bolsa *bag*
la bufanda *scarf*
la capa de agua *raincoat (Puerto Rico)*
la cartera *pocketbook, purse*
el chubasquero *raincoat (Spain)*
el collar *necklace*
la correa *belt*
el gorro *wool cap; hat*
los mahones *jeans (Puerto Rico)*
las pantallas *earrings (Puerto Rico)*
el peine *comb*
la peinilla *comb (Latin America)*
los pendientes *earrings*
la prenda *piece of clothing*
la pulsera *bracelet*
la sombrilla *parasol*
los vaqueros *jeans*
las zapatillas de tenis *sneakers; tennis shoes (Spain)*

Más palabras útiles/*More useful words*

de buena/mala calidad *good/poor quality*
de goma *(made of) rubber*
de lino *(made of) linen*
de manga corta/larga/media *short/long/half sleeve*
de nilón *nylon*
de oro *(made) of gold*
de plata *(made) of silver*
de platino *platinum*
de puntitos *polka dotted*

Para comprar ropa/*To go clothes shopping*

el escaparate *store window*
el/la dependiente/a *clerk*
la ganga *bargain*
la liquidación *clearance sale*
el maniquí *mannequin*
el mostrador *counter*
la oferta *offer; sale*
la rebaja *sale; discount*
el tacón alto/bajo *high/low heel*
la venta *clearance sale*
la vitrina *store window*
los zapatos planos/de cuña *flat/wedge shoes*

Unos adjetivos/*Some adjectives*

amplio/a *wide*
apretado/a *tight*

Unos verbos reflexivos/*Some reflexive verbs*

desvestirse (e → i → i) *to get undressed*

CAPÍTULO 9

El cuerpo humano/*The human body*

la arteria *artery*
el cabello *hair*
la cadera *hip*
la ceja *eyebrow*
el cerebelo *cerebellum*
el cerebro *brain*
la cintura *waist*
el codo *elbow*
la costilla *rib*
la frente *forehead*
el hombro *shoulder*
el hueso *bone*
el labio *lip*
la lengua *tongue*
las mejillas *cheeks*
la muñeca *wrist*
el músculo *muscle*
el muslo *thigh*
los nervios *nerves*
la pestaña *eyelash*
la piel *skin*
el pulmón *lung*
la rodilla *knee*
el talón *heel*
el trasero *buttocks (Spain)*
el tobillo *ankle*
la uña *nail*
las venas *veins*

Unas enfermedades y unos tratamientos médicos/*Some illnesses and medical treatments*

el alcoholismo *alcoholism*
la alta tensión *high blood pressure*
el ataque del corazón *heart attack*
la baja tensión *low blood pressure*
el cáncer *cancer*
la depresión *depression*
la diabetes *diabetes*
el dolor de cabeza *headache*
el/la drogadicto/a *drug addict*
la hipertensión *high blood pressure*
el infarto *heart attack*
la inflamación *inflammation*
el mareo *dizziness*
la narcomanía *drug addiction*
la presión alta/baja *high/low blood pressure*
la quemadura *burn*
el sarampión *measles*
el sida *AIDS*
la tirita *bandage*
la varicela *chicken pox*

Otros verbos útiles/*Other useful verbs*

contagiarse de *to catch (an illness)*
desmayarse *to faint*
desvanecerse *to faint*
doblarse *to sprain*
enyesar *to put on a cast*
fracturar(se) *to break; to fracture*
hacer gárgaras *to gargle*
hinchar *to swell*
pegársele *to catch something*
recetar *to prescribe*
respirar *to breathe*
sacar la sangre *to draw blood*
tomarle la presión *to take someone's blood pressure*
tomarle el pulso *to take someone's pulse*
tomarle la temperatura *to check someone's temperature*
torcerse *to sprain*
vomitar *to vomit*

Otras palabras útiles/*Other useful words*

las alergias *allergies*
el antihistamínico *antihistamine*
la camilla *stretcher*
la cura *cure*
la dosis *dosage*
la enfermedad *illness*
las gotas para los ojos *eyedrops*
los medicamentos *medicines*
las muletas *crutches*
operar *to operate*
el/la paciente *patient*
la penicilina *penicillin*
el pulso *pulse*
las pruebas médicas *medical tests*
la radiografía *X-ray*
el resultado *result*
retorcerse *to sprain*
el termómetro *thermometer*
la vacuna *vaccination*

CAPÍTULO 10

El transporte y otras palabras/*Transportation and other words*

el aparcamiento *parking lot*
el atasco *traffic jam*
el billete *ticket*
el camino *dirt road*
el camión *bus (Mexico)*
la camioneta *pickup truck; van; station wagon*
el carnet *driver's license (Spain)*
la carretera *highway*
enviar *to send; to dispatch*
la goma *tire (Latin America)*
la guagua *bus (Caribbean)*
el guía *steering wheel (Puerto Rico)*
el paso de peatones *crosswalk*
el seguro del coche *car insurance*
el tiquete *ticket*
la velocidad *speed*

Unas partes de un vehículo/*Some parts of a car*

el acelerador *accelerator; gas pedal*
el cinturón de seguridad *seat belt*
el claxon *horn*
el espejo retrovisor *rearview mirror*
los frenos *brakes*
las luces *lights*
el maletero *car trunk (Spain)*
el parachoques *bumper*
la transmisión *transmission*

Un verbo útile/*A useful verb*

perderse *to get lost*

El viaje/*Travel*

los cheques de viajero *traveler's checks*
la dirección *address*
el equipaje *luggage*
la estampilla *(postage) stamp*
la oficina de turismo *tourist office*
el paquete *package*
el pasaje de ida y vuelta *round-trip ticket*
los pasajes *(travel) tickets*
el sobre *the envelope*

El hotel/*The hotel*

el/la camarero/a *service maid*
el/la guardia de seguridad *security guard*
el/la portero/a *doorman/woman*
el/la recepcionista *receptionist*
el servicio *room service (cleaning)*
el/la telefonista *telephone operator*

CAPÍTULO 11

Unos animales/*Some animals*

la abeja *bee*
la ardilla *squirrel*
la ballena *whale*
la cabra *goat*
el cangrejo *crab*
el ciervo *deer*
el cochino *pig*
la culebra *snake*
el dinosaurio *dinosaur*
la foca *seal*
el gallo *rooster*
el gorila *gorilla*
la iguana *iguana*
la jirafa *giraffe*
el lobo *wolf*
el loro *parrot*
la mariposa *butterfly*
el marrano *pig*
el mono *monkey*
el nido *nest*
la oveja *sheep*
la paloma *pigeon; dove*
el pato *duck*
el puerco *pig*
el pulpo *octopus*
el puma *puma*
el rinoceronte *rhinoceros*
el saltamontes *grasshopper*
el tiburón *shark*
el tigre *tiger*
la tortuga *turtle*
el venado *deer*
el zorro *fox*

El medio ambiente/*The environment*

el aerosol *aerosol*
el agua subterránea *ground water*
la Antártida *Antarctica*
el Ártico *the Arctic*
la atmósfera *atmosphere*
el aumento *increase*
el bióxido de carbono *carbon dioxide*
el carbón *coal*
el central nuclear *nuclear plant*
el clorofluorocarbono *chlorofluorocarbon*
el combustible fósil *fossil fuel*
la cosecha *crop; harvest*
la descomposición *decomposition*
el desperdicio de patio *yard waste*
el ecosistema *ecosystem*
la energía *energy*
la energía eólica (molinos de viento) *wind power (windmills)*
la industria *industry*
insoportable *unbearable; unsustainable*
el medio ambiente *environment*
el oxígeno *oxygen*
el país *country*
el pesticida *pesticide*
el petróleo *petroleum*
la piedra *rock; stone*
las placas solares *solar panels*
la planta eléctrica *power plant*
el plomo *lead*
el polvo *dust*
el rayo de sol *ray of sunlight*
el rayo ultravioleta *ultraviolet ray*
el riesgo *risk*

Unos verbos/*Some verbs*

atrapar *to trap*
conseguir *to achieve*
corroer *to corrode*
dañar *to damage*
desarrollar *to evolve; to develop*
descongelarse *to melt; melt down*
destruir *to destroy*
hacer huelga *to go on strike*
hundirse *to sink*
luchar en contra *to fight against*
prevenir *to prevent*
realizar *to achieve*
tirar *to throw away (Spain)*

La política/*Politics*

la constitución *constitution*
la ciudadanía *citizenship*
el/la ciudadano/a *citizen*
el/la congresista *congressman/woman*
el gobierno *the government*
la monarquía constitucional *constitutional monarchy*
el paro general *general strike*
el/la primer/a ministro/a *prime minister*
el/la secretario/a de estado *secretary of state*

Las cuestiones políticas/*Political issues*

el aborto *abortion*
el abuso de menores *child abuse*
el derecho de trabajadores *workers' rights*
la eutanasia *euthanasia*
el genocidio *genocide*
la inmigración ilegal *illegal immigration*
la pena capital *death penalty*
la seguridad social *social security*
la violencia doméstica *domestic violence*

APPENDIX 4

SPANISH-ENGLISH GLOSSARY

A

a to; at (5, **11**); ~ **cambio** in exchange (4); ~ **causa de** as a result of (5); ~ **continuación** following (10); ~ **eso de** around (7); ~ **fin de** in order to (11); ~ **fines de** at the end of (8); ~ **la derecha de** to the right of (**3, 7, 11**); ~ **la izquierda de** to the left of (**3, 7, 11**); ~ **la parrilla** grilled (7); ~ **la vez** at the same time (4); ~ **la.../~ las...** at... o'clock (**PA**); ~ **lo mejor** maybe (5); ~ **mano** on hand (10); ~ **menudo** often (**2, 8**); ~ **principios de** at the beginning of (7); **¿~ qué hora?** at what time? (**PA**); ~ **través de** through (11); ~ **veces** sometimes; from time to time (**2, 4**); ~ **ver** let's see (2)
abajo below (9)
abarcar to encompass (5)
abolir to revoke; to repeal, to abolish (5)
Abra(n) el libro en la página... Open your book to page... (**PA**)
abrazo, el hug (PA)
abrigo, el overcoat (**8**)
abril April (**PA**)
abrir to open (**2**)
abuelo/a, el/la grandfather/ grandmother (**1**)
abuelos, los grandparents (**1**)
aburrido/a boring; bored (with **estar**) (**PB, 1, 2, 5**)
acabar con to end (4)
acabar de to have just (1, **9**)
acción, una película de action film (**5**)
aceite, el oil (**7**)
acerca de about (4, **11**)
acercarse to approach; to move near (4)
acierto, el match (11)
acompañar to accompany (6)
aconsejar to advise (12)
acontecimiento, el event (9)
acordarse de (ue) to remember (**8**)
acostarse (ue) to go to bed (**8**)
actor, el actor (**5**)
actriz, la actress (**5**)
adecuado/a suitable (10)
además in addition (1)
adentro inside (10)
Adiós. Good-bye. (**PA**)
adivinar to guess (4)
adjunto/a attached (10)
administración de empresas, la business administration (**2**)
¿Adónde? To where? (**2**)
advertir (ie, i) to warn (8)
aeropuerto, el airport (**10**)
afeitarse to shave (**8**)
afición, la interest (2)
aficionado/a, el/la fan (3, **5**)
afuera de outside of (**11**)
afueras, las outskirts (3)
agencia de viajes, la travel agency (6, **10**)
agente de viajes, el/la travel agent (**10**)
agosto August (**PA**)
agradable agreeable; pleasant (5)
agua, el water; ~ **(con hielo)** water (with ice) (5, 7); ~ **dulce** fresh water (5)
ahora now (4)
aire, el air (**11**); ~ **acondicionado** air conditioning (**10**)
ajo, el garlic (7)
al (contraction of **a** and **el**) to the; ~ **aire libre** in the open air (8); ~ **horno** baked (**7**); ~ **igual** the same as (3); ~ **lado de** beside; next to (3, 7, 11); ~ **revés** in reverse (8)
alabar to praise (11)
alborotado/a stirred up (11)
alcalde, el mayor (*masc.*) (**11**)
alcaldesa, la mayor (*fem.*) (**11**)
alegrarse to be happy (10)
alegre happy (5)
alemán/alemana German (**PA**)
alergia, tener to be allergic (**9**)
alfabetización, la literacy (8)
alfombra, la rug; carpet (**3**)
algo something (3, **4**)
algodón, el cotton (**8**)
alguien someone (**4**)
algún some/any (**4**)
alguno/a some/any (1, **4**)
alimento, el food (**7**)
aliviarse to alleviate (5)
allá over there (**6**)
allí there (4, **6**)
almacén, el department store (**4**)
almohada, la pillow (**3**)
almorzar (ue) to have lunch (**4, 7**)
almuerzo, el lunch (5, **7**)
alquilar to rent; to sublet (3)
alrededor around (9)
altillo, el attic (**3**)
altiplano, el high plateau (9)
alto/a tall (**1**)
altura, la altitud; height (9); **el mal de altura** altitude sickness (9)
aluminio, el aluminum (**11**)
amante, el/la lover (11)
amarillo/a yellow (**3**)
ambulante roving (4)
amenaza, la threat (8)
amigo/a, el/la friend (**1**)
amor, el love (4)
ampliar to increase (2)
amueblado/a furnished (**3**)
analizar to analyze (9)
ancho/a wide (7, **8**)
andar to walk (**7**)
anfibio, el amphibian (11)
anillo, el ring (5)
animado/a animated (**5**)
animal, el animal (**11**); ~ **doméstico** domesticated animal, pet (**11**); ~ **en peligro de extinción** endangered species (**11**); ~ **salvaje** wild animal (**11**)
anoche last night (**7**)
anotar to note; to jot down (5)
anteayer the day before yesterday (**7**)
antepasado/a, el/la ancestor (9)
antes de before (time/space) (2, **11**)
antiácido, el antacid (**9**)
antibiótico, el antibiotic (**9**)
antiguo/a old; ancient (2, **3**)
antipático/a unpleasant (**1**)
anuncio, el advertisement; flyer (1)
añadir to add (5)
año, el year (**PA**); ~ **pasado** last year (4, 7); **tener... años** to be... years old (**3**)
aparato doméstico, el appliance (8)
apariencia, la appearance (11)
apartado, el section (8)
apartamento, el apartment (**2**)
apartarse to move away (11)
apasionado/a passionate (**5**)
apellido, el last name (8)
apodo, el nickname (5)
apoyar to support (5, **11**); ~ **a un/a candidato/a** to support a candidate (**4**)
apoyo, el support (11)
aprender to learn (**2**)
aprobado/a approved (10)
aprobar (ue) to pass (a test) (10)
apropiado/a appropriate (5)
apuntes, los notes (**2**)
aquel/la that (way over there) (**5**)
aquél/la that one (way over there) (**5**)

aquellos/as those (way over there) (**5**)
aquéllos/as those ones (way over there) (**5**)
aquí here (1, **6**)
araña, la spider (5)
árbol, el tree (2,**11**)
arco iris, el rainbow (4)
armario, el armoire; closet; cabinet (**3**)
arquitectura, la architecture (**2**)
arreglar to straighten up; to arrange; to fix (**3**)
arreglar/hacer la maleta to pack a suitcase (**10**)
arreglarse to get ready (**8**)
arriesgado/a adventurous (**10**)
arroz, el rice (**7**)
arte, el art (**2**)
artesanía, la arts and crafts (2, **4**)
artículo, el article (5)
artista, el/la artist (**5**)
asado/a roasted; grilled (**7**)
asegurar to assure (10)
asesinar to murder (11)
asesor/a, el/la advisor (11)
asiento, el seat (10)
asignar to assign (4)
asistir to attend (11)
asociado/a associated (5)
asociar to associate (4)
áspero/a rough (11)
aspiradora, la vacuum cleaner (**3**); **pasar ~** to vacuum (**3**)
aspirina, la aspirin (**9**)
asunto, el subject; matter (1, 6)
asustado/a frightened (7)
asustar to scare (9)
atacar to attack (11)
atender (ie) to attend to; to assist (8)
aterrador/a frightening (9)
atletismo, el track and field (2)
atractivo/a appealing (**10**)
atraer to attract (8)
atravesado/a crossed (9)
atrevido/a daring (**8**)
atún, el tuna (5, **7**)
aumentar to grow (increase) (11)
aunque although; though (5)
autobús, el bus (**10**)
autopista, la freeway (**10**)
autoridad, la authority (5)
ave, el bird (11)
aventura, la adventure (2)
aventurero/a, el/la adventurer (10)
averiguar to find out (3)
aves, las poultry (**7**)
avión, el airplane (**10**)
ayer yesterday (**2, 7**)
ayuda, la help (1)
ayudante, el/la assistant (5)
ayudar to help (**3**)
azotar to whip (11)
azúcar, el sugar (**7**)
azul blue (**3**)

B

bahía, la bay (4)
bailar to dance (**2**)
baile, el dance (5)
bajar (de) to get down (from); to get off (of) (**10**)
bajo below; under (7)
bajo/a short (in stature) (**1**)
balcón, el balcony (**3**)
banana, la banana (**7**)
banco, el bank (**4**)
bandera, la flag (10)
bañarse to bathe (**8**)
bañera, la bathtub (**3**)
baño, el bathroom (**3**); **el traje de baño** swimsuit, bathing suit (**8**)
bar, el bar (**4**)
barato/a cheap (4, **7**)
barco, el boat (**10**)
barrio, el neighborhood (8)
barro, el clay (2)
basarse en to base one's judgment on (5)
básquetbol, jugar al to play basketball (**2**)
bastante rather; enough (3)
Bastante bien. Just fine. (**PA**)
bastar to be enough (8)
basura, la garbage (**11**); **sacar ~** to take out the garbage (**3**)
bata, la robe (**8**)
batata, la yam (7)
batería, la drums (**5**)
baterista, el/la drummer (**5**)
baúl, el trunk (**10**)
bebida, la beverage (**7**)
beige beige (**3**)
béisbol, jugar al to play baseball (**2**)
bello/a beautiful (10)
besito, el little kiss (PA)
beso, el kiss (1)
biblioteca, la library (**2**)
bicicleta, la bicycle (**10**)
bidet, el bidet (**3**)
bien good; well; **bastante ~** just fine (**PA**); **~ cocido/a** well done; well cooked (**7**); **~ hecho/a** well done; well cooked (**7**); **~ puesto** well set (7); **~, gracias.** Fine, thanks. (**PA**)
bienestar, el well-being; welfare (**11**)
bilingüe bilingual (1)
biología, la biology (**2**)
bistec, el steak (**7**)
blanco/a white (**3**)
bloque, el block (11)
blusa, la blouse (**8**)
boca, la mouth (**9**)
boda, la wedding (4)
boleto, el ticket (8, **10**); **~ de ida y vuelta** round-trip ticket (**10**)
bolígrafo, el ballpoint pen (**2**)
bolso, el bag; purse (7, **8**)
bondadoso/a kind (11)
bonito/a pretty (**1**)
borrador, el eraser (**2**)
bosque, el forest (4, **11**)
botar to throw away (**11**)
botas, las boots (**8**)
bote, el boat (4)
botella, la bottle (5,**11**)
botones, el bellman (**10**)
brazo, el arm (**9**)
broma, la joke (3)
¡Buen provecho! Enjoy your meal! (**7**)
Buenas: ~ noches. Good evening.; Good night. (**PA**); **~ tardes.** Good afternoon. (**PA**)
bueno/a good (**1**); **¡Qué ~!** That's great! (2)
Buenos días. Good morning. (**PA**)
bullicio, el hubbub (4)
buscar to look for (1, **4**)
búsqueda, la search (11)

C

caballo, el horse (**11**)
cabeza, la head (**9**); **tener dolor de cabeza** to have a headache (**9**)
cacique, el chief (9)
cada each; every (1)
cadena, la chain (3)
caer to fall (9)
café brown (**3**); **el ~** coffee (**4, 7**)
cafetería, la cafeteria (**2**)
caja (de cartón), la (cardboard) box (**11**)
cajero automático, el ATM machine (**4**)
calcetines, los socks (**8**)
calculadora, la calculator (**2**)
calefacción, la heater (**10**)
calidad, la quality (8, **11**)
caliente hot (temperature) (**7**)
calificado/a qualified (11)
callarse to get/keep quiet (**8**)
calle, la street (**3, 10**)
calor, tener to be hot (**3**)
cama, la bed (**3**); **hacer ~** to make the bed (**3**)
camarero/a, el/la waiter/waitress (**7**)
camarones, los shrimp (**7**)
cambiar to change (7, **10**); **~ de papel** to change roles (3)
caminar to walk; to go on foot (**2, 10**)
caminata, hacer una to take a walk (**4**)
camión, el truck (**10**)

camisa, la shirt (**8**)
camiseta, la T-shirt (**8**)
campamento de niños, el summer camp (**4**)
campaña, la campaign (**11**); **~ política** political campaign (**4**)
campesino/a, el/la farmer (11)
campo, el country (rural) (**3**)
canadiense Canadian (**PA**)
canción, la song (5)
candidato/a, el/la candidate (**11**)
canoa, la canoe (**4**)
cansado/a tired (**2**)
cantante, el/la singer (**5**)
cantar to sing (5)
capa de ozono, la ozone layer (**11**)
capaz capable (8)
capítulo, el chapter (6)
cara, la face (5, **9**)
característica física, la physical characteristic (**1**)
caracterizar to characterize (9)
carne, la meat (**7**)
caro/a expensive (3, **7**)
carrera, la career (1)
carreta, la cart (5)
carretera, la highway (10)
carro, el car (**10**)
carta, la letter (**4**)
casa, la house (1, **3**)
casado/a, estar to be married (1)
casarse to marry (7)
casi almost (**4**); **~ siempre** almost always (**8**)
caso, el case (10)
castillo, el castle (3)
catarata, la waterfall (8)
catarro, el cold (**9**); **tener (un) catarro** to have a cold (**9**)
catorce fourteen (**PA**)
CD, el compact disk (**2**)
cebolla, la onion (**7**)
cena, la dinner (**7**)
cenar to have dinner (**7**)
centavo, el cent (5)
centro, el downtown (**4**); **~ comercial** mall; business/shopping district (**4**); **~ estudiantil** student center; student union (**2**)
cepillarse (el pelo, los dientes) to brush (one's hair, teeth) (**8**)
cerámica, la ceramics (2)
cerca (de) close; near (**2, 7, 11**)
cerdo, el pork; pig (7, **11**)
cereal, el cereal (**7**)
cerebro, el brain (9)
cero zero (**PA**)
cerrado/a closed (3)
cerrar (ie) to close (**4**)
cerveza, la beer (PB, **7**)
cestería, la basket making (2)
chamán, el shaman (9)
Chao. Bye. (**PA**)
chaqueta, la jacket (**8**)
cheque, el bank check (**4**)
chicle, el gum (2)
chico/a, el/la boy/girl (**1**)
chile, el chili pepper (**7**)
chino/a Chinese (**PA**)
chisme, el gossip (7)
cibercafé, el Internet café (**4**)
ciclorruta, la bicycle path (10)
ciego/a blind (3)
cielo, el sky; heaven (**11**)
cien one hundred (**1, 2**); **~ mil** one hundred thousand (**3**); **~ millones** one hundred million (**3**)
ciencia ficción, una película de science fiction film (**5**)
ciencias, las science (**2**); **~ políticas** political science (2)
Cierre(n) el libro/los libros. Close your book/s. (**PA**)
cierto/a true (4)
cima, la top; summit (10)
cinco five (**PA**)
cincuenta fifty (**1**)
cine, el movie theater (**4**)
cintura, la waist (**9**)
cinturón, el belt (**8**)
circular to circulate (8); **~ una petición** to circulate a petition (**4**)
círculo, el circle (8)
cita, la appointment; date (4, 8)
ciudad, la city (1, **3, 4**)
claro of course (3)
claro/a light (colored) (**8**)
clase, la class; **la sala de clase** classroom (**2**)
clasificar to classify (5)
cliente/a, el/la customer (**7**)
clima, el climate (7)
club, el club (**4**); **~ campestre** country club (**4**)
coche, el car (**10**)
cocido/a boiled; baked (**7**)
cocina, la kitchen (**3**)
cocinar to cook (**3, 7**)
cocinero/a, el/la chef; cook (4, **7**)
cocodrilo, el crocodile (11)
código, el code (2)
cognado, el cognate (PA)
cola, la line (of people) (**10**)
colcha, la bedspread; comforter (**3**)
colegio, el high school (8)
colgar (ue) to hang up (7)
colibrí, el hummingbird (11)
colocar to place (11)
color, el color (**3**)
combatir to fight, to combat (**11**)
comedor, el dining room (**3**)
comentario, el comment (5)
comenzar (ie) to begin (2, **4**)
comer to eat (**2**)
cómico/a funny (**1**)
comida, la dinner; meal; food (PB, **7**); **repartir comidas** to hand out/deliver food (**4**)
como like (1); **tan… como** as… as (1)
¿Cómo? What?; How? (**PA, 2**); **¿~ andas?** How are you doing? (PA); **¿~ está usted?** How are you? (*for.*) (**PA**); **¿~ estás?** How are you? (*fam.*) (**PA**); **¿~ se dice… en español?** How do you say… in Spanish? (**PA**); **¿~ se escribe… en español?** How do you write… in Spanish? (**PA**); **¿~ se llama usted?** What is your name? (*for.*) (**PA**); **¿~ te llamas?** What is your name? (*fam.*) (**PA**)
cómodo/a comfortable (**8**)
compañero/a, el/la companion, colleage; **~ de clase** classmate (**2**); **~ de cuarto** roommate (**2**)
compañía, la company (8)
comparación, la comparison (10)
compartir to share (3)
competencia, la competition (7)
compilar to compile (11)
complejo, el complex (3)
composición, la composition (**2**)
comprar to buy (**2**)
compras, las shopping (4); **hacer ~** to go shopping (7); **ir de compras** to go shopping (**2**)
comprender to understand (1, **2**)
comprobar (ue) to check (3)
computadora, la computer (**2**)
común common (4)
con with (**2, 11**)
concierto, el concert (**5**); **dar un concierto** to give/perform a concert (**5**)
concursante, el/la contestant (8)
concurso, el contest (3)
condimento, el seasoning; condiment (**7**)
conducción, la driving (10)
conducir to drive (**7, 10**); **la licencia de ~** driver's license (**10**)
conejo, el rabbit (**11**)
confiar to trust (8)
congreso, el congress (**11**)
conjunto, el group; band; outfit (**5, 8**)
conmigo with me (8)
conmovedor/a moving, emotional (**5**)
conocer to know (**3**)
conocido/a known (4)
conocimiento, el knowledge (2)
conseguir (i, i) to get (7)
consejero/a, el/la counselor (**4**)
consejo, el advice (5)
conspiración, la conspiracy (7)
construir to construct (9)
consultorio, el doctor's office (9)

contagioso/a contagious (11)
contaminación, la pollution (**11**)
contaminar to pollute (**11**)
contar (ue) to tell (a story) (5)
contemporáneo/a contemporary (**3**)
contener (ie) to contain (7)
contenido, el content (9)
contento/a content, happy (**2**)
contestador automático, el answering machine (7)
contestar to answer (1, **2**)
Conteste(n). Answer. (**PA**)
contigo with you (7)
convencer to convince (5)
corazón, el heart (**9**)
corbata, la tie (**8**)
cordillera, la chain of mountains (7)
coro, el chorus (8)
corregir (i) to correct (3)
correo, el post office (**4**); **~ electrónico** e-mail (3); **la oficina de correos** post office (**4**)
correr to run (**2**)
cortar(se) to cut (oneself) (**9**)
cortejo, el courting (7)
cortesía, la courtesy, politeness (**PA**)
corto/a short (length) (**8, 10**)
cosa, la thing (**3**)
cosecha, la crop (7)
costa, la coast (4)
costar (ue) to cost (2, **4**)
costumbre, la custom (7)
costurera, la seamstress (8)
cotidiano/a daily (4)
crear to create (3)
creativo/a creative (**5**)
crecer to grow (8)
creer to believe (**2**)
crudo/a rare (meat); raw (**7**)
cruzar to cross (5)
cuaderno, el notebook (**2**)
cuadro, el square; picture; painting (**3**)
cuadros, de checked (**8**)
¿Cuál/es? Which (one/s)? (**2**)
¿Cuándo? When? (**2**)
¿Cuánto/a/os/as? How much?; How many? (**2**)
cuarenta forty (**1**)
cuarto, el room (**2, 3**); **~ doble** double room (**10**); **~ individual** single room (**10**)
cuarto/a fourth (**5**)
cuatro four (**PA**)
cuatrocientos four hundred (**2**)
cubano/a Cuban (**PA**)
cubrir to cover (7)
cuchara, la soup spoon; tablespoon (**7**)
cucharada, la spoonful (7)
cucharita, la teaspoon (**7**)
cuchillo, el knife (**7**)
cuello, el neck (**9**)
cuenta, la bill; account (**4**); **~, por favor.** The check, please. (**7**); **darse cuenta** to realize (9); **tener en cuenta** to keep in mind (**5**)
cuento, el story (5)
cuero, el leather (**8**)
cuerpo, el body (**9**)
cuestiones políticas, las political issues (**11**)
cueva, la cave (**11**)
cuidado, tener to be careful (**3**)
cuidadoso/a careful (**5**)
cuidar to take care of (9, **11**)
culpable guilty (8)
cumpleaños, el birthday (8)
cura, la cure (4)
curandero/a, el/la folk healer (4)
curar to cure (**9**)
curita, la adhesive bandage (**9**)
curso, el course (**2**)
cuyo/a/os/as whose (5)

D

daño, hacer to (do) damage (**11**)
dar to give (**3**); **~ con** to find (2); **~ un concierto** to give/perform a concert (**5**); **~ vida** to give life (5)
darse cuenta to realize (9)
dato, el data; information (9)
de of; from (1, **11**); **~ cuadros** checked (**8**); **~ la mañana** in the morning (**PA**); **~ la noche** in the evening (**PA**); **~ la tarde** in the afternoon (**PA**); **~ lunares** polka-dotted (**8**); **~ mal gusto** in poor taste (8); **~ manga larga** long sleeved (8); **~ nada.** You're welcome. (**PA**); **~ nuevo** again (4); **~ pronto** suddenly (4); **~ rayas** striped (**8**); **~ repente** suddenly (PB); **~ vez en cuando** once in a while (9)
debajo de under (**7, 11**)
deber ought to, should (1, **4**)
deber, el obligation; duty (**4**)
debido a owing to (8)
débil weak (**1**)
décimo/a tenth (**5**)
decir (i) to say (**3**)
decisión, la resolution (9)
dedicar to devote (3)
dedo, el finger (**9**); **~ del pie** toe (**9**)
defensa, la defense (**11**)
dejar to leave (7, **10**)
delante de in front of (7, **11**)
delgado/a thin (**1**)
delicia, la delight (11)
delincuencia, la crime (**11**)
demás, los the others (4)
demasiado too; too much (2)
democracia, la democracy (**11**)
demostrar (ue) to demonstrate (**4**)
dentro de inside of (3, **11**)
dependiente/a, el/la clerk (8)
deporte, el sport (**2**)
derecha de, a la to the right of (**3, 7, 11**)
derecho, el law; right (legal) (**2**)
derrame de petróleo, el oil spill (**11**)
desaparecer to disappear (5)
desaparecido/a missing (9)
desaparición, la disappearance (7)
desarrollado/a developed (7)
desarrollar to develop (11)
desastre, el disaster (4, **11**)
desayunar to have breakfast (**7**)
desayuno, el breakfast (**7**)
descansar to rest (7)
descifrar to decipher (9)
describir to describe (1)
descubrir to discover (4)
descuento, el discount (8)
desde from; since (3, 7, **11**)
desear to wish, to want (2)
desempleo, el unemployment (**11**)
desesperado/a desperate (11)
deshidratar to dehydrate (9)
desierto, el desert (9)
desigualdad, la inequality (10)
desordenado/a messy (**3**)
desorientador/a disorienting (9)
despedida, la farewell (**PA**)
despertador, el alarm clock (**2**)
despertarse (ie) to wake up; to awaken (**8**)
después de after (5, **6, 11**)
destacar to stand out (5)
destinatario, el addressee (5)
destino, el destination (8)
destrozado/a shattered; destroyed (10)
destrucción, la destruction (**11**)
detalle, el detail (6)
determinación, la resolution (11)
detrás de behind (**4, 11**)
deuda (externa), la (foreign) debt (**11**)
devolver (ue) to return (an object) (**4**)
día, el day (**PA**)
diálogo, el dialogue (4)
diario/a daily (4)
dibujar to draw (4)
dibujo, el drawing (3)
dicho, el saying (1)
diciembre December (**PA**)
dictador/a, el/la dictator (**11**)
dictadura, la dictatorship (**11**)
diecinueve nineteen (**PA**)
dieciocho eighteen (**PA**)
dieciséis sixteen (**PA**)
diecisiete seventeen (**PA**)

diente, el tooth (**9**); **cepillarse los dientes** to brush one's teeth (**8**)
diez ten (**PA**)
difícil difficult (1, **2**, **PB**, **10**)
dinero, el money (**2**)
diputado/a, el/la representative (**11**)
dirección, la address (8)
dirigir to conduct; to direct (3, 11)
discapacitado/a, el/la handicapped person (3)
disco compacto, el compact disk (**2**)
disculpa, la apology (10)
discurso, el speech (**11**)
discutir to discuss (4)
diseñador/a, el/la designer (8)
diseño, el design (4)
disfrutar to enjoy (5)
disponible available (10)
distraer to entertain; distract (5)
divertirse (ie, i) to enjoy oneself; to have fun (5, **8**)
dividido por divided by (**1**)
doblar to turn (**10**)
doce twelve (**PA**)
docena, la dozen (7)
doctor/a, el/la doctor (**9**)
documental, una película documentary film (**5**)
doler (ue) to hurt (**9**)
dolor, el pain (**9**); **~ de cabeza** headache (**9**); **~ de espalda** backache (**9**); **~ de estómago** stomachache (**9**); **~ de garganta** sore throat (**9**)
domingo, el Sunday (**PA**)
¿Dónde? Where? (**2**)
dormir (ue) to sleep (**4**)
dormirse (ue, u) to fall asleep (**8**)
dormitorio, el bedroom (**3**)
dos two (**PA**)
doscientos two hundred (**2**)
dramática, una película drama film (**5**)
ducha, la shower (**3**)
ducharse to shower (**8**)
duda, la doubt (5)
dulces, los candy; sweets (**7**)
duplicar to duplicate (10)
durante during (3)
durar to last (11)
duro/a hard; hard-boiled (**7**)
DVD, el DVD (**2**)

E

echar una siesta to take a nap (PB)
ecología, la ecology (**11**)
edad, la age (3)
edificio, el building (**2**)
efecto invernadero, el global warming (**11**)
ejemplo, el example (4)
ejercicio, el exercise (3); **hacer ejercicio** to exercise (**2**)
ejército, el army (5)
el the (**1**, **2**)
él he (**PA**, **2**)
elefante, el elephant (**11**)
elegante elegant (**8**)
elegir (i, i) to elect (9, **11**)
ella she (**PA**)
ellos/as they (**PA**)
emanar to emanate (11)
embarazada pregnant (9)
embriaguez, la intoxication (10)
emitido/a issued (10)
emoción, la emotion (**2**)
emocionado/a excited (4)
emocionante moving, emotional; exciting (**5**, **10**)
empezar (ie) to begin (**4**)
empleado/a, el/la attendant; employee (12)
emplear to employ (10)
empleo, el employment (3)
empresa, la company; firm (8)
empresario/a, el/la agent; manager (**5**)
en in (**11**); **~ punto** on the dot (1); **~ seguida** immediately (9); **~ vez de** instead of (8)
enamorarse to fall in love (11)
Encantado/a. Pleased to meet you. (**PA**)
encantar to love; to delight (**8**)
encender (ie) to turn on (light) (9)
encerrar (ie) to enclose (**4**)
encima (de) on top (of) (**3**, **7**, **11**)
encontrar (ue) to find; to meet (2, **4**)
encubierto/a undercover (11)
encuesta, la survey; poll (**11**)
endémico/a common (to a region) (11)
enero January (**PA**)
enfermar(se) to get sick (**9**)
enfermedad, la illness (**9**)
enfermero/a, el/la nurse (**9**)
enfermo/a ill; sick (**2**); **estar ~** to be sick (5, **9**)
enfocarse to focus (9)
enfrente (de) in front (of); across from; facing (2, **4**, **11**)
enhorabuena, la congratulations (11)
enojado/a angry (**2**)
enorme enormous (3)
ensalada, la salad (**7**)
ensayar to practice/rehearse (**5**)
ensayo, el essay (2)
enseñar to teach; to show (**2**)
ensuciar to dirty (11)
entender (ie) to understand (**4**)
enterarse to find out (8)
entero/a entire (3)
entonces then (5, **6**)
entrada, la ticket (**5**)
entrar to enter (2, **10**); **~ ganas** to get an urge (9)
entre among; between (2,**11**)
entregar to hand in (7)
entrenador/a, el/la trainer (4)
entretenerse (ie) to entertain oneself (8)
entretenido/a entertaining (**5**)
entrevista, la interview (3)
entrevistador/a, el/la interviewer (3)
enviar to send (8)
envolver (ue) to wrap (7)
épico/a epic (**5**)
episodio, el episode (3)
época, la epoch (4)
equilibrado/a balanced (7)
equipaje, el luggage (10)
equipo, el team (**2**)
equivocarse to be mistaken (9)
Es la.../Son las... It's... o'clock. (**PA**)
escalera, la staircase (**3**)
escaparse to escape (10)
escena, la scene (7)
esclavitud, la slavery (11)
escoger to choose (4)
esconder to hide (8)
Escriba(n). Write. (**PA**)
escribir to write (1, **2**)
escritor/a, el/la writer (6)
escritorio, el desk (**2**)
escuchar música to listen to music (**2**)
Escuche(n). Listen. (**PA**)
escudo, el coat of arms (3)
escuela, la school (4)
ese/a that (**5**)
ése/a that one (**5**)
esos/as that; those (3, **5**)
ésos/as those ones (**5**)
espacio, el space (3)
espalda, la back (**9**); **tener dolor de espalda** to have a backache (**9**)
espantoso/a scary (**5**)
español/a Spanish (**PA**)
especia, la spice (**7**)
especialidad, la major (1, **2**); **~ de la casa** specialty of the house (**7**)
especie, la species (11)
esperanza, la hope (11)
esperar to wait for; to hope (**2**)
esposo/a, el/la husband/wife (**1**)
Está nublado. It's cloudy. (**PA**)
estación, la season (**PA**); station (**10**); **~ (de tren, de autobús)** (train, bus) station (**10**); **~ de servicio/de gasolina** gas station (**10**)
estacionamiento, el parking (**10**)
estacionarse to park (**10**)
estadidad, la statehood (11)
estadio, el stadium (**2**)

estado, el state of being (**2**, **11**)
estadounidense (norteamericano/a) American (**PA**)
estafar to defraud (10)
estampado/a print; with a pattern or design (**8**)
estándar, el standard (11)
estante de libros, el bookcase (**3**)
estar to be (**2**); **~ casado/a** to be married (**1**); **~ de acuerdo** to agree (**4**); **~ enfermo/a** to be sick (5, **9**); **~ en huelga** to be on strike (**11**); **~ listo/a** to be ready (5); **~ nublado** to be cloudy (**PA**); **~ saludable** to be healthy (**9**); **~ sano/a** to be healthy (**9**)
este, el east (4)
este/a this (**5**)
éste/a this one (**5**)
estereotipo, el stereotype (2)
estilo, el style (5)
estimulante challenging (**10**)
esto this (3); **¿Qué es ~?** What's this? (**PA**)
estómago, el stomach (**9**); **tener dolor de estómago** to have a stomachache (**9**)
estornudar to sneeze (**9**)
estornudo, el sneeze (**9**)
estos/as these (**5**)
éstos/as these ones (**5**)
estrategia, la strategy (10)
estrecho/a narrow; tight (7, **8**)
estrella, la star (**5**)
estrenar una película to release a film/movie (**5**)
estreno, el opening (**5**)
estrés, el stress (4)
estudiante, el/la student (1, **2**)
estudiar to study (1, **2**)
estudio, el study (8)
estufa, la stove (**3**)
estupendo/a stupendous (**5**)
etapa, la stage (4)
evitar to avoid (**9**, **11**)
evolucionar to evolve (5)
examen, el exam (**2**); **~ físico** physical exam (**9**)
excursión, ir de to take a short trip (**4**)
exige más/menos more/less demanding (**10**)
exigente demanding (9)
éxito, tener to be successful (**3**)
expedido/a por completed by (10)
experimentar to experience (11)
explicar to explain (1)
expresión, la expression (**PA**)
extranjero, el abroad (**10**)
extraño/a strange (3)

F

fábrica, la factory (8)
fácil easy (**2**, **PB**)
falda, la skirt (**8**)
falso/a false (7)
faltar to miss (4)
fama, la fame (**5**)
familia, la family (**1**)
farmacéutico/a, el/la pharmacist (9)
farmacia, la pharmacy (**9**); **~ de turno/guardia** 24-hour pharmacy (9)
fascinar to fascinate (**8**)
febrero February (**PA**)
fecha, la date (5)
feliz happy (**2**)
feo/a ugly (**1**)
fiar to trust (10)
fiebre, la fever (**9**)
fiesta, la party (PB)
fila, la row (5)
fin, el end (11); **~ de semana** weekend (3); **~ de semana pasado** last weekend (**7**)
finalista, el/la finalist (3)
finalmente finally (**6**)
finca, la farm (**11**)
fino/a fine; delicate (**5**)
firma, la signature (3)
firmar to sign (3)
flor, la flower (8)
floreciente flourishing (8)
formal formal (**8**)
foto(grafía), la photograph (1)
francés/francesa French (**PA**)
frase, la sentence (4)
fraude, el fraud (6)
frecuencia, la frequency (4)
frecuentemente frequently (**8**)
fresco/a fresh (**7**)
frijoles, los beans (**7**)
frío, tener to be cold (**3**)
frito/a fried (**7**)
fruta, la fruit (**7**)
fuente, la source; fountain (3)
fuera de outside (4)
fuerte strong; loud (**1**)
fuerza, la force, strength (7)
fumar to smoke (10)
funcionar to work; to function (**10**)
fundado/a founded (11)
fútbol, el soccer (2); **~ americano** football (**2**)
futuro, el future (4)

G

galleta, la cookie (**7**)
gallina, la chicken, hen (7, **11**)
gallo, el rooster (7)
galopar to gallop (11)
ganar to win (3)
garaje, el garage (**3**)
garganta, la throat (**9**); **tener dolor de garganta** to have a sore throat (**9**)
gastar to spend (7)
gasto, el expense (10)
gato, el cat (10, **11**)
generalmente generally (**8**)
género, el genre (**5**)
gente, la people (**1**)
gimnasio, el gymnasium (**2**)
gira, la tour (**5**); **hacer una gira** to tour (**5**)
gobernador/a, el/la governor (**11**)
gobierno, el government (1, **11**)
golf, jugar al to play golf (**2**)
gordo/a fat (**1**)
gorra, la cap (**8**)
grabaciones, las recordings (**5**)
grabar to record (**5**)
Gracias. Thank you. (**PA**)
graduarse to graduate (4)
gramo, el gram (7)
grande big; large (**1**)
granja, la farm (**11**)
grano, el bean (4)
grasa, la fat (7)
gratis free (5)
gripe, la flu (**9**); **tener ~** to have the flu (**9**)
gris gray (**3**)
gritar to yell; to scream (8)
guantes, los gloves (**8**)
guapo/a handsome/pretty (**1**)
guardar to put away; to keep (**3**); **~ cama** to stay in bed (**9**)
guerra, la war (**11**); **una película de guerra** war film (**5**)
guía, la guide (4)
guitarra, la guitar (**5**)
guitarrista, el/la guitarist (**5**)
gustar to like (**PA**)

H

hábil skillful; capable (5)
habilidad, la ability (**5**)
habitación, la room (5)
hablar to speak (1, **2**)
Hace: ~ buen tiempo. The weather is nice. (**PA**); **~ calor.** It's hot. (**PA**); **~ frío.** It's cold. (**PA**); **~ mal tiempo.** The weather is bad. (**PA**); **~ sol.** It's sunny. (**PA**); **~ viento.** It's windy. (**PA**)
hacer to do; to make (**3**); **~ daño** to (do) damage (**11**); **~ falta** to need; to be lacking (**8**); **~ la cama** to make the bed (**3**); **~ las compras** to go shopping (7); **~ mímica** to

play charades (8); ~ **una caminata** to take a walk (**4**)
hambre, tener to be hungry (**3**)
hamburguesa, la hamburger (**7**)
hasta until (**2, 11**); ~ **luego.** See you later. (**PA**); ~ **mañana.** See you tomorrow. (**PA**); ~ **pronto.** See you soon. (**PA**)
hay there is; there are (**2**)
hecho/a de made from (9)
heladería, la ice cream shop (10)
helado, el ice cream (**7**)
helado/a iced (**7**)
herencia, la heritage (1)
herida, la wound (**9**)
hermano/a, el/la brother/sister (**1**)
hermanos, los brothers and sisters, siblings (**1**)
hermoso/a beautiful (4)
hervido/a boiled (**7**)
hielo, el ice (7); **el agua con hielo** ice water (5, 7)
hijo/a, el/la son/daughter (**1**)
hijos, los sons and daughters, children (**1**)
hispano/a Hispanic (PA)
hispanohablante, el/la Spanish speaker (1)
historia, la story (PB)
hogar, el home (8)
hoguera, la campfire (**4**)
hoja, la leaf (4)
hojalatería, la tin work (2)
¡Hola! Hi!; Hello! (**PA**)
hombre, el man (**1**)
honrado/a honorable (11)
hora, la hour (1); **¿Qué hora es?** What time is it? (**PA**)
horario (de clases), el (class) schedule (**2**)
hormiga, la ant (**11**)
hormiguero, el anthill (11)
hospital, el hospital (**9**)
hotel, el hotel (**10**)
hoy today (**2**); ~ **(en) día** today; nowadays (5)
hoyo, el hole (**11**)
huelga, la strike (**11**); **estar en huelga** to be on strike (**11**)
huevo, el egg (**7**)
humilde humble (**3**)
humor, una película de funny/comedy film (**5**)
huracán, el hurricane (**11**)

I

idioma, el language (**2**)
iglesia, la church (**4**)
igual que the same as (7)
igualdad, la equality (10)
Igualmente. Likewise. (**PA**)
imagen, la image (8)
imaginativo/a imaginative (**5**)
imitar to imitate (11)
imperio, el empire (9)
impermeable, el raincoat (**8**)
importar to matter; to be important (4, **8**)
impresionante impressive (3, **5**)
impuesto, el tax (**11**)
incendio, el fire (**11**)
incluir to include (4)
incluso including (4)
incómodo/a uncomfortable (9)
increíble incredible (8)
incumbir to concern (8)
indicar to indicate (4)
indígena indigenous (7)
ineficaz ineffectual (11)
infame infamous (11)
infancia, la childhood (12)
infección, tener una to have an infection (**9**)
inflación, la inflation (**11**)
influyente influential (11)
informal casual (**8**)
informática, la computer science (**2**)
informe, el report (9)
ingeniero/a, el/la engineer (10)
inglés/inglesa English (**PA**)
inodoro, el toilet (**3**)
insecto, el insect (**11**)
inteligente intelligent (**1**)
intentar to try (7)
intercambio, el exchange (4)
interesante interesting (**1, 10**)
interesar to interest (2)
intérprete, el/la interpreter (5)
intervenir (ie) to intervene (11)
inundación, la flood (**11**)
invertir (ie, i) to invest (11)
invierno, el winter (**PA**)
involucrado/a involved (11)
inyección, la shot (**9**)
ir to go (**4**); ~ **a pie** to walk; go on foot (**10**); ~ **de excursión** to take a short trip (**4**); ~ **de vacaciones** to go on vacation (7, **10**)
irse to go away; to leave (**8**); ~ **del hotel** to leave the hotel; to check out (**10**)
isla, la island (7)
izquierda de, a la to the left of (**3, 7, 11**)

J

jamás never (emphatic) (**4**)
jamón, el ham (**7**)
japonés/japonesa Japanese (**PA**)
jarabe, el cough syrup (**9**)
jardín, el garden (**3**)
jazz, el jazz (**5**)
jeans, los jeans (**8**)
jefe, el boss (9)
jerga, la jargon (8)
joven young (**1**)
joven, el/la young man/young woman (**1**)
joya, la jewel (9)
juego, el game (4)
jueves, el Thursday (**PA**)
jugador/a, el/la player (3)
jugar (ue) to play (**4**); ~ **al básquetbol** to play basketball (**2**); ~ **al béisbol** to play baseball (**2**); ~ **al fútbol** to play soccer (**2**); ~ **al fútbol americano** to play football (**2**); ~ **al golf** to play golf (**2**); ~ **al tenis** to play tennis (**2**)
jugo, el juice (**7**)
julio July (**PA**)
junio June (**PA**)
junto con along with, together with (2)
juntos/as together (3)

L

la the (**1**)
laboratorio, el laboratory (**2**)
lado, el side (2)
lago, el lake (5, **10, 11**)
lámpara, la lamp (**3**)
lana, la wool (**8**)
lápiz, el pencil (**2**)
largo/a long (7, **8, 10**)
las the (**1**)
lástima, la pity (11)
lastimar(se) to injure someone; (to get hurt; to hurt oneself) (**9**)
lata, la can (**11**)
latir to beat (heart) (9)
lavabo, el sink (**3**)
lavaplatos, el dishwasher (**3**)
lavar to wash (7); ~ **los platos** to wash the dishes (**3**)
lavarse to wash oneself (**8**)
Lea(n). Read. (**PA**)
lección, la lesson (5)
leche, la milk (4, **7**)
lechuga, la lettuce (**7**)
lectura, la reading (1)
leer to read (**2**)
lejos (de) far (from); far away (**2,11**)
lengua, la language (**5**)
lento/a slow (3, **5**)
león, el lion (**11**)
letra, la lyrics; letter (alphabet) (**5**)
levantarse to get up; to stand up (**8**)
ley, la law (2,**11**)
leyenda, la legend (9)
libre free (2)

librería, la bookstore (**2**)
libro, el book (1, 2); **Cierre(n) ~.** Close your book. (**PA**); **el estante de libros** bookcase (**3**)
licencia (de conducir), la driver's license (**10**); **sacar ~** to get a driver's license (**10**)
ligero/a light (weight) (5)
limón, el lemon (**7**)
limpiaparabrisas, el windshield wiper (**10**)
limpiar to clean (**3**)
limpio/a clean (**3**)
lío, el mess (muddle) (9)
liso/a solid-colored (**8**)
listo/a ready; **estar ~** to be ready (**5**)
literatura, la literature (**2**)
llamada, la phone call (7)
llamar to call (2)
llamarse to be called (**8**)
llanta, la tire (**10**)
llave, la key (7, **10**)
llegar to arrive (**2**)
llenar to fill (9, **10**)
llevar to wear; to take; to carry (5, **8**); **~ a alguien al médico** to take someone to the doctor (4);**~ a cabo** to carry out (**11**);**~ puesto** to wear; to have on (**8**)
llorar to cry (8)
Llueve. It's raining. (**PA**)
lluvia, la rain (**PA**); **~ ácida** acid rain (**11**)
lluvioso/a rainy (11)
lo: ¡~ odio! I hate it! (2); **~ que** what; that which (3); **~ sé.** I know. (**PA**); **~ siento** I'm sorry (10)
localizar to locate (5)
loco/a crazy (9)
loro, el parrot (11)
los the (**1**)
lucha libre, la wrestling (2)
luchar to fight; to combat (**11**)
luego later; then (3, **6**); **hasta ~** see you later (**PA**)
lugar, el place (**2**); **tener lugar** to take place (2)
lugareño/a, el local person; villager (4)
lujo, el luxury (10)
luna de miel, la honeymoon (10)
lunares, de polka-dotted (**8**)
lunes, el Monday (**PA**)
luz, la light (11)

M

madrastra, la stepmother (**1**)
madre, la mother (**1**)
maíz, el corn (**7**)
mal de altura, el altitude sickness (9)
mala suerte, la bad luck (4)
maleta, la suitcase (**10**); **arreglar/hacer ~** to pack a suitcase (**10**)
malo/a bad (**1**)
malvado/a evil (10)
mamá, la mom (**1**)
mamífero, el mammal (11)
mancha, la stain (9)
mandar to send (2); **~ una carta** to send/mail a letter (**4**)
mandato, el command (**PA**)
mandioca, la yucca (7)
manejar to drive (8, **10**)
manga larga, de long sleeved (8)
mano, la hand (1, **9**)
manta, la blanket (**3**)
mantel, el tablecloth (**7**)
mantener (ie) to maintain (9)
mantequilla, la butter (**7**)
manzana, la apple (4, **7**)
manzanilla, la chamomile (9)
mañana tomorrow (1, **2**); **de la ~** in the morning (**PA**); **hasta ~** see you tomorrow (**PA**)
mapa, el map (**2**)
maquillarse to put on make up (**8**)
mar, el sea (9)
maravilloso/a marvelous (7)
marcar to dial (9)
mareado/a nauseous (9)
mariscos, los seafood (**7**)
marrón brown (**3**)
martes, el Tuesday (**PA**)
marzo March (**PA**)
más plus; more (**1, 2**); **~ o menos.** So, so. (**PA**); **~ tarde que** later than (**7**); **~ temprano que** earlier than (**7**)
mascota, la pet (10)
matar to kill (10, **11**)
matemáticas, las mathematics (**2**)
materia, la subject (**2**)
mayo May (**PA**)
mayonesa, la mayonnaise (7)
mayor older; bigger (1, **10**); **el/la ~** the biggest (1, **10**)
mayordomo, el butler (10)
mayores, los elderly men/women (**4**); **las personas mayores** elderly men/women (**4**)
mayoría, la majority (7)
Me llamo… My name is… (**PA**)
medianoche, la midnight (**PA**)
medias, las stockings; hose (**8**)
medicamento, el medication (9)
medicina, la medicine (**2**)
médico/a, el/la doctor (**9**)
medio ambiente, el environment (**11**)
medio de transporte, el means of transportation (10)
mediodía, el noon (**PA**)
medir (i, i) to measure (11)
mejor better (5, **10**); **el/la ~** the best (1, **4, 10**)
mejorar(se) to get better; to improve (**9**)
melón, el melon (**7**)
mencionar to mention (4)
menor smaller (**10**); **el/la ~** the smallest (**10**)
menos minus; less (**1, 2**); **más o ~** so-so (**PA**); **por lo ~** at least (3)
mensaje, el message (3)
mentir (ie, i) to lie (**4**)
mentira, la lie (5)
menú, el menu (**7**)
mercado, el market (**4**)
merecer to deserve (11)
merendar (ie) to have a snack (**7**)
merienda, la snack (**7**)
mermelada, la jam; marmalade (**7**)
mes, el month (**PA**)
mesa, la table (**2**); **poner ~** to set the table (**3**)
meterse en política to get involved in politics (**11**)
metido/a en involved in (11)
método, el method (4)
metro, el subway (**10**)
mexicano/a Mexican (**PA**)
mezcla, la mixture (7)
mí me (**2**)
microondas, el microwave (**3**)
miedo, el fear (5); **tener miedo** to be afraid (**3**)
miembro, el member (4)
mientras while (2)
miércoles, el Wednesday (**PA**)
mil one thousand (**2, 3**)
milla, la mile (2)
millón one million (**3**)
mínimo, el minimum (5)
mío/a/os/as mine (**10**)
mirar to look at (3)
mi/s my (**1, 2**)
mismo/a/os/as, el/la/los/las same (1)
misterio, una película de mystery film (**5**)
mitad, la half (11)
mochila, la book bag; knapsack (**2**)
moda, la style; fashion (**8**)
modelo, el/la model (**8**)
moderno/a modern (**3**)
molestar to bother (**8**)
monarquía, la monarchy (**11**)
moneda, la money (1)
monstruo, el monster (9)
montaña, la mountain (8, **10, 11**)
montañoso/a mountainous (4)
montar: ~ a caballo to ride a horse (**11**); **~ en bicicleta** to ride a bike (**2**)

monte, el mountain (11)
montón, el pile (7)
morado/a purple (**3**)
morir (ue, u) to die (**4**)
mosca, la fly (**11**)
mosquito, el mosquito (**11**)
mostaza, la mustard (**7**)
mostrar (ue) to show (**4**)
moto(cicleta), la motorcycle (1, **10**)
motor, el motor; engine (**10**)
mover (ue) to move (10)
muchacho/a, el/la boy/girl (**1**)
muchas veces many times (**8**)
mucho a lot (**2, 8**); **~ gusto.** Nice to meet you. (**PA**)
mueble, el piece of furniture (**3**)
muerto/a dead (11)
mujer, la woman (**1**)
multa, la traffic ticket; fine (**10**)
mundo, el world (PA)
muñeca, la doll (8)
músculo, el muscle (9)
museo, el museum (**4**)
música, la music (**2, 5**); **~ clásica** classical music (**5**); **~ popular** pop music (**5**)
musical, una película musical film (**5**)
músico/a, el/la musician (**5**)
muy very (1); **~ bien.** Really well. (**PA**); **~ poco** very little (2)

N

nacer to be born (8)
nacido/a born (2)
nacionalidad, la nationality (**PA**)
nada nothing (3, **4**)
nadar to swim (**2**)
nadie no one, nobody (**4**)
naranja orange (*color*) (**3**); **la ~** orange (*fruit*) (**7**)
nariz, la nose (**9**)
narrar to narrate (6)
natación, la swimming (2)
natal native (3)
naturaleza, la nature (3, **11**)
náusea, la nausea (**9**)
necesitar to need (**2**)
negocio, el business (8)
negro/a black (**3**)
nervioso/a upset; nervous (**2**); **ponerse ~** to get nervous (**8**)
ni... ni neither... nor (3, **4**)
Nieva. It's snowing. (**PA**)
nieve, la snow (**PA**)
nigeriano/a Nigerian (**PA**)
ningún none (**4**)
ninguno/a none (**4**)
niño/a, el/la little boy/little girl (**1**); **el campamento de niños** summer camp (**4**)

nivel, el level (9)
No. No. (**PA**); **~ cabe duda** there is no doubt (9); **(~) comprendo.** I (don't) understand. (**PA**); **(~) es verdad.** It's (not) true. (1); (~) **lo sé.** I (don't) know. (**PA**); **~ obstante** however (11)
noche, de la in the evening (**PA**)
nombre, el name (1)
noreste, el northeast (2)
normalmente normally (**8**)
norte, el north (7)
norteamericano/a, el/la American (**PA**)
nosotros/as we (**PA**)
nota, la grade (4)
noticia, la news item (11)
novecientos nine hundred (**2**)
noveno/a ninth (**5**)
noventa ninety (**1**)
noviembre November (**PA**)
novio/a, el/la boyfriend/girlfriend (**1**)
nube, la cloud (**PA**)
nublado/a cloudy (**PA**); **está ~** it's cloudy (**PA**)
nuestro/a/os/as our/s (**1, 10**)
nueve nine (**PA**)
nuevo/a new (**3**)
número, el number (**PA**)
nunca never (**2, 4**)

O

o... o either... or (**4**)
objeto, el object (**3**)
obra, la work (3)
obtener (ie) to obtain (4)
occidental western (8)
océano, el ocean (**11**)
ochenta eighty (**1**)
ocho eight (**PA**)
ochocientos eight hundred (**2**)
octavo/a eighth (**5**)
octubre October (**PA**)
ocultar to hide (5)
ocupar to occupy (4)
ocurrir to occur (4, **9**)
oeste, el west (2)
oficina, la office (**3**); **~ de correos** post office (**4**)
ofrecer to offer (1)
oído, el inner ear (**9**)
oír to hear (**3**)
ojalá let's hope that; hopefully (11)
ojear las vitrinas to window-shop (8)
ojo, el eye (**9**)
olvidar to forget (7)
once eleven (**PA**)
ópera, la opera (**5**)
opinar to think, to express an opinion (1)

opinión, la opinion (4)
oportunidad, la opportunity (3)
opuesto, el opposite (4, 11)
oración, la sentence (3)
orden, el order (5)
oreja, la ear (**9**)
organizar to organize (**4**)
orgulloso/a proud (4)
origen, el origen (1)
orquesta, la orchestra (**5**)
oscuro/a dark (**8**)
oso, el bear (9, **11**)
otoño, el autumn, fall (**PA**)
otra vez again (4)
otro/a other (4)

P

paciente patient (**1**)
paciente, el/la patient (9)
padrastro, el stepfather (**1**)
padre, el father (**1**)
padres, los parents (**1**)
pagar to pay (**7**)
página, la page (2)
país, el country (1)
paisaje, el landscape (8)
pájaro, el bird (**11**)
palabra, la word (1)
pan, el bread (**7**)
pantalla, la screen (**5**)
pantalones, los pants (**8**); **~ cortos** shorts (**8**); **~ vaqueros** jeans (**8**)
papá, el dad (**1**)
papa, la potato (**7**); **las papas fritas** french fries; potato chips (**7**)
papel, el paper; role (**2, 11**); **hacer ~** to play the role (3)
paquete, el package (10)
par, el pair; couple (9)
para for; in order to (5, **11**)
parabrisas, el windshield (**10**)
parada, la bus stop (**10**)
paraguas, el umbrella (**8**)
parar to stop (PB)
pararse to stand (10)
parecer to seem (2)
parecido/a similar (7)
pared, la wall (**2**)
pareja, la pair (9)
pariente, el/la relative (PB)
parque, el park (**4**); **~ de atracciones** theme park (**10**)
párrafo, el paragraph (4)
partido, el game (9); **~ político** political party (**11**)
pasado/a last (**7**)
pasado, el past (4)
pasaje, el passage (9)
pasajero/a, el/la passenger (10)

pasaporte, el passport (**10**)
pasar: ~ la aspiradora to vacuum (**3**); **~ (por)** to pass (through); to happen (2, 3)
pasatiempo, el pastime (**2**)
pasear to take a walk (4)
paso, el step (3)
pastel, el pastry; pie (**7**)
pastilla, la pill (**9**)
patata, la potato (**7**)
patinar to skate (**2**)
paz, la peace (**5**)
peatón, el pedestrian (**10**)
pecho, el chest (**9**)
pedagogía, la education (**2**)
pedir (i) to ask for; to order (**4, 7**)
peinarse to comb one's hair (**8**)
película, la film; movie (3, **4, 5**); **~ de acción** action film (**5**); **~ de ciencia ficción** science fiction film (**5**); **~ documental** documentary (**5**); **~ dramática** drama film (**5**); **~ de guerra** war film (**5**); **~ de humor** funny/comedy film (**5**); **~ de misterio** mystery film (**5**); **~ musical** musical film (**5**); **~ romántica** romantic film (**5**); **~ de terror** horror film (**5**)
peligro, el danger (4)
peligroso/a dangerous (5, **10, 11**)
pelo, el hair (9); **cepillarse ~** to brush one's hair (**8**)
pelota, la ball (**2**)
pensar (ie) to think (**4**)
peor worse (**10**)
peor, el/la the worst (**4, 10**)
pequeño/a small (**1**)
pera, la pear (**7**)
perder (ie) to lose; to miss; to waste (**4, 10**)
perdido/a lost (4)
perezoso/a lazy (**1**)
periódico, el newspaper (7, **11**)
periodismo, el journalism (**2**)
periodista, el/la journalist (3)
pero but (**2**)
perro, el dog (8, **11**); **~ caliente** hot dog (4, **7**)
perseguir (i) to chase (**4**)
personaje, el character (PB)
personalidad, la personality (**1**)
personas mayores, las elderly men/women (**4**)
pertenecer to pertain (4)
pesadilla, la nightmare (8)
pesar to weigh (11)
pescado, el fish (**7**)
pésimo/a heavy, depressing (**5**)
peso, el weight (9)
petición, la request (11)
petróleo oil (**11**); **el derrame de petróleo** oil spill (**11**)
pez, el fish (**11**)
pianista, el/la pianist (**5**)
piano, el piano (**5**)
picadura, la bite (11)
picante spicy (**7**)
pie, el foot (**9**); **ir a pie** to go on foot (**10**)
pierna, la leg (**9**)
pijama, el pajamas (**8**)
pimienta, la pepper (**7**)
pintar to paint (2)
pintarse to dye (9)
pintura, la painting (8)
piscina, la pool (2)
pisco, el Peruvian brandy (7)
piso, el floor; story (in a building) (**3**); **el primer piso** second floor (**3**); **el segundo piso** third floor (**3**); **el tercer piso** fourth floor (**3**)
pista, la clue (5)
pistola, la pistol (8)
pizarra, la chalkboard (**2**); **Vayan a ~.** Go to the board. (**PA**)
placer, el pleasure (7)
plan, el plan (4)
planear to plan (6)
planeta, el planet (**11**)
planta, la plant (**3**); **~ baja** ground floor (**3**)
plantar to plant (**11**)
plástico, el plastic (**11**)
plátano, el banana (**7**)
plato, el plate; dish (4, **7**); **lavar los platos** to wash the dishes (**3**)
playa, la beach (4, **10**)
plaza, la town square (**4**)
población, la population (1)
pobre poor (**1**)
pobreza, la poverty (11)
poco, (un) a little; few (**1, 2**);
poco hecho/a rare (meat) (**7**)
poder to be able to (**3**); **el ~** power (9)
policía, el/la policeman/woman (**10**)
poliéster, el polyester (**8**)
política, la politics (**11**); **meterse en política** to get involved in politics (**11**)
pollo, el chicken (**7**)
poner to put; to place (**3**); **~ la mesa** to set the table (**3**)
ponerse: ~ la ropa to get dressed (**8**); **~ nervioso/a** to get nervous (**8**)
por times; by; for; through; because of (**1, 11**); **~ casualidad** by chance (10); **~ ciento** percent (**1**); **~ favor.** Please. (**PA**); **~ fin** finally (PA); **~ lo menos** at least (3); **¿~ qué?** Why? (2); **~ su cuenta** on their own (7); **~ supuesto** of course (3)
porcentaje, el percentage (7)
porque because (1)
portarse to behave (8)
portátil portable (4)
porteño/a person from Buenos Aires (8)
postre, el dessert (**7**)
potencia, la potency (11)
precio, el price (3)
predecir (i) to predict (4)
preferencia, la preference (4)
preferir (ie, i) to prefer (**4**)
pregunta, la question (**PA**)
preguntar to ask (**2**)
premio, el prize; award (3)
prenda, la garment (8)
prender to turn on (11)
preocupado/a worried (**2**)
preocuparse por to worry about; to concern oneself with (3, **11**)
preparar to prepare; to get ready (**2**); **~ la comida** to cook (**3**)
preparativo, el preparation (5)
presentación, la presentation (**PA**)
presentar una película to show a film/movie (**5**)
presentarse al juicio to go to court (10)
presentimiento, el premonition (4)
presidencia, la presidency (**11**)
presidente/a, el/la president (PB, **11**)
prestar to loan; to lend (8, **10**)
presupuesto, el budget (8)
previo/a previous (10)
primavera, la spring (**PA**)
primer piso, el second floor (**3**)
primer/o/a first (4, **5**)
primo/a, el/la cousin (**1**)
principal main (4)
prisa, la haste (7); **tener prisa** to be in a hurry (**3**)
profesor/a, el/la professor (**2**)
profundo/a deep (9)
programa, el platform (political) (11)
promedio average (5)
prometedor/a promising (5)
pronto soon (5); **hasta ~** see you soon (**PA**)
propina, la tip (**7, 10**)
propio/a own (6)
proponer to propose (5)
proporcionar to provide (8)
propósito, el purpose (7)
proteger to protect (7, **11**)
provincia, la province (**11**)
próximo/a next (PB)
prueba, la proof (10)
psicología, la psychology (**2**)
pueblo, el town (3, **4**)
puerta, la door (**2**)
puertorriqueño/a Puerto Rican (**PA**)

punto, el point (8)
puntual punctual (4)
puro/a pure (**11**)

Q

¿Qué? What? (2); **¡~ bueno!** That's great! (2); **¿~ es esto?** What is this? (**PA**); **¿~ hora es?** What time is it? (**PA**); **¿~ significa?** What does it mean? (**PA**); **¿~ tal?** How's it going? (**PA**); **¿~ tiempo hace?** What's the weather like? (**PA**)
quedar bien/mal to fit well/poorly (**8**)
quedarse to stay; to remain (**8**)
quehaceres, los chores (**3**)
quemar(se) to burn (oneself) (**9**)
querer (ie) to want; to love (2, **3**)
querido/a dear (1)
queso, el cheese (**7**)
¿Quién/es? Who? (**PA, 2**)
Quiero: ~ presentarle a... I would like to introduce you to...(*for.*) (**PA**); **~ presentarte a...** I would like to introduce you to...(*fam.*) (**PA**)
quince fifteen (**PA**)
quinientos five hundred (2)
quinto/a fifth (**5**)
quitarse (la ropa) to take off (one's clothes) (**8**)
quizás maybe (9)

R

radio, el/la radio (**2**)
raíz, la root (11)
rana, la frog (**11**)
rápido/a rapid (2)
raro/a strange; rare (7, 11)
rasgo, el characteristic (**1**)
rata, la rat (**11**)
ratón, el mouse (**11**)
rayas, de striped (**8**)
razón, la reason (3)
razón, tener to be right (**3**)
realizar to act out; to fulfill (7, 11)
recepción, la front desk (**10**)
receta, la recipe; prescription (7, **9**)
recetar to prescribe (9)
recibir to receive (1, **2**)
reciclar to recycle (**11**)
reclutar to recruit (10)
recoger to pick up; collect (3)
recomendar (ie) to recommend (**4**)
recompensa, la reward (11)
reconocer to recognize (8)
recordar (ue) to remember (**4**)
recuerdo, el memento; memory (3, 7)
recurso, el resource (**11**)
reforestar to reforest (**11**)
refrán, el saying (1)
refresco, el soft drink (**7**)
refrigerador, el refrigerator (**3**)
refugio, el refuge (11)
refutar to refute (8)
regalar to give (8)
regalo, el gift (7)
regatear to bargain; negotiate the price (7)
región, la region (**11**)
registrarse (en el hotel) to check in (**10**)
regla, la rule (8)
regresar to return (**2**)
Regular. So-so. (**PA**)
rehusar to refuse (**11**)
reina, la queen (**11**)
reír (i, i) to laugh (4)
relajante relaxing (**10**)
relajarse to relax (5)
reloj, el clock; watch (**2**)
remedio casero, el household remedy (7)
remordimiento, el remorse (10)
renombrar to rename (4)
renovar to renew (8)
repartir comidas to hand out/deliver food (**4**)
repasar to review (5)
repetir (i) to repeat (**4**)
Repita(n). Repeat. (**PA**)
reponer to replace (9)
reportaje, el report (10)
represa, la dam (7)
representar to perform (8)
reproductor de CD/DVD, el CD/DVD player (**2**)
requerir (ie) to require (11)
reseña, la review (5)
reserva, la reservation (**10**)
reservar una mesa to reserve a table (**7**)
resfriado, el cold (**9**); **tener un resfriado** to have a cold (**9**)
residencia, la residence; **~ de ancianos** nursing home/assisted living facility (**4**); **~ estudiantil** dormitory (**2**)
resolver (ue) to resolve (8, **11**)
respetar to respect (**5**)
respetuoso/a respectful (9)
respirar to breathe (9)
responsable responsible (**1**)
respuesta, la answer (**PA**)
restaurante, el restaurant (**4**)
resuelto/a resolved (10)
resultado, el result (4)
resumir to summarize (9)
resumen, el summary (9)
reunión, la meeting (2)
reunirse to get together; to meet (**8**)
reutilizar to reuse (11)
revisar to check; to overhaul (**10**)
revista, la magazine (5)
rey, el king (**11**)
rico/a rich (**1**)
riesgo, el risk (9)
río, el river (**11**)
ritmo, el rhythm (**5**)
rito, el rite (7)
robo, el robbery (7)
rock, el rock (music) (**5**)
rojo/a red (**3**)
romántica, una película romantic film (**5**)
rompecabezas, el riddle (7)
romper(se) to break (**9**)
ropa, la clothes (**3**); **~ interior** underwear (**8**); **ponerse ~** to get dressed (**8**); **quitarse ~** to take off one's clothes (**8**)
rosado/a pink (**3**)
roto/a broken (9)
rueda, la wheel (**10**)
ruido, el noise (3, **10**)
ruina, la ruin (9)

S

sábado, el Saturday (**PA**)
sábanas, las sheets (**3**)
saber to know (**4**)
sabor, el flavor (**5**)
sacar to get (a grade); to take out (2, 10); **~ la basura** to take out the garbage (**3**); **~ la licencia** to get a driver's license (**10**); **~ un CD** to release a CD (**5**)
sacudir el polvo to dust (3)
sal, la salt (**7**)
sala, la living room (**3**); **~ de clase** classroom (**2**); **~ de urgencias** emergency room (**9**)
salida, la exit (9)
salir to leave; to go out (**3, 10**)
salsa, la salsa (**5**); **~ de tomate** ketchup (**7**)
salud, la health (**9**)
saludable, estar to be healthy (**9**)
saludo, el greeting (**PA**)
salvar to save (8)
sandalias, las sandals (**8**)
sangre, la blood (**9**)
sano/a, estar to be healthy (**9**)
secarse to dry off (**8**)
sed, tener to be thirsty (**3**)
seda, la silk (**8**)
sede, la seat (of government) (9)
seguir (i) to follow; to continue (doing something) (**4**)
según according to (3, **11**)
segundo/a second (**5**)
segundo piso, el third floor (**3**)

seguramente surely (2)
seguridad, la security (2)
seguro/a sure (9)
seguro médico, el medical insurance (9)
seis six (**PA**)
seiscientos six hundred (**2**)
seleccionar to select (5)
sello, el postage stamp (**10**)
selva, la jungle (9, **11**); **~ tropical** (tropical) rain forest; jungle (**11**)
semáforo, el traffic light (**10**)
semana, la week (7); **~ pasada** last week (**7**)
sembrar (ie) to sow (**11**)
semejanza, la similarity (6)
semestre, el semester (**2**)
senado, el senate (**11**)
senador/a, el/la senator (**11**)
sencillo/a simple (10)
sentado/a seated (5)
sentarse (ie) to sit (**8**)
sentirse (ie, i) to feel (3, **8**)
señor (Sr.), el man, gentleman (**1**)
señora (Sra.), la woman; lady (**1**)
señorita (Srta.), la young woman; Miss (**1**)
septiembre September (**PA**)
séptimo/a seventh (**5**)
ser to be (**PA**); **~ alérgico/a** to be allergic (**9**); **el ~ humano** human being (11)
serenata, la serenade (11)
serio/a serious (9)
serpiente, la snake (**11**)
servilleta, la napkin (**7**)
servir (i) to serve (**4**)
sesenta sixty (**1**)
setecientos seven hundred (**2**)
setenta seventy (**1**)
sexto/a sixth (**5**)
si if (**2**)
sí yes (**PA, 2**)
siempre always (2, **3, 4, 8**)
sierra, la mountain range (9)
siete seven (**PA**)
siglo, el century (3)
significado, el meaning (8)
significar to mean (4)
siguiente following (3)
silla, la chair (**2**)
sillón, el armchair (**3**)
símbolo, el symbol (12)
simpático/a nice (**1**)
sin without (4, **11**); **~ embargo** nevertheless (2, **6**)
sino but rather (4)
síntoma, el symptom (9)
sitio, el site (11)
sobre over; about (5, **11**); **~ todo** above all (5)
sociedad, la society (8)
sofá, el sofa (**3**)
sol, el sun (**PA**)
solamente only (8)
soler (ue) to be accustomed to (10)
solicitar to solicit (11)
solicitud, la application (2)
sólo only (3)
solo/a only one; alone (7)
soltero, el bachelor (7)
solucionar to solve (5)
sombrero, el hat (**8**)
son equals (**1**)
sonar to ring (7)
sonido, el sound (5)
sopa, la soup (**7**)
soroche, el altitude (mountain) sickness (9)
sorprendente surprising (**5**)
sorpresa, la surprise (8)
sospechoso/a suspicious (2)
sótano, el basement (**3**)
Soy… I'm… (**PA**)
su/s his, her, its, your, their (**1**)
suave smooth (**5**)
subir (a) to go up; to get on (**10**)
subrayar to underline (7)
sucio/a dirty (**3**)
sudadera, la sweatshirt (**8**)
sudar to sweat (9)
suelo, el floor (**3**)
sueño, tener to be sleepy (**3**)
suerte, la luck (5); **la mala suerte** bad luck (4); **tener suerte** to be lucky (**3**)
suéter, el sweater (**8**)
sugerencia, la suggestion (10)
sujeto, el subject (8)
sunami, el tsunami (**11**)
supermercado, el supermarket (4)
sur, el south (7)
sureño/a southern (8)
surgir to emerge (8)
suspirar to sigh (11)
suspiro, el sigh (9)
sustituir to substitute (5)
suyo/a, el/la theirs (7)
suyo/a/os/as his, her/s, your/s (*for.*), their/s (3, **10**)

T

tacha, la mark (7)
tal vez perhaps (3)
tamaño, el size (9)
también too; also (1,2)
tambor, el drum (**5**)
tamborista, el/la drummer (**5**)
tampoco nor/neither (7)
tan… como as… as (1)
tanque, el gas tank (**10**)
tanto/a so much (9)
tantos/as so many (2)
tapas, las appetizers (3)
tardar en to take (time) (8)
tarde late (3); **de la ~** in the afternoon (**PA**); **más ~ que** later than (**7**)
tarea, la homework (**2**)
tarifa, la tariff; toll (5)
tarjeta, la card (4); **~ de crédito** credit card (**7**); **~ postal** postcard (**10**)
taxi, el taxi (**10**)
taza, la cup (**7**)
té (helado/caliente), el tea (iced/hot) (**7**)
teatro, el theater (**4**)
techo, el roof (**3**)
tela, la fabric (**8**)
televisión, la TV; **ver ~** to watch TV (**2**)
televisor, el TV set (**2**)
tema, el theme; topic (3)
temblar (ie) to tremble (7)
temer to fear (8)
temperatura, la temperature (**PA**)
templado/a temperate (8)
templo, el temple (**4**)
temprano early (3); **más ~ que** earlier than (**7**)
tenedor, el fork (**7**)
tener (ie) to have (**1**); **~ alergia** to be allergic (**9**); **~… años** to be… years old (**3**); **~ calor** to be hot (**3**); **~ un catarro** to have a cold (**9**); **~ cuidado** to be careful (**3**); **~ dolor de cabeza** to have a headache (**9**); **~ dolor de espalda** to have a backache (**9**); **~ dolor de estómago** to have a stomachache (**9**); **~ dolor de garganta** to have a sore throat (**9**); **~ en cuenta** to keep in mind (5); **~ éxito** to be successful (**3**); **~ frío** to be cold (**3**); **~ ganas de** + (infinitive) to feel like + (verb) (**3**); **~ (la/una) gripe** to have the flu (**9**); **~ hambre** to be hungry (3); **~ lugar** to take place (2); **~ miedo** to be afraid (**3**); **~ prisa** to be in a hurry (**3**); **~ que** + (infinitive) to have to + (verb) (**3**); **~ que ver con** to be related to (4); **~ razón** to be right (**3**); **~ suerte** to be lucky (**3**); **~ sueño** to be sleepy (**3**); **~ sed** to be thirsty (**3**); **~ tos** to have a cough (**9**); **~ vergüenza** to be embarrassed (**3**); **~ un virus** to have a virus (**9**); **~ una infección** to have an infection (**9**)
tenis, jugar al to play tennis (2)
tercer piso, el fourth floor (**3**)
tercer/o/a third (2, **5**)
terminar to finish; to end (**2**)
término medio medium (7)

terremoto, el earthquake (5, **11**)
terror, una película de horror film (**5**)
tesoro, el treasure (10)
tiburón, el shark (5)
tiempo, el weather; time (**PA**, 4); **¿Qué tiempo hace?** What's the weather like? (**PA**)
tienda, la store (**2**); **~ de campaña** tent (**4**)
tierra, la land; soil (5, **11**); **la Tierra** Earth (**11**)
tío/a, el/la uncle/aunt (**1**)
tirar to throw (8)
título, el title (7)
tiza, la chalk (2)
tocador, el dresser (**3**)
tocar to touch (**5**); **~ un instrumento** to play an instrument (2)
todavía still (3)
todo everything (2); **sobre ~** above all (5)
todos los días every day (**8**)
tomar to take; to drink (**2**); **~ el sol** to sunbathe (**2**)
tomate, el tomato (**7**); **la salsa de tomate** ketchup (**7**)
tónico/a stressed, emphasized (syllable) (10)
tonto/a silly; dumb (**1**)
tormenta, la storm (**11**)
tornado, el tornado (**11**)
torneo, el tournament (4)
toro, el bull (**11**)
torre, la tower (3)
torta, la cake (**7**)
tos, la cough (**9**);
tener tos to have a cough (**9**)
toser to cough (**9**)
tostada, la toast (**7**)
trabajador/a hard-working (**1**)
trabajar to work (**2**); **~ como voluntario/a** to volunteer (**4**)
trabajo, el work (1); **~ en prácticas** internship (8); **~ remunerado** job with a salary (4)
trabalenguas, el tongue twister (4)
tradicional traditional (**3**)
traducir to translate (11)
traer to bring (**3**)
tráfico, el traffic (**10**)
tragedia, la tragedy (**11**)
trágico/a tragic (**5**)
traje, el suit (5, **8**); **~ de baño** swimsuit; bathing suit (**8**)
tranquilizarse to calm down (9)
tranquilo/a calm; peaceful (5, **10**)
transitar to enter/exit (10)
transporte, el transportation (**10**); **el medio de transporte** means of transportation (10)
tratamiento, el treatment (**9**)
tratar to treat (9); **~ de** to try to (5, **9**)
tratarse de to deal with; to be about (8)
trece thirteen (**PA**)
treinta thirty (**PA**)
tren, el train (**10**)
tres three (**PA**)
trescientos three hundred (**2**)
tribu, la tribe (2)
triste sad (**2**)
trompeta, la trumpet (**5**)
trompetista, el/la trumpet player (**5**)
tú you (*fam.*) (**PA, 2**)
tu/s your (*fam.*) (**1, 2**)
turnarse to take turns (3)
tuyo/a/os/as yours (*fam.*) (**10**)

U

último/a last (5)
un/a a; one (**1**)
únicamente only (9)
único/a only (sole) (4)
unido/a close-knit (7)
uno one (**PA**)
unos/as some (**1**)
usar to use (**2**)
usted/es you (*for.*) (**PA**)
útil useful (**PA**)

V

vaca, la cow (**11**)
vacaciones, las vacation (**10**); **ir de vacaciones** to go on vacation (7, **10**)
valor, el value (6)
vaqueros, los jeans (**8**)
vaso, el glass (**7**)
Vaya(n) a la pizarra. Go to the board. (**PA**)
vecino/a, el/la neighbor (8)
vehículo, el vehicle (**10**)
veinte twenty (**PA**)
veinticinco twenty-five (**PA**)
veinticuatro twenty-four (**PA**)
veintidós twenty-two (**PA**)
veintinueve twenty-nine (**PA**)
veintiocho twenty-eight (**PA**)
veintiséis twenty-six (**PA**)
veintisiete twenty-seven (**PA**)
veintitrés twenty-three (**PA**)
veintiuno twenty-one (**PA**)
venda, la bandage (**9**)
vendaje, el bandage (**9**)
vendar(se) to bandage (oneself); to dress (a wound) (**9**)
vendedor/a, el/la seller; vendor (3)
vender to sell (7)
venir (ie) to come (**3**)
ventana, la window (**2**)
ver to see (**3**); **~ la televisión** to watch TV (**2**)
verano, el summer (**PA**)
verdad, la truth (3)
verdadero/a true (7)
verde green (**3**)
verdura, la vegetable (**7**)
vergüenza, tener to be embarrassed (**3**)
vertedero, el dump (**11**)
vestido, el dress (**8**)
vestirse (i, i) to get dressed (**8**)
vez, la time (5); **muchas veces** many times (**8**); **otra vez** again (4); **tal vez** perhaps (3)
viajar to travel (2, **10**)
viaje, el trip (8, **10**); **la agencia de viajes** travel agency (6, **10**); **el/la agente de viajes** travel agent (**10**); **ir de viaje** to go on a trip (**10**)
viajeros, los travelers (**10**)
vida, la life (2)
vidrio, el glass (**11**)
viejo/a old (**3**)
viento, el wind (**PA**)
viernes, el Friday (**PA**)
vigilar to watch (9)
vinagre, el vinegar (7)
vino, el wine (7)
virus, tener un to have a virus (**9**)
visitar to visit (**10**)
vivienda, la housing (3)
vivir to live (**2**)
vivo/a alive; living (**11**)
vocabulario, el vocabulary (1)
volante, el steering wheel (**10**)
volar (ue) to fly; to fly away (**10**)
volcán, el volcano (4)
voluntariado, el volunteerism (**4**)
volver (ue) to return (**4, 11**)
vosotros/as you (*fam. pl. Spain*) (**PA**)
votar to vote (**11**)
voto, el ballot (**11**)
voz, la voice (**5**)
vuelo, el flight (**10**)
vuestro/a/os/as your/s (*fam. pl. Spain*) (**1, 10**)

Y

y and (**2**); **¿ ~ tú?** And you? (*fam.*) (**PA**); **¿~ usted?** And you? (*for.*) (**PA**)
ya already (4); **~ no** no longer (5); **~ que** since (1)
yo I (**PA**)

Z

zapatillas, las slippers (**8**)
zapatos, los shoes (**8**); **~ de tenis** tennis shoes (**8**)

APPENDIX 5

ENGLISH-SPANISH GLOSSARY

A

a un/a (**1**)
a little (un) poco (**1, 2**)
a lot mucho (**2, 8**)
ability la habilidad (**5**)
able to, to be poder (3)
abolish, to abolir (5)
about acerca de; sobre (4, 5, **11**); **to be ~** tratarse de (8)
above all sobre todo (5)
abroad el extranjero (**10**)
accompany, to acompañar (6)
according to según (3, **11**)
account la cuenta (**4**)
accustomed to, to be soler (ue) (10)
acid rain la lluvia ácida (**11**)
across from enfrente de (**11**)
act out, to realizar (7)
action film la película de acción (**5**)
actor el actor (**5**)
actress la actriz (**5**)
add, to añadir (5)
address la dirección (8)
addressee el destinatario (5)
adhesive bandage la curita (**9**)
adventure la aventura (2)
adventurer el/la aventurero/a (10)
adventurous arriesgado/a (**10**)
advertisement el anuncio (1)
advice el consejo (5)
advise, to aconsejar (12)
advisor el/la asesor/a (11)
afraid, to be tener miedo (**3**)
after después de (5, **6, 11**)
afternoon: Good ~. Buenas tardes. (**PA**); **in the ~** de la tarde (**PA**)
again otra vez; de nuevo (4)
age la edad (3)
agency, travel la agencia de viajes (6, **10**)
agent el/la empresario/a (**5**); **travel ~** el/la agente de viajes (**10**)
agree, to estar de acuerdo (**4**)
agreeable agradable (5)
air el aire (**11**); **in the open ~** al aire libre (**8**)
air conditioning el aire acondicionado (**10**)
airplane el avión (**10**)
airport el aeropuerto (**10**)
alarm clock el despertador (**2**)
alive vivo/a (**11**)
allergic, to be ser alérgico/a; tener alergia (**9**)
alleviate, to aliviarse (5)
almost casi (**4**); **~ always** casi siempre (**8**)
alone solo/a (7)
along with junto con (2)
already ya (4)
also también (1, **2**)
although aunque (5)
altitude la altura (9); **~ (mountain) sickness** el soroche; el mal de altura (9)
aluminum el aluminio (**11**)
always siempre (2, **4, 8**)
American estadounidense (norteamericano/a) (**PA**)
among entre (2,**11**)
amphibian el anfibio (11)
analyze, to analizar (9)
ancestor el/la antepasado/a (9)
ancient antiguo/a (2)
and y (2); **~ you?** ¿Y usted? (*for.*); ¿Y tú? (*fam.*) (**PA**)
angry enojado/a (**2**)
animal el animal (**11**); **domesticated ~** el animal doméstico (**11**); **wild ~** el animal salvaje (**11**)
animated animado/a (**5**)
answer la respuesta (**PA**); **~.** Conteste(n). (**PA**); **to ~** contestar (1, **2**)
answering machine el contestador automático (7)
ant la hormiga (**11**)
antacid el antiácido (**9**)
anthill el hormiguero (11)
antibiotic el antibiótico (**9**)
apartment el apartamento (**2**)
apology la disculpa (10)
appealing atractivo/a (**10**)
appearance la apariencia (11)
appetizers las tapas (3)
apple la manzana (4, **7**)
appliance el aparato doméstico (8)
application la solicitud (2)
appointment la cita (4)
approach, to acercarse (4)
appropriate apropiado/a (5)
approved aprobado/a (10)
April abril (**PA**)
architecture la arquitectura (**2**)
arm el brazo (**9**)
armchair el sillón (**3**)
armoire el armario (**3**)
army el ejército (5)
around a eso de; alrededor (7, 9)
arrange, to arreglar (5)
arrive, to llegar (**2**)
art el arte (**2**)
article el artículo (5)
artist el/la artista (**5**)
arts and crafts la artesanía (2, **4**)
as: ~ a result of a causa de (5); **~ ... ~** tan... como (1)
ask, to preguntar (**2**); **~ for** pedir (i) (**4**)
aspirin la aspirina (9)
assign, to asignar (4)
assist, to atender (ie) (8)
assistant el/la ayudante (5)
assisted living facility la residencia de ancianos (**4**)
associate, to asociar (4)
associated asociado/a (5)
assure, to asegurar (10)
at a (5, **11**); **~ least** por lo menos (3); **~ the beginning** a principios de (7); **~ the end of** a fines de (8); **~ the same time** a la vez (4); **~ what time?** ¿A qué hora? (**PA**); **~ ... o'clock.** A la.../A las... (**PA**)
ATM machine el cajero automático (**4**)
attached adjunto/a (10)
attack, to atacar (11)
attend, to asistir (11); **~ to** atender (ie) (8)
attendant el/la empleado/a (12)
attic el altillo (**3**)
attract, to atraer (8)
August agosto (**PA**)
aunt la tía (**1**)
authority la autoridad (5)
autumn el otoño (**PA**)
available disponible (10)
average promedio (5)
avoid, to evitar (**9, 11**)
awaken, to despertarse (ie) (**8**)
award el premio (3)

B

bachelor el soltero (7)
back la espalda (**9**)
backache, to have a tener dolor de espalda (**9**)
bad malo/a (**1**); **~ luck** la mala suerte (4)
bag el bolso (7); **book ~** la mochila (**2**)
baked al horno; cocido/a (**7**)
balanced equilibrado/a (7)
balcony el balcón (**3**)
ball la pelota (**2**)
ballot el voto (**11**)
ballpoint pen el bolígrafo (**2**)
banana la banana; plátano (**7**)
band el conjunto (**5**)

bandage la venda; el vendaje (**9**); **adhesive ~** la curita (**9**); **to ~ (oneself)** vendar(se) (**9**)

bank el banco (**4**); **~ check** el cheque (**4**)

bar el bar (**4**)

bargain, to regatear (7)

base one's judgment on, to basarse en (5)

baseball, to play jugar al béisbol (**2**)

basement el sótano (**3**)

basket making la cestería (2)

basketball, to play jugar al básquetbol (**2**)

bathe, to bañarse (**8**)

bathing suit el traje de baño (**8**)

bathroom el baño (**3**)

bathtub la bañera (**3**)

bay la bahía (4)

be, to ser, estar (**PA, 2**)

beach la playa (4, **10**)

beans los frijoles (**7**)

bear el oso (9, **11**)

beat (heart), to latir (9)

beautiful hermoso/a; bello/a (4, 10)

because porque (1); **~ of** por (2, **11**)

bed la cama (**3**); **to go to ~** acostarse (ue) (**8**); **to make the ~** hacer la cama (**3**)

bedroom el dormitorio (**3**)

bedspread la colcha (**3**)

beer la cerveza (PB, **7**)

before (time/space) antes de (2, **11**)

begin, to comenzar (ie); empezar (ie) (2, **4**)

behave, to portarse (8)

behind detrás (de) (**4, 11**)

beige beige (**3**)

believe, to creer (**2**)

bellman el botones (**10**)

below bajo; abajo (7, 9)

belt el cinturón (**8**)

beside al lado de (**3, 7**)

better mejor (5, **10**)

between entre (2, **11**)

beverage la bebida (**7**)

bicycle la bicicleta (**10**); **~ path** la ciclorruta (10); **to ride a ~** montar en bicicleta (**2**)

bidet el bidet (**3**)

big grande (**1**)

bigger mayor (1, **10**)

bilingual bilingüe (1)

bill la cuenta (**4**)

biology la biología (**2**)

bird el pájaro; el ave (**11**)

birthday el cumpleaños (8)

bite la picadura (11)

black negro/a (**3**)

blanket la manta (**3**)

blind ciego/a (3)

block el bloque (11)

blood la sangre (**9**)

blouse la blusa (**8**)

blue azul (**3**)

boat el bote; el barco (4, **10**)

body el cuerpo (**9**)

boiled cocido/a; hervido/a (**7**)

book el libro (1, **2**); **~ bag** la mochila (**2**); **Close your ~.** Cierre(n) el libro. (**PA**); **Open your ~ to page …** Abra(n) el libro en la página… (**PA**)

bookcase el estante de libros (**3**)

bookstore la librería (**2**)

boots las botas (**8**)

bored aburrido/a (**2**)

boring aburrido/a (**PB, 1, 5**)

born nacido/a (2); **to be ~** nacer (8)

boss el jefe (9)

bother, to molestar (**8**)

bottle la botella (5, **11**)

box (cardboard) la caja (de cartón) (**11**)

boy el chico; el muchacho (**1**); **little ~** el niño (**1**)

boyfriend el novio (**1**)

brain el cerebro (9)

brandy, Peruvian el pisco (7)

bread el pan (**7**)

break, to romper(se) (**9**)

breakfast el desayuno (**7**); **to have ~** desayunar (**7**)

breathe, to respirar (9)

bring, to traer (**3**)

broken roto/a (9)

brother el hermano (**1**)

brown café; marrón (**3**)

brush (one's hair, teeth), to cepillarse (el pelo, los dientes) (**8**)

budget el presupuesto (8)

building el edificio (**2**)

bull el toro (**11**)

burn (oneself), to quemar(se) (**9**)

bus el autobús (**10**); **~ stop** la parada (**10**)

business el negocio (8); **~ administration** la administración de empresas (**2**); **~/shopping district** el centro comercial (**4**)

but pero (**2**); **~ rather** sino (4)

butler el mayordomo (10)

butter la mantequilla (**7**)

buy, to comprar (**2**)

by por (**1, 11**); **~ chance** por casualidad (10)

Bye. Chao. (**PA**)

C

cabinet el armario (**3**)

cafe el café (**4**); **Internet ~** el cibercafé (**4**)

cafeteria la cafetería (**2**)

cake la torta (**7**)

calculator la calculadora (**2**)

call: phone ~ la llamada (7); **to ~** llamar (2)

called, to be llamarse (**8**)

calm tranquilo/a (5, **10**); **to ~ down** tranquilizarse (9)

camp: summer ~ el campamento de niños (**4**)

campaign la campaña (**11**); **political ~** la campaña política (**4**)

campfire la hoguera (**4**)

can la lata (**11**)

Canadian canadiense (**PA**)

candidate el/la candidato/a (**11**); **to support a ~** apoyar a un/a candidato/a (**4**)

candy los dulces (7)

canoe la canoa (**4**)

cap la gorra (**8**)

capable hábil; capaz (5, 8)

car el coche; el carro (**10**)

card la tarjeta (4); **credit ~** la tarjeta de crédito (**7**)

career la carrera (1)

careful cuidadoso/a (**5**); **to be ~** tener cuidado (**3**)

carpet la alfombra (**3**)

carry, to llevar (5); **~ out** llevar a cabo (**11**)

cart la carreta (5)

case el caso (10)

castle el castillo (3)

casual informal (**8**)

cat el gato (10, **11**)

cave la cueva (**11**)

CD/DVD player el reproductor de CD/DVD (**2**)

cent el centavo (5)

century el siglo (3)

ceramics la cerámica (2)

cereal el cereal (**7**)

chain la cadena (3); **~ of mountains** la cordillera (7)

chair la silla (**2**)

chalk la tiza (**2**)

chalkboard la pizarra (**2**)

challenging estimulante (**10**)

chamomile la manzanilla (9)

change, to cambiar (7, **10**); **~ roles** cambiar de papel (3)

chapter el capítulo (6)

character el personaje (PB)

characteristic el rasgo (**1**); **physical ~** la característica física (**1**)

characterize, to caracterizar (9)
charades, to play hacer mímica (8)
chase, to perseguir (i) (**4**)
cheap barato/a (4, **7**)
check, to revisar; comprobar (ue) (3, **10**); **bank ~** el cheque (**4**); **The ~, please.** La cuenta, por favor. (**7**); **to ~ in** registrarse (en el hotel) (**10**); **to ~ out** irse del hotel (**10**)
checked de cuadros (**8**)
cheese el queso (**7**)
chef el/la cocinero/a (4)
chest el pecho (**9**)
chicken el pollo (meat); gallina (bird) (**7**)
chief el cacique (9)
childhood la infancia (12)
children los hijos (**1**)
chili pepper el chile (**7**)
Chinese chino/a (**PA**)
choose, to escoger; elegir (i, i) (4, 9)
chores los quehaceres (**3**)
chorus el coro (8)
church la iglesia (**4**)
circle el círculo (8)
circulate, to circular (8); **~ a petition** circular una petición (**4**)
city la ciudad (1, **3**, **4**)
classical music la música clásica (**5**)
classify, to clasificar (5)
classmate el/la compañero/a de clase (**2**)
classroom la sala de clase (**2**)
clay el barro (2)
clean limpio/a (**3**); **to ~** limpiar (**3**)
clerk el/la dependiente/a (8)
climate el clima (7)
clock el reloj (**2**); **alarm ~** el despertador (**2**)
close cerca (de) (**2**); **to ~** cerrar (ie) (**4**); **~ your book/s.** Cierre(n) el libro/los libros. (**PA**)
closed cerrado/a (3)
close-knit unido/a (7)
closet el armario (**3**)
clothes la ropa (**3**)
cloud la nube (**PA**)
cloudy, it's está nublado (**PA**)
club el club (**4**); **country ~** el club campestre (**9**)
clue la pista (5)
coast la costa (4)
coat of arms el escudo (3)
cocoa bean el grano de cacao (4)
code el código (2)
coffee el café (**7**)
cognate el cognado (PA)
cold el catarro; el resfriado (**9**); **it's ~** hace frío (**PA**); **to be ~** tener frío (**3**); **to have a ~** tener (un) catarro; tener un resfriado (**9**)
collect recoger (3)
color el color (**3**)
comb one's hair, to peinarse (**8**)
combat, to luchar; combatir (**11**)
come, to venir (ie) (**3**)
comfortable cómodo/a (**8**)
comforter la colcha (**3**)
command el mandato (**PA**)
comment el comentario (5)
common común (4); **~ (to a region)** endémico/a (11)
compact disk el disco compacto (el CD) (**2**)
company la compañía; la empresa (8)
comparison la comparación (10)
competition la competencia (7)
compile, to compilar (11)
completed by expedido/a por (10)
complex el complejo (3)
composition la composición (**2**)
computer la computadora (**2**); **~ science** la informática (**2**)
concern, to incumbir (8); **~ oneself with** preocuparse por (3, **11**)
concert el concierto (**5**); **to give/perform a ~** dar un concierto (**5**)
condiment el condimento (**7**)
conduct, to dirigir (3)
congratulations la enhorabuena (11)
congress el congreso (**11**)
conspiracy la conspiración (7)
construct, to construir (9)
contagious contagioso/a (11)
contain, to contener (ie) (7)
contemporary contemporáneo/a (**3**)
content contento/a (state of being); el contenido (**2**, 9)
contest el concurso (3)
contestant el/la concursante (8)
continue (doing something), to seguir (i) (**4**)
convince, to convencer (5)
cook el/la cocinero/a (**7**); **to ~** cocinar, preparar la comida (3, 7)
cookie la galleta (**7**)
corn el maíz (**7**)
correct, to corregir (i) (3)
cost, to costar (ue) (2, **4**)
cotton el algodón (**8**)
cough la tos (**9**); **~ syrup** el jarabe (**9**); **to ~** toser (**9**); **to have a ~** tener tos (**9**)
counselor el/la consejero/a (**4**)
country el país (nation); el campo (rural area) (1, **3**); **~ club** el club campestre (**4**)
couple el par (9)
course el curso (**2**)
courtesy la cortesía (**PA**)
courting el cortejo (7)
cousin el/la primo/a (**1**)
cover, to cubrir (7)
cow la vaca (**11**)
crazy loco/a (9)
create, to crear (3)
creative creativo/a (**5**)
credit card la tarjeta de crédito (**7**)
crime la delincuencia (**11**)
crocodile el cocodrilo (11)
crop la cosecha (7)
cross, to cruzar (5)
crossed atravesado/a (9)
cry, to llorar (8)
Cuban cubano/a (**PA**)
cup la taza (**7**)
cure la cura (4); **to ~** curar (**9**)
custom la costumbre (7)
customer el/la cliente/a (**7**)
cut (oneself), to cortar(se) (**9**)

D

dad el papá (**1**)
daily cotidiano/a; diario/a (4)
dam la represa (7)
damage, to (do) hacer daño (**11**)
dance el baile (5); **to ~** bailar (**2**)
danger el peligro (4)
dangerous peligroso/a (5, **10**, **11**)
daring atrevido/a (**8**)
dark oscuro/a (**8**)
data el dato (9)
date la fecha; la cita (5, 8)
daughter la hija (**1**)
day el día (**PA**); **the ~ before yesterday** anteayer (**7**)
dead muerto/a (11)
deal with, to tratarse de (8)
dear querido/a (1)
debt (foreign) la deuda (externa) (**11**)
December diciembre (**PA**)
decipher, to descifrar (9)
deep profundo/a (9)
defense la defensa (**11**)
defraud, to estafar (10)
dehydrate, to deshidratar (9)
delicate fino/a (**5**)
delight la delicia (11); **to ~** encantar (**8**)
demanding exigente (9); **more/less ~** exige más/menos (**10**)
democracy la democracia (**11**)
demonstrate, to demostrar (ue) (**4**)
department store el almacén (**4**)
depressing pésimo/a (**5**)
describe, to describir (1)
desert el desierto (9)
deserve, to merecer (11)
design el diseño (4)
designer el/la diseñador/a (8)

desk el escritorio (**2**); **front ~** la recepción (**10**)
desperate desesperado/a (11)
dessert el postre (**7**)
destination el destino (8)
destroyed destrozado/a (10)
destruction la destrucción (**11**)
detail el detalle (6)
develop, to desarrollar (11)
developed desarrollado/a (7)
devote, to dedicar (3)
dial, to marcar (9)
dialogue el diálogo (4)
dictator el/la dictador/a (**11**)
dictatorship la dictadura (**11**)
die, to morir (ue, u) (**4**)
difficult difícil (**2**, **PB**, **10**)
dining room el comedor (**3**)
dinner la cena; la comida (PB, **7**); **to have ~** cenar (**7**)
direct, to dirigir (11)
dirty sucio/a (**3**); **to ~** ensuciar (11)
disappear, to desaparecer (5)
disappearance la desaparición (7)
disaster el desastre (4, **11**)
discount el descuento (8)
discover, to descubrir (4)
discuss, to discutir (4)
dish el plato (4, **7**); **to wash the dishes** lavar los platos (**3**)
dishwasher el lavaplatos (**3**)
disorienting desorientador/a (9)
distract, to distraer (5)
divided by dividido por (**1**)
do, to hacer (**3**)
doctor el/la doctor/a; el/la médico/a (**9**); **~'s office** el consultorio (9)
documentary film el documental (**5**)
dog el perro (8, **11**)
doll la muñeca (8)
domesticated animal el animal doméstico (**11**)
door la puerta (**2**)
dormitory la residencia estudiantil (**2**)
double room el cuarto doble (**10**)
doubt la duda (5); **there is no ~** no cabe duda (**9**)
downtown el centro (**4**)
dozen la docena (7)
drama film la película dramática (**5**)
draw, to dibujar (4)
drawing el dibujo (3)
dress el vestido (**8**); **to ~ (a wound)** vendar(se) (**9**)
dresser el tocador (**3**)
drink, to tomar (**2**)
drive, to conducir; manejar (**7**, **10**)
driver's license la licencia (de conducir) (**10**)
driving la conducción (10)
drum el tambor (**5**)
drummer el/la baterista; el/la tamborista (**5**)
drums la batería (**5**)
dry off, to secarse (**8**)
dumb tonto/a (**1**)
dump el vertedero (**11**)
duplicate, to duplicar (10)
during durante (3)
dust, to sacudir el polvo (**3**)
duty el deber (**4**)
DVD el DVD (**2**)
dye, to pintarse (9)

E

each cada (1)
ear la oreja (**9**); **inner ~** el oído (**9**)
earlier than más temprano que (**7**)
early temprano (3)
Earth la Tierra (**11**)
earthquake el terremoto (5, **11**)
east el este (4)
easy fácil (**2**, **PB**)
eat, to comer (**2**)
ecology la ecología (**11**)
education la pedagogía (**2**)
egg el huevo (**7**)
eight ocho (**PA**); **~ hundred** ochocientos (**2**)
eighteen dieciocho (**PA**)
eighth octavo/a (**5**)
eighty ochenta (**1**)
either ... or o... o (**4**)
elderly men/women las personas mayores; los mayores (**4**)
elect, to elegir (i, i) (**11**)
elegant elegante (**8**)
elephant el elefante (**11**)
eleven once (**PA**)
e-mail el correo electrónico (3)
emanate, to emanar (11)
embarrassed, to be tener vergüenza (**3**)
emerge, to surgir (8)
emergency room la sala de urgencias (**9**)
emotion la emoción (**2**)
emotional emocionante; conmovedor/a (**5**)
empire el imperio (9)
employ, to emplear (10)
employee el empleado (12)
employment el empleo (3)
enclose, to encerrar (ie) (**4**)
encompass, to abarcar (5)
end el fin (11); **to ~** terminar; acabar con (**2**, 4)
endangered species el animal en peligro de extinción (**11**)
engine el motor (**10**)
engineer el/la ingeniero/a (10)
English inglés/inglesa (**PA**)
enjoy: ~ your meal! ¡Buen provecho! (**7**); **to ~** disfrutar (5); **to ~ oneself** divertirse (ie, i) (5, **8**)
enormous enorme (3)
enough bastante (3); **to be ~** bastar (8)
enter, to entrar (2, **10**); **~/exit** transitar (10)
entertain, to distraer (5); **~ oneself** entretenerse (ie) (8)
entertaining entretenido/a (**5**)
entire entero/a (3)
environment el medio ambiente (**11**)
epic épico/a (**5**)
episode el episodio (3)
epoch la época (4)
equality la igualdad (10)
equals son (**1**)
eraser el borrador (**2**)
escape, to escaparse (10)
essay el ensayo (2)
evening: Good ~. Buenas noches. (**PA**); **in the ~** de la noche (**PA**)
event el acontecimiento (9)
every cada (1); **~ day** todos los días (**8**)
everything todo (2)
evil malvado/a (10)
evolve, to evolucionar (5)
exam el examen (**2**); **physical ~** el examen físico (**9**)
example el ejemplo (4)
exchange el intercambio (4)
excited emocionado/a (4)
exciting emocionante (**10**)
exercise el ejercicio (3); **to ~** hacer ejercicio (**2**)
exit la salida (9)
expense el gasto (10)
expensive caro/a (3, **7**)
experience, to experimentar (11)
explain, to explicar (1)
express an opinion, to opinar (1)
expression la expresión (**PA**)
eye el ojo (**9**)

F

fabric la tela (**8**)
face la cara (5, **9**)
facing enfrente de (**11**)
factory la fábrica (8)
fall (season) el otoño (**PA**); **to ~** caer (9); **to ~ asleep** dormirse (ue, u) (**8**); **to ~ in love** enamorarse (11)
false falso/a (7)
fame la fama (**5**)

family la familia (**1**)
fan el/la aficionado/a (3, **5**)
far (from) lejos (de) (**2**,**11**)
farewell la despedida (**PA**)
farm la finca; la granja (**11**)
farmer el/la campesino/a (11)
fascinate, to fascinar (**8**)
fashion la moda (**8**)
fat gordo/a; la grasa (**1**, 7)
father el padre (**1**)
fear el miedo (5); **to ~** temer (8)
February febrero (**PA**)
feel, to sentirse (ie, i) (3, **8**); **~ like +** ***(verb)*** tener ganas de + *(infinitive)* (**3**)
fever la fiebre (**9**)
few poco (**2**)
fifteen quince (**PA**)
fifth quinto/a (**5**)
fifty cincuenta (**1**)
fight, to luchar; combatir (**11**)
fill, to llenar (9, **10**)
film la película (**5**); **action ~** la película de acción (**5**); **documentary ~** el documental (**5**); **drama ~** la película dramática (**5**); **funny/comedy ~** la película de humor (**5**); **horror ~** la película de terror (**5**); **musical ~** la película musical (**5**); **mystery ~** la película de misterio (**5**); **romantic ~** la película romántica (**5**); **science fiction ~** la película de ciencia ficción (**5**); **to release a ~** estrenar una película (**5**); **to show a ~/movie** presentar una película (5); **war ~** la película de guerra (**5**)
finalist el/la finalista (3)
finally por fin; finalmente (PA, **6**)
find, to dar con; encontrar (ue) (2, **4**); **~ out** averiguar; enterarse (3, 8)
fine fino/a; la multa (**5**, **10**); **~, thanks.** Bien, gracias. (**PA**)
finger el dedo (**9**)
finish, to terminar (**2**)
fire el incendio (**11**)
first primer/o/a (4, **5**)
fish el pescado; el pez (**7**, **11**)
fit well/poorly, to quedar bien/mal (**8**)
five cinco (**PA**); **~ hundred** quinientos (2)
fix, to arreglar (5)
flag la bandera (10)
flavor el sabor (**5**)
flight el vuelo (**10**)
flood la inundación (**11**)
floor el piso; el suelo (**3**); **fourth ~** el tercer piso (**3**); **ground ~** la planta baja (**3**); **second ~** el primer piso (**3**); **third ~** el segundo piso (**3**)
flourishing floreciente (8)
flower la flor (8)
flu la gripe (**9**); **to have the ~** tener (la/una) gripe (**9**)
fly la mosca (**11**); **to ~** volar (ue) (**10**)
flyer el anuncio (3)
focus, to enfocarse (9)
folk healer el/la curandero/a (4)
follow, to seguir (i) (**4**)
following siguiente; a continuación (3, 10)
food la comida; el alimento (PB, **7**)
foot el pie (**9**); **to go on ~** caminar; ir a pie (**10**)
football, to play jugar al fútbol americano (**2**)
for para; por (2, 5, **11**)
force la fuerza (7)
forest el bosque (4, **11**); **rain (tropical) ~** la selva tropical (**11**)
forget, to olvidar (7)
fork el tenedor (**7**)
formal formal (**8**)
forty cuarenta (**1**)
founded fundado/a (11)
fountain la fuente (3)
four cuatro (**PA**); **~ hundred** cuatrocientos (**2**)
fourteen catorce (**PA**)
fourth cuarto/a (**5**); **~ floor** el tercer piso (**3**)
fraud el fraude (6)
free libre; gratis (2, 5)
freeway la autopista (**10**)
French francés/francesa (**PA**); **~ fries** las papas fritas (**7**)
frequency la frecuencia (4)
frequently frecuentemente (**8**)
fresh fresco/a (**7**); **~ water** el agua dulce (5)
Friday el viernes (**PA**)
fried frito/a (**7**)
friend el/la amigo/a (**1**)
frightened asustado/a (7)
frightening atterador/a (9)
frog la rana (**11**)
from de, desde (3, **11**)
from time to time a veces (**2**)
front desk la recepción (**10**)
fruit la fruta (**7**)
fulfill, to realizar (11)
fun, to have divertirse (ie, i) (5, **8**)
function, to funcionar (**10**)
funny cómico/a (**1**); **~/comedy film** la película de humor (**5**)
furnished amueblado/a (**3**)
furniture los muebles; **piece of ~** el mueble (**3**)
future el futuro (4)

G

gallop, to galopar (11)
game el juego; el partido (4, 9)
garage el garaje (**3**)
garbage la basura (**11**); **to take out the ~** sacar la basura (**3**)
garden el jardín (**3**)
garlic el ajo (7)
garment la prenda (8)
gas: ~ station la estación de servicio/de gasolina (**10**); **~ tank** el tanque (**10**)
generally generalmente (**8**)
genre el género (**5**)
gentleman el señor (Sr.) (**1**)
German alemán/alemana (**PA**)
get, to conseguir (i, i) (7); **~ (a grade)** sacar (2); **~ (dressed)** ponerse (la ropa); vestirse (i, i) (**8**); **~ (nervous)** ponerse (nervioso/a) (**8**); **~ a driver's license** sacar la licencia (**10**); **~ an urge** entrar ganas (9); **~ better** mejorar(se) (**9**); **~ down (from)** bajar (de) (**10**); **~ involved in politics** meterse en política (**11**); **~ off (of)** bajar (de) (**10**); **~ on** subir (a) (**10**); **~ ready** preparar; arreglarse (**2**, **8**); **~ sick** enfermar(se) (**9**); **~ together** reunirse (**8**); **~ up** levantarse (**8**); **~/keep quiet** callarse (**8**)
gift el regalo (7)
girl la chica, la muchacha (**1**); **little ~** la niña (**1**)
girlfriend la novia (**1**)
give, to dar; regalar (**3**, 8); **~ life** dar vida (5); **~/perform a concert** dar un concierto (**5**)
glass el vaso; el vidrio (**7**, **11**)
global warming el efecto invernadero (**11**)
gloves los guantes (8)
go, to ir (**4**); **Go to the board.** Vaya(n) a la pizarra. (**PA**); **to ~ away** irse (**8**); **to ~ on a trip** ir de viaje (**10**); **to ~ on foot** caminar; ir a pie (**10**); **to ~ on vacation** ir de vacaciones (7, **10**); **to ~ out** salir (**3**); **to ~ shopping** ir de compras; hacer las compras (**2**); **to ~ to bed** acostarse (ue) (**8**); **to ~ to court** presentarse al juicio (10); **to ~ up** subir (a) (**10**)
golf, to play jugar al golf (**2**)
good bueno/a (**1**); **~ afternoon.** Buenas tardes. (**PA**); **~ evening/night.** Buenas noches. (**PA**); **~ morning.** Buenos días. (**PA**); **~-bye.** Adiós. (**PA**)
gossip el chisme (7)

government el gobierno (1, **11**)
governor el/la gobernador/a (**11**)
grade la nota (4)
graduate, to graduarse (4)
gram el gramo (7)
grandfather el abuelo (**1**)
grandmother la abuela (**1**)
grandparents los abuelos (**1**)
gray gris (**3**)
green verde (**3**)
greeting el saludo (**PA**)
grilled a la parrilla; asado/a (**7**)
ground floor la planta baja (**3**)
group el conjunto (**5**)
grow, to crecer; aumentar (8, 11)
guess, to adivinar (4)
guide la guía (4)
guilty culpable (8)
guitar la guitarra (**5**)
guitarist el/la guitarrista (**5**)
gum el chicle (2)
gymnasium el gimnasio (**2**)

H

hair el pelo (**9**)
half la mitad (11)
ham el jamón (**7**)
hamburger la hamburguesa (**7**)
hand la mano (1, **9**); **on ~** a mano (10); **to ~ in** entregar (7)
hand out/deliver food, to repartir comidas (**4**)
handicapped person el/la discapacitado/a (3)
handsome guapo/a (**1**)
hang up, to colgar (ue) (7)
happen, to pasar (3)
happy contento/a; feliz; alegre (**2**, 5); **to be ~** alegrarse (10)
hard: ~-boiled duro/a (**7**); **~-working** trabajador/a (**1**)
haste prisa (7)
hat el sombrero (**8**)
have, to tener (**1**); **~ a backache** tener dolor de espalda (**9**); **~ a cold** tener (un) catarro; tener un resfriado (**9**); **~ a cough** tener tos (**9**); **~ a headache** tener dolor de cabeza (**9**); **~ a snack** merendar (ie) (**7**); **~ a sore throat** tener dolor de garganta (**9**); **~ a stomachache** tener dolor de estómago (**9**); **~ a virus** tener un virus (**9**); **~ an infection** tener una infección (**9**); **~ breakfast** desayunar (7); **~ dinner** cenar (**7**); **~ fun** divertirse (ie, i) (5, **8**); **~ just** acabar de (1, **9**); **~ lunch** almorzar (ue) (**4, 7**); **~ the flu** tener (la/una) gripe (**9**); **~ to + *(verb)*** tener que + *(infinitive)* (**3**)
he él (**PA, 2**)
head la cabeza (**9**)
headache, to have a tener dolor de cabeza (**9**)
health la salud (**9**)
healthy, to be estar saludable; estar sano/a (**9**)
hear, to oír (**3**)
heart el corazón (**9**)
heater la calefacción (**10**)
heaven el cielo (**11**)
height la altura (9)
Hello! ¡Hola! (**PA**)
help la ayuda (1); **to ~** ayudar (**3**)
hen la gallina (7, **11**)
her su/s (**1**); **~/s** suyo/a/os/as (**10**)
here aquí (1, **6**)
heritage la herencia (1)
Hi! ¡Hola! (**PA**)
hide, to ocultar; esconder (5, 8)
high: ~ plateau el altiplano (9); **~ school** el colegio (8)
highway la carretera (10)
his su/s; suyo/a/os/as (**1, 10**)
Hispanic hispano (PA)
hole el hoyo (**11**)
home el hogar (8); **nursing ~** la residencia de ancianos (**4**)
homework la tarea (**2**)
honeymoon la luna de miel (10)
honorable honrado/a (11)
hope la esperanza (11); **let's ~ that** ojalá (11); **to ~** esperar (**2**)
hopefully ojalá (11)
horror film la película de terror (**5**)
horse el caballo (**11**); **to ride a ~** montar a caballo (**11**)
hospital el hospital (**9**)
hot (temperature) caliente (7); **~ dog** el perro caliente (4, 7); **It's ~.** Hace calor. (**PA**); **to be ~** tener calor (**3**)
hotel el hotel (**10**); **to leave the ~** irse del hotel (**10**)
hour la hora (1)
house la casa (1, **3**)
household remedy el remedio casero (7)
housing la vivienda (3)
How? ¿Cómo? (**PA, 2**); **~ are you doing?** ¿Cómo andas? (**PA**); **~ are you?** ¿Cómo está usted? (*for.*); ¿Cómo estás? (*fam.*) (**PA**); **~ do you say... in Spanish?** ¿Cómo se dice... en español? (**PA**); **~ do you write... in Spanish?** ¿Cómo se escribe... en español? (**PA**); **~ much/many?** ¿Cuánto/a/os/as? (**2**); **~'s it going?** ¿Qué tal? (**PA**)
however no obstante (11)
hubbub el bullicio (4)
hug el abrazo (PA)
human being el ser humano (11)
humble humilde (**3**)
hummingbird el colibrí (11)
hungry, to be tener hambre (**3**)
hurricane el huracán (**11**)
hurry, to be in a tener prisa (**3**)
hurt, to doler (ue) (**9**); **~ oneself** lastimar(se) (**9**)
husband el esposo (**1**)

I

I yo (**PA**); **~ (don't) understand.** (No) comprendo. (**PA**); **~ don't know.** No lo sé. (**PA**); **~ hate it!** ¡Lo odio! (2); **~ know.** Lo sé. (**PA**); **~ would like to introduce you to...** Quiero presentarle a... (*for.*); Quiero presentarte a... (*fam.*) (**PA**); **~'m...** Soy... (**PA**); **~'m sorry** lo siento (10)
ice el hielo (**7**); **~ cream** el helado (**7**); **~ cream shop** la heladería (10)
iced helado/a (**7**)
if si (**2**)
ill enfermo/a (**2**)
illness la enfermedad (**9**)
image la imagen (8)
imaginative imaginativo/a (**5**)
imitate, to imitar (11)
immediately en seguida (9)
important, to be importar (4, **8**)
impressive impresionante (3, **5**)
improve, to mejorar(se) (**9**)
in en (**11**); **~ addition** además (1); **~ exchange** a cambio (4); **~ front (of)** enfrente (de); delante de (2, **4, 11**); **~ order to** para, a fin de (5,**11**); **~ poor taste** de mal gusto (8); **~ reverse** al revés (8); **~ the afternoon** de la tarde (**PA**); **~ the evening** de la noche (**PA**); **~ the morning** de la mañana (**PA**); **~ the open air** al aire libre (8)
include, to incluir (4)
including incluso (4)
increase, to ampliar (2)
incredible increíble (8)
indicate, to indicar (4)
indigenous indígena (7)
ineffectual ineficaz (11)
inequality la desigualdad (10)
infamous infame (11)
infection, to have an tener una infección (**9**)
inflation la inflación (**11**)
influential influyente (11)
information el dato (9)
injure someone, to lastimar (**9**)
inner ear el oído (**9**)

insect el insecto (**11**)
inside adentro (10); **~ of** dentro de (3, **11**)
instead of en vez de (8)
instrument, to play an tocar; tocar un instrumento (**2, 5**)
insurance, medical el seguro médico (9)
intelligent inteligente (**1**)
interest la afición (2)
interest, to interesar (2)
interesting interesante (**1, 10**)
Internet café el cibercafé (**4**)
internship el trabajo en prácticas (8)
interpreter el/la intérprete (5)
intervene, to intervenir (ie) (11)
interview la entrevista (3)
interviewer el/la entrevistador/a (3)
intoxication la embriaguez (10)
invest, to invertir (ie, i) (11)
involved involucrado/a (11); **~ in** metido/a en (11)
island la isla (7)
issued emitido/a (10)
issues, political las cuestiones políticas (**11**)
It's: ~ (not) true. (No) es verdad. (1); **~ cloudy.** Está nublado. (**PA**); **~ cold.** Hace frío. (**PA**); **~ hot.** Hace calor. (**PA**); **~ raining.** Llueve. (**PA**); **~ snowing.** Nieva. (**PA**); **~ sunny.** Hace sol. (**PA**); **~ windy.** Hace viento. (**PA**); **~ … o'clock.** Es la…/Son las… (**PA**)
its su/s

J

jacket la chaqueta (**8**)
jam la mermelada (**7**)
January enero (**PA**)
Japanese japonés/japonesa (**PA**)
jargon la jerga (8)
jazz el jazz (**5**)
jeans los jeans; los (pantalones) vaqueros (**8**)
jewel la joya (9)
job with a salary el trabajo remunerado (4)
joke la broma (3)
jot down, to anotar (5)
journalism el periodismo (**2**)
journalist el/la periodista (3)
juice el jugo (**7**)
July julio (**PA**)
June junio (**PA**)
jungle la selva, la selva tropical (9, **11**)
Just fine. Bastante bien. (**PA**)

K

keep, to guardar (**3**); **~ in mind** tener en cuenta (5)
ketchup la salsa de tomate (**7**)
key la llave (7, **10**)
kill, to matar (10, **11**)
kind bondadoso/a (11)
king el rey (**11**)
kiss el beso (1); **little ~** el besito (PA)
kitchen la cocina (**3**)
knapsack la mochila (**2**)
knife el cuchillo (**7**)
know, to conocer; saber (**3, 4**)
knowledge el conocimiento (2)
known conocido/a (4)

L

laboratory el laboratorio (**2**)
lacking, to be hacer falta (**8**)
lady la señora (Sra.) (**1**)
lake el lago (5, **10, 11**)
lamp la lámpara (**3**)
land la tierra (5, **11**)
landscape el paisaje (8)
language el idioma; la lengua (**2, 5**); **languages** los idiomas (**2**)
large grande (**1**)
last último/a; pasado/a (5, 7); **~ name** el apellido (8); **~ night** anoche (**7**); **~ week** la semana pasada (**7**); **~ weekend** el fin de semana pasado (**7**); **~ year** el año pasado (4, **7**); **to ~** durar (11)
late tarde (3)
later luego (3); **~ than** más tarde que (**7**)
laugh, to reír (i, i) (4)
law el derecho; la ley (**2, 11**)
lazy perezoso/a (**1**)
leaf la hoja (4)
learn, to aprender (**2**)
leather el cuero (**8**)
leave, to salir; irse; salir; dejar (**3, 8, 10**); **~ the hotel** irse del hotel (**10**)
left of, to the a la izquierda de (**3, 7, 11**)
leg la pierna (**9**)
legend la leyenda (9)
lemon el limón (**7**)
lend, to prestar (8, **10**)
less menos (**2**)
lesson la lección (5)
let's: ~ see a ver (2); **~ hope that** ojalá (11)
letter la carta; la letra (alphabet) (**4**, 5); **to mail/send a ~** mandar una carta (**4**)
lettuce la lechuga (**7**)
level el nivel (9)
library la biblioteca (**2**)
license: driver's ~ la licencia (de conducir) (**10**)
lie la mentira (5); **to ~** mentir (ie) (**4**)
life la vida (2)
light claro/a (light in color); ligero/a (light in weight); la luz (5, **8**, 11); **traffic ~** el semáforo (**10**)
like como (1); **to ~** gustar (**PA**)
Likewise. Igualmente. (**PA**)
line (of people) la cola (**10**)
lion el león (**11**)
Listen. Escuche(n). (**PA**); **to ~ to music** escuchar música (**2**)
literacy la alfabetización (8)
literature la literatura (**2**)
little: ~ boy/girl el/la niño/a (**1**); **~ kiss** el besito (PA)
live, to vivir (**2**)
living vivo/a (**11**); **~ room** la sala (**3**)
loan, to prestar (8, **10**)
local person el lugareño/a (4)
locate, to localizar (5)
long largo/a (7, **8, 10**); **~ sleeved** de manga larga (8)
look: to ~ at mirar (1); **to ~ for** buscar (1, **4**)
lose, to perder (ie) (**4, 10**)
lost perdido/a (4)
loud fuerte (3)
love el amor (4); **to ~** querer (ie); encantar (**3, 8**); **to fall in ~** enamorarse (11)
lover el/la amante (11)
luck la suerte (5)
lucky, to be tener suerte (**3**)
luggage el equipaje (10)
lunch el almuerzo (5, **7**); **to have ~** almorzar (ue) (**4, 7**)
luxury el lujo (10)
lyrics la letra (**5**)

M

machine, answering el contestador automático (7)
made from hecho/a de (9)
magazine la revista (5)
mail/send a letter, to mandar una carta (**4**)
main principal (4)
maintain, to mantener (ie) (9)
major la especialidad (1, **2**)
majority la mayoría (7)
make, to hacer (**3**); **~ the bed** hacer la cama (**3**)
make up el maquillaje; **to put on ~** maquillarse (**8**)
mall el centro comercial (**4**)

mammal el mamífero (11)
man el hombre; el señor (Sr.) (**1**); **elderly men/women** las personas mayores; los mayores (4); **young ~/woman** el/la joven (**1**)
manager el/la empresario/a (**5**)
many: ~ times muchas veces (**8**); **so ~/much** tanto/a/os/as (2, 9)
map el mapa (**2**)
March marzo (**PA**)
mark la tacha (7)
market el mercado (**4**)
marmalade la mermelada (**7**)
married, to be estar casado/a (1)
marry, to casarse (7)
marvelous maravilloso/a (7)
match el acierto (11)
mathematics las matemáticas (**2**)
matter el asunto (6); **to ~** importar (4, **8**)
May mayo (**PA**)
maybe quizás; a lo mejor (5, 9)
mayonnaise la mayonesa (**7**)
mayor el alcalde; la alcadesa (**11**)
me mí (**2**)
meal la comida (PB, **7**)
mean, to significar (4)
meaning el significado (8)
means of transportation el medio de transporte (10)
measure, to medir (i, i) (11)
meat la carne (**7**)
medical insurance el seguro médico (9)
medication el medicamento (9)
medicine la medicina (**2**)
medium término medio (**7**)
meet, to encontrar (ue); reunirse (4, **8**)
meeting la reunión (2)
melon el melón (**7**)
member el miembro (4)
memento el recuerdo (3)
memory el recuerdo (7)
mention, to mencionar (4)
menu el menú (**7**)
mess (muddle) el lío (9)
message el mensaje (3)
messy desordenado/a (**3**)
method el método (4)
Mexican mexicano/a (**PA**)
microwave el microondas (**3**)
midnight la medianoche (**PA**)
mile la milla (2)
milk la leche (4, **7**)
mine mío/a/os/as (**10**)
minimum el mínimo (5)
minus menos (**1**)
Miss la señorita (Srta.) (**1**)
miss, to faltar; perder (ie) (4, 7, **10**)
missing desaparecido/a (9)
mistaken, to be equivocarse (9)
mixture la mezcla (7)
model el/la modelo (**8**)
modern moderno/a (**3**)
mom la mamá (**1**)
monarchy la monarquía (**11**)
Monday el lunes (**PA**)
money el dinero; la moneda (1, **2**)
monster el monstruo (9)
month el mes (**PA**)
more más (**2**); **~/less demanding** exige más/menos (**10**)
morning: Good ~. Buenos días. (**PA**); **in the ~** de la mañana (**PA**)
mosquito el mosquito (**11**)
mother la madre (**1**)
motor el motor (**10**)
motorcycle la moto(cicleta) (1, **10**)
mountain la montaña; el monte (8, **10, 11**); **~ range** la sierra (9)
mountainous montañoso/a (4)
mouse el ratón (**11**)
mouth la boca (**9**)
move, to mover (ue) (10); **~ away** apartarse (11); **~ near** acercarse (4)
movie la película (3,4, **5**); **~ theater** el cine (**4**)
moving conmovedor/a; emocionante (**5**)
murder, to asesinar (11)
muscle el músculo (9)
museum el museo (**4**)
music la música (**2, 5**); **classical ~** la música clásica (**5**); **listen to ~** escuchar música (**2**); **pop ~** la música popular (**5**)
musical film la película musical (**5**)
musician el/la músico/a (**5**)
mustard la mostaza (**7**)
my mi/s (**1, 2**); **~ name is...** me llamo... (**PA**)
mystery film la película de misterio (**5**)

N

name el nombre (1); **last ~** apellido (8); **What is your ~?** ¿Cómo se llama usted? (*for.*); ¿Cómo te llamas? (*fam.*) (**PA**)
nap, to take a echar una siesta (PB)
napkin la servilleta (**7**)
narrate, to narrar (6)
narrow estrecho/a (7, **8**)
nationality la nacionalidad (**PA**)
native natal (3)
nature la naturaleza (3, **11**)
nausea la náusea (**9**)
nauseous mareado/a (9)
near cerca (de) (**2, 7, 11**)
neck el cuello (**9**)
need, to necesitar; hacer falta (**2, 8**)
negotiate the price, to regatear (7)
neighbor el/la vecino/a (8)
neighborhood el barrio (8)
neither... nor ni... ni (3, **4**)
nervous nervioso/a (**2**)
never nunca; jamás (emphatic) (**2, 4**)
nevertheless sin embargo (2, **6**)
new nuevo/a (**3**)
news item la noticia (11)
newspaper el periódico (7, **11**)
next próximo/a (PB); **~ to** al lado de (**3, 7, 11**)
nice simpático/a (**1**); **~ to meet you.** Mucho gusto. (**PA**)
nickname el apodo (5)
Nigerian nigeriano/a (**PA**)
night: Good ~. Buenas noches. (**PA**); **last ~** anoche (**7**)
nightmare la pesadilla (8)
nine nueve (**PA**); **~ hundred** novecientos (**2**)
nineteen diecinueve (**PA**)
ninety noventa (**1**)
ninth noveno/a (**5**)
no no (**PA**); **~ longer** ya no (5); **~ one** nadie (**4**)
nobody nadie (**4**)
noise el ruido (3, **10**)
none ningún; ninguno/a (**4**)
noon el mediodía (**PA**)
nor/neither tampoco (7)
normally normalmente (**8**)
north el norte (7)
northeast el noreste (2)
nose la nariz (**9**)
note, to anotar (5)
notebook el cuaderno (**2**)
notes los apuntes (**2**)
nothing nada (3, **4**)
November noviembre (**PA**)
now ahora (4)
nowadays hoy (en) día (5)
number el número (**PA**)
nurse el/la enfermero/a (**9**)
nursing home la residencia de ancianos (**4**)

O

object el objeto (**3**)
obligation el deber (**4**)
obtain, to obtener (ie) (4)
occupy, to ocupar (4)
occur, to ocurrir (4, **9**)
ocean el océano (**11**)
October octubre (**PA**)
of de (1, **11**); **~ course** por supuesto; claro (3)
offer, to ofrecer (1)
office la oficina (**3**); **post ~** la oficina de correos; correos (**4**)

often a menudo (**2, 8**)
oil el aceite (7); **~ spill** el derrame de petróleo (**11**)
old antiguo/a; viejo/a (2, **3**)
older mayor (1, **10**)
on: ~ hand a mano (10); **~ the dot** en punto (1); **~ their own** por su cuenta (7); **~ top (of)** encima (de) (**3, 7, 11**)
once in a while de vez en cuando (9)
one uno; un/a (**PA, 1**); **~ hundred** cien (**1, 2**); **~ hundred million** cien millones (**3**); **~ hundred thousand** cien mil (**3**); **~ million** un millón (3); **~ thousand** mil (**2, 3**)
onion la cebolla (**7**)
only sólo; único/a; solamente; únicamente (3, 4, 8, 9); **~ one** solo/a (7)
open, to abrir (**2**); **Open your book to page...** Abra(n) el libro en la página... (**PA**)
opening el estreno (**5**)
opera la ópera (**5**)
opinion la opinión (4)
opportunity la oportunidad (3)
opposite opuesto/a; el opuesto (4, 11)
orange naranja (color); la naranja (fruit) (**3, 7**)
orchestra la orquesta (**5**)
order el orden (5); **to ~** pedir (**7**)
organize, to organizar (**4**)
origen el origen (1)
other otro/a (4)
others, the los demás (4)
ought to/should deber (1, **4**)
our/s nuestro/a/os/as (**1, 10**)
outfit el conjunto (**8**)
outside of (a)fuera de (4, **11**)
outskirts las afueras (3)
over sobre (5, **11**); **~ there** allá (**6**)
overcoat el abrigo (**8**)
overhaul, to revisar (**10**)
owing to debido a (8)
own propio/a (6); **on their ~** por su cuenta (7)
ozone layer la capa de ozono (**11**)

P

pack a suitcase, to arreglar/hacer la maleta (**10**)
package el paquete (10)
page la página (2)
pain el dolor (**9**)
paint, to pintar (2)
painting el cuadro; la pintura (**3**, 8)
pair la pareja; el par (9)
pajamas el pijama (**8**)
pants los pantalones (**8**)
pantyhose las medias (**8**)
paper el papel (**2, 11**)
paragraph el párrafo (4)
parents los padres (**1**)
park el parque (**4**); **theme ~** el parque de atracciones (**10**); **to ~** estacionarse (**10**)
parking el estacionamiento (**10**)
parrot el loro (11)
party la fiesta (PB); **political ~** el partido político (**11**)
pass: to ~ (a test) aprobar (ue) (10); **to ~ (through)** pasar (por) (2)
passage el pasaje (9)
passenger el/la pasajero/a (10)
passionate apasionado/a (**5**)
passport el pasaporte (**10**)
past el pasado (4)
pastime el pasatiempo (**2**)
pastry el pastel (**7**)
patient paciente; el/la paciente (**1**, 9)
pay, to pagar (**7**)
peace la paz (**5**)
peaceful tranquilo/a (5, **10**)
pear la pera (**7**)
pedestrian el peatón (**10**)
pen, ballpoint el bolígrafo (**2**)
pencil el lápiz (**2**)
people la gente (**1**)
pepper la pimienta (**7**); **chili ~** el chile (**7**)
percent por ciento (**1**)
percentage el porcentaje (7)
perform, to representar (8)
perhaps tal vez (3)
person: handicapped ~ el/la discapacitado/a (3); **local ~** el lugareño (4); **~ from Buenos Aires** porteño/a (8)
personality la personalidad (**1**)
pertain, to pertenecer (4)
Peruvian brandy el pisco (7)
pet la mascota; el animal doméstico (10, **11**)
pharmacist el/la farmacéutico/a (9)
pharmacy la farmacia (**9**); **24-hour ~** la farmacia de turno/guardia (9)
phone call la llamada (7)
photograph la foto(grafía) (1)
physical: ~ characteristic la característica física (**1**); **~ exam** el examen físico (**9**)
pianist el/la pianista (**5**)
piano el piano (**5**)
pick up, to recoger (3)
picture el cuadro (**3**)
pie el pastel (**7**)
piece of furniture el mueble (**3**)
pig el cerdo (**11**)
pile el montón (7)
pill la pastilla (**9**)
pillow la almohada (**3**)
pink rosado/a (**3**)
pistol la pistola (8)
pity la lástima (11)
place el lugar (**2**); **to ~** poner; colocar (**3**, 11)
plan el plan (4); **to ~** planear (6)
planet el planeta (**11**)
plant la planta (**3**); **to ~** plantar (**11**)
plastic el plástico (**11**)
plate el plato (**7**)
platform (political) el programa (11)
play, to jugar (ue) (**4**); **~ an instrument** tocar; tocar un instrumento (**2, 5**); **~ baseball** jugar al béisbol (**2**); **~ basketball** jugar al básquetbol (**2**); **~ charades** hacer mímica (8); **~ football** jugar al fútbol americano (**2**); **~ soccer** jugar al fútbol (**2**); **~ tennis** jugar al tenis (**2**); **~ the role** hacer el papel (3)
player el/la jugador/a (3); **CD/DVD ~** el reproductor de CD/DVD (**2**); **trumpet ~** el/la trompetista (**5**)
pleasant agradable (5)
Please. Por favor. (**PA**)
Pleased to meet you. Encantado/a. (**PA**)
pleasure el placer (7)
plus más (**1**)
point el punto (8)
policeman/woman el/la policía (**10**)
politeness la cortesía (**PA**)
political: ~ campaign la campaña política (**4**); **~ issues** las cuestiones políticas (**11**); **~ party** el partido político (**11**); **~ platform** el programa (11); **~ science** las ciencias políticas (2)
politics la política (**11**)
polka-dotted de lunares (**8**)
poll la encuesta (**11**)
pollute, to contaminar (**11**)
pollution la contaminación (**11**)
polyester el poliéster (**8**)
pool la piscina (2)
poor pobre (**1**)
pop music la música popular (**5**)
population la población (1)
pork el cerdo (7)
portable portátil (4)
post office la oficina de correos; correos (**4**)
postage stamp el sello (**10**)
postcard la tarjeta postal (**10**)
potato la papa; la patata (**7**); **~ chips** las papas fritas (**7**)
potency la potencia (11)
poultry las aves (**7**)
poverty la pobreza (11)

power el poder (9)
practice/rehearse, to ensayar (**5**)
praise, to alabar (11)
predict, to predecir (i) (4)
prefer, to preferir (ie) (**4**)
preference la preferencia (4)
pregnant embarazada (9)
premonition el presentimiento (4)
preparation el preparativo (5)
prepare, to preparar (**2**)
prescribe, to recetar (9)
prescription la receta (**9**)
presentation la presentación (**PA**)
presidency la presidencia (**11**)
president el/la presidente/a (PB, **11**)
pretty bonito/a; guapo/a (**1**)
previous previo/a (10)
price el precio (3); **to negotiate the ~** regatear (7)
print (with a pattern or design) estampado/a (**8**)
prize el premio (3)
professor el/la profesor/a (**2**)
promising prometedor/a (5)
proof la prueba (10)
propose, to proponer (5)
protect, to proteger (7, **11**)
proud orgulloso/a (4)
provide, to proporcionar (8)
province la provincia (**11**)
psychology la psicología (**2**)
Puerto Rican puertorriqueño/a (**PA**)
punctual puntual (4)
pure puro/a (**11**)
purple morado/a (**3**)
purpose el propósito (7)
purse el bolso (**8**)
put, to poner (**3**); **~ away** guardar (**3**); **~ on make up** maquillarse (**8**)

Q

qualified calificado/a (11)
quality la calidad (8, **11**)
queen la reina (**11**)
question la pregunta (**PA**)

R

rabbit el conejo (**11**)
radio el/la radio (**2**)
rain la lluvia (**PA**); **acid ~** la lluvia ácida (**11**); **(tropical) ~ forest** la selva tropical (**11**)
rainbow el arco iris (4)
raincoat el impermeable (**8**)
raining, it's llueve (**PA**)
rainy lluvioso/a (11)
raise, to subir (11)
rapid rápido (2)
rare poco hecho/a, crudo/a (meat); raro/a (**7, 11**)
rat la rata (**11**)
rather bastante (3)
raw crudo/a (**7**)
read, to leer (**2**); **Read.** Lea(n). (**PA**)
reading la lectura (1)
ready, to be estar listo/a (5)
realize, to darse cuenta (9)
Really well. Muy bien. (**PA**)
reason la razón (3)
receive, to recibir (1, **2**)
recipe la receta (7)
recognize, to reconocer (8)
recommend, to recomendar (ie) (**4**)
record, to grabar (**5**)
recordings las grabaciones (**5**)
recruit, to reclutar (10)
recycle, to reciclar (**11**)
red rojo/a (**3**)
reforest, to reforestar (**11**)
refrigerator el refrigerador (**3**)
refuge el refugio (11)
refuse, to rehusar (**11**)
refute, to refutar (8)
region la región (**11**)
rehearse, to ensayar (**5**)
related to, to be tener que ver con (4)
relative el/la pariente (PB)
relax, to relajarse (5)
relaxing relajante (**10**)
release: to ~ a CD sacar un CD (**5**); **to ~ a film/movie** estrenar una película (**5**)
remain, to quedarse (**8**)
remedy, household el remedio casero (7)
remember, to recordar (ue); acordarse de (ue) (**4, 8**)
remorse el remordimiento (10)
rename, to renombrar (4)
renew, to renovar (8)
rent, to alquilar (3)
repeal, to abolir (5)
repeat, to repetir (i) (4); **Repeat.** Repita(n). (**PA**)
replace, to reponer (9)
report el informe; el reportaje (9, 10)
representative el/la diputado/a (**11**)
request la petición (11)
require, to requerir (ie) (11)
reservation la reserva (**10**)
reserve a table, to reservar una mesa (**7**)
resolution la decisión; la determinación (9, 11)
resolve, to resolver (ue) (8, **11**)
resolved resuelto/a (10)
resource el recurso (**11**)
respect, to respetar (**5**)
respectful respetuoso/a (9)
responsible responsable (**1**)
rest, to descansar (7)
restaurant el restaurante (**4**)
result el resultado (4)
return, to regresar; devolver (an object); volver (ue) (**2, 4, 11**)
reuse, to reutilizar (11)
review la reseña (5); **to ~** repasar (5)
revoke, to abolir (5)
reward la recompensa (11)
rhythm el ritmo (**5**)
rice el arroz (**7**)
rich rico/a (**1**)
riddle el rompecabezas (7)
ride, to montar; **~ a bike** montar en bicicleta (**2**); **~ a horse** montar a caballo (**11**)
right (legal) el derecho (**2**); **to be ~** tener razón (**3**); **to the ~ of** a la derecha de (**3, 7, 11**)
ring el anillo (5); **to ~** sonar (7)
risk el riesgo (9)
rite el rito (7)
river el río (**11**)
roasted asado/a (**7**)
robbery el robo (7)
robe la bata (**8**)
rock (music) el rock (**5**)
role el papel (3)
romantic film la película romántica (**5**)
roof el techo (**3**)
room el cuarto; la habitación (**2, 3**, 5); **dining ~** el comedor (3); **double ~** el cuarto doble (**10**); **emergency ~** la sala de urgencias (**9**); **single ~** el cuarto individual (**10**)
roommate el/la compañero/a de cuarto (**2**)
rooster el gallo (7)
root la raíz (11)
rough áspero/a (11)
round-trip ticket el boleto de ida y vuelta (**10**)
roving ambulante (4)
row la fila (5)
rug la alfombra (**3**)
ruin la ruina (9)
rule la regla (8)
run, to correr (**2**)

S

sad triste (**2**)
salad la ensalada (**7**)
salsa la salsa (**5**)
salt la sal (**7**)
same el/la/los/las mismo/a/os/as (1); **the ~ as** al igual; igual que (3, 7)

sandals las sandalias (**8**)
Saturday el sábado (**PA**)
save, to salvar (8)
say, to decir (i) (**3**)
saying el dicho; el refrán (1)
scare, to asustar (9)
scary espantoso/a (**5**)
scene la escena (7)
schedule el horario (de clases) (**2**)
school la escuela (4)
science las ciencias (**2**); **~ fiction film** la película de ciencia ficción (**5**); **computer ~** la informática (**2**); **political ~** las ciencias políticas (2)
scream, to gritar (8)
screen la pantalla (**5**)
sea el mar (9)
seafood los mariscos (**7**)
seamstress la costurera (8)
search la búsqueda (11)
season la estación (**PA**)
seasoning el condimento (**7**)
seat la sede (of government); el asiento (9, 10)
seated sentado/a (5)
second segundo/a (**5**); **~ floor** el primer piso (**3**)
section el apartado (8)
security la seguridad (2)
see: ~ you later. Hasta luego. (**PA**); **~ you soon.** Hasta pronto. (**PA**); **~ you tomorrow.** Hasta mañana. (**PA**); **to ~** ver (**3**)
seem, to parecer (2)
select, to seleccionar (5)
sell, to vender (7)
seller el/la vendedor/a (3)
semester el semestre (**2**)
senate el senado (**11**)
senator el/la senador/a (**11**)
send, to mandar; enviar (2, 8); **~/mail a letter** mandar una carta (**4**)
sentence la oración; la frase (3, 4)
September septiembre (**PA**)
serenade la serenata (11)
serious serio/a (9)
serve, to servir (i) (**4**)
set the table, to poner la mesa (**3**)
seven siete (**PA**); **~ hundred** setecientos (2)
seventeen diecisiete (**PA**)
seventh séptimo/a (**5**)
seventy setenta (**1**)
shaman el chamán (9)
share, to compartir (3)
shark el tiburón (5)
shattered destrozado/a (10)
shave, to afeitarse (**8**)
she ella (**PA**)
sheets las sábanas (**3**)
shirt la camisa (**8**)
shoe el zapato (**8**); **tennis shoes** los zapatos de tenis (**8**)
shop, to comprar; **to window-shop** ojear las vitrinas (8)
shopping las compras (4); **~ district** el centro comercial (**4**); **to go ~** ir de compras, hacer las compras (**2**)
short bajo/a (in stature); corto/a (in length) (**1, 8, 10**)
shorts los pantalones cortos (**8**)
shot la inyección (**9**)
should (ought to) deber (1, **4**)
show, to enseñar; mostrar (ue) (**2, 4**); **~ a film/movie** presentar una película (**5**)
shower la ducha (**3**); **to ~** ducharse (**8**)
shrimp los camarones (**7**)
siblings los hermanos (**1**)
sick enfermo/a (**2**); **to be ~** estar enfermo/a (5, **9**)
side el lado (2)
sigh el suspiro (9) suspirar (9, 11)
sign, to firmar (3)
signature la firma (3)
silk la seda (**8**)
silly tonto/a (**1**)
similar parecido/a (7)
similarity la semejanza (6)
simple sencillo/a (10)
since ya que; desde (1, 7)
sing, to cantar (5)
singer el/la cantante (**5**)
single room el cuarto individual (**10**)
sink el lavabo (**3**)
sister la hermana (**1**)
sit, to sentarse (ie) (**8**)
site el sitio (11)
six seis (**PA**); **~ hundred** seiscientos (2)
sixteen dieciséis (**PA**)
sixth sexto/a (**5**)
sixty sesenta (**1**)
size el tamaño (9)
skate, to patinar (**2**)
skillful hábil (5)
skirt la falda (**8**)
sky el cielo (**11**)
slavery la esclavitud (11)
sleep, to dormir (ue) (**4**)
sleepy, to be tener sueño (**3**)
slippers las zapatillas (**8**)
slow lento/a (3, **5**)
small pequeño/a (**1**)
smaller menor (**10**)
smallest, the el/la menor (**10**)
smoke, to fumar (10)
smooth suave (**5**)
snack la merienda (7); **to have a ~** merendar (ie) (**7**)
snake la serpiente (**11**)
sneeze el estornudo (9); **to ~** estornudar (**9**)
snow la nieve (**PA**)
snowing, it's nieva (**PA**)
so: ~ many/much tanto/a/os/as (2, 9); **~-~.** Más o menos.; Regular. (**PA**)
soccer, to play jugar al fútbol (**2**)
society la sociedad (8)
socks los calcetines (**8**)
sofa el sofá (**3**)
soft drink el refresco (**7**)
soil la tierra (5, **11**)
solicit, to solicitar (11)
solid-colored liso/a (**8**)
solve, to solucionar (5)
some unos/as (**1**)
some/any algún; alguno/a (1, **4**)
someone alguien (**4**)
something algo (3, **4**)
sometimes a veces (**2, 4**)
son el hijo (**1**)
song la canción (5)
soon pronto (5)
sore throat, to have a tener dolor de garganta (**9**)
sound el sonido (5)
soup la sopa (**7**); **~ spoon** la cuchara (**7**)
source la fuente (3)
south el sur (7)
southern sureño/a (8)
sow, to sembrar (ie) (**11**)
space el espacio (3)
Spanish español/a (**PA**); **~ speaker** el/la hispanohablante (1)
speak, to hablar (1, **2**)
specialty of the house la especialidad de la casa (**7**)
species la especie (11); **endangered ~** el animal en peligro de extinción (**11**)
speech el discurso (**11**)
spend, to gastar (7)
spice la especia (**7**)
spicy picante (**7**)
spider la araña (5)
spill, oil el derrame de petróleo (**11**)
spoon la cuchara (**7**); **soup ~** la cuchara (**7**)
spoonful la cucharada (7)
sport el deporte (**2**)
spring la primavera (**PA**)
square el cuadro (3)
stadium el estadio (**2**)
stage la etapa (4)
stain la mancha (9)
staircase la escalera (**3**)
stamp, postage el sello (**10**)
stand, to pararse (10); **~ out** destacar (5); **~ up** levantarse (**8**)

standard el estándar (11)
star la estrella (**5**)
state el estado (9, **11**); **~ of being** el estado (**2**)
statehood la estadidad (11)
station (train, bus) la estación (de tren, de autobús) (**10**); **gas ~** la estación de servicio/de gasolina (**10**)
stay, to quedarse (**8**); **~ in bed** guardar cama (**9**)
steak el bistec (**7**)
steering wheel el volante (**10**)
step el paso (3)
stepfather el padrastro (**1**)
stepmother la madrastra (**1**)
stereotype el estereotipo (2)
still todavía (3)
stirred up alborotado/a (11)
stockings las medias (**8**)
stomach el estómago (**9**)
stomachache, to have a tener dolor de estómago (**9**)
stop: bus ~ la parada (**10**); **to ~** parar (PB)
store la tienda (**2**); **department ~** el almacén (**4**)
storm la tormenta (**11**)
story la historia; el cuento; el piso (in a building) (PB, **3**, 5)
stove la estufa (**3**)
straighten up, to arreglar (**3**)
strange extraño/a; raro/a (3, 7)
strategy la estrategia (10)
street la calle (**3, 10**)
strength la fuerza (7)
stress el estrés (4)
stressed (emphasized) tónico/a (10)
strike la huelga (**11**); **to be on ~** estar en huelga (**11**)
striped de rayas (**8**)
strong fuerte (**1**)
student el/la estudiante (1, **2**); **~ center/union** el centro estudiantil (**2**)
study el estudio (8); **to ~** estudiar (**1, 2**)
stupendous estupendo/a (**5**)
stupid tonto/a (3)
style el estilo; la moda (5, **8**)
subject el asunto; la materia; el sujeto (1, **2**, 8)
sublet, to alquilar (3)
substitute, to sustituir (5)
subway el metro (**10**)
successful, to be tener éxito (**3**)
suddenly de repente; de pronto (PB, 4)
sugar el azúcar (**7**)
suggestion la sugerencia (10)
suit el traje (5, **8**); **bathing ~** el traje de baño (**8**)
suitable adecuado/a (10)
suitcase la maleta (**10**); **to pack a ~** arreglar/hacer la maleta (**10**)
summarize, to resumir (9)
summary el resumen (9)
summer el verano (**PA**); **~ camp** el campamento de niños (4)
summit la cima (10)
sun el sol (**PA**)
sunbathe, to tomar el sol (**2**)
Sunday el domingo (**PA**)
sunny, it's hace sol (**PA**)
supermarket el supermercado (**4**)
support el apoyo (11); **to ~** apoyar (5, **11**); **to ~ a candidate** apoyar a un/a candidato/a (**4**)
sure seguro/a (9)
surely seguramente (2)
surprise la sorpresa (8)
surprising sorprendente (**5**)
survey la encuesta (**11**)
suspicious sospechoso (2)
sweat, to sudar (9)
sweater el suéter (**8**)
sweatshirt la sudadera (**8**)
sweets los dulces (**7**)
swim, to nadar (**2**)
swimming la natación (2)
swimsuit el traje de baño (**8**)
symbol el símbolo (12)
symptom el síntoma (9)

T

table la mesa (**2**); **to reserve a ~** reservar una mesa (**7**); **to set the ~** poner la mesa (**3**)
tablecloth el mantel (**7**)
tablespoon la cuchara (**7**)
take, to tomar; llevar (**2**, 5); **~ a nap** echar una siesta (PB); **~ a short trip** ir de excursión (**4**); **~ a walk** hacer una caminata; pasear (**4**); **~ care of** cuidar (9, **11**); **~ off (one's clothes)** quitarse (la ropa) (**8**); **~ out the garbage** sacar la basura (**3**); **~ out** sacar (10); **~ place** tener lugar (2); **~ someone to the doctor** llevar a alguien al médico (**4**); **~ (time)** tardar en (8); **~ turns** turnarse (3)
tall alto/a (**1**)
tariff la tarifa (5)
tax el impuesto (**11**)
taxi el taxi (**10**)
tea (iced/hot) el té (helado/caliente) (**7**)
teach, to enseñar (**2**)
team el equipo (**2**)
teaspoon la cucharita (**7**)
tell (a story), to contar (ue) (5)
temperate templado/a (8)
temperature la temperatura (**PA**)
temple el templo (**4**)
ten diez (**PA**)
tennis: ~ shoes los zapatos de tenis (**8**); **to play ~** jugar al tenis (**2**)
tent la tienda de campaña (4)
tenth décimo/a (**5**)
Thank you. Gracias. (**PA**)
that ese/a (**5**); **~ (way over there)** aquel/la (**5**); **~ one** ése/a (**5**); **~ one (way over there)** aquél/la (**5**); **~ which** lo que (3); **~'s great!** ¡Qué bueno! (2)
the el, los, la, las (**1, 2**); **~ best** el/la mejor (1, **4, 10**); **~ biggest** el/la mayor (1, **10**); **~ check, please.** La cuenta, por favor. (**7**); **~ day before yesterday** anteayer (**7**); **~ same as** al igual; igual que (3, 7); **~ smallest** el/la menor (**10**); **~ weather is bad.** Hace mal tiempo. (**PA**); ~ weather is nice. Hace buen tiempo. (PA); **~ worst** el/la peor (**4, 10**)
theater el teatro (**4**); **movie ~** el cine (**4**)
their su/s (**1**)
theirs suyo/a/os/as (7, **10**)
theme el tema (3); **~ park** el parque de atracciones (**10**)
then entonces; luego (5, **6**)
there allí (4, **6**); **~ is no doubt** no cabe duda (9); **~ is/are** hay (**2**); **over ~** allá (**6**)
these estos/as (**5**); **~ ones** éstos/as (**5**)
they ellos/as (**PA**)
thin delgado/a (**1**)
thing la cosa (**3**)
think, to opinar; pensar (ie) (1, **4**)
third tercer/o/a (2, **5**); **~ floor** el segundo piso (**3**)
thirsty, to be tener sed (**3**)
thirteen trece (**PA**)
thirty treinta (**PA**)
this (one) esto (neuter); este/a; éste/a (this one) (3, **5**)
those esos/as; ésos/as (those); aquellos/as; aquéllos/as (those way over there) (3, **5**)
though aunque (5)
threat la amenaza (8)
three tres (**PA**); **~ hundred** trescientos (**2**)
throat la garganta (**9**); **to have a sore ~** tener dolor de garganta (**9**)
through por, a través de (2, **11**)
throw, to tirar (8); **~ away** botar (**11**)
Thursday el jueves (**PA**)

ticket la entrada, el boleto (**5, 10**); **round-trip ~** el boleto de ida y vuelta (**10**); **traffic ~** la multa (**10**)
tie la corbata (**8**)
tight estrecho/a (7, **8**)
time el tiempo; la vez (4, 5); **from ~ to ~** a veces (**2**); **many times** muchas veces (**8**); **What ~ is it?** ¿Qué hora es? (**PA**)
times por (**1**)
tin work la hojalatería (2)
tip la propina (**7, 10**)
tire la llanta (**10**)
tired cansado/a (**2**)
title el título (7)
to a (**11**); **~ where?** ¿Adónde? (**2**)
toast la tostada (**7**)
today hoy (**2**)
toe el dedo del pie (**9**)
together juntos/as (3); **~ with** junto con (2)
toilet el inodoro (**3**)
toll la tarifa (5)
tomato el tomate (**7**)
tomorrow mañana (1, **2**)
tongue twister el trabalenguas (4)
too también; demasiado (1, **2**); **~ much** demasiado (2)
tooth el diente (**9**)
top la cima (10); **on ~ (of)** encima (de) (**3, 7, 11**)
topic el tema (3)
tornado el tornado (**11**)
tour la gira (**5**); **to ~** hacer una gira (**5**)
tournament el torneo (4)
tower la torre (3)
town el pueblo (3, **4**); **~ square** la plaza (**4**)
track and field el atletismo (2)
traditional tradicional (**3**)
traffic el tráfico (**10**); **~ light** el semáforo (**10**); **~ ticket** la multa (**10**)
tragedy la tragedia (**11**)
tragic trágico/a (**5**)
train el tren (**10**)
trainer el/la entrenador/a (4)
translate, to traducir (11)
transportation el transporte (**10**); **means of ~** el medio de transporte (10)
travel: ~ agency la agencia de viajes (6, **10**); **~ agent** el/la agente de viajes (**10**); **to ~** viajar (2, **10**)
travelers los viajeros (**10**)
treasure el tesoro (10)
treat, to tratar (9)
treatment el tratamiento (**9**)
tree el árbol (2, **11**)
tremble, to temblar (ie) (7)
tribe la tribu (2)
trip el viaje (8, **10**); **to go on a ~** ir de viaje (**10**); **to take a (short) ~** ir de excursión (**4**)
truck el camión (**10**)
true cierto/a; verdadero/a (4, 7); **It's (not) ~.** (No) es verdad. (**1**)
trumpet la trompeta (**5**); **~ player** el/la trompetista (**5**)
trunk el baúl (**10**)
trust, to confiar; fiar (8, 10)
truth la verdad (3)
try, to intentar; tratar de (to try to) (5, 7, **9**)
T-shirt la camiseta (**8**)
tsunami el sunami (**11**)
Tuesday el martes (**PA**)
tuna el atún 5, **7**
turn, to doblar (**10**); **~ on** encender (ie); prender (9, 11)
TV set el televisor (**2**)
twelve doce (**PA**)
twenty veinte (**PA**); **~-eight** veintiocho (**PA**); **~-five** veinticinco (**PA**); **~-four** veinticuatro (**PA**); **~-nine** veintinueve (**PA**); **~-one** veintiuno (**PA**); **~-seven** veintisiete (**PA**); **~-six** veintiséis (**PA**); **~-three** veintitrés (**PA**); **~-two** veintidós (**PA**)
two dos (**PA**); **~ hundred** doscientos (**2**)

U

ugly feo/a (**1**)
umbrella el paraguas (**8**)
uncle el tío (**1**)
uncomfortable incómodo/a (9)
under bajo; debajo de (**7, 11**)
undercover encubierto/a (11)
underline, to subrayar (7)
understand, to comprender; entender (ie) (1, **2, 4**)
underwear la ropa interior (**8**)
unemployment el desempleo (**11**)
unpleasant antipático/a (**1**)
until hasta (**2, 11**)
upset nervioso/a (**2**)
use, to usar (**2**)
useful útil (**PA**)

V

vacation las vacaciones (**10**); **to go on ~** ir de vacaciones (7, **10**)
vacuum, to pasar la aspiradora (**3**)
value el valor (6)
vegetable la verdura (**7**)
vehicle el vehículo (**10**)
vendor el/la vendedor/a (3)
very muy (**1**); **~ little** muy poco (2)
villager el lugareño/a (4)
vinegar el vinagre (**7**)
virus, to have a tener un virus (**9**)
visit, to visitar (**10**)
vocabulary el vocabulario (1)
voice la voz (**5**)
volcano el volcán (4)
volunteer, to trabajar como voluntario/a (**4**)
volunteerism el voluntariado (**4**)
vote, to votar (**11**)

W

waist la cintura (**9**)
wait for esperar (**2**)
waiter el camarero (**7**)
waitress la camarera (**7**)
wake up, to despertarse (ie) (**8**)
walk: to take a ~ hacer una caminata; pasear (**4**); **to ~** caminar; andar; ir a pie (**2, 7, 10**)
wall la pared (**2**)
want, to desear; querer (ie) (2, **3**)
war la guerra (**11**); **~ film** la película de guerra (**5**)
warn, to advertir (ie, i) (8)
wash, to lavar (7); **~ oneself** lavarse (**8**); **~ the dishes** lavar los platos (**3**)
waste, to perder (ie) (**4**)
watch el reloj (2); **to ~** vigilar (9); **to ~ TV** ver la televisión (**2**)
water: ~ with ice el agua con hielo (5, 7); **fresh ~** el agua dulce (5)
waterfall la catarata (8)
we nosotros/as (**PA**)
weak débil (**1**)
wear, to llevar; llevar puesto (5, **8**)
weather el tiempo (**PA**); **The ~ is nice/bad.** Hace buen/mal tiempo. (**PA**); **What's the ~ like?** ¿Qué tiempo hace? (**PA**)
wedding la boda (4)
Wednesday el miércoles (**PA**)
week la semana (**7**); **last ~** la semana pasada (**7**)
weekend el fin de semana (3); **last ~** el fin de semana pasado (**7**)
weigh, to pesar (11)
weight el peso (9)
welfare el bienestar (**11**)
well: Really ~. Muy bien. (**PA**); **~ done/cooked** bien cocido/a; bien hecho/a (**7**); **~ set** bien puesto (7); **~-being** el bienestar (**11**)
west el oeste (2)
western occidental (8)
what lo que (3)

What? ¿Qué? (**2**); ¿Cómo? (**PA, 2**); ~ **does it mean?** ¿Qué significa? (**PA**); ~ **is this?** ¿Qué es esto? (**PA**); ~ **is your name?** ¿Cómo se llama usted? (*for.*); ¿Cómo te llamas? (*fam.*) (PA); ~ **time is it?** ¿Qué hora es? (PA); ~**'s the weather like?** ¿Qué tiempo hace? (**PA**)
wheel la rueda (**10**); **steering** ~ el volante (**10**)
When? ¿Cuándo? (**2**)
Where? ¿Dónde? (**2**); **to** ~**?** ¿adónde? (**2**)
Which (one/s)? ¿Cuál/es? (2)
while mientras (2); **once in a** ~ de vez en cuando (9)
whip, to azotar (11)
white blanco/a (**3**)
Who? ¿Quién? ¿Quiénes? (**PA, 2**)
whose cuyo/a/os/as (5)
Why? ¿Por qué? (**2**)
wide ancho/a (7, **8**)
wife la esposa (**1**)
wild animal el animal salvaje (**11**)
win, to ganar (3)
wind el viento (**PA**)
window la ventana (**2**); **to** ~**-shop** ojear las vitrinas (8)
windshield el parabrisas (**10**); ~ **wiper** el limpiaparabrisas (**10**)
windy, it's hace viento. (**PA**)
wine el vino (**7**)
winter el invierno (**PA**)
wish, to desear (2)
with con (**2, 11**); ~ **me** conmigo (8); ~ **you** contigo (7)
without sin (4, **11**)
woman la mujer; la señora (Sra.) (**1**); **young** ~ la joven (**1**); la señorita (Srta.) (**1**)
wool la lana (**8**)
word la palabra (1)
work el trabajo; la obra (1, 3); **to** ~ trabajar; funcionar (**2, 10**)
world el mundo (PA)
worried preocupado/a (**2**)
worry about, to preocuparse por (3, **11**)
worse peor (**10**)
worst, the el/la peor (**4, 10**)
wound la herida (**9**)
wrap, to envolver (ue) (7)
wrestling la lucha libre (2)
write, to escribir (1, **2**); **Write.** Escriba(n). (**PA**)
writer el/la escritor/a (6)

Y

yam la batata (7)
year el año (**PA**); **last** ~ el año pasado (4, **7**); **to be... years old** tener... años (**3**)
yell, to gritar (8)
yellow amarillo/a (3)
Yes. Sí. (**PA, 2**)
yesterday ayer (**2, 7**)
you usted/es (*for.*); tú (*fam.*); vosotros/as (*fam. pl. Spain*) (**PA, 2**)
You're welcome. De nada. (**PA**)
young joven (**1**); ~ **man** el joven (**1**); ~ **woman** la joven, la señorita (Srta.) (**1**)
your tu/s (*fam.*); su/s (*for.*); vuestro/a/os/as (*fam. pl. Spain*) (**1, 2**)
yours tuyo/a/os/as (*fam.*); suyo/a/os/as (*for.*); vuestro/a/os/as (*fam. pl. Spain*) (**10**)
yucca la mandioca (7)

Z

zero cero (**PA**)

CREDITS

PHOTO CREDITS

Cover Donald Nausbaum/Getty Images, Inc. – Stone Allstock; **p. 3** clockwise from top: Mehau Kuluk/Photo Researchers, Inc.; Stevie Grand/Science Photo Library/Photo Researchers, Inc.; Maximilian Stock LTD/Phototake NYC; Jose Luis Pelaez/Corbis/Bettmann; **p. 4** Demetrio Carrasco/Dorling Kindersley Media Library; Getty Images – Stockbyte; Glow Images/AGE Fotostock America, Inc.; **p. 7** Creatas/AGE Fotostock America, Inc.; Robert Fried/Robert Fried Photography; Photo Researchers, Inc.; **p. 17** Jeffrey Mayer/Getty Images – WireImage.com; Chad Rachman/AP Wide World Photos; Micheline Pelletier/Corbis/Sygma; Dirck Halstead/Getty Images – Time Life Pictures; **p. 22** Jan Persson/Lebrecht Music & Arts Photo Library; The Art Archive/Picture desk, Inc./Kobal Collection; Lebrecht Music & Arts Photo Library; George Stroud/Getty Images, Inc. – Hulton Archive Photos; **p. 31** Blend Images/Superstock; **p. 36** N. Frank/Viesti Associates, Inc.; **p. 47** Ryan McVay/Getty Images, Inc. – Photodisc; **p. 48** Wolfgang Kaehler Photography; **p. 50** Erin Baiano/Pearson Education/PH College; **p. 52** clockwise from upper left: Russell Kaye/Getty Images – Stone Allstock; Kayte M. Deioma/PhotoEdit, Inc.; Paul Fusco/Magnum Photos, Inc.; Jeffrey Allan Salter/Corbis/SABA Press Photos, Inc.; Kathy Willens/AP Wide World Photos; **p. 52** Erin Baiano/Pearson Education/PH College; **p. 54** Erin Baiano/Pearson Education/PH College; **p. 56** Erin Baiano/Pearson Education/PH College; **p. 61** Juan O'Gorman/The Bridgeman Art Library International; **p. 64** left to right: NASA/Liaison/Getty Images, Inc; Andrew Brusso/Corbis/Outline; Jason Szenes/Corbis/Sygma; PA/Topham/The Image Works; **p. 70** David Young-Wolff/PhotoEdit, Inc.; **p. 74** EPA/Bureau of Engraving/AP Wide World Photos; Corbis/Bettmann; Matthew Ward/Dorling Kindersley Media Library; Jimmy Dorantes/Latin Focus Photo Agency; **p. 83** clockwise from upper left: Henry Romero/Corbis/Reuters America LLC; David Young-Wolff/PhotoEdit, Inc.; Michael Newman/PhotoEdit, Inc.; Chad Ehlers/The Stock Connection; Russell Gordon/Odyssey Productions, Inc.; Getty Images – Stockbyte; **p. 85** AFP Photo/John Gibson/Getty Images, Inc. – Agence Frances Presse; **p. 87** David Young-Wolff/PhotoEdit, Inc.; **p. 90** top: Robert Frerck/Odyssey Productions, Inc.; bottom: Francesca Yorke/Dorling Kindersley Media Library; **p. 91** clockwise from top: Robert Fried/Robert Fried Photography; Getty Images, Inc. – Hulton Archive Photos; John Mitchell; AFP Photo/Jorge Uzon/Getty Images, Inc. – Agence France Presse; **p. 99** Jean-Luc Bohin/SuperStock, Inc.; **p. 103** 1. David Young-Wolff/PhotoEdit, Inc.; 2. Gilbert Martinez/The Stock Connection; 3. Steve Kaufman/Corbis/Bettman; 4. Robert Fried/Robert Fried Photography; 5. James Brunker/Magical Andes Photography; 6. Santiago Fernandez/AGE Fotostock American, Inc.; **p. 108** top: Kim Sayer/Dorling Kindersley Media Library; bottom: Emma Lee/Getty Images, Inc. – Photodisc; **p. 110** Ian Aitken/Rough Guides/Dorling Kindersley; **p. 114** left: Victor Rojas/AFP/Getty Images, Inc. – Agence France Presse; right: Egales Editorial; **p. 115** clockwise from upper left: Max Alexander/Dorling Kindersley Media Library; Simon Harris/Robert Harding World Imagery; Robert Fried/Robert Fried Photography; Peter Bowater/Photo Researchers, Inc.; Paco Feria/Das Fotoarchiv/Peter Arnold, Inc.; Juna Manuel Borrero/Nature Picture Library; Robin Smith/Photolibrary.com; **p. 116** David Buffington/Getty Images, Inc./Photodisc; Agencja Fotograficzna Caro Sp. z.o.o.; **p. 121** left to right: Jean-Luc Bohin/age footstock/SuperStock, Inc.; John Connell/Photolibrary.com; Elio Montes/AGE Fotostock America, Inc.; Wolfgang Kaehler Photography; **p. 124** Amy Etra/PhotoEdit Inc.; **p. 126** Robert Frerck Odyssey/Odyssey Productions, Inc.; Art Resource, NY; L. Mangino/The Image Works; Paul Conkin/PhotoEdit Inc.; **p. 127** Clive Streeter/Dorling Kindersley Media Library; Fran Fernandez Photography; Ellen Rooney/Robert Harding World Imagery; Robert Fried/Robert Fried Photography; **pp. 128, 130** Erin Baiano/Pearson Education/PH College; **p. 135** D. Donne Bryant Stock Photography; **p. 138** Peter Wilson/Dorling Kindersley Media Library; First Light/Image State/International Stock Photography Ltd.; Bill Bachman/Creative Eye/MIRA.com; **p. 139** Robert Frerck/Woodfin Camp & Associates, Inc.; Robert Fried/Robert Fried Photography; **p. 141** Rob Crandall/The Stock Connection; **p. 143** Jeff Greenberg/PhotoEdit, Inc.; **p. 146** Getty Images – Digital Vision; Alamy Images; **p. 148** Photolibrary.com; **p. 150** Chad Ehlers/The Stock Connection; **p. 153** Will Hart; Michael Newman/PhotoEdit, Inc.; **p. 155** Corbis RF; **p. 158** Jose Vincenti Resino; **p. 161** Robert Fried/Robert Fried Photography; Dagli Ortis/PictureDesk/Kobal Collection; Derrick Furlong/Robert Harding World Imagery; **p. 162** Jeff Joiner Photography, LLC; D. Donne Bryant Stock Photography; Robert Fried/Robert Fried Photography; **p. 163** Robert Fried/Robert Fried Photography; Luis Romero/AP Wide World Photos; Ken Hively/NewsCom; **pp. 164, 166** Erin Baiano/Pearson Education/PH College; **p. 171** Alejandro Bolivar/EFE/SIPA Press; **p. 175** Michael A. Keller/Corbis/Bettmann; Julia Ardon; El Nuevo Diario; **p. 179** CiroCesar/La Opinion; Frank Micelotta/Getty Images; Ricky Davila/Cover; Eliseo Fernandez/NewsCom; Telarc/Heads Up International; **p. 187** Mitchell Gerber/Corbis/Bettmann; Stephane Cardinale/Corbis/Sygma; Vincent Kessler/Corbis/Reuters America LLC; Nancy Kaszerman/Corbis NY; **p. 192** Jim Whitmer Photography; Bob Riha, Jr./Getty Images, Inc. – Liaison; **p. 195** Getty Images, Inc. – Photodisc; Peter Chartrand/D. Donne Bryant Stock Photography; Ariel Leon/AP Wide World Photos; **p. 196** Tony Freeman/PhotoEdit Inc.; Jeff Greenberg/PhotoEdit Inc.; Sabine Vielmo/Peter Arnold, Inc.; Juan Carlos Ulate/Corbis/Reuters America LLC; **p. 197** Michael Newman/PhotoEdit Inc.; Keven Schafer/Corbis/Bettmann; Jeff Greenberg/PhotoEdit Inc.; **pp. 198, 200** Erin Baiano/Pearson Education/PH College; **p. 205** clockwise from upper left: Paul Fusco/Magnum Photos Inc.; National Geographic Image Collection; Paul Conkin/PhotoEdit Inc.; Robert Fried/Robert Fried Photography; **p. 207** N. Frank/Viesti Associates, Inc.; David Young-Wolff/PhotoEdit Inc.; Ryan McVay/Getty Images, Inc. – Photodisc; **p. 208** left to right: David Young-Wolff/PhotoEdit Inc.; Robert Frerck, Odyssey Productions, Inc.; Robert Frerck, Odyssey Productions, Inc.; Robert Fried/Robert Fried Photography; Jeff Joiner Photography, LLC; Robert Fried/Robert Fried Photography;/Getty Images, Inc. – Photodisc; Tony Freeman/PhotoEdit Inc.; Michael Newman/PhotoEdit Inc.; **p. 210** Jeff Greenberg/PhotoEdit Inc.; **p. 212** Steve Mason/Getty Images, Inc. – Photodisc; **p. 213** George Widman/Corbis NY; **p. 215** Nancy Johnson Black; **pp. 216, 217** Erin Baiano/Pearson Education/PH College; **p. 218** Photofest; Martin Heitner/The Stock Connection; Peter Pawinski/Getty Images, Inc. – Agence France Presse;

p. 219 ¿Lo sabes? photos: Robert Frerck/Getty Images, Inc./Stone Allstock; Santiago Fdez Fuentes/age footstock/SuperStock; Robert Crandall/The Stock Connection; Getty Images – De Agostini Editore Picture Library; Robert Fried/Robert Fried Photography; Ellen Rooney/Robert Harding World Imagery; Dagli Orti/Picture Desk, Inc./Kobal Connection; Robert Frerck/ Odyssey Productions, Inc.; ¿Lo sabes? Doble photos: Getty Images – De Agostini Editore Picture Library; Sheperd Sherbell/Corbis/ SABA Press Photos, Inc.; José Fuste Raga/AGE Fotostock America, Inc.; Harvey Lloyd/Getty Images, Inc. – Taxi; Luis Romero/AP Wide World Photos; Peter Chartrand/D. Donne Bryant Stock Photography; Juan Carlos Ulate/Corbis/Reuters America LLC; Jeff Greenberg/PhotoEdit Inc.; **p. 220** Gabe Palmer/Corbis/Bettmann; **p. 223** top to bottom: Michael Newman/PhotoEdit Inc.; Jeff Greenberg/PhotoEdit Inc.; Emma Lee/Getty Images, Inc. – Photodisc; **p. 224** Rob Lewine/Corbis/Bettmann; Corbis Royalty Free; Jack Hollingsworth/Getty Images, Inc. – Photodisc; **p. 225** Creatas/Dynamic Graphics; **p. 232** Jeffrey Greenberg/Photo Researchers, Inc.; Andrea Booher/Getty Images, Inc. – Stone Allstock; **p. 235** Martin Heitner/The Stock Collection; Gary Ombler/Dorling Kindersley Media Library; Ira Montgomery/Getty Images, Inc./Image Bank; Doug Scott/AGE Fotostock America, Inc.; Pia Tryde/ Dorling Kindersley Media Library; **p. 236**/Getty Images, Inc. – Photodisc;/Getty Images, Inc. – Photodisc; Carroll Seghers, II, The Stock Connection; **p. 238** Mary Kate Denny//PhotoEdit Inc.; **p. 239** Photolibrary.com; **p. 242** BSIP/Phototake NYC; **p. 243** Odile Noel/Lebrecht Music & Arts Photo Library; Corbis/Stock Market; **p. 246** Susan Van Etten/PhotoEdit Inc.; Newscom; **p. 247** Jeff Greenberg/PhotoEdit Inc.; **p. 251** Masterfile Corporation; **p. 256** PhotoEdit Inc.; **p. 265** Miki Katsman/Corbis/Bettmann; **p. 274** Dirk Wyse/D. Donne Bryant Stock Photography; **p. 276** clockwise from upper left: Barbara Penoyar/Getty Images, Inc. – Photodisc; Rhonda Klevansky/Getty Images, Inc. – Stone Allstock; Alamy Images; Alison Parks-Whitfield Photography; **p. 277** David R. Frazier Photolibrary, Inc.; Pearson Learning Photo Studio; Itaipu Binacional; Stuart Westmoreland/Danita Delimont Photography; **pp. 278, 280** Erin Baiano/Pearson Education/PH College; **p. 285** Kathy Willens/AP Wide World Photos; **p. 288** Bruon Morandi/AGE Fotostock America, Inc.; Patrick Luethy/Latinphoto.org; **p. 289** left: Jeff Greenberg/PhotoEdit Inc.; right: Shaun Best/Corbis NY; **p. 291** James Leynse/Corbis/SABA Press Photos, Inc.; **p. 296** left to right: Corbis/Bettmann; Stephanie Cardinale/Corbis/Sygma; Alpha London/Globe Photos, Inc.; Laurie Lewis/Lebrecht Music & Arts Photo Library; The Granger Collection; Roberta Parkin/Retna Ltd.; Sorel/SMPSP/Photofest; Sergio Larrain/Magnum Photos, Inc.; **p. 306** Walter Bibikow/Stock Boston; **p. 308** Oscar Kersenbaum/Getty Images, Inc. – Hulton Archive Photos; **p. 310** David Young-Wolff/ PhotoEdit Inc.; **p. 312** David R. Frazier Photolibrary, Inc.; Corbis Royalty free; George Haling/Getty Images – Stone Allstock; Chad Ehlers/Getty Images, Inc. – Stone Allstock; **p. 313** Hans Neleman/Getty Images, Inc.; Anna Zuckerman-Vdovenko/PhotoEdit Inc.; Max and Bea Hunn/D. Donne Bryant Stock Photography; Alison Parks-Whitfield Photography; **pp. 314, 316** Erin Baiano/Pearson Education/PH College; **p. 321** Getty Images – Stockbyte; **p. 324** Stephen Schildbach/Getty Images, Inc. – Artville LLC; **p. 330** Hubert Stadler/Corbis/Bettmann; **p. 331** Getty Images – Stockbyte; **p. 336** Danny Lehman/Corbis NY; **p. 340** Bob Daemmrich/The Image Works; Robert Fried/Robert Fried Photography; **p. 343** Erin Baiano/Pearson Education/PH College; **p. 345** Richard Lord/PhotoEdit Inc.; José Fuste Raga/AGE Fotostock America, Inc.; Willam Albert Allard/National Geographic Image Collection; **p. 346** Lonely Planet Images/Photo 20-20; Angelo Cavalli/Getty Images, Inc. – Image Bank; SGM/The Stock Connection; **p. 347** Robert Fried Photography; Dorling Kindersley/Dorling Kindersley Media Library; V. Englebert; Robert Harding World Imagery; **pp. 348, 350** Erin Baiano/Pearson Education/PH College; **p. 355** Stock Portfolio/The Stock Connection; **p. 365** Mikael Karlsson/Arresting Images; **p. 366** Lino Wchima Photography; Daniel Ciccone; **p. 367** Robert Fried Photography; Richard Megna/Fundamental Photographs, NYC; **p. 370** M Stock/The Stock Connection; **p. 371** Jacques Jangoux/The Stock Connection; La Samanna; Kevin Schafer/Stone/Getty Images, Inc./Getty News; **p. 379** Getty Images, Inc. – Stockbyte; **p. 381** Getty Images, Inc. – Stockbyte; REUTERS/Daniel Munoz/Corbis NY; Ricardo Mazalan/AP Wide World Photos; **p. 382** Victor Englebert; Steve Starr/Corbis NY; Michelle Lyman/Omni-Photo Communications, Inc.; **pp. 383, 386** Erin Baiano/Pearson Education/PH College; **p. 391** NASA; **p. 398** Topham/The Image Works; **p. 402** National Geographic Image Collection; **p. 415** Kevin Peterson/ Getty Images, Inc. – Photodisc; **p. 417** Stewart Cohen/Getty Images, Inc. – Stone Allstock; Heidi Grassley/Dorling Kindersley Media Library; Bill Bachmann/PhotoEdit Inc.; Paolo Pulga/Dorling Kindersley Media Library; **p. 418** Esbin Anderson/Omni-Photo Communications, Inc.; Steve Dunwell/Getty Images, Inc./Image Bank; Kevin Schafer/Corbis/Bettmann; David Parker/Photo Researchers, Inc.; **p. 419** Jeff Greenberg/Omni-Photo Communications, Inc.; Catherine Karnow/Woodfin Camp & Associates, Inc.; Tom & Susan Bean, Inc.; Martin Rogers/Stock Boston; **pp. 420, 422** Erin Baiano/Pearson Education/PH College; **p. 427** clockwise from upper left: Catherine Karnow/Woodfin Camp & Associates; Alamy Images; Chad Ehlers/Getty Images – Stone Allstock; William Albert Allard/National Geographic Image Collection; **p. 429** Juan Silva Productions/Getty Images, Inc. – Image Bank; Elizabeth Crews Photography; Push Pictures/Corbis NY; **p. 430** SuperStock, Inc.; Getty Images – Stockbyte; **p. 431** Getty Images – Stockbyte; Amy Etra/PhotoEdit Inc.; **p. 433** Robert Brenner/PhotoEdit Inc.; Getty Images – Stockbyte; Gary Buss/Getty Images – Taxi; Luxner News, Inc.; **p. 434** Daniel Rivademar/Odyssey Productions, Inc.; Chris Anderson/Aurora & Quanta Productions, Inc.; Dennis MacDonald/PhotoEdit Inc.; **p. 435** David Young-Wolff/PhotoEdit Inc.; Robert Fried Photography; **p. 437** Ryan McVay/ Getty Images, Inc./Photodisc; D. Berry/Getty Images, Inc./Photodisc; Alan Keohane/Dorling Kindersley Media Library; Spencer Grant/PhotoEdit Inc.; **p. 438** Barbara Penoyar/Getty Images, Inc. – Photodisc; David R. Frazier Photolibrary, Inc.; David R. Frazier Photolibrary, Inc.; Hans Neleman/Getty Images, Inc.; Richard Lord/PhotoEdit Inc.; Lonely Planet Images/Photo 20-20; Robert Fried Photography; Getty Images – Stockbyte; Victor Englebert; Stewart Cohen/Getty Images – Stone Allstock; Esbin Aderson/ Omni-Photo Communications; Michael Newman/PhotoEdit Inc.; **p. 439** left to right: Walter Bibikow/Getty Images – Taxi; Getty Images – De Agostini Editore Picture Library; Larry Dale Gordon/Getty Images, Inc./Image Bank; Ken Welsh/AGE Fotostock America, Inc.; Luxner News, Inc.; Spectrum Photofile; Pablo Corral Vega/Corbis/Bettmann; José Enrique Molina/AGE Fotostock America, Inc.; Robert Frerck/Getty Images, Inc./Stone allsstock; Nacho Moro/SuperStock, Inc.; Mark Bacon/Latin Focus Photo Agency; **p. 440** Lisa Thompson/NewsCom; Stuart Cohen/The Image Works; National Geographic Image Collection; Jupiter Images; **p. 441** Erin Baiano/Pearson Education/PH College.

INDEX

M

N

O

P

Q

R

S

T

U

V

W

Y

Z